To obtain more information, or to order bulk purchases for
educational or business uses, please contact

National Review Books
215 Lexington Avenue
4th Floor
New York, NY 10016

www.nationalreview.com

The Temptation of Wilfred Malachey © 1985 by William F. Buckley, Jr.
Reprinted here by permission of the author

ISBN: 0-9627841-5-X

Jacket Design by Luba Myts

PRINTED IN THE UNITED STATES OF AMERICA

The National Review

TREASURY
OF
CLASSIC
CHILDREN'S
LITERATURE

CONTENTS

Acknowledgments

ST. NICHOLAS MAGAZINE, the renowned children's monthly magazine that was published from 1874 until 1941, when it finally succumbed to the Great Depression, was—and still is—a treasure trove of wonderful, beautifully written literature for children.

Engaging, entertaining, instructive (without being preachy), and at times almost magical, *St. Nicholas Magazine* was so distinct and unique—so special (to employ an over-used word)—that it became a major influence on an ensuing generation of writers. It soared, and every month took countless children along to unsurpassed heights.

During its "golden years," which experts on children's literature regard as being from its founding through 1918 (much of which time it thrived under the editorial guidance of the great Mary Mapes Dodge), *St. Nicholas* was home to the best and most enduring writers of literature—whether it be "children's" or any other genre.

This volume gives a new home to these classic works, many of them at risk of being forgotten.

Except for Howard Pyle's "The Three Fortunes" (originally published in *Harper's Young People*—another superior publication of the time) and the sole work of children's literature by William F. Buckley Jr., *The Temptation of Wilfred Malachey* (first published in 1985), the stories and artwork in this collection were all taken from original editions of *St. Nicholas Magazine*.

The text and pictures in *The National Review Treasury of Classic Children's Literature* were scanned, processed, and reformatted from the pages of the original magazine issues, in all cases found in annual or semiannual bound volumes (spines cracked, leather covers flaking, pages dulled with a brown patina, and exuding a somewhat sweet, earthy aroma).

Converting a magazine article, printed on a page that in some cases is now over 125 years old, to "electronic" text—so that it can be formatted, edited, corrected, etc.—is a cumbersome process, and a sad one too: The page must be cut out of the volume. 'Tis a bibliophile's nightmare.

But then, the opportunity to share the wonderful stories on those pages with a new generation of children more than offsets that sadness.

For those interested, the mechanics behind this book worked thus: The page is taken from the volume and scanned at a high dot-per-inch (DPI) resolution, so that the details of illustrations are enhanced. At this point the image is regarded by the computer as just that—an image. The text on the page is nothing more than a picture, the letters nothing more than lines and curves. In order to convert the words of that image into electronic text, an optical character recognition (OCR) software program—now quite commonly used—is applied: It "reads" the text on a scanned page and converts it into an electronic format that can be edited and corrected.

But the OCR process is not faultless. For example, the letters "r" and "n," when next to each other, as in the word "barn," can, to the OCR processing software, be viewed as an "m"—producing "bam" instead of "barn." Similarly, a contraction such as "I'll" was regularly deemed by the OCR process to be "1 11." So converting an image of words into electronic text, as wonderful a process as it may be, is far from infallible.

Enter the humans.

Without question this book would not exist were it not for *National Review* Associate Editor Julie Crane, our proofreader supreme, who has read, re-read, and then read again all the stories in *The National Review Treasury of Classic Children's Literature*. Not only did she find and correct a myriad of inelegant ellipses and puzzling punctuations, Julie also was of great help in the process of nominating stories from which Bill Buckley selected those that made our final cut.

Of critical assistance along the way were the delightful Rachel Zabarkes, *NR's* 2002 summer intern, who spent many hours back-stopping our efforts, and Associate Editor Sarah Maserati, who also graced our efforts with her considerable proofreading talents. Good ladies, we are in your debt. As we are to Kevin Longstreet, Assistant to *NR's* Publisher, who helped out in many ways, as did *National Review* techno-whizzes, George Vara and Aaron Bailey.

A very special thank you goes to *NR's* Art Director, Luba Myts. Handed a myriad of computer disks clogged with scores of stories and hundreds of illustrations, she took all the material given her and worked her magic, weaving the bytes of information into this volume that we find so pleasing to the eye. Luba designed the book's layout and its cover art, converted the electronic text into its pages, re-scanned, cleaned up, and formatted much of the book's artwork (our previous efforts in this area did not meet her high standards). And she did all this on top of her usual day-to-day efforts with the magazine. *Brava!*

The éminence grise of this book is *NR* Publisher Ed Capano. His advice and direction and pushing and cajoling throughout the past two years were critical to the project's fruition. And, of course, what you hold in your hands comes to you courtesy of *NR* Editor-at-Large William F. Buckley Jr., who read scores upon scores of stories, graded them, and then finally selected those that are contained herein. ¡Muchas gracias, jefes!

And finally, a word of thanks to my family, several of whom were conscripted into this project. Early on in the process, my dear wife, Sharon, and my sainted mother, Angela Fowler, both proofread and offered their views on the merits of particular stories. And my two eldest children, James and Mary, often had to endure their father asking them, on the spur of the moment, to "read this story and tell me what you think." They cost a lot less than a focus group. Their wisdom was priceless. Father, husband, and son thanks all.

Happy and enjoyable reading!

Jack Fowler
NR Associate Publisher
September 2002

Introduction

BY WILLIAM F. BUCKLEY JR.

THESE WORDS ARE in part autobiographical, but that, I think, may be forgiven under the circumstances. To read through stories that were written for children inevitably recasts the workaday perspectives of the adult. One's memory goes back to when these stories were first read, and reading them now revives stimulations experienced in childhood. When you were young. When I was . . . very young.

We were a very large household. I was the sixth child, always struggling to achieve the sophistication and immunities of child #5. Let alone #4. As it happened, #3 was enviable not only because she was an august 15, but because the children's stories matriculated in her imagination and stayed there with remarkable tenure. I am talking about Priscilla Buckley, and the perspective on her in 1936 when, as her eleven-year-old brother, I wondered if any phenomenon existed anywhere to match her ongoing mastery of all the *St. Nicholas Magazine* stories. She would recall antecedent authors and events and, with the eye-twinkle that charmed everyone during her professional career, she'd correct me when I passed callow judgment on her favorites.

Moreover, she had a special advantage. The two oldest of our siblings, ages 17 and 19, were scornful of our reading habits. Not because they had outgrown *St. Nicholas* but because they thought it correct, as advanced teenagers, to relegate the literature as belonging exclusively to younger boys and girls. It required my sister Aloïse and my brother John some years before true sophistication set in, permitting them to enjoy, as we do now, that which is enjoyable irrespective of the age at which one first reads it, or of the age of the children for whom it was intended.

St. Nicholas Magazine was mailed directly to my sister Priscilla, who read the issue on arrival, forthwith. She would also bring home bound volumes, stacked in the Sharon Library, dating back over the turn of the century. The future managing editor of *National Review* would then hand her copy down, next in seniority, to Jim, future senator from New York and judge of the Court of Appeals. Jim paid special attention to those stories that gave prominence even to such awful creatures as were featured in Charles Lummis's "The First of the Rattlesnakes." He was especially devoted to stories by Rudyard Kipling and Frances Hodgson Burnett. Jim would pass on the issue of the magazine to Jane, 13, worldly, beautiful, poised. I thought her the essence of sophistication as she would pass along the magazine, advising me which of the stories she found especially important. When she recommended Lewis Carroll's "Bruno's Revenge," she carefully pointed out that the author was the same "author" who had written *Alice in Wonderland*. I remember pretending that I understood what special distinction this gave him. I had no idea that *Alice*, like Dante's *Inferno*, had intellectual levels of narrative, taxing the most inquisitive and urbane minds, then as now.

Trish, future managing editor of *Triumph* magazine, was my special playmate. She was deferential only in the way that juniors defer to older siblings. She was resolute, shaking her red pigtails, in affirming her own favorite stories. If I hadn't resolved not to stretch autobiographical license too far, I'd wax on at this point that my disagreeing with my beloved Trish about one story or another was an indication of combative inclinations, to which I gave lifelong exercise for fifty years after reading my first issue of *St. Nicholas Magazine*.

In any event, there was always something in the magazine to talk about. After my sister Trish, in family sequence, came brother Reid, now an illustrious author and teacher. But he was much younger than the 1.5 year interval separating the rest of us would have decreed. Accordingly, we didn't think of Reid even prospectively as in the loop that began with Priscilla and reached down, terminally, to Trish, age ten. Five devotees of children's stories, and special addicts of *St. Nicholas Magazine*.

THE CHILDREN'S STORIES, you will find, are extraordinarily varied. There are also the fairy tales, into which children's minds gladly slid in those days. When we read the Oz books, we had no difficulty at all in fancying ourselves as mingling with Real People. The movie made after the book, *The Wizard of Oz*, is viewed by American children over the age of ten as palpable romance. Tell-it-to-the-Marines wasn't by any means the attitude we brought to such tales.

I remember a book in the Oz series called *The Magic of Oz*. That book disclosed a word, a mastery of the correct pronunciation of which endowed the apprentice with the power to transform himself/herself into any animal on earth. I spent a great deal of time endeavoring to master that magical word. It read something on the order of PYRZQXGL. I must have tried to order the syllables and attempt their pronunciation out loud 500 times, slightly varying the accentuation in order to activate the efficacious phonemes that would permit my reincarnation as a tiger. On achieving this, I would end forever any presumption, in our household, that because I was a mere eleven, anyone older could belittle me *and hope to survive!*

The magic word never quite worked for me, but maybe I owe to that delirious obsession some sense of the enchanting mystery of the morphology of words: *Get words right.* I reflected on the misusage phenomenon when I served in the United Nations and had to sit down in my delegate's chair to listen to a speech by the ambassador from the "German Democratic Republic." There is no magical incantation, I reminded myself, that could make the man I was listening to pass himself off persuasively as either a democrat or a republican.

Some illusions, as with all of those references for fifty years to the "democratic" states of Communist Europe, are noxious, crying out to be put down. But the illusions of this volume's storytellers—many initially selected by Mary Mapes Dodge, founding editor of *St. Nicholas Magazine*, and author of the imperishable *Hans Brinker, or The Silver Skates*—stimulate awe, wonder, delight, fear, reassurance. There are no children's tales in this collection of a kind that would have stimulated base appetites. I wonder what Adolf Hitler read as a child?

Which brings me to use a much rejected word, secretly cherished by me but which I use, out of cowardice, infrequently, and mostly in the closet. It is "wholesome." In the modern age people tend to think that wholesome goes with Cream of Wheat, marshmallows, and Kool-Aid, inducing tedium soon, nausea later. It is difficult to conceive of a movie these days that would advertise itself as "wholesome." Imagine recommending to Hollywood producers a rating of PG-6.

Well, these are wholesome stories, but some of them come with bite and wit and cunning, and one is not to be thrown off by such a title as Thornton Burgess's "Tommy and the Meadow Mice." The story survives a title all but inconceivable in modern times.

Concerning which (modern times) I should say something about my own contribution to the lore. Fifteen years ago I was asked to write a children's book. I thought the idea challenging and provocative. How old, I asked, would the children be to whom I'd be addressing my book?

Oh, the publisher said, "Thirteen, 14, maybe even 15."

I told my agent that I was handicapped by not knowing anybody 14 years old, my son having passed that age twenty years earlier. Nobody who knows my agent, Lois Wallace, will be surprised to learn that, after making a date for tea, she came along and produced for my inspection her 14-year-old son and his playmate. I could start with them, in my struggle to devise a story that might hold their attention. In further conversation with my publisher I pressed for more of the rules, and he said that the story should present 1) miscreancy, 2) an element of fantasy, and 3) final reconciliation.

Zap! *The Temptation of Wilfred Malachey*—see page 484. It is, to quote the publisher, a rollicking good children's story, will make you tremble, exult, laugh, weep, and maybe reach out for your mother's hand.

She is there, solid in the imagination, as she was in real life.

WFB
Stamford, Connecticut
September 2002

The Brownies' Friendly Turn

WRITTEN AND ILLUSTRATED BY PALMER COX

One night while snow was lying deep
On level plain and mountain steep,
A sheltered nook the Brownies found,
Where conversation might go 'round.
Said one: "The people hereabout
Their wood supply have taken out;
But while they stripped the timber lot,
The village parson they forgot.
Now odds and ends, the story goes,
Must cook his meals and warm his toes."

Another spoke: "The way is clear
To show both skill and courage here.
You're not the sort, I know, to shirk;
And coward-like to flee from work.
You act at once whenever you find
A chance to render service kind,
Nor wait to see what others do
In matters that appeal to you.
This task in waiting must be done
Before another day has run.

The signs of change are in the air;
A storm is near though skies are fair;
As oft when smiles the broadest lie,
The tears are nearest to the eye.
To work let every Brownie bend,
And prove tonight the parson's friend.
We'll not take oxen from the stall,
That through the day must pull and haul,
Nor horses from the manger lead;
But let them take the rest they need.

Since mystic power is at our call,
By our own selves we'll do it all.
Our willing arms shall take the place
Of clanking chain and leathern trace,
And 'round the door the wood we'll strew
Until we hide the house from view."

At once the Brownies sought the ground
Where fuel could with ease be found—

While more from under drifts of snow
Removed old trees, and made them go
Like plows along the icy street,
With half their limbs and roots complete.

The wind that night was cold and keen,
And frosted Brownies oft were seen.
They clapped their hands and stamped their to
They rubbed with snow each numbing nose,

A place where forest fires had spread,
And left the timber scorched and dead.
And there through all the chilly night
They tugged and tore with all their might;
Some bearing branches as their load;
With lengthy poles still others strode,
Or struggled, till they scarce could see,
With logs that bent them like a V;

And drew the frost from every face
Before it proved a painful case.
And thus, in spite of every ill,
The work was carried forward still.
Around the house some stayed to pile
The gathered wood in proper style;
Whichever harder work they found
As high and higher rose the mound.

Above the window-sill it grew,
And next, the cornice hid from view;
And, ere the dawn had forced a stop,
The pile o'erlooked the chimney-top.

That morning, when the parson rose,
Against the pane he pressed his nose,
And tried the outer world to scan
To learn how signs of weather ran.
But, 'round the house, behind, before,
In front of window, shed, and door,

The wood was piled to such a height
But little sky was left in sight!
When next he climbed his pulpit stair,
He touched upon the strange affair,
And asked a blessing rich to fall
Upon the heads and homes of all
Who through the night had worked so hard
To heap the fuel 'round the yard.
His hearers knew they had no claim
To such a blessing, if it came,
But whispered: "We don't understand—
It must have been a Brownie Band."

First published in the May 1885 edition of *St. Nicholas Magazine*

Tabby's Table-Cloth

from the "Spinning-Wheel" series

BY LOUISA MAY ALCOTT

THE STORM KEPT on all night, and next morning the drifts were higher, the wind stronger, and the snow falling faster than ever. Through the day the children roved about the great house, amusing themselves as best they could; and, when evening came, they gathered around the fire again, eager for the promised story from Grandmamma.

"I've a little cold," said the old lady, "and am too hoarse for talking, my dears; but Aunt Elinor has looked up a parcel of old tales that I've told her at different times and which she has written down. You will like to hear her reading better than my dull way of telling them, and I can help Minnie and Lotty with their work, for I see they are bent on learning to spin."

The young folk were well pleased with Grandma's proposal; for Aunt Nell was a favorite with all, being lively and kind and fond of children, and the only maiden aunt in the family. Now, she smilingly produced a faded old portfolio, and, turning over a little pile of manuscripts, said in her pleasant way:

"Here are all sorts, picked up in my travels at home and abroad; and in order to suit all of you, I have put the names on slips of paper into this basket, and each can draw one in turn. Does that please my distinguished audience?"

"Yes, yes. Geoff's the oldest, let him draw first," cried the flock, fluttering like a flight of birds before they settle.

"Girls come first," answered the boy, with a nod toward the eldest girl cousin.

Lotty put in her hand and, after some fumbling, drew out a paper on which was written, "*Tabby's Table-Cloth.*"

"Is that a good one?" she asked, for Geoff looked disappointed.

"More fighting, though a girl is still the heroine," answered Aunt Nell, searching for the manuscript.

"I think two revolutions will be enough for you, General," added Grandmamma, laughing.

"Do we beat in both?" asked the boy, brightening up at once.

"Yes."

"All right, then. I vote for 'Dolly's Dish-Cloth,' or whatever it is; though I don't see what it can possibly have to do with war," he added.

"Ah, my dear, women have their part to play as well as men at such times, and do it bravely, though one does not hear so much about their courage. I've often wished some one would collect all that can be found about these forgotten heroines, and put it in a book for us to read, admire, and emulate when our turn comes."

Grandma looked thoughtfully at the fire as she spoke, and Lotty said, with her eye on the portfolio: "Perhaps Aunt Nell will do it for us. Then history won't be so dry, and we can glorify our foremothers as well as fathers."

"I'll see what I can find. Now spin away, Minnie, and sit still, boys—if you can."

Then, having settled Grandma's foot-stool, and turned up the lamp, Aunt Nell read the tale of

TABBY'S TABLE-CLOTH

ON THE 20TH day of March, 1775, a little girl was trudging along a country road with a basket of eggs on her arm. She seemed in a great hurry, and looked anxiously about her as she went; for those were stirring times, and Tabitha Tarbell lived in a town that took a famous part in the Revolution. She was a rosy-faced, bright-eyed lass of fourteen, full of vigor, courage, and patriotism, and just then much excited by the frequent rumors which reached Concord that the British were coming to destroy the stores sent there for safe keeping while the enemy occupied Boston. Tabby glowed with wrath at the idea, and (metaphorically speaking) shook her fist at august King George, being a stanch little Rebel, ready to fight and die for her country rather than submit to tyranny of any kind.

In nearly every house something valuable was hidden. Colonel Barrett had six barrels of powder; Ebenezer Hubbard, sixty-eight barrels of flour; axes, tents, and spades were at Daniel Cray's; and Captain David Brown had guns, cartridges, and musket balls. Cannon were hidden in the woods; firearms were being manufactured at Barrett's Mills; cartouch-boxes, belts, and holsters, at Reuben Brown's; saltpetre at Josiah Melvin's; and much oatmeal was prepared at Captain Timothy Wheeler's. A morning gun was fired, a guard of ten men patrolled the town at night, and the brave farmers were making ready for what they felt must come.

There were Tories in the town who gave the enemy all the information they could gather; therefore, much caution was necessary in making plans, lest these enemies should betray them. Pass-words were adopted, secret signals used, and messages sent from house to house in all sorts of queer ways. Such a message lay hidden under the eggs in Tabby's basket, and the brave little girl was going on an important errand from her uncle, Captain David Brown, to Deacon Cyrus Hosmer, who lived at the other end of the town, by the South Bridge. She had been employed several times before in the same way, and had proved herself quick-witted, stout-hearted, and light-footed. Now, as she trotted along in her scarlet cloak and hood, she was wishing she could still further distinguish herself by some great act of heroism; for good Parson Emerson had patted her on the head and said, "Well done, child!" when he heard how she ran all the way to Captain Barrett's, in the night, to warn him that Doctor Lee, the Tory, had been detected sending information of certain secret plans to the enemy.

"I would do more than that, though it was a fearsome run through the dark woods. Wouldn't those two like to know all I know about the stores? But I wouldn't tell 'em, not if they drove a bayonet through me. I'm not afeared of 'em;" and Tabby tossed her head defiantly, as she paused to shift her basket from one arm to the other.

But she evidently was "afeared" of something, for her ruddy cheeks turned pale and her heart gave a thump as two men came in sight, and stopped suddenly on seeing her. They were strangers; and though nothing in their dress indicated it, the girl's quick eye saw that they were soldiers; step and carriage betrayed it, and the rapidity with which these martial gentlemen changed into quiet travelers roused her suspicions at once. They exchanged a few whispered words; then they came on, swinging their stout sticks, one whistling, the other keeping a keen lookout along the lonely road before and behind them.

"My pretty lass, can you tell me where Mr. Daniel Bliss lives?" asked the younger, with a smile and a salute.

Tabby was sure now that they were British; for the voice was deep and full, and the face a ruddy English face, and the man they wanted was a well-known Tory. But she showed no sign of alarm beyond the modest color in her cheeks, and answered civilly: "Yes, sir, over yonder a piece."

"Thanks, and a kiss for that," said the young man, stooping to bestow his gift. But he got a smart box on the ear, and Tabby ran off in a fury of indignation.

With a laugh they went on, never dreaming that the little Rebel was going to turn spy herself, and get the better of them. She hurried away to Deacon Hosmer's, and did her errand, adding thereto the news that strangers were in town. "We must know more of them," said the Deacon. "Clap a different suit on her, wife, and send her with the eggs to Mrs. Bliss. We have all we want of them, and Tabby can look well about her, while she rests and gossips over there. Bliss must be looked after smartly, for he is a knave and will do us harm."

Away went Tabby in a blue cloak and hood, much pleased with her mission; and, coming to the Tory's house about noon smelt afar off a savory odor of roasting meat and baking pies.

Stepping softly to the back door, she peeped through a small window, and saw Mrs. Bliss and her handmaid cooking away in the big kitchen, too busy to heed the little spy, who slipped around to the front of the house to take a general survey before she went in. All she saw confirmed her suspicions; for in the keeping-room a table was set forth in great style, with the silver tankards, best china, and the fine damask table-cloth, which the housewife kept for holidays. Still another peep through the lilac bushes before the parlor windows showed her the two strangers closeted with Mr. Bliss, all talking earnestly, but in too low a tone for a word to reach even her sharp ears.

"I *will* know what they are at. I'm sure it is mischief, and I won't go back with only my walk for my pains," thought Tabby; and marching into the kitchen, she presented her eggs with a civil message from Madam Hosmer.

"They are mighty welcome, child. I've used a sight for my custards, and need more for the flip. We've company to dinner unexpected, and I'm much put about," said Mrs. Bliss, who seemed to be concerned about something besides the dinner, and in her flurry forgot to be surprised at the unusual gift; for the neighbors shunned them, and the poor woman had many anxieties on her husband's account, the family being divided—one brother a Tory and one a Rebel.

"Can I help, ma'am? I'm a master hand at beating eggs, Aunt Hitty says. I'm tired, and wouldn't mind sitting a bit if I'm not in the way," said Tabby, bound to discover something more before she left.

"But you be in the way. We don't want any help, so you'd better be steppin' along home, else suthin' besides eggs may git whipped. Tale-bearers aren't welcome here," said old Puah, the maid, a sour spinster, who sympathized with her master, and openly declared she hoped the British would put down the Yankee rebels soon and sharply.

Mrs. Bliss was in the pantry, and heard nothing of this little passage of arms; for Tabby hotly resented the epithet of "tale-bearer," though she knew that the men in the parlor were not the only spies on the premises.

"When you are all drummed out of town and this house burnt to the ground, you may be glad of my help, and I wish you may get it. Good-day, old crab-apple," answered saucy Tabby; and, catching up her basket, she marched out of the kitchen with her nose in the air.

But as she passed the front of the house, she could not resist another look at the fine dinner table; for in those days few had time or heart for feasting, and the best napery and china seldom appeared. One window stood open, and as the girl leaned in, something moved under the long cloth that swept the floor. It was not the wind, for the March day was still and sunny, and in a minute out popped a gray cat's head, and puss came purring to meet the new-comer whose step had roused him from a nap.

"Where one tabby hides another can. Can I dare to do it? What would become of me if found out? How wonderful it would be if I could hear what these men are plotting. I will."

A sound in the next room decided her; and, thrusting the basket among the bushes, she leaped lightly in and vanished under the table, leaving puss calmly washing her face on the window-sill.

As soon as it was done Tabby's heart began to flutter; but it was too late to retreat, for at that moment in hustled Mrs. Bliss, and the poor girl could only make herself as small as possible, quite hidden under the long folds that fell on all sides from the wide, old-fashioned table. She discovered nothing from the women's

The children gathered around the fire, eager for the promised story.

chat, for it ran on sage cheese, egg-nog, roast pork, and lamentations over a burnt pie. By the time dinner was served, and the guests called in to eat it, Tabby was calm enough to have all her wits about her, and pride gave her courage to be ready for the consequences, whatever they might be.

For a time the hungry gentlemen were too busy eating to talk much; but when Mrs. Bliss went out, and the flip came in, they were ready for business. The window was shut, whereat Tabby exulted that she was inside; the talkers drew closer together, and spoke so low that she could only catch a sentence now and then, which caused her to pull her hair with vexation; and they swore a good deal, to the great horror of the pious little maiden curled up at their feet. But she heard enough to prove that she was right; for these men were Captain Brown and Ensign De Bernicre, of the British army, come to learn where the supplies were stored and how well the town was defended, She heard Mr. Bliss tell them that some of the "Rebels," as he called his neighbors, had sent him word that he should not leave the town alive, and he was in much fear for his life and property. She heard the Englishmen tell him that if he came with them they would protect him; for they were armed, and three of them together could surely get safely off, as no one knew the strangers had arrived but the slip of a girl who showed them the way. Here "the slip of a girl" nodded her head savagely, and hoped the speaker's ear still tingled with the buffet she gave it.

Mr. Bliss gladly consented to this plan and told them he would show them the road to Lexington, which was a shorter way to Boston than through Weston and Sudbury, the road they came.

"These people won't fight, will they?" asked Ensign De Bernicre.

"There goes a man who will fight you to the death," answered Mr. Bliss, pointing to his brother Tom, busy in a distant field.

The Ensign swore again, and gave a stamp that brought his heavy heel down on poor Tabby's hand as she leaned forward to catch every word. The cruel blow nearly forced a cry from her; but she bit her lips and never stirred, though faint with pain. When she could listen again, Mr. Bliss was telling all he knew about the hiding places of the powder, grain, and cannon the enemy wished to capture and destroy. He could not tell much, for the secrets had been well kept; but if he had known that our young Rebel was taking notes of his words under his own table, he might have been less ready to betray his neighbors. No one suspected a listener, however, and all Tabby could do was to scowl at three pairs of muddy boots, and wish she were a man that she might fight the wearers of them.

She very nearly had a chance to fight or fly; for just as they were preparing to leave the table a sudden sneeze nearly undid her. She thought she was lost, and hid her face, expecting to be dragged out to instant death, perhaps, by the wrathful men of war.

"What's that?" exclaimed the Ensign, as a sudden pause followed that fatal sound.

"It came from under the table," added Captain Brown, and a hand lifted a corner of the cloth.

A shiver went through Tabby, and she held her breath, with her eye upon that big, brown hand; but the next moment she could have laughed with joy, for pussy saved her. The cat had come to doze on her warm skirts, and when the cloth was raised, fancying he was to be fed by his master, Puss rose and walked out purring loudly, tail erect, with its white tip waving like a flag of truce.

"'Tis but the old cat, gentlemen. A good beast, and, fortunately for us, unable to report our conference," said Mr. Bliss, with an air of relief, for he had started guiltily at the bare idea of an eavesdropper.

"He sneezed as if he were as great a snuff-taker as an old woman of whom we asked our way above here," laughed the Ensign, as they all rose.

"And there she is now, coming along as if our grenadiers were after her!" exclaimed the Captain, as the sound of steps and a wailing voice came nearer and nearer.

Tabby took a long breath, and vowed that she would beg or buy the dear old cat that had saved her from destruction. Then she forgot her own danger in listening to the poor woman, who came in crying that her neighbors said she must leave town at once, for they would tar and feather a body for showing spies the road to a Tory's house.

"Well for me I came and heard their plots, or I might be sent off in like case," thought the girl, feeling that the more perils she encountered, the greater heroine she would be.

Mr. Bliss comforted the old soul, bidding her stay there till the neighbors forgot her, and the officers gave her some money to pay for the costly service she had done them. Then they left the room, and after some delay the three men set off; but Tabby was compelled to stay in her hiding-place till the table was cleared, and the women deep in gossip as they washed dishes in the kitchen. Then the little spy crept out softly, and raising the window with great care, ran away as fast as her stiff limbs would carry her.

By the time she reached the Deacon's, however, and told her tale, the Tories were well on their way, Mr. Bliss having provided them with horses that his own flight might be the speedier.

So they escaped; but the warning was given, and Tabby received great praise for her hour under the table. The towns-people hastened their preparations, and had time to remove the most valuable stores to neighboring towns; to mount their cannon and drill their minute-men; for these resolute farmers meant to resist oppression, and the world knows how well they did it when the hour came.

Such an early spring had not been known for years; and by the 19th of April fruit trees were in bloom, winter grain was up, and the stately elms that fringed the river and overarched the village streets were budding fast. It seemed a pity that such a lovely world should be disturbed by strife; but liberty was dearer than prosperity or peace, and the people leaped from their beds when young Dr. Prescott came, riding for his life, with the message Paul Revere brought from Boston in the night:

"Arm! arm! the British are coming!"

Like an electric spark the news ran from house to house, and men made ready to fight, while the brave women bade them go, and did their best to guard the treasure confided to their keeping. A little later, word came that the British were at Lexington, and blood had been shed. Then the farmers shouldered their guns with few words but stern faces, and by sunrise a hundred men stood ready with good Parson Emerson at their head. More men were coming in from the neighboring towns, and all felt that the hour had arrived when patience ceased to be a virtue and rebellion was just.

Great was the excitement everywhere; but at Captain David Brown's one little heart beat high with hope and fear as Tabby stood at the door, looking across the river to the town, where drums were beating, bells ringing, and people hurrying to and fro.

"I can't fight, but I *must* see," she said; and catching up her cloak, she ran over the North Bridge, promising her aunt to return and bring her word as soon as the enemy appeared.

"What news—are they coming?" called the people from the Manse and the few houses that then stood along that road. But Tabby could only shake her head and run the faster in her eagerness to see what was happening on that memorable day. When she reached the middle of the town she found that the little company had gone along the Lexington road to meet the enemy. Nothing daunted, she hurried in that direction and, climbing a high bank, waited to catch a glimpse of the British grenadiers, of whom she had heard so much.

About seven o'clock they came, the sun glittering on the arms of eight hundred English soldiers marching toward the hundred stout-hearted farmers, who waited till they were within a few rods of them.

"Let us stand our ground; and if we die, let us die here," said brave Parson Emerson, still among his people, ready for anything but surrender.

"Nay," said a cautious Lincoln man, "it will not do for us to *begin* the war."

So they reluctantly fell back to the town, the British following slowly, being weary with their seven-mile march over the hills from Lexington. Coming to a little brown house perched on the hillside, one of the thirsty officers spied a well, with the bucket swinging at the end of the long pole. Running up the bank, he was about to drink, when a girl, who was crouching behind the well, sprang up, and with an energetic gesture, flung the water in his face, crying:

"That's the way we serve spies!"

Before Ensign De Bernicre—for it was he, acting as guide to the enemy—could clear his eyes and dry his drenched face, Tabby was gone over the hill with a laugh and a defiant gesture toward the red-coats below.

In high feather at this exploit, she darted about the town, watching the British at their work of destruction. They cut down and burnt the liberty pole, broke open sixty barrels of flour, flung five hundred pounds of balls into the mill-pond and wells, and set the court-house on fire. Other parties were ordered to different quarters of the town to ransack houses and destroy all the stores they found. Captain Parsons was sent to take possession of the North Bridge, and De Bernicre led the way, for he had taken notes on his former visit, and was a good guide. As they marched, a little scarlet figure went flying on before them, and vanished at the turn of the road. It was Tabby hastening home to warn her aunt.

"Quick child, whip on this gown and cap and hurry into bed. These prying fellows will surely have pity on a sick girl, and respect this room if no other," said Mrs. Brown, briskly helping Tabby into a short night-gown and round cap, and tucking her well up when she was laid down, for between the plump feather beds were hidden many muskets, the most precious of their stores. This had been planned beforehand, and Tabby was glad to rest and tell her tale while Aunty Brown put physic bottles and glasses on the table, set some evil-smelling herbs to simmer on the hearth, and, compromising with her conscience, concocted a nice little story to tell the invaders.

Presently they came, and it was well for Tabby that the Ensign remained below to guard the doors while the men ransacked the house from garret to cellar, for he might have recognized the saucy girl who had twice maltreated him.

"These are feathers; lift the covers carefully or you'll be half smothered, they fly about so," said Mrs. Brown, as the men came to some casks of cartridges and flints, which she had artfully ripped up several pillows to conceal.

Quite deceived, the men gladly passed on, leaving the very things they most wanted to destroy. Coming to the bed-room, where more treasures of the same valuable sort were hidden in various nooks and corners, the dame held up her finger, saying, with an anxious glance toward Tabby:

"Step softly, please. You wouldn't harm a poor, sick girl. The doctor thinks it is small-pox, and a fright might kill her. I keep the chamber as fresh as I can with herbs, so I guess there isn't much danger of catching it."

The men reluctantly looked in, saw a flushed face on the pillow (for Tabby was red with running, and her black eyes wild with excitement), took a sniff at the wormwood and motherwort, and with a hasty glance into a closet or two where sundry clothes concealed hidden doors, hastily retired to report the danger and get away as soon as possible.

They would have been much disgusted at the trick played upon them if they had seen the sick girl fly out of bed and dance a jig of joy as they tramped away to Barrett's Mills. But soon Tabby had no heart for merriment as she watched the Minute-Men gather by the bridge, saw the British march down on the other side, and when their first volley killed brave Isaac Davis and Abner Hosmer, of Acton, she heard Major Buttrick give the order, "Fire, fellow-soldiers; for God's sake, fire!"

For a little while shots rang, smoke rose, shouts were heard, and red and blue coats mingled in the struggle on the bridge. Then the British fell back, leaving two dead soldiers behind them. These were buried where they fell; and the bodies of the Acton men were sent home to their poor wives, Concord's first martyrs for liberty.

No need to tell more of the story of that day; all children know it, and many have made a pilgrimage to see the old monument set up where the English fell, and the bronze *Minute-Man*, standing on his granite pedestal to mark the spot where the brave Concord farmers fired the shot that made the old North Bridge immortal.

We must follow Tabby, and tell how she got her table-cloth. When the fight was over, the dead buried, the wounded cared for, and the prisoners exchanged, the Tories were punished. Dr. Lee was confined to his own farm on penalty of being shot if he left it, and the property of Daniel Bliss was confiscated by government. Some things were sold at auction, and Captain Brown bought the fine cloth and gave it to Tabby, saying heartily:

"There, my girl, that belongs to you, and you may well be proud of it; for thanks to your quick wits and eyes and ears we were not taken unawares, but sent the red-coats back faster than they came."

And Tabby *was* proud of it, keeping it carefully, displaying it with immense satisfaction when she told the story, and spinning busily to make a set of napkins to go with it. It covered the table when her wedding supper was spread, was used at the christening of her first boy, and for many a Thanksgiving and Christmas dinner through the happy years of her married life.

Then it was preserved by her daughters as a relic of their mother's youth, and long after the old woman was gone, the well-worn cloth still appeared on great occasions, till it grew too thin for anything but careful keeping, to illustrate the story so proudly told by the grandchildren, who found it hard to believe that the feeble old lady of ninety could be the lively lass who played her little part in the Revolution with such spirit.

In 1861, Tabby's table-cloth saw another war, and made an honorable end. When men were called for, Concord responded "Here!" and sent a goodly number, led by another, brave Colonel Prescott. Barretts, Hosmers, Melvins, Browns, and Wheelers stood shoulder to shoulder, as their grandfathers stood that day to meet the British by the bridge. Mothers said, "Go, my son," as bravely as before, and sisters and sweethearts smiled with wet eyes as the boys in blue marched away again, cheered on by another noble Emerson. More than one of Tabby's descendants went, some to fight, some to nurse; and for four long years the old town worked and waited, hoped and prayed, burying the dear dead boys sent home, nursing those who brought back honorable wounds, and sending more to man the breaches made by the awful battles that filled both North and South with a wilderness of graves.

The women knit and sewed, Sundays as well as week days, to supply the call for clothes; the men emptied their pockets freely, glad to give, and the minister, after preaching like a Christian soldier, took off his coat and packed boxes of comforts like a tender father.

"More lint and bandages called for, and I do believe we've torn and picked up every old rag in the town," said one busy lady to another, as several sat together making comfort-bags in the third year of the long struggle.

"I have cleared my garret of nearly everything in it, and only wish I had more to give," answered one of the patriotic Barrett mothers.

"We can't buy anything so soft and good as worn-out sheets and table-cloths. New ones won't do, or I'd cut up every one of mine," said a newly married Wheeler, sewing for dear life, as she remembered the many cousins gone to the war.

"I think I shall have to give our Revolutionary table-cloth. It's old enough, and soft as silk, and I'm sure my blessed grandmother would think that it couldn't make a better end," spoke up white-headed Madam Hubbard, for Tabby Tarbell had married one of that numerous and worthy race.

"Oh, you wouldn't cut up that famous cloth, would you?" cried the younger woman.

"Yes, I will. It's in rags, and when I'm gone no one will care for it. Folks don't seem to remember what the women did in those days, so it's no use keeping relics of 'em," answered the old lady, who would have owned herself mistaken if she could have looked forward to 1876, when the town celebrated its centennial, and proudly exhibited the little scissors with which Mrs. Barrett cut paper for cartridges, among other ancient trophies of that earlier day.

So the ancient cloth was carefully made into a box-full of the finest lint and softest squares to lay on wounds, and sent to one of the Concord women who had gone as a nurse.

"Here's a treasure!" she said, as she came to it among other comforts newly arrived from home. "Just what I want for my brave Rebel and poor little Johnny Bullard."

The "brave Rebel" was a Southern man who had fought well and was badly wounded in many ways, yet never complained; and in the midst of great suffering was always so courteous, patient, and courageous, that the men called him "our gentleman," and tried to show how much they respected so gallant a foe. John Bullard was an English drummer boy, who had been through several battles, stoutly drumming away in spite of bullets and cannon-balls; cheering many a camp-fire with his voice, for he sang like a blackbird, and was always merry, always plucky, and so great a favorite in his regiment, that all mourned for "little Johnny" when his right arm was shot off at Gettysburg. It was thought he would die; but he pulled through the worst of it, and was slowly struggling back to health, still trying to be gay, and beginning to chirp feebly now and then, like a convalescent bird.

"Here, Johnny, is some splendid lint for this poor arm, and some of the softest compresses for Carrol's wound. He is asleep, so I'll begin with you, and while I work I'll amuse you with the story of the old table-cloth this lint came from," said Nurse May, as she stood by the bed where the thin, white face smiled at her, though the boy dreaded the hard quarter of an hour he had to endure every day.

"Thanky, mum. We 'aven't 'ad a story for a good bit. I'm 'arty this mornin', and think I'll be hup by this day week, won't I?"

"I hope so. Now shut your eyes and listen; then you won't mind the twinges I give you, gentle as I try to be," answered the nurse, beginning her painful task.

Then she told the story of Tabby's table-cloth, and the boy enjoyed it immensely, laughing out at the slapping and the throwing water in the ensign's face, and openly rejoicing when the red-coats got the worst of it.

"As we've beaten all the rest of the world, I don't mind our 'aving bad luck that time. We har' friends now, and I'll fight for you, mum, like a British bull-dog, if I hever get the chance," said Johnny, when the tale and dressing were ended.

"So you shall. I like to turn a brave enemy into a faithful friend, as I hope we shall yet be able to do with our southern brothers. I admire their courage and their loyalty to what they believe to be right; and we are all suffering the punishment we deserve for waiting till this sad war came, instead of settling the trouble years ago, as we might have done if we had loved honesty and honor more than money and power."

As she spoke, Miss Hunt turned to her other patient, and saw by the expression of his face that he had heard both the tale and the talk.

He smiled, and said, "Good morning," as usual, but when she stooped to lay a compress of the soft, wet damask on the angry wound in his breast, he whispered, with a grateful look:

"You *have* changed one 'southern brother' from an enemy into a friend. Whether I live or die, I never can forget how generous and kind you have all been to me."

"Thank you! It is worth months of anxiety and care to hear such words. Let us shake hands, and do our best to make North and South as good friends as England and America now are," said the nurse, offering her hand.

"Me, too! I've got one 'and left, and I give it ye with all me 'art. God bless ye, sir, and a lively getting hup for the two of us!" cried Johnny, stretching across the narrow space that divided the beds, with a beaming face and true English readiness to forgive a fallen foe when he had proved a brave one.

The three hands met in a warm shake, and the act was a little lesson more eloquent than words to the lookers-on; for the spirit of brotherhood that should bind us all together worked the miracle of linking these three by the frail threads spun a century ago. So Tabby's table-cloth did make a beautiful and useful end at last.

First published in the February 1884 edition of *St. Nicholas Magazine*

Onawandah

from the "Spinning-Wheel" series

BY LOUISA MAY ALCOTT

LONG AGO, WHEN hostile Indians haunted the great forests, and every settle-ment had its fort for the protection of the inhabitants, in one of the towns on the Connecticut River lived Parson Bain and his little son and daughter. The wife and mother was dead; but an old servant took care of them, and did her best to make Reuben and Eunice good children. Her direst threat, when they were naughty, was, "The Indians will come and fetch you, if you don't behave." So they grew up in great fear of the red men. Even the friendly Indians, who sometimes came for food or powder, were regarded with suspicion by the people. No man went to work with-out his gun near by. On Sundays, when they trudged to the rude meeting-house, all carried the trusty rifle on the shoulder, and while the pastor preached, a sentinel mounted guard at the door, to give warning if canoes came down the river or a dark face peered from the wood.

One autumn night, when the first heavy rains were falling and a cold wind whistled through the valley, a knock came at the minister's door and, opening it, he found an Indian boy, ragged, hungry, and foot-sore, who begged for food and shelter. In his broken way, he told how he had fallen ill and been left to die by ene-mies who had taken him from his own people, months before; how he had wan-dered for days till almost sinking; and that he had come now to ask for help, led by the hospitable light in the parsonage window.

"Send him away, Master, or harm will come of it. He is a spy, and we shall all be scalped by the murdering Injuns who are waiting in the wood," said old Becky, harshly; while little Eunice hid in the old servant's ample skirts, and twelve-year-old Reuben laid his hand on his cross-bow, ready to defend his sister if need be.

But the good man drew the poor lad in, saying, with his friendly smile: "Shall not a Christian be as hospitable as a godless savage? Come in, child, and be fed; you sorely need rest and shelter."

Leaving his face to express the gratitude he had no words to tell, the boy sat by the comfortable fire and ate like a famished wolf, while Becky muttered her fore-bodings and the children eyed the dark youth at a safe distance. Something in his pinched face, wounded foot, and eyes full of dumb pain and patience, touched the little girl's tender heart, and, yielding to a pitiful impulse, she brought her own basin of new milk and, setting it beside the stranger, ran to hide behind her father, suddenly remembering that this was one of the dreaded Indians.

"That was well done, little daughter. Thou shalt love thine enemies, and share thy bread with the needy. See, he is smiling; that pleased him, and he wishes us to be his friends."

But Eunice ventured no more that night, and quaked in her little bed at the thought of the strange boy sleeping on a blanket before the fire below. Reuben hid his fears better, and resolved to watch while others slept; but was off as soon as his curly head touched the pillow, and dreamed of tomahawks and war-whoops till morning.

Next day, neighbors came to see the waif, and one and all advised sending him away as soon as possible, since he was doubtless a spy, as Becky said, and would bring trouble of some sort.

"When he is well, he may go whither-soever he will; but while he is too lame to walk, weak with hunger, and worn out with weariness, I will harbor him. He can not feign suffering and starvation like this. I shall do my duty, and leave the consequences to the Lord," answered the parson, with such pious firmness that the neighbors said no more.

But they kept a close watch upon Onawandah, when he went among them, silent and submissive, but with the proud air of a captive prince, and sometimes a fierce flash in his black eyes when the other lads taunted him with his red skin. He was very lame for weeks, and could only sit in the sun, weaving pretty baskets for Eunice, and shaping bows and arrows for Reuben. The children were soon his friends, for with them he was always gentle, trying in his soft language and expressive gestures to show his good will and gratitude; for they defended him against their ruder playmates, and, following their father's example, trusted and cherished the homeless youth.

When he was able to walk, he taught the boy to shoot and trap the wild creatures of the wood, to find fish where others failed, and to guide himself in the wilderness by star and sun, wind and water. To Eunice he brought little offerings of bark and feathers; taught her to make moccasins of skin, belts of shells, or pouches gay with porcupine quills and colored grass. He would not work for old Becky—who plainly showed her distrust—saying: "A brave does not grind corn and bring wood; that is squaw's work. Onawandah will hunt and fish and fight for you, but no more." And even the request of the parson could not win obedience in this, though the boy would have died for the good man.

"We can not tame an eagle as we can a barn-yard fowl. Let him remember only kindness of us, and so we turn a foe into a friend," said Parson Bain, stroking the sleek, dark head, that always bowed before him, with a docile reverence shown to no other living creature.

Winter came, and the settlers fared hardly through the long months, when the drifts rose to the eaves of their low cabins, and the stores, carefully harvested, failed to supply even their simple wants.

But the minister's family never lacked wild meat, for Onawandah proved himself a better hunter than any man in the town, and the boy of sixteen led the way on his snow-shoes when they went to track a bear to its den, chase the deer for miles, or shoot the wolves that howled about their homes in the winter nights.

But he never joined in their games, and sat apart when the young folk made merry, as if he scorned such childish pastimes and longed to be a man in all things. Why he stayed when he was well again, no one could tell, unless he waited for spring to make his way to his own people. But Reuben and Eunice rejoiced to keep him; for while he taught them many things, he was their pupil also, learning English rapidly, and proving himself a very affectionate and devoted friend and servant, in his own quiet way.

"Be of good cheer, little daughter; I shall be gone but three days, and our brave Onawandah will guard you well," said the parson, one April morning, as he mounted his horse to visit a distant settlement, where the bitter winter had brought sickness and death to more than one household.

The boy showed his white teeth in a bright smile as he stood beside the children, while Becky croaked, with a shake of the head:

"I hope you mayn't find you've warmed a viper in your bosom, Master."

Two days later, it seemed as if Becky was a true prophet, and that the confiding minister *had* been terribly deceived; for Onawandah went away to hunt, and, that night, the awful war-whoop woke the sleeping villagers to find their houses burning, while the hidden Indians shot at them by the light of the fires kindled by dusky scouts. In terror and confusion the whites flew to the fort; and, while the men fought bravely, the women held blankets to catch arrows and bullets, or bound up the hurts of their defenders.

It was all over by daylight, and the red men sped away up the river, with several prisoners, and such booty as they could plunder from the deserted houses. Not till all fear of a return of their enemies was over, did the poor people venture to leave the fort and seek their ruined homes. Then it was discovered that Becky and the parson's children were gone, and great was the bewailing, for the good man was much beloved by all his flock.

Suddenly the smothered voice of Becky was heard by a party of visitors, calling dolefully:

"I am here, betwixt the beds. Pull me out, neighbors, for I am half dead with fright and smothering."

The old woman was quickly extricated from her hiding-place, and with much energy declared that she had seen Onawandah, disguised with war-paint, among the Indians, and that he had torn away the children from her arms before she could fly from the house.

"He chose his time well, when they were defenseless, dear lambs! Spite of all my warnings, Master trusted him, and this is the thanks we get. Oh, my poor master! How can I tell him this heavy news?"

There was no need to tell it; for, as Becky sat moaning and beating her breast on the fireless hearth, and the sympathizing neighbors stood about her, the sound of a horse's hoofs was heard, and the parson came down the hilly road like one riding for his life. He had seen the smoke afar off, guessed the sad truth, and hurried on, to find his home in ruins and to learn by his first glance at the faces around him that his children were gone.

When he had heard all there was to tell, he sat down upon his door-stone with his head in his hands, praying for strength to bear a grief too deep for words. The wounded and weary men tried to comfort him with hope, and the women wept with him as they hugged their own babies closer to the hearts that ached for the lost children. Suddenly a stir went through the mournful group, as Onawandah came from the wood with a young deer upon his shoulders, and amazement in his face as he saw the desolation before him. Dropping his burden, he stood an instant looking with eyes that kindled fiercely; then he came bounding toward them, undaunted by the hatred, suspicion, and surprise plainly written on the countenances before him. He missed his playmates, and asked but one question:

"The boy? the little squaw?—where gone?"

His answer was a rough one, for the men seized him and poured forth the tale, heaping reproaches upon him for such treachery and ingratitude. He bore it all in proud silence till they pointed to the poor father whose dumb sorrow was more eloquent than all their wrath. Onawandah looked at him, and the fire died out of his eyes as if quenched by the tears he would not shed. Shaking off the hands that held him, he went to his good friend, saying with passionate earnestness:

"Onawandah is *not* traitor! Onawandah remembers. Onawandah grateful! You believe?"

The poor parson looked up at him, and could not doubt his truth; for genuine love and sorrow ennobled the dark face, and he had never known the boy to lie.

"I believe and trust you still, but others will not. Go, you are no longer safe here, and I have no home to offer you," said the parson, sadly, feeling that he cared for none, unless his children were restored to him.

"Onawandah has no fear. He goes; but he comes again to bring the boy, the little squaw."

Few words, but they were so solemnly spoken that the most unbelieving were impressed; for the youth laid one hand on the gray head bowed before him, and lifted the other toward heaven, as if calling the Great Spirit to hear his vow.

A relenting murmur went through the crowd, but the boy paid no heed, as he turned away, and with no arms but his hunting knife and bow, no food but such as he could find, no guide but the sun by day, the stars by night, plunged into the pathless forest and was gone.

Then the people drew a long breath, and muttered to one another:

"He will never do it, yet he is a brave lad for his years."

"Only a shift to get off with a whole skin, I warrant you. These varlets are as cunning as foxes," added Becky, sourly.

The parson alone believed and hoped, though weeks and months went by, and his children did not come.

MEANTIME, REUBEN AND EUNICE were far away in an Indian camp, resting as best they could, after the long journey that followed that dreadful night. Their captors were not cruel to them, for Reuben was a stout fellow and, thanks to Onawandah, could hold his own with the boys who would have tormented him if he had been feeble or cowardly. Eunice also was a hardy creature for her years, and when her first fright and fatigue were over, made herself useful in many ways among the squaws, who did not let the pretty child suffer greatly; though she was neglected, because they knew no better.

Life in a wigwam was not a life of ease, and fortunately the children were accustomed to simple habits and the hardships that all endured in those early times. But they mourned for home till their young faces were pathetic with the longing, and their pillows of dry leaves were often wet with tears in the night. Their clothes grew ragged, their hair unkempt, their faces tanned by sun and wind. Scanty food and exposure to all weathers tried the strength of their bodies, and uncertainty as to their fate saddened their spirits; yet they bore up bravely, and said their prayers faithfully, feeling sure that God would bring them home to father in His own good time.

One day, when Reuben was snaring birds in the wood—for the Indians had no fear of such young children venturing to escape—he heard the cry of a quail, and followed it deeper and deeper into the forest, till it ceased, and, with a sudden rustle, Onawandah rose up from the brakes, his finger on his lips to prevent any exclamation that might betray him to other ears and eyes.

"I come for you and little Laraka"—(the name he gave Eunice, meaning "Wild Rose"). "I take you home. Not know me yet. Go and wait."

He spoke low and fast; but the joy in his face told how glad he was to find the boy after his long search, and Reuben clung to him, trying not to disgrace himself by crying like a girl, in his surprise and delight.

Lying hidden in the tall brakes they talked in whispers, while one told of the capture, and the other of a plan of escape; for, though a friendly tribe, these Indians were not Onawandah's people, and they must not suspect that he knew the children, else they might be separated at once.

"Little squaw betray me. You watch her. Tell her not to cry out, not speak me any time. When I say come, we go—fast—in the night. Not ready yet."

These were the orders Reuben received, and, when he could compose himself, he went back to the wigwams, leaving his friend in the wood, while he told the good news to Eunice, and prepared her for the part she must play.

Fear had taught her self-control, and the poor child stood the test well, working off her relief and rapture by pounding corn in the stone mortar till her little hands were blistered, and her arms ached for hours afterward.

Not till the next day did Onawandah make his appearance, and then he came limping into the village, weary, lame, and half starved after his long wandering in the wilderness. He was kindly welcomed, and his story believed, for he told only the first part, and said nothing of his life among the white men. He hardly glanced at the children when they were pointed out to him by their captors, and scowled at poor Eunice, who forgot her part in her joy, and smiled as she met the dark eyes, that till now had always looked kindly at her. A touch from Reuben warned her, and she was glad to hide her confusion by shaking her long hair over her face, as if afraid of the stranger.

Onawandah took no further notice of them, but seemed to be very lame with the old wound in his foot, which prevented his being obliged to hunt with the men. He was resting and slowly gathering strength for the hard task he had set himself, while he waited for a safe time to save the children. They understood, but the suspense proved too much for little Eunice, and she pined with impatience to be gone. She lost appetite and color, and cast such appealing glances at Onawandah, that he could not seem quite indifferent, and gave her a soft word now and then, or did such acts of kindness as he could perform unsuspected. When she lay awake at night thinking of home, a cricket would chirp outside the wigwam, and a hand slip in a leaf full of berries, or a bark-cup of fresh water for the feverish little mouth. Sometimes it was only a caress or a whisper of encouragement, that reassured the childish heart, and sent her to sleep with a comfortable sense of love and protection, like a sheltering wing over a motherless bird.

Reuben stood it better, and entered heartily into the excitement of the plot, for he had grown tall and strong in these trying months, and felt that he must prove himself a man to sustain and defend his sister. Quietly he put away each day a bit of dried meat, a handful of parched corn, or a well-sharpened arrowhead, as provision for the journey; while Onawandah seemed to be amusing himself with making moccasins and a little vest of deer-skin for an Indian child about the age of Eunice.

At last, in the early autumn, all the men went off on the war-path, leaving only boys and women behind. Then Onawandah's eyes began to kindle, and Reuben's heart to beat fast, for both felt that their time for escape had come.

All was ready, and one moonless night the signal was given. A cricket chirped shrilly outside the tent where the children slept with one old squaw. A strong hand cut the skin beside their bed of fir boughs, and two trembling creatures crept out to follow the tall shadow that flitted noiselessly before them into the darkness of the wood. Not a broken twig, a careless step, or a whispered word betrayed them, and they vanished as swiftly and silently as hunted deer flying for their lives.

Till dawn they hurried on, Onawandah carrying Eunice, whose strength soon failed, and Reuben manfully shouldering the hatchet and the pouch of food. At sunrise they hid in a thicket by a spring and rested, while waiting for the friendly night to come again. Then they pushed on, and fear gave wings to their feet, so that by another morning they were far enough away to venture to travel more slowly and sleep at night.

If the children had learned to love and trust the Indian boy in happier times, they adored him now, and came to regard him as an earthly Providence, so faithful, brave, and tender was he; so forgetful of himself, so bent on saving them. He never seemed to sleep, ate the poorest morsels, or went without any food when provision failed; let no danger daunt him, no hardship wring complaint from him; but went on through the wild forest, led by guides invisible to them, till they began to hope that home was near.

Twice he saved their lives. Once, when he went in search of food, leaving Reuben to guard his sister, the children, being very hungry, ignorantly ate some poisonous berries which looked like wild cherries, and were deliciously sweet. The boy generously gave most of them to Eunice, and soon was terror-stricken to see her grow pale and cold and deathly ill. Not knowing what to do, he could only rub her hands and call wildly for Onawandah.

The name echoed through the silent wood, and, though far away, the keen ear of the Indian heard it, his fleet feet brought him back in time, and his knowledge of wild roots and herbs made it possible to save the child when no other help was at hand.

"Make fire. Keep warm. I soon come," he said, after hearing the story and examining Eunice, who could only lift her eyes to him, full of childish confidence and patience.

Then he was off again, scouring the woods like a hound on the scent, searching everywhere for the precious little herb that would counteract the poison. Any one watching him would have thought him crazy as he rushed hither and thither, tearing up the leaves, creeping on his hands and knees that it might not escape him, and when he found it, springing up with a cry that startled the birds, and carried hope to poor Reuben, who was trying to forget his own pain in his anxiety for Eunice, whom he thought dying.

"Eat, eat, while I make drink. All safe now," cried Onawandah, as he came leaping toward them with his hands full of green leaves, and his dark face shining with joy.

Suddenly he rose, and in his own musical
language prayed to the Great Spirit.

The boy was soon relieved, but for hours they hung over the girl, who suffered sadly, till she grew unconscious and lay as if dead. Reuben's courage failed then, and he cried bitterly, thinking how hard it would be to leave the dear little creature under the pines and go home alone to father. Even Onawandah lost hope for a while, and sat like a bronze statue of despair, with his eyes fixed on his Wild Rose, who seemed fading away too soon.

Suddenly he rose, stretched his arms to the west, where the sun was setting splendidly, and in his own musical language prayed to the Great Spirit. The Christian boy fell upon his knees, feeling that the only help was in the Father who saw and heard them even in the wilderness. Both were comforted, and when they turned to Eunice there was a faint tinge of color on the pale cheeks, as if the evening red kissed her, the look of pain was gone, and she slept quietly without the moans that had made their hearts ache before.

"He hears! he hears!' cried Onawandah, and for the first time Reuben saw tears in his keen eyes, as the Indian boy turned his face to the sky full of a gratitude that no words were sweet enough to tell.

All night, Eunice lay peacefully sleeping, and the moon lighted Onawandah's lonely watch, for the boy Reuben was worn out with suspense, and slept beside his sister.

In the morning she was safe, and great was the rejoicing; but for two days the little invalid was not allowed to continue the journey, much as they longed to hurry on. It was a pretty sight, the bed of hemlock boughs spread under a green tent of woven branches, and on the pillow of moss the pale child watching the flicker of sunshine through the leaves, listening to the babble of a brook close by, or sleeping tranquilly, lulled by the murmur of the pines. Patient, loving, and grateful, it was a pleasure to serve her, and both the lads were faithful nurses. Onawandah cooked birds for her to eat, and made a pleasant drink of the wild raspberry leaves to quench her thirst. Reuben snared rabbits, that she might have nourishing food, and longed to shoot a deer for provision, that she might not suffer hunger again on their journey. This boyish desire led him deeper into the wood than it was wise for him to go alone, for it was near nightfall, and wild creatures haunted the forest in those days. The fire, which Onawandah kept constantly burning, guarded their little camp where Eunice lay; but Reuben, with no weapon but his bow and hunting knife, was beyond this protection when he at last gave up his vain hunt and turned homeward. Suddenly, the sound of stealthy steps startled him, but he could see nothing through the dusk at first, and hurried on, fearing that some treacherous Indian was following him. Then he remembered his sister, and resolved not to betray her resting-place if he could help it, for he had learned courage of Onawandah, and longed to be as brave and generous as his dusky hero.

So he paused to watch and wait, and soon saw the gleam of two fiery eyes, not behind, but above him, in a tree. Then he knew that it was an "Indian devil," as they called a species of fierce wildcat that lurked in the thickets and sprang on its prey like a small tiger.

"If I could only kill it alone, how proud Onawandah would be of me," thought Reuben, burning for the good opinion of his friend.

It would have been wiser to hurry on and give the beast no time to spring; but the boy was over bold, and, fitting an arrow to the string, aimed at the bright eye-ball and let fly. A sharp snarl showed that some harm was done, and, rather daunted by the savage sound, Reuben raced away, meaning to come back next day for the prize he hoped he had secured.

But soon he heard the creature bounding after him, and he uttered one ringing shout for help, feeling too late that he had been foolhardy. Fortunately he was nearer camp than he thought. Onawandah heard him and was there in time to receive the wildcat, as, mad with the pain of the wound, it sprung at Reuben. There was no time for words, and the boy could only watch in breathless interest and anxiety the fight which went on between the brute and the Indian.

It was sharp but short, for Onawandah had his knife, and as soon as he could get the snarling, struggling beast down, he killed it with a skillful stroke. But not before it had torn and bitten him more dangerously than he knew; for the dusk hid the wounds, and excitement kept him from feeling them at first. Reuben thanked him heartily, and accepted his few words of warning with grateful docility; then both hurried back to Eunice, who till next day knew nothing of her brother's danger.

Onawandah made light of his scratches, as he called them, got their supper, and sent Reuben early to bed, for tomorrow they were to start again.

Excited by his adventure, the boy slept lightly, and waking in the night, saw by the flicker of the fire Onawandah binding up a deep wound in his breast with wet moss and his own belt. A stifled groan betrayed how much he suffered; but when Reuben went to him, he would accept no help, said it was nothing, and sent him back to bed, preferring to endure the pain in stern silence, with true Indian pride and courage.

Next morning, they set out and pushed on as fast as Eunice's strength allowed. But it was evident that Onawandah suffered much, though he would not rest, forbade the children to speak of his wounds, and pressed on with feverish haste, as if he feared that his strength might not hold out. Reuben watched him anxiously, for there was a look in his face that troubled the boy and filled him with alarm, as well as with remorse and love. Eunice would not let him carry her as before, but trudged bravely behind him, though her feet ached and her breath often failed as she tried to keep up; and both children did all they could to comfort and sustain their friend, who seemed glad to give his life for them.

In three days they reached the river, and, as if Heaven helped them in their greatest need, found a canoe, left by some hunter, near the shore. In they sprang, and let the swift current bear them along, Eunice kneeling in the bow like a little figure-head of Hope, Reuben steering with his paddle, and Onawandah sitting with arms tightly folded over his breast, as if to control the sharp anguish of the neglected wound. He knew that it was past help now, and only cared to see the children safe; then, worn out but happy, he was proud to die, having paid his debt to the good parson, and proved that he was not a liar nor a traitor.

Hour after hour they floated down the great river, looking eagerly for signs of home, and when at last they entered the familiar valley, while the little girl cried for joy, and the boy paddled as he had never done before, Onawandah sat erect with his haggard eyes fixed on the dim distance, and sang his death-song in a clear, strong voice—though every breath was pain—bent on dying like a brave, without complaint or fear.

At last they saw the smoke from the cabins on the hillside and, hastily mooring the canoe, all sprung out, eager to be at home after their long and perilous wandering. But as his foot touched the land, Onawandah felt that he could do no more, and stretching his arms toward the parsonage, the windows of which glimmered as hospitably as they had done when he first saw them, he said, with a pathetic sort of triumph in his broken voice: "Go. I can not—tell the good father, Onawandah not lie, not forget. He keep his promise."

Then he dropped upon the grass and lay as if dead, while Reuben, bidding Eunice keep watch, ran as fast as his tired legs could carry him to tell the tale and bring help.

The little girl did her part tenderly, carrying water in her hands to wet the white lips, tearing up her ragged skirt to lay fresh bandages on the wound that had been bleeding the brave boy's life away, and, sitting by him, gathered his head into her arms, begging him to wait till father came.

But poor Onawandah had waited too long; now he could only look up into the dear, loving, little face bent over him, and whisper wistfully: "Wild Rose will remember Onawandah?" as the light went out of his eyes, and his last breath was a smile for her.

When the parson and his people came hurrying up full of wonder, joy, and good-will, they found Eunice weeping bitterly, and the Indian boy lying like a young warrior smiling at death.

"Ah, my neighbors, the savage has taught us a lesson we never can forget. Let us imitate his virtues, and do honor to his memory," said the pastor, as he held his little daughter close and looked down at the pathetic figure at his feet, whose silence was more eloquent than any words.

All felt it, and even old Becky had a remorseful sigh for the boy who had kept his word so well and given back her darlings safe.

They buried him where he lay; and for years the lonely mound under the great oak was kept green by loving hands. Wild roses bloomed there, and the murmur of the Long River of Pines was a fit lullaby for faithful Onawandah.

First published in the April 1884 edition of *St. Nicholas Magazine*

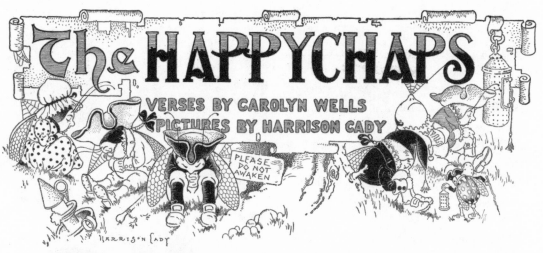

O LD Woodchopper Chip was brave and strong,
Old Woodchopper Chip was good;
And he always whistled a gay little song,
And merrily smiled as he strode along
Through the Adirondack wood.
And whenever he'd stop,
And go "chippity-chop,"
Before you knew it a tree would drop!
Elm and maple and beech and ash,
Under his ax would fall down, *crash!*
The chips would fly
'most up to the sky,
Old Woodchopper Chip was so strong and spry.
One day he thought 'twould be a good joke
To chop down the old "Centennial Oak."
Now, that tree, as Chip had been frequently told,
Was several more than a hundred years old;

*They heard the sound
of bursting bombs.*

They slept and slept in the old hollow oak.

'Way back in the days of the Revolution,
'Twas an old time-honored institution.
It rose so high, and it spread so wide,
'Twas easily king of the countryside,
But Chip didn't care, and he laughed
with glee,
As he chippity-chopped at the old oak
tree.
Now, this is the strange part. In days
long gone,
A hundred or so
Of years ago,
While the Revolution was going on,
The dear little, queer little Happychaps,
(You never have heard that name,
perhaps,
But they were the teeniest, weeniest
race
That ever lived in any place.)

Then the tree fell down with a crashing loud,
And the Happychaps all swarmed out in a crowd.

When they heard the sound
Of the guns all 'round,
The rolling drums,
And the bursting bombs,
The cannon's flash,
And the "bang! boom!! crash!!!"
They shook and shivered,
And quaked and quivered,
For a Revolution in full swing,
Is a noisier noise than anything!

Now, what do you think these
Happychaps did?
To the old oak tree they ran and hid;
And the good old oak
Thought it quite a joke
To shelter the staid little, 'fraid little
folk.
They scrambled in by pairs and dozens,
Fathers and mothers and aunts and
cousins;
Helter-skelter they crowded in,
And thus shut out the war's loud din.

General Happychap spoke up loud.

General Happychap meets Sir Horace Hoptoad.

But in that great big hollow tree,
There was nothing to do, and so you see,
Each Happychap
Took off shoes and cap,
And lay down for a cozy, dozy nap.
Then what do you think those
Happychaps did?
So well they were sheltered, so snug
they were hid
They slept and slept in the old hollow
oak,
And they never awoke
When morning broke;
The days went by, and still they slept;
The weeks and months into seasons
crept;
Summer and winter and spring and fall—
They just forgot to wake up at all!
The long years into a century rolled,
They slept, regardless of heat or cold,
They slept away,
Till the fateful day,
When Woodchopper Chip came by their
way.
When his big, sharp ax
With resounding whacks,
On the old oak tree made swift attacks,
Each Happychap's eyes flew open wide;
"What's that?" each Happychap loudly
cried.
Chip! chop!! the blows fell fast and thick,

The Happychaps bounced out of bed
right quick.
Then the tree fell down with a crashing
loud,
And the Happychaps all swarmed out in
a crowd.
They tumbled around and they jumped
about,
Beyond all doubt
They were glad to be out!
They sang and they danced,
They capered and pranced,
They frolicked,
And rollicked,
And all seemed entranced
To see once more the shining sun,
And they thought another day had
begun!

Professor Happychap, old and wise,
Tweaked his nose and blinked his eyes;
He listened for boom of cannon or gun,
And hearing none,
He cried, "What fun!
That noisy old war is certainly over,

General Happychap is measured
for a suit of clothes.

And now, my friends, we can live in
clover!"
Then General Happychap spoke up loud,
And made a speech to the listening
crowd.

"Dear fellow Happychaps," he began,
"It seems to me,
That it would be
A thoroughly wise and enjoyable
plan
To invite all the Happychaps, far
and near,
To come and hold a reunion here.
Our present raiment, as you may
see,
Rather worn and faded seems to be,
So I propose
That we get new clothes,
And I hope you'll all agree."

The Happychaps visit Tailor Cricket.

As the General waited for their reply,
Sir Horace Hoptoad came hopping by;
His costume was gorgeous and gay and
grand,
With a smile quite bland,
He held out his hand;
To General Happychap, bowing low,
He said, "I'm glad to see you, but oh!

Who are you, sir, and why are you here?
And these people near,
With their garments queer,
I haven't seen such for many a year!"
"Well, well!" said the General, "you
don't say!
Are these things not the style today?
Then show us the way
To a tailor, I pray,
And we'll gladly purchase some new
array."
Then by Sir Horace Hoptoad led,
To Cricket, the Tailor, the Happychaps
fled.

He measured them carefully, one by one,
And promised their garments by set of
sun.
All sorts of uniforms, all sorts of suits,
Sashes, surtouts,
Bonnets and boots,
Tailor Cricket declared he would have
them done.

The Happychaps then in great elation
Began to make plans for the
celebration;
They planned most wonderful,
marvelous things,
As big as a circus with three or four
rings!
And the story of that, they announce to
their friends,
Will surely be seen
In next month's magazine;
But just here, dear reader, this first
chapter ends.

First published in the January 1908 edition of *St. Nicholas Magazine*

The Proud Little Grain of Wheat

BY FRANCES HODGSON BURNETT

THERE ONCE WAS a little grain of wheat which was very proud indeed. The first thing it remembered was being very much crowded and jostled by a great many other grains of wheat, all living in the same sack in the granary. It was quite dark in the sack, and no one could move about, and so there was nothing to be done but to sit still and talk and think. The proud little grain of wheat talked a great deal, but did not think quite so much, while her next neighbor thought a great deal and only talked when it was asked questions it could answer. It used to say that when it thought a great deal it could remember things which it seemed to have heard a long time ago.

"What is the use of our staying here so long doing nothing, and never being seen by anybody?" the proud little grain once asked.

"I don't know," the learned grain replied. "I don't know the answer to that. Ask me another."

"Why can't I sing like the birds that build their nests in the roof? I should like to sing, instead of sitting here in the dark."

"Because you have no voice," said the learned grain.

This was a very good answer indeed.

"Why didn't someone give me a voice, then—why didn't they?" said the proud little grain, getting very cross.

The learned grain thought for several minutes.

"There might be two answers to that," she said, at last. "One might be that nobody had a voice to spare, and the other might be that you have nowhere to put one if it were given to you."

"Everybody is better off than I am," said the proud little grain. "The birds can fly and sing, the children can play and shout. I am sure I can get no rest for their shouting and playing. There are two little boys who make enough noise to deafen a whole sackful of us."

"Ah! I know them," said the learned grain. "And it's true they are noisy. Their names are Lionel and Arthur. There is a thin place, in the side of the sack through which I can see them. I would rather stay where I am than have to do all they do. They have long yellow hair, and when they stand on their heads the straw sticks in it and they look very curious. I heard a strange thing through listening to them the other day."

"What was it?" asked the proud grain.

"They were playing in the straw, and someone came to them—it was a lady who had brought them something on a plate. They began to dance and shout: 'It's cake! It's cake! Nice little mamma for bringing us cake.' And then they each sat down with a piece and began to take great bites out of it. I shuddered to think of it afterward."

"Why?"

"Well, you know they are always asking questions, and they began to ask questions of their mamma, who lay down in the straw near them. She seemed to be used to it. These are the questions Arthur asked:

"'Who made the cake?'

"'The cook.'

"'Who made the cook?'

"'God.'

"'What did he make her for?'

"'Why didn't he make her white?'

"'Why didn't he make you black?'

"'Did he cut a hole in heaven and drop me through when he made me?'

"'Why didn't it hurt me when I tumbled such a long way?'

"She said she 'didn't know' to all but the two first, and then he asked two more.

"'What is the cake made of?'

"'Flour, sugar, eggs, and butter.'

"'What is flour made of?'

"It was the answer to that which made me shudder."

"What was it?" asked the proud grain.

"She said it was made of—wheat! I don't see the advantage of being rich."

"Was the cake rich?" asked the proud grain.

"Their mother said it was. She said, 'Don't eat it so fast—it is very rich.'"

"Ah!" said the proud grain. "I should like to be rich. It must be very fine to be rich. If I am ever made into cake, I mean to be so rich that no one will dare to eat me at all."

"Ah!" said the learned grain. "I don't think those boys would be afraid to eat you, however rich you were. They are not afraid of richness."

"They'd be afraid of me before they had done with me," said the proud grain. "I am not a common grain of wheat. Wait until I am made into cake. But gracious me! there doesn't seem much prospect of it while we are shut up here. How dark and stuffy it is, and how we are crowded, and what a stupid lot the other grains are! I'm tired of it, I must say."

"We are all in the same sack," said the learned grain, very quietly.

It was a good many days after that, that something happened. Quite early in the morning, a man and a boy came into the granary, and moved the sack of wheat from its place, wakening all the grains from their last nap.

"What is the matter?" said the proud grain. "Who is daring to disturb us?"

"Hush!" whispered the learned grain, in the most solemn manner. "Something is going to happen. Something like this happened to somebody belonging to me long ago. I seem to remember it when I think very hard. I seem to remember something about one of my family being sown."

"What is sown?" demanded the other grain.

"It is being thrown into the earth," began the learned grain.

Oh, what a passion the proud grain got into! "Into the earth?" she shrieked out. "Into the common earth? The earth is nothing but dirt, and I am *not* a common grain of wheat. I won't be sown! I will *not* be sown! How dare any one sow me against my will! I would rather stay in the sack."

But just as she was saying it, she was thrown out with the learned grain and some others into another dark place, and carried off by the farmer, in spite of her temper; for the farmer could not hear her voice at all, and wouldn't have minded it if he had, because he knew she was only a grain of wheat, and ought to be sown, so that some good might come of her.

Well, she was carried out to a large field in the pouch which the farmer wore at his belt. The field had been ploughed, and there was a sweet smell of fresh earth in the air; the sky was a deep, deep blue, but the air was cool and the few leaves on the trees were brown and dry, and looked as if they had been left over from last year.

"Ah!" said the learned grain. "It was just such a day as this when my grandfather, or my father, or somebody else related to me, was sown. I think I remember that it was called Early Spring."

"As for me," said the proud grain, fiercely, "I should like to see the man who would dare to sow me!"

At that very moment, the farmer put his big, brown hand into the bag and threw her, as she thought, at least half a mile from him.

He had not thrown her so far as that, however, and she landed safely in the shadow of a clod of rich earth, which the sun had warmed through and through. She was quite out of breath and very dizzy at first, but in a few seconds she began to feel better and could not help looking around, in spite of her anger, to see if there was any one near to talk to. But she saw no one, and so began to scold as usual.

"They not only sow me," she called out, "but they throw me all by myself, where I can have no company at all. It is disgraceful."

Then she heard a voice from the other side of the clod. It was the learned grain, who had fallen there when the farmer threw her out of his pouch.

"Don't be angry," it said, "I am here. We are all right so far. Perhaps, when they cover us with the earth, we shall be even nearer to each other than we are now."

"Do you mean to say they will cover us with the earth?" asked the proud grain.

"Yes," was the answer. "And there we shall lie in the dark, and the rain will moisten us, and the sun will warm us, until we grow larger and larger, and at last burst open!"

"Speak for yourself," said the proud grain; "I shall do no such thing!"

But it all happened just as the learned grain had said, which showed what a wise grain it was, and how much it had found out just by thinking hard and remembering all it could.

Before the day was over, they were covered snugly up with the soft, fragrant, brown earth, and there they lay day after day.

One morning, when the proud grain wakened, she found herself wet through and through with rain which had fallen in the night, and the next day the sun shone down and warmed it so that it really began to be afraid that it would be obliged to grow too large for its skin, which felt a little tight for it already.

It said nothing of this to the learned grain, at first, because it was determined not to burst if it could help it; but after the same thing had happened a great many times, it found, one morning, that it really was swelling, and it felt obliged to tell the learned grain about it.

"Well," it said, pettishly, "I suppose you will be glad to hear that you were right. I *am* going to burst. My skin is so tight now that it doesn't fit me at all, and I know I can't stand another warm shower like the last."

"Oh!" said the learned grain, in a quiet way (really learned people always have a quiet way), "I knew I was right, or I shouldn't have said so. I hope you don't find it very uncomfortable. I think I myself shall burst by tomorrow."

"Of course I find it uncomfortable," said the proud grain. "Who wouldn't find it uncomfortable to be two or three sizes too small for oneself! Pouf! Crack! There I go! I have split all up my right side, and I must say it's a relief."

"Crack! Pouf! So have I," said the learned grain. "Now we must begin to push up through the earth. I am sure my relation did that."

"Well, I shouldn't mind getting out into the air. It would be a change at least."

So each of them began to push her way through the earth as strongly as she could, and, sure enough, it was not long before the proud grain actually found herself out in the world again breathing the sweet air, under the blue sky, across which fleecy white clouds were drifting, and swift-winged, happy birds darting.

"It really is a lovely day," were the first words the proud grain said. She couldn't help it. The sunshine was so delightful, and the birds chirped and twittered so merrily in the bare branches, and, more wonderful than all, the great field was brown no longer, but was covered with millions of little, fresh green blades, which trembled and bent their frail bodies before the light wind.

"This *is* an improvement," said the proud grain.

Then there was a little stir in the earth beside it, and up through the brown mould came the learned grain, fresh, bright, green, like the rest.

"I told you I was not a common grain of wheat," said the proud one.

"You are not a grain of wheat at all now," said the learned one, modestly. "You are a blade of wheat, and there are a great many others like you."

"See how green I am!" said the proud blade.

"Yes, you are very green," said its companion. "You will not be so green when you are older."

The proud grain, which must be called a blade now, had plenty of change and company after this. It grew taller and taller every day, and made a great many new acquaintances as the weather grew warmer. These were little gold and green beetles living near it, who often passed it, and now and then stopped to talk a little about their children and their journeys under the soil. Birds dropped down from the sky sometimes to gossip and twitter of the nests they were building in the apple-trees, and the new songs they were learning to sing.

Once, on a very warm day, a great golden butterfly floating by on his large lovely wings, fluttered down softly and lit on the proud blade, who felt so much prouder when he did it that she trembled for joy.

"He admires me more than all the rest in the field, you see," she said, haughtily. "That is because I am so green."

"If I were you," said the learned blade, in its modest way, "I believe I would not talk so much about being green. People will make such ill-natured remarks when one speaks often of oneself."

"I am above such people," said the proud blade. "I can find nothing more interesting to talk of than myself."

As time went on, it was delighted to find that it grew taller than any other blade in the field, and threw out other blades; and at last there grew out of the top of its stalk ever so many plump, new little grains, all fitting closely together, and wearing tight little green covers.

"Look at me!" she said then. "I am the queen of all the wheat. I have a crown."

"No," said its learned companion. "You are now an ear of wheat."

And in a short time all the other stalks wore the same kind of crown, and it found out that the learned blade was right, and that it was only an ear, after all.

And now the weather had grown still warmer and the trees were covered with leaves, and the birds sang and built their nests in them and laid their little blue eggs, and in time, wonderful to relate, there came baby birds, that were

always opening their mouths for food, and crying "peep, peep," to their fathers
and mothers. There were more butterflies floating about on their amber and purple wings, and the gold and green beetles were so busy they had no time to talk.

"Well!" said the proud ear of wheat (you remember it was an ear by this time)
to its companion one day. "You see, you were right again. I am not so green as I
was. I am turning yellow—but yellow is the color of gold, and I don't object to looking like gold."

"You will soon be ripe," said its friend.

"And what will happen then?"

"The reaping-machine will come and cut you down, and other strange things
will happen."

"There I make a stand," said the proud ear, "I will *not* be cut down." But it was
just as the wise ear said it would be. Not long after, a reaping-machine was brought
and driven back and forth in the field, and down went all the wheat ears before the
great knives. But it did not hurt the wheat, of course, and only the proud ear felt
angry.

"I am the color of gold," it said, "and yet they have dared to cut me down.
What will they do next, I wonder?"

What they did next was to bunch it up with other wheat and tie it and stack it
together, and then it was carried in a wagon and laid in the barn.

Then there was a great bustle after a while. The farmer's wife and daughters
and her two servants began to work as hard as they could.

"The thrashers are coming," they said, "and we must make plenty of things for
them to eat."

So they made pies and cakes and bread until their cupboards were full; and
surely enough the thrashers did come with the thrashing-machine, which was
painted red, and went "Puff! puff! puff! rattle! rattle!" all the time. And the proud
wheat was thrashed out by it, and found itself in grains again and very much out
of breath.

"I look almost as I was at first," she said; "only there are so many of me. I am grander
than ever now. I was only one grain of wheat at first, and now I am at least fifty."

When it was put into a sack, it managed to get all its grains together in one
place, so that it might feel as grand as possible. It was so proud that it felt grand,
however much it was knocked about.

It did not lie in the sack very long this time before something else happened.
One morning it heard the farmer's wife saying to the helper:

"Take this yere sack of wheat to the mill, Jerry. I want to try it when I make that
thar cake for the boarders. Them two children from Washington city are powerful
hands for cake."

So Jerry lifted the sack up and threw it over his shoulder, and carried it out into the spring-wagon.

"Now we are going to travel," said the proud wheat. "Don't let us be separated."

At that minute, there were heard two young voices, shouting: "Jerry, take us in the wagon! Let us go to mill, Jerry! We want to go to mill."

And these were the very two boys who had played in the granary and made so much noise the summer before. They had grown a little bigger, and their yellow hair was longer, but they looked just as they used to, with their strong little legs and big brown eyes, and their sailor hats set so far back on their heads that it was a wonder they stayed on. And gracious! how they shouted and ran.

"What does yer mar say?" asked Jerry.

"Says we can go!" shouted both at once, as if Jerry had been deaf, which he wasn't at all—quite the contrary.

So Jerry, who was very good-natured, lifted them in, and cracked his whip, and the horses started off. It was a long ride to the mill, but Lionel and Arthur were not too tired to shout again when they reached it. They shouted at the sight of the creek and the big wheel turning round and round slowly, with the water dashing and pouring and foaming over it.

"What turns the wheel?" asked Arthur.

"The water, honey," said Jerry.

"What turns the water?"

"Well now, honey," said Jerry, "you hev me thar. I don't know nuffin 'bout it. What a boy you is fur axin' dif 'cult questions."

Then he carried the sack in to the miller, and said he would wait until the wheat was ground.

"Ground!" said the proud wheat. "We are going to be ground? I hope it is agreeable. Let us keep close together."

They did keep close together, but it wasn't very agreeable to be poured into a hopper and then crushed into fine powder between two big stones.

"Makes nice flour," said the miller, rubbing it between his fingers.

"Flour!" said the wheat—which was wheat no longer. "Now I am flour, and I am finer than ever. How white I am! I really would rather be white than green or gold color. I wonder where the learned grain is, and if it is as fine and white as I am."

But the learned grain and her family had been laid away in the granary for seed wheat.

Before the wagon reached the house again, the two boys were fast asleep in the bottom of it, and had to be helped out just as the sack was, and carried in.

The sack was taken into the kitchen at once and opened, and even in its wheat days the flour had never been so proud as it was when it heard the farmer's wife say:

"I'm going to make this into cake."

"Ah!" it said; "I thought so. Now I shall be rich, and admired by everybody."

The farmer's wife then took some of it out in a large white bowl, and after that she busied herself beating eggs and sugar and butter all together in another bowl: and after a while she took the flour and beat it in also.

"Now I am in grand company," said the flour. "The eggs and butter are the color of gold, the sugar is like silver or diamonds. This is the very society for me."

"The cake looks rich," said one of the daughters.

"It's rather too rich for them children," said her mother. "But I dunno, neither. Nothin' don't hurt 'em. I reckon they could eat a panel of rail fence and come to no harm."

"I'm rich," said the flour to itself. "That is just what I intended from the first. I am rich and I am cake."

Just then, a pair of big brown eyes came and peeped into it. They belonged to a round little head with a mass of tangled curls all over it—they belonged to Arthur.

"What's that?" he asked.

"Cake."

"Who made it?"

"I did."

"I like you," said Arthur. "You're such a nice woman. Who's going to eat any of it? Is Lionel?"

"I'm afraid it's too rich for boys," said the woman, but she laughed and kissed him.

"No," said Arthur. "I'm afraid it isn't."

"I shall be much too rich," said the cake, angrily. "Boys, indeed. I was made for something better than boys."

After that, it was poured into a cake-mold, and put into the oven, where it had rather an unpleasant time of it. It was so hot in there that if the farmer's wife had not watched it carefully, it would have been burned.

"But I am cake," it said. "And of the richest kind, so I can bear it, even if it is uncomfortable."

When it was taken out, it really was cake, and it felt as if it was quite satisfied. Every one who came into the kitchen and saw it, said:

"Oh, what nice cake! How well your new flour has done!"

But just once, while it was cooling, it had a curious, disagreeable feeling. It found, all at once, that the two boys, Lionel and Arthur, had come quietly into the kitchen and stood near the table looking at the cake with their great eyes wide open and their little red mouths open, too.

"Dear me," it said. "How nervous I feel—actually nervous. What great eyes they have, and how they shine! And what are those sharp white things in their mouths? I really don't like them to look at me in that way. It seems like something personal. I wish the farmer's wife would come."

Such a chill ran over it, that it was quite cool when the woman came in, and she put it away in the cupboard on a plate.

But, that very afternoon, she took it out again and set it on the table on a glass cake-stand. She put some leaves around it to make it look nice, and it noticed that there were a great many other things on the table, and they all looked fresh and bright.

"This is all in my honor," it said. "They know I am rich."

Then several people came in and took chairs around the table.

"They all come in to sit and look at me," said the vain cake. "I wish the learned grain could see me now."

There was a little high-chair on each side of the table, and at first these were empty, but in a few minutes the door opened and in came the two little boys. They had pretty, clean outfits on, and their "bangs" and curls were bright with being brushed.

"Even they have been dressed up to do me honor," thought the cake.

But, the next minute, it began to feel quite nervous again. Arthur's chair was near the glass stand, and when he had climbed up and seated himself, he put one elbow on the table and rested his fat chin on his fat hand, and, fixing his eyes on the cake, sat and stared at it in such an unnaturally quiet manner for some seconds, that any cake might well have felt nervous.

"There's the cake," he said, at last, in such a deeply thoughtful voice that the cake felt faint with anger.

Then a remarkable thing happened. Some one drew the stand toward them and took a knife and cut out a large slice of the cake.

"Go away!" said the cake, though no one heard it. "I am cake! I am rich! I am not for boys! How dare you!"

Arthur stretched out his hand; he took the slice; he lifted it up, and then the cake saw his red mouth open—yes, open wider than it could have believed possible—wide enough to show two dreadful rows of little sharp white things.

"Good gra—" it began.

But it never said "cious." Never at all. For in two minutes Arthur had eaten it!!

And there was an end of its airs and graces.

First published in the January 1880 edition of *St. Nicholas Magazine*

The Spring Cleaning

As Told by Queen Crosspatch

BY FRANCES HODGSON BURNETT

ILLUSTRATIONS BY HARRISON CADY

It is just the hundreds and thousands of things I have to do for people that makes it impossible for me to attend to my literary work. Of course nothing ever would get told if I didn't tell it, and how is a person to find time for stories when she works seventy-five hours a day. You may say that there are not seventy-five hours in a day, but I know better. I work seventy-five hours every day whether they are there or not.

—Queen Crosspatch

PART ONE

OF COURSE YOU don't understand what I mean by my Spring Cleaning. That is because you know next to nothing about Fairy ways. I suppose you think that Spring comes just because April comes and you imagine I have nothing to do with it. There's where you are mistaken. April might come and stay for a year and nothing would happen if I did not set things going. In the Autumn I put everything to bed and in the Spring I and my Green Workers waken everything up—and a nice time we have of it. After it is all over my Green Workers are so tired I let them go to sleep for a month.

Last Spring was a very tiresome one. It was so slow and obstinate that there were days when I thought I wouldn't have any Spring at all and would just begin with Summer. I have done it before and I'll do it again if I'm aggravated.

I would have done it then but for Bunch. Bunch was the little girl who lived at the vicarage and she was called Bunch because when she was a very fat baby with a great many short frilly petticoats sticking out all round her short legs, she was so cozy and good-tempered that someone said she was nothing but a bunch of sweetness, and very soon everyone called her Bunch. She was eight years old, and she was little, and chubby, and funny, but she was always laughing, or had just stopped laughing, or was just going to begin to laugh, and that's the kind of child I like—it's the kind Fairies always like—Green Workers and all. Her father was the vicar of a very old church in a very old English village where a good many poor people

*I and my Green Workers
waken everything up.*

lived, and all the cottagers liked her. Old Mrs. Wiggles, who was bedridden, always stopped grumbling when Bunch came to see her, and old Daddy Dimp, who was almost stone deaf, always put his hand behind his ear and bent down sideways so that she could stand on tiptoe and shout out to him:

"How are your rheumatics today, Daddy? I've brought you a package of mints." Because she never had more than a halfpenny she could not bring him more than a few twisted up in a bit of paper, but I can tell you he did like it and he used to chuckle, and grin, and rub his old hands and say:

"Thank 'ee, Miss. 'Ere's a bit o' comfort," and he would be as pleased as Punch.

Bunch was always cheerful. For instance, she was never the least bit cross or unhappy because she never had a new hat in the Summer, but always had to have her old leghorn one pressed out and never knew what was going to be put on it by way of trimming. Sometimes it was a piece of second-hand ribbon her Aunt Jinny had worn the year before, and sometimes it was a wreath of rather shabby flowers her mama found in an old box and straightened the leaves of, and once it was a bunch of cherries and some lace which had been her grandmama's dress cap. But Bunch used always to say, "Well, it *is* a nice one this year, isn't it?" and go to church and sit in the vicarage pew as cheerfully as if the little children from the Hall, whose pew was next to hers, were not as grand as could be in their embroidered frocks and hats with white plumes and fresh carnations, or daisies, or roses. The little Bensons—who were the Hall children—loved her and her hat and were always so excited on the Sunday when the new trimming appeared that they couldn't sit still on their seats and wriggled shamefully. If they had not had a nice governess they would have been frowned at during the service and

"How are your rheumatics today, Daddy?"

The Primrose World

scolded on the way home and perhaps not allowed to have any pudding, at least two Sundays in a year—the Sunday when Bunch's hat came to church in its Summer trimmings and the Sunday when it came out disguised for Winter, either with steamed and cleaned velvet bows, or covered with a breadth of a relation's old silk dress. The time Aunt Jinny had given her mother a piece of a blue silk party frock just big enough to cover the hat all over and leave something for rosettes, I can tell you Bunch *was* grand and the little Bensons were so delighted that they whispered to each other, and Jack Benson even winked at her over the top of their pew. Three-year-old Billie Benson, who had been brought to church for the first time, actually clapped his hands and spoke out loud:

"Bunchy boofle boo hat!" he said, and he was only stopped by his eldest sister Janey seizing his hand and saying into his ear in a hollow whisper:

"People never speak in church! They *never* do! They'll think you are a baby."

I am telling you about the hat because it will show you how little money Bunch had and how if she did anything for poor people she had to do it without spending anything, and I and my Green Workers had to help her. That was how it happened that my Spring Cleaning was so important that year.

At the back of the vicarage garden there was a place which was so lovely in the Springtime that when you saw it first you simply could not bear to stand still. Bunch called it the Primrose World. It was a softly sloping hill with a running stream at its foot and a wood at the other side of the stream, and in March and April it blossomed out into millions of primroses—not thousands, but millions— and it was all one carpet of pale yellow flowers from top to bottom. Never was anything so beautiful. You could go out with a basket and

Bunch

pick, and pick, and pick, and carry your basket home and bring back another one and pick, and pick, and pick, and you could bring all your friends and pick, and pick, and pick, and you could get your little spades and dig up clumps, and dig up clumps, and dig up clumps, and plant them in your own garden, or your friends' gardens and still the Primrose World would look as if no one had ever touched it and the carpet of pale yellow blossoms would be as thick and wonderful as ever.

Now it happened that year that the Primrose World was more important to Bunch than it had ever been before. As soon as the thick yellow carpet was spread she was going to have a party—a Primrose party. Just let me tell you about it. There is a day in England which is called Primrose Day in memory of a great man whose favorite flower was the primrose. On that day people go about with bunches of primroses on their dresses, and even horses have primroses decorating their ears. The great man's statue is hung and wreathed and piled about with primroses, and primroses are carried everywhere. Tons of them must be brought to Covent Garden Flower Market, and all the street-corner flower sellers sit with their baskets full to sell to passers-by.

It happened that the year before last Bunch was taken to London by her Aunt Jinny. The hat was done up and Aunt Jinny put some real primroses in it for fun, and Bunch carried a large primrose bouquet in her hand, and had some pinned on her coat. I myself—Queen Crosspatch—went with her on the bouquet because I thought she might need a Fairy.

She enjoyed herself very much.

"It looks as if the Primrose World had taken a ticket at the station and come to London for a holiday," she said.

She and Aunt Jinny did ever so many nice things, but my business is just to tell you about the one thing that happened that made the Spring Cleaning so important.

It was a rather cold and windy English Spring day and as we were waiting for a bus, suddenly a torn, shabby, old straw hat came flying across the street and danced about on the pavement.

"There's a hat!" Bunch cried out. "The wind has blown it off some little girl's head," and she bounced forward and picked it up before it could get away again.

"I wonder who it belongs to," said Bunch.

"Look across the street," I whispered to her. She was one of the children who can hear Fairies speaking though they don't know they hear them. They imagine that a Fairy's voice is their own thoughts.

She looked across the street, which was crowded with people, and cabs, and carriages, and omnibuses, and there on the other side was a thin, bare-headed little flower girl looking up and down and everywhere for her hat. She looked so worried and unhappy that Bunch said:

"Oh! I do wish a Fairy would take me across the street to her!"

That minute I made the big policeman hold up his hand and the omnibuses, and carts, and carriages, and cabs, all stopped as if a giant had ordered them to do it, and Bunch and Aunt Jinny scurried across with the rest of the people, and of course I went over on the biggest primrose in the bouquet.

The thin little flower girl was looking all about, and tears had come into her eyes. She was a forlorn looking child and had a battered basket on her arm with a few shabby bunches of primroses in it which were as forlorn as herself.

Bunch ran to her quite out of breath with hurry.

"Here's your hat," she cried out. "The wind carried it across the street and I picked it up."

The thin little girl looked as delighted as if it had been as beautiful as Janey Benson's hat with the long ostrich feather.

"Oh, my! I am glad!" she said. "Thank yer, Miss."

"Look at her shabby primroses," I whispered in Bunch's ear, and she looked and saw she had only a few little wilted miserable bouquets.

"Do you sell primroses for a living?" she asked the flower girl.

"Yes, Miss."

"You haven't many, have you?" said Bunch.

"They was dear, this year, Miss, 'cos the Spring is so late. These was all I could get an' nobody wants to buy them. I've not 'ad no luck."

Bunch put her big fresh bouquet into the basket, and unpinned those on her coat, and whisked those out of her hat in a minute.

"These are nice ones," she said. "Sell them. They came out of my Primrose World."

The thin little flower girl was so glad she could scarcely speak, and that instant I beckoned to a gentleman who was passing by. He did not know that a Fairy—and Queen Crosspatch at that—had beckoned to him, but he stopped and spoke.

"Hello!" he said. "Those look as if they came from the country. I'll take them all."

"They came from the Primrose World," Bunch said. "Thank you for buying them."

"Those look as if they came from the country."

"The Primrose World?" he said. I could see he was a nice man. "There must be Fairies there." And he picked up the flowers and after he had looked from Bunch to the thin little flower girl, and from the thin little flower girl to Bunch, he actually threw into the basket a whole five-shilling piece, which was about five times as much as they were worth. I flew onto his shoulder and told him he must do it.

The thin little flower girl stared at Bunch as if she thought *she* was a Fairy.

"Miss!" she gasped. "Is that Primrose World true?"

Then I whispered in Bunch's ear and she caught hold of Aunt Jinny's coat. She imagined she had a new thought of her own—but *I* had made her think it.

"Aunt Jinny," she said in great excitement, "next year when the Primrose World is all out, couldn't this little girl come to the vicarage, and couldn't we go and pick, and pick, and pick, and couldn't the Bensons come and help us to pick, and pick, and pick, and couldn't the village children come and pick, and pick, and pick, until she had as many primroses as ever anybody could sell?" She was a sudden child, and she whirled round to the flower girl again.

"What's your name?" she asked.

"Jane Ann Biggs," the girl answered.

"Couldn't she—couldn't we—couldn't they, Aunt Jinny?" cried Bunch. "Wouldn't father let us?"

Aunt Jinny laughed as she often laughed at Bunch. "We'll take Jane Ann Biggs's address and talk it over when we go home," she answered.

And that was the beginning of the Primrose party. Of course I was the person who talked it over with the vicar and his wife, though they could neither see me nor hear my voice. *I* arranged it all. The next year, the day before Primrose Day, Jane Ann Biggs was to come down from London very early in the morning, and as many primroses as could be picked were to be sent back with her in a hamper so that she would have enough to make shillings, and shillings, and shillings by selling them.

The little Bensons nearly danced their legs off with joy at the thought of the fun they were going to have, and the fun the thin little flower girl was going to have. The village children who were asked to help could think of nothing else, until a great many of them actually forgot their multiplication tables and said that twice four was twenty-two, and things like that. As to Bunch, she dreamed of the Primrose party three nights a week and she cheered up old Mrs. Wiggles and Daddy Dimp by telling them about it until they forgot to think of their legs and backs and felt quite young and sprightly.

"Bless us! Bless us! Bless us!" they said, in the most joyful manner. And Daddy Dimp even said that he believed "come Springtime" he would "go and take a pick himself, same as if he wasn't more than seventy."

You can just see how important it was that my Spring Cleaning should be done

and all the Primrose World be in bloom the day
before Primrose Day so that everything would be
ready for the party.

I began to be anxious and watch things
almost as soon as Christmas was over. I called all
my Green Workers together and gave them a
good talking to.

"Now," I said, "You must get new frost brooms
and have your tools sharpened and your tuggers
in order, and be ready at a moment's notice.
There is to be no loitering this year and no saying
that your brooms are worn out, or your tuggers
want mending." (A tugger is a little green rope
the Green Workers tug at the slow flowers with
when they won't come up. The Green Workers

Jane Ann Biggs

have a great many tools human beings don't know anything about. Mine have a
flower opener which I could recommend to any Fairy.)

But that Spring *was* stubborn and slow. I thought it would never come. Snow
kept falling when it had no right to fall, and the Frost Imps had added millions to
their Standing Army and they would not stop working in the night. But one morning in March when they had spread out a frost I felt sure it was late enough to be
the very last one and I knew there was no time to lose—not a minute. So I called
out my Green Workers with their brooms.

"Begin the Spring Cleaning at once," I ordered. "Sweep every particle of frost
off the grass and all the evergreens, and polish up the shrubs and trees. If there are
any bits of ice on the twigs where buds may be thinking of pushing through, be sure
to knock them off. Go round to all the violets and crocuses and daffodils and knock
at their doors. Call the dormice and don't let them roll up into balls and go to sleep
again. Tell them I won't have it. Summon the birds and let them know that I expect
all the nests to be built with the modern improvements."

They flew off in flocks so fast that they made a whizzing sound in the air. Then
I flew over the fields to the very oldest elm tree and called on the Reverend Cawker
Rook. Of course I found him sitting huddled up on a top branch, dozing, with his
head sunk on his shoulder.

"Is your surplice clean?" I shouted out. "And where is your prayer book?"

He shuffled and blinked and winked sleepily.

"Eh! Eh! Eh!" he stuttered. "You do startle a person so with your sudden ways!"

"Eh! Eh! Eh!" I answered. "If you would be a little sudden yourself now and then,
business would be better attended to. I have begun my Spring Cleaning and it is time

*Queen Crosspatch and the
Reverend Cawker Rook*

for you to prepare for the bird weddings."

He is a slow old thing but I stirred him up and left him fumbling about in the hole in the tree where he kept his surplice and prayer-book.

I stirred everything up that day—flower roots and trees and birds and dormice and by afternoon the Green Workers had swept off all the frost, until everything was as neat as could be. I put on my cap and apron and helped them myself.

When the day was over I was glad enough to tuck myself up in my moss bed in my winter palace under the rose garden, and I slept till morning without once turning over. When daylight came and I got up and put on my field-mouse fur coat and hood and gloves, and went outside, what do you suppose had happened! The Frost Imps had brought their army out again and had been working all night, and things were worse than ever. The grass was white and glittering, the dormice had rolled themselves up into balls and gone to sleep again, the gentlemen and lady birds were turning their backs on one another, and the Reverend Cawker Rook had shuffled his book and his surplice back into the hole in the tree trunk and he was huddled up on the topmost branch, dozing, with his head sunk in his shoulders.

"I shall lose my temper in a minute," I said.

PART TWO

THE MOMENT AFTER I exclaimed "I shall lose my temper in a minute!" I suddenly remembered I hadn't any Temper to lose, because I had lost the only one I had (just before I decided to write *The Troubles of Queen Silverbell*, but that is quite another story for which we have no time now!) and I had never found him since. So as I felt that I must lose something I lost my pocket handkerchief instead. I flew over to the Primrose World in such a hurry that I was quite out of breath when I got there. It was covered with dead leaves and the dead leaves were covered with frost and you could not believe it had ever even *heard* of a primrose. I stamped about and *stamped* about. Of course I knew that if this sort of thing went on I never, never could get it ready in time for Bunch and the party and Jane Ann Biggs.

And while I was stamping about I heard a rustling of the dead leaves and there was Bunch herself, and I could see she was neither laughing, nor was just going to laugh, and she had not just finished laughing either. She did not look like Bunch in the least.

"There is another frost," she said. "The primroses will never come at all."

I flew on to her arm and called out to her as loud as I could:

"Don't be frightened. I will manage it somehow." And of course she felt as if she had had a cheerful thought, and a smile began to curl up her nice red mouth.

"I won't be frightened," she said. "I will believe that somehow they will come up—even if Fairies have to come and pull them."

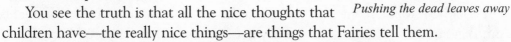

Pushing the dead leaves away

You see the truth is that all the nice thoughts that children have—the really nice things—are things that Fairies tell them.

She went down on her knees and began to push the dead leaves away from a place where she saw a bit of green sticking up. The bit of green was the new leaf of a primrose and she uncovered it and found two or three more—very little and very cold.

"Oh! you darling fings," she said, talking baby talk to them. "You darling fings!" And she stooped and kissed them and kissed them. "Do come up," she said, patting the earth round them with her warm little hand. "Do come up. Try and try and try. Jane Ann Biggs does so want you."

I could not stand it a minute longer. I left her and flew across the Primrose World and into the wood on the other side of the stream. I alighted on the top of a tree and put my golden trumpet to my lips and called out just as I did that day on the Huge Green Hill when I was reforming the Cozy Lion. This was what I called out this time:

> *Green Workers! Green Workers! Halloa!*
> *Green Workers! Green Workers! Ho! Ho!*
> *Come East and come West,*
> *Come o'er the hill crest,*
> *Come ready for friend or for foe!*
> *Come ready to polish and sweep!*
> *Come ready to crawl and to creep!*
> *Come ready to sing*
> *While you clean for the Spring,*
> *Come ready to bound, hop and leap!*

In two minutes the air was all green and buzzy with them. They came this way and that, and that way and this. They came in flocks, they came in clouds, they nearly knocked each other down they came so fast. The fact is some of them had guessed they were being called to do something for Bunch and they all liked her.

The wood was full of them, they crowded together on the ground and hung in clusters from the branches. And they all chanted together:

> *All steady—all steady fly we,*
> *All ready—all ready you see!*
> *From East and from West*
> *To do your behest*
> *Whatever it chances to be.*

I could not wait a moment. I told them the whole story about Bunch and Jane Ann Biggs and the Primrose party. They got so excited that the wood buzzed as if fifty million beehives had been upset in it.

"What shall we do?! What shall we do?! This is work for us—s-s-s-s-s-s-!" they said, in their tiny voices.

"This is what you will do," I answered. "Never until the Primrose World is ready

A Frost Imp

must you go to bed. You must stay up and watch every single night. Then when the Frost Imps come out to do their work you must all gather in a long line behind them and sweep off the frost as fast as they put it on. At this time of the year they are very tired of their winter work, and they really want to go to bed for their summer sleep. If you undo their work they will get discouraged and not come any more. The great thing is that Frost Imps cannot turn round because their necks are made of icicles and would break, and they won't know what is happening behind them. They can only see when the army is turned to march home."

The Green Workers shrieked and laughed and rolled about with delight. They were not only fond of Bunch, but they did not like the Frost Imps because they interfered with fun.

That night they were ready dressed in their warmest green smocks, and carrying their brooms. We were all hiding in the Primrose World when Bunch came out to look at it. She had on her little red cloak and hood and was mournful.

"It is so cold," she sighed. "I am afraid there will be another frost tonight."

If she could have heard Fairies she would have heard the Green Workers just squeal as they rolled about under the dead leaves and thought of the fun they were going to have.

When it was quite dark and every one was in bed and the Primrose World was as still as still could be, we heard the Frost Imps creeping along. They came to the top of the slope and stretched their whole army in a long line. Then their general gave his orders in an icy voice, saying slowly:

> Frost, frost, begin to freeze
> Grass and moss and buds and trees,
> Leave nothing peeping.
> Pinch, nip, and bind them fast,
> Till each bud when you have passed
> Stiff and cold lies sleeping.

Then the army marched forward and began. They worked as hard as they could, fastening the ice crystals on everything and even putting ice sheaths on some poor things. But my Green Workers were spread out in a line behind them— a Green Worker behind each Frost Imp, and as fast as an Imp covered a bud, or a twig, or a peeping green primrose leaf, the Green Workers behind him swept off the crystals or broke off the ice sheaths. I never saw them work quite as fast. They were so excited and hot that they melted ice crystals just by coming near them. They thought it would be such fun when the Imps turned round to march home and found all their work undone—and serve them right! They hopped and rushed about so that they made a noise and as the Imps could not turn their icicle necks they began to feel frightened. They knew something must be behind them and they could not tell *what* was going to happen to them.

When they were nearly at the foot of the hill they began to make little groans and sighs, and at last all along the line you could hear them saying this in a kind of creepy chant:

> What is the meaning of this?
> Behind us something rustles.
> What is the meaning of this?

Behind us something bustles.
What is the meaning of this?
Behind us something hustles.
It's something very queer and very bold.
What is the meaning of this?
Behind us things are sweeping.
What is the meaning of this?
Behind us things are leaping.
What is the meaning of this?
Behind us things are creeping.
It really makes MY BLOOD RUN COLD!

And by that time they had reached the bottom of the hill and wheeled round all in a line ready to march home. And there were my Green Workers spread out in *their* line face to face with them. And their work was all undone and it startled them so and made them so hot that they gave one wild shriek and their icicle necks broke, their heads fell off, and the whole army melted away—General Freeze and all.

After that night we never left the primroses a minute. They had been cold so long that they were half dead with sleep. So the Green Workers never stopped going round from one to the other to knock at their doors and tell them they *must* wake up. They told them about Bunch and the party and Jane Ann Biggs. They called it out, they sang it, they shouted it. They knocked on their doors, they thumped on their doors, they kicked on their doors. The primroses were not really lazy, but the cold had stupefied them, and when they were wakened they just drawled out, "In a min-ute" and fell asleep again, and the Green Workers had to thump and kick on their doors again. When they did waken at last they were so stiff that they could hardly move. It took them so long to push a green leaf through the earth and when they got one through they could not get it any further.

Bunch used to come down with the little Bensons and say:

My Green Workers spread out their
line face to face with them.

"They are so slow in growing. I never saw them so slow. Look what weenty leaves."

So we brought out the Green Delvers and the Green Tuggers. The Delvers brought their tiny spades and dug the earth loose round all the roots, and the Tuggers brought their ropes and fastened them round every least bit of a leaf they saw, and pulled and tugged, and tugged and pulled until they dragged them up into the light so that they grew in spite of themselves.

But there was such a short time to do it in and Bunch and the Bensons sometimes looked so frightened, and one day they brought a letter with them and

Pulling the Spring plants

it was from Jane Ann Biggs and this was what it said:

DERE MIS
wil the primrosses bee reddy
Jane ann bigs

It was bad spelling but Jane Ann had never been to school. There was only a week more to work and I should nearly have gone crazy, only Fairies never do. And suddenly one night I thought of hot-water bags.

"Get two or three million fairy hot-water bags," I said to my head Green Workers, Skip and Trip and Flip and Nip. "Get them at once."

They got them before sunset and all that night the whole army of Green Workers ran from one clump of primroses to the other putting the hot-water bags close to the roots and keeping them almost as warm as if they had been in a green-house. The next morning the sun came out and kept them warm all day and more green leaves and more green leaves began to show above the earth every few minutes.

"Hooray! Hooray!" the Workers shouted all together. "Now we have got them."

The next night we used more hot-water bags and the next day the sunshine was warmer still and the green leaves thrust themselves up on every side and began to uncurl.

The letter from Jane Ann Biggs

*Putting hot water bags at
the roots of primroses*

Dear me! How we did work for four nights and how the primroses did work in the daytime. And on the fourth day Bunch and all the little Bensons came out together and in two minutes after they bent down to look at the clumps of green leaves they sprang up shouting:

"There are buds! There are buds! There are buds! And lots of them are yellow!"

They ran about up and down the Primrose World, darting here and there and screaming for joy and at last they joined hands and danced and danced in a ring round a huge cluster which had on it a dozen wide-open pale yellow primroses.

"I believe the Fairies did it," said Bunch. "I just believe it!"

"I just believe it!"

There was such excitement that the very trees got interested and began pushing out leaves and leaves as fast as they could, everything began to push out leaves, birds began to sit on boughs together and propose to each other with the loudest trills and twitters, dormice waked up and rabbits and squirrels began to frisk about and whisk tails. Old Cawker Rook shuffled on his surplice and fussed about with his book in such a flurry to do something that he married birds who hadn't asked him—married them the minute he saw them. He was quite out of breath with marrying, and on the fifth day he accidentally married a squirrel to a lady woodpecker just because they chanced to be on the same tree and he was in such a hurry that he dropped his spectacles and did not know what he was doing. If I had not been on the spot to unmarry them at once, it would have been most unfortunate, for as it was the lady woodpecker was so provoked that she nearly pecked the squirrel's eyes out.

Well, on two days before Primrose Day the Primrose World was a sight to behold. It had seventeen million more primroses on it then than it had ever had before and they were all twice as big and twice as lovely.

When Jane Ann Biggs came and was brought out by Bunch and the little Bensons her eyes looked like saucers and she sat very suddenly flat down on the ground.

"Miss," said Jane Ann Biggs to Bunch, "is this 'ere the earth an' 'ave I died an' gone to 'eving?"

Bunch and the Bensons pulled her up and made her dance round with them.

"No!" they shouted. "You're alive! You're alive! You're really alive! And this is the Primrose World."

Then the village children came to help and every one had a basket and they picked and picked and picked and picked and picked and picked and picked and Daddy Dimp came and picked and picked and picked and picked and Mrs. Wiggles's grandson brought her in a wheelbarrow and when she sat down and began to pick I made her forget all about her legs and she stood up and found that they were quite well and she need never be bedridden or need never grumble any more.

My Green Workers picked as well. The children could not understand why their baskets filled so soon.

It was the most beautiful party that I ever went to. The vicarage cook made perfectly delightful things to eat and the vicarage housemaid and the boy who weeds the garden brought them out and spread them on beds of primroses and everybody was so hungry and happy that Jane Ann Biggs clutched Bunch's sleeve twelve times and said:

"Oh! Miss! Are yer sure it's not 'eving?"

The vicar had arranged about sending the primroses to town in hampers so that they would be all fresh in the morning. He was such a nice vicar and only preached quite short sermons and they were only about things you can really do—like being cheerful and loving one another.

So hampers and hampers of primroses went to town and Jane Ann Biggs sold them to men in Covent Garden Market and kept a hamper to sell at big houses herself. She really made quite a little fortune—for a thin flower girl. And the best of it was that she and Bunch and the Bensons were such friends that it was arranged that she should come to the Primrose World every single Spring so she would have it to look forward to all the year.

> *Now that's the story of just ONE of my Spring Cleanings, and if it does not show you how much I have to do and how nothing could happen without me, you must be rather stupid.*
>
> —Queen Crosspatch

First published in the December 1908 and January 1909 editions of *St. Nicholas Magazine*

The Story of Prince Fairyfoot

BY FRANCES HODGSON BURNETT

PART ONE

ONCE UPON A TIME, in the days of the fairies, there was in the far west country a kingdom which was called by the name of Stumpinghame. It was a rather curious country in several ways. In the first place, the people who lived there thought that Stumpinghame was all the world; they thought there was no world at all outside of Stumpinghame. And they thought that the people of Stumpinghame knew everything that could possibly be known, and that what they did not know was of no consequence at all.

One idea common in Stumpinghame was really very unusual indeed. It was a peculiar taste in the matter of feet. In Stumpinghame the larger a person's feet were, the more beautiful and elegant he or she was considered; and the more aristocratic and nobly born a man was, the more immense were his feet. Only the very lowest and most vulgar persons were ever known to have small feet. The King's feet were simply huge; so were the Queen's; so were those of the young princes and princesses. It had never occurred to anyone that a member of such a royal family could possibly disgrace himself by being born with small feet. Well, you may imagine, then, what a terrible and humiliating state of affairs arose when there was born into that royal family a little son, a prince, whose feet were so very small and slender and delicate that they would have been considered small even in other places than Stumpinghame. Grief and confusion seized the entire nation. The Queen fainted six times a day; the King had black rosettes fastened upon his crown; all the flags were at half-mast; and the court went into the deepest mourning. There had been born to Stumpinghame a royal prince with small feet, and nobody knew how the country could survive it!

Yet the disgraceful little prince survived it and did not seem to mind it at all. He was the prettiest and best-tempered baby the royal nurse had ever seen. But for his small feet, he would have been the flower of the family. The royal nurse said so herself, and privately told his little royal highness's chief bottle-washer that she "never see a hinfant as took notice so, and sneezed as hintelligent." But of course the King and Queen could see nothing but his little feet, and very soon they made up their minds to send him away. So one day they had him bundled up and carried where they thought he might be quite forgotten. They sent him to the hut of a swineherd who lived deep, deep in a great forest which seemed to end nowhere.

They gave the swineherd some money, and some clothes for Fairyfoot, and told him that if he would take care of the child, they would send money and clothes every year. As for themselves, they only wished to be sure of never seeing Fairyfoot again.

This pleased the swineherd well enough. He was poor, and he had a wife and ten children, and hundreds of swine to take care of, and he knew he could use the little prince's money and clothes for his own family, and no one would find it out. So he let his wife take the little fellow, and as soon as the King's messengers had gone, the woman took the royal clothes off the Prince and put on him a coarse little night-gown, and gave all his things to her own children. But the baby prince did not seem to mind that—he did not seem to mind anything, even that he had no name but Prince Fairyfoot, which had been given him in contempt by the disgusted courtiers. He grew prettier and prettier every day, and long before the time when other children begin to walk, he could run about on his fairy feet.

The swineherd and his wife did not like him at all; in fact, they disliked him because he was so much prettier and so much brighter than their own clumsy children. And the children did not like him because they were ill-natured and only liked themselves.

So as he grew older year by year, the poor little prince was more and more lonely. He had no one to play with, and was obliged to be always by himself. He dressed only in the coarsest and roughest clothes; he seldom had enough to eat, and he slept on straw in a loft under the roof of the swineherd's hut. But all this did not prevent his being strong and rosy and active. He was as fleet as the wind, and he had a voice as sweet as a bird's; he had lovely sparkling eyes, and bright golden hair; and he had so kind a heart that he would not have done a wrong or cruel thing for the world. As soon as he was big enough, the swineherd made him go out into the forest every day to take care of the swine. He was obliged to keep them together in one place, and if any of them ran away into the forest, Prince Fairyfoot was beaten. And as the swine were very wild and unruly, he was very often beaten, because it was almost impossible to keep them from wandering off; and when they ran away, they ran so fast, and through places so tangled, that it was almost impossible to follow them.

The swineherd is well pleased to receive the little Prince and the money.

The forest in which he had to spend the long days was a very beautiful one, however, and he could take pleasure in that. It was a forest so great that it was like a world in itself: There were in it strange, splendid trees, the branches of which interlocked overhead, and when their many leaves moved and rustled, it seemed as if they were whispering secrets. There were bright, swift, strange birds, that flew about in the deep golden sunshine, and when they rested on the boughs, they too seemed telling one another secrets. There was a bright, clear brook, with water as sparkling and pure as crystal, and with shining shells and pebbles of all colors lying in the gold and silver sand at the bottom. Prince Fairyfoot always thought the brook knew the forest's secret also and sang it softly to the flowers as it ran along. And as for the flowers, they were beautiful; they grew as thickly as if they had been a carpet, and under them was another carpet of lovely green moss. The trees and the birds, and the brook and the flowers, were Prince Fairyfoot's friends. He loved them, and never was very lonely when he was with them; and if his swine had not run away so often, and if the swineherd had not beaten him so much, sometimes— indeed, nearly all summer—he would have been almost happy. He used to lie on the fragrant carpet of flowers and moss, and listen to the soft sound of the running water, and to the whispering of the waving leaves, and to the songs of the birds; and he would wonder what they were saying to one another, and if it were true, as the swineherd's children said, that the great forest was full of fairies. And then he would pretend it was true, and would tell himself stories about them, and make believe they were his friends, and that they came to talk to him and let him love them. He wanted to love something or somebody, and he had nothing to love— not even a little dog.

One day he was resting under a great green tree, feeling really quite happy because everything was so beautiful. He had even made a little song to chime in with the brook's, and he was singing it softly and sweetly, when suddenly, as he lifted his curly, golden head to look about him, he saw that all his swine were gone. He sprang to his feet, feeling very much frightened, and he whistled and called, but he heard nothing. He could not imagine how they all could have disappeared so quietly, without making any sound; but not one of them was anywhere to be seen. Then his poor little heart began to beat fast with trouble and anxiety. He ran here and there; he looked through the bushes and under the trees; he ran, and ran, and ran, and called, and whistled, and searched; but nowhere—nowhere was one of those swine to be found! He searched for them for hours, going deeper and deeper into the forest than he had ever been before. He saw strange trees and strange flowers, and heard strange sounds, and at last the sun began to go down and he knew he would soon be left in the dark. His little feet and legs were scratched with brambles, and were so tired that they would scarcely carry him; but he dared not go back to the swineherd's hut without finding the swine. The only comfort he had on all the long way was that the little brook had run by his side and sung its song to him; and sometimes he had stopped and bathed his hot face in it, and had said, "Oh, little brook, you are so kind to me! You are my friend, I know. It would be so lonely without you!"

When, at last, the sun did go down, Prince Fairyfoot had wandered so far that he did not know where he was, and he was so tired that he threw himself down by the brook, and hid his face in the flowery moss, and said: "Oh, little brook, I am so tired I can go no further! And I can never find them!"

While he was lying there in despair, he heard a sound in the air above him, and looked up to see what it was. It sounded like a little bird in some trouble. And surely enough, there was a huge hawk darting after a plump little brown bird with a red breast. The little bird was uttering sharp, frightened cries, and Prince Fairyfoot felt so sorry for it that he sprung up and tried to drive the hawk away. The little bird saw him at once, and straightway flew to him, and Fairyfoot covered it with his cap. And then the hawk flew away in a great rage.

When the hawk was gone, Fairyfoot sat down again and lifted his cap, expecting, of course, to see the brown bird with the red breast. But, instead of a bird, out stepped a little man, not much higher than your little finger—a plump little man in a brown suit with a bright red vest, and with a cocked hat on.

"Why!" exclaimed Fairyfoot, "I'm surprised!"

"So am I!" said the little man, cheerfully. "I never was more surprised in my life, except when my great-aunt's grandmother got into such a rage, and changed me into a robin-redbreast. I tell you, that surprised me!"

"I should think it might," said Fairyfoot. "Why did she do it?"

"Mad," answered the little man. "That was what was the matter with her. She was always losing her temper like that, and turning people into awkward things, and then being sorry for it, and not being able to change them back again. If you are a fairy, you have to be careful. If you'll believe me, that woman once turned her second cousin's sister-in-law into a mushroom, and somebody picked her and she was made into a sauce—which is a thing no man likes to have happen in his family."

"Of course not," said Fairyfoot, politely.

"The difficulty is," said the little man, "that some fairies don't graduate. They learn how to turn people into things, but they don't learn how to unturn them; and then, when they get mad in their families—you know how it is about getting mad in families—there is confusion. Yes, seriously, confusion arises. It arises. That was the way with my great-aunt's grandmother. She was not a cultivated old person, and she did not know how to unturn people, and now you see the result. Quite accidentally I trod on her favorite corn; she got mad and changed me into a robin and regretted it ever afterward. I could only become myself again by a kind-hearted person's saving me from a great danger. You are that person. Give me your hand."

Fairyfoot held out his hand. The little man looked at it.

"On second thought," he said, "I can't shake it—it's too large. I'll sit on it, and talk to you."

With these words, he hopped upon Fairyfoot's hand, and sat down, smiling and clasping his own hands about his tiny knees.

"I declare, it's delightful not to be a robin," he said. "Had to go about picking up worms, you know. Disgusting business. I always did hate worms. I never ate them myself—I drew the line there; but I had to get them for my family."

Suddenly he began to giggle, and to hug his knees up tight.

"Do you wish to know what I'm laughing at?" he asked Fairyfoot.

"Yes," Fairyfoot answered.

The little man giggled more than ever.

"I'm thinking about my wife," he said—"the one I had when I was a robin. A nice rage she'll be in when I don't come home tonight! She'll have to hustle around and pick up worms for herself, and for the children, too—and it serves her right. She had a temper that would embitter the life of a crow—much more a simple robin. I wore myself to skin and bone taking care of her and her brood, and how I did hate 'em!—bare, squawking things, always with their throats gaping open. They seemed to think a parent's sole duty was to bring worms for them."

"It must have been unpleasant," said Fairyfoot.

"It was more than that," said the little man. "It used to make my feathers stand on end. There was the nest, too! Fancy being changed into a robin, and being obliged to build a nest at a moment's notice! I never felt so ridiculous in my life. How was I to know how to build a nest! And the worst of it was the way she went on about it."

"She?" said Fairyfoot.

"Oh, her, you know," replied the little man, ungrammatically; "my wife. She'd always been a robin, and she knew how to build a nest; she liked to order me about, too: she was one of that kind. But, of course, I wasn't going to own that I didn't know anything about nest-building; I could never have done anything with her in the world, if I'd let her think she knew as much as I did. So I just put things together in a way of my own, and built a nest that would have made you weep! The bottom fell out of it the first night. It nearly killed me."

"Did you fall out, too?" inquired Fairyfoot.

"Oh, no," answered the little man. "I meant that it nearly killed me to think the eggs weren't in it at the time."

"What did you do about the nest?" asked Fairyfoot.

The little man winked in the most improper manner.

"Do?" he said. "I got mad, of course, and told her that if she hadn't interfered, it wouldn't have happened; said it was exactly like a hen to fly around giving advice and unsettling one's mind, and then complain if things weren't right. I told her she might build the nest herself, if she thought she could build a better one. She did it, too!" And he winked again.

"Was it a better one?" asked Fairyfoot.

The little man actually winked a third time. "It may surprise you to hear that it was," he replied; "but it didn't surprise me. By the bye," he added, with startling suddenness, "what's your name and what's the matter with you?"

"My name is Prince Fairyfoot," said the boy, "and I have lost my master's swine."

"My name," said the little man, "is Robin Goodfellow, and I'll find them for you."

He had a tiny scarlet silk pouch hanging at his waist, and he put his hand into it and drew forth the smallest golden whistle you ever saw.

"Blow that," he said, giving it to Fairyfoot, "and take care that you don't swallow it. You are such a tremendous creature!"

Fairyfoot took the whistle and put it very delicately to his lips. He blew, and there came from it a high, clear sound that seemed to pierce the deepest depths of the forest.

"Blow again," commanded Robin Goodfellow. Again Prince Fairyfoot blew, and again the pure clear sound rang through the trees, and the next instant he heard a loud rushing and tramping and squeaking and grunting, and all the great drove of swine came tearing through the bushes and formed themselves into a circle and stood staring at him as if waiting to be told what to do next.

"Oh! Robin Goodfellow! Robin Goodfellow!" cried Fairyfoot, "how grateful I am to you!"

"Not as grateful as I am to you," said Robin Goodfellow. "But for you I should be disturbing that hawk's digestion at the present moment, instead of which, here I am, a respectable fairy once more, and my late wife (though I ought not to call her that, for goodness knows she was early enough hustling me out of my nest before day-break, with an unpleasant proverb about the early bird catching the worm!)—I suppose I should say my early wife—is at this juncture a widow. Now, where do you live?"

Fairyfoot told him, and told him also about the swineherd, and how it happened that, though he was a prince, he had to herd swine and live in the forest.

"Well, well!" said Robin Goodfellow, "that is a disagreeable state of affairs. Perhaps I can make it rather easier for you. You see that is a fairy whistle."

"I thought so," said Fairyfoot.

"Well," continued Robin Goodfellow, "you can always call your swine with it, so you will never be beaten again. Now are you ever lonely?"

"Sometimes I am very lonely indeed," answered the Prince. "No one cares for me, though I think the brook is sometimes sorry, and tries to tell me things."

"Of course," said Robin. "They all like you. I've heard them say so."

"Oh, have you?" cried Fairyfoot, joyfully.

"Yes; you never throw stones at the birds, or break the branches of the trees, or trample on the flowers, when you can help it."

"The birds sing to me," said Fairyfoot, "and the trees seem to beckon to me and whisper; and when I am very lonely, I lie down in the grass and look into the eyes of the flowers and talk to them. I would not hurt one of them for all the world!"

"Humph!" said Robin, "you are a rather good little fellow. Would you like to go to a party?"

"A party!" said Fairyfoot. "What is that?"

"This sort of thing," said Robin; and he jumped up and began to dance around and to kick up his heels gayly in the palm of Fairyfoot's hand. "Wine, you know, and cake, and all sorts of fun. It begins at twelve tonight, in a place the fairies know of; and it lasts until just two minutes and three seconds and a half before daylight. Would you like to come?"

"Oh," cried Fairyfoot, "I should be so happy if I might!"

"Well, you may," said Robin; "I'll take you. They'll be delighted to see any friend of mine. I'm a great favorite; of course you can easily imagine that! It was a great blow to them when I was changed; such a loss, you know! In fact, there were several lady fairies, who—but no matter." And he gave a slight cough, and began to arrange his necktie with a disgracefully consequential air, though he was trying very hard not to look conceited; and while he was endeavoring to appear easy and gracefully careless, he began accidentally to hum "See the Conquering Hero Comes," which was not the right tune, under the circumstances.

"But for you," he said next, "I couldn't have given them the relief and pleasure of seeing me this evening. And what ecstasy it will be to them, to be sure! I shouldn't be surprised if it broke up the whole thing. They'll faint so—for joy, you know— just at first—that is, the ladies will. The men won't like it at all; and I don't blame 'em. I suppose I shouldn't like it—to see another fellow sweep all before him. That's what I do; I sweep all before me." And he waved his hand in such a fine large gesture that he overbalanced himself and turned a somersault. But he jumped up after it, quite undisturbed.

"You'll see me do it, tonight," he said, knocking the dents out of his hat— "sweep all before me." Then he put his hat on, and his hands on his hips, with a swaggering, man-of-society air. "I say," he said, "I'm glad you're going. I should like you to see it."

"And I should like to see it," replied Fairyfoot.

"Well," said Mr. Goodfellow, "you deserve it, though that's saying a great deal. You've restored me to them. But for you, even if I'd escaped that hawk, I should have had to spend the night in that beastly robin's nest, crowded into a corner by those squawking things, and domineered over by her! I wasn't made for that! I'm superior to it. Domestic life doesn't suit me. I was made for society. I adorn it. She never appreciated me. She couldn't soar to it. When I think of the way she treated me!" he exclaimed, suddenly getting into a rage, "I've a great mind to turn back into a robin, and soundly flap her beak!"

"Would you like to see her now?" asked Fairyfoot innocently.

Mr. Goodfellow glanced behind him in great haste, and suddenly sat down.

"No, no!" he exclaimed in a tremendous hurry; "by no means! She has no del-icacy. And she doesn't deserve to see me. And there's a violence and uncertainty about her movements which is annoying beyond anything you can imagine. No, I don't want to see her! I'll let her go unpunished for the present. Perhaps it's punishment enough for her to be deprived of me. Just pick up your cap, wont you? and if you see any birds lying about, throw it at them, robins particularly."

"I think I must take the swine home, if you'll excuse me," said Fairyfoot. "I'm late now."

"Well, let me sit on your shoulder and I'll go with you, and show you a short way home," said Goodfellow; "I know all about it, so you needn't think about yourself again. In fact, we'll talk about the party. Just blow your whis-tle, and the swine will go ahead." Fairyfoot did so, and the swine rushed through the forest before them, and Robin Goodfellow perched himself on the prince's shoulder and chatted as they went.

"Let me sit on your shoulder and I'll go with you," said Robin Goodfellow.

IT HAD TAKEN Fairyfoot hours to reach the place where he had found Robin, but some-

Robin waits for Fairyfoot.

how it seemed to him only a very short time before they came to the open place near the swineherd's hut; and the path they had walked in had been so pleasant and flowery that it had been delightful all the way.

"Now," said Robin when they stopped, "if you will come here tonight at twelve o'clock, when the moon shines under this tree, you will find me waiting for you. Now I'm going. Good-bye!" And he was gone before the last word was quite finished.

Fairyfoot went toward the hut, driving the swine before him, and suddenly he saw the swineherd come out of his house and stand staring stupidly at the pigs. He was a very coarse, hideous man with bristling yellow hair, and little eyes, and a face rather like a pig's, and he always looked stupid, but just now he looked more stupid than ever. He seemed dumb with surprise.

"What's the matter with the swine?" he asked in his hoarse voice, which was rather piglike too.

"I don't know," answered Fairyfoot, feeling a little alarmed. "What *is* the matter with them?"

"They are four times fatter and five times bigger and six times cleaner and seven times heavier and eight times handsomer than they were when you took them out," the swineherd said.

"I've done nothing to them," said Fairyfoot. "They ran away, but they came back again."

The swineherd went lumbering back into the hut and called his wife. "Come, and look at the swine," he said.

And then the woman came out, and stared first at the swine and then at Fairyfoot.

"He has been with the fairies," she said at last to her husband; "or it is because he is a king's son. We must treat him better if he can do wonders like that."

PART TWO

IN WENT THE swineherd's wife and she prepared quite a good supper for Fairyfoot, and gave it to him. But Fairyfoot was scarcely hungry at all, he was so eager for night to come, so that he might see the fairies. When he went to his loft under the roof, he thought at first he could not sleep; but suddenly his hand touched the fairy whistle and he fell asleep at once, and did not waken again until a moonbeam fell brightly upon his face and aroused him. Then he jumped up and ran to the hole in the wall to look out, and he saw that the hour had come, and that the moon was so low in the sky that its slanting light had crept under the oak tree. He slipped downstairs so lightly that his master heard nothing, and then he found himself out in the beautiful night with the moonlight so bright that it was lighter than daytime. And there was Robin Goodfellow waiting for him under the tree! He was so finely dressed that, for a moment, Fairyfoot scarcely knew him. His suit was made out of the purple velvet petals of a pansy, which was far finer than any ordinary velvet, and he wore plumes, and tassels, and a ruffle around his neck, and in his belt was thrust a tiny sword, not half as big as the finest needle.

"Take me on your shoulder," he said to Fairyfoot, "and I will show you the way."

Fairyfoot took him up, and they went their way through the forest. And the strange part of it was that though Fairyfoot thought he knew all the forest by heart, every path they took was new to him, and more beautiful than anything he had ever seen before. The moonlight seemed to grow brighter and purer at every step, and the sleeping flowers sweeter and lovelier, and the moss greener and thicker. Fairyfoot felt so happy and gay that he forgot he had ever been sad and lonely in his life.

Robin Goodfellow, too, seemed to be in very good spirits. He related a great many stories to Fairyfoot, and, singularly enough, they all were about himself and divers and sundry fairy ladies who had been so very much attached to him that he scarcely expected to find them alive at the present moment. He felt quite sure they must have died of grief in his absence.

"I have caused a great deal of trouble in the course of my life," he said, regretfully, shaking his head. "I have sometimes wished I could avoid it, but that is impossible. Ahem!—When my great-aunt's grandmother rashly and inopportunely changed me into a robin, I was having a little flirtation with a little creature who was really quite attractive. I might have decided to engage myself to her. She was very charming. Her name was Gauzita. Tomorrow I shall go and place flowers on her tomb."

"I thought fairies never died," said Fairyfoot.

"Only on rare occasions and only from love," answered Robin. "They needn't die unless they wish to. They have been known to do it through love. They frequently wish they hadn't afterward—in fact, invariably—and then they can come to life again. But Gauzita—"

"Are you quite sure she is dead?" asked Fairyfoot.

"Sure!" cried Mr. Goodfellow, in wild indignation. "Why, she hasn't seen me for a couple of years. I've molted twice since last we met. I congratulate myself that she didn't see me then," he added in a lower voice. "Of course she's dead," he added, with solemn emphasis—"as dead as a door nail."

Just then Fairyfoot heard some enchanting sounds, faint but clear. They were sounds of delicate music and of tiny laughter, like the ringing of silver bells.

"Ah!" said Robin Goodfellow, "there they are! But it seems to me they are rather gay, considering they have not seen me for so long. Turn into the path."

Almost immediately they found themselves in a beautiful little dell, filled with moonlight, and with glittering stars in the cup of every flower; for there were thousands of dewdrops, and every dewdrop shone like a star. There were also crowds and crowds of tiny men and women, all beautiful, all dressed in brilliant, delicate dresses, all laughing or dancing or feasting at the little tables, which were loaded with every dainty the most fastidious fairy could wish for.

"Now," said Robin Goodfellow, "you shall see me sweep all before me. Put me down."

Fairyfoot put him down, and stood and watched him while he walked forward with a very grand manner. He went straight to the gayest and largest group he could see. It was a group of gentlemen fairies who were crowding around a lily of the valley, on the bent stem of which a tiny lady fairy was sitting, airily swaying herself to and fro, and laughing and chatting with all her admirers at once.

She seemed to be enjoying herself immensely; indeed, it was disgracefully plain that she was having a great deal of fun. One gentleman fairy was fanning her, one was holding her programme, one had her bouquet, another her little scent bottle, and those who had nothing to hold for her were scowling furiously at the rest. It was evident that she was very popular and that she did not object to it at all; in fact, the way her eyes sparkled and danced was distinctly reprehensible.

"You have engaged to dance the next waltz with every one of us!" said one of her adorers. "How are you going to do it?"

"Did I engage to dance with all of you?" she said, giving her lily stem the sauciest little swing, which set all the bells ringing. "Well, I am not going to dance it with all."

"Not with *me?*" the admirer with the fan whispered in her ear.

She gave him the most delightful little look, just to make him believe she wanted to dance with him but really couldn't. Robin Goodfellow saw her. And then she smiled sweetly upon all the rest, every one of them. Robin Goodfellow saw that too.

"I am going to sit here and look at you and let you talk to me," she said; "I do so enjoy brilliant conversation."

All the gentlemen fairies were so much elated by this that they began to brighten up, and settle their ruffs, and fall into graceful attitudes, and think of sparkling things to say; because every one of them knew from the glance of her eyes in his direction, that he was the one whose conversation was brilliant; every one knew there could be no mistake about its being himself that she meant. The way she looked just proved it. Altogether, it was more than Robin Goodfellow could stand, for it was Gauzita who was deporting herself in this unaccountable manner, swinging on lily stems and "going on," so to speak, with several partners at once in a way to chill the blood of any proper young lady fairy—who hadn't any partner at all. It was Gauzita herself.

He made his way into the very center of the group.

"Gauzita!" he said. He thought, of course, she would drop right off her lily stem. But she didn't. She simply stopped swinging a moment, and stared at him.

"Gracious!" she exclaimed. "And who are you?"

"Who am I?" cried Mr. Goodfellow severely. "Don't you remember me?"

"No," she said coolly; "I don't, not in the least."

Robin Goodfellow almost gasped for breath. He had never met with anything so outrageous in his life.

"You don't remember *me*," he cried. "*Me!* Why, it's impossible!"

"Is it?" said Gauzita with a touch of dainty impudence. "What's your name?"

Robin Goodfellow was almost paralyzed. Gauzita took up a midget of an eyeglass which she had dangling from a thread of a gold chain, and she stuck it in her eye and tilted her impertinent little chin and looked him over. Not that she was nearsighted—not a bit of it—it was just one of her tricks and manners.

"Dear me!" she said. "You do look a trifle familiar. It isn't, it can't be, Mr. —, Mr. —," then she turned to the adorer who held her fan—"it can't be Mr. —, the one who was changed into a robin, you know," she said. "Such a ridiculous thing to be changed into! What was his name?"

"Oh, yes! I know whom you mean. Mr. —ah—Goodfellow!" said the fairy with the fan.

"So it was," she said, looking Robin over again. "And he has been pecking at trees and things, and hopping in and out of nests ever since, I suppose. How absurd! And we have been enjoying ourselves so much since he went away! I think I never *did* have so lovely a time as I have had during these last two years. I began to know you," she added, in a kindly tone, "just about the time he went away."

Robin Goodfellow is disappointed.

"You have been enjoying yourself?" almost shrieked Robin Goodfellow.

"Well," said Gauzita, in unexcusable slang, "I must smile." And she did smile.

"And nobody has pined away and died?" cried Robin.

"I haven't," said Gauzita, swinging herself and ringing her bells again. "I really haven't had time."

Robin Goodfellow turned around and rushed out of the group. He regarded this as insulting. He went back to Fairyfoot in such a hurry that he tripped on his sword and fell and rolled over so many times that Fairyfoot had to stop him and pick him up.

"Is she dead?" asked Fairyfoot.

"No," said Robin; "she isn't!"

He sat down on a small mushroom and clasped his hands about his knees and looked mad—just mad. Angry or indignant wouldn't express it.

"I have a great mind to go and be a misanthrope," he said.

"Oh, I wouldn't," said Fairyfoot. He didn't know what a misanthrope was; but he thought it must be something unpleasant.

"Wouldn't you?" said Robin, looking up at him.

"No," answered Fairyfoot.

"Well," said Robin, "I guess I won't. Let's go and have some fun. They are all that way. You can't depend on any of them. Never trust one of them. I believe that creature has been engaged as much as twice since I left. By a singular coincidence," he added, "I have been married twice myself—but of course that's different. I'm a man, you know, and—well, it's different. We won't dwell on it. Let's go and dance. But wait a minute first." He took a little bottle from his pocket.

"If you remain the size you are," he continued, "you will tread on whole sets of lanciers and destroy entire brigades. If you drink this, you will become as small as we are; and then when you are going home, I will give you something to make you large again." Fairyfoot drank from the little flagon, and immediately he felt himself growing smaller and smaller until at last he was as small as his companion.

"Now, come on!" said Robin.

On they went and joined the fairies, and they danced and played fairy games and feasted on fairy dainties, and were so gay and happy that Fairyfoot was wild with joy. Everybody made him welcome and seemed to like him, and the lady fairies were simply delightful, especially Gauzita, who took a great fancy to him. Just before the sun rose, Robin gave him something from another flagon, and he grew large again, and two minutes and three seconds and a half before daylight the ball broke up, and Robin took him home and left him, promising to call for him the next night.

Every night throughout the whole summer the same thing happened. At midnight he went to the fairies' dance; and at two minutes and three seconds and a half before dawn he came home. He was never lonely any more, because all day long he could think of what pleasure he would have when the night came; and besides that, all the fairies were his friends. But when the summer was coming to an end, Robin Goodfellow said to him: "This is our last dance—at least, it will be our last for some time. At this time of the year we always go back to our own country, and we don't return until spring."

This made Fairyfoot very sad. He did not know how he could bear to be left alone again, but he knew it could not be helped; so he tried to be as cheerful as possible, and he went to the final festivities and enjoyed himself more than ever before, and Gauzita gave him a tiny ring for a parting gift. But the next night, when Robin did not come for him, he felt very lonely indeed, and the next day he was so sorrowful that he wandered far away into the forest in the hope of finding something to cheer him a little. He wandered so far that he became very tired and thirsty, and he was just making up his mind to go home, when he thought he heard the sound of falling water. It seemed to come from behind a thicket of climbing roses; and he went toward the place and pushed the branches aside a little so that he could look through. What he saw was a great surprise to him. Though it was the end of the summer, inside the thicket the roses were blooming in thousands all around a pool as clear as crystal, into which the sparkling water fell from a hole in a rock above. It was the most beautiful, clear pool that Fairyfoot had ever seen, and he pressed his way through the rose branches, and, entering the circle they enclosed, he knelt by the water and drank.

Almost instantly his feeling of sadness left him, and he felt quite happy and refreshed. He stretched himself on the thick perfumed moss and listened to the tinkling of the water, and it was not long before he fell asleep.

When he awakened, the moon was shining, the pool sparkled like a silver plaque crusted with diamonds, and two nightingales were singing in the branches over his head. And the next moment he found out that he understood their language just as plainly as if they had been human beings instead of birds. The water with which he had quenched his thirst was enchanted, and had given him this new power.

"Poor boy!" said one nightingale, "he looks tired. I wonder where he came from."

"Why, my dear," said the other; "is it possible you don't know that he is Prince Fairyfoot?"

"What!" said the first nightingale—"the King of Stumpinghame's son who was born with small feet?"

"Yes," said the second. "And the poor child has lived in the forest, keeping the swineherd's pigs, ever since. And he is a very nice boy, too—never throws stones at birds or robs nests."

"What a pity he doesn't know about the pool where the red berries grow!" said the first nightingale.

PART THREE

"WHAT POOL—AND what red berries?" asked the second nightingale.

"Why, my dear," said the first, "is it possible you don't know about the pool where the red berries grow—the pool where the poor, dear Princess Goldenhair met with her misfortune?"

"Never heard of it," said the second nightingale rather crossly.

"Well," explained the other, "you have to follow the brook for a day and three-quarters and then take all the paths to the left until you come to the pool. It is very ugly and muddy, and bushes with red berries on them grow around it."

"Well, what of that?" said her companion; "and what happened to the Princess Goldenhair?"

"Don't you know that, either?" exclaimed her friend.

"No."

"Ah!" said the first nightingale, "it was very sad. She went out with her father, the King, who had a hunting party; and she lost her way and wandered on and on until she came to the pool. Her poor little feet were so hot that she took off her gold-embroidered satin slippers, and put them into the water—her feet, not the slippers—and the next minute they began to grow and grow, and to get larger and larger, until they were so immense she could hardly walk at all; and though all the physicians in the kingdom have tried to make them smaller, nothing can be done, and she is perfectly unhappy."

"What a pity she doesn't know about this pool!" said the other bird. "If she just came here and bathed them three times in the water, they would be smaller and more beautiful than ever, and she would be more lovely than she has ever been."

"It is a pity," said her companion; "but you know if we once let people know what this water will do, we should be overrun with creatures bathing themselves beautiful, and trampling our moss and tearing down our rose-trees, and we should never have any peace."

"That is true," agreed the other.

Very soon after, they flew away, and Fairyfoot was left alone. He had been so excited while they were talking that he had been hardly able to lie still. He was so sorry for the Princess Goldenhair, and so glad for himself. Now he could find his way to the pool with the red berries, and he could bathe his feet in it until they were large enough to satisfy Stumpinghame; and he could go back to his father's court, and his parents would perhaps be fond of him. But he had so good a heart that he could not think of being happy himself and letting others remain unhappy, when he could help them. So the first thing was to find the Princess Goldenhair, and tell her about the nightingales' fountain. But how was he to find her? The nightingales had not told him. He was very much troubled, indeed. How was he to find her?

Suddenly, quite suddenly, he thought of the ring Gauzita had given him. When she had given it to him she had made an odd remark.

"When you wish to go anywhere," she had said, "hold it in your hand, turn around twice with closed eyes, and something queer will happen."

He had thought it was one of her little jokes, but now it occurred to him that at least he might try what would happen. So he rose up, held the ring in his hand, closed his eyes, and turned around twice.

What did happen was that he began to walk, not very fast, but still passing along as if he were moving rapidly. He did not know where he was going, but he guessed that the ring did, and that if he obeyed it, he should find the Princess Goldenhair. He went on and on, not getting in the least tired, until about daylight he found himself under a great tree, and on the ground beneath it was spread a delightful breakfast which he knew was for him. He sat down and ate it, and then got up again and went on his way once more. Before noon he had left the forest behind him and was in a strange country. He knew it was not Stumpinghame, because the people had not large feet. But they all had sad faces, and once or twice, when he passed groups of them who were talking, he heard them speak of the Princess Goldenhair, as if they were sorry for her and could not enjoy themselves while such a misfortune rested upon her.

"So sweet, and lovely, and kind a princess!" they said; "and it really seems as if she would never be any better."

The sun was just setting when Fairyfoot came in sight of the palace. It was built of white marble and had beautiful pleasure-grounds about it, but somehow there seemed to be a settled gloom in the air. Fairyfoot had entered the great pleasure-garden and was wondering where it would be best to go first, when he saw a love-ly white fawn, with a golden collar around its neck, come bounding over the flower-beds, and he heard, at a little distance, a sweet voice saying sorrowfully, "Come back, my fawn; I can not run and play with you as once I used to. Do not leave me, my little friend."

And soon from behind the trees came a line of beautiful girls, walking two by two, all very slowly; and at the head of the line, first of all, came the loveliest princess in the world, dressed softly in pure white, with a wreath of lilies on her long golden hair, which fell almost to the hem of her white gown.

She had so fair and tender a young face, and her large, soft eyes yet looked so sorrowful, that Fairyfoot loved her in a moment, and he knelt on one knee, taking off his cap and bending his head until his own golden hair almost hid his face.

"Beautiful Princess Goldenhair, beautiful and sweet Princess, may I speak to you?" he said.

The princess stopped and looked at him, and answered him softly. It surprised her to see one so poorly dressed kneeling before her, in her palace-gardens, among the brilliant flowers; but she always spoke softly to everyone.

"What is there that I can do for you, my friend?" she said.

"Beautiful Princess," answered Fairyfoot, blushing, "I hope very much that I may be able to do something for you."

"For me!" she exclaimed. "Thank you, friend; what is it you can do? Indeed, I need a help I am afraid no one can ever give me."

"Gracious and fairest lady," said Fairyfoot, "it is that help, I think—nay, I am sure—that I bring to you."

"Oh!" said the sweet princess. "You have a kind face and most true eyes, and when I look at you—I do not know why it is, but I feel a little happier. What is it you would say to me?"

Still kneeling before her, still bending his head modestly, and still blushing, Fairyfoot told his story. He told her of his own sadness and loneliness, and of why he was considered so terrible a disgrace to his family. He told her about the fountain of the nightingales and what he had heard there, and how he had journeyed through the forest, and beyond it into her own country, to find her. And while he told it, her beautiful face changed from red to white, and her hands closely clasped themselves together.

"Oh!" she said when he had finished, "I know that this is true, from the kind look in your eyes. And I shall be happy again. And how can I thank you for being so good to a poor little princess whom you had never seen?"

"Only let me see you happy once more, most sweet Princess," answered Fairyfoot, "and that will be all I desire—only if, perhaps, I might once—kiss your hand."

She held out her hand to him with so lovely a look in her soft eyes that he felt happier than he had ever been before, even at the fairy dances. This was a different kind of happiness. Her hand was as white as a dove's wing and as soft as a dove's breast. "Come," she said; "let us go at once to the King."

Within a few minutes the whole palace was in an uproar of excitement. Preparations were made to go to the fountain of the nightingales immediately. Remembering what the birds had said about not wishing to be disturbed, Fairyfoot asked the King to take only a small party. So no one was to go but the King himself, the Princess, in a covered chair carried by two bearers, the Lord High Chamberlain, two Maids of Honor, and Fairyfoot.

Before morning they were on their way; and the day after, they reached the thicket of roses, and Fairyfoot pushed aside the branches and led the way into the dell.

The Princess Goldenhair sat down upon the edge of the pool, and put her feet

The marriage of . . .

into it. In two minutes, they began to look smaller. She bathed them once, twice, three times, and, as the nightingales had said, they became smaller and more beautiful than ever. As for the Princess herself, she really could not be more beautiful than she had been; but the Lord High Chamberlain—who had been an exceedingly ugly old gentleman—after washing his face, became so young and handsome that the first Maid of Honor immediately fell in love with him. Whereupon she washed her face, and became so beautiful that he fell in love with her, and they were engaged upon the spot.

The Princess could not find any words to tell Fairyfoot how grateful she was and how happy. She could only look at him again and again with her soft, radiant eyes, and again and again give him her hand that he might kiss it.

She was so sweet and gentle that Fairyfoot could not bear the thought of leaving her; and when the King begged him to return to the palace with them and live there always, he was more glad than I can tell you. To be near this lovely Princess, to be her friend, to love and serve her and look at her every day was such happiness that he wanted nothing more. But first he wished to visit his father and mother and sisters and brothers in Stumpinghame; so the King and Princess and their attendants went with him to the pool where the red berries grew; and after he had bathed his feet in the water, they were so large that Stumpinghame contained nothing like them, even the King's and Queen's seeming small in comparison. And when, a few days later, he arrived at the Stumpinghame Palace, attended in great state by the magnificent retinue with which the father of the Princess Goldenhair had provided him, he was received with unbounded rapture by his parents. The King and Queen felt that to have a son with feet of such a size was something to be proud of, indeed. They could not admire him sufficiently, although the whole country was illuminated and feasting continued throughout his visit.

But though he was glad to be no longer a disgrace to his family, it can not be

. . . Prince Fairyfoot and Princess Goldenhair

said that he enjoyed the size of his feet very much on his own account. Indeed, he much preferred being Prince Fairyfoot, as fleet as the wind and as light as a young deer, and he was quite glad to go to the fountain of the nightingales after his visit was at an end, and bathe his feet small again, and to return to the palace of the Princess Goldenhair with the soft and tender eyes. There every one loved him, and he loved every one, and was four times as happy as the day is long.

He loved the Princess more dearly every day, and of course, as soon as they were old enough, they were married. And of course, too, they used to go in the summer to the forest and dance in the moonlight with the fairies, who adored them both.

When they went to visit Stumpinghame, they always bathed their feet in the pool of the red berries; and when they returned, they made them small again in the fountain of the nightingales.

They were always great friends with Robin Goodfellow, and he was always very confidential with them about Gauzita, who continued to be as pretty and saucy as ever.

"Some of these days," he used to say severely, "I'll marry another fairy, and see how she'll like that—to see some one else basking in my society! I *will* get even with her!"

But he *never* did.

First published in the December 1886 and January and
February 1887 editions of *St. Nicholas Magazine*

The Judge and the Cur

BY TEMPLE BAILEY

ONY'S STAND WAS on the coldest corner of the wind-swept street. In summer this was very fortunate, for Tony could catch the occasional coolness of such breezes as straggled up from the river; but in winter Tony's fingers grew red and his nose blue in the chill, searching blasts.

There was consolation, however, in the peanut-roaster. By hugging very close to it, Tony could keep himself warm on one side at least.

In the bitterest weather Tony kept his fruit covered. The man who owned the stand did not wish to have the fruit freeze, but he was not so careful of Tony. He came every morning to see that all was in order, to scold Tony until the boy was stubbornly resentful, and then to leave him through all the tiresome hours until night came on, when he returned and sent Tony home to a poor little supper and a poor little bed.

Tony could not have stood it if it had not been for Smuggler. Smuggler was a dog. Tony had named him Smuggler because he had to be smuggled into odd corners whenever the man who owned the stand came around; and Smuggler, like the wise, small tramp of the streets that he was, took refuge under his piece of carpet beneath the stand whenever the dog-catchers or a policeman of unfriendly aspect walked by or stopped at the peanut-roaster.

The big policeman on the corner, however, kept his eyes and ears closed to the fact that there was an unlicensed cur on his beat. Now and then the proprietor of a little restaurant across the street treated Tony to a bowl of soup—thick, hot soup, with two slices of bread.

So, with these occasional feasts, and with the nights of comfort when he and Smuggler lay curled close together, Tony managed to live without running away, and even to be a little happy.

But the dog-catchers had their eyes on Smuggler. One very cold morning they swept up the street with nets ready, but Smuggler disappeared at the first sound of the yelping, barking wagon-load, and there was nothing to be seen under the stand but an innocent piece of old carpet. When, however, the dog-catchers had vanished around the corner, Tony gave a little whistle, the carpet became suddenly animated, a scrubby head emerged, and, with a glad bark of freedom, Smuggler charged down on the sparrows in the street.

And it was then that the Judge drove up. "It's just such curs, Johnson," he said, looking at Smuggler with great disfavor, as the small vagabond darted under the horses' feet, "that make dogs a menace to the community. A good dog," he continued, with his hand on the head of Emperor II, "is a precious possession, but I haven't any use for common canines."

"No, sir," grinned the coachman, as he climbed down. "Those are fine oranges, sir. A dozen, did you say, sir?"

"Yes," said the Judge.

Emperor II sat quietly in front of the Judge. Between the two there was the dignified understanding that exists when the dog is of noble breed and the master of noble instincts. They were both of them gentlemen of the old school, and if Emperor II rarely received a caress from the old man's hand, he knew every inflection of the testy, kind old voice, and his tail would wave slightly at the mere sound of his master's name.

Tony was putting up the fruit stolidly. He could not understand why people wanted fruit in such weather, nor could he understand why so fine a gentleman should be buying fruit at his stand instead of patronizing one of the fashionable and high-priced fruit-stores up town. Why didn't he get one of the hot pies at the little restaurant across the way? If Tony had money, he would buy ten hot pies at one time, and then he and Smuggler would eat and eat—

Just then the determined dog-catchers executed a flank movement. They had spotted Smuggler, and they had moved away merely to allay suspicion.

"Good!" said the Judge, as he saw the man with the net making for Smuggler.

Tony dropped the bag of oranges and opened his arms to his little dog; but the man with the net ran between them and reached for Smuggler, who was huddled up under the stand. Then, suddenly, there was the rush of a big grayish body, and Emperor II, in spite of the Judge's efforts to hold him, leaped to the rescue of Smuggler—poor, frightened, cowering Smuggler.

Tony dropped the bag of oranges and opened his arms to his little dog.

The old dog laid his head on his master's knee and looked at him.

Emperor stood in front of him, his massive old head raised, his white teeth show-ing in menace, defying any one to touch him—him who wore on his massive sil-ver-mounted collar the tag that made him a free dog within the limits of the city.

At this the dog-catcher stopped. "Call off your dog, sir," he said to the Judge, respectfully but firmly.

Tony stood with his two small red hands clasped closely together, his miserable, imploring face turned up to the Judge.

"Please, please!" he gasped, and the tears made dirty little rivers down his cheeks.

"Oh, by George!" said the Judge.

The big policeman had strolled up and a small crowd had gathered.

"Fine mastiff, sir," said the big policeman, as he looked at grand old Emperor II, who still held the catchers at bay, "but you will have to call him off."

"Emperor, boy, come here!" commanded the Judge, reluctantly.

Then Emperor's head drooped. He looked from the shivering little cur in the corner to his master. Then, seeing no sign of relenting in the Judge's face, he went to the carriage and leaped in, with ears down—a disappointed knight-errant.

The dog-catchers then carried off the struggling, yelping Smuggler, and Tony, seeing that remonstrance was useless, with dulled, unquestioning submission to more suffering, went on putting the fruit into bags.

The big policeman strolled over to the side of the carriage. "Poor little chap!" he said. "The dog was all he had."

The Judge cleared his throat. "Such dogs are a nuisance," he began; but his voice wavered a little, and Emperor, noting the kinder tone, turned on his master two beautiful, pleading eyes, and put a paw on the Judge's knee.

"There's nothing to be done, I suppose?" mused the Judge, with his eyes on the distant wagon of the dog-catchers.

"No; unless you could go to the pound and pay his tax."

"Humph!" said the Judge, testily. "My dinner is waiting"; and then Johnson climbed in with the fruit, and they drove away.

The big policeman tried to comfort Tony, and went over to the restaurant, and soon a waiter brought him a bowl of soup and a hot pie; but the boy was dumb with misery.

Whirling around in his brain was but one thought: Smuggler was gone, and he would never see his little dog again. After that nothing mattered. He didn't care whether he took care of the stand or not. He would go away somewhere and never come back. When the man who owned the stand came that night, he scolded and fussed, and finally struck at the boy, but the big policeman interfered. "Stop that," he said, "I'll run you in."

All night long, in his miserable bed, the boy sobbed and slept, and dreamed that Smuggler was back again, and woke to find his arms empty. He thought of Smuggler with the other yelping, downcast, condemned dogs at the pound. He hoped they would not hurt him. He wondered if he missed his little master, and then he sobbed again as he yearned for the small warm body that had lain for so many nights at his side. Smuggler might not be beautiful, but he was loving, and "He was all I had," groaned Tony, with heavy weeping, as he sank into troubled slumber.

In the morning he had made up his mind that he would run away. There was country somewhere, and perhaps he could find it, and sleep in some barn on the hay. No one cared for him, no one but Smuggler, and perhaps even now Smuggler was about to die.

Then, in the gray dawn, he went back to the fruit-stand, to sit with his head in his hands. Toward noon, as he crouched shivering and unhappy in his cold corner, there came the sound of swift trotting horses, and Tony was conscious all at once of a picture in which the Judge, with his big fur overcoat, was the main feature. At his feet was the great mastiff, his head up, his eyes blazing with joyous excitement.

And what was that in the corner of the seat? Something small and yellow and scrubby! Tony gasped, but before he could cry out, the carriage stopped, and the small yellow scrubby object bolted out of it straight into Tony's arms!

It was Smuggler! Little Smuggler, with a collar studded with silver nails, in every-

Tony and Smuggler

thing but size just like the one around Emperor's lordly neck, and hanging from the collar was the precious tag that made him a licensed dog!

The Judge's face was beaming as he explained, but he could scarcely make himself heard, for the little dog was barking, and Emperor bayed excitedly as he leaped back and forth from the Judge to Tony.

"We had a time, I tell you," laughed the Judge. "We went to the pound this morning. I couldn't tell which was your dog, but Emperor knew him, and we paid the fine, and got the license, and bought a collar, and here we are!"

But the Judge did not tell of his troubled conscience of the night before, when, in his easy-chair before a glowing fire, with Emperor II stretched full length on the rug, the thought of the lonely little figure on the windy corner had come between him and his book. And when the old dog had laid his head on his master's knee and looked at him with inquiring, loving eyes, the Judge had made a decision. "We'll do it the first thing in the morning, old fellow," he had said, and Emperor gave him his paw, and they shook hands on it.

At first Tony could not thank the Judge. He simply stood there with a glorified look on his swarthy face, the wriggling, happy dog in his arms, and said over and over again:

"Smuggler, Smuggler, Smuggler!"

The Judge's eyes were watery. He took a bill out of his pocket.

"Here, boy," he said; "spend this on yourself and the dog."

Tony went over to the carriage and put one arm around Emperor's great neck.

"Thank you both—thank you," he began.

But all at once the Judge was in a great hurry. "There, there," he said sharply; "I'll be late at my office." But he smiled as Johnson gathered up the reins. Then, as he drove off, he gave a backward glance at the thin little figure and the yellow cur, and he laid his hand on Emperor's head with one of his rare caresses.

"By George!" he said huskily. "By George!"

First published in the February 1904 edition of *St. Nicholas Magazine*

Casperl

BY HENRY CULYER BUNNER

CASPERL WAS A wood-chopper, and the son of a wood-chopper, and although he was only eighteen when his father died, he was so strong and active, that he went on chopping and hauling wood for the whole neighborhood, and people said he did it quite as well as his father, while he was certainly a great deal more pleasant in his manner and much more willing to oblige others.

It was a poor country, however, for it was right in the heart of the Black Forest, and there were more witches and fairies and goblins there than healthy human beings. So Casperl scarcely made a living, for all he worked hard and rose up early in the morning, summer and winter. His friends often advised him to go to some better place, where he could earn more money; but he only shook his head and said that the place was good enough for him.

He never told any one, though, why he loved his poor hut in the depths of the dark forest, because it was a secret which he did not wish to share with strangers. For he had discovered, a mile or two from his home, in the very blackest part of the woods, an enchanted mountain. It was a high mountain, covered with trees and rocks and thick, tangled undergrowth, except at the very top, where there stood a castle surrounded by smooth, green lawns and beautiful gardens, which were always kept in the neatest possible order, although no gardener was ever seen.

This enchanted mountain had been under a spell for nearly two hundred years. The lovely Princess who lived there had once ruled the whole country. But a powerful and wicked magician disguised himself as a prince, and professed love to her. At first the Princess loved her false suitor; but one day she found out that he was not what he pretended to be, and she told him to leave her and never to come near her again.

"For you are not a prince," she said. "You are an impostor, and I will never wed any but a true prince."

"Very well," said the magician, in a rage. "You shall wait for your true prince, if there is such a thing as a true prince; and you shall marry no one till he comes."

And then the magician cast a spell upon the beautiful castle on the top of the mountain, and the terrible forest sprang up about it. Rocks rose up out of the earth and piled themselves in great heaps among the tree-trunks. Saplings and brush and twisted, poisonous vines came to fill up every crack and crevice, so that no mortal man could possibly go to the summit, except by one path, which was purposely left clear. And in that path there was a gate that the strongest man could not open, it was so heavy. Farther up the mountain-slope, the trunk of a tree lay right across the way—a magic tree, that no one could climb over or crawl under or cut through. And beyond the gate and the tree was a dragon with green eyes that frightened away every man that looked at it.

And there the beautiful Princess was doomed to live until the true prince should arrive and overcome these three obstacles.

Now, although none of the people in the forest, except Casperl, knew of the mountain or the Princess, the story had been told in many distant countries, and year after year young princes came from all parts of the earth to try to rescue the lovely captive and win her for a bride. But one after the other, they all tried and failed—the best of them could not so much as open the gate.

And so there the Princess remained, as the years went on. But she did not grow any older, or any less beautiful, for she was still waiting for the True Prince, and she believed that some day he would come.

This was what kept Casperl from leaving the Black Forest. He was sorry for the Princess, and he hoped some day to see her rescued and wedded to the True Prince.

Every evening, when his work was done, he would walk to the foot of the mountain, and sit down on a great stone, and look up to the top, where the Princess was walking in her garden. And as it was an enchanted mountain, he could see her clearly, although she was so far away. Yes, he could see her face as well as though she were close by him, and he thought it was truly the loveliest face in the world.

There he would sit and sadly watch the princes who tried to climb the hill. There was scarcely a day that some prince from a far country did not come to make the attempt. One after another, they would arrive with gorgeous trains of followers, mounted on fine horses, and dressed in costumes so magnificent that a plain cloth-of-gold suit looked shabby among them. They would look up to the mountain-top and see the Princess walking there, and they would praise her beauty so warmly that Casperl, when he heard them, felt sure he was quite right in thinking her the loveliest woman in the world.

But every prince had to make the trial by himself. That was one of the conditions which the magician made when he laid the spell upon the castle; although Casperl did not know it.

And each prince would throw off his cloak, and shoulder a silver- or gold-handled ax, and fasten his sword by his side, and set out to climb the hill, and open the gate, and cut through the fallen tree, and slay the dragon, and wed the Princess.

Up he would go, bright and hopeful, and tug away at the gate until he found that he could do nothing with it, and then he would plunge into the tangled thickets of underbrush, and try his best to fight his way through to the summit.

But every one of them came back, after a while, with his fine clothes torn and his soft skin scratched, all tired and disheartened and worn out. And then he would look spitefully up at the mountain, and say he didn't care so much about wedding the Princess, after all; that she was only a common enchanted princess, just like any other enchanted princess, and really not worth so much trouble.

This would grieve Casperl, for he couldn't help thinking that it was impossible that any other woman could be as lovely as *his* Princess. You see, he called her *his* Princess, because he took such an interest in her, and he didn't think there could be any harm in speaking of her in that way, just to himself. For he never supposed she could even know that there was such a humble creature as poor young Casperl, the wood-chopper, who sat at the foot of the hill and looked up at her.

And so the days went on, and the unlucky princes came and went, and Casperl watched them all. Sometimes he saw his Princess look down from over the castle parapets, and eagerly follow with her lovely eyes the struggles of some brave suitor through the thickets, until the poor Prince gave up the job in despair. Then she would look sad and turn away. But generally she paid no attention to the attempts that were made to reach her. That kind of thing had been going on so long that she was quite used to it.

By and by, one summer evening, as Casperl sat watching, there came a little prince with a small train of attendants. He was rather undersized for a prince; he didn't look strong, and he did look as though he slept too much in the morning and too little at night. He slipped off his coat, however, and climbed up the road, and began to push and pull at the gate.

Casperl watched him carelessly for a while, and then, happening to look up, he saw that the Princess was gazing sadly down on the poor little Prince as he tugged and toiled.

And then a bold idea came to Casperl. Why shouldn't he help the Prince? He was young and strong; he had often thought that, if he were a prince, a gate like that should not keep him away from the Princess. Why, indeed, should he not give his strength to help to free the Princess? And he felt a great pity for the poor little Prince, too.

So he walked modestly up the hill and offered his services to the Prince.

"Your Royal Highness," he said, "I am only a wood-chopper; but, if you please, I am a strong wood-chopper, and perhaps I can be of use to you."

"But why should you take the trouble to help me?" inquired the Prince. "What good will it do you?"

"Oh, well!" said Casperl, "it's helping the Princess, too, don't you know?"

"No, I don't know," said the Prince. "However, you may try what you can do. Here, put your shoulder to this end of the gate, and I will stand right behind you."

"Courage, your Royal Highness!" said Casperl.

Now, Casperl did not know that it was forbidden to any suitor to have help in his attempt to climb the hill. The Prince knew it, though, but he said to himself, "When I am through with this wood-chopper I will dismiss him, and no one will know anything about it. I can never lift this gate by myself. I will let him do it for me, and thus I shall get the Princess, and he will be just as well satisfied, for he is only a wood-chopper."

So Casperl put his broad shoulder to the gate and pushed with all his might. It was very heavy, but after a while it began to move a little.

"Courage, your Royal Highness!" said Casperl. "We'll move it, after all."

But if he had looked over his shoulder, he would have seen that the little Prince was not pushing at all, but that he had put on his cloak, and was standing idly by, laughing to himself at the way he was making a wood-chopper do his work for him.

After a long struggle, the gate gave way, and swung open just wide enough to let them through. It was a close squeeze for the Prince; but Casperl held the gate open until he slipped through.

"Dear me," said the Prince, "you're quite a strong fellow. You really were of some assistance to me. Let me see, I think the stories say something about a tree, or some such thing, farther up the road. As you are a wood-chopper, and as you have your ax with you, perhaps you might walk up a bit and see if you can't make yourself useful."

Casperl was quite willing, for he began to feel that he was doing something for the Princess, and it pleased him to think that even a wood-chopper could do her a service.

So they walked up until they came to the tree. And then the Prince drew out his silver ax, and sharpened it carefully on the sole of his shoe, while Casperl picked up a stone and whetted his old iron ax, which was all he had.

"Now," said the Prince, "let's see what we can do."

But he really didn't do anything. It was Casperl who swung his ax and chopped hard at the magic tree. Every blow made the chips fly; but the wood grew instantly over every cut, just as though he had been cutting into water.

For a little while the Prince amused himself by trying first to climb over the tree, and then to crawl under it. But he soon found that whichever way he went, the tree grew up or down so fast that he was shut off. Finally he gave it up, and went and lay down on his back on the grass, and watched Casperl working.

And Casperl worked hard. The tree grew fast; but he chopped faster. His forehead was wet and his arms were tired, but he worked away and made the chips fly in a cloud. He was too busy to take the time to look over his shoulder, so he did not see the Prince lying on the grass. But every now and then he spoke cheerily, saying, "We'll do it, your Royal Highness!"

And he did it, in the end. After a long, long while, he got the better of the magic tree, for he chopped quicker than it could grow, and at last he had cut a gap right across the trunk.

The Prince jumped up from the grass and leaped nimbly through, and Casperl followed him slowly and sadly, for he was tired, and it began to occur to him that the Prince hadn't said anything about the Princess, which made him wonder if he were the True Prince, after all. "I'm afraid," he thought, "the Princess won't thank me if I bring her a prince who doesn't love her. And it really is very strange that this Prince hasn't said a word about her."

So he ventured to remark, very meekly:

"Your Royal Highness will be glad to see the Princess."

"Oh, no doubt," said the Prince.

"And the Princess will be very glad to see your Royal Highness," went on Casperl.

"Oh, of course!" said the Prince. "And your Royal Highness will be very good to the Princess," said Casperl further, by way of a hint.

"I think," said the Prince, "that you are talking altogether too much about the Princess. I don't believe I need you any more. Perhaps you would better go home. I'm much obliged to you for your assistance. I can't reward you just now, but if you will come to see me after I have married the Princess, I may be able to do something for you."

Casperl turned away, somewhat disappointed, and was going down the hill, when the Prince called him back.

"Oh, by the way!" he said; "There's a dragon, I understand, a little farther on. Perhaps you'd like to come along and see me kill him?"

Casperl thought he would like to see the Prince do something for the Princess, so he followed meekly on. Very soon they came to the top of the mountain, and

"I am sure you are a Prince," said the Princess.

saw the green lawns and beautiful gardens of the enchanted castle—and there was the dragon waiting for them.

The dragon reared itself on its dreadful tail, and flapped its black wings; and its great green, shining, scaly body swelled and twisted, and it roared in a terrible way.

The little Prince drew his jeweled sword and walked slowly up to the monster. And then the great beast opened its red mouth and blew out one awful breath, that caught the Prince up as if he were a feather, and whisked him clear off the mountain and over the tops of the trees in the valley, and that was the last anyone ever saw of him.

Then Casperl grasped his old ax and leaped forward to meet the dragon, never stopping to think how poor his weapon was. But all of a sudden the dragon vanished and disappeared and was gone, and there was no trace of it anywhere; but the beautiful Princess stood in its place and smiled and held out her white hand to Casperl.

"My Prince!" she said, "so you have come at last!"

"I beg your gracious Highness's pardon," said Casperl; "but I am no Prince."

"Oh, yes, you are!" said the Princess; "how did you come here, if you are not my True Prince? Didn't you come through the gate and across the tree, and haven't you driven the dragon away?"

"I only helped—" began Casperl.

"You did it all," said the Princess, "for I saw you. Please don't contradict a lady."

"But I don't see how I could—" Casperl began again.

"People who are helping others," said the Princess, "often have a strength beyond their own. But perhaps you didn't come here to help me, after all?"

"Oh, your gracious Highness," cried Casperl, "there's nothing I wouldn't do to help you. But I'm sure I'm not a Prince."

"And I am sure you are," said the Princess, and she led him to a fountain near by, and when he looked at his reflection in the water, he saw that he was dressed more magnificently than any prince who ever yet had come to the enchanted mountain.

And just then the wedding-bells began to ring, and that is all I know of the fairy story, for Casperl and the Princess lived so happily ever after in the castle on top of the mountain, that they never came down to tell the rest of it.

First published in the April 1886 edition of *St. Nicholas Magazine*

In Yeddo Bay

BY JACK LONDON

SOMEWHERE ALONG THEATER Street he had lost it. He remembered being hustled somewhat roughly on the bridge over one of the canals that cross that busy thoroughfare. Possibly some light-fingered pickpocket was even then enjoying the fifty-odd yen his purse had contained. And then again, he thought, he might have lost it himself, just lost it carelessly.

Hopelessly, and for the twentieth time, he searched in all his pockets for the missing purse. It was not there. His hand lingered in his empty hip-pocket, and he woefully regarded the voluble and vociferous restaurant-keeper, who insanely clamored: "Twenty-five sen! You pay now! Twenty-five sen!"

"But my purse!" the boy said. "I tell you I've lost it somewhere."

Whereupon the restaurant-keeper lifted his arms indignantly and shrieked: "Twenty-five sen! Twenty-five sen! You pay now!"

Quite a crowd had collected, and it was growing embarrassing for Alf Davis.

It was so ridiculous and petty, Alf thought. Such a disturbance about nothing! And, decidedly, he must be doing something. Thoughts of diving wildly through that forest of legs, and of striking out at whomsoever opposed him, flashed through his mind; but, as though divining his purpose, one of the waiters, a short and chunky chap with an evil-looking cast in one eye, seized him by the arm.

"You pay now! You pay now! Twenty-five sen!" yelled the proprietor, hoarse with rage.

Alf was red in the face, too, from mortification; but he resolutely set out on another exploration. He had given up the purse, pinning his last hope on stray coins. In the little change-pocket of his coat he found a ten-sen piece and five copper sen; and remembering having recently missed a ten-sen piece, he cut the seam of the pocket and resurrected the coin from the depths of the lining. Twenty-five sen he held in his hand, the sum required to pay for the supper he had eaten. He turned them over to the proprietor, who counted them, grew suddenly calm, and bowed obsequiously—in fact, the whole crowd bowed obsequiously and melted away.

Alf Davis was a young sailor, just turned sixteen, on board the *Annie Mine*, an American sealing-schooner which had run into Yokohama to ship its season's catch of skins to London. And in this his second trip ashore he was beginning to catch his first puzzling glimpses of the Oriental mind. He laughed when the bowing and kowtowing was over, and turned on his heel to confront another problem. How was he to get aboard ship? It was eleven o'clock at night, and there would be no ship's boats ashore, while the outlook for hiring a native boatman, with nothing but empty pockets to draw upon, was not particularly inviting.

Keeping a sharp lookout for shipmates, he went down to the pier. At Yokohama there are no long lines of wharves. The shipping lies out at anchor, enabling a few hundred of the locals to make a livelihood by carrying passengers to and from the shore.

A dozen sampan men and boys hailed Alf and offered their services. He select-ed the most favorable-looking one, an old and beneficent-appearing man with a withered leg. Alf stepped into his sampan and sat down. It was quite dark and he could not see what the old fellow was doing, though he evidently was doing noth-ing about shoving off and getting under way. At last he limped over and peered into Alf's face.

"Ten sen," he said.

"Yes, I know, ten sen," Alf answered him careless-ly. "But hurry up. American schooner."

"Ten sen. You pay now," the old fellow insisted.

Alf felt himself grow hot all over at the hateful words "pay now." "You take me to American schooner; then I pay," he said.

But the man stood up patiently before him, held out his hand, and said, "Ten sen. You pay now."

Alf tried to explain. He had no money. He had lost his purse. But he would pay. As soon as he got aboard the American schooner, then he would pay. No, he would not even go aboard the American schooner. He

Quite a crowd had collected, and it was growing embarrassing for Alf Davis.

would call to his shipmates, and they would give the sampan man the ten sen first. After that he would go aboard. So it was all right, of course.

To all of which the beneficent-appearing old man replied; "You pay now. Ten sen." And, to make matters worse, the other sampan men squatted on the pier-steps, listening.

Alf, chagrined and angry, stood up to step ashore. But the old fellow laid a detaining hand on his sleeve. "You give shirt now. I take you 'Merican schooner," he proposed.

Then it was that all of Alt's American independence flamed up in his breast. He had a born dislike of being imposed upon, and to Alf this was sheer robbery! Ten sen was equivalent to six American cents, while his shirt, which was of good quality and was new, had cost him two dollars.

He turned his back on the man without a word, and went out to the end of the pier, the crowd, laughing with great gusto, following at his heels. The majority of them were heavy-set, muscular fellows, and the July night being one of sweltering heat, they were clad in the least possible raiment. The water-people of any race are rough and turbulent, and it struck Alf that to be out at midnight on a pier-end with such a crowd of wharfmen, in a big Japanese city, was not as safe as it might be.

One burly fellow, with a shock of black hair and ferocious eyes, came up. The rest shoved in after him to take part in the discussion.

"Give me shoes," the man said. "Give me shoes now. I take you 'Merican schooner."

Alf shook his head; whereat the crowd clamored that he accept the proposal. He was so constituted that to brow-beat or bully him was the last way under the sun of getting Alf to do any certain thing. He would dare willingly, but he would not permit himself to be driven. So this attempt of the boat-men to force Alf only aroused all his dogged stubbornness. The same qualities were in him that are in men who lead forlorn hopes; and there, under the stars, on the lonely pier, encircled by the jostling and shouldering gang, he resolved that he would die rather than submit to the indignity of being robbed of a single stitch of clothing. Not value, but principle, was at stake.

Then somebody thrust roughly against him from behind. He whirled about with flashing eyes, and the circle involuntarily gave ground. But the crowd was growing more boisterous. Each and every article of clothing he had on was demanded by one or another, and these demands were shouted simultaneously at the tops of very healthy lungs.

Alf had long since ceased to say anything, but he knew that the situation was getting dangerous, and that the only thing left to him was to get away. His face was set doggedly, his eyes glinted like points of steel, and his body was firmly and confidently poised. This air of determination sufficiently impressed the boat-men to make them give way before him when he started to walk toward the shore-end of the pier. But they trooped along beside him and behind him, shouting and laughing more noisily than ever. One of the youngsters, about Alf's size and build, impudently snatched his cap from his head; but before he could put it on his own head, Alf struck out from the shoulder, and sent the fellow rolling on the stones.

The cap flew out of his hand and disappeared among the many legs. Alf did some quick thinking; his sailor pride would not permit him to leave the cap in their hands. He followed in the direction it had sped, and soon found it under the bare foot of a stalwart fellow, who kept his weight stolidly upon it. Alf tried to get the cap out by a sudden jerk, but failed. He shoved against the man's leg, but the man only grunted. It was challenge direct, and Alf accepted it. Like a flash one leg was behind the man and Alf had thrust strongly with his shoulder against the fellow's chest. Nothing could save the man from the fierce vigorousness of the trick, and he was hurled over and backward.

Next, the cap was on Alf's head and his fists were up before him. Then Alf whirled about to prevent attack from behind, and all those in that quarter fled precipitately. This was what he wanted. None remained between him and the shore end. The pier was narrow. Facing them and threatening with his fist those who attempted to pass him on either side, he continued his retreat. It was exciting work, walking backward and at the same time checking that surging mass of men. But they feared sailor's fists; and it was the battles fought by many sailors, more than his own war-like front, that gave Alf the victory.

Where the pier adjoins the shore was the station of the harbor police, and Alf backed into the electric-lighted office, very much to the amusement of the dapper lieutenant in charge. The sampan men, grown quiet and orderly, clustered like flies by the open door, through which they could see and hear what passed.

Alf explained his difficulty in few words, and demanded, as the privilege of a stranger in a strange land, that the lieutenant put him aboard in the police-boat. The lieutenant, in turn, who knew all the "rules and regulations" by heart, explained that the harbor police were not ferrymen, and that the police-boats had other functions to perform than that of transporting belated and penniless sailor-men to their ships. He also said he knew the sampan men to be natural-born robbers, but that so long as they robbed within the law he was powerless. It was their right to collect fares in advance, and who was he to command them to take a passenger and collect fare at the journey's end? Alf acknowledged the justice of his remarks, but suggested that while he could not command he might persuade. The lieutenant was willing to oblige, and went to the door, from where he delivered a speech to the crowd. But they, too, knew their rights, and, when the officer had finished, shouted in chorus their abominable "Ten sen! You pay now! You pay now!"

"You see, I can do nothing," the lieutenant said, who spoke perfect English.

"But I have warned them not to harm or molest you, so you will be safe, at least. The night is warm and half over. Lie down somewhere and go to sleep. I would permit you to sleep here in the office were it not against the rules and regulations."

Alf thanked him for his kindness and courtesy; but the sampan men had aroused all his pride and doggedness, and the problem could not be solved that way. To sleep out the night on the stones was an acknowledgment of defeat.

"The sampan men refuse to take me out?"

The lieutenant nodded.

"And you refuse to take me out?"

Again the lieutenant nodded.

"Well, then, it's not in the rules and regulations that you can prevent my taking myself out?"

The lieutenant was perplexed. "There is no boat," he said.

"That's not the question," Alf proclaimed hotly. "If I take myself out, everybody's satisfied and no harm done?"

"Yes; what you say is true," persisted the puzzled lieutenant, "But you cannot take yourself out."

"You just watch me," was the retort.

Down went Alf's cap on the office floor. Right and left he kicked off his low-cut shoes. Trousers and shirt followed.

"Remember," he said in ringing tones, "I, as a citizen of the United States, shall hold you, the city of Yokohama, and the government of Japan responsible for those clothes. Good night."

He plunged through the doorway, scattering the astounded boatmen to either side, and ran out on the pier. But they quickly recovered and ran after him, shouting with glee at the new phase the situation had taken on. It was a night long remembered among the water-folk of Yokohama town. Straight to the end Alf ran, and, without pause, dived off cleanly and neatly into the water. He struck out with a lusty, single-overhand stroke till curiosity prompted him to halt for a moment. Out of the darkness, from where the pier should be, voices were calling to him. He turned on his back, floated, and listened.

"All right! All right!" he could distinguish from the babel. "No pay now; pay bime by! Come back! Come back now; pay bime by!"

"No, thank you," he called back. "No pay at all. Good night."

Then he faced about in order to locate the *Annie Mine*. She was fully a mile away, and in the darkness it was no easy task to get her bearings. First, he settled upon a blaze of lights which he knew nothing but a man-of-war could make. That must be the United States war-ship *Lancaster*. Somewhere to the left and beyond should be the *Annie Mine*. But to the left he made out three lights close together. That could not be the schooner. For the moment he was confused. He rolled over on his back and shut his eyes, striving to construct a mental picture of the harbor as he had seen it in daytime. With a snort of satisfaction he rolled back again. The three lights evidently belonged to the big English tramp steamer. Therefore the schooner must lie somewhere between the three lights and the *Lancaster*. He gazed long and steadily, and there, very dim and low, but at the point he expected, burned a single light—the anchor-light of the *Annie Mine*.

And it was a fine swim under the starshine. The air was warm as the water, and the water as warm as tepid milk. The good salt taste of it was in his mouth, the tingling of it along his limbs; and the steady beat of his heart, heavy and strong, made him glad for living.

But beyond being glorious, the swim was uneventful. On the right hand he passed the many-lighted *Lancaster*, on the left hand the English tramp, and ere long the *Annie Mine* loomed large above him. He grasped the hanging rope-ladder and drew himself noiselessly on deck. There was no one in sight. He saw a light in the galley, and knew that the

Straight to the end Alf ran, and, without pause, dived off cleanly and neatly into the water.

captain's son, who kept the lonely anchor-watch, was making coffee. Alf went forward to the forecastle. The men were snoring in their bunks, and in that confined space the heat seemed to him insufferable. So he put on a thin cotton shirt and a pair of dungaree trousers, tucked blanket and pillow under his arm, and went up on deck and out on the forecastle-head.

Hardly had he begun to doze when he was roused by a boat coming alongside and hailing the anchor-watch. It was the police-boat, and to Alf it was given to enjoy the excited conversation that ensued. Yes, the captain's son recognized the clothes. They belonged to Alf Davis, one of the seamen. What had happened? No; Alf Davis had not come aboard. He was ashore. He was not ashore? Then he must be drowned. Here both the lieutenant and the captain's son talked at the same time, and Alf could make out nothing. Then he heard them come forward and rouse out the crew. The crew grumbled sleepily and said that Alf Davis was not in the forecastle; whereupon the captain's son waxed indignant at the Yokohama police and their ways, and the lieutenant quoted rules and regulations in despairing accents.

Alf rose up from the forecastle-head and extended his hand, saying:

"I guess I'll take those clothes. Thank you for bringing them so promptly."

"I don't see why he couldn't have brought you aboard inside of them," said the captain's son.

And the police lieutenant said nothing, though he turned the clothes over somewhat sheepishly to their rightful owner.

The next day, when Alf started to go ashore, he found himself surrounded by shouting and gesticulating, though very respectful, sampan men, all extraordinarily anxious to have him for a passenger. Nor did the one he selected say, "You pay now," when he entered his boat. When Alf prepared to step out on to the pier, he offered the man the customary ten sen. But the man drew himself up and shook his head. "You all right," he said. "You no pay. You never no pay. You bully boy and all right."

And for the rest of the Annie Mine's stay in port, the sampan men refused money at Alf Davis's hand. Out of admiration for his pluck and independence, they had given him the freedom of the harbor.

First published in the February 1903 edition of St. Nicholas Magazine

To Repel Boarders

BY JACK LONDON

"NO; HONEST, NOW, Bob, I'm sure I was born too late. The twentieth century's no place for me. If I'd had my way—"

"You'd have been born in the sixteenth," I broke in, laughing, "with Drake and Hawkins and Raleigh and the rest of the sea-kings."

"You're right!" Paul affirmed. He rolled over upon his back on the little after-deck, with a long sigh of dissatisfaction.

It was a little past midnight, and, with the wind nearly astern, we were running down Lower San Francisco Bay to Bay Farm Island. Paul Fairfax and I went to the same school, lived next door to each other, and "chummed it" together. By saving money, by earning more, and by each of us foregoing a bicycle on his birthday, we had collected the purchase price of the *Mist*, a beamy twenty-eight-footer, sloop-rigged, with baby topsail and center-board.

Paul's father was a yachtsman himself, and he had conducted the business for us, poking around, overhauling, sticking his penknife into the timbers, and testing the planks with the greatest care. In

Paul's father was a yachtsman himself.

fact, it was on his schooner the *Whim* that Paul and I had picked up what we knew about boat-sailing, and now that the *Mist* was ours, we were hard at work adding to our knowledge.

The *Mist*, being broad of beam, was comfortable and roomy. A man could stand upright in the cabin, and what with the stove, cooking-utensils, and bunks, we were good for trips in her of a week at a time. And we were just starting out on the first of such trips, and it was because it was the first trip that we were sailing by night. Early in the evening we had beaten out from Oakland, and we were now off the mouth of Alameda Creek, a large salt-water estuary which fills and empties San Leandro Bay.

"Men lived in those days," Paul said, so suddenly as to startle me from my own thoughts. "In the days of the sea-kings, I mean," he explained.

I said "Oh!" sympathetically, and began to whistle "Captain Kidd."

"Now, I've my ideas about things," Paul went on. "They talk about romance and adventure and all that, but I say romance and adventure are dead. We're too civilized. We don't have adventures in the twentieth century. We go to the circus—"

"But—" I strove to interrupt, though he would not listen to me.

"You look here, Bob," he said. "In all the time you and I've gone together what adventures have we had? True, we were out in the hills once, and didn't get back till late at night, and we were good and hungry, but we weren't even lost. We knew where we were all the time. It was only a case of walk. What I mean is, we've never had to fight for our lives. Understand? We've never had a pistol fired at us, or a cannon, or a sword waving over our heads, or—or anything.

"You'd better slack away three or four feet of that main-sheet," he said in a hopeless sort of way, as though it did not matter much anyway. "The wind's still veering around.

"Why, in the old times the sea was one constant glorious adventure," he continued. "A boy left school and became a midshipman, and in a few weeks was cruising after Spanish galleons or locking yard-arms with a French privateer, or—doing lots of things."

"Well—there *are* adventures today," I objected.

But Paul went on as though I had not spoken:

"And today we go from school to high school, and from high school to college, and then we go into the office or become doctors and things, and the only adventures we know about are the ones we read in books. Why, just as sure as I'm sitting here on the stern of the sloop *Mist*, just so sure am I that we wouldn't know what to do if a real adventure came along. Now, would we?"

"Oh, I don't know," I answered non-committally.

"Well, you wouldn't be a coward, would you?" he demanded.

I was sure I wouldn't, and said so.

"But you don't have to be a coward to lose your head, do you?"

I agreed that brave men might get excited.

"Well, then," Paul summed up, with a note of regret in his voice, "the chances are that we'd spoil the adventure. So it's a shame, and that's all I can say about it."

"The adventure hasn't come yet," I answered, not caring to see him down in the mouth over nothing. You see, Paul was a peculiar fellow in some things, and I knew him pretty well. He read a good deal, and had a quick imagination, and once in a while he'd get into moods like this one. So I said, "The adventure hasn't come yet, so there's no use worrying about its being spoiled. For all we know, it might turn out splendidly."

Paul didn't say anything for some time, and I was thinking he was out of the mood, when he spoke up suddenly:

"Just imagine, Bob Kellogg, as we're sailing along now, just as we are, and never mind what for, that a boat should bear down upon us with armed men in it, what would you do to repel boarders? Think you could rise to it?"

"What would *you* do?" I asked pointedly. "Remember, we haven't even a single shotgun aboard."

"You would surrender, then?" he demanded angrily. "But suppose they were going to kill you?"

"I'm not saying what I'd do," I answered stiffly, beginning to get a little angry myself. "I'm asking what you'd do, without weapons of any sort?"

"I'd find something," he replied—rather shortly, I thought.

I began to chuckle. "Then the adventure wouldn't be spoiled, would it? And you've been talking rubbish."

Paul struck a match, looked at his watch, and remarked that it was nearly one o'clock—a way he had when the argument went against him. Besides, this was the nearest we ever came to quarreling now, though our share of squabbles had fallen to us in the earlier days of our friendship. I had just seen a little white light ahead when Paul spoke again.

"Anchor-light," he said. "Funny place for people to drop the hook. It may be a scow-schooner with a dinky astern, so you'd better go wide."

I eased the *Mist* several points, and, the wind puffing up, we went plowing along at a pretty fair speed, passing the light so wide that we could not make out what manner of craft it marked. Suddenly the *Mist* slacked up in a slow and easy way, as though running upon soft mud. We were both startled. The wind was blowing stronger than ever, and yet we were almost at a standstill.

"Mud-flats out here! Never heard of such a thing!"

So Paul exclaimed with a snort of unbelief, and, seizing an oar, shoved it down over the side. And straight down it went till the water wet his hand. There was no bottom! Then we were dumfounded. The wind was whistling by, and still the Mist was moving ahead at a snail's pace. There seemed something dead about her, and it was all I could do at the tiller to keep her from swinging up into the wind.

"Listen!" I laid my hand on Paul's arm. We could hear the sound of rowlocks, and saw the little white light bobbing up and down and now very close to us. "There's your armed boat," I whispered in fun. "Beat the crew to quarters and stand by to repel boarders!"

We both laughed, and were still laughing when a wild scream of rage came out of the darkness, and the approaching boat shot under our stern. By the light of the lantern it carried we could see the two men in it distinctly. They were angry-looking fellows with sun-bronzed faces, and with knitted tam-o'-shanters perched seaman fashion on their heads. Bright-colored woolen sashes were around their waists, and long sea-boots covered their legs.

I remember yet the cold chill which passed along my backbone as I noted the tiny gold ear-rings in the ears of one. For all the world they were like pirates stepped out of the pages of romance.

And, to make the picture complete, their faces were distorted with anger, and each flourished a long knife. They were both shouting, in high-pitched voices, some foreign jargon we could not understand.

One of them, the smaller of the two, and if anything the more vicious-looking, put his hands on the rail of the Mist and started to come aboard.

Quick as a flash Paul placed the end of the oar against the man's chest and shoved him back into his boat. He fell in a heap, but scrambled to his feet, waving the knife and shrieking:

"You break-a my net-a! You break-a my net-a!"

And he held forth in the jargon again, his companion joining him, and both preparing to make another dash to come aboard the Mist.

"They're Italian fishermen," I cried, the facts of the case breaking in upon me. "We've run over their smelt-net, and it's slipped along the keel and fouled our rudder. We're anchored to it."

"Yes, and they're murderous chaps, too," Paul said, sparring at them with the oar to make them keep their distance.

"Say, you fellows!" he called to them. "Give us a chance and we'll get it clear for you! We didn't know your net was there. We didn't mean to do it, you know!"

"You won't lose anything!" I added. "We'll pay the damages!"

But they could not understand what we were saying, or did not care to understand.

"You break-a my net-a! You break-a my net-a!" the smaller man, the one with the ear-rings, screamed back, making furious gestures. "I fix-a you! You-a see, I fix-a you!"

This time, when Paul thrust him back, he seized the oar in his hands, and his companion jumped aboard. I put my back against the tiller, and no sooner had he landed, and before he had caught his balance, than I met him with another oar, and he fell heavily backward into the boat. It was getting serious, and when he arose and caught my oar, and I realized his strength, I confess that I felt a goodly tinge of fear. But though he was stronger than I, instead of dragging me over-board when he wrenched on the oar, he merely pulled his boat in closer; and when I shoved, the boat was forced away. Besides, the knife, still in his right hand, made

him awkward and some-what counterbalanced the advantage his superior strength gave him. Paul and his enemy were in the same situation—a sort of deadlock, which contin-ued for several seconds, but which could not last. Several times I shouted that we would pay for whatever damage their net had suffered, but my words seemed to be with-out effect.

Then my man began to tuck the oar under his arm, and to come up along it, slowly, hand over hand. The small man did the same with Paul. Moment by moment they came closer and closer, and we knew that the end was only a question of time.

"Hard up, Bob!" Paul called softly to me.

I gave him a quick

Moment by moment they came closer and closer.

glance, and caught an instant's glimpse of what I took to be a very pale face and a very set jaw.

"Oh, Bob," he pleaded, "hard up your helm! Hard up your helm, Bob!"

And his meaning dawned upon me. Still holding to my end of the oar, I shoved the tiller over with my back, and even bent my body to keep it over. As it was the *Mist* was nearly dead before the wind, and this maneuver was bound to force her to jibe her mainsail from one side to the other. I could tell by the "feel" when the wind spilled out of the canvas and the boom tilted up. Paul's man had now gained a footing on the little deck, and my man was just scrambling up.

"Look out!" I shouted to Paul. "Here she comes!"

Both he and I let go the oars and tumbled into the cockpit. The next instant the big boom and the heavy blocks swept over our heads, the main-sheet whipping past like a great coiling snake and the *Mist* heeling over with a violent jar. Both men had jumped for it, but in some way the little man either got his knife-hand jammed or fell upon it, for the first sight we caught of him, he was standing in his boat, his bleeding fingers clasped close between his knees and his face; all twisted with pain and helpless rage.

"Now's our chance!" Paul whispered. "Over with you!"

And on either side of the rudder we lowered ourselves into the water, pressing the net down with our feet, till, with a jerk, it went clear. Then it was up and in, Paul at the main-sheet and I at the tiller, the *Mist* plunging ahead with freedom in her motion, and the little white light astern growing small and smaller.

"Now that you've had your adventure, do you feel any better?" I remember asking when we had changed our clothes and were sitting dry and comfortable again in the cockpit.

"Well, if I don't have the nightmare for a week to come"—Paul paused and puckered his brows in judicial fashion—"it will be because I can't sleep, that's one thing sure!"

First published in the June 1902 edition of *St. Nicholas Magazine*

The Voyage of the
Northern Light

BY JOHN TOWNSEND TROWBRIDGE

I HAD JUST completed my sophomore year at Harvard when I narrowly escaped having my college course cut short in the middle by the strange thing that happened to me that summer.

I passed my vacation in Canada chiefly on Cape Breton and Prince Edward Island and in the month of August found myself at Charlottetown, undecided as to the route by which I should return to the United States. There, one afternoon, as I was sauntering about the harbor, I fell in with the captain of a coasting schooner, the *Northern Light*, who was getting his craft ready for sea.

He was bluff and blunt, but good-natured, and easily drawn into conversation. He told me he was bound for Boston; and when I remarked that he couldn't have much freight aboard, the schooner's sides rising high out of the water, he answered, with a significant quirk of the mouth which provoked my curiosity: "She'll wet 'em 'fore ever she gets out of the Strait, if freight is all that's wanted."

He went on to say that he was waiting for a wind to run over to a small port on the south shore, where he was to take in building-stone from the Nova Scotia quar-

ries. He showed me his cabin, which, for the cabin of a coaster, was neat and comfortable; and interested me so much in the life he led, and in his own simple, genial character, that I said impulsively:

"If it was by daylight, and you would take a passenger, I might be tempted to try a voyage with you, as far as the south shore."

"I can give you a bunk, and we've got a decent sort of a cook," he replied. "You'll be welcome, if you won't mind roughing it."

I said it would be just what I should like.

"Then you'd better come aboard this evening," he went on. "We can't beat out into the Strait with this light southerly breeze; but if I know the signs, it will shift about and freshen 'fore morning, and the sunrise will see our sheets taut and sails bellying."

There was a touch of poetry in the man's nature, in piquant contrast with his weather-roughened visage and chubby form.

In the evening I went on board with my valise—a little to his surprise, I thought, for he had evidently expected my heart would fail me at the last moment; and after watching the moonlight on the water, for a while, took possession of the berth allotted me in the small cabin. I slept soundly, and did not waken until noises on deck and the harsh creak-creak of the hoisting-tackle warned me that we were getting under sail.

I hurried on my clothing, and putting my head out over the gangway saw that the schooner was spreading her white wings, like some huge croaking crane preparing to take flight. We had already swung off into the stream, heading down the harbor; the wind had freshened, and got into the northwest; the canvas filled, the masts swayed, the lightly ballasted hull yielded and careened, and we were off, with the dim shores flitting away from us, and the waves gurgling under our wales. The east brightened behind over the hills, and we had hardly passed the point and entered the open Strait when the clouds on the horizon broke into fiery flakes, and the first beams of the sunrise gilded our spars.

I had a keen appetite for the cook's good breakfast of fried bacon and potatoes, and enjoyed the passage with as fine a zest as I had felt for anything so far in my vacation. It took us about five hours to run over to the landing on the north coast of Nova Scotia, where our cargo, from a neighboring sandstone quarry, was to be taken aboard. We drifted into a little cove, and the mate stood ready to fling a line to the pier, when my attention was called to a boy who came forward to catch it.

He had a singularly solemn countenance for a boy of his age (he could hardly have been more than seventeen), bare feet and legs, and a brown neck, exposed by his coarse woolen shirt wide open at the throat. He had on an old straw hat with a ripped crown, showing the top of his uncombed head through the gap.

"Wide awake, Jake!" called out the captain.

"Jake's wide awake," the boy answered, extending his hands to catch the line.

"Good for you, Jake!" cried the captain, as the hawser was hauled in from the schooner.

"I know what's good," said Jake, simply.

"You know better than some folks that think they know a great deal more. Here—ketch that!" cried the captain. Then, as the boy stooped to pick up a Canadian copper flung to him on the wharf, he added:

"Jake never'll dam the St. Lawrence, but he's good as gold all through."

My voyage over had been so delightful that I was much inclined to accept an invitation from the captain to take the trip to Boston with him; although he warned me that the *Northern Light* wouldn't sail so dashingly with heavy freight as she did with light ballast. Anyhow, I would spend the time on shore, while the schooner was lading, visit the quarries, and explore the country a little. There were a few houses in sight, grouped about the cove.

As I stepped to the wharf with my valise, I asked Jake to show me a good boarding-place.

"Want a place to stop?" he said in his solemn, earnest way. "Ma'll let you in. I'll tell her. Come on," and he took my valise.

He went on before. I followed him, amid piles of quarry-stone, and along a path that led over a high bank to a dingy little house on the terrace of the hills. It commanded a fine view of the coast and the sea, but nothing else could be said in its favor. I shrank back, feeling that I had made an awkward mistake in

accepting Jake's guidance; but he threw the door open, calling out: "Ma, here's a man come to stop with us! I said you'd let him in."

The surprised face of a stooping little gray-haired woman peered out.

"Why, Jakey," she said, "how could you!" She gave me a kindly but distressed smile. "I'd like to be hospitable, but I hain't a speck of room, nor a spare bed."

"He can sleep with me," said Jake, generously; "or I'll sleep on the floor."

I relieved her embarrassment by saying, "Jake is altogether too kind. If he will show the way to some house you can recommend, I shall be as much obliged to him as if I turned him out of his bed."

"Oh, yes," she exclaimed quickly; "Mr. Kendall's. Jakey will go with you." Her voice softened as she added, with a tearful sort of smile, "Jakey is good-hearted as you ever see, but he don't always use good judgment. Go along with the gentleman, Jakey dear."

Jake appeared disappointed that they were not to have me as a guest; he backed up the offer of his bed with a proposal to "ketch a lunker" for my dinner, by which a big fish was meant; then, as even that failed to tempt me, he faced about abruptly, and, with a curt "Come on!" he set off to guide me to the nearest farm-house.

I saw a good deal of him while I stayed in the neighborhood. I took him with me in my excursions, and enjoyed his quaint and often shrewd sayings, and his simple kind-heartedness. The Kendalls, with whom I lodged, gave him credit for the gift of second-sight, inherited from his Scotch ancestry; and told a curious story of his having seen a certain coaster go down in the Strait three days before it actually did go down, and in the way he described. I concluded, however, that he made more misses than hits in his predictions, as forecasters of the future commonly do; and that the gift had been attributed to him on account of an abrupt and sententious way of saying things.

Having decided to make the voyage to Boston with Captain Cameron, I wrote to assure my friends at home that they would have no cause for anxiety if they missed my letters for a few days, or failed to see me as soon as they expected. Then one afternoon I sat on the wharf, watching the last of the building-blocks as they were lowered by the derrick through the schooner's main hatch into the hold.

"We'll be off by sundown, if the wind stays to the west'ard," said the captain; "just a jolly breeze for running out of the Strait!"

That was joyful news to me, but not so to Jake, who came and sat by my side.

"I shall hate to have you go," he exclaimed earnestly. And when I asked him why: "'Cause you've been good to me. Some folks poke fun at me; but you never do that. I don't like to have fun poked at me, more 'n anybody does, though I know I ain't bright," he said, with a pathos that was touching, it was so simple and unconscious.

I was trying to frame some comforting reply to this affecting speech, when he said, "I'm going to make you a present," and handed out to me an old pocket-knife with a much-worn blade and a cracked horn handle.

I couldn't help smiling as I asked how he could think of parting with such a treasure.

"You've made me presents," he replied; "you give me this hat, and the shoes I've got on; and you lost your knife when we was out in the boat fishing."

This was true; and he had heard me lament that I couldn't buy another good knife at the country store where I had purchased his hat and shoes.

"But, you dear fellow," I exclaimed, "I can't take your knife!"

He was evidently hurt, seeming to think I had slighted his humble offering. After a moment's silence he said, still holding the knife in his open palm—and I remember just how it looked, with one end of the whitish horn handle broken away at a rivet, showing the polished iron rim, and how I had to wink the glimmering moisture from my eyes in order to see it at all:

"Time'll come, and 'twon't be long first"—he spoke slowly and earnestly—"when you'll be glad to give a thousand dollars for a jack-knife no better 'n that. Then you'll think of what I tell ye."

"I haven't got a thousand dollars in the world," I said, laughing: "so give it to me." And I took it to please him.

But I knew how much he prized the poor old battered thing, and felt guilty of a heartless robbery when I thought of carrying it off in my pocket. So, as he was accompanying me to the schooner an hour later, I left him to walk on with my valise, while I stopped at his mother's door to bid her good-by.

"And here is the knife which your son gave me," I said. "It was very, very kind in him; but of course I can't keep it."

She said she was "afraid Jakey would feel awful bad" if I didn't, and she took it with reluctance.

"Hide it away from him awhile," I said; "then some day put it where he will find it, and perhaps he will have forgotten all about giving it away."

"I'll do just as you wish," she replied, tears rising in her eyes as I shook her hand with sincere cordiality. "I know 'twa'n't no sort of a present for him to make to a person like you; but, as I said to you once before, and as you've had a chance to find out for yourself, my poor boy don't always use good judgment." I tried to say something reassuring, but faltered, and she went on: "You've been dreadful good to him, and I know how he'll miss you!"

I hurried away, and bade Jake good-by on board the schooner.

"Wish I was going with you," he said. "I would in a minute, if 'twa'n't for ma."

"She needs you," I answered. "You're a great comfort to her, Jake; and I hope you never will leave her. Now go ashore, my good Jake, and good-by!"

Without a word he walked to the wharf and dropped down on a block of stone, where he remained seated, sadly watching us as we made sail and got under way— as pathetic a picture of Patience on a monument as you can well imagine. His disconsolate, motionless figure grew indistinct across the tossing waves, until a jutting headland hid him from view.

We went out with a good breeze, but the schooner was laden and her progress was prosaic enough compared with the fine dash she had made in coming over from the island. But I was altogether at my ease on board. The captain was good company; I had in my valise two or three interesting books which, so far on my trip, I had not taken time to read; and I did not easily tire of watching the waves, the gulls, the clouds, and the shores, which were sometimes quite near.

We passed through the Gulf of Canso partly by daylight, and were becalmed in Chedabucto Bay until a strong east wind sprang up, against which we had a rather dull time beating out into the Atlantic. The captain took good fortune and bad with equal cheerfulness, and when I expressed a wish that the wind would change back again to the westward, he said:

"Be patient, young man! We can't have everything our own way. Let the wind hold, and after we pass Cape Canso it will give us a straight run to Massachusetts Bay."

Night came on—our second night—and we were still knocking about inside the cape. The schooner heaved on the long swells that came rolling in from the Atlantic; but the evening, though cool, was fine; and I was glad to keep the deck with the captain.

He told tales of his seafaring life, one of which I had good reason to remember, from the bearing it had upon my own subsequent strange adventure. It was of a brother of his, who sailed with him as his mate a few years before, and was lost overboard and drowned under his very eyes, when he might have been saved if there had been any convenient object at hand to fling after him so as to keep him afloat till a boat could be lowered.

"Since then," he said, "I have always kept a life-buoy ready for the man at the wheel to cast overboard, in case of such an accident. We have never had to use it yet, and I hope we never shall; but there it is, and there it will always be found as long as I walk the deck."

I had noticed it, a circular life-preserver, with a sort of line attached, such as one often sees on passenger steamers, but rarely on board of a common sailing-vessel. Buoy and line were held together by a smaller cord which a quick pull at a bow-knot would untie, and the whole was hung securely on a cleat under the stern-rail.

I was sitting on the box over the steering-gear, and the captain was himself at the wheel; our own green and red lights were in the rigging, when we noticed, off our port bow, the lights of a steamer coming in sight around the cape. She was evidently entering the bay, and as we were directly in her path I expressed some anxiety as to her course.

"We have the right of way," said the captain; "she sees our lights, and she'll pass astern of us. That's what she's doing," he added, after a minute's careful observation.

He called the mate to the wheel, while he himself stood watching the stranger. There was something mysterious and awe-inspiring in the gradual approach of her lights, like two great eyes, one green and one red, in the immense darkness; and in the slow, far-off, monotonous clank of her machinery, growing upon the silence of the night and of the sea.

The ship's bell rang, and a steam-signal responded, booming across the water. Soon I could make out a dim object looming on the horizon; at the same time there was a gradual veering of the steamer's lights.

"She's changing her course!" cried the captain. "What does that mean?" It was the first time I had heard him speak in a tone indicating any excitement.

"She means to cross our bows," said the mate.

"She can't do that!" the captain exclaimed. "She'll be aboard of us, sure as fate!"

Moments of terrible uncertainty ensued. The ship's bell clanged. The sailors in the forecastle came tumbling up on deck. We were all on our feet, every man getting ready to obey whatever orders were called out to him in the emergency: a never-to-be-forgotten scene of hurry and apprehension, lighted by the lanterns in the shrouds over our heads.

On came the great black hull, towering above us—for we were comparatively low in the water—and rushing down upon our port bow. Our captain roared out at her, and there was all at once a wild movement of human figures visible along her rail. She veered again, and the schooner at the same time fell off from her course, both vessels endeavoring to bear away from each other, but it was too late. There was a tremendous crash, and I thought for a moment the steamer was actually walking over us. I could see her prow rise out of the water, as if she had struck a ledge. She recoiled, settled back, and immediately drifted away from us, disappearing in the darkness.

The schooner made a horrible lurch under the shock, then rolled back in the other direction, lifting barrels of water on her bow, and spilling it across the deck. I hurried forward with the captain to see what damage had been done. The steamer had cut us down to the top layer of blocks of stone that composed our freight, and the sea was spouting in through the gap.

There was but one chance of saving her—to check the incoming torrent by means of objects thrust down over the crushed side, while she was headed for the shore, in the hope of running her aground before she sank. Planks, hatch-covers, potato-bags, the cabin door—wrenched off in mad haste—hammer and spikes, a rope to support a sailor, up to his waist in the water, over her side—every available object was used, and every effort made, but all to no purpose; the flood rushed in beneath and around and through the obstructions; then a great wave swept by, undoing all that had been done.

Meanwhile the schooner was steadily settling in that direction, and the farther she went over the faster the sea poured in.

"No use!" cried the captain. "We must try to launch the boat."

There was but one, and it had not been hanging from the stern davits at any time during the voyage, it had been carried lying bottom up on deck, against the bulwarks that were cut down by the collision. The steamer's stem had struck it and shoved it from its position, giving it a bad wrench, but without crushing it; and there was hope that it would still prove seaworthy.

But no sooner was it lowered by ropes over the side than it began to fill with water.

A sort of panic followed, but the captain did not once lose his head.

"Don't pile into her!" he shouted to the sailors scrambling overboard. "Keep her afloat! Hold on to her rail till she's bailed out and the leak stanched! Get her off, so she won't be sucked down!"

I knew what that meant. Until then I had hardly realized that the danger was so imminent. I had such confidence in the captain that I stood eagerly watching him, and waiting to obey his orders or follow his example.

He and I were alone on the deck by this time. We looked down upon a tumultuous scene, half in shadow and half lighted by the ship's lanterns, one man in the boat with a bucket bailing with all his might; another trying to stuff burlaps into the opened seams; two or three up to their shoulders in the water, clinging to the gunwales, and endeavoring, by swimming and by pushing with an oar, to get her away from the schooner. But few words were uttered, and those in quick, half-stifled tones, like the voices of men in a death-struggle.

"You are doing well, boys!" the captain called out cheerily. "And you!"—he caught me roughly by the arm, and turned my face toward the stern—"the life-buoy for you! And be quick!"

I had thought of that, but still had hopes that the boat would be emptied and saved and brought back alongside before the schooner went down.

"And you, captain?" I said; "take the life-buoy yourself!"

"Start!" he exclaimed. "Don't you see we are sinking?"

I lost no more precious moments, but ran for the life-buoy, released it from its fastenings, put my feet through it, and slipped it up under my arms. I gave one glance at the captain as his stumpy form disappeared over the schooner's side, then threw the loosened coils of the buoy-line overboard, and jumped after it.

In my excitement I didn't much mind the shock of the immersion, although the water was very cold and I was unaccustomed to sea-bathing. I could swim a little, but I knew well that without some support I couldn't have kept my head above the waves many minutes.

What did I think about? I can hardly tell. In that frightful crisis I suppose my past life should have flashed before my mind, and I ought to have thought of my friends at home; for I was well aware that, even with my life-preserver on, I might perish before I could be rescued.

But, incredible as it may seem, some of my thoughts were facetious, and it is chiefly those that I remember. Whether I could read the name on the stern or not (it seems to me now that I could), I looked up to where it was, and said to myself, "The *Northern Light* will soon be quenched!"

Then, "Where was Moses when the light went out?" It was the jocularity of terrible excitement, something like Hamlet's after the interview with his father's ghost.

It could hardly have lasted half a minute. Things were rushing to a climax faster than I can tell them. I had drifted a few yards away from the stern, and was paddling to increase the distance, when I discovered that the line attached to the life-buoy did not come free when I pulled at it. On the contrary, I was pulling myself back to the schooner. In short, the line had caught on something when I flung it over; it was spliced to the buoy, and I was in the buoy. As I continued pulling in one direction, the schooner began pulling in the other—she was making her final, wallowing, gurgling plunge to the bottom drawing me down with her!

It was impossible to untie or break the line, though I might have cut it, even while I felt myself hauled rapidly after the wreck.

I struggled frantically, and I believe I shrieked out, just as my head was going under:

"A THOUSAND DOLLARS FOR A JACK-KNIFE!"

How far down I was drawn I haven't the slightest notion. It seemed to me a long way, and what was probably but a few seconds of agony appeared many minutes. I remember a ringing in my head, and vivid flashes of light; then all at once there was nothing for me to struggle against, and I rose rapidly to the surface.

I had succeeded in freeing myself from the buoy.

Something was floating near. I grasped it. It was a ship's fender. Then a boat bore down upon me, pulled by plashing oars; if I hadn't shrieked out, it might have passed over me. It was a boat from the steamer that had run us down. I was quickly pulled in over the gunwale; and afterward the captain and all our crew were picked up from the foundering boat and other floating objects.

The steamer was also injured by the collision, but not disabled; and we received the kindest treatment on board.

It was impossible to untie or break the line.

The captain had strangely mistaken our distance when he attempted to cross our bows; we were much nearer than he supposed. She was a tramp steamer, but her owners were responsible; and as we were not in any way at fault, they had heavy damages to pay. I was told that if I put in a personal claim, it would be settled; but I never did.

And as for Jake's prediction, which was so singularly fulfilled? I have related the circumstances as I remember them, and am willing to leave the question of prophecy or coincidence to anybody's unbiased judgment. Some very strange things happen in this world of ours—things it is useless to argue much about; and this I regard as one of them.

Oh!—well, yes; I reached home in time to get ready for the fall term, and completed my college course.

First published in the December 1896 edition of *St. Nicholas Magazine*

Nöll and Antoonje

And How They Entertained the Beggars

BY MRS. ERNEST ATKINS

ANTOONJE SAT BY his own hearthstone one Monday evening, enjoying his supper. It was a good supper. "The cheese has a great smell," thought Antoonje, sniffing. He was glad that he was a rich man and could buy such cheeses as that. And the firelight danced on the silver teaspoons which Lys kept so bright and shining.

"A fine thing to have real silver teaspoons," thought Antoonje.

He lifted his cup, noticing how fine it was, with the rosy light of the fire glowing through it.

"A fine thing to have such chinaware as that," said Antoonje to himself. He rose from the table, and stretched himself and yawned. How he hated to leave the warm fire! Lys helped him on with his greatcoat, and he opened the door.

Whisht! how the wind blew! B-r-r-h-h! how cold it was! It made Antoonje shiver, although his coat was lined with fur. He turned up his collar and tramped off over the snow to the barns. The cows and sheep were huddled together for warmth.

"A fine thing to have such a grand lot of sheep and kine," said Antoonje.

"That it is, sir," said a voice.

Antoonje gave a start of surprise. He lifted his lantern, and there, huddled up in a corner, was a beggar man, who looked like nothing so much as a bundle of rags, with a red-nosed face sticking out of the top.

"Well, old rags and bones!" said Antoonje, curtly. "What are you doing here, I'd like to know?"

"What a fine coat you have, Mynheer!" said the beggar. "I should like to be hugging it round me. Summer-time is the beggars' holiday, Mynheer—what with the good sun a-shining and costing ne'er a penny, and the warm breezes fluttering and flapping the rags and tags so gaily; with berries on every bush, and a concert in every tree-top! Yes, summer-time is the beggars' holiday, Mynheer Antoonje. But winter's a bad time."

"What's all that got to do with me, I'd like to know!" said Antoonje, in his harsh voice. "There are poor and there are rich in this world, and I'm this and you're that. Move on, now! I can't have a strange fellow in my barn."

"Here I am in a pretty fix," said the beggar, cheerily. "And all because of having such a tongue in my head! 'Tis better to shiver in a barn corner than to be wandering across the snow with your toes like ice in your shoes."

"Some have warm shoes and some haven't," said Antoonje. "It's the way of the world. I'm going in and to bed now. But first I'll see you gone, and the barn door locked. Go over there and toast your toes at Nöll's fire, if you like!"

And with that, Antoonje gave the poor beggar a shove with his foot, and turned him out-of-doors.

"B-r-r-h-h!" said Antoonje, as he turned toward the house. "How cold it is—cold enough for two coats!" He was glad to get indoors again and sit by the fire with his pipe between his teeth, and watch Lys knitting warm stockings for the children. Antoonje and Lys had

"What a fine coat you have . . .

four children. They were early tucked in bed with warm coverlets over them up to the tips of their noses, so that they dreamed it was summer-time, and that they were running races down the hot, dusty road.

"Nöll is a silly!" said Antoonje.

"His children have no best frocks for Sunday," said Lys, scornfully.

"I am glad we are so well off, Antoonje, and that you are so clever."

NOW THE BEGGAR trotted across the snow toward the light gleaming in Nöll's window. The wind flapped his rags of garments, and whistled down his collar, and played a tune in his long, loose hair. Nöll's house was a small one, not at all as fine as Brother Antoonje's. The beggar went up to the very front door and knocked. Nöll stuck his head out.

"Come in! come in! whoever you are!" roared he, in his hearty voice, "Such a night to be out in!"

. . . Mynheer!" said the beggar.

You might have thought the beggar was a real prince in a velvet dress, so hospitable was Nöll.

"Kaatje! Kaatje!" he called, "bring in the hot tea and a loaf of bread, for here's a man who's been playing tag with Jack Frost!"

And pulling up the best chair to the fire, Nöll brushed the snow off the beggar's shoulders. In bustled Kaatje with the tea and the loaf.

"Eat all you can," said Nöll, "and warm yourself without and within."

"Too bad we haven't a bit of cheese, isn't it, Nöll?" said Kaatje.

"You should have stopped at my brother's house over yonder," said Nöll. "He always has a cheese as big as a house in the larder, with the grandest smell to it."

Just then, the door opened a little, creaking on its hinges.

"Ho! ho! who is this?" said the beggar, for there was a little head in the crack.

"Dortchen! Dortchen!" exclaimed Mother Kaatje, with uplifted finger; "why are you not in bed and asleep, along with your sister Franzje?"

"My toes are so cold, Mother," said Dortchen. "I dreamed I was walking bare-footed in the snow. Franzje is not in bed, either!"

And she stepped into the room with Franzje just behind her.

"Franzje! Franzje!" said her mother; "why are you not in bed and asleep? Your brother Piet is a good boy."

"My ears are so cold, Mother," said Franzje. "I dreamed the north wind was whispering to me, and his words froze in my ears. And Piet is not in bed, either!" And she crept up to the fire, with Piet following.

"Piet! Piet!" said his mother; "why are you not asleep? Little Jan is the best of you all, for he sleeps till cockcrow."

"My nose is so cold, Mother," said Piet. "I dreamed I was a snow man. And little Jan is not in bed, either!"

"Oh, little Jan," said Mother Kaatje, "why are you not sleeping?"

"My hands are so cold, Mother," said little Jan. "I dreamed I had icicles as long as *that* on every finger."

"What naughty children you are!" said Kaatje, with her face all laughing wrinkles.

She let them curl up on the warm hearth, and their eyes grew large and round as they watched the beggar. It seemed as if they could not stop looking at him. At last Piet said, "What makes the bright light round your head?"

The beggar laughed. "The glow from the fire, I suppose," he said. "It makes your own hair shine like gold, Mr. Snow Man."

"And you have on gold shoes!" cried Dortchen.

"Your own toes are warm now, little Dortchen," said the beggar, "and you are now dreaming warm dreams instead of cold ones!"

"I thought you were a beggar," said Franzje, breathlessly. "But you are wearing grand clothes that shine like the rainbow! How your cloak rustles! Like Aunt Lys's silk gown on Sundays!"

"What nonsense!" said the beggar, chuckling. "I think you must move nearer to the fire, for you are not yet awake. The north wind still whispers in your ears, and pretends he is a silk cloak."

Then little Jan had something to say.

"I felt your cloak," said he, "when you weren't looking: It *is* silk inside and velvet outside, like the grand parlor curtains at my uncle's house over yonder."

"Ho! ho!" said the beggar. "How can a boy with icicles on every finger-tip know the difference between silk and velvet, I'd like to know! Let us make more room for little Jan by the fire. For his dream, like yours, is not yet over!"

"'Sh, 'sh, 'sh!" said Mother Kaatje. "You have all talked more than you should. And such fancies! No wonder you're half awake!"

And, addressing the beggar, she said: "I would not tell it to many—but you, perhaps, are even poorer than ourselves. The coverlets are so thin! Poor children! Wood is to be had for the cutting, summer and winter, but blankets do not grow on the trees. Pile on more logs, Nöll. If we are to keep warm, we must sit up all night by the fire. What a night it is! Do you not hear the wind roar?"

"The children are asleep," said the beggar. "What eyes they have, for seeing what is not—gold shoes and the like!"

"Yes, yes," said Kaatje. "Their nonsense keeps us merry in spite of hard times."

SOON ALL WAS quiet, except for Nöll snoring in his chair. A log fell crumbling into coals and made Kaatje start in her sleep. The children did not stir, they were so warm and comfortable. Yes, all were asleep—all except the beggar.

"What a pity it is," said he to himself, "that men can't see the fairies—only little children now and then, before the dust of the highways has got into their eyes. I should like to know what Kaatje thinks of the cut of this cloak, for instance. She's a woman of sense. She'd know whether rainbow silk would wear as well as plain rose-color!"

He walked up and down the room in the dim firelight, the fairy who, to most dull eyes, was only a poor ragged beggar with a nose red from the cold. His clothes glittered with fairy jewels, and his velvet cloak was lined with rainbow silk, which rustled ever so gently. And his shoes were of gold, as Dortchen had said. He was as busy as could be about something—lifting a chair-cushion here and a table-cover there, and opening boxes and cupboards.

Then he settled himself down to nap in his chair. How the wind roared down the chimney! It stirred the fire, and blew a sprinkling of warm ashes out upon the hearthstone.

"What good folk Nöll and Kaatje are!" said the beggar, looking at their kind, sleeping faces.

Then he curled his legs up under him, and leaned his head upon his hand, and slept, like anybody else, while the fire glowed warm and red.

He had thought himself just asleep when the dawn came, and the cock crowed.

"I must be going on now," said he. "The sun is shining, and the wind has died down."

But they would not let him go until he had eaten a great bowl of porridge.

"Your clothes are none too warm, my man," said Nöll.

"There is your other coat hanging behind the door, Nöll," said Kaatje. "It would help to keep some of the cold out."

"That is so," said Nöll, "though there's little choice between the best coat and the worst, if the truth is told. But such as it is, you are welcome to it, and God speed you!"

He helped the beggar into the coat, saying, "It had been best for you had you stopped at Brother Antoonje's house over there. He has warm great-coats and to spare, Antoonje; a new one every winter, and each one finer than the last."

So the beggar went away (at least Nöll and Kaatje thought he was a beggar). But the children knew better.

"He is a fairy prince," said they to each other. Now Mother Kaatje said to herself: "The sun is shining. I will take up the carpets and give them a good beating. Then I will open all the windows wide, and do a little scrubbing. It is a pity to waste such a fine house-cleaning day." So she began to bustle about, humming to herself.

Then something quite astonishing happened! She lifted a cushion and found five gold coins underneath it.

"What's this, Nöll?" she cried, for she could hardly believe her eyes.

Here was enough to buy bread and cheese for all the rest of the year.

Nöll was quite as astonished as Kaatje was. He went to the cupboard to get his tobacco jar. He knew it was almost empty. He was saving what was left for a special occasion. Truly this *was* one! He lifted the lid and stuck his hand in, and his fingers touched gold coins. The tobacco jar was filled up to the top with them.

"Kaatje! Kaatje! Luck has come to us!" cried Nöll.

"Oh, deary me!" said Kaatje, and she went to the chest of drawers to get a clean handkerchief, for she was near weeping.

And right on top of the clean clothes was a pile of money too. At that, Kaatje sobbed aloud. And in putting her handkerchief to her eyes, she knocked over a little vase Antoonje had given her on her wedding-day. Out of it rolled scores of bright coins, falling upon the floor with a great clatter.

Even Nöll was frightened. His tongue became so parched that he could hardly swallow. So he bethought himself of a drink of water, and went to the shelf to get a cup. The cups were all filled with money, even little Jan's birthday mug!

"Why, we are richer than Antoonje!" cried Kaatje.

"Ten times over!" said Nöll.

"Just to think of it, Nöll!" said Kaatje, wiping her eyes.

"Are we dreaming, or is this real gold?" said Nöll. "Where did all this money come from?"

"I'm sure I don't know what to think," replied Kaatje. "But let us call the children, Nöll. They will know whether or not we are awake."

When the children came in, they were amazed to see their own mother sitting there with a lapful of gold money.

"Is this real?" cried she. "Are my eyes open or shut? Pinch me, Dortchen, for I am afraid I am still asleep."

"This is real money," said Piet, "and gold money, too. Uncle Antoonje once let

She knocked over the little vase Antoonje had given her.

me hold a gold coin in my hand, and it was just like this one, with the picture of the king on it."

"Where did the money come from, Mother?" said Dortchen. "And can we have new dresses?"

"The money was lying here and there about the house," said Mother Kaatje. "New dresses—yes! And shoes, too!"

"Why, we can get lots of things," said Franzje, jumping up and down. "Dolls, and gold rings, and tulip bulbs, and lace caps, and cheese, and warm covers for our beds!"

"But however in the world this money came to us, I cannot guess!" said Nöll.

"I know, Father," said little Jan. "It was the fairy prince!"

"What are you talking about, little Jan?" said Kaatje, taking his fat round face between her two hands. "Are you children dreaming, too, after all?"

"It's the beggar man Jan means," said Franzje. "If you had only looked, Mother! Or listened! It *was* a velvet cloak with a silk lining!"

"And such pretty gold shoes!" exclaimed Dortchen.

"And shiny hair!" said Piet.

WELL, THE FACT of the matter was, the money was there; and it was real money which did not vanish overnight, either. Nöll and Kaatje could not stop wondering that such good fortune had come to them, and all because they had warmed a poor beggar by the fire on a cold night. Said Kaatje: "To think that he was really a fairy!"

"To think of giving my second best coat to a fairy prince!" exclaimed Nöll. "Think of the patches, Kaatje! And bread without cheese, too!"

"'Twas little, Nöll," said Kaatje, "but it was the best we had, after all."

The next day, Kaatje put on her bonnet and went into the town. She bought some of the things she had longed for all her life, and presents for everybody all around.

And of course the news got to Brother Antoonje, over in the great house, that Nöll had come upon prosperous days.

"He was always a silly!" said Antoonje to Lys.

But he put on his hat to go over and see wherefore and whence Nöll had got his good fortune.

So he knocked at Nöll's door, and it was the first time in many years. For Antoonje wasn't one to go hunting up poor relations, not he! But this was a different matter, when Brother Nöll had dropped a gold coin in the plate at church on Sunday; and Kaatje was wearing a new cap with real lace frills; and the children in new frocks, and shoes that squeaked all the way up the aisle. This was worth looking into, thought Antoonje.

He came in and sat down by the fire, and said: "'Tis a fine day, truly. We'll soon be thinking of crops—that is, if you're at all interested in crops, Brother Nöll! Perhaps you're too rich now to care whether the season is good or bad!"

And he drummed on the arm of the chair, and waited to hear what Nöll had to say.

"Oh, there's plenty of use for money in this world," said Nöll, "if only to keep bread and cheese in the pantry for the beggar who knocks at your door."

"I always thought you were a fool, Nöll," said Antoonje, cheerfully, "and now I know it. Bread and cheese, indeed! There was a beggar in my barn last Monday night. I sped him on his way with the toe of my boot, that I did!"

"What did he look like, Antoonje?" said Nöll.

"Oh, he was only a bundle of rags," said Antoonje, "and he had a great lot of yellow hair, which hung down to his shoulders."

"Well, well," said Nöll, "I didn't know he called at your house, too. You turned away good luck from your door that time, Brother. For the gold was real gold, and 'twas he who left it at this house. That beggar was a fairy prince, Antoonje! And we gave him bread, plain bread without cheese, and my second best coat!"

"You don't say so!" said Antoonje, six times over.

He was *that* crestfallen to think that he had kicked out good luck at the toe of his boot!

He went home as glum as could be, and drove the cat out-of-doors, and scolded the children, and grumbled at the supper. And all because he envied Nöll his good fortune. He sat in the chimney-corner that night and never said a word. Lys knew better than to ask him what he was thinking about, too. No, he didn't say a word that night.

But the next morning, he said: "Buy the best and biggest cheese in the market—and a cake with white frosting—and a jug of schnapps. And roast a fowl, Lys, and put it away cold on the shelf."

And then he never said another word all morning.

At noon he said: "Lys, make up the bed in the spare room. And mind you put on the lace quilt and the best feather pillows."

And then he never said another word all afternoon.

At supper-time, he said: "Get out my last winter's coat, Lys, and give it a good brushing."

Then he went to bed, but not to sleep. He was getting up all night and popping his head out of the window.

Once he said, "I thought I heard the gate squeak on its hinges." And another time he said, "The dogs barked. They always bark at beggars."

And the next time he said, "Was that a knock at the door?"

And then it was morning.

Lys bustled about her tasks. But Antoonje sat on the gate all day long, swinging his heels, and looking up and down the road, as if there was nothing else quite so important. Then, just as Lys was setting the table for supper (with the fine linen cloth, and the silver teaspoons, and the china cups and saucers), the door opened, and in walked Antoonje, arm in arm with a beggar!

"What have we for supper?" cried Antoonje, jovially. "Bring in the cold fowl, Lys, and the cheese, and the frosted cake, and the schnapps."

Then he called little Willemin to fetch his own warm slippers, and bade the guest put them on.

"What a shabby coat, man!" said Antoonje, turning the beggar about.

And he sent Daughter Neltje running to the clothes-press to bring out his Sunday suit for the beggar to wear. Mother Lys was a little surprised at that, I can tell you. But she was a wise woman, and kept her own thoughts to herself. As for the beggar, all he did was to grin behind his hand.

So they sat down to supper, and it was an extra good supper—what with the fine cheese and the cold fowl and the frosted cake and the jug of schnapps. Antoonje wasn't doing things by halves, either. He treated the beggar as if he were a real prince.

It was, "Have this, sir," and, "Have that, sir," and every time Antoonje spoke, the sly beggar grinned behind his hand. But all the same he ate a good supper.

Afterward as they sat by the fire, Willemin spoke up. Her eyes were as round as saucers. "What makes you look like our cat, just when she's going to catch a mouse?"

"Go to bed, Willemin," said Antoonje, crossly. "The very idea! I can't think what's come over the child!"

"But you do look like one," cried Neltje. "A tiger-cat!"

"Not another word!" roared Antoonje, stamping his foot.

"I tell you what you look like," said Blaas, jumping up. "You look like a pirate! I shouldn't wonder if you had a gun on you! Tell me, *are* you a pirate?"

"Hold your tongue!" shouted Antoonje. "Off with the whole pack of you!"

"Oh, he isn't a pirate, Father," said little Mies, sticking his head in at the door. "He's a robber, for he doesn't make any noise when he walks!"

At that, Antoonje leaped to his feet. "Off to your beds!" he fairly screamed.

They were gone, scampering along the passage. Antoonje wiped his forehead.

"I hope you'll overlook this, sir," he said politely. "What things children do say. Dear me! I hope this hasn't caused you too much annoyance."

"Oh, no," said the beggar, grinning behind his hand.

He stuck out his toes to the warm fire. He felt warm, and comfortable, and happy. He liked being treated like a prince, I can tell you. He was so contented that it made him sleepy, and he began to yawn great, wide yawns.

"Ah, bed's the best place," said Antoonje.

He led the beggar off to the spare room, and lit the candles and turned down the covers.

"Happy dreams, sir," said he, politely.

And then he, too, went to bed with great satisfaction.

As he turned over and pulled the covers up to his ears, he said to himself, "Nöll isn't the only one who invites good luck in at the front door!"

Then he went to sleep.

NOW WHEN ALL was quiet in the middle of the night, the beggar jumped up (he had gone to bed wearing Antoonje's best Sunday suit), and he spread Lys's handsome lace quilt on the floor. Then he went out to the kitchen as if he were walking on eggs, and took the rest of the big cheese and the frosted cake, and went back and laid them down on the lace quilt.

Then he tiptoed into the parlor and had a look around. He took a pair of silver candlesticks off the table, and a branch of pink coral, and a gold ink-pot, and the gold snuff-box which had belonged to Antoonje's grandfather. And back he trotted and laid them down on the lace quilt.

Then he went to the sitting-room and took all the fine silver teaspoons, and the linen table-cloth, and the china cups and saucers. Then he went to the cupboard and took Antoonje's tobacco jar and his best pipe; and to the linen press, where he took all of Lys's best handkerchiefs and her lace cap. And these, too, he added to his store.

All the time, he grinned and glanced all about with his small, keen eyes, so that he shouldn't miss anything. He did look like a cat, as Willemin and Neltje had said, and he moved quite as softly in his stocking-feet,

All the time, he glanced around with small, keen eyes,
so that he shouldn't miss anything.

right into Antoonje's bedroom, where he took the gold watch from under his pillow, and the big silver ring off his finger, and all his savings in the left-hand corner of the second bureau drawer. And out of the top drawer, he took Lys's gold hoop earrings and her big agate brooch.

"Now I'll be moving along," said he.

So he drank all the cream off the top of the milk, and buttoned Antoonje's best Sunday suit over his chest, and took his fur-lined greatcoat off the hook in the hall. And he put on his wooden shoes again, and off he went across the fields with the handsome lace quilt and all the good things it contained in a bundle over his shoulder.

Yes, he looked like a robber, and he *was* one, too, as you know without being told.

WHEN THE COCK crowed next morning, Antoonje jumped out of bed. "Now we'll see," said he, "whether Brother Nöll is the only fellow who knows how to entertain a fairy prince!"

Then he felt under his pillow for his gold watch to see the time of day. And of course the watch was gone! Then he missed his silver ring, and his hair rose on his head, for he was smart enough, was Antoonje, to see which way the wind was blowing.

"Lys! Lys!" called he, as he opened the second bureau drawer, and turned all the clothes topsy-turvy. "Where are all my savings, Lys?"

(But he knew without being told where they had gone.)

"And your earrings and agate brooch?"

So they began to fly around the house and find that one thing and another were gone.

"The silver candlesticks, Lys!"

"The frosted cake, Antoonje!"

"My tobacco jar, Lys!"

"My best handkerchiefs, Antoonje!"

"And my gold ink-pot!"

"And my lace cap!"

"The silver teaspoons!"

"And the cream for breakfast!"

They shouted about the house until they were hoarse, for, truth to tell, there wasn't much of anything that hadn't gone off bundled up in that handsome lace quilt.

The children came to see what was the matter.

"There! I said he was a cat," said Willemin.

"I said he was a tiger-cat!" said Neltje.

"I told you he was a pirate," cried Blaas.

"But I was right," said little Mies. "I *knew* he was a robber!"

"I've a mind to give every one of you a good beating!" shouted Antoonje.

That was *his* way of taking things.

WHEN NÖLL HEARD the news, he came over the way and knocked at Antoonje's door.

"How do you do?" said he, when Lys opened it.

But all Lys said was, "My best table-cloth!"

"Well," said Nöll, sitting down in a chair, "I hear your beggar wasn't a fairy prince, Brother Antoonje."

"It's all your fault!" said Antoonje, crossly.

"How so, Brother?"

"Oh, you know well enough."

Nöll thought for a long time. Then he said aloud what was in his mind.

"You asked that beggar in to sup and sleep not so much because your heart was warm, but because you thought to profit by it, Antoonje!"

That was a blunt speech for Nöll, to be sure.

"Maybe yes, and maybe no," said Antoonje.

But all the same he knew Nöll was right.

"Hist! What is that?" said Nöll.

"Only the children crying," said Antoonje. "I've promised them a good beating. I'll give them something to cry *for!*"

"Antoonje," said Nöll, "why do you beat the children when it's only your own ill temper? Look here! I've a bargain to strike with you. Half my gold money if you'll let them off without a whipping. Don't you know they see what's what sometimes, and know a robber from a fairy prince? As for the money, I'm not used to having so much lying about the house, and that's the truth. It clutters up things!"

"How silly you are, Nöll!" said Antoonje. "I always thought you were a fool. Now I know it!"

That was the way he had always talked to Brother Nöll. But, all the same, he accepted the bargain and the gold money that went with it.

Nöll went home as well pleased as could be, because he was kind and generous, and knew that it was more fun to go halves than to keep everything for himself.

First published in the February 1913 edition of St. *Nicholas Magazine*

Between Sea and Sky

BY HJALMAR HJORTH BOYESEN

"ICELAND IS THE most beautiful land the sun doth shine upon," said Sigurd Sigurdson to his two sons.

"How can you know that, Father," asked Thoralf, the elder of the two boys, "when you have never been anywhere else?"

"I know it in my heart," said Sigurd devoutly.

"It is, after all, a matter of taste," observed the son. "I think, if I were hard pressed, I might be induced to put up with some other country."

"You ought to blush with shame," his father rejoined warmly. "You do not deserve the name of an Icelander, when you fail to see how you have been blessed in having been born in so beautiful a country."

"I wish it were less beautiful and had more things to eat in it," muttered Thoralf. "Salted codfish, I have no doubt, is good for the soul, but it rests very heavily on the stomach, especially when you eat it three times a day."

"You ought to thank God that you have codfish, and are not a naked savage on some South Sea isle, who feeds like an animal on the herbs of the earth."

"But I like codfish much better than smoked puffin," remarked Jens, the younger brother, who was carving a pipe-bowl. "Smoked puffin always makes me sea-sick. It tastes like cod liver oil."

Sigurd smiled, and, patting the younger boy on the head, entered the cottage.

"You shouldn't talk so to Father, Thoralf," said Jens, with superior dignity; for his father's caress made him proud and happy. "Father works so hard, and he does not like to see anyone discontented."

"That is just it," replied the elder brother; "he works so hard, and yet barely manages to keep the wolf from the door. That is what makes me impatient with the country. If he worked so hard in any other country he would live in abundance, and in America he would become a rich man."

This conversation took place one day, late in the autumn, outside of a fisherman's cottage on the northwestern coast of Iceland. The wind was blowing a gale down from the very ice-engirdled pole, and it required a very genial temper to keep one from getting blue. The ocean, which was but a few hundred feet distant, roared like an angry beast, and shook its white mane of spray, flinging it up against the black clouds. With every fresh gust of wind, a shower of salt water would fly hissing through the air and whirl about the chimney-top, which was white on the windward side from dried deposits of brine. On the turf-thatched roof big pieces of driftwood, weighted down with stones, were laid lengthwise and cross-wise, and along the walls fishing-nets hung in festoons from wooden pegs. Even the low door was draped, as with decorative intent, with the folds of a great drag-net, the clumsy cork-floats of which often dashed into the faces of those who attempted to enter. Under a driftwood shed which projected from the northern wall was seen a pile of peat, cut into square blocks, and a quantity of the same useful material might be observed down at the beach, in a boat which the boys had been unloading when the storm blew up. Trees no longer grow on the island, except the crippled and twisted dwarf-birch, which creeps along the ground like a snake, and, if it ever dares lift its head, rarely grows more than four or six feet high. In the olden time, which is described in the so-called sagas of the twelfth and thirteenth centuries, Iceland had very considerable forests of birch and probably also of pine. But they were cut down; and the climate has gradually been growing colder, until now even the hardiest tree, if it be induced to strike root in a sheltered place, never reaches maturity. The Icelanders therefore burn peat, and use for building their houses driftwood, which is carried to them by the Gulf Stream from Cuba and the other well-wooded isles along the Mexican Gulf.

"If it keeps blowing like this," said Thoralf, fixing his weather eye on the black horizon, "we shan't be able to go a-fishing; and Mother says the larder is very nearly empty."

"I wish it would blow down an Englishman or something on us," remarked the younger brother; "Englishmen always have such lots of money, and they are willing to pay for everything they look at."

"While you are a-wishing, why don't you wish for an American? Americans have mountains and mountains of money, and they don't mind a bit what they do with it. That's the reason I should like to be an American."

"Yes, let us wish for an American or two to make us comfortable for the winter. But I am afraid it is too late in the season to expect foreigners."

The two boys chatted together in this strain, each working at some piece of wood-carving which he expected to sell to some foreign traveler. Thoralf was sixteen years old, tall of growth, but round-shouldered, from being obliged to work when he was too young. He was rather a handsome lad, though his features were square and weather-beaten, and he looked prematurely old. Jens, the younger boy, was fourteen years old, and was his mother's darling. For even up under the North Pole mothers love their children tenderly, and sometimes they love one a little more than another; that is, of course, the merest wee bit of a fraction of a trifle more. Icelandic mothers are so constituted that when one child is a little weaker and sicklier than the rest, and thus seems to be more in need of petting, they are apt to love their little weakling above all their other children, and to lavish the tenderest care upon that one. It was because little Jens had so narrow a chest, and looked so small and slender by the side of his robust brother, that his mother always singled him out for favors and caresses.

ALL NIGHT LONG the storm danced wildly about the cottage, rattling the windows, shaking the walls, and making fierce assaults upon the door, as if it meant to burst in. Sometimes it bellowed hoarsely down the chimney, and whirled the ashes on the hearth, like a gray snowdrift, through the room. The fire had been put out, of course; but the dancing ashes kept up a fitful patter, like that of a pelting rainstorm, against the walls; they even penetrated into the sleeping alcoves and powdered the heads of their occupants. For in Iceland it is only well-to-do people who can afford to have separate sleeping-rooms; ordinary folk sleep in little closed alcoves, along the walls of the sitting-room; masters and servants, parents and children, guests and wayfarers, all retiring at night into square little holes in the walls, where they undress behind sliding trapdoors which may be opened again, when the lights have been put out, and the supply of air threatens to become exhausted. It was in a little closet of this sort that Thoralf and Jens were lying, listening to the roar of the storm. Thoralf dozed off occasionally, and tried gently to extricate himself from his frightened brother's embrace; but Jens lay with wide-open eyes, staring into the dark, and now and then sliding the trapdoor aside and peeping out, until a blinding shower of ashes would again compel him to slip his head under the sheepskin coverlet.

When at last he summoned courage to peep out, he could not help shuddering. It was terribly cheerless and desolate. And all the time, his father's words kept ringing ironically in his ears: "Iceland is the most beautiful land the sun doth shine upon."

For the first time in his life he began to question whether his father might not possibly be mistaken, or, perhaps, blinded by his love for his country. But the boy immediately repented of this doubt, and, as if to convince himself in spite of everything, kept repeating the patriotic motto to himself until he fell asleep.

It was yet pitch dark in the room, when he was awakened by his father, who stood stooping over him.

"Sleep on, child," said Sigurd; "it was your brother I wanted to wake up, not you."

"What is the matter, Father? What has happened?" cried Jens, rising up in bed, and rubbing the ashes from the corners of his eyes.

"We are snowed up," said the father quietly. "It is already nine o'clock, I should judge, or thereabouts, but not a ray of light comes through the windows. I want Thoralf to help me open the door."

Thoralf was by this time awake, and finished his primitive toilet with much dispatch. The darkness, the damp cold, and the unopened window-shutters impressed him ominously. He felt as if some calamity had happened or were about to happen. Sigurd lighted a piece of driftwood and stuck it into a crevice in the wall. The storm seemed to have ceased; a strange, tomb-like silence prevailed without and within. On the low hearth lay a small snowdrift which sparkled with a starlike glitter in the light.

"Bring the snow shovels, Thoralf," said Sigurd. "Be quick; lose no time."

"They are in the shed outside," answered Thoralf.

"That is very unlucky," said the father; "now we shall have to use our fists."

The door opened outward, and it was only with the greatest difficulty that father and son succeeded in pushing it ajar. The storm had driven the snow with such force against it that their efforts seemed scarcely to make any impression upon the dense white wall which rose up before them.

"This is of no earthly use, Father," said the boy; "it is a day's job at the very least. Let me rather try the chimney."

"But you might stick in the snow and perish," objected the father anxiously.

"Weeds don't perish so easily," said Thoralf.

"Stand up on the hearth, Father, and I will climb up on your shoulders," urged the boy.

Sigurd half reluctantly complied with his son's request, who crawled up his father's back, and soon planted his feet on the paternal shoulders. He pulled his knitted woolen cap over his eyes and ears so as to protect them from the drizzling soot which descended in intermittent showers. Then, groping with his toes for a little projection of the wall, he gained a securer foothold, and, pushing boldly on, soon thrust his sooty head through the snow-crust. A chorus as of a thousand howling wolves burst upon his bewildered sense; the storm raged, shrieked, roared, and nearly swept him off his feet. Its biting breath smote his face like a sharp whip-lash.

"Give me my sheepskin coat," he cried down into the cottage; "the wind chills me to the bone."

The sheepskin coat was handed to him on the end of a pole, and seated upon the edge of the chimney, he pulled it on and buttoned it securely. Then he rolled up the edges of his cap in front and cautiously exposed his eyes and the tip of his nose. It was not a pleasant experiment, but one dictated by necessity. As far as he could see, the world was white with snow, which the storm whirled madly around, and swept now earthward, now heavenward. Great funnel-shaped columns of snow danced up the hillsides and vanished against the black horizon. The prospect before the boy was by no means inviting, but he had been accustomed to battle with dangers since his earliest childhood, and he was not easily dismayed. With much deliberation, he climbed over the edge of the chimney, and rolled down the slope of the roof in the direction of the shed. He might have rolled a great deal farther, if he had not taken the precaution to roll against the wind. When he had made sure that he was in the right locality, he checked himself by spreading his legs and arms; then, judging by the outline of the snow where the door of the shed was, he crept along the edge of the roof on the leeward side. He looked more like a small polar bear than a boy, covered, as he was, with snow from head to foot. He was prepared for a laborious descent, and raising himself up he jumped with all his might, hoping that his weight would carry him a couple of feet down. To his utmost astonishment he accomplished considerably more. The snow yielded under his feet as if it had been eider-down, and he tumbled head-long into a white cave right at the entrance to the shed. The storm, while it had packed the snow on the windward side, had naturally scattered it very loosely on the leeward, which left a considerable space unfilled under the projecting eaves.

Thoralf picked himself up and entered the shed without difficulty. He made up a large bundle of peat, which he put into a basket which could be carried, by means of straps, upon the back. With a snow-shovel he then proceeded to dig a tunnel to the nearest window. This was not a very hard task, as the distance was not great. The window was opened and the basket of peat, a couple of shovels, and two pairs of skis (to be used in case of emergency) were handed in. Thoralf himself, who was hungry as a wolf, made haste to avail himself of the same entrance. And it occurred to him as a happy afterthought that he might have saved himself much trouble if he had selected the window instead of the chimney, when he sallied forth on his expedition. He had erroneously taken it for granted that the snow would be packed as hard everywhere as it was at the front door. The mother, who had been spending this exciting half-hour in keeping little Jens warm, now lighted a fire and made coffee: and Thoralf needed no coaxing to do justice to his breakfast, even though it had, like everything else in Iceland, a flavor of salted fish.

FIVE DAYS HAD passed, and still the storm raged with unabated fury. The access to the ocean was cut off, and, with that, access to food. Already the last handful of flour had been made into bread, and of the dried cod which hung in rows under the ceiling only one small and skinny specimen remained. The father and the mother sat with mournful faces at the hearth, the former reading in his hymn-book, the latter stroking the hair of her youngest boy. Thoralf, who was carving at his everlasting pipe-bowl (a corpulent and short-legged Turk with an enormous mustache), looked up suddenly from his work and glanced questioningly at his father.

"Father," he said abruptly, "how would you like to starve to death?"

"God will preserve us from that, my son," answered the father devoutly.

"Not unless we try to preserve ourselves," retorted the boy earnestly. "We can't tell how long this storm is going to last, and it is better for us to start out in search of food now, while we are yet strong, than to wait until later, when, as likely as not, we shall be weakened by hunger."

"But what would you have me do, Thoralf?" asked the father sadly. "To venture out on the ocean in this weather would be certain death."

"True; but we can reach the Pope's Nose on our skis, and there we might snare or shoot some auks and gulls. Though I am not partial to that kind of diet myself, it is always preferable to starvation."

"Wait, my son, wait," said Sigurd earnestly. "We have food enough for today, and by tomorrow the storm will have ceased, and we may go fishing without endangering our lives."

"As you wish, Father," the son replied, a trifle hurt at his father's unresponsive manner; "but if you will take a look out of the chimney, you will find that it looks black enough to storm for another week."

The father, instead of accepting this suggestion, went quietly to his bookcase, took out a copy of Livy, in Latin, and sat down to read. Occasionally he looked up a word in the lexicon (which he had borrowed from the public library at Reykjavik), but read nevertheless with apparent fluency and pleasure. Though he was a fisherman, he was also a scholar, and during the long winter evenings he had taught himself Latin and even a smattering of Greek. In Iceland the people have to spend their evenings at home; and especially since their millennial celebration in 1876, when American scholars presented the people with a large library, books are their unfailing resource. In the case of Sigurd Sigurdson, however, books had become a kind of dissipation, and he had to be weaned gradually of his predilection for Homer and Livy. His oldest son especially looked upon Latin and Greek as a vicious indulgence, which no man with a family could afford to foster. Many a day when Sigurd ought to have been out in his boat casting his nets, he stayed at home reading. And this, in Thoralf's opinion, was the chief reason why they would always remain poor and run the risk of starvation, whenever a stretch of bad weather prevented them from going to sea.

The next morning—the sixth since the breaking of the storm—Thoralf climbed up to his post of observation on the chimney top, and saw, to his dismay, that his prediction was correct. It had ceased snowing, but the wind was blowing as fiercely as ever, and the cold was intense.

"Will you follow me, Father, or will you not?" he asked, when he had accomplished his descent into the room. "Our last fish is now eaten, and our last loaf of bread will soon follow suit."

"I will go with you, my son," answered Sigurd, putting down his Livy reluctantly. He had just been reading for the hundredth time about the expulsion of the Tarquins from Rome, and his blood was aglow with sympathy and enthusiasm.

"Here is your coat, Sigurd," said his wife, holding up the great sheepskin garment, and assisting him in putting it on.

"And here are your skis and your mittens and your cap," cried Thoralf, eager to seize the moment when his father was in the mood for action.

Muffled up like Eskimos to their very eyes, armed with bows and arrows and long poles with nooses of horse-hair at the ends, they sallied forth on their skis. The wind blew straight into their faces, forcing their breaths down their throats and compelling them to tack in zigzag lines like ships in a gale. The promontory called "The Pope's Nose" was about a mile distant; but in spite of their knowledge of the land, they went twice astray, and had to lie down in the snow, every now and then, so as to draw breath and warm the exposed portions of their faces. At the end of nearly two hours, they found themselves at their destination, but to their unutterable astonishment, the ocean seemed to have vanished, and as far as their eyes could reach, a vast field of packed ice loomed up against the sky in fantastic bastions, turrets, and spires. The storm had driven down this enormous arctic wilderness from the frozen precincts of the pole; and now they were blockaded on all sides, and cut off from all intercourse with humanity.

"We are lost, Thoralf," muttered his father, after having gazed for some time in speechless despair at the towering icebergs; "we might just as well have remained at home."

"The wind, which has blown the ice down upon us, can blow it away again too," replied the son with forced cheerfulness.

"I see no living thing here," said Sigurd, spying anxiously seaward.

"Nor do I," rejoined Thoralf; "but if we hunt, we shall. I have brought a rope, and I am going to pay a little visit to those auks and gulls that must be hiding in the sheltered nooks of the rocks."

He climbed over the edge of the chimney.

"Are you mad, boy?" cried the father in alarm. "I will never permit it!"

"There is no help for it, Father," said the boy resolutely. "Here, you take hold of one end of the rope; the other I will secure about my waist. Now, get a good strong hold, and brace your feet against the rock there."

Sigurd, after some remonstrance, yielded, as was his wont, to his son's resolution and courage. Stepping off his skis, which he stuck endwise into the snow, and burrowing his feet down until they reached the solid rock, he tied the rope around his waist and twisted it about his hands, and at last, with quaking heart, gave the signal for the perilous enterprise. The promontory, which rose abruptly to a height of two or three hundred feet from the sea, presented a jagged wall full of nooks and crevices glazed with frozen snow on the windward side, but black and partly bare to leeward.

"Now, let go!" shouted Thoralf; "and stop when I give a slight pull at the rope."

"All right," replied his father.

And slowly, slowly, hovering in mid-air, now yielding to an irresistible impulse of dread, now brave, cautious, and confident, Thoralf descended the cliff, which no human foot had ever trod before. He held in his hand the pole with the horse-hair noose, and over his shoulder hung a fox-skin hunting-bag. With alert, wide-open eyes he spied about him, exploring every cranny of the rock, and thrusting his pole into the holes where he suspected the birds might have taken refuge. Sometimes a gust of wind would have flung him violently against the jagged wall if he had not, by means of his pole, warded off the collision. At last he caught sight of a bare ledge, where he might gain a secure foothold; for the rope cut him terribly about the waist, and made him anxious to relieve the strain, if only for a moment. He gave the signal to his father, and by the aid of his pole swung himself over to the projecting ledge. It was uncomfortably narrow, and, what was worse, the remnants of a dozen auk's nests had made the place extremely slippery. Nevertheless, he seated himself, allowing his feet to dangle, and gazed out upon the vast ocean, which looked in its icy grandeur like a forest of shining towers and minarets. It struck him for the first time in his life that perhaps his father was right in his belief that Iceland was the fairest land the sun doth shine upon; but he could not help reflecting that it was a very unprofitable kind of beauty. The storm whistled and howled overhead, but under the lee of the sheltering rock it blew only in fitful gusts with intermissions of comparative calm. He knew that in fair weather this was the haunt of innumerable seabirds, and he concluded that even now they could not be far away. He pulled up his legs, and crept carefully on hands and feet along the slippery ledge, peering intently into every nook and crevice. His eyes, which had been half-blinded by the glare of the snow, gradually recovered their power of vision. There! What was that? Something

seemed to move on the ledge below. Yes, there sat a long row of auks, some erect
as soldiers, as if determined to face it out; others huddled together in clusters,
and comically woe-begone. Quite a number lay dead at the base of the rock,
whether from starvation or as the victims of fierce fights for the possession of the
sheltered ledges could scarcely be determined. Thoralf, delighted at the sight of
anything eatable (even though it was poor eating), gently lowered the end of his
pole, slipped the noose about the neck of a large, military-looking fellow, and,
with a quick pull, swung him out over the ice-field. The auk gave a few ineffectual flaps with his useless wings, and expired. His picking off apparently occasioned no comment whatever in his family, for his comrades never uttered a
sound nor stirred an inch, except to take possession of the place he had vacated.
Number two met his fate with the same listless resignation; and numbers three,
four, and five were likewise removed in the same noiseless manner, without
impressing their neighbors with the fact that their turn might come next. The
birds were half-benumbed with hunger, and their usually alert senses were drowsy
and stupefied. Nevertheless, number six, when it felt the noose about its neck,
raised a hubbub that suddenly aroused the whole colony, and, with a chorus of
wild screams, the birds flung themselves down the cliffs or, in their bewilderment,
dashed headlong down upon the ice, where they lay half stunned or helplessly
sprawling. So through all the caves and hiding-places of the promontory the
commotion spread, and the noise of screams and confused chatter mingled with
the storm and filled the vault of the sky. In an instant, a great flock of gulls was
on the wing, and circled with resentful shrieks about the head of the daring
intruder who had disturbed their wintry peace. The wind whirled them about,
but they still held their own, and almost brushed with their wings against his
face, while he struck out at them with his pole. He had no intention of catching
them; but, by chance, a huge burgomaster gull got its foot into the noose. It made
an ineffectual attempt to disentangle itself, then, with piercing screams, flapped
its great wings, beating the air desperately. Thoralf, having packed three birds
into his hunting-bag, tied the three others together by the legs, and flung them
across his shoulders. Then, gradually trusting his weight to the rope, he slid off
the rock, and was about to give his father the signal to hoist him up. But, greatly to his astonishment, his living captive, by the power of its mighty wings,
pulling at the end of the pole, swung him considerably farther into space than he
had calculated. He would have liked to let go both the gull and the pole, but he
perceived instantly that if he did, he would, by the mere force of his weight, be
flung back against the rocky wall. He did not dare take that risk, as the blow
might be hard enough to stun him. A strange, tingling sensation shot through his
nerves, and the blood throbbed with a surging sound in his ears. There he hung

suspended in mid-air, over a terrible precipice—and a hundred feet below was the jagged ice-field with its sharp, fiercely-shining steeples! With a powerful effort of will, he collected his senses, clenched his teeth, and strove to think clearly. The gull whirled wildly eastward and westward, and he swayed with its every motion like a living pendulum between sea and sky.

He began to grow dizzy, but again his powerful will came to his rescue, and he gazed resolutely up against the brow of the precipice and down upon the project-ing ledges below, in order to accustom his eye and his mind to the sight. By a strong effort he succeeded in giving a pull at the rope, and expected to feel him-self raised upward by his father's strong arms. But to his amazement, there came no response to his signal. He repeated it once, twice, thrice; there was a slight tug-ging at the rope, but no upward movement. Then the brave lad's heart stood still, and his courage well-nigh failed him.

"Father!" he cried, with a hoarse voice of despair; "why don't you pull me up?"

His cry was lost in the roar of the wind, and there came no answer. Taking hold once more of the rope with one hand, he considered the possibility of climbing; but the miserable gull, seeming every moment to redouble its efforts at escape, deprived him of the use of his hands unless he chose to dash out his brains by col-lision with the rock. Something like a husky, choked scream seemed to float down from above, and staring again upward, he saw his father's head projecting over the brink of the precipice.

"The rope will break," screamed Sigurd. "I have tied it to the rock."

Thoralf instantly took in the situation. By the swinging motion, occasioned both by the wind and his fight with the gull, the rope had become frayed against the sharp edge of the cliff, and his chances of life, he coolly concluded, were now not worth a sixpence. Curiously enough, his agitation suddenly left him, and a great calm came over him. He seemed to stand face to face with eternity; and as nothing else that he could do was of any avail, he could at least steel his heart to meet death like a man and an Icelander.

"I am trying to get hold of the rope below the place where it is frayed," he heard his father shout during a momentary lull in the storm.

"Don't try," answered the boy; "you can't do it, alone. Rather, let me down on the lower ledge, and let me sit there until you can go and get some one to help you."

His father, accustomed to take his son's advice, reluctantly lowered him ten or twenty feet until he was on a level with the shelving ledge below, which was broad-er than the one upon which he had first gained foothold. But—oh, the misery of it!—the ledge did not project far enough! He could not reach it with his feet! The rope, of which only a few strands remained, might break at any moment and—he dared not think what would be the result! He had scarcely had time to consider, when a brilliant device shot through his brain. With a sudden thrust he flung away the pole, and the impetus of his weight sent him inward with such force that he landed securely upon the broad shelf of rock.

The gull, surprised by the sudden weight of the pole, made a somersault, strove to rise again, and tumbled, with the pole still depending from its leg, down upon the ice-field.

It was well that Thoralf was warmly clad, or he could never have endured the terrible hours while he sat through the long afternoon, hearing the moaning and shrieking of the wind and seeing the darkness close about him. The storm was chilling him with its fierce breath. One of the birds he tied about his throat as a sort of scarf, using the feet and neck for making the knot, and the dense, downy feathers sent a glow of comfort through him, in spite of his consciousness that every hour might be his last. If he could only keep awake through the night, the chances were that he would survive to greet the morning.

A stout rope was dangling in mid-air and slowly approaching him.

He hit upon an ingenious plan for accomplishing this purpose. He opened the bill of the auk which warmed his neck, cut off the lower mandible, and placed the upper one (which was as sharp as a knife) so that it would inevitably cut his chin in case he should nod. He leaned against the rock and thought of his mother and the warm, comfortable chimney-corner at home. The wind probably resented this thought, for it suddenly sent a biting gust right into Thoralf's face, and he buried his nose in the downy breast of the auks until the pain had subsided. The darkness had now settled upon sea and land; only here and there white steeples loomed out of the gloom. Thoralf, simply to occupy his thought, began to count them. But all of a sudden one of the steeples seemed to move, then another—and another.

The boy feared that the long strain of excitement was depriving him of his reason. The wind, too, after a few wild arctic howls, acquired a warmer breath and a gentler sound. It could not be possible that he was dreaming. For in that case he would soon be dead. Perhaps he was dead already, and was drifting through this strange icy vista to a better world. All these imaginings flitted through his mind, and were again dismissed as improbable. He scratched his face with the foot of an auk in order to convince himself that he was really awake. Yes, there could be no doubt of it; he was wide awake. Accordingly he once more fixed his eyes upon the ghostly steeples and towers, and—it sent cold shudders down his back—they were still moving. Then there came a fusillade as of heavy artillery, followed by a salvo of lighter musketry; then came a fierce grinding, and cracking, and creaking sound, as if the whole ocean were of glass and were breaking to pieces. "What," thought Thoralf, "if the ice is breaking to pieces!"

In an instant, the explanation of the whole spectral panorama was clear as the day. The wind had veered round to the southeast, and the whole enormous ice-floe was being driven out to sea. For several hours—he could not tell how many—he sat watching this superb spectacle by the pale light of the aurora borealis, which toward midnight began to flicker across the sky and illuminated the northern horizon. He found the sight so interesting that for a while he forgot to be sleepy. But toward morning, when the aurora began to fade and the clouds to cover the east, a terrible weariness was irresistibly stealing over him. He could see glimpses of the black water beneath him; and the shining spires of ice were vanishing in the dusk, drifting rapidly away upon the arctic currents with death and disaster to ships and crews that might happen to cross their paths.

It was terrible at what a snail's pace the hours crept along! It seemed to Thoralf as if a week had passed since his father left him. He pinched himself in order to keep awake, but it was of no use; his eyelids would slowly droop and his head would incline—horrors! what was that? Oh, he had forgotten; it was the sharp mandible of the auk that cut his chin. He put his hand up to it, and felt something warm and clammy on his fingers. He was bleeding. It took Thoralf several minutes to stay the blood—the wound was deeper than he had bargained for; but it occupied him and kept him awake, which was of vital importance.

At last, after a long and desperate struggle with drowsiness, he saw the dawn break faintly in the east. It was a mere feeble promise of light, a remote suggestion that there was such a thing as day. But to the boy, worn out by the terrible strain of death and danger staring him in the face, it was a glorious assurance that rescue was at hand. The tears came into his eyes—not tears of weakness, but tears of gratitude that the terrible trial had been endured. Gradually the light spread like a pale, grayish veil over the eastern sky, and the ocean caught faint reflections of the presence of the unseen sun. The wind was mild, and thousands of birds that had been imprisoned by the ice in the crevices of the rocks whirled triumphantly into the air and plunged with wild screams into the tide below. It was hard to imagine where they all had been, for the air seemed alive with them, the cliffs teemed with them; and they fought, and shrieked, and chattered, like a howling mob in times of famine. It was owing to this unearthly tumult that Thoralf did not hear the voice which called to him from the top of the cliff. His senses were half-dazed by the noise and by the sudden relief from the excitement of the night. Then there came two voices floating down to him—then quite a chorus. He tried to look up, but the beetling brow of the rock prevented him from seeing anything but a stout rope, which was dangling in mid-air and slowly approaching him.

With all the power of his lungs he responded to the call; and there came a wild cheer from above—a cheer full of triumph and joy. He recognized the voices of Hunding's sons, who lived on the other side of the promontory; and he knew that even without their father they were strong enough to pull up a man three times his weight. The difficulty now was only to get hold of the rope, which hung too far out for his hands to reach it.

"Shake the rope hard," he called up; and immediately the rope was shaken into serpentine undulations; and after a few vain efforts, he succeeded in catching hold of the knot. To secure the rope about his waist and to give the signal for the ascent was but a moment's work. They hauled vigorously, those sons of Hunding—for he rose, up, along the black walls—up—up—up—with no uncertain motion.

At last, when he was at the very brink of the precipice, he saw his father's pale and anxious face leaning out over the abyss. But there was another face too! Whose could it be? It was a woman's face. It was his mother's. Somebody swung him out into space; a strange, delicious dizziness came over him, his eyes were blinded with tears; he did not know where he was. He only knew that he was inexpressibly happy.

There came a tremendous cheer from somewhere—for Icelanders know how to cheer—but it penetrated but faintly through his bewildered senses. Something cold touched his forehead; it seemed to be snow; then warm drops fell, which were tears. He opened his eyes; he was in his mother's arms. Little Jens was crying over him and kissing him. His father and Hunding's sons were standing with folded arms, gazing joyously at him.

First published in the February 1887 edition of *St. Nicholas Magazine*

The Brownies and the Spinning-Wheel

WRITTEN AND ILLUSTRATED BY PALMER COX

One evening, with the falling dew,
Some Brownies 'round a cottage drew,
And, while they strolled about the place
Or rested from their recent race,
Said one: "I've learned the reason why
We miss the 'Biddy, Biddy!' cry,
That every morning brought a score
Of fowls around this cottage door;

'Tis rheumatism most severe
That keeps the widow prisoned here.
And brushes, brooms, and mops around,
An unaccustomed rest have found.
Her sheep go bleating through the field,
In quest of salt no herb can yield,
To early roost the fowls withdraw
With drooping wings and empty craw,

While sore neglect you may discern
On every side, where'er you turn.

Her neighbors' eyes, at times like these,
Seem troubled with some sad disease

That caught the branches overhead,
And round her heels the gravel spread.
The oily rolls are somewhere nigh,
And waiting for the spindle lie.
On these we might our skill have shown,
But trouble never flies alone;
Her spinning-wheel is lying there
In fragments quite beyond repair.
It happened in this tragic way:
While standing out at close of day,
A passing goat, with manners bold,
Mistook it for a rival old,
And knocked it 'round for half an hour
With all his noted butting power.
They say it was a striking scene,

That robs them of the power to spy
Beyond where private interests lie.
If help she finds in time of need,
From Brownies' hands it must proceed."
Another said: "The wool, I know,
Went through the mill a month ago.
I saw her when she bore the sack
Up yonder hill, a wondrous pack

That twilight conflict on the green;
The wheel was resting on the shed,
The frame around the garden spread,
Before he seemed to gain his sight,
And judge the article aright."

A third remarked: "I call to mind
Another wheel that we may find,

Though somewhat worn by use and time,
It seems to be in order prime;
Now, night is but a babe as yet,
The dew has scarce the clover wet;
By running fast and working hard
We soon can bring it to the yard;
Then stationed here in open air
The widow's wool shall be our care,
And all we meet with, high or low,
We'll leave in yarn before we go."

Across the tail-race of a mill,
And through a churchyard on the hill.

They found the wheel, with head and feet,
And band and fixtures, all complete;
And soon beneath the trying load
Were struggling on the homeward road.

They had some trouble, toil, and care,
Some hoisting here, and hauling there;

This suited all, and soon with zeal
They started off to find the wheel;
Their course across the country lay
Where great obstructions barred the way;
But Brownies seldom go around
However rough or wild the ground.
O'er rocky slope and marshy bed,
With one accord they pushed ahead—

At times, the wheel upon a fence
Defied them all to drag it thence,
As though determined to remain
And serve the farmer, guarding grain.
But patient head and willing hand
Can wonders work in every land;
And cunning Brownies never yield,
But aye as victors leave the field.

Some ran for sticks, and some for pries,
And more for blocks on which to rise,
That every hand or shoulder there,
In such a pinch might do its share.
Before the door they set the wheel,
And near at band the winding reel,

Their mode of action and their skill
With wonder might a spinster fill;
No forward step or two, then back,
With now a pull and now a slack,
But out across the yard entire
They spun the yarn like endless wire—

That some might wind while others spun,
And thus the task be quickly done.
No time was wasted, now, to find
What best would suit each hand or mind,
But here and there, with common bent,
In busy groups to work they went.
Some through the cottage crept about
To find the wool and pass it out.
With some to turn, and some to pull,
And some to shout, "The spindle's full!"
The wheel gave out a droning song—
The work in hand was pushed along.

Beyond the well with steady haul,
Across the patch of beans and all,
Until the walls, or ditches wide,
A greater stretch of wool denied.
The widow's yarn was quickly wound
In tidy balls, quite large and round.
And ere the night began to fade,
The borrowed wheel at home was laid,
And none the worse for rack or wear,
Except some bruises here and there,
A spindle bent, a broken band,
The owner failed to understand.

First published in the May 1885 edition of *St. Nicholas Magazine*

Sir Marrok

BY ALLEN FRENCH

CHAPTER ONE

In Sherwood, many a hundred year
Ere Robin Hood first saw the light,
There was a knight, famed far and near,
By witchery brought to woeful plight.
The Lay of Sir Marrok

SHERWOOD FOREST WAS once called Bedegraine, strange, mysterious, dark. There the last Druids held their rites and sacrificed human lives. There witches and warlocks worked ill on all the countryside, feeding their lean and wasted bodies on the belongings of the poor people. Into those forest fastnesses withdrew robbers, emerging to plunder travelers, even to pillage villages and towns.

The word came to Uther in his hall—Uther Pendragon, King of Britain. 'Twas not the first complaint—it should be the last. His crown lost honor when pagan, sorcerer, robber, lived safe from him. He looked about from the dais, and out of the throng of his knights called forth Marrok, the newest companion of the Table Round. Marrok knelt before the throne.

"Marrok, thou hast asked a quest."

"Yea, my liege."

"Instead, take thou a fief. Go, put in order my land of Bedegraine."

'Twas banishment. What of that? Kings were in those days the instruments of God, men the instruments of kings. Marrok went, and toiled long at the task. He gathered men. His castle rose at the edge of the wood; under its shadow settled the weary peasants of the region, glad at last of peace. By little and little he swept a larger circle through the wood. At last Bedegraine, through its extent, stood clear, for, as says the bard whose ballad has come down to us in fragments,

Marrok the knight left no place of rest
For witch or warlock or pagan pest,
And burned to ashes each robber nest.

Then throughout Bedegraine were to be seen here and there the thresholds and chimneys of the dwellings of witches, the charred logs of the strong houses of the robbers, and the deserted stone rings of the Druids. But at the forest's rim rose villages, and the sheep and cattle wandered safe, and the swine were herded even in the wood, for Marrok—fighting finished—took to hunting, and the beasts of prey were his quarry. Beneath the branches of beech and oak no wolf lurked, but far to the north the harried packs fled at his coming.

Then the old roads through Bedegraine were cleared, and traffic once more flowed along its leafy arteries. Monks came; Marrok gave them land and workmen, and they built a monastery. Not far away knights built castles, each like an outpost to Marrok's own. The land grew rich, and in peace was happy.

Marrok himself was happy. He had won a wife long before, and when the days of war were ended she blessed him with a son. Then she died, and her loss was his one grief. His life was simple. Mornings, in the castle hall, he judged causes, listened to the reports of his underlings, and directed what should be done. Afternoons, he rode out, looked at the farms and buildings, saw that everything was in order, planned changes, remedied defects. Or he rode far through the wood, hunting the deer. And in the evening, by the great fireplace, in the hall, he listened to the songs of minstrels or heard the tales of travelers, to shelter whom was his delight.

One morning Marrok sat in the great hall and judged the causes of his people. Small quarrels and great were brought before him; he settled them all. Before his keen eye and quiet smile truth was laid bare. When he spoke all listened, all agreed. His word was law because it was right. His calm face, his hair just turning gray, his great, strong frame, and his sinewy hand, seemed to his people the attributes of unvarying justice. In those dark days of the early world, at least one corner held light.

There sounded a bugle at the gate. The porter announced a herald. The travel-stained man stood before the dais, bearing on his tabard the insignium of the king, the fabled beast Pendragon. Marrok commanded to bring meat and drink.

"Nay," said the herald. "To Sir Marrok, knight of the Table Round, bring I a message. Then must I forward on my journey."

"Say on."

The herald drew himself up. "Arthur Pendragon—"

"Arthur?" cried Marrok. "Not Uther?"

"Arthur Pendragon, King of England, to Marrok, knight, sends greeting. Son am I to Uther, lately dead. Since lords and knights in evil council do deny my kingship and combine against my kingdom, now I, Arthur, do command thee, Marrok, straightway to London. Take arms and arm thy men; set thy affairs in order; leave in thy lands some sure steward, and come thyself, with all force and speed, to join my army."

There was silence in the hall. The herald stood waiting.

"Of Arthur," said Marrok at last, "heard I never."

Sir Marrok receives the herald of the King.

"Merlin the magician," said the herald, "also sends thee greeting. By the great Pendragon, by thy knighthood, by thy vow as member of the Table Round, he bids thee come. By every sacred sign doth he swear: Arthur is son of Uther, by his wife Igraine, long kept in secret, bred under Merlin's eye. And if thou come not—"

"Peace," said Marrok. "Against Arthur who are arrayed?"

"King Lot of Orkney, the King of the Hundred Knights, King Carados, and King Nentres of Garloth."

"And with Arthur?"

"King Bors of Gaul and King Ban of Benwick."

"I will come."

One stood ready with a salver and a goblet of wine. The herald took the vessel. "To thee, Marrok, to us all, I drink." He set the empty goblet down, turned, and was gone.

Dead silence reigned in the crowded hall. Suitors and henchmen stood waiting. Marrok, his head sunk upon his breast, his hands gripping the arms of his chair, sat long. But then he groaned aloud.

His people answered with a sudden cry. Some kneeled; all began to pray him: "Lord, go not. Stay with us. Let war go on. Defend us, thyself, thy son, and leave us not!"

Marrok rose and raised his hand. There was silence. They gazed with wonder and fear upon his face, where pain sat visible.

"It has come," he said. "War has come. Our peaceful fields, our happy homes, will be swept upon, trampled down, destroyed. But I must go—else were I no true knight. Go now. Go all. Let every man set his house in order. On the third day each one who can bear arms bringing sword or shield, bow or spear, on horse or foot shall come here to the castle, ready to go or stay as I direct."

They left the hall. With sobs and tears they hastened to their homes. Marrok, alone, turned his face upward. "What shall I do?" he murmured, "how shall I find a loyal one to guard this land, this people, and my son?"

CHAPTER TWO: HOW AGATHA THE NURSE ADVISED MARROK, AND OF WHAT THE KNIGHT DID

Now Irma was a lady wise,
And Irma was a lady fair,
And unto Bedegraine she came,
To live within the forest there.
The Lay of Sir Marrok

MARROK SAT THOUGHTFUL, even sad. He knew what was to come. For himself he cared not. To go where he was sent, to do as he was bidden, to fight—even to die—was a part of his duty toward his lord. But to leave his people, whom he regarded as his children, was hard. He had reclaimed Bedegraine; he had made happiness possible in the land. Should war in his absence sweep over Bedegraine, all which he had built up would be destroyed, like tender plants stamped into the ground. And to leave his son—that was the worst pang of all.

Someone came into the empty hall—Agatha the nurse, leading his seven-year-old son. "Oh, my lord," she cried, "what is this I hear? You will leave us?"

"I must."

She ran and knelt at his feet; she made the boy, who knew nothing of it all, kneel and clasp his little hands. She knew it was of no use, knew that Marrok must go; but Agatha was ever an actress. And Marrok, irritated at the useless plea, took the child in his arms. Wise man that he was, in only one thing was he ever at fault—in his judgment of women. Good women he knew, thanks to his wife. But of Agatha sometimes he suspected that she was not good.

"Peace, woman," he said.

She rose and stood before him humbly. "Oh, my lord," she said, "now truly I see that thou must go. Tell me, then, what wilt thou do for the safety of us here left behind, and of thy little son?"

"Agatha," said Marrok, "it is even that which troubles me sorest. There are Father John and old Bennet, and I can perhaps leave behind one of my men-at-arms."

"Thy neighbors?" asked Agatha.

"Nay," said Marrok. "The nearest is ten miles away—what succor could he be in time of need? Moreover, all must do as I—gird on armor and fight for the king."

"'Tis true," said Agatha.

"If but my wife were alive!" said Marrok. "She had the mind of a man. I can leave behind none but a priest and an old man to guard my people. But, Agatha, thou art wise, and thou art of the council of Morgan le Fay. I pray you, think, and devise a scheme."

Now in those early days, before the coming of Arthur to his own, it was not known what Morgan le Fay truly was. Daughter of Igraine and half-sister of Arthur, she was known as a wise princess and honored. But in truth she was a sorceress of great and terrible powers, whose magic arts, in after years, were like to wreck the kingdom of Britain. And already she was spreading her nets throughout the island.

"Oh," said Agatha, sighing, "if but my lady were alive, then should we all have safety in thy absence. Truly could she defend the castle and administer the lands.

And, my lord, I see but one way to leave us in equal safety. For Father John and old Bennet are but weak bulwarks against misfortune."

"What is thy plan?"

"To marry again."

"Marry? But whom?"

"The Lady Irma."

Then Marrok rose to his feet and cried, "Never!" For when Agatha first proposed he should marry he smiled in contempt, and when he heard the name, and saw that the Lady Irma was the one person who in his absence could take his place, he rebelled at the idea of placing her in his wife's place.

"Truly," said Agatha, "the idea seems to me good. The Lady Irma is discreet and wise. Moreover, she hath a firm hand to keep thy lands in order. And again, she liveth alone in her moated grange within Bedegraine, where is no protection against danger. It would at least be courteous to offer her the shelter of this castle."

One more reason Agatha had, which she did not offer, namely, that Irma was also of the council of Morgan le Fay.

Then Marrok bowed his head and said: "Leave me, and the child with me." Agatha, turning at the door of the hall, saw how his fingers drummed upon the arm of his chair, and went away smiling, content. But Marrok sat and thought, moving not and saying nothing, until his child slept in his arms. At last, when it was near sunset, he rose from his seat. Sorely against his will, he had decided to give his son another guardian and his people a protectress. He laid the sleeping child in Agatha's arms, ordered his horse to be saddled, and rode away in the wonderful summer evening.

Beautiful was Bedegraine with the last light lingering among its leaves. But Marrok, thoughtful, saw nothing of the beauty as he guided the horse along the little-used path. He stopped before the lonely dwelling of the Lady Irma. The moat of the ancient house was grown with grass, the palisades were insecure, and the grange seemed ready to fall from age. When he was admitted, and stood waiting in a chamber, the dim shapes and shadows seemed strange and even awesome.

There were odd hangings on the walls, broidered with histories which his unlettered skill could not interpret. Had he but known it, they represented the sorceries of Medea, the magic of Circe, and the weird, mysterious rites of Isis. Vessels of curious shape hung from the rafters, books stood on shelves, and vials with many-colored contents were ranged against the wall. But Marrok knew that Irma was a wise woman to whom such things were as playthings, and he puzzled not over their use. In truth, before he had long time to think, a bright little figure ran into the room and caught him by the knees. He knew it was Irma's daughter Gertrude.

Then Irma herself stood before him, grave and beautiful and tall. Dark were her hair and eyes, her skin was as the olive of the South. Graceful was her form, and courteous the words and gestures with which she bade him welcome. Marrok, as he stooped and lifted the child from the ground, noted that she was different from her mother in everything—in golden hair, blue eyes, and cheek as fair as a rose-petal. He held her within the crook of his arm, and spoke to her mother from out his open, manly nature.

"My Lady Irma," he said, "this day heard I news—the saddest for this kingdom that have come in many years. Uther is dead, and over his throne has arisen strife. The realm of Britain will be rent in twain."

"Sir Marrok," cried the lady, as in surprise, "I grieve." But in truth she was not surprised, nor did she grieve; for as to the news, she had known it for many days; and as to what she hoped Marrok should say to her, she had wished it long.

"My lady," said Marrok, "we may all grieve, for war is the most dreadful thing on this earth, and of what may happen to our poor people here in Bedegraine, I tremble to think. Two days hence must I forth to the war, and leave behind all that I love."

"Nay," said Irma, "is it sooth? And who, Sir Marrok, will guard your people and your lands till you return?"

"My lady," answered Marrok, "let this child, your little Gertrude, appeal to your own heart and let you know my fears for my son, and for my vassals, who are as my children. And as for what I shall say to you, if it come hastily and blunt, I beg you to pardon my lack of courtliness, remembering that I am but a rough knight, and that there is no time for delay."

"Sir Marrok," replied the lady, "I pray you speak without fear of my opinion."

She stood waiting for his words. But Marrok, as he tried to speak, felt that something tied his tongue. Beautiful as Irma was, and strong of character likewise, he would not ask her to be his wife. Marriage without love was impossible to him, and this was not at all a matter of love. Remembering how, on bended knee, he had begged his wife for her hand, his face grew red and he stood speechless.

The lady glanced at his face quickly, and thought that she read all that was written there plainly as in a book. Then she dropped her eyes and stood waiting, while the little girl cooed and stroked with her soft hand Marrok's cheek. Finally he found voice and spoke.

"My lady," he said, "I beg you to leave this place and come to my castle, and in my absence rule over my people and my lands. It is much that I ask; but in the castle is safety, and this will be a place of danger. Also will you earn much gratitude from all." Remembering what he had come to say, his voice died away and he looked at the floor.

But the lady's face flushed and her eyes flashed, for she had expected a proposal of marriage. Had he been looking at her, he must have perceived her anger. Yet she controlled it quickly, and thought how she should answer: whether (and here her anger would rule), with irony, that she was his vassal and would obey; or (and this would be with craft) that she was thankful for his thought of her. And she said to herself: "To wait is wise, for to those who wait power comes in the end." And she answered him humbly and sweetly:

"You honor me much, Sir Marrok, and in deep gratitude I accept your offer."

Then Marrok bowed and thanked her from his heart, and for a time they spoke together, planning when she should come to the castle. The knight was much pleased, for in all she said Irma showed great understanding, and he thought that now everything would go well. As he took his leave he said, for the lovely child had touched his heart: "Who knows the future, my lady? Perhaps after us our children may marry, and rule long happily in Bedegraine!" Then he mounted his horse and rode homeward cheerfully.

On the third day, early in the morning, came the people to the castle of Bedegraine. Long lines of men, in armor and with weapons, horsed or on foot, thronged the ways that led to the castle. Even the women of the nearer hamlets came to take farewell of their lord. And conspicuous among the poorer sort came horses and carts, laden with the possessions of the Lady Irma, her books and her strange utensils, while the lady herself rode on a mule, with her little daughter beside her.

Marrok with sad heart ordered the men as they came, and set them in companies, some to go and some to stay. When the lady came he went to meet her. And Father John appeared, all in his richest priestly robes. At last, where an altar was erected in the great hall, and the chief vassals crowded about—while the two children, Gertrude and Walter, Marrok's silent son, stood behind their parents—then the lady vowed solemnly that she would administer Marrok's lands truly, and cherish his little son. And after that Marrok stood upon the dais, with the lady at his side.

"Hear ye," he cried, "and let it be known throughout Bedegraine that I, Marrok, give into the hands of the Lady Irma, the keys of my castle, and authority over all my possessions. In my absence everything shall be hers—the ordering of all things. She shall adjudge causes, she shall receive rents. And all shall obey her word."

Then the vassals, one and one, swore allegiance to the lady, placing their hands within hers. And she, standing upright, said no word, but looked with ever-brightening eyes.

Then came the time for departure. Sir Marrok kissed his son and little Gertrude, and pressed his lips to the hand of the lady. Quickly he gave the word, and sprang into the saddle. And man and horse followed, even to the animals with packs, bearing food, and arms for the campaign. Women wept and cried farewell, and with their hearts full of fear for the future, both those that went and those that stayed said good-by. Within the castle all hastened to the battlements, to catch the last glimpse of those departing. The train slowly disappeared in the forest, while on the highest turret the Lady Irma, and Agatha the nurse, and the two children waved their hands. Little Gertrude laughed and did not understand; yet Walter knew, and while from his habit he said nothing, he wept.

But the Lady Irma seemed to smile.

CHAPTER THREE: HOW IT FARED IN BEDEGRAINE WITH MARROK AWAY

The news came flying from the south,
A fearful word for all, I ween;
In haste it passed from month to month,
And sadder folk were never seen.
The Lay of Sir Marrok

THE FOREST OF Bedegraine was of great extent. On its southern border was the castle of Marrok, with its wealthy lands. But the great battle which was fought in Bedegraine, between the king and his rebellious vassals, was many miles to the north, and only stragglers came to Marrok's land. And the castle of Bedegraine, of the siege of which we read in Malory, was only a little watch-tower near the battle-field. Then the war swept far away, and of it Bedegraine heard only murmurs. For Arthur, having made himself secure in Britain, led his armies overseas and marched upon Rome.

How he sped, and what wonders he accomplished, read in Malory. Marrok was with him, fought in the great battles, and won much praise. But let us turn our eyes upon Bedegraine, where, though there was peace, greater harm could not have come in war.

When Marrok was gone there was great welcoming and many kisses between Agatha and the Lady Irma. The strange books of the new mistress of the castle, with her vials and mysterious instruments, they set in a little room within the keep, where the thickest walls gave greatest safety. None but Irma and Agatha might enter therein, and at times—often in the night, at the dark of the moon—they retired there for hours. Yet at first, when the armies of the king were still within England, the lady ruled in Bedegraine as Marrok himself, with such clear judgment and steady hand that the people marveled at her.

At these times the Lady Irma consulted much with Father John the priest, and with Bennet the old squire, the trustiest of the servants of Marrok. From them she learned all the ways of Bedegraine, its riches, and its people. With Agatha she spoke much in secret, and with her she went publicly among the people, until, like Marrok, she knew each house and its inmates.

But when Arthur took ship for Brittany, and left only Sir Bawdwin and Sir Constantine to govern England, there came a change at Bedegraine. Slowly the Lady Irma began new ways. First of all she sent away, one by one, the old castle servants, so that at last cooks and serving-maids, grooms and men-at-arms, were new in the castle. Some were from the lands round about, and, oddly, were those that had never found favor in the eyes of Marrok. And some were new in Bedegraine. And when the second year was but half gone, of the former servants none remained but Agatha and old Bennet and Father John.

Bennet was old, but, like an oak, he was sturdy. Cross was he, but, like a watchdog, was honest and kind at heart. His advice had ever been heeded, and in the ordering of the men of the castle he had always been the chief. In devotion to the lords of the castle he never failed, even to the peril of his life, and once he saved the life of the Lady Irma when, in the courtyard, a caged bear broke loose and would have killed her. From that encounter old Bennet lay a month in his bed, and for the rest of his life could use his left arm but stiffly; and yet his devotion helped him nothing.

For the loose manners and careless words of the new servants angered him much. Most of all, Hugh, the young and careless cup-bearer, irritated Bennet, so that one morning the old man gave the younger a cuff on the ear. Hugh went bawling to the hall, and soon Bennet was summoned before the lady.

"What hast thou done?" asked Irma, with bent brows. "This man is my servant, subject to the orders of none but me."

"Nay," said Bennet; "he came among the grooms in the courtyard and gave orders contrary to mine. If such things are to be, then serve I no longer in the castle."

This he said with confidence, for he believed he could not be spared. But the lady answered quickly, glad at heart: "Then pack thy belongings and go. Old art thou and useless, and shalt stay no longer here."

Bennet stood open-mouthed, staring. All the new servants winked and nudged one another, and even Hugh, despite his aching jaw, smiled with delight. Only Father John started out to protest, and cried: "My lady!"

But Irma answered: "Peace. The man shall go."

Then Bennet, with angry head held high, said, "Well, I will go." He packed his few possessions and left; but when he crossed the castle drawbridge his head drooped, and he sought his daughter's home in the near-by village, nigh heart-broken.

Father John stayed behind at the castle, and sought still to move hearts to the good. But among the new servants he found none who listened, and at last it happened that when he rang for daily prayers no one came. Mindful of the fate of Bennet, he made no complaint, but turned his hopes toward the two children, Gertrude and Walter. And them, throughout a month, he taught the rudiments of knowledge and principles of religion. But once, as he was teaching them, and they at his knee attended, each according to character—for Gertrude asked many questions, and Walter said nothing, but thought—once he turned and saw behind him the Lady Irma, with Agatha and Hugh the cup-bearer, listening at the door.

The lady came forward and spoke, and in her eyes Father John saw the light that was in them when she dismissed Bennet. "Father John," she said, "I have listened to thy teaching, and it is not good. Saidst thou not: 'a child should love the commands of God above the desires of men, and obey God even rather than a parent'?"

"Ay," said the priest; and he saw what was coming.

Then the lady stamped her foot, and her eyes flashed. "But I say that submission is the virtue of a child, to every word that its parent commandeth. How shall a child think for itself against the wishes of its parent? False priest, begone, and take thy teachings elsewhere!"

Father John saw on the lips of Agatha and Hugh smiles such as he saw when Bennet went away. He himself smiled—a smile so strange that the others sobered, not knowing what it meant. But the priest stooped and kissed each child, and, as he was, with neither scrip nor cloak, went down the stairs to the gate of the castle. There, with sign and word, he blessed it and its inmates, and went away.

Thus Bennet and Father John went to the village outside the castle, there to dwell. To the people Bennet became a great helper, being wise in all things worldly, whether as regards the work in the fields, or the building of houses, or the care of animals, or the making and use of arms. But Father John became a spiritual guide, and people came to him every day for help and counsel. They built him a church and a manse. Because in the castle the lady now seldom sat to judge causes, and her justice had become injustice, the disputes of the vassals were at last brought to the priest for settlement, and by him wisely adjudged.

And daily in the castle were music and singing and great merriment. Yet on the face of the child Walter were seldom seen smiles, for though but nine years of age he was not happy, with his father and Bennet and Father John all away. Only with Gertrude, when they two were alone, could he be merry. And the Lady Irma, viewing his sober face, felt as if he were watching her acts, to remember them against her. She grew to hate him.

It came at last to the autumn of the second year since Marrok's departure, and winter was coming on. One day the lady and her archers were outside the castle wall, and to give her pleasure the men shot at a mark. Of them all Hugh, now their captain, was the best, and, as the lady's favorite, received many smiles. Gertrude and Walter played near, from the edge of the forest gathering colored leaves to make themselves garlands. At a little distance, above the trees, rose the smoke from village chimneys.

Along the forest road came spurring a rider on a jaded horse. He wore a herald's tabard, and as he neared he blew a horn. Archers and women, even the children also, gathered around the Lady Irma, and all heard the words of the messenger as he sat upon his steed.

"My Lady Irma," said the messenger, "I crave the reward of a bearer of news."

"Thou shalt have it," said the lady.

"But give it me now," said the rider, "for my news is ill, and thou mayst forget."

Then the lady, smiling lightly, gave money from the purse at her belt—broad silver pieces. From a cask of wine that stood near for refreshment she commanded to bring drink for the man. He thanked, and drank, and delivered the message.

"My Lady Irma," he said, "my news is sooth, and all London weeps at it. In Lombardy, hard by Pavia, Arthur the king was slain, and all of his great lords. And Sir Marrok was among the slain."

Then the lady rose and laughed aloud. From her girdle she took her purse, all bejeweled, and gave it to the messenger. "Callst thou such news ill?" she cried. "Better heard I never!"

The messenger smiled, for he was shrewd and loved money. The archers that stood about smiled also, and nudged each the other, and whispered, "Now our good times begin." But Agatha and Hugh smiled broadest of all, and Hugh fell upon his knee and kissed the lady's hand, saying, "Fair lady, I give you joy."

At these words the children, that had stood staring, began to cry. At first none noticed them, till the Lady Irma, hearing the sound of weeping, called them to her. Gertrude's chin she took between thumb and finger, and raising her face upward, she looked with a severe expression into the child's eyes.

"Gertrude," said she, "this news is naught to thee. Go then to thy room until thou art thyself again."

Then the lady called Walter, and she looked into his face as she had into her daughter's. The boy was still, but he defied her. He looked into the lady's eyes manfully, and she saw that she had over him no such power as over gentle Gertrude. With her glance she insisted, trying to make him yield, but still his eyes looked at her unsubdued. No word passed between them, but she knew he did not fear her, and grew angry.

"Come down, Sir Messenger," she cried, "from your jaded steed. He is spent and spoiled; you shall have another." The messenger dismounted. Then the lady's eyes flashed, and she spoke to her men. "Bind this boy upon the horse's back! Tie his feet beneath the saddle, his hands behind him!"

It was done. Walter made no protest, uttered no cry. When he was bound upon the horse he looked at the lady, and the glance of the silent boy was more than she could bear. "Whip the horse into the wood!" she cried.

Then Agatha, laughing, flung her scarf across the boy's breast. "Wear this for my sake," she said in jest. And the archers urged the beast toward the forest; but it would move only slowly. At last Hugh, taking his bow, shot an arrow into the horse's croup. With a great cry of pain the steed sprang forward into the wood. He disappeared, but all, listening, heard his hoof-beats upon the turf until at last they died away.

It was three days before the news reached the village. Then Bennet and Father John, with what few able-bodied men remained from the war, with old men, boys, and even women, went forth into Bedegraine to search. They found nothing. Snow came and drove them homeward; the night was bitter cold. Hugh mounted upon his horse, guarded by the archers, met them on the return. He spoke scornfully:

"Fools, know ye not that wolves have come again to Bedegraine?"

And in proof came at that moment a long howl from the forest.

CHAPTER FOUR: OF MARROK'S RETURN, AND OF THE MAGIC OF THE LADY IRMA

> She mixed the spices and the wine,
> She made the waxen image small,
> She lit three candles at the shrine,
> And on the evil powers did call.
> *The Lay of Sir Marrok*

IT WAS THE seventh year since Marrok's departure. Britain was at peace; Arthur was secure upon his throne. All the neighbor-countries did him homage. His barons and knights that had so well fought for him returned unto their homes. A little train, much smaller than had left it, rode toward Bedegraine, and their leader, spurring out before the others, reached it first.

But as he passed along the road his countenance overclouded, and his heart grew heavy. Gone were the waving fields of grain, the acres of prosperous crops. Changed indeed were the neat and smiling villages. The houses were squalid, the streets dirty. At his coming he saw people look, then hide from sight. In the fields the scanty hay-crop rotted ungathered, and hosts of sapling oak and beeches invaded lands which the peasants once had plowed. The warrior bowed his head. "Woe is me!" he cried. "War hath swept over Bedegraine!"

Then he spurred faster, anxious for sight of the castle. "My son!" he thought. But presently he cried, "God be praised!" Serene and strong, the castle lifted its rugged head above the trees. When he had it in full view he knew no harm had come to it. "At least," he thought, "that hath been spared. But oh! my poor people!"

It was evening. The castle drawbridge was raised. The knight blew his horn, and a warder looked over the battlement. "What aileth you all?" cried the knight. "Hath no news of peace come to Bedegraine? Let down the bridge."

"Who are you," asked the churl, "that you speak so high?"

"Go to the lady," answered the knight. "Tell her that Sir Marrok hath returned."

The warder laughed. "Go to!" he cried. "Sir Marrok is dead."

"Send for the lady," said the knight, again. "Tell her that one who calls himself Sir Marrok is at the gate."

The warder would have laughed again, but from the knight spoke dignity and authority. "If it should be true," he muttered, "then are we all sped!—I go," he said, and went.

The knight waited. "They have supposed me dead! But what of that? My poor people! Fire and sword have swept my fields."

And yet that desolation in Bedegraine came not from the torch and ax of a pillaging army. The wicked, careless woman within the castle had caused it all, with over-great taxes, with seizure of cattle, and with exaction of severe labor.

At last upon its hinges creaked the bridge, and the chains rattled. The bridge sank, the portcullis rose, and the great gate opened. The knight rode forward. The courtyard was bright with torches; the archers stood about, each with a flaming knot. Among them stood the Lady Irma with white face.

The knight drew rein and looked about him. The lady he saw, Agatha he saw. The rest were strangers all. "Lady Irma," he said, "gladly I see you again. Agatha, too. But where are Bennet and Father John, and where is my little son?"

"Sir Marrok," said the lady, "it is you in sooth?"

"It is!"said the knight:

"Bennet is in the woods for deer," said the lady; "he hath not returned. But, Marrok, thy child is sick, and lieth in the turret chamber, and there Father John watcheth, for he is a good leech [physician]."

Marrok sprang from his steed, and his armor clanged in the courtyard. "Is the boy ill?" he cried. "Is he in danger? Then will I to him at once."

"Nay, Sir Marrok," said the lady. "There is no danger. But the lad sleepeth and the priest saith he must not be disturbed. Rest thou here. Hast thou no word for me?"

Then Marrok bent over the lady's hand, and spoke to Agatha, and began to inquire of the castle servants. For Hugh he knew not, but he missed Christopher and Ronald and the dozen others he had left behind. But the lady interrupted, and ordered the servants to unarm him. They hastened to remove his helmet and his

"Sir Marrok," said the Lady, "it is you in sooth?"

armor; they bore away his sword, and led the steed to the stable. And Marrok gladly gave up his arms and wrapped himself in the rich mantle which Agatha brought. Then the lady ordered food. With much talk and laughter she led him to the table in the hall.

But a thought was heavy on Marrok's mind, and he broke into her talk. "My Lady Irma, my heart was sad as I rode hither. For I perceived clearly that war hath visited my lands and spoiled my vassals of prosperity. Tell me, I pray you, when it happened, and how many were killed, and who are yet left. Glad am I that the castle escaped."

But she hung upon his arm, and smiled, and said: "Nay, my lord; of these things ask not tonight. Tomorrow will be time for sorrowful tidings. But now let me go and with my skill brew thee a drink that will cure thy fatigue, and make thee glad to be once more in thine own castle." Then she slipped away, laughing back over her shoulder, so that Marrok was pleased, and with a smile sat in the hall, watching the servants spread a table, and waiting her return.

The lady went quickly to her chamber, and shut herself in. She took wax and softened it over a brazier; then with deft fingers she kneaded it and made of it a figure. A wolf she made, so small as to stand upon the hand. She put it within a little cabinet upon the wall, and before it lit three candles, one burning with a green flame, one with red, and one with blue. Then she took her vials, and quickly compounded a drink, mixing it in a golden chalice. And all the time she said strange words for spells and charms.

She left the room, and gave orders that the servants should leave their work and all go into the servants' hall. Agatha she sent to see that the gate of the castle, and the drawbridge, stood free. Alone she entered the hall, and, pausing before Marrok, offered him the golden chalice, that he might drink.

He took it and pledged her. "May thy wishes prosper," he said.

"May thy wish come true," she answered; and she watched him keenly.

He sipped the wine and smiled at her. "A noble taste!" he cried.

"Drink it all," she said.

Then he drank the drink, glad at heart. But as he took the chalice from his mouth, smiling and about to speak, lo! words would not come! And a strange change came over him. For gray hair sprang on his hands and face, and his face became a snout, and his arms and legs were as those of an animal. The chalice fell to the ground. Then the Lady Irma struck at him with her hand, and laughed, and cried: "Down, beast!"

Anon Marrok fell upon all fours, and behold, he was a wolf, long, and lank, and gray. The lady, with delight, pointed him to a mirror. There with horror he saw himself. Then she cried, "Out!"

Amazed he fled from the hall, down the stairs, over the drawbridge, and out into the night. In deadly fear he sought the forest and hid in its depths. And though his men came home, and his people watched and waited long, Marrok was seen not again, and none knew what had become of him.

CHAPTER FIVE: HOW THE GREAT OPPORTUNITY CAME TO MARROK

By baleful deed, on woeful day,
Sir Morcar sought to win a bride,
And thus to Marrok showed the way
For him to help the weaker side.
The Lay of Sir Marrok

TRULY IT SEEMS sometimes that injustice and cruelty triumph in the world, and innocence and right are trampled. And now, when the Lady Irma and her minions carried it with a high hand in the castle, and Marrok, in wolfish shape, cowered in the forest, did it especially so seem.

Sad and pitiful were the feelings of Marrok. Deep in the woods he hid himself, and with shame and dread avoided the sight of all living things. Even the birds that sang in the branches caused him to start, and as for the deer that fled at his coming, their fear could not be greater than his. For weeks he lay close, living on the scantiest of food, and grew thin with starvation and with hatred of himself.

What was there left him in the world? Only as a wolf to hunt food in the wood, miserably to live as a beast in the forest, hated of men. And he cried to God from the depths of his heart, "Kill me and let this life finish!" But no such merciful end was sent.

Sometimes he would steal to the edge of the forest and look out upon the homes of men. Sometimes he would creep close to the castle and lie long in wait, hoping for a sight of his son. But though he saw the lady and her retainers, richly clothed and making merry, he saw neither the boy Walter, nor Bennet, nor Father John. And when he looked at the village he saw the poverty of his people. No longer they fed in the forest their rich herds of swine, for wolves lurked in the coverts and the swine were nearly all killed. And only in little hidden patches the peasants tilled the ground, for the lady sometimes sent her servants and seized the greater part of what they had.

In the forest Marrok spied upon the wolves and counted their numbers. It seemed they were as many as when he first came to Bedegraine. Here and there he found the abodes of witches and warlocks, workers of ill. And once he came to the roadside where men lay dead upon the ground, where horses and mules strayed masterless, and chests lay strewn, open and plundered. Marrok knew this for the sign of robbers.

Then his heart almost burst within him, and he cried: "Bedegraine is again but a savage place, and all the work of my life is made nothing!"

One day he was upon a height. Bedegraine lay before him like the green ocean, the wind moving the leaves in waves. In one place he could see the towers of his castle, in another a village, and in another the open land and wooden house of old Sir Simon, once his friend.

And as he watched, behold! he saw new proof that evil reigned. For he saw fighting before the house of Sir Simon, and the servants of the old knight driven within pell-mell. Then he saw arrows tipped with fire fly to the roof of the house, and marked besiegers battering at the door. Before long the ancient grange burned brightly at all its four corners. Then suddenly those within came rushing out, in the attempt to save their lives by flight. Marrok saw women in the midst of a valiant little band. On horseback they pushed their way, and made for the wood. But many fell; one, who from his knightly bearing seemed Sir Simon, sank at last from many wounds. Then suddenly the distant struggle became flight and pursuit along the forest road, with a girl, as it seemed, ahead on her steed, with but a boy to defend her, and armed men thundering along behind. And thus they disappeared within the screen of leaves.

Marrok rushed from his place and plunged into the forest.

Now it was Agnes, the daughter of Sir Simon, who fled so hastily, and her brother who defended her. Behind came hurrying the men of Sir Morcar, with the knight himself, at their head. And the reason of it was that Agnes was pledged in marriage to Sir Roger, who lived far away across Bedegraine, and she had refused the offer of Morcar.

Her brother, unhelmeted, bade her not fear. But she knew by the laboring breath of her horse that the poor beast was wounded and could not run far. In fact, when they were scarce a mile within the forest, it stopped and stood trembling. The pursuers were close behind. Her brother cried, "Into the woods!" and, turning, rode to meet his death that he might delay her pursuers.

She waited till she saw him fall, sprang to the ground, and slipped into the covert. Behind her she heard shouts, and men crashing through the bushes. She ran the faster. Then pattering on the fallen leaves came steps at her very side, and there, as she ran, was a wolf trotting with her. She feared him less than the men, and ran on. But at last she stopped breathless and sank on a stone. The wolf placed himself before her, listening to the sounds of her pursuers.

Men beat the forest to right and left. But only one came where they lurked, and he, with the wolf at his throat, died before he could raise sword to strike. Then, gaining breath, the maiden said, as if to a friend, "I can go on," and she followed the wolf away. Deeper and deeper they went among the trees, until no sounds came from behind. Safe, the maiden fell on her knees, and wept and prayed.

There, as they delayed, night fell, and Marrok watched her troubled sleep. He heard a human voice again, and from her broken words learned the story. "Nay, father," she cried earnestly, "not Morcar—Roger do I love. Him only can I wed." Then words of thanks, as to her father yielding to her request, and then, waking to the forest night, she clung eagerly to her preserver, wet his fur with her tears, and lying close slept again, only to wake once more, crying, "Mercy, Morcar, spare my father!" Then she lay long awake, moaning: "Roger—Roger! How shall I find him?"

And Marrok, once more appealed to, once more trusted, trembled with joy at the touch of her arms, the moisture of her tears. Understanding her words, he knew what to do.

On the third morning thereafter Sir Roger of the Rock went forth early into the wood, wishing, in the happiness of his heart, to see the coming of bright day and hear the birds sing. He wandered on the turf under the trees, and made himself a song and a tune, and he sang them. The song, say the chronicles, runs thus:

> My Lady Agnes, fair and bright,
> Happy I who am your knight—
> Happy that tomorrow morn
> I shall no more be alone.
> For today I ride to marry
> My lady fair
> With golden hair,
> And shall no longer tarry.

But of the tune to this song we know nothing.

Thus ever smiling to himself, and at times singing, Sir Roger went farther into the wood, until he was nearly a mile from his castle. Thinking upon his lady, and how fair and sweet she was, he went farther than he meant. At last he remembered the hour. He was to ride that morning to the house of Sir Simon, and there take the Lady Agnes to wife. So he turned himself about and started to return.

But there, right there under an oak-tree, lay a lady, young, it seemed, and perhaps fair, but he could not see her face. At her side couched a wolf, the largest ever seen, grim and terrible of aspect, but fast asleep. Sir Roger thought: "The beast hath slain the lady!" But on looking, lo, her breast was moving gently, and she also slept. Sir Roger stood marveling.

At last he thought, "I must slay the wolf and save the lady." With all quietness he drew his sword and stole upon the beast, meaning to strike. The eyes of the wolf opened and he rose to his feet, and Sir Roger was astonished at his size. But seeing the lady move, he said to himself, "Haste!" and gripped his sword for the attack. Then he heard a voice cry, "Roger!" It sounded as the voice of his love. In truth, the lady who had been sleeping stepped between him and the wolf, and it was Agnes, his betrothed.

Then doubly he feared for her life, and cried: "Agnes, beware the wolf at your back!" He sought to pass her, and struck eagerly at the beast. But the lady caught his arm, and the wolf, turning away, vanished among the trees of the forest.

"Oh, Roger," said Agnes, in tears, "now is he gone! My life hath he saved. Leagues hath he led me in the forest, even, when I was tired, bearing me upon his back." And she told him her story. Then he joined her in searching for the wolf; but he was indeed gone.

Now as to the revenge which Sir Roger took upon Sir Morcar for the sake of his wife, that is too long a tale to be told in this story. But Marrok, leaving the lovers together, went away rejoicing. Once more he had been of use in the world. And since he had defended Agnes against the men of Morcar, and then against wolves, and then against robbers (but these stories are also too long to be told here), at last he knew his power, and knew how he should use it.

CHAPTER SIX: OF MARROK AND THE WOLVES, AND HOW HE SERVED THE WITCHES WHO DWELT WITHIN BEDEGRAINE

For what is Brute but body strong?
And what is strong in Man but brain?
And Marrok, to thee still belong
The powers to make thee man again.
The Lay of Sir Marrok

MANY WERE THE wolves of Bedegraine, and fierce. They hunted in great packs, and to them day and night were the same, for none opposed them. That Marrok alone should war upon them seemed madness.

But one day, where more than twenty lay sodden, gorged upon two does and their fawns, Marrok walked into the pack. Slowly, with anger at the intrusion but with no alarm, they straggled to their feet and faced him. One by one he measured them with his eye. He was longest of limb, deepest of chest, firmest of muscle, but he knew that without his fertile human brain he could do little against twenty. The plan of his brain was ready.

He singled as the leader the wolf who growled quickest and loudest of all. Now, animals have no speech, and no words could pass; but signs are much, defiance is easy of expression, and the cool, slow stare of the intruder enraged the leader-wolf.

He challenged first, then sprang—and in an instant lay with broken back.

Marrok moved slowly from the circle, contemptuous. Another of the pack leaped at him, to be flung headlong. Then the whole, recovering from their amazement, hurled themselves blindly on his footsteps, and followed him furiously into the bushes as he began his easy run. In the long chase that then commenced, again and again the fugitive turned, and the first pursuer, from a single snap of iron jaws, gasped out his life amid the leaves. From the pursuit but ten returned.

So began Marrok's hunting. On the second day the terrible wolf sought out the remnant of the pack, attacked, fled, and killed the pursuers singly, till at the last three in their turn fled before him, and but one escaped. Confident, Marrok sought the survivor in the very center of the pack in which it had found refuge, killed it there, and then the leader also of this new band. That night he lay down wounded, but six more wolves were dead, and the shuddering rumor of his deeds passed through the forest. Two months more, and a pack of thirty fled at his coming.

Then gradually he herded them northward, from side to side ranging the forest and sweeping it clear. His animal senses were so keen that nothing could deceive him. Here a band of six, there a pack of a dozen, broke back to their old haunts. He hunted them down, every one, and again commenced his northward drive. Each time, when their panic left them and the wolves sought to return, he appeared among them, however numerous, and slew without mercy. Neither spared he himself. Gaunt, haggard, sore from wounds, stiff from hard fights, tired from long running—his hunt began each morning at dawn, rested only at dark, and ceased not, day after day. At last, and for good, the wolves fled across the open lands to the forests far beyond. Forever it was known among them: no wolf might live in Bedegraine.

The year came round again, and Bedegraine was free. Yet Marrok, scarred and weary, might not rest. The second pest of his lands must go. He had marked each house of warlock or witch, had listened at their doors and spied upon their actions. The old Witch of the Marsh was the most potent of all—who, with snakes and cats as familiars, brewed evil nightly in her squalid hut. To her abode he went.

Within she crooned a spell:

> "Ye marshy imps and goblins rude,
> Whose powers I do fortify
> And serve yon with your food,
> Come feed ye here at my repast,
> And when ye well have broken fast
> Give each a drop of blood."

Listening, Marrok cowered. The sounds in the air seemed from the invisible wings of spirits whose powers might blight him where he stood. Yet he made with clumsy paw the sign of the cross, and then with all his force pushed at the door.

The Witch of the Marsh saw a wolf on the threshold, and forgot her spells. Her herbs fell from her hands into the fire, and flamed out; she retired into the corner. Hissing, her snakes sought safety, and her cats, with great tails, sprang on the shelves. The white fangs of the wolf showed as in a smile. "She fears me," thought Marrok, and advanced. He seized a brand from the hearth.

The witch screamed. "Out!" she cried. "Imp of Satan—beast of the pit—out! Will ye fire my house? Out!" Feebly she threw at him a dish.

"If I am of Satan," thought Marrok, "why should she fear me? Then would we both be of the Evil One, and so cousins." But he paused not to puzzle. "She throws but a dish. I had feared spells."

He thrust the brand into a heap of flax in the corner. Barely did the Witch of the Marsh escape with her life from the destruction of the hut.

"Her snakes and cats are dead and her belongings burned," thought Marrok. "I will not kill her." He left her wailing in the night.

That night three other huts went up in flames.

The next night more followed. Only the warlock of the Druids' Ring, who lived among the fallen stones of the ancient altar, could retire into his house and defy fire. Marrok scratched at the stone slab that made the door, but could not seize to lift it. Then he pushed at a tottering stone that stood near, until it fell across the slab. Imprisoned for days, the warlock at length dug his way out, then fled far from Bedegraine.

But his fellows gathered at the castle and begged protection of the Lady Irma. "We have served you," they said, with quavering voices and shaking hands. "Do thou now help us."

The lady in her silken robes looked at the witches and warlocks dressed in rags. Long hair and matted beards, lean bodies and shrunk limbs—such were the rewards of all their spells.

She sneered. "Get ye hence," she said. "Out of my castle!"

They fell on their knees. "We all are of the same origin," they cried. "Sorcerers are we all. The great should help the small." Their shrill cries smote upon the lady's ear.

"You offend me," she answered. "Get ye forth. Ho, archers, drive them hence!"

As the archers whipped them away Agatha plucked the lady's sleeve. "Truly," she said, "we are witches as are they. Shall we destroy them?"

"They are but carrion," said the lady. "I despise them."

"They have served us."

"But can serve us no longer and no injury can they do us."

"But this wolf of which they speak?"

"Believe you such a tale? The forest wolves are hungry and bold. The witches have been frightened; that is all."

So the witches were driven forth, and wandered up and down the roads, sleeping in the ditches, till at last, in other regions, they found new homes. Irma, as she had said, took from them no harm. And yet—their story of the wolf! Irma could not forget it.

Outside, in the forest, Marrok hesitated before beginning his next task. To fight men! But one day he met a robber alone in the wood.

The man laughed. "A royal wolf!" he cried. "Standeth at gaze! Sith he runs not, I must e'en have his skin." And he began to string his bow.

The distance was short between them; the man had no sword. Marrok saw his chance, and on his third task made a beginning there and then.

CHAPTER SEVEN: HOW THE DOINGS OF THE WOLF CAME TO THE EARS OF IRMA

"Peter the robber," the lady said,
"What of the tribute you used to pay?
Speak the truth or beware thine head!"
But when he spoke she was in dismay.
The Lay of Sir Marrok

IRMA SAT IN the hall, and her vassals paid their tithes. The peasants, one by one, brought in their produce and laid it, sighing, at her feet. Servants bore it away to the store-rooms after the lady, with keen eyes, had measured each man's share.

To none she gave praise, to none thanks; but when all was finished she commanded them to stand before her again.

"Knaves," she cried, "your produce is still bad. What oats are these? what fruit? what meat? Lean meats and musty grain have ye brought, now, for the fourth year. For the last time I say it, bring better, or ye leave your farms."

With the cold hand of fear on their hearts they went away. Then from where he stood within a bay she beckoned forward one who had been waiting—a strong man, fierce of face.

"Peter," she said, "thou also hast come. Little hast thou brought of late. How much bringest thou now?"

"My lady," he said—and he bowed low even as the peasants—"here is the tale of my tribute: forty golden crowns, and two hundred of silver; seventy yards of silken cloth, ninety of woolen, a hundred ten of linen bleached, and a packet of fine lace."

A smile came upon the lady's face—a smile at which her archers were uneasy and the man before her quailed.

"Peter," she said, "Peter the Robber, thou hidest in my woods, thou robbest travelers on my lands. Half thy gains are mine. I laugh at these trifles you bring. Seek you to deceive me?"

"Lady," said the surly robber, "I bring you fair half—nay, more. For misfortune has come among us. My men are frightened; they will scarcely forth to rob even a rich train. One hardly dares go forty yards from another, for fear of the wolf. Even I, lady—"

The lady bent forward. "The wolf, sayst thou?" She waved her hand to her archers. "Clear the hall!"

The hall was cleared. Irma, Agatha, Peter, alone remained. "Now," said the lady, "speak plainly. If thou liest, 'tis at peril of thy head. A wolf, thou saidst?"

"Ay," said the robber, "a wolf. My lady, 'tis two months now since my men began to fail me—going out to hunt, returning not. Three, then six, were missed. Then we came on one lying dead. A beast had killed him as with one bite. More men were missed, we found more bodies. Then one day—I saw it with my own eyes— as my best man walked not the length of this hall away from us, a wolf rose out of a thicket and killed him on the instant."

"Nay!" said the lady.

"We were all there," cried Peter. "Forty of us within a javelin's cast. Since then more men are lost. He follows, attacks even openly. The men fear. I fear, I myself."

"A single wolf?"

"One wolf alone. Lady, there has been war among the wolves. Many have died. Now see we none except this wolf."

"He is large?"

"The largest of any."

"And strong?"

"Can break a man's neck. And cunning as a cat."

"And so," said the lady, "ye fear him as old women fear the tale of a witch! Call ye yourselves men?"

"Men are we," said Peter, stoutly. "Naught human do we fear. But, my lady, listen. This fortnight past heard we news of the coming of a train of wealthy merchants through from the south. Them had we seized, we all were rich. I laid my men in ambush on the road; the trap was sure. I heard the distant bells on the mules coming along the road, when sudden fell a panic among our men. My lady, 'twas the wolf!"

"Ay!" cried Irma, angrily.

"Hear me, my lady," begged Peter. "He slew the farthest quietly; three were dead before the rest were ware. Then sprang he right among us."

"And you fled?"

"Ay, quickly, and he on our heels. 'Twas twenty minutes before we drew together against him."

"And the merchants?"

"Passed through scatheless."

The lady rose and stamped her foot. "Peter," she said, "ye may speak sooth. But go; bring me the skin of the wolf!"

"My lady!" cried he.

"Go; come not again without it."

"He is a werewolf!" gasped Peter. "We cannot slay him." But he went.

Then Agatha and the lady looked at each other long, without speaking, and in the faces of both was alarm.

CHAPTER EIGHT: HOW BENNET AND FATHER JOHN WERE DRIVEN FROM THEIR HOMES

> Though Bennet hunted as he could,
> Old was he now and maimed beside,
> And there for very lack of food
> In Bedegraine they might have died.
> *The Lay of Sir Marrok*

THERE CAME TO the Lady Irma the news that the peasants were more prosperous. She set about to find the reason.

In fact, the peasants were fatter and more content. Now their dependence, as in the days of Marrok, was in their swine and their crops.

"Truly, madam," said Hugh, "in hunting I have seen larger herds of the villains' swine, and they are beginning to cut down the saplings that were springing in their fallow land."

"Send out," quoth the lady, "and catch me a peasant."

Presently one was brought in, trembling properly at a horse's tail, a rope around his neck.

"Hark ye, villain," said the lady. "Tell me of thy fellows. How is it that ye have more swine?"

"Lady," answered the fellow, in fear, "there are less wolves in the forest."

"How," she asked, "hath that aught to do with thy swine and their number?"

"Two years agone," he said, "I had but two. Last year but three young swine grew up. But this year I have raised in safety two great litters—sixteen in all."

"And that is because there are few wolves?"

"This twelvemonth, lady, have I seen not one, save the great gray wolf that doth no harm."

"Go," said the lady. "See that thou bringest, within the week, six of thy young porkers, killed and dressed."

The peasant went, wringing his hands. The lady caught more, and learned more things. There were surely no wolves to do harm.

Peter the Robber said so, also. The peasants even dared to pasture their milch-cows, most valuable of their belongings, on the fine herbage that grew at the edge of the forest.

"Thus the cows are growing fat and give more milk, and the calves are stronger," said Peter. "The peasants are becoming sturdier, with more milk and meat. This also have I learned, lady: 'tis Bennet and Father John that have set the peasants at saving their old lands; this spring and summer at least a hundred of the old acres are again under the plow."

"And the great gray wolf?" asked the lady, looking into Peter's eyes.

Peter became confused. "The wolf—my lady—we have killed him not yet."

"So," sneered Irma, "my valiant robbers are afeard."

"My lady," he cried, "surely it is no beast. The wolf is human. We dare go about only by threes. With two it is not safe. The wolf killeth one, and escapes before the other can raise his bow."

"Not an arrow in him yet?"

"Not one."

"Nay," cried the lady, in anger, "but I see ye are all cowards. Hark ye. Hunt him the more. Follow him! Track him! Give him no sleep!"

"But he is swifter than a horse," muttered Peter. "He leaveth no trail, and none know his lair."

"Find it," said the lady. "Begone, and act. And you," quoth she, turning to Hugh, "take archers and go to the village. Rout me that old villain Bennet from his daughter's house, where he liveth now these seven year. Take Father John from his manse by the church. Too long have these men comforted and counseled the peasants. Bid them leave my lands. Proclaim it death for any to harbor them. They work against me secretly. I will be rid of them."

And so that evening, while within Bedegraine Peter and his men again laid their heads together to catch the gray wolf, in the village women wept, and children wailed, and men knitted brows and clenched their fists. For Father John and Bennet were driven away, and had no place to go except into the forest.

But there, as he turned to the altar, stood a great gray wolf and looked at them.

They found the house of the warlock of the Druids' Ring, and made it habit-able for themselves. On the heathen stones Father John hourly offered prayer. But old Bennet, though he hunted long, brought in no food.

"There is game in plenty," he grumbled. It was the third day, and both were faint with hunger. "But I cannot shoot as I used. This left arm, that I injured sav-ing the Lady Irma from the bear, permits me not to draw the bow."

"It is well," said Father John. "The Lord, who fed his prophet with his ravens, will feed us also. Let us ask him for help."

But there, as he turned to the altar, stood a great gray wolf and looked at them. Bennet put hand to knife.

"Stir not," said the priest. "'Tis the wolf of which the peasants tell. He will not harm us." And he knelt.

But as he prayed he watched the wolf.

"O Lord," he said, "whose land this is, we pray thee take us in thy care. And first, we pray thee, send Marrok, our beloved master, to rule over us again."

At these words the wolf trembled.

"Or, if this cannot be, bring us the boy Walter, to take his father's place, and grow into a man, and rule over us. Yet, since we have not seen him from that day when he was driven forth, a child, bound upon a horse's back, here into the win-try forest—grant us, if he be dead, to find his bones, that we may give them Christian burial."

At this the wolf dropped his head, and great tears rolled from his eyes and fell upon the sod.

"But if we ask too much," said Father John, "stretch forth at least thy hand over these poor people, and lift them up. Give again swine and cattle, crops and fruit. And soften the heart of the lady of the castle, that she may do justice and her cruelties may cease."

The wolf gritted his teeth, his bristles rose, and he looked so fierce that the priest almost feared to proceed. With a weaker voice he concluded:

"And send food, we pray thee, to us thy two servants, who starve here helpless."

"Thank Heaven," cried Bennet, "the wolf is gone!"

He had indeed vanished in the bushes. But at the end of half an hour the thicket cracked, and lo! there was the wolf again, over his back a fresh-killed fawn. This he dropped before the priest.

"Praised be the Lord," cried Father John, "who hath sent us a helper! Make fire, Bennet, and cook the meat."

"If only the beast spring not upon my back," grumbled Bennet. And he made the fire, ever ready to clap his hand upon his weapon. But the wolf lay and watched, and when the crisp meat was done he drew near, as if himself ready to eat.

"Mayhap he will partake," said the priest, and he laid a collop [a small piece of meat] before the wolf. "Look, he eateth, and daintily, unlike an animal."

"He seemeth to like cooked food," whispered Bennet—which was true.

Then daily the wolf brought food to the two men, and they lived in comfort. But also he searched the forest from end to end and side to side. Yet never found he, whether in thicket or in grove, bones of horse or boy.

CHAPTER NINE: OF THE ABBEY OF BEDEGRAINE, AND WHO BECAME ABBOT IN ANSELM'S STEAD

"Now Richard to the west hath hied,
And Anselm he is like to dee.
Ride, Peter, ride!" the lady cried,
"And bring the prior speedily."
The Lay of Sir Marrok

THE PEASANTS OF Bedegraine continued to prosper. The fame of the gray wolf spread. In irritation the lady oppressed the peasants more, and planned many a hunt for the wolf. But to no purpose.

For the swine and cattle multiplied, and the crops grew plentiful. And when men beat the forest for the wolf he was not to be found.

When packs of hounds were brought and put upon his trail, he fled from them, and turning, killed the first pursuer, till all were slain—which has been the method of one against many since the time of the Horatii. So, when the lady could find no more hounds, she ceased hunting in this manner.

But the news came to her ears that the wolf abode with Bennet and Father John and fed them daily. The sanctity of the priest became multiplied in the eyes of the peasants, and they reverenced him greatly. Then the lady laid a plan to catch the wolf. Yet when the men of Peter's band closed in, one morn, around the Druids' Ring, the wolf slipped out through a gap in their line, and, turning on their backs, slew three.

The godliness of the priest began to make him friends, and in the Abbey of Bedegraine raised him up followers. Marrok had founded the abbey, endowed it with rich lands, and gave it many privileges. But the influence of the Lady Irma had worked even there, and in the years of Marrok's absence abbot and prior and many of the priests came to lead wicked and disorderly lives. Their peasants were oppressed, their lands began to waste.

But the good among the monks took heart of grace at the story of Father John and the wolf. Surely this priest, Marrok's chaplain, was a saintly man, and in a land of darkness shone like a ray of good. Among them secretly spread a strong resolve to imitate him, and to wait and watch and pray.

Now one day came to the Lady Irma a monk in haste. "My lady, the abbot lies at the point of death, and the prior is far away."

"What matters that to me?"

"This: that the lesser monks are murmuring. Unless the prior can be brought back before the abbot dies, they will make Father John abbot, and then—"

And then farewell drinking, and fat feeding, and merrymaking, and all good things. That was the monk's idea. But the lady saw further. She frowned. "Send for Peter the Robber!"

Peter came, with sword and bow and dagger, and a hunted light in his eyes.

"Nay, Peter," quoth the lady, when she had gazed upon him, "thou lookest strange."

"Strange I feel, and strange feel we all, not knowing whom the wolf will take next."

"A pest on him!" cried the lady, and wished it true; for while in the castle she worked spells and tried to cast them on the wolf, he was out of her power until he should return into her sight. But she never saw him, though he often saw her.

"Peter," said the lady, "here is a letter which take thou to the Prior Richard. Three days ago went he to the west. Seek him out and bring him back."

"Nay," said Peter. "Give me a horse. Afoot will I not travel without my fellows."

The lady commanded to give him a horse, and Peter rode forth into Bedegraine and took the forest road. His horse was fresh and fleet, he was well armed. Wayside flowers bloomed along the ancient turfy road, and the great trees of the forest were calm. Bright shone the sun, yet Peter's mood was dark and fearsome. He scanned the forest on either hand, and urged his horse, that he might quickly pass the three leagues of the forest. And though he was so high on his horse, he rode with knife in hand, to defend his life.

But nothing showed among the trees except the dun deer. And though the bright sun, the warm air, the beauties of the forest, were nothing to Peter, he was a stout carle [peasant], and at last gained heart. When but a league of the road was left he slipped his knife into its sheath. "Ho!" he said, "I meet not the gray wolf today."

Then as he rode he hummed a catch, to prove his courage. And he sat easier on his horse, cocked his bonnet, and thought of his reward, for the lady had promised many crowns. But out of a thicket shot suddenly the great gray wolf, and sprang on the horse's croup.

Peter screamed, felt for his knife, and struck with his spurs. The wolf seized him by the neck from behind. Rearing, the horse flung them both to the ground. The wolf leaped up, but Peter lay still. His neck was broken.

Then the wolf, pawing and nuzzling, drew the letter out of Peter's doublet, for

The wolf spread the letter out, and stood with wrinkled forehead, scanning the lines.

he knew that not without purpose did Peter ride on horseback. He broke the seal and spread the letter out, and stood with wrinkled forehead, scanning the lines. Then he took the letter in his mouth and sped away among the trees.

He came to where Father John and Bennet had celebrated their daily mass. At the priest's feet he laid the letter. The priest read the screed:

> To PRIOR RICHARD: Why wanderest thou in the west? Anselm the abbot lieth on his death-bed, and the monks murmur. If thou returnest not in haste, not thou wilt be abbot, but the hedge-priest, Father John, who with his werewolf mightily impresseth all here in Bedegraine. And if that happeneth thou wilt not even be prior. Return, therefore, and guard thy interests and mine. This by the hands of Peter, the Robber, from thy lady
>
> IRMA

Then Father John arose, and took his staff and scrip, and said: "I go to the abbey. Bennet, lead thou me by the straightest way."

But Bennet cried: "The way lies past the castle!"

Then Father John, with ready wit, turned to the wolf and said: "O noble wolf, much hast thou done for this land! Canst thou now not lead us quickly to the abbey?"

The wolf, at such a pace that the priest and Bennet might follow, led them through the forest. By devious ways he brought them until at last, when they left the shelter of the trees, the abbey towers were close in front. Bennet thundered at the gate and demanded admittance.

"But who are ye?" asked the warder. "Our abbot lieth dying, and we are all in fear."

"I am Father John," said the priest, "and I come to shrive the abbot."

When that was heard within the abbey, monks came running. The gate was opened, and Bennet and the father went in. But Marrok watched outside, and would not enter.

On his bed lay Anselm the abbot, sick to death. Had Prior Richard been there, no thought of repentance would have stirred the abbot's mind. But lying in his cell alone, thinking of his past life, fear came to him. He had heard of Father John. Once he had laughed; now he welcomed him. And Father John, standing by the bed, confessed the abbot of all his sins, and shrived him. Then the abbot commanded the monks to come to the door of his cell. As they stood in the passage outside, he commanded them that they should immediately make Father John abbot in his place. Then he begged for their prayers, and died.

Anon in full chapter—all being there but the Prior Richard and the monk that had gone to the lady—they elected Father John abbot, but expelled Richard from the brotherhood. When this was done the new abbot went to the gate, and the wolf started out of the edge of the forest where he had watched.

"O wolf," said Father John, "now am I abbot, thanks to thee. Come within these walls, and spend at rest the remainder of thy days."

But the wolf, having heard this news, went away. He returned to Bedegraine, knowing that Peter's men, so soon as they found the body, would be in confusion. They were so already. Fright had fallen on them. By twos and threes they fled away, nor stopped for their treasure. And the wolf was content to scare away those that would have sought refuge in the castle. None did he slay, for he was weary of killing.

Thus was Bedegraine cleared of outlaws, and we hear of no more until the time of Robin Hood. But then Bedegraine was called Sherwood.

When the Lady Irma heard the news, she laughed bitterly, and hid her chagrin with scornful words. Nevertheless she knew that two of the props of her strength were gone.

And Bennet, stoutly refusing to be made priest, dwelt in the abbey and became overseer of the lands. Soon as he might, he began to train the peasants to arms, meaning some day to take revenge on the lady. And sometimes he stole at night to the castle of the lady, looking to see how strict guard was kept, and whether in any place the walls of the castle were weak.

CHAPTER TEN: THE HUNTING OF SIR MARROK

> Sir Tristam was a well-versed knight
> In harping and in minstrelsy.
> In hunting took he great delight,
> And best of all the hounds had he.
> *The Lay of Sir Marrok*

THE LADY IRMA puzzled much about the great wolf. She laid her spells to bewitch him; her archers hunted him. In vain. But one day seemed promised her her heart's desire.

A knight came riding to the castle. He was tall and fair, with flowing locks and open, joyous face. A squire and two servants attended him, with horses and dogs. Six dogs there were, great hounds for the chase, and with them two little bratchets [hunting dogs]. On his shield the knight bore the arms of Cornwall.

The lady met him in the court, and bade him welcome. The servants she sent to the servants' hall, the knight she led to her own table, where she charmed him with her hospitality and her conversation. At last she asked him his name—"if you are under no vow to conceal it," she said, for to that all knights were much given.

"Lady," he said, "my name is Sir Tristram of Lyonesse."

"Nay," she cried, "and is it true? See I in my hall the noble Tristram, greatest of the knights of Britain?"

"My lady," he said, "there are better knights than I—Launcelot and Sir Lamorak."

"Forgive me, sir," she said. "Your modesty is beyond praise, but also your worth. Known are you everywhere for a noble knight, and a sweet singer, and the greatest of all hunters. Known is your fight against Sir Marhaus of Ireland, and your many valiant deeds."

And she flattered him to his face, but so sweetly that Sir Tristram was pleased. Then she begged him to sing, and sat as rapt in delight, but really she was thinking deeply. When he had finished she sighed.

"Lady," he asked, "why sigh you?"

"Ah, Sir Tristram," she answered, "thy harping and singing were so sweet that I had forgotten my troubles. When you finished I remembered them again. Therefore did I sigh."

"Truly, lady," he responded, "if you have troubles, tell them to me; for the heart becomes lighter by confidence."

Irma had put Gertrude into a deep sleep in her chamber, and she now sent Agatha to busy the squire and Hugh with pleasant chat. Then, knowing she could speak freely, she began her tale to Sir Tristram.

"Saw ye," she said, "my lands as ye rode hither? What thought you of them?"

"'Tis a rich land," he said, "with prosperous and happy peasants. Lady, to them thou art a benefactress."

Irma sighed. "Truly I seek to be to them as their dead lord" (but she mentioned not Marrok's name), "and my peasants have been happy. But lately has come a plague into my land that is beginning to waste our substance."

"What is it?" he asked. For Tristram was a noble knight, and, as Irma meant, he started at the hope of adventure.

"These four years," she said, "hath there lived a wolf in my forest. He killeth swine and cattle; he devoureth children. And now hath it come to such a pass that two must work always in the field together, for one man dares not work alone."

Thereat Tristram laughed a mighty laugh. "Lady, is that all? Ere tomorrow's sun is set lay I this wolf dead."

"How?" she asked. "With thy dogs?"

"With my dogs, and my fleet steed, and my javelin," was the knight's confident answer.

"But this wolf is strong; he pulls down one by one the dogs that pursue him."

"Yet will he not pull down my dogs, and should he, he will not escape my bratchets."

The lady's eyes sparkled. "'Oh, Sir Tristram, if thou deliverest this land, my people will bless thee, and I more than they! A great pest and unbearable has this wolf become."

"Lady," he said, "fear not. But now let me to bed, for I have traveled far; and in the morning will I hunt the wolf."

The lady led him to his chamber, and gave orders that his squire and men should be well served. Then she and Agatha and Hugh rejoiced together, for Tristram was renowned as the mightiest hunter in the world.

In the morning Tristram mounted his steed at the castle gate, and Gouvervail his squire mounted his, and Hugh, who would go too, mounted his. The dogs were loosed, eager for the chase, and all moved into the forest. Before long the lady, listening, heard Sir Tristram's horn, and knew that the dogs had found the scent.

But Marrok, couched in the forest, heard the horn, and groaned. "That," said he, "is the horn of Sir Tristram." For he knew Sir Tristram well, and since no one in the world could blow the horn so well as the knight of Lyonesse, Marrok knew the blast. And he groaned again, for he believed his end had come.

But he ran a good race, doing as he had done before. For the great hounds of Sir Tristram, the fleetest and strongest in all Britain, one by one he slew. The swiftest first, the slowest last, one by one they lay dead. And Marrok thought for one instant, "Perhaps now I am free."

Then he heard the baying of the bratchets, which so long as the hounds bayed were silent, but now gave tongue. And he knew that against bratchets he could do nothing, for they were small and slight, quick to turn and dodge, and he could never take them. He stood a moment in despair, and they came upon him among the trees, and waited and barked. Then Marrok saw the fair-haired knight coming upon his white horse, and turned and ran.

Minstrel and gleeman chanted of that chase for full four hundred years. Northward first fled Marrok, through the forest, till he reached its border. Then he turned west, and through the roughest country he led his pursuers. Then he ran south, then east, till the fair towers of Sir Roger of the Rock shone upon his sight. For a moment he was minded to flee there for protection. But the bratchets and the knight came upon him—all else were left behind—and Marrok fled south once more.

Then in despair he was minded to stay in the bushes and wait the knight and attack him. For ever, whether through swamp or thicket, or over knoll, or among rocks, Sir Tristram followed close. But Marrok could not slay his friend, and he ran on. His heart grew heavy in his breast, his lungs and mouth were dry, and his legs weary. Then he thought at last: "I will die among my people."

He turned toward the village of Bedegraine, and with his last strength fled thither. One bratchet fell and died, but the other and Sir Tristram followed on. And Marrok, almost spent, reached the village, ran into a yard, stood, and panted. The last bratchet, at the entrance, fell, and the horse stopped for weariness. But Sir Tristram leaped to the ground, his javelin in his hand, and walked up to Sir Marrok.

Marrok looked him in the eye and thought: "Better die from friend's hand than from foe's." He budged not, but waited for the blow. And Sir Tristram admired him, and said: "'Tis pity, brave wolf; but thy end hath come at last."

He raised his javelin. But a little flitting figure came in between, and behold, there was a child by the side of the wolf! She threw her arms about his neck and covered him with her body; and looking over her shoulder with sparkling eyes, she cried to the knight: "Thou shalt not slay him!"

"Stand aside!" cried Sir Tristram. "Child, he will kill thee!" And he sought to find place for a blow. But he might not hurl his weapon without striking the child, and as he hesitated the men of the house came running, and with scythes and pitchforks confronted Sir Tristram. "Sir Knight," cried they all, in one voice, "hold thy hand!"

Sir Tristram stood in amazement. "This," he cried, "is the wolf ye all hate."

"But we love him!" they answered.

"He killeth your swine and cattle."

"Nay," they protested. "Since he has come to the land our kine [cows] feed in peace."

"But he beareth away children."

The oldest man stood out before the others and spoke: "Sir Knight, listen. Last winter was a snow-storm, great and terrible; and the child that thou seest here was bewildered in the storm, and though we sought for hours, we might not find her, and the cold and snow drove us within doors to save our own lives. While we waited and lamented, we heard a scratching at the door. We opened, sir, and there was the child in the drift at the door, and this wolf stood a little way off. In the snow were no other marks than his. He had brought her home on his back."

"Is this truth?" queried Sir Tristram, greatly puzzled. "The lady said—"

"Oh, the lady!" cried they all. And Sir Tristram heard things that astonished him.

At last he mounted again his wearied steed, and gave gold to the peasants so that they should bury his bratchet. And while the wolf, weary and yet glad, made his way to the wood, Sir Tristram took the road to the castle. As he went he met his squire and men; but Hugh, fearing to remain in the forest, had returned to the castle. Tristram rode thither.

From the castle battlements the Lady Irma spoke to Tristram; but reading much in his face, she kept the gate barred.

"How now, Sir Tristram," she asked, as if eagerly, "is the wolf slain?"

"Lady," he answered, "the wolf hath escaped."

"Alas," she responded, "my peasants will lament!"

"Out upon thee, traitress," cried Sir Tristram, fiercely. "Deceiver art thou truly, and oppressor of thy people. Would thou wert a man!"

She laughed without words.

He turned his horse's head away. "Lady," he said, "I shall tell of thy deeds among knights."

But the lady still laughed serenely. Tristram was not of Arthur's court, and none but Arthur did she fear.

CHAPTER ELEVEN: OF HUGH WHO WOULD HAVE SLAIN THE WOLF, AND OF AGATHA THE NURSE

He armed himself at break of dawn,
Beneath his coat a shirt of mail.
"Let the wolf stand, though I go alone,
And to me the beast shall fall."
The Lay of Sir Marrok

GERTRUDE, THE DAUGHTER of Irma, grew tall and beautiful. She lived in the castle like a flower in a moss-grown wall, and lighted it by her presence. Therefore it came naturally that Hugh, the captain of the archers, wished her for his wife.

Hugh was stout of body and bold of deed, cruel and hateful. He served the Lady Irma in her own spirit, and she trusted him. He called himself knight, but he was none, nor yet a gentleman born, being the son of a peasant. So for a while the lady denied him the hand of Gertrude, putting him off from time to time.

But one day Hugh came to her and said: "My lady, what wish ye most in the world?"

She answered: "The death of the wolf."

"Lady Irma," he asked, "if I slay the wolf, wilt thou give me thy daughter Gertrude to wife?"

The lady thought, but not long. She answered: "I will."

Hugh said with joy: "Make ready the bridal dress, for the wolf dieth soon."

Now Hugh had learned that Marrok slept at the Druids' Ring, in the hut of the warlock, where Father John and Bennet once lived. Loving the Lady Gertrude greatly, he dared a deed. "I will go alone," he thought, "and seek him out. If I wear my shirt of mail, he cannot harm me."

He put on beneath his doublet a fine shirt of chain-mail. In the bright day he rode out from the castle and went to the Druids' Ring. There Marrok lay sleeping; but he waked at the tramp of the horse. When Hugh appeared among the great stones, the wolf stood looking at him.

Hugh cast a javelin, and missed. Then Marrok, hearing the chink of chain-mail and seeing it was useless to attack, turned limping, and slipped away into the forest. "He is lame!" cried Hugh, in delight, and gave chase. The horse with his heavy burden could go but slowly among the trees. But the wolf seemed wounded and sore, and Hugh kept him in sight. He urged his horse with the spurs, and rode eagerly. "Nay," he cried, "the wolf is mine."

But Hugh, thrown from the saddle, was hurled into the depths.

But go as he might, Hugh could not gain until he came out upon a great ledge, all rocks, which overhung the forest. Below, fifty feet, were jagged stones. The ledge was broad and mossy, and the wolf seemed so near, limping in front, that Hugh gave a shout and beat the horse with the flat of his sword. "I have him!" he cried. "I have him!" And the horse, lumbering into full speed, lessened the distance between them.

Then the wolf, just as the horse was close behind, and Hugh leaned forward to strike, leaped nimbly to one side. His lameness vanished. For one instant he waited, until the horse was quite abreast. Then he sprang under the horse's body, avoiding the blow of the sword, and caught the steed by the further forefoot. Quickly he wrenched backward, and the steed, tripped as with a noose, plunged and fell at the edge of the crag. But Hugh, thrown from the saddle, was buried into the depths.

The steed, in great fear, scrambled to his feet and fled headlong. The wolf stood listening. From below he heard a mighty crash. And then was silence.

THAT VERY DAY, soon after noon, Agatha wandered into the mead to watch for Hugh. She picked crocuses, and at the edge of the wood waited long, to wish him joy of his success.

Then she spied flowers in the forest, earliest snow-drops, and went into the wood to pick them. She heard a sound behind her, and turned. Almost she fainted from fright, for there stood the wolf, gray and great. He advanced upon her slowly. "Marrok!" she cried, and fell on her knees for mercy.

Still he advanced, and she gained strength from despair. She sprang up and ran away, ever deeper into the forest. Behind her trotted the wolf, and at each glimpse of him she ran faster. He kept between her and the castle, and she had no chance to return, but ran always farther from safety. When she had gone a mile, she came upon the forest road.

There at the edge of the trees was a horse all ready saddled, cropping the turf. And Agatha ran to him in hope. He let her seize the bridle and mount. "'Tis Hugh's horse. Hugh must be dead," she thought, "but I shall escape." She headed the horse to the north, and urged him to start.

Then into the road came the wolf, and the horse started indeed. Snorting with fear, he ran, and the wolf for a little way followed. Then Agatha, looking back, saw that he fell farther behind.

At last he stopped, satisfied, for he knew she would not return. In truth she rode eagerly, far away, into the country of the north. Never was she seen again in Bedegraine.

CHAPTER TWELVE: OF THE STRANGER KNIGHT WHO CAME FROM THE NORTH, WHICH BRINGETH AN END TO THIS TALE

'Tis far the outcast lad may flee,
And wide the wanderer may roam,
But soon or late, before he die,
He finds the way to his father's home.
The Lay of Sir Marrok

HUGH AND AGATHA came no more, and a new life began for the Lady Irma—a lonely, irksome life.

She was shut in and companionless. Her one-time friends were gone, for Sir Roger had slain Sir Morcar, and Father John ruled in the abbey. No longer might she ride thither for merrymaking. And in the castle were none but her serving-maids, her archers, and her daughter Gertrude.

Between Gertrude and her mother was no affection, but only tyranny and mistrust. The mother kept the daughter close, watched her, checked her, commanded her. Therefore she received not love, but patient service. Also there was no heartiness, for Gertrude could not but dislike her mother's ways. She sat silent in her presence, and Irma complained angrily of her sullenness. Yet it was not sullenness—merely timidity and repression; for Gertrude was sweet and gentle.

Thus Irma, bored and wrathful, chafed in her castle. And another cause for irritation there was—that the peasants refused her all supplies, but beat off her archers when they were sent for tithes. The lady might not send to the abbey; neither could she depend upon traveling merchants. For the road from the south was through the village, and the peasants warned all travelers away, lest they should pay heavy toll. Sir Roger stopped the eastern road, and the abbey the western. The wolf himself guarded the road from the north.

It was lucky for Irma that Marrok had built the castle as a very granary, holding food for five years' siege. The great chambers had always been kept full, and there was store of gold and wine. So the lady lived secure, but she bit her fingers in impatience and vowed vengeance on all. When a luckless trader chanced into her clutches, she fleeced him. If she caught a peasant, she made him a slave. And when knights fell into her hands, she held them long time for ransom. She feared nothing, and laughed away the forebodings that sometimes came, telling her the end was drawing near.

One day there rode through the forest a young knight, coming from the north. Strong and handsome he was, brown-haired and blue-eyed. It was in May. He hung his helmet on his saddle-bow and looked about in the beautiful wood. The birds sang sweetly among the trees, the sky was blue, the turf was green, and the first daisies, Chaucer's darling flowers, nodded by the wayside. His heart laughed and his eyes danced. Another knight would have caroled gaily; but the young man was silent by nature, and he said no word.

He came to a cross-road, and behold, across the southern road lay a great wolf, gray and shaggy and scarred. The horse snorted with fear, but the knight urged him on. There lay his road. Then the wolf rose and fawned on the young man, as if to turn him to the right or left. But the knight, greatly wondering, kept the horse's head to the southern way, and would not be turned from his course.

Then the wolf stood in the path and growled; but the young man had no fear. He raised his javelin and threatened. The wolf, crying as with a human voice, vanished in the forest; and his cry sounded often as the knight pursued his way, coming now from the right, now from the left. But the sound ceased when the knight came to a great mead, in the midst of which stood a castle.

Perhaps the crying of the wolf, perhaps the whispers of the forest, had called strange voices to the young knight's heart, speaking to him of the past. It was more than the mere beauty of the scene, as he drew rein at the edge of the wood, that made the castle seem to him familiar, kindly. "Mayhap," he said, "my search is ended." With childish memories stirring, and hope rising fast, he gave no heed to the last call of the wolf, that seemed to say: "Back! Back!" He rode forward to the castle.

It was near nightfall, and the knight blew his horn at the castle gate. He was admitted; a lady, beautiful and gracious, met him in the court. "Welcome, fair knight," Irma cried. "Dismount and unarm thyself, and come to the feast. I am the Lady Irma of Castle Bedegraine, and thou art welcome."

The knight, with slow, grave smile, answered with few words: "Lady, thou art kind." He dismounted.

The archers took his arms and armor, a groom his horse. The lady led him to a great hall, where the young man paused and looked about. "Nay, my lady," he said, with brightening face. "Were it not for these hangings and yonder great banner, I should think I had ended my search. I pray thee, under the banner is there not a shield carved in stone, and thereon a lion sleeping?"

Now under the banner was the shield indeed, the arms of Marrok, which the lady had covered with the banner. Yet she answered: "Nay, there is no carving there." And her heart leaped in her breast, for she knew from his slow speech, and from his question, that the knight was Walter, Marrok's son.

Now Gertrude had come into the hall, and stood at her mother's back, but Irma did not see her. And Walter, looking at the banner, sighed and said: "Almost it seems the same hall. Lady, I seek my birthplace, the home of my father, whence years agone I was cruelly driven. The castle's name I know not, nor my father's; but I recall the hall with the carved shield, and I should know my own little room."

Then Gertrude caught her breath, and they both saw her. But while Walter, in the midst of his disappointment, looked on her with a sudden strange delight, thinking her the most beautiful girl he had ever seen, Irma was frightened and angry. She cast on Gertrude the old glance of command, and the daughter, shuddering, knew that she must obey her mother, even to the words she spoke.

"Gertrude," asked Irma, "thou art not well?"

"Nay, mother."

"Then go to thy chamber." And Gertrude, struggling to stay, to speak, went from the hall.

Irma turned to Walter. "Sir Knight," she said, "I pray thee forgive my daughter's intrusion. She is ill-mannered. But for yourself, prithee wait here a little space. I will bring a spiced drink for welcome, and will order for thee a bath and fresh robes." She left the young man wondering at the vision he had seen, and sought her secret chamber.

At its door was Gertrude, who marked the look on her mother's face, and fell at her feet. "Mother," she cried, "what go you to do?"

"Gertrude," said Irma, "I bade you go to your chamber."

"Mother," cried Gertrude, "I cannot. The young man is Walter. What wilt thou do to him?"

Irma strove to fix her with her glance, but she failed. Gertrude, summoning her will, threw off Irma's power, even at this late time.

"I will go," she said, "to warn him."

And she turned away.

But Irma seized her suddenly by the arms. By force she drew Gertrude to her chamber, thrust her in, and locked the door. "Now," she said, ignoring Gertrude's cries, "do thy worst."

Gertrude leaned from the window, and there, far below in the dusk, under the wall, she saw the figure of a man. "Ho!" she cried, "who is there?"

"My Lady Gertrude," answered a cautious voice, "is it thou? I am old Bennet."

"Bennet," cried Gertrude, "fly for help. Here within is Walter, Marrok's son. He knoweth my mother not, and I fear for his life."

But though she saw Bennet hasten toward the village, she despaired. The village was a half-mile thence, and it would take time to gather men.

Meanwhile Irma went to the secret chamber and shut herself in. She took wax and warmed it at the brazier, and as she warmed it she thought. Should she make Walter a cat, or a dog, or a snake? Remembering the unexpected deeds of the wolf, she thought any of these too dangerous. Out of spite, she would not kill him. So when the wax was warmed she modeled with it swiftly the figure of an owl—the small brown horned owl. She put the figure on the little shrine on the wall, and lit before it three candles, one red, one blue, and one green. "There," quoth she; "he can hoot in the forest and catch mice."

Then she took her vials and compounded a drink, and all the while she muttered charms and spells. And bearing the drink in a golden chalice, she went down to the banqueting-hall.

Now without, in the forest, the wolf mourned for the young man. Seven years he had lived in Bedegraine, but never had he felt so drawn toward human being as to this stranger knight. A great sadness seized him, and he wandered, striving to throw it off. Instead, it grew upon him. He could think of nothing but the young man lying dead. He cried at last, "Let death come to me, not to him!" And he ventured all.

He went to a thicket in the wood, and entering, came upon an iron door among rocks.

Then Marrok pushed upon a hidden lever, and the door swung inward. He entered and shut the door, and went forward in darkness. But he knew the way, for he had built it himself against a time of danger to the castle. The passage led straight, then curved, and Marrok came upon a wall. He found a spring and pushed, and the solid stones moved upward.

This time he was on a stair, up which he clambered. Again he came on the solid rock, but again it moved at his touch on a spring, and let him pass. And there he was in a little chamber, lit by a lamp. There were hangings on the walls, books on shelves, and vials within cupboards. In one place hung a suit of armor. Upon the wall was a little shrine, and a waxen figure of an owl thereon, and three candles, red, blue, and green, burning before it.

Then he understood everything, and hastily rearing, he reached at the shrine with clumsy forefoot, meaning to destroy the figure of the owl. The shrine swayed at his touch, the candles guttered, and the figure, rolling away, hid under the hangings. The wax was still warm and tough, and it did not break. But from within the shrine fell out another figure, and broke in two upon the stone flags of the floor. And it was the figure of a wolf.

Then Marrok, standing there upright, felt a change come over him. The fur vanished from his body, his paws became hands and feet, and his limbs were those of a man. Behold, he was himself again, clothed in the robes he wore when he became a wolf!

He knew the change, and uttered a great cry of joy. But pausing not, he seized from the wall his sword, and casting down the scabbard, hastened from the room. Down the stone stair he hurried, till he came to the banqueting-hall, and stood at the door.

Marrok turned to his son, dropped his sword, and held out his arms.

Within were Irma and the stranger knight, and Marrok heard her words:

"Thou art Walter, son of Marrok, and thy father's castle is not far from here. Pledge me in this wine, Sir Knight, and I will tell thee where to find him."

The young knight, with sparkling eyes, took the chalice from her. "Lady," he said, "a thousand times I thank thee. I pledge thee."

But Marrok strode forward from the door, and cried, "Drink not!" And Walter, seeing a man with drawn sword, put down the wine hastily upon the table, and seized his dagger.

Then Marrok turned to Irma and cried in triumph, "Traitress, thou hast failed!" He raised his sword to strike the cup to the floor.

But she, thinking he meant to slay her, snatched quickly at the chalice, and drained the drink to the dregs. Then she looked the knight in the face, and dropped the chalice.

"Marrok! Marrok!" These were her last words. For she changed quickly into a little owl, circled upward, found an open window, and flew hooting into the night.

Marrok turned to his son, dropped his sword, and held out his arms. "Walter," he cried, "she was a sorceress. But I am Marrok, thine own father!"

Long was their embrace and loving, and then they sat and told each other many things. But after a while they heard a great commotion in the castle, and each seized his sword, fearing the servants of Irma.

Yet it was Bennet that they heard, who had come with help. For while the old man mustered men in the village, but all too slowly, there had ridden up Sir Roger of the Rock, and Father John, each with retainers. All together hastened to the castle and forced the gate. Bennet sent the peasants to the servants' hall to surprise the archers. Great and complete was the vengeance that the peasants took. But Bennet himself, and Sir Roger, and Father John, with the men-at-arms, rushed to the banquet-hall, and it was they who burst in the door upon Sir Marrok and his son.

Joyous was the greeting, and deep was the delight of all. Gertrude they brought from her chamber. She hung upon Sir Marrok's neck, and Walter was delighted with the sight. And the peasants, thronging into the hall, fell upon their knees and gave thanks at the sight of their lord.

Of Irma, who had become an owl, nothing more was heard. But Walter, the son of Marrok, married Gertrude, the daughter of Irma, some six months from that day. And all the land of Bedegraine was happy, except that the peasants lamented that they saw the great gray wolf no more. For since the return of Marrok the wolf was never again seen. And Marrok told to no one that he had been the wolf, except to Walter and Gertrude and to Father John. And Father John, growing old, wrote all this in a chronicle, whence came the song that minstrels sang, from which was written the story that is printed here.

First published in the May 1902 edition of *St. Nicholas Magazine*

"HAPPYCHAPS and Skiddoodles! Lend me your ears!"
Said old Hiram Hoppergrass, loudly;
Some frightened Skiddoodles hid under their beds,
For most of them hadn't an ear to their heads!
But the Happychaps offered theirs proudly.
   "Ho! Ho!" cried old Hoppergrass, laughing aloud,
   As he noticed the scurrying Skiddoodle crowd,
   "Hey! don't run away!
   Come back here and stay!
   Don't think for a moment I mean a *real* ear!
   That's a figure of speech. I mean: listen and hear!"
   Much relieved, the Skiddoodles came back to their places,
   With smiles of content on their dear little faces,
   And listened with eager and earless attention
   To whatever the eloquent Hiram might mention.
   I must tell you the scene

Was the big village green;
And Skiddoodles and Happychaps came to find out,
What old Hoppergrass could be talking about.
You see Jollipopolis proudly could boast
Of a green that could hold a million, at most!
For its citizens (as you well know) weren't big,
And they crowded together like seeds in a fig.
Well, on a great stand
(The kind they call grand)
Hiram Hoppergrass made a big speechification
Recommending a Fourth of July celebration.
"We Skiddoodles," he said, "have always done this;
And I think an omission would be quite amiss."
Then General Happychap, handsome and bland,
Exclaimed: "I am sure that you all understand
The Day that we celebrate all over this land,
And 'twill be a new thing to Happychap folk,

A pleasant conversation

The Crack Regiment of Jollipopolis

For, you see, we were housed in Centennial Oak
Ever since this triumphant American nation
Made cause for a Fourth of July Celebration.
And, indeed, and forsooth,
To tell you the truth,
I cannot deny,
No notion have I
Of what ought to be done on the Fourth of July!"
The Skiddoodles their laughter could scarcely contain,
But as they were polite, they tried to refrain
From making the blunder
Of showing their wonder;
And at Hiram's admonishment
Hid their astonishment;
And yet their surprise
Could be seen in their eyes.
To think anybody 'most half an inch high
Didn't know how to celebrate Fourth of July!
"Of course," said old Hiram, with courteous tact,
"We Skiddoodles well know that it is a fact
That all of you Happychaps
Were very nappy chaps;
And being in bed for more than a century,
You were just as 'shut in,' as in some penitentiary."
"Quite so," said the General; "now, I propose
That the whole of the day, from its dawn to its close,
Hoppergrass takes the whole celebration in charge,
And I hope that he'll make it both brilliant and large."

Timothy Terrapin sets off a rocket.

Whiz! Rattle-te-bang!
Boom! Clingety-clang!
The cannons went off, and the village bells rang.
With a snap and a snort,
And a deafening report,
Sounded rifles and guns of every sort.
And as they exploded,
Again they were loaded,
And then they went off with a boom and a roar,
With just the same hubbub they kicked up before!
A flicker and flash!
A clang and a clash!
A clatter and clamor! a crack! and a crash!
And what was the cause of this hullaballoo?
Why, Fourth of July! and the Red, White, and Blue!
'Twas just about—nearly—'most daybreak. At least,
The sun had just poked his nose up in the east,
And Skiddoodles and Happychaps sprang from their beds,
Tightly (for safety's sake) holding their heads,
And gallantly marching right past their front yards,
They saw the white-plumed Jollipopolis Guards!
A crack regiment, this,
With nothing amiss;
From their spurs to their helmets the pink of perfection,
For General Happychap made the selection.
The trills and the toots
Of their fifes and their flutes,
Were mingled with firing of noisy salutes.
While the blare of the trumpets and roll of the drums,
Could be heard o'er the banging and bursting of bombs.
Well, in just half a jiffy, as you may suppose,

A part of the Fourth of July parade

Happychaps and Skiddoodles jumped into their clothes.
They hustled their feet
In a manner quite fleet,
And in less than a jiffy were down in the street.
Some Happychaps
Had pistols with caps;
Some had fire-crackers,
And some snicker-snackers.
But all men and women and all girls and boys,
Had firearms of some sort to make a loud noise.
So the racket and fun
On the Fourth was begun;
Though the panes of the Fireflies' House broke, one by one,
Outside of that, little damage was done.
Old Chief Dewdrop, for instance, was thrown from his horse,
When a big cracker went off with terrible force.
The cracker went off—and Dewdrop did, too!
But he only jumped up and cried: "Whoop-a-ma-roo!"

Reading the news

*Timothy saves the lives
of the balloon passengers.*

An American flag was proudly unfurled,
The noblest, most glorious flag in the world.
To Jollipopolitans it was endeared,
And its stars and its stripes were exultingly cheered!

Celebrating the Fourth in Jollipopolis

There took place in the morning a "Horribles' Parade"!
And all sorts of jokes on the people were made.
Ridiculous floats
Represented queer boats;
And showed up the foibles of this one or that,
Hoppergrass very thin, and Hoptoad extra fat.
Even General Happychap had to be guyed,
As, covered with medals and puffed up with pride,
Percy Porcupine threw quills, in hopes they'd stick in,
But they harmlessly lit on old Tim Terrapin.
A game of golf Duncan McHappychap tried;
But he broke his sticks and his strokes all went wide.
Poor Toots got a jar
As he fell from his car,
And wearily dragged the machine from afar.
Professor Happychap, solemn and wise,
Was made up as an owl, with great, blinking eyes;
Messenger Happychap
Received many a clap
As old Rip Van Winkle, enjoying his nap!
In glee they applauded each float and each raft,
For nobody minded how much he was chaffed.

*Old Hiram Hoots after
the celebration*

And as the procession went lumbering by,
The Rah-Rah Boys shouted Hip-Hip-Hooray! Hi!!
For the afternoon there was planned an ascension
Of a monster balloon of wondrous dimension.
Some shouted "Hurrah!"
When this sight they saw;
But others just held their breath with awe.
The balloon soared high,
'Most up to the sky;
But it was a fire-balloon, you see,
And as it sailed higher,
It somehow took fire,
And then all were scared as could be!
Then Timothy Terrapin, clever old fellow!
Calmly opened his "umberellow,"
And holding it like a parachute,
To the balloonists, said simply, "Scoot!"
They all jumped into the queer life-boat,
And thus to earth they could safely float.

*A Happychap
takes a ride.*

Though some little Skiddoodles fell out
in the dirt,
No one was injured and no one was hurt.
But you all know how newspapers act,
And that funny old *Daily Buzz* (for a
fact!)
Got out an "Extra!" and newsboys
screamed:
"Balloon on fire!
Disaster dire!
Great holocaust!
All lives are lost!
Happychaps burned!
Details not learned!
But those we cherished,
In flames must have perished!"
An awful thing it seemed!
But would you believe those newsboys'
capers?
They rushed right off to sell their papers—
Without waiting to hear of Timothy's
"flight"
And that no one was killed the leastest
mite,
And how everybody came down all right.
In the evening, fireworks were all the go,
And they were a sparkling, spectacular
show.

Bombs and rockets and Catharine-
wheels,
Flower-pots and sizzling snakes and eels;
And gay Greek fire,
Like a blazing pyre;
And Roman candles whose stars went
high,
And mixed with the others up in the
sky.
Then the fireflies swarmed,
And quickly formed
Themselves in a glittering "set piece,"
bright,
Whose sparkling pattern spelled
"Good night!"

Then the Star-Spangled Banner streamed
out from its pole,
And a thrill went through each little
patriot soul;
"And the rockets' red glare,
The bombs bursting in air,
Gave proof through the night that our
flag was still there!"
For all Happychaps and all the
Skiddoodles,
Are loyal, true-hearted, and brave
Yankee Doodles!

First published in the July 1908 edition of *St. Nicholas Magazine*

Bruno's Revenge

BY LEWIS CARROLL

IT WAS A very hot afternoon—too hot to go for a walk or do anything—or else it wouldn't have happened, I believe.

In the first place, I want to know why fairies should always be teaching *us* to do our duty, and lecturing *us* when we go wrong, and we should never teach *them* anything. You can't mean to say that fairies are never greedy, or selfish, or cross, or deceitful, because that would be nonsense, you know. Well, then, don't you agree with me that they might be all the better for a little scolding and punishing now and then?

I really don't see why it shouldn't be tried, and I'm almost sure (only *please* don't repeat this loud in the woods) that if you could only catch a fairy, and put it in the corner, and give it nothing but bread and water for a day or two, you'd find it quite an improved character; it would take down its conceit a little, at all events.

The next question is, what is the best time for seeing fairies? I believe I can tell you all about that.

The first rule is, that it must be a *very* hot day—that we may consider as settled; and you must be just a *little* sleepy—but not too sleepy to keep your eyes open, mind. Well, and you ought to feel a little—what one may call "fairyish"—the Scotch call it "eerie," and perhaps that's a prettier word; if you don't know what it means, I'm afraid I can hardly explain it; you must wait till you meet a fairy, and then you'll know.

And the last rule is, that the crickets shouldn't be chirping. I can't stop to explain that rule just now—you must take it on trust for the present.

So, if all these things happen together, you've a good chance of seeing a fairy— or at least a much better chance than if they didn't.

The one I'm going to tell you about was a real, naughty little fairy. Properly speaking, there were two of them, and one was naughty and one was good, but perhaps you would have found that out for yourself.

Now we really *are* going to begin the story.

It was Tuesday afternoon, about half-past three—it's always best to be particular as to dates—and I had wandered down into the wood by the lake, partly because I had nothing to do, and that seemed to be a good place to do it in, and partly (as I said at first) because it was too hot to be comfortable anywhere, except under trees.

The first thing I noticed, as I went lazily along through an open place in the wood, was a large beetle lying struggling on its back, and I went down directly on one knee to help the poor thing on its feet again. In some things, you know, you can't be quite sure what an insect would like; for instance, I never could quite settle, supposing I were a moth, whether I would rather be kept out of the candle, or be allowed to fly straight in and get burnt; or, again, supposing I were a spider, I'm not sure if I should be *quite* pleased to have my web torn down, and the fly let loose; but I feel quite certain that, if I were a beetle and had rolled over on my back, I should always be glad to be helped up again.

So, as I was saying, I had gone down on one knee, and was just reaching out a little stick to turn the beetle over, when I saw a sight that made me draw back hastily and hold my breath, for fear of making any noise and frightening the little creature away.

Not that she looked as if she would be easily frightened; she seemed so good and gentle that I'm sure she would never expect that any one could wish to hurt her. She was only a few inches high, and was dressed in green, so that you really would hardly have noticed her among the long grass; and she was so delicate and graceful that she quite seemed to belong to the place, almost as if she were one of the flowers. I may tell you, besides, that she had no wings (I don't believe in fairies with wings), and that she had quantities of long brown hair and large, earnest brown eyes, and then I shall have done all I can to give you an idea of what she was like.

Sylvie (I found out her name afterward) had knelt down, just as I was doing, to help the beetle; but it needed more than a little stick for *her* to get it on its legs again; it was as much as she could do, with both arms, to roll the heavy thing over; and all the while she was talking to it, half-scolding and half-comforting, as a nurse might do with a child that had fallen down.

"There, there! You needn't cry so much about it; you're not killed yet—though if you were, you couldn't cry, you know, and so it's a general rule against crying, my dear! And how did you come to tumble over? But I can see well enough how it was—I needn't ask you that—walking over sand-pits with your chin in the air, as usual. Of course if you go among sand-pits like that, you must expect to tumble; you should look."

The beetle murmured something that sounded like "I *did* look," and Sylvie went on again:

"But I know you didn't! You never do! You always walk with your chin up— you're so dreadfully conceited. Well, let's see how many legs are broken this time. Why, none of them, I declare! though that's certainly more than you deserve. And what's the good of having six legs, my dear, if you can only kick them all about in the air when you tumble? Legs are meant to walk with, you know. Now, don't be cross about it, and don't begin putting out your wings yet; I've some more to say.

Go down to the frog that lives behind that buttercup—give him my compliments—Sylvie's compliments—can you say 'compliments'?"

The beetle tried, and, I suppose, succeeded.

"Yes, that's right. And tell him he's to give you some of that salve I left with
him yesterday. And you'd better get him to rub it in for you; he's got rather cold
hands, but you mustn't mind that."

I think the beetle must have shuddered at this idea, for Sylvie went on in a
graver tone:

"Now, you needn't pretend to be so particular as all that, as if you were too
grand to be rubbed by a frog. The fact is, you ought to be very much obliged to him.
Suppose you could get nobody but a toad to do it, how would you like that?"

There was a little pause, and then Sylvie added:

"Now you may go. Be a good beetle, and don't keep your chin in the air."

And then began one of those performances of humming, and whizzing, and
restless banging about, such as a beetle indulges in when it has decided on flying,
but hasn't quite made up its mind which way to go. At last, in one of its awkward
zigzags, it managed to fly right into my face, and by the time I had recovered from
the shock, the little fairy was gone.

I looked about in all directions for the little creature, but there was no trace of
her—and my "eerie" feeling was quite gone off, and the crickets were chirping
again merrily, so I knew she was really gone.

And now I've got time to tell you the rule about the crickets. They always leave
off chirping when a fairy goes by, because a fairy's a kind of queen over them, I suppose; at all events, it's a much grander thing than a cricket; so whenever you're
walking out, and the crickets suddenly leave off chirping, you may be sure that
either they see a fairy, or else they're frightened at your coming so near.

I walked on sadly enough, you may be sure. However, I comforted myself with
thinking, "It's been a very wonderful afternoon, so far; I'll just go quietly on and
look about me, and I shouldn't wonder if I come across another fairy somewhere."

Peering about in this way, I happened to notice a plant with rounded leaves,
and with queer little holes cut out in the middle of several of them. "Ah! the leaf-
cutter bee," I carelessly remarked; you know I am very learned in natural history
(for instance, I can always tell kittens from chickens at one glance); and I was passing on, when a sudden thought made me stoop down and examine the leaves more
carefully.

Then a little thrill of delight ran through me, for I noticed that the holes were
all arranged so as to form letters; there were three leaves side by side, with "B," "R,"
and "U" marked on them, and after some search I found two more, which contained an "N" and an "O."

By this time the "eerie" feeling had all come back again, and I suddenly observed that no crickets were chirping; so I felt quite sure that "Bruno" was a fairy, and that he was somewhere very near.

And so indeed he was—so near that I had very nearly walked over him without seeing him; which would have been dreadful, always supposing that fairies *can* be walked over; my own belief is that they are something of the nature of will-o'-the-wisps, and there's no walking over *them*.

Think of any pretty little boy you know, rather fat, with rosy cheeks, large dark eyes, and tangled brown hair, and then fancy him made small enough to go comfortably into a coffee-cup, and you'll have a very fair idea of what the little creature was like.

"What's your name, little fellow?" I began, in as soft a voice as I could manage. And, by the way, that's another of the curious things in life that I never could quite understand—why we always begin by asking little children their names; is it because we fancy there isn't quite enough of them, and a name will help to make them a little bigger? You never thought of asking a real large man his name, now, did you? But, however that may be, I felt it quite necessary to know *his* name; so, as he didn't answer my question, I asked it again a little louder. "What's your name, my little man?"

"What's yours?" he said, without looking up.

"My name's Lewis Carroll," I said, quite gently, for he was much too small to be angry with for answering so uncivilly.

"Duke of Anything?" he asked, just looking at me for a moment, and then going on with his work.

"Not Duke at all," I said, a little ashamed of having to confess it.

"You're big enough to be two Dukes," said the little creature. "I suppose you're Sir Something, then?"

"No," I said, feeling more and more ashamed. "I haven't got any title."

The fairy seemed to think that in that case I really wasn't worth the trouble of talking to, for he quietly went on digging, and tearing the flowers to pieces as fast as he got them out of the ground. After a few minutes I tried again:

"*Please* tell me what your name is."

"B'uno," the little fellow answered, very readily. "Why didn't you say 'please' before?"

"That's something like what we used to be taught in the nursery," I thought to myself, looking back through the long years (about a hundred and fifty of them) to the time when I used to be a little child myself. And here an idea came into my head, and I asked him, "Aren't you one of the fairies that teach children to be good?"

"Well, we have to do that sometimes," said Bruno, "and a d'eadful bother it is."

As he said this, he savagely tore a heart's-ease in two, and trampled on the pieces.

"What *are* you doing there, Bruno?" I said.

"Spoiling Sylvie's garden," was all the answer Bruno would give at first. But, as he went on tearing up the flowers, he muttered to himself, "The nasty c'oss thing—wouldn't let me go and play this morning, though I wanted to ever so much—said I must finish my lessons first—lessons, indeed! I'll vex her finely, though!"

"Oh, Bruno, you shouldn't do that!" I cried. "Don't you know that's revenge? And revenge is a wicked, cruel, dangerous thing!"

"River-edge?" said Bruno. "What a funny word! I suppose you call it cooel and dangerous because, if you went too far and tumbled in, you'd get d'owned."

"No, not river-edge," I explained; "rev-enge" (saying the word very slowly and distinctly). But I couldn't help thinking that Bruno's explanation did very well for either word.

"Oh!" said Bruno, opening his eyes very wide, but without attempting to repeat the word.

"Come! try and pronounce it, Bruno!" I said, cheerfully. "Rev-enge, rev-enge."

But Bruno only tossed his little head, and said he couldn't; that his mouth wasn't the right shape for words of that kind. And the more I laughed, the more sulky the little fellow got about it.

"Well, never mind, little man!" I said. "Shall I help you with the job you've got there?"

"Yes, please," Bruno said, quite pacified. "Only I wish I could think of something to vex her more than this. You don't know how hard it is to make her ang'y!"

"Now listen to me, Bruno, and I'll teach you quite a splendid kind of revenge!"

"Something that'll vex her finely?" Bruno asked with gleaming eyes.

"Something that'll vex her finely. First, we'll get up all the weeds in her garden. See, there are a good many at this end—quite hiding the flowers."

"But *that* won't vex her," said Bruno, looking rather puzzled.

"After that," I said, without noticing the remark, "we'll water the highest bed—up here. You see it's getting quite dry and dusty,"

Bruno looked at me inquisitively, but he said nothing this time.

"Then, after that," I went on, "the walks want sweeping a bit; and I think you might cut down that tall nettle; it's so close to the garden that it's quite in the way—"

"What *are* you talking about?" Bruno impatiently interrupted me. "All that won't vex her a bit!"

"Won't it?" I said, innocently. "Then, after that, suppose we put in some of these colored pebbles—just to mark the divisions between the different kinds of flowers, you know. That'll have a very pretty effect."

Bruno turned round and had another good stare at me. At last there came an odd little twinkle in his eye, and he said, with quite a new meaning in his voice:

"V'y well—let's put 'em in rows—all the 'ed together, and all the blue together."

"That'll do capitally," I said; "and then—what kind of flowers does Sylvie like best in her garden?"

Bruno had to put his thumb in his mouth and consider a little before he could answer. "Violets," he said, at last.

"There's a beautiful bed of violets down by the lake—"

"Oh, let's fetch 'em!" cried Bruno, giving a little skip into the air. "Here! Catch hold of my hand, and I'll help you along. The g'ass is rather thick down that way."

I couldn't help laughing at his having so entirely forgotten what a big creature he was talking to.

"No, not yet, Bruno," I said; "we must consider what's the right thing to do first. You see we've got quite a business before us."

"Yes, let's consider," said Bruno, putting his thumb into his mouth again, and sitting down upon a stuffed mouse.

"What do you keep that mouse for?" I said. "You should bury it, or throw it into the lake."

"Why, it's to measure with!" cried Bruno. "How ever would you do a garden without one? We make each bed th'ee mouses and a half long, and two mouses wide."

I stopped him, as he was dragging it off by the tail to show me how it was used, for I was half afraid the "eerie" feeling might go off before we had finished the garden, and in that case I should see no more of him or Sylvie.

"I think the best way will be for *you* to weed the beds, while *I* sort out these pebbles, ready to mark the walks with."

"That's it!" cried Bruno. "And I'll tell you about the caterpillars while we work."

"Ah, let's hear about the caterpillars," I said, as I drew the pebbles together into a heap, and began dividing them into colors.

And Bruno went on in a low, rapid tone, more as if he were talking to himself. "Yesterday I saw two little caterpillars, when I was sitting by the brook, just where you go into the wood. They were quite g'een, and they had yellow eyes, and they didn't see *me*. And one of them had got a moth's wing to carry—a g'eat b'own moth's wing, you know, all d'y, with feathers. So he couldn't want it to eat, I should think—perhaps he meant to make a cloak for the winter?"

"Perhaps," I said, for Bruno had twisted up the last word into a sort of question, and was looking at me for an answer.

One word was quite enough for the little fellow, and he went on, merrily:

"Well, and so he didn't want the other caterpillar to see the moth's wing, you know; so what must he do but t'y to carry it with all his left legs, and he t'ied to walk on the other set. Of course, he toppled over after that."

"After what?" I said, catching at the last word, for, to tell the truth, I hadn't been attending much.

"He toppled over," Bruno repeated, very gravely, "and if *you* ever saw a caterpillar topple over, you'd know it's a serious thing, and not sit g'inning like that— and I shan't tell you any more."

"Indeed and indeed, Bruno, I didn't mean to grin. See, I'm quite grave again now."

But Bruno only folded his arms and said, "Don't tell *me*. I see a little twinkle in one of your eyes—just like the moon."

"Am *I* like the moon, Bruno?" I asked.

"Your face is large and round like the moon," Bruno answered, looking at me thoughtfully. "It doesn't shine quite so bright—but it's cleaner."

I couldn't help smiling at this. "You know I wash *my* face, Bruno. The moon never does that."

"Oh, doesn't she though!" cried Bruno; and he leaned forward and added in a solemn whisper, "The moon's face gets dirtier and dirtier every night, till it's black all ac'oss. And then, when it's dirty all over—so—" (he passed his hand across his own rosy cheeks as he spoke) "then she washes it."

"And then it's all clean again, isn't it?"

"Not all in a moment," said Bruno. "What a deal of teaching you want! She washes it little by little—only she begins at the other edge."

By this time he was sitting quietly on the mouse, with his arms folded, and the weeding wasn't getting on a bit. So I was obliged to say:

"Work first and pleasure afterward; no more talking till that bed's finished."

After that we had a few minutes of silence, while I sorted out the pebbles, and amused myself with watching Bruno's plan of gardening. It was quite a new plan to me: he always measured each bed before he weeded it, as if he was afraid the weeding would make it shrink; and once, when it came out longer than he wished, he set to work to thump the mouse with his tiny fist, crying out, "There now! It's all 'ong again! Why don't you keep your tail st'aight when I tell you!"

"I'll tell you what I'll do," Bruno said in a half-whisper, as we worked: "I'll get you an invitation to the king's dinner-party. I know one of the head-waiters."

I couldn't help laughing at this idea. "Do the waiters invite the guests?" I asked.

"Oh, not *to sit down!*" Bruno hastily replied. "But to help, you know. You'd like that, wouldn't you? To hand about plates, and so on."

"Well, but that's not so nice as sitting at the table, is it?"

"Of course it isn't," Bruno said, in a tone as if he rather pitied my ignorance; "but if you're not even Sir Anything, you can't expect to be allowed to sit at the table, you know."

I said, as meekly as I could, that I didn't expect it, but it was the only way of going to a dinner-party that I really enjoyed. And Bruno tossed his head, and said, in a rather offended tone, that I might do as I pleased—there were many he knew that would give their ears to go.

"Have you ever been yourself, Bruno?"

"They invited me once last year," Bruno said, very gravely. "It was to wash up the soup-plates—no, the cheese-plates I mean—that was g'and enough. But the g'andest thing of all was, I fetched the Duke of Dandelion a glass of cider!"

"That *was* grand!" I said, biting my lip to keep myself from laughing.

"Wasn't it!" said Bruno, very earnestly. "You know it isn't every one that's had such an honor as *that!*"

This set me thinking of the various queer things we call "an honor" in this world, which, after all, haven't a bit more honor in them than what the dear little Bruno enjoyed (by the way, I hope you're beginning to like him a little, naughty as he was) when he took the Duke of Dandelion a glass of cider.

I don't know how long I might have dreamed on in this way if Bruno hadn't suddenly roused me.

"Oh, come here quick!" he cried, in a state of the wildest excitement. "Catch hold of his other horn! I can't hold him more than a minute!"

He was struggling desperately with a great snail, clinging to one of its horns, and nearly breaking his poor little back in his efforts to drag it over a blade of grass.

I saw we should have no more gardening if I let this sort of thing go on, so I quietly took the snail away, and put it on a bank where he couldn't reach it. "We'll hunt it afterward, Bruno," I said, "if you really want to catch it. But what's the use of it when you've got it?"

"What's the use of a fox when you've got it?" said Bruno. "I know you big things hunt foxes."

I tried to think of some good reason why "big things" should hunt foxes, and he shouldn't hunt snails, but none came into my head: so I said at last, "Well, I suppose one's as good as the other. I'll go snail-hunting myself, some day."

"I should think you wouldn't be so silly," said Bruno, "as to go snail-hunting all by yourself. Why, you'd never get the snail along, if you hadn't somebody to hold on to his other horn!"

"Of course I sha'n't go alone," I said, quite gravely. "By the way, is that the best kind to hunt, or do you recommend the ones without shells?"

"Oh no! We never hunt the ones without shells," Bruno said, with a little shudder at the thought of it. "They're always so c'oss about it; and then, if you tumble over them, they're ever so sticky!"

By this time we had nearly finished the garden. I had fetched some violets, and Bruno was just helping me to put in the last, when he suddenly stopped and said, "I'm tired."

"Rest, then," I said; "I can go on without you."

Bruno needed no second invitation: he at once began arranging the mouse as a kind of sofa. "And I'll sing you a little song," he said as he rolled it about.

"Do," said I: "there's nothing I should like better."

"Which song will you choose?" Bruno said, as he dragged the mouse into a place where he could get a good view of me. "'Ting, ting, ting,' is the nicest."

There was no resisting such a strong hint as this: however, I pretended to think about it for a moment, and then said, "Well, I like 'Ting, ting, ting,' best of all."

"That shows you're a good judge of music," Bruno said, with a pleased look. "How many bluebells would you like?" And he put his thumb into his mouth to help me to consider.

As there was only one bluebell within easy reach, I said very gravely that I thought one would do *this* time, and I picked it and gave it to him. Bruno ran his hand once or twice up and down the flowers—like a musician trying an instrument—producing a most delicious delicate tinkling as he did so. I had never heard flower-music before—I don't think one can unless one's in the "eerie" state—and I don't know quite how to give you an idea of what it was like, except by saying that it sounded like a peal of bells a thousand miles off.

When he had satisfied himself that the flowers were in tune, he seated himself on the mouse (he never seemed really comfortable anywhere else), and, looking up at me with a merry twinkle in his eyes, he began. By the way, the tune was rather a curious one, and the words went so:

> "Rise, oh, rise! The daylight dies:
> The owls are hooting, ting, ting, ting!
> Wake, oh, wake! Beside the lake
> The elves are fluting, ting, ting, ting!
> Welcoming our fairy king
> We sing, sing, sing."

He sang the first four lines briskly and merrily, making the bluebells chime in time with the music; but the last two he sang quite slowly and gently, and merely waved the flowers backward and forward above his head. And when he had finished the first verse, he left off to explain.

"The name of our fairy king is Obberwon" (he meant Oberon, I believe), "and he lives over the lake—*there*—and now and then he comes in a little boat—and then we go and meet him—and then we sing this song, you know."

"And then you go and dine with him?" I said, mischievously.

"You shouldn't talk," Bruno hastily said; "it interrupts the song so."

I said I wouldn't do it again.

"I never talk myself when I'm singing," he went on, very gravely; "so you shouldn't either."

Then he tuned the bluebells once more, and sung:

> "Hear, oh, hear! From far and near
> A music stealing, ting, ting, ting!
> Fairy bells adown the dells
> Are merrily pealing, ting, ting, ting!
> Welcoming our fairy king
> We ring, ring, ring.
>
> "See, oh, see! On every tree
> What lamps are shining, ting, ting, ting!
> They are eyes of fiery flies
> To light our dining, ting, ting, ting!
> Welcoming our fairy king
> They swing, swing, swing.
> "Haste, oh, haste! to take and taste
> The dainties waiting, ting, ting, ting!
> Honey-dew is stored—"

"Hush, Bruno!" I interrupted, in a warning whisper. "She's coming!"

Bruno checked his song only just in time for Sylvie not to hear him; and then, catching sight of her as she slowly made her way through the long grass, he suddenly rushed out headlong at her like a little bull, shouting, "Look the other way! Look the other way!"

"Which way?" Sylvie asked, in rather a frightened tone, as she looked round in all directions to see where the danger could be.

"*That* way!" said Bruno, carefully turning her round with her face to the wood. "Now, walk backward—walk gently—don't be f'ightened; you sha'n't t'ip!"

But Sylvie did "t'ip," notwithstanding; in fact he led her, in his hurry, across so many little sticks and stones, that it was really a wonder the poor child could keep on her feet at all. But he was far too much excited to think of what he was doing.

I silently pointed out to Bruno the best place to lead her to, so as to get a view of the whole garden at once; it was a little rising ground, about the height of a potato, and, when they had mounted it, I drew back into the shade that Sylvie mightn't see me.

I heard Bruno cry out triumphantly, "*Now* you may look!" and then followed a great clapping of hands, but it was all done by Bruno himself. Sylvie was quite silent; she only stood and gazed with her hands clasped tightly together, and I was half afraid she didn't like it after all.

Bruno, too, was watching her anxiously, and when she jumped down from the mound, and began wandering up and down the little walks, he cautiously followed her about, evidently anxious that she should form her own opinion of it all, without any hint from him. And when at last she drew a long breath, and gave her verdict—in a hurried whisper, and without the slightest regard to grammar—"It's the loveliest thing as I never saw in all my life before!" the little fellow looked as well pleased as if it had been given by all the judges and juries in England put together.

"And did you really do it all by yourself, Bruno?" said Sylvie. "And all for me?"

"I was helped a bit," Bruno began, with a merry little laugh at her surprise. "We've been at it all the afternoon; I thought you'd like—" and here the poor little fellow's lip began to quiver, and all in a moment he burst out crying, and, running up to Sylvie, he flung his arms passionately round her neck, and hid his face on her shoulder.

There was a little quiver in Sylvie's voice too, as she whispered, "Why, what's the matter, darling?" and tried to lift up his head and kiss him.

But Bruno only clung to her, sobbing, and wouldn't be comforted till he had confessed all.

"I tried—to spoil your garden—first—but—I'll never—never—" and then came another burst of tears which drowned the rest of the sentence. At last he got out the words. "I liked—putting in the flowers—for *you*, Sylvie—and I never was so happy before," and the rosy little face came up at last to be kissed, all wet with tears as it was.

Sylvie was crying too by this time, and she said nothing but "Bruno dear!" and "*I* never was so happy before;" though why two children who had never been so happy before should both be crying was a great mystery to me.

I, too, felt very happy, but of course I didn't cry; "big things" never do, you know—we leave all that to the fairies. Only I think it must have been raining a little just then, for I found a drop or two on my cheeks.

After that they went through the whole garden again, flower by flower, as if it were a long sentence they were spelling out, with kisses for commas, and a great hug by way of a full-stop when they got to the end.

"Do you know, that was my river-edge, Sylvie?" Bruno began, looking solemnly at her.

Sylvie laughed merrily. "What *do* you mean?" she said, and she pushed back her heavy brown hair with both hands, and looked at him with danc-ing eyes in which the big tear-drops were still glittering.

Bruno drew in a long breath, and made up his mouth for a great effort.

"I mean rev—enge," he said; "now you under'tand." And he looked so happy and proud at having said the word right at last that I

"It's the loveliest thing as I never saw in all my life before!"

quite envied him. I rather think Sylvie didn't "under'tand" at all; but she gave him a little kiss on each cheek, which seemed to do just as well.

So they wandered off lovingly together, in among the buttercups, each with an arm twined round the other, whispering and laughing as they went, and never so much as once looked back at poor me. Yes, once, just before I quite lost sight of them, Bruno half turned his head, and nodded me a saucy little good-bye over one shoulder. And that was all the thanks I got for *my* trouble.

I know you're sorry the story's come to an end—aren't you?—so I'll just tell you one thing more. The very last thing I saw of them was this: Sylvie was stooping down with her arms round Bruno's neck, and saying coaxingly in his ear, "Do you know, Bruno, I've quite forgotten that hard word; do say it once more. Come! Only this once, dear!"

But Bruno wouldn't try it again.

First published in the December 1877 edition of *St. Nicholas Magazine*

The Three Fortunes

WRITTEN AND ILLUSTRATED
BY HOWARD PYLE

ONCE THERE WERE three brothers, and there was nothing in the world they might call their own except a cherry tree.

One morning the three brothers went to look at their cherry tree, and, lo! the birds had been there before them, and the ripest and best cherries were gone.

So it was settled that the three should watch the cherry-tree, turn and turn about, to guard the fruit from the little thieves of the sky.

Well, first it was the eldest brother's turn, and by-and-by who should come trudging along the dusty road but an old man.

"Dear friend," said the old man to the lad in the cherry-tree, "will you not give a poor old body a cherry or two, for my throat is parched and dry with the dust of the road, and it is nothing that I have had to eat for the whole morning?"

It was a good heart that beat under the eldest brother's jacket. "Yes," said he, "you may take what you want; only you must be careful not to touch any of those that belong to my brothers."

So the old man laid aside his staff, and ate his fill of the plump cherries.

The next day it was the second brother's turn, and by-and-by who should come along but the same old man that had walked there the day before, and what he wanted was a few more cherries.

The second brother was as soft-hearted as the first.

"Yes," said he, "you may eat your fill, only you must touch none that belong to my brothers."

So the old man ate and ate; and then he said, "Thank you," and traveled the same way he had gone the day before.

He was an old man no longer, but a blessed angel.

The third day the youngest brother watched the cherry-tree, and then the same thing happened that had happened twice before: along came the old man, and got all the cherries that he wanted, and when he had finished there were not enough cherries upon the tree to feed a black-bird.

"Never mind," said the three brothers as they talked the matter over that night; "we have two strong hands apiece, and that is enough to keep body and soul together out in the wide world."

Just then the door opened, and who should come walking into the house but the old man who had eaten the cherries: only he was an old man no longer, but a blessed angel with wings as white as snow, and a face that shone like the full-moon at midnight.

"It was a good market that you took your cherries to," said he. "Come along with me, and I will make the fortunes of all of you."

The three brothers were glad enough to do that, for there was nothing at all to be made by staying at home.

Well, they traveled on and on without a stop, until they were so weary that they could scarcely drag one foot after the other. By-and-by, when the day broke and the birds began to sing, they came to the foot of a great high mountain, and when the eldest brother saw it, his courage all ran away like water from a sieve.

"I can go no further," said he, "for my feet are as heavy as lead already."

"Very well, then," said the angel; "you shall stay where you are; only ask what you want, and you shall have it."

Now in a field close by was a great lot of wild pigeons, so many of them that it would take three men to count them.

"See!" said the eldest brother. "I would like to have a great drove of cattle—as many of them as there are pigeons in the field yonder."

"That you shall have," said the angel. He waved the palm leaves he carried over the pigeons, and there stood a great drove of cattle, every one of them as white as milk. He touched the stocks and stones that lay scattered all about, and there stood drovers and dairy-maids enough to attend the whole drove. After that they said "Good-by," and shook hands all round, and then the two brothers and the angel went on their way, leaving the eldest behind with his cattle and peace and plenty.

Up the hill they went, and on and on until they reached the very top, and there the second brother gave out just as the first had done.

"See!" said he. "I can go no further, even if it were to find a mountain of gold and silver."

"Very well," said the angel. "Then you shall stay here. Only ask for what you want, and you shall have it."

Now on the top of the hill grew more thistles than your grandmother can talk about. "I should like," said the second brother, "to have as many vines bearing grapes as there are thistles growing about us here."

"Very well," said the angel; "you shall have your wish." He waved his palm branch over the thistles, and there stood that many vines, all loaded down with grapes. He touched the stocks and stones that lay round about them, and there stood so many vine-dressers. After that the angel and the youngest brother said "Good-by," and trudged away.

*The angel and the youngest brother said
"Good-by," and trudged away.*

On they went, and on they went, and ever so far, and by-and-by they came to where an old dusty hat lay in the middle of the road.

"Look," said the angel. "Yonder is something that is worth the having."

"Tut!" said the lad. "And what would I do with an old tattered thatch like that?"

The angel only smiled. He picked up the hat and set it upon his head; and then the lad rubbed his eyes, for look as he might, he could see nothing but thin air. Then the angel took the hat off his head, and there he stood just as before.

"And now," said he, "will you take it?"

Oh yes, the lad would take it now, and be glad to have it, for he could see with half an eye that it was a magical cap. After that they went on again.

"Look," said the angel, after awhile, "there is something worth having too"; and it was nothing but an old rusty nail.

"Pooh!" said the lad, "what do I want with an old rusty nail?"

The angel only smiled, just as he had done before. He stooped and picked it up, and, lo! it was a splendid dagger, with a hilt of gold studded over with gems.

"Listen," said the angel. "It will pierce whatsoever you strike, and nobody but you can draw it forth again. And now will you take it?"

"Yes, yes," said the lad, "that I will, and be glad to have it."

And the angel gave it to him.

On they went again; and when for the third time the angel stopped, it was because they had come upon an old pair of shoes lying by the road-side, and they were as green with must and mildew as though they had been lying in Father Time's garret in damp weather.

"And what do I want with such a pair of shoes as that?" said the lad. But the angel only smiled just as he had done twice before. He stooped and drew the shoes upon his feet. Then he took a step, and, whisk! he was out of sight as quick as a wink. He took another step, and he was back again like a flash. "And now," said he, "will you have them?"

Oh yes, the lad would take them now, and gladly; and well he might, for they were of the kind that carry one seven miles at a step, and across the water as well as across the land.

Then the angel pointed over the hills and far away.

"Yonder," said he, "lies a good town, and there you will find your fortune; and now I must return whence I came, for my time here is at an end." So saying, he spread his great white wings and leaped up into the air. Up and up he flew until he twinkled out of sight like a star in the morning, and all the lad could do was to stand and gape after him.

But by-and-by his wits came back to earth again, and then he put on his cap of darkness and his shoes of speed, and turned his toes whither the angel had pointed, for the evening was coming on, and not a house in sight.

He took sixteen steps, and, plump! there he was in the midst of a great town, and nobody could see him, because he had his magical cap upon his head.

Just in front of him was a great palace. Into the palace he went, and up and down through this room and that; but all the time he kept his cap tight upon his head, and not a soul saw hide or hair of him. By-and-by he came to a little room, and there lay a Princess fast asleep.

But the lad stood there as if he had been turned to stone, and just looked, for he had never seen such a beauty in his life before. Her hair was like spun gold, and her cheeks like ripe apples and milk.

Then suddenly, as he stood there, a great, ugly, poisonous snake crept out of a hole in the wall near by where the Princess lay sleeping. As soon as the lad saw it he whipped out his golden dagger, and with one blow pinned the serpent through the head and fast to the wall, where it hung wriggling and squirming. Then he wrote some words upon a piece of paper, and tied it fast to the handle of the dagger, and this was what they said:

"Who draws me forth struck me home"

Then he kissed the Princess as she lay sleeping, and went his way, and nobody was the wiser for his coming or his going.

But the next morning, when the Princess awoke, there was the dead snake

A great ugly, poisonous snake crept out of a hole in the wall.

and the dagger and the piece of paper; then what a hubbub there was in the palace! As for the Princess, she said she would marry whoever would draw the dagger out of the wall into which it had been thrust.

It did not take long for the news of that saying to get abroad. Before the week was out came crowds of princes and nobles, pushing and elbowing to have a try at pulling out the dagger, for the Princess was the most beautiful in the whole world.

But as for pulling out the blade, why, bless you! not one of them could budge it so much as a hair's breadth; so there the dagger stuck for all their trying.

All this time the lad lived about the castle, though no one could see him because of his cap. But one day he fell asleep out in the garden, and the hat fell off his head, and there he lay.

And then it was the Princess's turn to look and look, for she thought she had never seen such a handsome fellow.

Down the stairs she ran and out under the trees, so quietly that when the lad opened his eyes and jumped up, there she stood before him, with the dark cap in her hands.

"And was it you," said she, "who struck the dagger into the snake's head and into the wall up yonder?"

"Yes," said the lad; "it was I."

"Then come with me," said she, "and draw it out again." So saying, she took him by the hand, and led him up the steps and into the castle.

Then when the King, her father, and all the lords and nobles had gathered together, the lad just stepped up to the dagger, and laying his hands upon it, drew it forth with hardly a pull.

But, dear, dear, what a fume the King was in, to be sure! Was it for the Princess to marry the likes of such a one as the lad, with his old hat and his dusty, musty shoes? No, no; he should be paid for killing the snake; but as for marrying the Princess, why, that was a tune with another sort of a dance.

"Very well," said the lad, "we shall see about that" and so saying, he clapped his dark cap upon his head, and picked up the Princess, and, whisk! away he went, seven miles at a step.

On he went, and on he went, until he came to a country where everybody grazed sheep, and it was not long until he found one who wanted a shepherd, and there he and the Princess settled themselves to live. Every morning he drove the sheep over the hill, while the Princess stayed at home in a little hut in the valley, and mended his jacket, and knit stockings for cold weather.

So passed a year and a day, and then the angel came down to the earth again in the guise of an old man. He journeyed until he came to the place where the eldest brother lived.

Up came the angel, and knocked at a grand house, and it was the eldest brother himself who opened to him.

"Will you not give a poor old man a jug of milk and a lump of cheese?" said the angel.

But the eldest brother had grown rich and proud in the time that had passed, and, like many of the rest of us, he did not know an angel when he saw one.

"Prut!" says he; "if I give milk and cheese to every beggar who comes to my door, there will soon be none left for myself."

"Then all these things are not for you," said the angel. He waved his staff over the herd of fine cattle, and quick as a wink they were changed into white pigeons, and away they flew. As for the drovers and dairy-maids, they were changed again into stocks and stones.

After that there was nothing left for the man to do but to trudge back to the old home again.

But the angel went on, until by-and-by he came to where the second brother dwelt, with a fine vineyard growing all over the top of the hill. "And will you," said he, "give a poor old body a bunch of grapes and a glass of wine?"

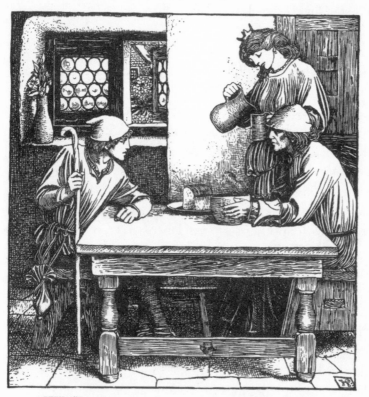

They set before him a loaf of bread and a bowl of milk.

The second brother knew the angel no better than the first had done. "Prut!" said he; "and if I give grapes and wine to every beggar who comes asking them, I shall soon have none for myself."

"Then," said the angel, "the vineyard is not for you."

And so saying, he waved his palm branch, and there stood so many thistles instead of fruitful vines, and so many stocks and stones instead of vine dressers, and nothing was left for the second brother to do but to trudge away home and join the other.

On went the angel until at last he rapped at the door of the little hut under the hill where the youngest brother lived. "Will you," said he, "give a bite to eat and a place to rest the soles of his feet to an old body who has come a long way today and is very tired?"

Yes, indeed, the poor old man should have the best that was to be had in the house. So the Princess and the youngest brother brought the angel into the house and set before him a loaf of bread and a bowl of milk, which was all they had. The young fellow sat down along with him at the table, and made things as pleasant for him as he was able, and the Princess waited on him with her own hands.

Then the angel threw off the likeness of an old man, and the lad wondered that he had not known him before.

"Ask what you want," said the angel, "and you shall have it."

But the lad only shook his head. "We want nothing in this house," said he, "that we have not already."

"Then you must come along with me," said the angel, "for they who want nothing themselves must give to other folk."

So saying, he took the Princess by one hand and the lad by the other, and, whisk! before they knew it, there they were back in the King's castle again; and if anybody in the world was glad it was the old King, for what he had said he had said in haste, and he loved the Princess as the apple of his eye.

But when he heard all the ins and outs of the business, he gave the youngest brother half of his kingdom to rule over, for a body should do what a body can when an angel tells a body thus and so.

But the other brothers? Why, listen!

When the youngest heard how they were living at the old home, with nothing but the cherry-tree to keep body and soul together, he just sent a grand coach for them and brought them to his own house, and there they lived back of the stove in the warm palace, and in peace and comfort, and never again grudged a body anything as long as they lived.

For when one's white cows and grape-vines have been turned into pigeons and thistles, one is apt to put on one's thinking cap and turn wise.

First published in the July 24, 1888, issue of *Harper's Young People*

The Soldiering of
Beniah Stidham

WRITTEN AND ILLUSTRATED
BY HOWARD PYLE

WHEN YOU LOOK at a very old man, it seems hard to imagine that he was ever once a boy, full of sport and mischief like the boys whom we know nowadays.

There is a "daguerreotype" of Beniah Stidham that was taken about the year 1850. It is the picture of a very, very old man, with a bald, bony forehead, and a face full of wrinkles and furrows. His lips are sucked in between his toothless gums, and his nose is hooked down as though to meet his lean chin beneath.

In the picture he wears a swallow-tailed coat with a rolling collar and with buttons that look like brass. The cuffs of his long, wrinkled coat-sleeves come down almost to the knotted knuckles, and one skinny hand rests upon the top of a hooked cane. It does not seem possible that he could ever have been a boy, but he was—though it was away back in the time of the Revolutionary War.

He was about fifteen years old at the time of the battle of Brandywine—that was in the year 1777. He was then an apprentice in Mr. Connelly's cooper-shops near Brandywine. His father, Amos Stidham, kept a tin-store, and sometimes peddled tinware and buckets down in the lower counties and up through Pennsylvania. At that time Beniah was a big, awkward, loose-jointed, over-grown lad; he shot up like a weed, and his clothes were always too small for him. His hands stuck far out from his sleeves. They were splay and red, and they were big like his feet. He stuttered when he talked, and everybody laughed at him for it.

Most people thought that he was slack-witted, but he was not; he was only very shy and timid. Sometimes he himself felt that he had as good sense as anybody if he only had a chance to show it. These things happened in Delaware, which in those days was almost like a part of Pennsylvania. There was a great deal of excitement in Wilmington at the time of the beginning of the trouble in Boston, the fight at

Lexington, and the battle at Bunker Hill. There were enlisted for the war more than twenty young fellows from Wilmington and Brandywine; they used to drill every evening in a field at the foot of Quaker Hill, where the Meetinghouse stood and not far from the William Penn Inn. A good many people—especially the boys—used to go in the evening to see them drill. It seemed to Beniah that if he could only go for a soldier he might stand a great deal better chance of getting along than he had in Wilmington, where everyone laughed at him and seemed to think that he was lacking in wits.

He had it in his mind a great many times to speak to his father about going for a soldier, but he could not quite find courage to do so, for he felt almost sure that he would be laughed at.

One night he did manage to speak of it, and when he did, it was just as he thought it would be. It was just after supper, and they still sat at table, in the kitchen. He was nervous, and when he began speaking he stuttered more than usual.

"I wo-wo-wo-wo-wish you'd l-let me go fer a sis-sis-sis-sis-sis-sis-soldier, Father," said he.

His sister Debby burst out laughing. "A sis-sis-sis-sis-soldier!" she mocked.

"A what!" said Beniah's father. "You a soldier? You would make a pretty soldier, now, wouldn't you? Why, you wouldn't be able to say 'Who goes there?' fer stutterin'!" and then Debby laughed again, and when she saw that it made Beniah angry, she laughed still more.

So Beniah did not go soldiering that time.

AFTER THE BATTLE of Brandywine, Lord Howe's fleet of war-ships came up into the Delaware from the Chesapeake Bay, and everybody was anxious and troubled, for there was talk that the enemy would bombard the town. You could see the fleet coming up the bay from the hills back of the town—the sails seemed to cover the water all over; that was in the afternoon, just before supper. That evening a good many people left town, and others sent their china and silver up into the country for safe-keeping.

After supper the bellman went through the streets calling a meeting at the Town Hall. Captain Stapler was at home at that time and spoke to the people. He told them that there was no danger of the fleet bombarding the town, for the river was

two miles away, and the cannon could not carry that far. He showed them that the only way that the enemy could approach the town was up the Christiana River, and that if the citizens would build a redoubt at the head of the marsh the place would be perfectly defended.

The people found a good deal of comfort in what he said; but the next morning the *Roebuck* and *Liverpool* ships of war were seen to be lying, with their tenders and two transports, opposite the town; and once more all the talk was that they were going to bombard.

There was a great deal said that morning at the cooper-shops about all this. Some opined that the ships were certainly going to bombard, but others held that what they would do would be to send a regiment of Hessians up the creek to burn down the town.

They used to drill every evening.

During the morning, old Billy Jester came up from Christiana village, and said that the towns-people were building a mud fort down at the Rocks below the Old Swedes' Church, and that they expected two cannon and some soldiers to come down from Fort Mifflin in the afternoon. This was a great comfort to everybody, for the time.

About eleven o'clock in the morning the enemy suddenly began firing. Boom!—the sudden startling noise sounded dull and heavy, like the falling of some great weight; the windows rattled—boom!—boom!—boom!—and then again, after a little pause—boom!—boom! There was a little while,

a few seconds of breathless listening, and then Tom Pierson, the foreman of the shop, shouted:

"By gum! they're bombarding the town!"

Then he dropped his adze, and ran out of the door without waiting to take his hat. As he ran, there sounded again the same dull, heavy report—boom! boom!

There was no more work in the cooper-shops that day. Beniah ran all the way home. His father was just then away in the lower counties, and Beniah did not know what was going to happen to Debby and his mother. Maybe he would find the house all knocked to pieces with cannon-balls. Boom! boom! sounded the cannon again, and Beniah ran faster and faster, his mouth all dry and clammy with fear and excitement. The streets were full of people hurrying toward the hills. When he got home he found that no harm had happened, but the house was shut and all the doors locked. He met Mrs. Frist, and she told him that his mother and Debby had gone up to Quaker Hill.

He found them there a little while later, but by that time the war-ships had stopped firing, and after a while everybody went back home.

In the afternoon it was known that they had not been firing at the town at all, but at some people who had gone down on the neck to look at them, and whom, no doubt, they took to be militia or something of the kind.

Just before supper it was reported that one of Jonas Stidham's cows had been killed by a cannon-ball. Jonas Stidham was Beniah's uncle, and in the evening he went over to look at the cow. He met several others going on the same errand— two men and three or four boys. There was quite a crowd gathered about the place. The cow lay on its side, with its neck stretched out. There was a great hole in its side, made by the cannon-ball, and there was blood upon the ground. It looked very dreadful, and seemed to bring the terrors of war very near; and everybody stood about and talked in low voices.

After he had seen the dead cow, Beniah went down to where they were building the mud fort. They were just putting the cannon into place, and Captain Stapler was drilling a company of young men of the town who had enlisted for its defense. Beniah wished that he was one of them. After the drill was over, Captain Stapler came up to him and said: "Don't you want to enlist, Beniah?"

Beniah would not have dared to enlist if his father had been at home, but his father was away, and he signed his name to the roll-book!

That was the way that he came to go soldiering.

THAT NIGHT BENIAH did not go home, for he had to stay with the others who had enlisted. They were quartered at the barn just back of the mud fort. But he sent word by Jimmy Rogers that he was not coming home, because he had enlisted in Captain Stapler's company.

However, Captain Stapler let him go home the next morning for a little while. He found that all the boys knew that he had enlisted, and that he was great among them. He had to tell each one he met all about the matter. They all went along with him—fifteen or twenty of them—and waited in the street outside while he was talking with his family within. His mother had gone out, but his sister Debby was in the kitchen.

"Oh, but you'll catch it when Daddy comes home!" said she.

Beniah pretended not to pay any attention to her.

"When is he coming home?" said he, after a while.

"I don't know, but, mark my words, you'll catch it when he does come," said Debby.

That night they set pickets along the edge of the marsh, and then Beniah really began to soldier. He took his turn at standing guard about nine o'clock. There was no wind, but the night was very raw and chill. At first Beniah rather liked the excitement of it, but by and by he began to get very cold. He remembered his father's overcoat that hung back of the door in the entry, and he wished he had brought it with him from home; but it was too late to wish for that now. And then it was very lonesome and silent in the darkness of the night. A mist hung all over the marsh, and in the still air the voices of the men who were working upon the redoubt by lantern-light, and of the volunteers at their quarters in the barn where they had kindled a fire, sounded with perfect clearness and distinctness in the stillness. The tide was coming in, and the water gurgled and rippled in the ditches, where the reeds stood stark and stiff in the gloom. The reed-birds had not yet flown south, and their sleepy "cheep, cheeping" sounded incessantly through the darkness.

The moon was about rising, and the sky, to the east, was lit with a milky paleness. Toward it the marsh stretched away into the distance, the thin tops of the nearer reeds just showing above the white mysterious veil of mist that covered the water. It was all very strange and lonesome, and when Beniah thought of home and how nice it would be to be in his warm bed, he could not help wishing that he had not enlisted. And then he certainly would "catch it" when his father came home, as Debby had said he would. It was not a pleasant prospect.

By and by the moon rose, and at the same time a breeze sprang up. It grew colder than ever, and presently the water began to splash and dash against the river-bank beyond. The veil of mist disappeared, and the water darkled and flashed with broken shadows and sparks of light. Beniah's fingers holding the musket felt numb and dead. He wondered how much longer he would have to stay on guard; he felt as though he had been there a long time already. He crouched down under the lee of the riverbank and in the corner of a fence which stood there to keep the cows off of the marsh.

He had been there maybe five minutes, and was growing very sleepy with the cold, when he suddenly heard a sharp sound, and instantly started wide awake. It was the sound as of an oar striking against the side of a boat. There was something very strange in the sharp rap ringing through the stillness, and whoever had made it had evidently not intended to do so, for the after stillness was unbroken.

Beniah crouched in the fence-corner, listening breathlessly, intensely. He had forgotten all about being cold and sleepy and miserable. He felt that his heart was beating and leaping unevenly, and his breath came quickly, as though he had been running. Was the enemy coming? What should he do?

He did not move; he only crouched there, trying to hold his breath and to still the beating of his heart with his elbow pressed against his ribs. He was afraid that if there was another sound he might miss hearing it because of his labored breathing and the pulses humming in his ears. He gripped his musket with straining fingers.

There was a pause of perfect stillness. Then suddenly he heard a faint splash as though some one had stepped incautiously into the water. Again there was stillness. Then something moved in the reeds—maybe it was a regiment of Hessians! Beniah crouched lower, and poked his musket through the bars of the fence. What would happen next? He wondered if it was all real—if the enemy was actually coming.

Suddenly the reeds stirred again. Beniah crouched down still lower. Then he saw something slowly rise above the edge of the river-bank, sharp-cut and black against the milky sky. It was the head of a man, and it was surmounted by a tall conical cap—it was the sort of a cap that the British soldiers wore. As Beniah gazed, it seemed to him as though he had now stopped breathing altogether. The head remained there motionless for a while, as though listening; then the body that belonged to it slowly rose as though from the earth, and stood, from the waist up black against the sky.

Beniah tried to say, "Who goes there?" and then he found that what his father had said was true; he could not say the words for stuttering. He was so excited that he could not utter a sound; he would have to shoot without saying, "Who goes there?" There was nothing else to do. He aimed his eye along the barrel of his musket, but it was so dark that he could not see the sights of the gun very well. Should he shoot? He hesitated for an intense second or two—then came a blinding flash of resolve.

He drew the trigger. Bang!

For a moment he was deafened and bewildered by the report and the blinding flash of light. Then the cloud of pungent gunpowder-smoke drifted away, and his senses came back to him. The head and body were gone from against the sky.

Beniah sprang to his feet and flew back toward the mud fort, yelling he knew not what. It seemed as though the whole night was peopled with enemies. But nobody followed him. Suddenly he stopped in his flight, and stood again listening. Were the British follow- ing him? No, they were not. He heard alarmed voices from the fort, and the shouting of the pickets. A strange impulse seized him that he could not resist: he felt that he must go back and see what he had shot. He turned and crept slowly back, step by step, pausing now and then, and listening intently. By and by he came to where the figure had stood, and, craning his neck, peeped cautiously over the river-bank. The moon shone bright on the rippling water in a little open place in the reeds. There was something black lying in the water, and as Beniah continued looking at it, he saw it move with a wallowing splash. Then he ran away shouting and yelling.

CAPTAIN STAPLER THOUGHT that an attack would surely be made, but it was not; and, after a while, he ordered a company from the mud fort out along the river-bank, to see who it was that Beniah had shot. They took a lantern along with them, and Beniah went ahead to show them where it was.

"Yonder's the place," said he; "and I fu-fired my gi-gi-gi-gi-gun from the fa-fa- fence, ja-just here."

Captain Stapler peered down among the reeds. "By gum!" said he, "he's shot something, sure enough." He went cautiously down the bank; then he stooped over, and soon lifted something that lay in the water. Then there was a groan.

"Come down here, two or three of you!" called out Captain Stapler. "Beniah's actually shot a man, as sure as life!"

A number of the men scrambled down the bank; they lifted the black figure; it groaned again as they did so. They carried it up and laid it down upon the top of the bank. The clothes were very muddy and wet, but the light of the lantern twin- kled here and there upon the buttons and braid of a uniform. Captain Stapler bent over the wounded man. "By gracious!" said he, "it's a Hessian—like enough he's a spy." Beniah saw that the blood was running over one side of the wet uniform, and he was filled with a sort of terrible triumph. They carried the wounded man to the barn, and Dr. Taylor came and looked at him. The wound was in the neck, and it was not especially dangerous. No doubt the man had been stunned by the ball when it struck him.

The Hessian was a young man. "*Sprechen Sie Deutsch?*" asked he, but nobody understood him.

THE NEXT MORNING Beniah's father came home. He did not stop to ungear the horse, but drove straight down to the mud fort in his cart. He was very angry.

"What're you doing here, anyhow?" said he to Beniah; and he caught him by the collar and shook him till Beniah's hat slipped down over one eye. "What're you doin' here, anyhow—killin' and shootin' and murtherin' folks? You come home with me, Beniah—you come home with me!" and he shook him again.

"He can't go," said Captain Stapler. "You can't take him, Amos. He's enlisted, and he's signed his name upon the roll-book."

"I don't care a rap what he's signed," said Amos. "He hain't goin' to stay here shootin' folks. He's got to come home along with me, he has." And Beniah went.

Nobody knows what happened after he got home, and Beniah did not tell, but next day he went back to work at the cooper-shops again. All the boys seemed glad to see him, and wanted to know just how he shot the Hessian.

A good many people visited the wounded Hessian down in the barn the day he had been shot. Among others came "Dutch Charlie," the cobbler. He could understand what the Hessian said. He told Captain Stapler that the man was not a spy, but a deserter from the transport-ship in the river. It seemed almost a pity that the man had not been a spy; but, after all, it did not make any great difference in the way people looked on what Beniah Stidham had done; for the fact remained that he was a Hessian. And nobody thought of laughing at Beniah, even when he stuttered in telling how he shot him.

After a while the Hessian got well, and then he started a store in Philadelphia. He did well, and made money, and the queerest part of the whole business was that he married Debby Stidham—in spite of its having been Beniah who shot him in the neck.

This is the story of Beniah Stidham's soldiering. It lasted only two nights and a day, but he got a great deal of glory by it.

First published in the December 1892 edition of *St. Nicholas Magazine*

Baby Sylvester

BY BRET HARTE

IT WAS AT a little mining camp in the California Sierras that he first dawned upon me in all his grotesque sweetness.

I had arrived early in the morning, but not in time to intercept the friend who was the object of my visit. He had gone "prospecting"—so they told me on the river—and would not probably return until late in the afternoon. They could not say what direction he had taken; they could not suggest that I would be likely to find him if I followed. But it was the general opinion that I had better wait.

I looked around me. I was standing upon the bank of the river; and, apparently, the only other human beings in the world were my interlocutors, who were even then just disappearing from my horizon down the steep bank toward the river's dry bed. I approached the edge of the bank.

Where could I wait?

Oh, anywhere; down with them on the river-bar, where they were working, if I liked! Or I could make myself at home in any of those cabins that I found lying round loose. Or, perhaps it would be cooler and pleasanter for me in my friend's cabin on the hill. Did I see those three large sugar-pines? And, a little to the right, a canvas roof and chimney over the bushes? Well, that was my friend's—that was Dick Sylvester's cabin. I could stake my horse in that little hollow, and just hang round there till he came. I would find some books in the shanty; I could amuse myself with them. Or I could play with the baby.

Do what?

But they had already gone. I leaned over the bank and called after their vanishing figures:

"What did you say I could do?"

The answer floated slowly up on the hot, sluggish air:

"Pla-a-y with the ba-by."

The lazy echoes took it up and tossed it languidly from hill to hill, until Bald Mountain opposite made some incoherent remark about the baby, and then all was still.

I must have been mistaken. My friend was not a man of family; there was not a woman within forty miles of the river camp; he never was so passionately devoted to children as to import a luxury so expensive. I must have been mistaken.

I turned my horse's head toward the hill. As we slowly climbed the narrow trail, the little settlement might have been some exhumed Pompeian suburb, so deserted and silent were its habitations. The open doors plainly disclosed each rudely-furnished interior—the rough pine table, with the scant equipage of the morning meal still standing; the wooden bunk, with its tumbled and disheveled blankets. A golden lizard—the very genius of desolate stillness—had stopped breathless upon the threshold of one cabin; a squirrel peeped impudently into the window of another; a woodpecker, with the general flavor of undertaking which distinguishes that bird, withheld his sepulchral hammer from the coffin-lid of the roof on which he was professionally engaged, as we passed. For a moment, I half-regretted that I had not accepted the invitation to the river-bed; but, the next moment, a breeze swept up the long, dark canyon, and the waiting files of the pines beyond bent toward me in salutation. I think my horse understood as well as myself that it was the cabins that made the solitude human, and therefore unbearable, for he quickened his pace, and with a gentle trot brought me to the edge of the wood and the three pines that stood like sentries before the Sylvester outpost.

Unsaddling my horse in the little hollow, I unslung the long *riata* [lariat] from the saddle-bow, and tethering him to a young sapling, turned toward the cabin. But I had gone only a few steps when I heard a quick trot behind me, and poor Pomposo, with every fibre tingling with fear, was at my heels. I looked hurriedly around. The breeze had died away, and only an occasional breath from the deep-chested woods, more like a long sigh than any articulate sound, or the dry singing of a cicada in the heated canyon, were to be heard. I examined the ground carefully for rattlesnakes, but in vain. Yet here was Pomposo shivering from his arched neck to his sensitive haunches, his very flanks pulsating with terror. I soothed him as well as I could, and then walked to the edge of the wood and peered into its dark recesses. The bright flash of a bird's wing, or the quick dart of a squirrel, was all I saw. I confess it was with something of superstitious expectation that I again turned toward the cabin. A fairy child, attended by Titania and her train, lying in an expensive cradle, would not have surprised me; a Sleeping Beauty, whose awakening would have repeopled these solitudes with life and energy, I am afraid I began to confidently look for, and would have kissed without hesitation.

But I found none of these. Here was the evidence of my friend's taste and refinement in the hearth swept scrupulously clean, in the picturesque arrangement of the fur skins that covered the floor and furniture, and the striped *serape* [a fine Mexican blanket] lying on the wooden couch. Here were the walls fancifully papered with illustrations from the *London News*; here was the wood-cut portrait of Mr. Emerson over the chimney, quaintly framed with blue jays' wings; here were his few favorite books on the swinging shelf; and here, lying upon the couch, the latest copy of *Punch*. Dear Dick! The flour-sack was sometimes empty, but the gentle satirist seldom missed his weekly visit.

I threw myself on the couch and tried to read. But I soon exhausted my interest in my friend's library, and lay there staring through the open door on the green hillside beyond. The breeze again sprang up, and a delicious coolness, mixed with the rare incense of the woods, stole through the cabin. The slumbrous droning of bumble-bees outside the canvas roof, the faint cawing of rooks on the opposite mountain, and the fatigue of my morning ride, began to droop my eyelids. I pulled the *serape* over me, as a precaution against the freshening mountain breeze, and in a few moments was asleep.

I do not remember how long I slept. I must have been conscious, however, during my slumber, of my inability to keep myself covered by the *serape*, for I awoke once or twice, clutching it with a despairing hand as it was disappearing over the foot of the couch. Then I became suddenly aroused to the fact that my efforts to retain it were resisted by some equally persistent force, and, letting it go, I was horrified at seeing it swiftly drawn under the couch. At this point I sat up completely awake; for immediately after, what seemed to be an exaggerated muff began to emerge from under the couch. Presently it appeared fully, dragging the *serape* after it. There was no mistaking it now—it was a baby bear. A mere suckling, it was true—a helpless roll of fat and fur—but, unmistakably, a grizzly cub.

I cannot recall anything more irresistibly ludicrous than its aspect as it slowly raised its small wondering eyes to mine. It was so much taller on its haunches than its shoulders—its fore-legs were so disproportionately small—that in walking, its hind-feet invariably took precedence. It was perpetually pitching forward over its pointed, inoffensive nose, and recovering itself always, after these involuntary somersaults, with the gravest astonishment. To add to its preposterous appearance, one of its hind-feet was adorned by a shoe of Sylvester's, into which it had accidentally and inextricably stepped. As this somewhat impeded its first impulse to fly, it turned to me; and then, possibly recognizing in the stranger the same species as its master, it paused. Presently, it slowly raised itself on its hind-legs, and vaguely and deprecatingly waved a baby paw, fringed with little hooks of steel. I took the paw and shook it gravely. From that moment we were friends. The little affair of the *serape* was forgotten.

Nevertheless, I was wise enough to cement our friendship by an act of delicate courtesy. Following the direction of his eyes, I had no difficulty in finding, on a shelf near the ridge-pole, the sugar-box and the square lumps of white sugar that even the poorest miner is never without. While he was eating them I had time to examine him more closely. His body was a silky, dark, but exquisitely modulated grey, deepening to black in his paws and muzzle. His fur was excessively long, thick, and soft as eider down; the cushions of flesh beneath, perfectly infantine in their texture and contour. He was so very young that the palms of his half-human feet were still tender as a baby's. Except for the bright blue, steely hooks, half-sheathed in his little toes, there was not a single harsh outline or detail in his plump figure. He was as free from angles as one of Leda's offspring. Your caressing hand sank away in his fur with dreamy languor. To look at him long was an intoxication of the senses; to pat him was a wild delirium; to embrace him, an utter demoralization of the intellectual faculties.

When he had finished the sugar, he rolled out of the door with a half-diffident,

There was no mistaking it now—it was a baby bear.

half-inviting look in his eye, as if he expected me to follow. I did so, but the sniffing and snorting of the keen-scented Pomposo in the hollow not only revealed the cause of his former terror, but decided me to take another direction. After a moment's hesitation, he concluded to go with me, although I am satisfied, from a certain impish look in his eye, that he fully understood and rather enjoyed the fright of Pomposo. As he rolled along at my side, with a gait not unlike a drunken sailor, I discovered that his long hair concealed a leather collar around his neck, which bore for its legend the single word, "Baby"! I recalled the mysterious suggestion of the two miners. This, then, was the "baby" with whom I was to "play."

How we "played"; how Baby allowed me to roll him down hill, crawling and puffing up again each time, with perfect good humor; how he climbed a young sapling after my Panama hat, which I had "shied" into one of the topmost branches; how after getting it he refused to descend until it suited his pleasure; how when he did come down he persisted in walking about on three legs, carrying my hat, a crushed and shapeless mass, clasped to his breast with the remaining one; how I missed him at last, and finally discovered him seated on a table in one of the tenantless cabins, with a bottle of syrup between his paws, vainly endeavoring to extract its contents—these and other details of that eventful day I shall not weary the reader with now. Enough that when Dick Sylvester returned, I was pretty well fagged out, and the baby was rolled up, an immense bolster at the foot of the couch, asleep. Sylvester's first words after our greeting were:

"Isn't he delicious?"

"Perfectly. Where did you get him?"

"Lying under his dead mother, five miles from here," said Dick, lighting his pipe. "Knocked her over at fifty yards; perfectly clean shot—never moved afterwards! Baby crawled out, scared but unhurt. She must have been carrying him in her mouth, and dropped him when she faced me, for he wasn't more than three days old, and not steady on his pins. He takes the only milk that comes to the settlement—brought up by Adams Express at seven o'clock every morning. They say he looks like me. Do you think so?" asked Dick, with perfect gravity, stroking his hay-colored moustachios, and evidently assuming his best expression.

I took leave of the baby early the next morning in Sylvester's cabin, and out of respect to Pomposo's feelings, rode by without any postscript of expression. But the night before I had made Sylvester solemnly swear, that in the event of any separation between himself and Baby, it should revert to me. "At the same time," he had added, "it's only fair to say that I don't think of dying just yet, old fellow, and I don't know of anything else that would part the cub and me."

Two months after this conversation, as I was turning over the morning's mail at my office in San Francisco, I noticed a letter bearing Sylvester's familiar hand. But it was post-marked "Stockton," and I opened it with some anxiety at once. Its contents were as follows:

O, FRANK!—Don't you remember what we agreed upon about the baby? Well, consider me as dead for the next six months, or gone where cubs can't follow me—East. I know you love the baby; but do you think, dear boy—now, really, do you think you could be a father to it? Consider this well. You are young, thoughtless, well-meaning enough; but dare you take upon yourself the functions of guide, genius, or guardian to one so young and guileless? Could you be the mentor to this Telemachus? Think of the temptations of a metropolis. Look at the question well, and let me know speedily, for I've got him as far as this place, and he's kicking up an awful row in the hotel-yard, and rattling his chain like a maniac. Let me know by telegraph at once.

—SYLVESTER

P. S.—Of course he's grown a little, and doesn't take things always as quietly as he did. He dropped rather heavily on two of Watson's "purps" last week, and snatched old Watson himself, bald-headed, for interfering. You remember Watson: for an intelligent man, he knows very little of California fauna. How are you fixed for bears on Montgomery Street—I mean in regard to corrals and things? S.

P. P. S.—He's got some new tricks. The boys have been teaching him to put up his hands with them. He slings an ugly left.—S.

I am afraid that my desire to possess myself of Baby overcame all other considerations, and I telegraphed an affirmative at once to Sylvester. When I reached my lodgings late that afternoon, my landlady was awaiting me with a telegram. It was two lines from Sylvester:

All right. Baby goes down on night-boat. Be a father to him.—S.

It was due, then, at one o'clock that night. For a moment I was staggered at my own precipitation. I had as yet made no preparations—had said nothing to my landlady about her new guest. I expected to arrange everything in time; and now, through Sylvester's indecent haste, that time had been shortened twelve hours.

Something, however, must be done at once. I turned to Mrs. Brown. I had great reliance in her maternal instincts; I had that still greater reliance, common to our sex, in the general tender-heartedness of pretty women. But I confess I was alarmed. Yet, with a feeble smile, I tried to introduce the subject with classical ease and lightness. I even said, "If Shakespeare's Athenian clown, Mrs. Brown, believed that a lion among ladies was a dreadful thing, what must—" But here I broke down, for Mrs. Brown, with the awful intuition of her sex, I saw at once was more occupied with my manner than my speech. So I tried a business brusquerie, and, placing the telegram in her hand, said hurriedly, "We must do something about this at once. It's perfectly absurd, but he will be here at one tonight. Beg thousand pardons, but business prevented my speaking before—" and paused, out of breath and courage.

Mrs. Brown read the telegram gravely, lifted her pretty eyebrows, turned the paper over and looked on the other side, and then, in a remote and chilling voice, asked me if she understood me to say that the mother was coming also.

"Oh dear, no," I exclaimed, with considerable relief; "the mother is dead, you know. Sylvester—that is my friend, who sent this—shot her when the Baby was only three days old—" But the expression of Mrs. Brown's face at this moment was so alarming, that I saw that nothing but the fullest explanation would save me. Hastily, and I fear not very coherently, I told her all.

She relaxed sweetly. She said I had frightened her with my talk about lions. Indeed, I think my picture of poor Baby—albeit a trifle highly-colored—touched her motherly heart. She was even a little vexed at what she called Sylvester's "hard-heartedness." Still, I was not without some apprehension. It was two months since I had seen him, and Sylvester's vague allusion to his "slinging an ugly left" pained me. I looked at sympathetic little Mrs. Brown, and the thought of Watson's pups covered me with guilty confusion.

Mrs. Brown had agreed to sit up with me until he arrived. One o'clock came, but no Baby. Two o'clock—three o'clock passed. It was almost four when there was a wild clatter of horses' hoofs outside, and with a jerk a wagon stopped at the door. In an instant I had opened it and confronted a stranger. Almost at the same moment, the horses attempted to run away with the wagon.

The stranger's appearance was, to say the least, disconcerting. His clothes were badly torn and frayed; his linen sack hung from his shoulders like a herald's apron; one of his hands was bandaged; his face scratched, and there was no hat on his disheveled head. To add to the general effect, he had evidently sought relief from his woes in drink, and he swayed from side to side as he clung to the door-handle; and, in a very thick voice, stated that he had "suthin" for me outside. When he had finished, the horses made another plunge.

Mrs. Brown thought they must be frightened at something.

"Frightened!" laughed the stranger, with bitter irony. "Oh no! Hossish aint frightened! On'y ran away four timesh comin' here. Oh no! Nobody's frightened. Everythin's all ri'. Aint it, Bill?" he said, addressing the driver. "On'y been overboard twish; knocked down a hatchway once. Thash nothin'! On'y two men unner doctor's han's at Stockton. Thash nothin'! Six hunner dollarsh cover all dammish."

I was too much disheartened to reply, but moved toward the wagon. The stranger eyed me with an astonishment that almost sobered him.

"Do you reckon to tackle that animile yourself?" he asked, as he surveyed me from head to foot.

I did not speak, but, with an appearance of boldness I was far from feeling, walked to the wagon and called "Baby!"

"All ri'. Cash loose them straps, Bill, and stan' clear."

The straps were cut loose, and Baby—the remorseless, the terrible—quietly tumbled to the ground, and rolling to my side, rubbed his foolish head against me.

I think the astonishment of the two men was beyond any vocal expression. Without a word the drunken stranger got into the wagon and drove away.

And Baby? He had grown, it is true, a trifle larger; but he was thin, and bore the marks of evident ill-usage. His beautiful coat was matted and unkempt, and his claws—those bright steel hooks—had been ruthlessly pared to the quick. His eyes were furtive and restless, and the old expression of stupid good humor had changed to one of intelligent distrust. His intercourse with mankind had evidently quickened his intellect without broadening his moral nature.

I had great difficulty in keeping Mrs. Brown from smothering him in blankets and ruining his digestion with the delicacies of her larder; but I at last got him completely rolled up in the corner of my room and asleep. I lay awake some time later with plans for his future. I finally determined to take him to Oakland, where I had built a little cottage and always spent my Sundays, the very next day. And in the midst of a rosy picture of domestic felicity, I fell asleep.

When I awoke it was broad day. My eyes at once sought the corner where Baby had been lying. But he was gone. I sprang from the bed, looked under it, searched the closet, but in vain. The door was still locked; but there were the marks of his blunted claws upon the sill of the window, that I had forgotten to close. He had evidently escaped that way—but where? The window opened upon a balcony, to which the only other entrance was through the hall. He must be still in the house.

My hand was already upon the bell-rope, but I stayed it in time. If he had not made himself known, why should I disturb the house? I dressed myself hurriedly, and slipped into the hall. The first object that met my eyes was a boot lying upon the stairs. It bore the marks of Baby's teeth; and as I looked along the hall, I saw too plainly that the usual array of freshly-blackened boots and shoes before the lodgers' doors was not there. As I ascended the stairs I found another, but with the blacking carefully licked off. On the third floor were two or three more boots, slightly mouthed; but at this point Baby's taste for blacking had evidently palled. A little further on was a ladder, leading to an open hatch. I mounted the ladder, and reached the flat roof, that formed a continuous level over the row of houses to the corner of the street. Behind the chimney on the very last roof something was lurking. It was the fugitive Baby. He was covered with dust and dirt and fragments of glass. But he was sitting on his hind-legs, and was eating an enormous slab of peanut candy, with a look of mingled guilt and infinite satisfaction. He even, I fancied, slightly stroked his stomach with his disengaged fore-paw, as I approached.

He knew that I was looking for him, and the expression of his eye said plainly, "The past, at least, is secure."

I hurried him, with the evidences of his guilt, back to the hatch, and descended on tip-toe to the floor beneath. Providence favored us; I met no one on the stairs, and his own cushioned tread was inaudible. I think he was conscious of the dangers of detection, for he even forebore to breathe, or much less chew the last mouthful he had taken; and he skulked at my side, with the syrup dropping from his motionless jaws. I think he would have silently choked to death just then, for my sake: and it was not until I had reached my room again, and threw myself panting on the sofa, that I saw how near strangulation he had been. He gulped once or twice, apologetically, and then walked to the corner of his own accord, and rolled himself up like an immense sugar-plum, sweating remorse and treacle at every pore.

I locked him in when I went to breakfast, when I found Mrs. Brown's lodgers in a state of intense excitement over certain mysterious events of the night before, and the dreadful revelations of the morning. It appeared that burglars had entered the block from the hatch; that being suddenly alarmed, they had quitted our house without committing any depredation, dropping even the boots they had collected in the halls; but that a desperate attempt had been made to force the till in the confectioner's shop on the corner, and that the glass show-cases had been ruthlessly smashed. A courageous servant in No. 4 had seen a masked burglar, on his hands and knees, attempting to enter their hatch; but on her shouting, "Away wid yees," he instantly fled.

I sat through this recital with cheeks that burned uncomfortably; nor was I the less embarrassed on raising my eyes to meet Mrs. Brown's fixed curiously and mischievously on mine. As soon as I could make my escape from the table, I did so; and running rapidly up stairs, sought refuge from any possible inquiry in my own room. Baby was still asleep in the corner. It would not be safe to remove him until the lodgers had gone downtown; and I was revolving in my mind the expediency of keeping him until night veiled his obtrusive eccentricity from the public eye, when there came a cautious tap at my door. I opened it. Mrs. Brown slipped in quietly, closed the door softly, stood with her back against it and her hand on the knob, and beckoned me mysteriously towards her. Then she asked, in a low voice:

"Is hair—dye poisonous?"

I was too confounded to speak. "Oh, do! You know what I mean," she said, impatiently. "This stuff." She produced suddenly from behind her a bottle with a Greek label—so long as to run two or three times spirally around it from top to bottom. "He says it isn't a dye; it's a vegetable preparation, for invigorating—"

"Who says?" I asked, despairingly.

"Why, Mr. Parker, of course," said Mrs. Brown, severely, with the air of having repeated the name a great many times—"the old gentleman in the room above. The simple question I want to ask," she continued, with the calm manner of one who has just convicted another of gross ambiguity of language, "is only this: If some of this stuff were put in a saucer and left carelessly on the table, and a child or a baby or a cat, or any young animal, should come in at the window and drink it up— a whole saucer full—because it had a sweet taste, would it be likely to hurt them?"

I cast an anxious glance at Baby, sleeping peacefully in the corner, and a very grateful one at Mrs. Brown, and said I didn't think it would.

"Because," said Mrs. Brown, loftily, as she opened the door, "I thought if it was poisonous, remedies might be used in time. Because," she added suddenly, abandoning her lofty manner and wildly rushing to the corner, with a frantic embrace of the unconscious Baby, "because if any nasty stuff should turn its boofull hair a horrid green or a naughty pink, it would break its own muzzer's heart, it would!"

But before I could assure Mrs. Brown of the inefficiency of hair-dye as an internal application, she had darted from the room.

That night, with the secrecy of defaulters, Baby and I decamped from Mrs. Brown's. Distrusting the too emotional nature of that noble animal, the horse, I had recourse to a hand-cart, drawn by a stout Irishman, to convey my charge to the ferry. Even then, Baby refused to go unless I walked by the cart, and at times rode in it.

"I wish," said Mrs. Brown, as she stood by the door wrapped in an immense shawl, and saw us depart, "I wish it looked less solemn—less like a pauper's funeral."

I must admit, that as I walked by the cart that night, I felt very much as if I were accompanying the remains of some humble friend to his last resting-place; and that, when I was obliged to ride in it, I never could entirely convince myself that I was not helplessly overcome by liquor, or the victim of an accident, en route to the hospital. But, at last, we reached the ferry. On the boat I think no one discovered Baby except a drunken man, who approached me to ask for a light for his cigar, but who suddenly dropped it and fled in dismay to the gentlemen's cabin, where his incoherent ravings were luckily taken for the earlier indications of delirium tremens.

It was nearly midnight when I reached my little cottage on the outskirts of Oakland; and it was with a feeling of relief and security that I entered, locked the door, and turned him loose in the hall, satisfied that henceforward his depredations would be limited to my own property. He was very quiet that night, and after he had tried to mount the hat-rack, under the mistaken impression that it was intended for his own gymnastic exercise, and knocked all the hats off, he went peaceably to sleep on the rug.

In a week, with the exercise afforded him by the run of a large, carefully boarded enclosure, he recovered his health, strength, spirits, and much of his former beauty. His presence was unknown to my neighbors, although it was noticeable that horses invariably "shied" in passing to the windward of my house, and that the baker and milk-man had great difficulty in the delivery of their wares in the morning, and indulged in unseemly and unnecessary profanity in so doing.

At the end of the week, I determined to invite a few friends to see the Baby, and to that purpose wrote a number of formal invitations. After descanting, at some length, on the great expense and danger attending his capture and training, I offered a programme of the performances of the "Infant Phenomenon of Sierran Solitudes," drawn up into the highest professional profusion of alliteration and capital letters. A few extracts will give the reader some idea of his educational progress:

1. He will, rolled up in a Round Ball, roll down the Wood Shed, Rapidly, illustrating His manner of Escaping from His Enemy in His Native Wilds.

2. He will Ascend the Well Pole, and remove from the Very Top a Hat, and as much of the Crown and Brim thereof as May be Permitted.

3. He will perform in a pantomime, descriptive of the Conduct of the Big Bear, The Middle-Sized Bear, and The Little Bear of the Popular Nursery Legend.

4. He will shake his chain Rapidly, showing his Manner of striking Dismay and Terror in the Breasts of Wanderers in Ursine Wildernesses.

The morning of the exhibition came, but an hour before the performance the wretched Baby was missing. The Chinese cook could not indicate his whereabouts. I searched the premises thoroughly, and then, in despair, took my hat and hurried out into the narrow lane that led toward the open fields and the woods beyond. But I found no trace nor track of Baby Sylvester. I returned, after an hour's fruitless search, to find my guests already assembled on the rear verandah. I briefly recounted my disappointment, my probable loss, and begged their assistance.

"Why," said a Spanish friend, who prided himself on his accurate knowledge of English, to Barker, who seemed to be trying vainly to rise from his reclining position on the verandah, "Why do you not disengage yourself from the verandah of our friend? And why, in the name of Heaven, do you attach to yourself so much of this thing, and make to yourself such unnecessary contortion? Ah," he continued, suddenly withdrawing one of his own feet from the verandah with an evident effort, "I am myself attached! Surely it is something here!"

It evidently was. My guests were all rising with difficulty—the floor of the verandah was covered with some glutinous substance. It was—syrup!

I saw it all in a flash. I ran to the barn; the keg of "golden syrup," purchased only the day before, lay empty upon the floor. There were sticky tracks all over the enclosure, but still no Baby.

"There's something moving the ground over there by that pile of dirt," said Barker.

He was right; the earth was shaking in one corner of the enclosure like an earthquake. I approached cautiously. I saw, what I had not before noticed, that the ground was thrown up; and there, in the middle of an immense grave-like cavity, crouched Baby Sylvester, still digging, and slowly, but surely, sinking from sight in a mass of dust and clay.

What were his intentions? Whether he was stung by remorse, and wished to hide himself from my reproachful eyes, or whether he was simply trying to dry his syrup-besmeared coat, I never shall know, for that day, alas! was his last with me.

He was pumped upon for two hours, at the end of which time he still yielded a thin treacle. He was then taken and carefully enwrapped in blankets and locked up in the store-room. The next morning he was gone! The lower portion of the window sash and pane were gone too. His successful experiments on the fragile texture of glass at the confectioner's, on the first day of his entrance to civilization, had not been lost upon him. His first essay at combining cause and effect ended in his escape.

Where he went, where he hid, who captured him if he did not succeed in reaching the foot-hills beyond Oakland, even the offer of a large reward, backed by the efforts of an intelligent police, could not discover. I never saw him again from that day until—

Did I see him? I was in a horse-car on Sixth Avenue, a few days ago, when the horses suddenly became unmanageable and left the track for the sidewalk, amid the oaths and execrations of the driver. Immediately in front of the car a crowd had gathered around two performing bears and a showman. One of the animals—thin, emaciated, and the mere wreck of his native strength—attracted my attention. I endeavored to attract his. He turned a pair of bleared, sightless eyes in my direction, but there was no sign of recognition. I leaned from the car-window and called, softly, "Baby!" But he did not heed. I closed the window. The car was just moving on, when he suddenly turned, and, either by accident or design, thrust a callous paw through the glass.

"It's worth a dollar-and-a-half to put in a new pane," said the conductor, "if folks will play with bears!—"

First published in the July 1874 edition of *St. Nicholas Magazine*

The Magic Clocks

BY HELEN HUNT JACKSON

PART ONE

ONE DAY, AS four children—Frank, James, Helen, and Elizabeth—were playing in front of their father's house, a queer thing happened. They had not heard the sound of approaching footsteps; but suddenly they saw a little old man standing in front of the gate, leaning over it and looking at them.

He carried upon his back a big box strapped with leather bands, and held in place by a wide band passing across his chest.

"Why, there's a peddler!" exclaimed Frank.

"Mamma never buys anything from peddlers, you know," said Elizabeth. "She always tells Bridget to send them right away without calling her."

"You need not come in," shouted James; "peddlers never sell anything here."

The old man did not move nor speak, but stood still, with his eyes fixed on the children, looking first at one, then at another.

"What an odd old man!" said Helen in a whisper, coming up closer to her brother Frank. "I wish he would go away. What makes him stare so at us?"

"Why doesn't he speak?" said James.

"Perhaps he is deaf and dumb, poor man," said Elizabeth; and she took a few hesitating steps toward the gate.

At this the old man smiled. When he smiled, his face became beautiful. A sort of light spread all over it. As soon as the children saw the smile, they all began to walk toward him. He seemed to draw them, insensibly. They were half afraid, and yet they could not stay away from him.

"No, dear children," he said; "I am not deaf and dumb. I was only looking at your faces to see whether I should leave some of my magic clocks with you."

At the word "magic," Frank was at once all attention. He had a passion for conjurors' tricks and for anything that was mystical. He thought he would rather be a prestidigitator than anything else in the world.

"What is there magical about your clocks?" he asked eagerly. "I never heard of a magic clock."

"We couldn't buy any, Frank," whispered Elizabeth. "Mamma wouldn't let us."

"They are not for sale, little lady," said the old man, smiling again.

He had overheard her whisper. At this second smile the children drew still nearer him. They almost loved him.

"Oh, do show them to us!" cried Frank.

"I thought you said you were thinking whether you could leave some of them here," said Helen, pettishly; "and now you say they are not for sale. Then how could you leave them here?"

All the answer the old man made to this was to nod his head and say, as if to himself, "She needs one!" And with that he slipped his box off his shoulders, set it down on the ground, and began to undo the leathern buckles.

All the time that he was doing this, he kept repeating to himself some strange words that the children could not understand. It sounded like poetry; but the language did not resemble any the children had ever heard.

"What are you saying? Do talk English! can't you," exclaimed Helen hastily. She was a very quick-tempered little girl, and often said things that sounded as if she were very cross, even when she was not cross at all, but only impatient.

This time the old man looked at her sternly before he nodded his head.

"Yes," he said—"she needs one badly!"

At this, Helen slipped behind Frank and, pulling his jacket, whispered: "Do make him go away, Frank! He frightens me."

"Be quiet!" said Frank angrily, pushing her back. "Don't be so foolish! I want to see the clocks!"

"So, ho! He needs one, too!" said the old man, without looking up, as he went on unbuckling strap after strap.

"What does he mean?" said Elizabeth to James in a low tone. "I am afraid he is crazy. Poor old man; what will become of him?"

At this the old man gave a smile that seemed to light up the whole place like a great sunbeam; and he nodded his head three or four times; and he fixed his eyes on Elizabeth's face with so beautiful an expression of good-will and affection, that she was ashamed of having thought he must be crazy.

"Good girl! good girl!" he said, and lifted out of his box a beautiful little white alabaster clock, not more than six inches high, and handed it to Elizabeth.

"Oh, what a beauty!" she cried.

"But what is magical about it?" asked Frank. "It looks just like other clocks."

"No, not like other clocks," replied the old man, handing another one to Frank, and one to James, and one to Helen. They all were alike—pure white alabaster, with gold faces, and wreaths of red roses painted on them.

"I wonder if he stole them," whispered Helen to James.

"Bang! bang! bang!" went the clock in her hands! You wouldn't have thought so loud and harsh a note could come from so tiny a little clock. Helen was so frightened that she dropped it on the ground.

"Oh!" cried Elizabeth, springing to catch it. "It will be broken!"

The children watch their magic clocks.

"How could you say so unkind a thing, Helen?"

"Kling! kling! kling!" went the clock in Elizabeth's hands, with a note as sweet as a canary's voice; but she was as frightened as Helen had been, and dropped her clock just as quickly on the ground at her feet.

But they were not broken or cracked, and the old man, who seemed strangely nimble for his age, picked them both up before the two girls could reach them. Handing them back, he said, still smiling:

"Magic clocks will stand a great many hard knocks without breaking."

All this time Frank was turning his over and over, and looking at a little glass set in the back, through which the machinery could be seen. Frank knew something about the construction of clocks and watches. He had an old silver watch of his own that he had more than once taken to pieces and put together again.

"Humph! There isn't anything magical about these clocks," he declared at last, rather rudely. "I can see all the wheels. They're just such as are always in clocks."

"Dong! dong! dong!" struck the clock in his hands in a sharp, squeaking tone, not so loud and harsh as Helen's, but disagreeable enough to make Frank start and cry out with surprise. He did not let go of the clock, however, but held it even tighter, and began to look at it more closely.

"Magic clocks! magic clocks!" said the old man; and as he spoke these words, he disappeared from sight. Big box, leathern straps, old man, sunny smile—all had vanished from under the children's very eyes, as suddenly as if the earth had opened and swallowed him up.

"Why! where's he gone?" cried Elizabeth.

Helen began to cry.

"He's a witch," she said.

"Not a witch! you little goose," said James, who was rather scared himself. "You mean a wizard—a witch is a woman!"

"Bang! bang! bang!" went James's clock, just as Helen's had done when she spoke unkindly.

James set it down on the ground, close to the fence, and stepped away from it a few feet. Helen and Elizabeth put theirs down in a line with it. Frank still held his in his hands, and was looking all about for the old man; up and down the street, even into the sky overhead.

But there was not a trace of a human being in the street; not a cloud in the sky overhead. "Well, it does look like magic!" he said, "that's a fact. Anyhow, we have the clocks, and we didn't have to pay the old fellow anything."

"Dong! dong! dong!" said his clock, in a loud, discordant note. This time Frank himself was a little frightened. He put his clock down a little apart from the others, stepped back a few paces, thrust his hands into his pockets and began to whistle.

"They seem to strike every few minutes," he said, "without any sort of time about it. That's queer."

"Let's keep perfectly still and watch them," said James, "and see if they'll do anything."

Five minutes, ten, fifteen passed. Not a sound from the clocks. Not a sound from the children.

"I've been thinking—" began Elizabeth, gently.

"Well, of course you have," broke in Helen; "we all have been thinking! we're not ninnies."

"Whang! whang! whang!" went Helen's clock in a tone so spiteful and hateful that all four of the children jumped.

"That's it! I knew it!" said Elizabeth. "I know what the magic is. The clocks will strike in that harsh way when we say mean, hateful things, and they'll make a musical sound when we say pleasant things, and that'll remind us all the time."

"I believe that's so," said Frank, thoughtfully. I wish the old man hadn't gone. We don't know how to wind them up. They're real beauties."

"There isn't any keyhole in them," said James, who had been looking his over again, with close scrutiny.

"I believe they don't need to be wound up," said Elizabeth. "I think they'll keep on going always. They aren't really clocks at all."

"They are just magic things, like the things in the *Arabian Nights*."

"That's so," said Frank. "Let's take them into the house, and show them to Mamma. I wonder if she will let us keep them."

"I think she will," said Helen, who was quite subdued by this time. "I think she'll be glad to keep anything that will make me speak pleasantly when I feel cross; and, as long as I live, I never want to hear another sound like that last loud one that my clock gave."

"Nor I," said Frank.

"Nor I," said James.

"I liked the sound mine made," said Elizabeth; "it was just like music."

"Well, I suppose it always will be, Lizzie," said the other children, all speaking together; "because you are always so sweet and good-natured, you know."

Upon which all four of the clocks struck together three notes, so musical and sweet you would have said fairy-bells must have been ringing in the air.

What the children's mother said when she saw the clocks, I do not know; but she thought the children had imagined all about the clocks striking; for it was a very queer thing, that no matter how loudly the clocks struck, nobody but their owners could hear the sounds. At first this used to frighten the children, especially Helen, whose clock, I am sorry to say, had to strike loudly and harshly many times in a week. But more and more they came to feel that the clocks were their friends; and that in some mysterious way which they could not understand, the old man who had brought them must be their friend too.

"I think he'll be back again some day," said Elizabeth, one evening when they all had been having a fine play together, and each one of them had been trying to make all the others have a good time, and the little clocks had all rung out together a lovely chime of sweet "Kling-a-ling-lings." "I think he'll come back to see whether we've been helped by the clocks or not."

"I think so, too," said Frank; "and if he does, I tell you, I'm going to grip his coat, and hold him tight till he's answered all our questions."

"I'll be afraid to see him," sighed poor little Helen. "I have such a dreadful temper. But I do try very hard to conquer it, nobody knows how hard, and I don't mean ever to stop trying."

"Kling-a-kling-ling! kling-ling! ling! ling," said Helen's clock, which she had under her arm. She hardly ever stirred without it—she was so anxious to be reminded always when she spoke crossly.

"There! That's a comfort!" she exclaimed. "It hasn't made so sweet a sound as that for three days."

"No wonder," said Frank, thoughtlessly; "you've been a perfect spit-fire these last three days; I've wondered what ailed you."

Helen's eyes filled with tears, and she was just about to make some angry reply, when "Bang! bang! bang!" came from Frank's chamber window, which stood wide open. His clock was standing on the window-sill.

"I was caught that time," said Frank. "Never mind, Helen. I didn't mean to make you feel badly. I am very sorry I said it."

"Kling-a-ling," said the little clock, in a gentle, soft note.

"Doesn't it sound like 'all right,' when they ring that way?" said Elizabeth. "It is almost like a real voice speaking. I just wish the old man would come back!" she continued. "I'd like to thank him. We never thanked him, you know. He vanished so quickly."

"I think he'll come," replied Frank. "Magicians always do come back, in fairy stories. Don't you know, in so many stories it says, 'And the magician re-appeared?'"

"That's so!" echoed James, "I'm sure he'll come back."

PART TWO

AFTER A LONG time, almost a year, the old man really did come back. It was in the pleasant springtime that he had come at first, and the last snow was just melting away when he came the second time.

The children had a big snow-man in their yard; they made him in February, and the cold weather had continued so steadily that he had lasted away into April, much to the children's delight. He was a giant snow-man; fully six feet high. They called him the Colossus of Rhodes, after a picture their father had shown to them of a great statue which stood astride a gulf of water, hundreds and hundreds of years ago.

So splendid a snow-man had never before been seen in the town, and the children had two months' solid fun with him—piecing him, putting big elbows on him, sticking red woolen caps on his head, tying comforters around his neck, fastening placards on his breast, such as "Pity the sorrows of a poor blind man," "I am cold," or "Fresh from the North Pole." This last was Helen's device. She also made a bright blue and white flag, out of two old silk pocket-handkerchiefs, and on the white half she worked, in big blue letters, "The Ice Captain." This she sewed on the end of an old hearth-brush handle, and stuck it into the snow-man's right hand. The brush handle was bright red and yellow, and the effect of the whole was very gay.

But the days of the snow-man were fast drawing to a close. In the last week of March he began to sink in stature. Each day he settled down more and more, and grew shorter, and shorter, until even Elizabeth could reach his head by standing on tip-toe. Finally, his right arm fell off and made a big snow pile down by his side; then a mischievous town boy stoned off his head, and the children decided that they would finish up the job of destroying him themselves. So that was what they were at, the morning their old friend the Magic-Clock man returned.

It was just as it had been the first time. They did not hear a footstep, or a sound of any kind, until suddenly they looked around and saw the old man standing at the gate. He had the same big box on his back, and the same pleasant smile on his face, and he looked at them steadily, as before, without speaking.

"Oh, there is the old man!" exclaimed Elizabeth, joyfully.

"I told you he would come," said Frank, and they all ran to the gate as fast as they could go; only Helen lagged a little, and shyly hung her pretty head, for fear the old man would say something stern to her. She, more than any of the others, believed that the old man was really a magician, and that he would know all she had done during the whole year, and how that very morning, when her nurse hurt her head a little, combing the tangles out of her curly hair, she had spoken so snappishly to her that the little white clock had rung out in as loud and disapproving a tone as ever, and poor Helen had thought to herself: "Dear me! I shall never, never learn to keep my temper!"

But, strange to say, there was not one of the children who received so loving and friendly a glance from the old man as that which he gave to Helen. He waited until she had come up before he spoke a word; then, stretching out his hand, he laid it on her curls, and vigorously nodding his head, he said, smiling all the while like a sunbeam:

"Tangle Locks—magic clocks. How did they go, little one?"

Helen could not speak; but the other three all cried out at once:

"Oh, they are lovely! We thank you ever so much."

Frank, true to his resolution, had already taken firm hold of the old man's coat-tail and begun with his questioning:

"We want to know, sir—" He did not get any farther with his question. Interrupting him in a kindly but firm tone, the old man said:

"I am going to tell you all you can know about it. The things you were going to ask me are things you can not be told."

"How did he know what I was going to ask him?" thought Frank. "He is a great magician, I do believe. But I think he might tell me what makes the clocks strike, and why they don't need any winding up."

The old man was unstrapping his box from his shoulders. As he set it upon the ground, the children gathered closer around him, with eager looks. They thought he was going to open it, and perhaps give them some new kind of magic gift. But he only smiled, and shook his head.

"No, no," he said, seating himself on the box, "I have nothing for you in my box. It is full of just the same sort of magic clocks that I gave you. I never carry anything else. My only business is to go about the world, giving them to boys and girls.

Then, after they have had the clocks a year, I come again to see what use they have made of them."

Here he fixed his eyes on Helen, who grew very red in the face, and tried to hide behind Frank. But the old man reached out a very long arm, and, drawing her forward, took her between his knees, and again patted her golden curls.

"We should like to know, sir," again began Frank, who still kept a corner of one of the old man's coat-tails tightly grasped in his hand. "We should like to know, sir—"

He did not get any farther in his question. Interrupting him in the same gentle, kindly voice, the old man continued speaking as if he had not heard Frank at all.

"I have not brought you any presents this year, but I am going to tell you something which will be better than any present in the world."

The children all crowded closer, their eyes full of wonder and interest. But Frank did not let go the coat-tail.

"I don't care," he was saying to himself; "he sha'n't slip away from me this time till I find out about the wheels."

"The thing I am going to tell you now," continued the old man, "is even more wonderful than the clocks. I tell it only to such children as have made good use of their clocks, and have tried to obey the warnings given them. I see that you have done so. I can tell as soon as I look at children's faces whether they have tried or not."

At this Helen lifted up her face, encouraged; and, looking directly into the old man's kind, gray eyes, whispered:

"I have tried very hard."

The old man nodded, and patted her curls, as he went on:

"I did not tell you, when I was here before, anything about these clocks. Now, I shall explain to you what makes them strike."

"Ha!" thought Frank, "now we're coming to it. That's something like!" and in his eager delight he dropped the coat-tail and crowded up closer in front of the old man.

"There is a fairy inside of each clock," said the old man; "a fairy so small that no human eyes can see her."

Helen caught her breath. "Oh, a real live fairy?" she said. "Will she never come out and speak to us?"

"The way they speak is by striking the clocks," replied the old man. "That is all they are there for—to keep watch over all you do, and to call out to you, by striking the clocks, to warn you when you do wrong, and to praise you when you do right. These fairies live in the clocks; but they can come out of them whenever they like. And part of their work has to be done outside of the clocks. Where do you think?"

Here he paused for an answer; but the children were too excited to make any answer.

"Outside the clocks!" shouted Frank.

"Yes, outside the clocks," continued the old man. "Outside the clocks; on—your—faces!"

Here he paused and looked smilingly at the children, almost laughing at the bewilderment he saw in their eyes.

"On—our—faces!" repeated Elizabeth, thoughtfully, rubbing her cheek with her hand as she spoke. "Oh, I guess—"

"Yes, you can guess, perhaps," the old man said; "but I shall tell the others, and you will see if you guessed right. The work the fairies do on your faces is this: They are obliged to keep a written record there, of every time the clocks strike."

"Every time!" exclaimed Elizabeth. She thought she must have guessed wrongly. "Our faces would be all marked up then!"

"So they are!" replied the old man, "all marked up; and people who understand the fairies' writing can read the records as soon as they look at you. That is the way I knew, as soon as I looked at you, today, that you had been making a good use of your clocks this whole year—that you had been growing better and better children all the time."

At this the tears rolled down Helen's cheek. "Oh, no," she said; "you didn't read it right on my face; for only this morning I was as cross as ever to my nurse, because my hair was snarled."

"That's nothing!" spoke up Frank. "You did read it right, sir; she's grown to be kind and good almost all the time. We all think so, don't we?" and he looked at the others.

"Yes, indeed," said Elizabeth; and, "Yes, indeed!" echoed James.

The old man nodded. "I'm never mistaken," he said. "There is no such thing as mistaking that kind of writing on faces. Every time the clock strikes for a mean act or a cross word, out flies the fairy and draws a line about the mouth or about the eyes that says, 'mean!' 'cross!' or 'untrue!' just as plain as plain English. And every time the clock strikes for a pleasant, kind, generous, loving, true act or word, out flies the fairy, so happy and glad, and draws the lines which mean, 'pleasant,' 'kind,' 'generous,' 'loving,' 'true,' on the face. And these lines never die out. It isn't like any other writing. Writing in ink or with pencil—all such writing fades; and the paper it is written on is destroyed in a thousand ways— torn, burned up, lost. All such writing comes to an end, and disappears sooner or later. But the writing on faces never fades. It grows clearer and clearer the longer you live; and you can never get a new face till you die; the one that you are born with must last you to the end of life! And if you allow your face to become written all over with ugly lines, of dishonest, mean, unkind, ill-natured actions, almost before you know it, you will have what is called 'a bad face.' You often hear people say of a man, 'he has a bad face,' or 'he has a good face.' That is what the fairies who write on faces have done, to let the whole world know what sort of a man or woman the person is."

"Some people are born pretty, Nurse says," interrupted Helen, timidly; "she says you can't spoil a pretty face."

"Nurse is mistaken," said the old man energetically. "That is a great mistake. The prettiest face in the world can be made frightful to look at, simply by being written full of hateful actions and words; and the plainest face in the world can be made to look beautiful by being written full of love and kindness and truth."

"That's like Mamma's face," said Elizabeth.

"Yes! yes!" cried all the children.

"Then your mamma has been all her life doing kind things, and speaking pleasant words," said the old man.

"That's so," said Frank.

"Will being cross a few times, spoil one's face?" asked poor Helen anxiously.

"Oh, no! dear child," the old man answered, "luckily for everybody. If that were so, the fairies would be discouraged with their writing, for they hate to make bad faces. Whatever lines are in the majority, as the days go by, will show on the faces. If there are ten pleasant lines to one ill-natured one, the ill-natured one will be so crossed out that it will not show."

"Ten to one," sighed Helen; "that's a great many."

"Pshaw!" cried Frank, "you have twenty to one, on your face, Helen; you're pleasant twenty times, nowadays, where you are cross once."

The old man gave a queer sort of chuckle.

"You'll do, children," he said, rising, and putting Helen down on the ground. "You'll do! I wish all my children understood it all as well as you seem to."

"But we should like to know, sir," began Frank, catching hold of the old man's coat-tail once more. "Before you go, we should like to know, sir—"

He did not get any farther with his question. As suddenly as he vanished the first time, the old man had vanished now. Big box, straps, sunny smile, old man— all gone, like a puff of smoke! Not a sign of a living creature in the street; not a trace of a cloud in the sky.

The children rubbed their eyes, and gazed up and down, and at each other, too astonished to speak.

Frank first found his voice.

"I never saw anything like it!" he said. "It's too provoking. The next time he comes, I sha'n't drop his coat-tail one single second. I'm determined to find out about those wheels."

"I think he's told us all he means to," said Elizabeth. "I don't believe he'll ever come back again."

What is the old man's name? And where are his clocks to be found? Guess!

First published in the November and December 1885 editions of *St. Nicholas Magazine*

Ben's Sister

BY MARIA L. POOL

THE SNOW WAS more than a foot deep on a level, and Naomi could not estimate the depths of the drifts that were piled here and there.

"However," she said gayly, "the crust will bear you; and I only wish I were going, too. Tell Auntie her jelly was divine and her cake transcendent."

"Divine and tranthendent," lisped the child, who, although a boy of eight years, had been arrayed in his sister's heavy woolen jacket, which was the warmest garment available. He had on a cloth cap without a visor, and this cap was fastened down with many windings of a white "cloud." Rubber boots nearly enveloped his short legs, and leathern mittens were on his hands, in one of which was grasped a six-quart tin pail. His bright, rosy face might have been that of a girl, and both in size and countenance he appeared younger than he really was.

Naomi used to say that when she felt very much in need of a sister, she called Ben a girl, but when she wanted a protector, she admitted that he was a boy.

"You'll go by the cart path, of course," spoke up a woman who was leaning back in a large chair, and whose pale, thin face bore a resemblance to the faces of the children before her, and showed that she was their mother and an invalid.

"Yeth, ma'am," said Ben. "Now I'm off. Remember, 'Omi, bithcuit for thupper."

"Don't break the eggs as you go, and don't spill the milk as you come!" called out Naomi at the door.

She stood an instant watching the boy's figure as it trudged along over the crust. She shivered as she looked, for the air was biting cold and swept down from the north.

The whole sky was covered by a light haze, such as often in New England precedes one of those snow-storms in which the flakes sift down with a sharp persistence that makes one breathless who tries to battle against them.

A sudden anxiety came to the girl, and she called after her brother:

"Remember, Ben, I allow you three hours—one to go, one to stay, and one to come home. Then it'll be four o'clock. After that I shall begin to worry."

"All right!" shouted the boy. "You'll be very thilly to worry, though!"

Naomi glanced at the thermometer, which hung by the door. It marked five degrees above zero.

Then she went into the room where her mother sat, and put more wood into the cracked cook-stove. She was uneasy. She had an impulse to go out and run after her brother, but she remained quiet, and told herself how foolish she was.

She took up a book and read aloud for an hour, her mother placidly braiding straw the while. By that time a few flakes began to drift about in the air, whirling, apparently with no intention of falling.

Naomi started up and flung her book on the table. "Mother," she exclaimed; "I'm sorry we let Ben go!"

"Ben knows the way perfectly; and he will be home by dusk," replied her mother.

Nevertheless, Mrs. Dunlap looked out of the window, marked the ominous light gray of the heavens, and knew well that a heavy snowstorm was beginning. It might be a week before the sun shone again. Still it really was "thilly," as Ben had said, to worry about him.

The wind kept shrieking around the corner of the house. Naomi put on an old coat, hood, and mittens, and went out to bring in wood. She filled the woodbox and made a pile along the floor by the stove.

As she did so, a big Newfoundland dog came from a corner of the woodhouse and followed her back and forth. "Roy," she said, reprovingly, "you ought to have gone with Ben."

Roy wagged his tail seriously, as if to say, he had more weighty things to attend to than trotting after a boy.

When Naomi had finished her work, she walked toward the pine wood through which Ben had gone. She did not quite know how cold it was until she turned to come back, and faced the icy wind that made her coat feel as if it were but a rag.

How desolate and alone the small brown house, which was her home, looked now to her! It stood in the midst of snow, with the snow flying about it.

The Dunlaps were very poor, as their home plainly showed. Naomi's mother was a widow, and had been unable to walk for two years. You can imagine that Naomi, at fifteen, felt as if she were heavily burdened.

She had been obliged to give up school just when school had become very interesting to her. She did the housework, and both she and Ben helped their mother with the straw work, which once a week was brought to the house from Farnborough, in a long, odd wagon.

In the season there were always piles of men's and boys' hats growing under Mrs. Dunlap's busy fingers. Even little Ben, on Saturdays and in the spare hours of the long spring days, had to make "top-pieces."

But there were dull weeks in which the Farnborough wagon did not come to the house, and the Dunlaps lived closer than ever.

Perhaps you think Naomi was melancholy and somber under this life. But she was not. Sometimes there was a great deal of fun in that bit of a house on "Goose Hill," and Ben often said that if any other boy had a sister who was more of a "brick," he should just like to see that fellow.

It was three o'clock when Naomi came in and announced that the mercury had fallen two degrees more, and she thought she would begin making the biscuit.

The boy had gone to an aunt's with eggs, and was to bring back some milk.

"There is no danger of his spilling the milk," remarked Naomi, measuring baking-powder. "It will be frozen as solid as a rock."

At half-past four it was dark, of course. Naomi's biscuits were done and placed on the hearth, wrapped in a towel.

"Ben should not have stopped a moment longer than we told him," said his mother, severely. "But, Naomi, you must not worry; there's no good in worrying."

Nevertheless, the girl knew that her mother was worrying more and more, with every moment that passed.

It was snowing faster than ever now, as Naomi discovered when she stood on the doorstep and peered about her. She could see nothing. A blinding, cutting swirl was in the air and shut off all vision.

As she stood there, Roy thrust his nose into her hand and whined. She went in directly and put a light where it shone mistily out toward the pine wood.

The cold was increasing so fast that she doubted if it could continue snowing much longer. But the wind would drive the snow from the ground and the drifts as blindingly as though the storm held on.

As Naomi went back into the kitchen where her mother sat, her face was pale but determined.

The thought of her little brother struggling alone, in such a storm, was no longer endurable.

"Mother," she said resolutely, "I am going out to the pine woods. I shall take a lantern, and Roy will go with me. Ben must be near home. I will meet him, and bring him in."

Mrs. Dunlap pressed her hands tightly together. In spite of her calm comments, she was half wild with anxiety.

She looked helplessly at her daughter, who was pulling on long rubber boots. There was no neighbor within half a mile.

"Then you will both be in the storm," said the mother feebly; "and I can do nothing."

Naomi came to her mother's side and kissed her.

"You have the worst of it," she said cheerfully, though her heart was like lead. "But I shall be back in half an hour. With my lantern and Roy, I shall be well armed."

She tied shawls over the very shabby coat, which was all she had. She wheeled her mother's chair so that the good woman might be able to keep the stove full of wood.

"Don't worry, Mother, but please have a hot stove when we come back," Naomi said, as she took up her lantern and, followed by Roy, hurried out into the storm.

The wind swept into the entry, and howled so that the anxious woman within shuddered.

It was comparatively easy for Naomi to go toward the pines, for the wind was at her back, and she ran on over the snow-crust, swinging her lantern before her, and calling her brother's name in her fresh young voice, that went forward on the rushing air.

It was terribly cold, though, even with the wind behind her! Her hands and feet began to sting and ache.

She had not, as she believed, been going in the path toward the wood five minutes, when, in some unaccountable way, the wind was no longer behind her. It was rushing down upon her right, and she felt as if she were going downhill.

She stood perfectly still, but trembling with a thrill of terrible alarm. She lifted her lantern; but from the first, the light had been of little service. It made a small luminous halo, while beyond was a blank, impenetrable white wall that seemed to rush and roar about her—a wall that moved.

She screamed "Benny!" at the top of her voice.

"Oh, he *must* hear me!" she exclaimed to herself. "Roy, where is Ben?"

The dog had kept near to her all the time. Now he lifted his broad, snow-sprinkled head, and pressed still nearer as if he said:

"I am going to take care of *you*."

"Go!" cried Naomi, fiercely. "Find him! Find him! Don't stay with me! Find Ben!"

The dog galloped away from her as she gave the command. When he had gone, she felt an unreasoning and almost helpless terror.

She stood still, for she knew now that she had not the least idea which way to turn. She was like one in a dream, and still she must not dare to remain quiet. There was that demon of the cold waiting for her if she were to cease moving.

Her feet and hands ached so that from sheer pain she could hardly keep the tears back.

She went on, only trying to keep the wind behind her, for that was all she had to guide her in the right direction, and she was fully aware how poor a guide that was.

Where was the courage with which she had started? She felt utterly subdued now, and her only thought was the thought of her brother.

She stamped her feet and swung her arms; then, as well as she could with her stiff lips, she whistled to the dog, but he did not answer.

She went staggering on, whither she knew not.

As often as she could spare her breath, she shouted "Ben!" and when no answer came, she felt as if she were calling that name in a great, cruel world that had nothing in it but storm.

Even the dog had left her. He had never been carefully trained. Perhaps he had gone home. Mechanically she kept jumping about in the snow; for she dared not go far in any direction.

All at once, above the roar about her, she heard Roy's bark, short and quick. The sound was like an elixir of life in her veins. She sprang forward. The dog, she found, was but a few yards away. Naomi soon discovered him pulling at something in the snow. She dashed down beside that something, and began furiously to brush the snow from it.

"Ith 'at you, 'Omi?" asked a sleepy voice.

The girl began to cry, but she did not stop working.

"Don't bother a fellow!" said Ben, drowsily, "I'm all right. I'm only rethting."

"Resting!" repeated Naomi shrilly. "You are freezing! Get up! You *shall* get up!"

She took hold of his collar and jerked him to his feet, the exertion sending a glow through her frame.

"Now, thop that! I tell you, I'm all right. I wath cold, but I got warm."

His voice sank as he tried to loose her hold and fall back. She shook him again. She put down her lantern, and held him with one hand while she beat him with the other. She did not know that this was her own salvation, too; but she knew that it was the only way to save Benny.

"You lazy thing! You wicked boy!" she shouted, not caring what she said. "Take hold of my hand. We'll make Roy go home, and we'll follow him."

She kept at work. She slapped the boy's face. She was not in the least particular as to how or where she struck him.

In a moment, to her great joy, he began to resent her treatment. He struck out at her in return.

"Do you think I'm going to thtand thith?" he cried.

Naomi stopped her tears and stood up to the fight. She taunted him. She said the most irritating things.

From utter helplessness, the boy gradually became roused to amazement and anger. What had come over his sister?

If she had come ten minutes later, she probably never could have brought him back to life.

"Now come home with me," she said when she was so weary she could keep up the battle no longer. She tried to pull him after her. But he began to whimper, and said:

"I tell you I can't go! There 'th thomething the matter with my legth. They are jutht like plugth of wood. That 'th why you knocked me down tho eathy. Gueth you couldn't have done it if they hadn't been thtiff!"

Naomi's blood went back chokingly to her heart. But she said with determination:

"For all that, you've got to come!"

She pulled him, his feet shuffling and dragging, Roy walking close to her gravely. She stepped, panting, desperate.

"Ben," she said, in a voice that went through the boy's numb, half-frozen senses like a knife, "do you want to die? You are freezing! If you don't try with all your might, we shall both freeze! Think of Mother waiting for us!"

Ben tried and struggled. In all his little life, he had never made such an effort before.

He sank back, crying out in an agony:

"Oh, no; I *can't* walk! You'd better go home to Mother!"

He sobbed and clung to her.

Naomi stood upright a moment, holding her brother and trying to think, while the dog lay down in the snow.

But nothing came clearly to her mind save the picture of her mother, helpless,

sitting by the kitchen stove, waiting and listening.

She must waste no time. It seemed as if every instant froze a drop of blood.

Which way should she try to move?

In the cloud of snow, and the hurtling of the wind, was there a strange, dim radiance ahead?

Naomi peered forward, distrusting her own eyesight, holding Ben in her arms the while.

Roy, as if he had known all the time where he was, now arose, and he began to walk slowly forward.

She lifted her lantern, but the light was of little service.

The very next moment, the girl heard— for the wind brought the words straight from the speaker:

"Naomi! Ben! My children!"

Roy barked with delight.

Naomi knew then that they were close to their own home; the light was the one that she herself had put in the window, and it was her mother's voice that was calling.

Inspired, empowered by a strength beyond her own, she lifted Ben and staggered forward toward the light.

Stumbling, slipping, she struggled on.

She knew not how, conscious only that she was still going

toward the light which all the time grew more and more distinct.

Soon she saw that her mother was leaning from an open window—and she cried out huskily:

"Mother! Mother! Here we are!"

Naomi knew afterward that her mother crawled—Mrs. Dunlap could not tell how—to the door and opened it, and that in some way she herself reached the warm kitchen with her burden. There the heat seemed to stop her breath, and she fainted, dimly feeling the dog's soft, warm tongue on her face as her last sensation.

When she came to life again, the doors were still open, and the sharp wind was blowing in, for Mrs. Dunlap knew that a warm room was not the place for frost-bitten people. She had been rubbing their temples and hands with snow, sitting on the floor beside them.

Naomi, naturally strong and well, soon revived and began earnestly to care for Benny, working over him as her mother directed; and her commands were so wise that the boy received no permanent injury, though his feet were but "poor things," he said, all that winter.

The storm did not last very long.

The next day the sun shone, and Naomi went out toward the pine wood, and at the very edge, nearest the house, she found Ben's tin pail; the cover was off, and in the frozen milk was a deep hole, evidently made by Roy, who, as he had already tasted the milk, received the rest of it as a gift.

Not far off was the lantern, which Naomi had thrown aside when she found Ben. She was now sure she had been no more than a few rods from the house at any time.

"Perhaps I went around and around," she said to herself, as she took up the lantern. "But if I hadn't gone out for him, Ben would have died."

With this, she pressed back the somewhat hysterical sobs that were rising, and hurried home with the pail and lantern.

"You needn't try to make fun of it all," said Ben in the dusk of the next evening. He caught his sister's hand closely as he sat bolstered in a big chair by the stove. "I know what you did, you thaved me. I knew you were a brick!" Here there came a little quiver in his voice. "Well," he said, beginning again, "Mother thaid I ought to thank Heaven for you; and if I really wath thankful, you know, I thould try to be the kind of a brother you'd alwayth be proud of all your life."

"And so you will," said Naomi. "I do believe you will!"

First published in the April 1886 edition of *St. Nicholas Magazine*

Tom Sawyer Abroad

BY HUCK FINN

"EDITED" BY MARK TWAIN

CHAPTER ONE

DO YOU RECKON Tom Sawyer was satisfied after all them adventures? I mean the adventures we had down the river, and the time we set the darky Jim free and Tom got shot in the leg. No, he wasn't. It only just p'isoned him for more. That was all the effect it had. You see, when we three came back up the river in glory, as you may say, from that long travel, and the village received us with a torch-light procession and speeches, and everybody hurrah'd and shouted, it made us heroes, and that was what Tom Sawyer had always been hankering to be.

For a while he *was* satisfied. Everybody made much of him, and he tilted up his nose and stepped around the town as though he owned it. Some called him Tom Sawyer the Traveler, and that just swelled him up fit to bust. You see he laid over me and Jim considerable, because we only went down the river on a raft and came back by the steamboat, but Tom went by the steamboat both ways. The boys envied me and Jim a good deal, but land! they just knuckled to the dirt before Tom.

Well, I don't know; maybe he might have been satisfied if it hadn't been for old Nat Parsons, which was postmaster, and powerful long and slim, and kind o' good-hearted and silly, and bald-headed, on account of his age, and about the talkiest old cretur I ever see. For as much as thirty years he'd been the only man in the village that had a reputation—I mean a reputation for being a traveler, and of course he was mortal proud of it, and it was reckoned that in the course of that thirty years he had told about that journey over a million times and enjoyed it every time. And now comes along a boy not quite fifteen, and sets everybody admiring and gawking over *his* travels, and it just give the poor old man the high strikes. It made him sick to listen to Tom, and hear the people say "My land!" "Did you ever!" "My goodness sakes alive!" and all such things; but he couldn't pull away from it, any more than a fly that's got its hind leg fast in the molasses. And always when Tom come to a rest, the poor old cretur would chip in on *his* same old travels and work them for all they were worth, but they were pretty faded, and didn't go for much, and it was pitiful to see. And then Tom would take another innings, and then the old man again—and so on, and so on, for an hour and more, each trying to beat out the other.

You see, Parsons' travels happened like this: When he first got to be postmaster and was green in the business, there come a letter for somebody he didn't know, and there wasn't any such person in the village. Well, he didn't know what to do, nor how to act, and there the letter stayed and stayed, week in and week out, till the bare sight of it give him a conniption. The postage wasn't paid on it, and that was another thing to worry about. There wasn't any way to collect that ten cents, and he reckon'd the Gov'ment would hold him responsible for it and maybe turn him out besides, when they found he hadn't collected it. Well, at last he couldn't stand it any longer. He couldn't sleep nights, he couldn't eat, he was thinned down to a shadder, yet da'sn't ask anybody's advice, for the very person he asked for advice might go back on him and let the Gov'ment know about the letter. He had the letter buried under the floor, but that did no good; if he happened to see a person standing over the place it'd give him the cold shivers, and loaded him up with suspicions, and he would sit up that night till the town was as still and dark, and then he would sneak there and get it out and bury it in another place. Of course people got to avoiding him and shaking their heads and whispering, because, the way he was looking and acting, they judged he had killed somebody or done something terrible, they didn't know what, and if he had been a stranger they would've lynched him.

Well, as I was saying, it got so he couldn't stand it any longer; so he made up his mind to pull out for Washington, and just go to the President of the United States and make a clean breast of the whole thing, not keeping back an atom, and then fetch the letter out and lay it before the whole Gov'ment, and say, "Now, there she is—do with me what you're a mind to; though as heaven is my judge I am an innocent man and not deserving of the full penalties of the law and leaving behind me a family that must starve and yet hadn't had a thing to do with it, which is the whole truth and I can swear to it."

So he did it. He had a little wee bit of steamboating, and some stage-coaching, but all the rest of the way was horseback, and it took him three weeks to get to Washington. He saw lots of land and lots of villages and four cities. He was gone 'most eight weeks, and there never was such a proud man in the village as when he got back. His travels made him the greatest man in all that region, and the most talked about; and people come from as much as thirty miles back in the country, and from over in the Illinois bottoms, too, just to look at him—and there they'd stand and gawk, and he'd gabble. You never see anything like it.

Well, there wasn't any way, now, to settle which was the greatest traveler; some said it was Nat, some said it was Tom. Everybody allowed that Nat had seen the most longitude, but they had to give in that whatever Tom was short in longitude he had made up in latitude and climate. It was about a stand-off; so both of them had to whoop up their dangerous adventures, and try to get ahead *that* way. That bullet-wound in Tom's leg was a tough thing for Nat Parsons to buck against, but he bucked the best he could; and at a disadvantage, too, for Tom didn't set still as he'd orter done, to be fair, but always got up and sauntered around and worked his limp while Nat was painting up the adventure that *he* had in Washington; for Tom never let go that limp when his leg got well, but practised it nights at home, and kept it good as new right along.

Nat's adventure was like this; I don't know how true it is; maybe he got it out of a paper, or somewhere, but I will say this for him, that he *did* know how to tell it. He could make anybody's flesh crawl, and he'd turn pale and hold his breath when he told it, and sometimes women and girls got so faint they couldn't stick it out. Well, it was this way, as near as I can remember:

He come a-loping into Washington, and put up his horse and shoved out to the President's house with his letter, and they told him the President was up to the Capitol, and just going to start for Philadelphia—not a minute to lose if he wanted to catch him. Nat 'most dropped, it made him so sick. His horse was put up, and he didn't know what *to* do. But just then along comes a darky driving an old ram-shackly hack, and he see his chance. He rushes out and shouts: "A half a dollar if you git me to the Capitol in half an hour, and a quarter extra if you do it in twenty minutes!"

"Done!" says the darky.

Nat he jumped in and slammed the door, and away they went a-ripping and a-tearing over the roughest road a body ever see, and the racket of it was something awful. Nat passed his arms through the loops and hung on for life and death, but pretty soon the hack hit a rock and flew up in the air, and the bottom fell out, and when it come down Nat's feet was on the ground, and he see he was in the most desperate danger if he couldn't keep up with the hack. He was horrible scared, but he laid into his work for all he was worth, and hung tight to the arm-loops and made his legs fairly fly. He yelled and shouted to the driver to stop, and so did the crowds along the street, for they could see his legs spinning along under the coach, and his head and shoulders bobbing inside, through the windows, and he was in awful danger; but the more they all shouted the more the darky whooped and yelled and lashed the horses and shouted, "Don't you fret, I's gwine to git you dah in time, boss; I's gwine to do it, sho'!" for you see he thought they were all hurrying him up, and of course he couldn't hear anything for the racket he was making. And so they went ripping along, and everybody just petrified to see it, and when they got to the Capitol at last it was the quickest trip that ever was made, and everybody said so. The horses laid down, and Nat dropped, all tuckered out, and he was all dust and rags and barefooted; but he was in time and just in time, and caught the President and give him the letter, and everything was all right, and the

President give him a free pardon on the spot, and Nat give the darky two extra quarters instead of one because he could see that if he hadn't had the hack he wouldn't 'a' got there in time, nor anywhere near it.

It *was* a powerful good adventure, and Tom Sawyer had to work his bullet-wound mighty lively to hold his own against it.

Well, by and by Tom's glory got to paling down gradly, on account of other things turning up for the people to talk about—first a horse-race, and on top of that a house afire, and on top of that the circus, and on top of that the eclipse; and that started a revival, same as it always does, and by that time there wasn't any more talk about Tom, so to speak, and you never see a person so sick and disgusted.

Pretty soon he got to worrying and fretting right along day in and day out, and when I asked him what *was* he in such a state about, he said it 'most broke his heart to think how time was slipping away, and him getting older and older, and no wars breaking out and no way of making a name for himself that he could see. Now that is the way boys is always thinking, but he was the first one I ever heard come out and say it.

So then he set to work to get up a plan to make him celebrated; and pretty soon he struck it, and offered to take me and Jim in. Tom Sawyer was always free and generous that way. There's a plenty of boys that's mighty good and friendly when *you*'ve got a good thing, but when a good thing happens to come their way they don't say a word to you, and try to hog it all. That warn't ever Tom Sawyer's way, I can say that for him. There's plenty of boys that will come hankering and groveling around you when you've got an apple, and beg the core off of you; but when they've got one, and you beg for the core and remind them how you give them a core one time, they say thank you 'most to death, but there ain't a-going to be no core. But I notice they always git come up with; all you got to do is to wait.

Well, we went out in the woods on the hill, and Tom told us what it was. It was a crusade.

"What's a crusade?" I says.

He looked scornful the way he's always done when he was ashamed of a person, and says—

"Huck Finn, do you mean to tell me you don't know what a crusade is?"

"No," says I, "I don't. And I don't care to, nuther. I've lived till now and done without it, and had my health, too. But as soon as you tell me, I'll know, and that's soon enough. I don't see any use in finding out things and clogging up my head with them when I mayn't ever have any occasion to use 'em. There was Lance Williams, he learned how to talk Choctaw here till one come and dug his grave for him. Now, then, what's a crusade? But I can tell you one thing before you begin; if it's a patent-right, there's no money in it. Bill Thompson he—"

We went out in the woods on the hill, and Tom told us what it was. It was a crusade.

"Patent-right!" says he. "I never see such an idiot. Why, a crusade is a kind of war."

I thought he must be losing his mind. But no, he was in real earnest, and went right on, perfectly ca'm:

"A crusade is a war to recover the Holy Land from the pagans."

"Which Holy Land?"

"Why, *the* Holy Land—there ain't but one."

"What do *we* want of it?"

"Why, can't you understand? It's in the hands of the pagans, and it's our duty to take it away from them."

"How did we come to let them git hold of it?"

"We didn't come to let them git hold of it. They always had it."

"Why, Tom, then it must belong to them, don't it?"

"Why of course it does. Who said it didn't?"

I studied over it, but couldn't seem to git at the right of it, no way. I says:

"It's too many for me, Tom Sawyer. If I had a farm and it was mine, and another person wanted it, would it be right for him to—"

"Oh, shucks! you don't know enough to come in when it rains, Huck Finn. It ain't a farm, it's entirely different. You see, it's like this. They own the land, just the mere land, and that's all they *do* own; but it was our folks, our Jews and Christians, that made it holy, and so they haven't any business to be there defiling it. It's a shame, and we ought not to stand it a minute. We ought to march against them and take it away from them."

"Why, it does seem to me it's the most mixed-up thing I ever see! Now if I had a farm and another person—"

"Don't I tell you it hasn't got anything to do with farming? Farming is business, just common low-down business; that's all it is, it's all you can say for it; but this is higher, this is religious, and totally different."

"Religious to go and take the land away from people that owns it?"

"Certainly; it's always been considered so."

Jim he shook his head, and says:

"Mars Tom, I reckon dey's a mistake about it somers—dey mos' sholy is. I's religious myself, en I knows plenty religious people, but I hain't run across none dat acts like dat."

It made Tom hot, and he says:

"Well, it's enough to make a body sick, such mullet-headed ignorance! If either of you'd read anything about history, you'd know that Richard Cur de Loon, and the Pope, and Godfrey de Bulleyn, and lots more of the most noble-hearted and pious people in the world, hacked and hammered at the paynims for more than two hundred years trying to take their land away from them, and swum neck-deep in blood the whole time—and yet here's a couple of sap-headed country yahoos out in the backwoods of Missouri, setting themselves up to know more about the rights and wrongs of it than they did! Talk about cheek!"

Well, of course, that put a more different light on it, and me and Jim felt pretty cheap and ignorant, and wished we hadn't been quite so chipper. I couldn't say nothing, and Jim he couldn't for a while; then he says:

"Well, den, I reckon it's all right; beca'se ef dey didn't know, dey ain't no use for po' ignorant folks like us to be trying to know; en so, ef it's our duty, we got to go en tackle it en do de bes' we can. Same time, I feel as sorry for dem paynims as Mars Tom. De hard part gwine to be to kill folks dat a body hain't 'quainted wid and dat hain't done him no harm. Dat's it, you see. Ef we wuz to go 'mongst 'em, jist we three, en say we's hungry, en ast 'em for a bite to eat, why, maybe dey's jist like yuther people. Don't you reckon dey is? Why, dey'd give it, I know dey would, en den—"

"Then what?"

"Well, Mars Tom, my idea is like dis. It ain't no use, we can't kill dem po' strangers dat ain't doin' us no harm, till we've had practice—I knows it perfectly well, Mars Tom—'deed I knows it perfectly well. But ef we takes a' ax or two, jist you en me en Huck, en slips across de river tonight arter de moon's gone down, en

*He would 'a' raised a couple of thousand knights
and brushed the whole paynim outfit into the sea.*

kills dat sick fam'ly dat's over on the Sny, en burns dey house down, en—"

"Oh, you make me tired!" says Tom. "I don't want to argue any more with people like you and Huck Finn, that's always wandering from the subject, and ain't got any more sense than to try to reason out a thing that's pure theology by the laws that protect real estate!"

Now that's just where Tom Sawyer warn't fair. Jim didn't mean no harm, and I didn't mean no harm. We knowed well enough that he was right and we was wrong, and all we was after was to get at the *how* of it, and that was all; and the only reason he couldn't explain it so we could understand it was because we was ignorant—yes, and pretty dull, too, I ain't denying that; but, land! that ain't no crime, I should think.

But he wouldn't hear no more about it—just said if we had tackled the thing in the proper spirit, he would 'a' raised a couple of thousand knights and put them in steel armor from head to heel, and made me a lieutenant and Jim a sutler, and took the command himself and brushed the whole paynim outfit into the sea like flies and come back across the world in a glory like sunset. But he said we didn't know enough to take the chance when we had it, and he wouldn't ever offer it again. And he didn't. When he once got set, you couldn't budge him.

But I didn't care much. I am peaceable, and don't get up rows with people that ain't doing nothing to me. I allowed if the paynim was satisfied I was, and we would let it stand at that.

Now Tom he got all that notion out of Walter Scott's book, which he was always reading. And it *was* a wild notion, because in my opinion he never could've raised the men, and if he did, as like as not he would've got licked. I took the books and read all about it, and as near as I could make it out, most of the folks that shook farming to go crusading had a mighty rocky time of it.

CHAPTER TWO

WELL, TOM GOT up one thing after another, but they all had tender spots about 'em somewheres, and he had to shove 'em aside. So at last he was about in despair. Then the St. Louis papers begun to talk a good deal about the balloon that was going to sail to Europe, and Tom sort of thought he wanted to go down and see what it looked like, but couldn't make up his mind. But the papers went on talking, and so he allowed that maybe if he didn't go he mightn't ever have another chance to see a balloon and next, he found out that Nat Parsons was going down to see it, and that decided him, of course.

He wasn't going to have Nat Parsons coming back bragging about seeing the balloon, and him having to listen to it and keep quiet. So he wanted me and Jim to go too, and we went.

It was a noble big balloon, and had wings and fans and all sorts of things, and wasn't like any balloon you see in pictures. It was away out toward the edge of town, in a vacant lot, corner of Twelfth street; and there was a big crowd around it, making fun of it, and making fun of the man—a lean pale feller with that soft kind of moonlight in his eyes, you know—and they kept saying it wouldn't go. It made him hot to hear them, and he would turn on them and shake his fist and say they was animals and blind, but some day they would find they had stood face to face with one of the men that lifts up nations and makes civilizations, and was too dull to know it; and right here on this spot their own children and grandchildren would build a monument to him that would outlast a thousand years, but his name would outlast the monument. And then the crowd would burst out in a laugh again, and yell at him, and ask him what was his name before he was married, and what he would take to not do it, and what was his sister's cat's grandmother's name, and all the things that a crowd says when they've got hold of a feller that they see they can plague. Well, some things they said *was* funny—yes, and mighty witty too, I ain't denying that—but all the same it warn't fair nor brave, all them people pitching on one, and they so glib and sharp, and him without any gift of talk to answer back with. But, good land! what did he want to sass back for? You see, it couldn't do him no good, and it was just nuts for them. They *had* him, you know. But that was his way. I reckon he couldn't help it; he was made so, I judge. He was a good-enough sort of cretur, and hadn't no harm in him, and was just a genius, as the papers said, which wasn't his fault. We can't all be sound: we've got to be the way we're made. As near as I can make out, geniuses think they know it all, and so they won't take people's advice, but always go their own way, which makes everybody forsake them and despise them, and that is perfectly natural. If they was humbler, and listened and tried to learn, it would be better for them.

The part the professor was in was like a boat, and was big and roomy, and had water-tight lockers around the inside to keep all sorts of things in, and a body could sit on them, and make beds on them, too. We went aboard, and there was twenty people there, snooping around and examining, and old Nat Parsons was there, too. The professor kept fussing around, getting ready, and the people went ashore, drifting out one at a time, and old Nat he was the last. Of course it wouldn't do to let him go out behind *us*. We mustn't budge till he was gone, so we could be last ourselves.

But he was gone now, so it was time for us to follow. I heard a big shout, and turned around—the city was dropping from under us like a shot! It made me sick all through, I was so scared. Jim turned gray and couldn't say a word, and Tom didn't say nothing, but looked excited. The city went on dropping down, and down, and down; but we didn't seem to be doing nothing but just hang in the air and stand still. The houses got smaller and smaller, and the city pulled itself together, closer and closer, and the men and wagons got to looking like ants and bugs crawling around, and the streets like threads and cracks; and then it all kind of melted together, and there wasn't any city any more: it was only a big scar on the earth, and it seemed to me a body could see up the river and down the river about a thousand miles, though of course it wasn't so much. By and by the earth was a ball—just a round ball, of a dull color, with shiny stripes wriggling and winding around over it, which was rivers. The Widder Douglas always told me the earth was round like a ball, but I never took any stock in a lot of them superstitions o' hers, and of course I paid no attention to that one, because I could see myself that the world was the shape of a plate, and flat. I used to go up on the hill, and take a look around and prove it for myself, because I reckon the best way to get a sure thing on a fact is to go and examine for yourself, and not take anybody's say-so. But I had to give in, now, that the widder was right. That is, she was right as to the rest of the world, but she warn't right about the part our village is in; that part is the shape of a plate, and flat, I take my oath!

The professor had been quiet all this time, as if he was asleep; but he broke loose now, and he was mighty bitter. He says something like this:

"Idiots! They said it wouldn't go; and they wanted to examine it, and spy around and get the secret of it out of me. But I beat them. Nobody knows the secret but me. Nobody knows what makes it move but me; and it's a new power—a new power, and a thousand times the strongest in the earth! Steam's foolishness

He said he would sail his balloon around the globe, just to show what he could do.

to it! They said I couldn't go to Europe. To Europe! Why, there's power aboard to last five years, and feed for three months. They are fools! What do they know about it? Yes, and they said my air-ship was flimsy. Why, she's good for fifty years! I can sail the skies all my life if I want to, and steer where I please, though they laughed at that, and said I couldn't. Couldn't steer! Come here, boy; we'll see. You press these buttons as I tell you."

He made Tom steer the ship all about and every which way, and learnt him the whole thing in nearly no time; and Tom said it was perfectly easy. He made him fetch the ship down 'most to the earth, and had him spin her along so close to the Illinois prairies that a body could talk to the farmers, and hear everything they said perfectly plain; and he flung out printed bills to them that told about the balloon, and said it was going to Europe. Tom got so he could steer straight for a tree till he got nearly to it, and then dart up and skin right along over the top of it. Yes, and he showed Tom how to land her; and he done it first-rate, too, and set her down in the prairies as soft as wool. But the minute we started to skip out the Professor says, "No, you don't!" and shot her up in the air again. It was awful. I begun to beg, and so did Jim; but it only give his temper a rise, and he begun to rage around and look wild out of his eyes, and I was scared of him.

Well, then he got on to his troubles again, and mourned and grumbled about the way he was treated, and couldn't seem to git over it, and especially people's saying his ship was flimsy. He scoffed at that, and at their saying she warn't simple and would be always getting out of order. Get out of order! That graveled him; he said that she couldn't any more get out of order than the solar sister.

He got worse and worse, and I never see a person take on so. It give me the cold shivers to see him, and so it did Jim. By and by he got to yelling and screaming, and then he swore the world shouldn't ever have his secret at all now, it had treated him so mean. He said he would sail his balloon around the globe just to show what he could do, and then he would sink it in the sea, and sink us all along with it, too. Well, it was the awfullest fix to be in, and here was night coming on!

He give us something to eat, and made us go to the other end of the boat, and he laid down on a locker, where he could boss all the works, and put his old pepper-box revolver under his head, and said if anybody come fooling around there trying to land her, he would kill him.

We set scrunched up together, and thought considerable, but didn't say much—only just a word once in a while when a body had to say something or bust, we was *so* scared and worried. The night dragged along slow and lonesome. We was pretty low down, and the moonshine made everything soft and pretty, and the farm-houses looked snug and homeful, and we could hear the farm sounds, and wished we could be down there; but, laws! we just slipped along over them like a ghost, and never left a track.

Away in the night, when all the sounds was late sounds, and the air had a late feel, and a

And here was night coming on!

late smell, too—about a two-o'clock feel, as near as I could make out—Tom said the Professor was so quiet this time he must be asleep, and we'd better—

"Better what?" I says in a whisper, and feeling sick all over, because I knowed what he was thinking about.

"Better slip back there and tie him, and land the ship," he says.

I says: "No, sir! Don't you budge, Tom Sawyer."

And Jim—well, Jim was kind o' gasping, he was so scared. He says:

"Oh, Mars Tom, *don't!* Ef you teches him, we's gone—we's gone sho'! I ain't gwine anear him, not for nothin' in dis worl'. Mars Tom, he's plumb crazy."

Tom whispers and says: "That's *why* we've got to do something. If he wasn't crazy I wouldn't give shucks to be anywhere but here; you couldn't hire me to get out—now that I've got used to this balloon and over the scare of being cut loose from the solid ground—if he was in his right mind. But it's no good politics, sailing around like this with a person that's out of his head, and says he's going round the world and then drown us all. We've *got* to do something, I tell you, and do it before he wakes up, too, or we mayn't ever get another chance. Come!"

But it made us turn cold and creepy just to think of it, and we said we would-n't budge. So Tom was for slipping back there by himself to see if he couldn't get at the steering-gear and land the ship. We begged and begged him not to, but it warn't no use; so he got down on his hands and knees, and begun to crawl an inch at a time, we a-holding our breath and watching. After he got to the middle of the boat he crept slower than ever, and it did seem like years to me. But at last we see him get to the Professor's head, and sort of raise up soft and look a good spell in his face and listen. Then we see him begin to inch along again toward the Professor's feet where the steering-buttons was. Well, he got there all safe, and was reaching slow and steady toward the buttons, but he knocked down something that made a noise, and we see him slump down flat an' soft in the bottom, and lay still. The Professor stirred, and says, "What's that?" But everybody kept dead still and quiet, and he begun to mutter and mumble and nestle, like a person that's going to wake up, and I thought I was going to die, I was so worried and scared.

Then a cloud slid over the moon, and I 'most cried, I was so glad. She buried herself deeper and deeper into the cloud, and it got so dark we couldn't see Tom. Then it began to sprinkle rain, and we could hear the Professor fussing at his ropes and things and abusing the weather. We was afraid every minute he would touch Tom, and then we would be goners, and no help; but Tom was already on his way back, and when we felt his hands on our knees my breath stopped sudden, and my heart fell down 'mongst my other works, because I couldn't tell in the dark but it might be the Professor, which I thought it *was.*

Dear! I was so glad to have him back that I was just as near happy as a person

could be that was up in the air that way with a deranged man. You can't land a balloon in the dark, and so I hoped it would keep on raining, for I didn't want Tom to
go meddling any more and make us so awful uncomfortable. Well, I got my wish. It
drizzled and drizzled along the rest of the night, which wasn't long, though it did
seem so; and at daybreak it cleared, and the world looked mighty soft and gray and
pretty, and the forests and fields so good to see again, and the horses and cattle
standing sober and thinking. Next, the sun come a-blazing up gay and splendid,
and then we began to feel rusty and stretchy, and first we knowed we was all asleep.

CHAPTER THREE

WE WENT TO sleep about four o'clock, and woke up about eight. The professor
was setting back there at his end, looking glum. He pitched us some breakfast, but
he told us not to come abaft the midship compass. That was about the middle of
the boat. Well, when you are sharp-set, and you eat and satisfy yourself, everything
looks pretty different from what it done before. It makes a body feel pretty near
comfortable, even when he is up in a balloon with a genius. We got to talking
together.

There was one thing that kept bothering me, and by and by I says:

"Tom, didn't we start east?"

"Yes."

"How fast have we been going?"

"Well, you heard what the professor said when he was raging round.
Sometimes, he said, we was making fifty miles an hour, sometimes ninety, sometimes a hundred; said that with a gale to help he could make three hundred any
time, and said if he wanted the gale, and wanted it blowing the right direction, he
only had to go up higher or down lower to find it."

"Well, then, it's just as I reckoned. The professor lied."

"Why?"

"Because if we was going so fast we ought to be past Illinois, oughtn't we?"

"Certainly."

"Well, we ain't."

"What's the reason we ain't?"

"I know by the color. We're right over Illinois yet. And you can see for yourself
that Indiana ain't in sight."

"I wonder what's the matter with you, Huck. You know by the *color?*"

"Yes, of course I do."

"What's the color got to do with it?"

"It's got everything to do with it. Illinois is green, Indiana is pink. You show me any pink down here, if you can. No, sir; it's green."

"Indiana *pink?* Why, what a lie!"

"It ain't no lie; I've seen it on the map, and it's pink."

You never see a person so aggravated and disgusted. He says:

"Well, if I was such a numskull as you, Huck Finn, I would jump over. Seen it on the map! Huck Finn, did you reckon the States was the same color out of doors as they are on the map?"

"Tom Sawyer, what's a map for? Ain't it to learn you facts?"

"Of course."

"Well, then, how's it going to do that if it tells lies? That's what I want to know."

"Shucks, you muggins! It don't tell lies."

"It don't, don't it?"

"No, it don't."

"All right, then; if it don't, there ain't no two States the same color. You git around *that*, if you can, Tom Sawyer."

He see I had him, and Jim see it too; and I tell you, I felt pretty good, for Tom Sawyer was always a hard person to git ahead of. Jim slapped his leg and says:

"I tell *you!* dat's smart, dat's right down smart. Ain't no use, Mars Tom; he got you *dis* time, sho!" He slapped his leg again, and says, "My *lan!*, but it was smart one!"

I never felt so good in my life; and yet *I* didn't know I was saying anything much till it was out. I was just mooning along, perfectly careless, and not expecting anything was going to happen, and never *thinking* of such a thing at all, when, all of a sudden, out it come. Why, it was just as much a surprise to me as it was to any of them. It was just the same way it is when a person is munching along on a hunk of corn-pone, and not thinking about anything, and all of a sudden bites into a di'- mond. Now all that *he* knows first off is that it's some kind of gravel he's bit into; but he don't find out it's a di'mond till he gits it out and brushes off the sand and crumbs and one thing or another, and has a look at it, and then he's surprised and glad—yes, and proud too; though when you' come to look the thing straight in the eye, he ain't entitled to as much credit as he would 'a' been if he'd been *hunting* di'monds. You can see the difference easy if you think it over. You see, an accident, that way, ain't fairly as big a thing as a thing that's done a-purpose. Anybody could find that di'mond in that corn-pone; but mind you, it's got to be somebody that's got *that kind of a corn-pone*. That's where that feller's credit comes in, you see; and that's where mine comes in. I don't claim no great things—I don't reckon I could 'a' done it again—but I done it that time; that's all I claim. And I hadn't no more idea I could do such a thing, and warn't any more thinking about it or trying to, than you be this minute. Why, I was just as cam, a body couldn't be any cammer, and yet, all of a sudden, out it come. I've often thought of that time, and I can remember just the way everything looked, same as if it was only last week. I can see it all: beautiful rolling country with woods and fields and lakes for hundreds and hundreds of miles all around, and towns and villages scattered everywheres under us, here and there and yonder; and the professor mooning over a chart on his little table, and Tom's cap flopping in the rigging where it was hung up to dry. And one thing in particular was a bird right alongside, not ten foot off, going our way and trying to keep up, but losing ground all the time; and a railroad train doing the same thing down there, sliding among the trees and farms, and pouring out a long cloud of black smoke and now and then a little puff of white; and when the white was gone so long you had almost forgot it, you would hear a little faint toot, and that was the whistle. And we left the bird and the train both behind, 'way behind, and done it easy too.

But Tom he was huffy, and said me and Jim was a couple of ignorant blatherskites, and then he says:

"Suppose there's a brown calf and a big brown dog, and an artist is making a picture of them. What is the *main* thing that that artist has got to do? He has got to paint them so you can tell them apart the minute you look at them, hain't he? Of course. Well, then, do you want him to go and paint *both* of them brown? Certainly you don't. He paints one of them blue, and then you can't make no mistake. It's just the same with the maps. That's why they make every State a different color; it ain't to deceive you, it's to keep you from deceiving yourself."

But I couldn't see no argument about that, and neither could Jim. Jim shook his head, and says:

"Why, Mars Tom, if you knowed what chuckleheads dem painters is, you'd wait a long time before you'd fetch one er *dem* in to back up a fac'. I's gwine to tell you, den you kin see for youself. I see one of 'em a-paintin' away, one day, down in ole Hank Wilson's back lot, en I went down to see, en he was paintin' dat old brindle cow wid de near horn gone—you knows de one I means. En I ast him what he's paintin' her for, en he say when he git her painted, de picture's wuth a hundred dollars. Mars Tom, he could a got de cow fer fifteen, en I *tole* him so. Well, sah, if you'll b'lieve me, he jes' shuck his head, dat painter *did*, en went on a-dobbin'. Bless you, Mars Tom, *dey* don't know nothin'."

Tom he lost his temper. I notice a person 'most always does that's got laid out in an argument. He told us to shut up, and maybe we'd feel better. Then he see a town clock away off down yonder, and he took up the glass and looked at it, and then looked at his silver turnip, and then at the clock, and then at the turnip again, and says:

"That's funny! That clock's near about an hour fast."

So he put up his turnip. Then he see another clock, and took a look, and it was an hour fast too. That puzzled him.

"That's a mighty curious thing," he says. "I don't understand it."

Then he took the glass and hunted up another clock, and sure enough it was an hour fast too. Then his eyes began to spread and his breath to come out kinder gaspy like, and he says:

"Ger-reat Scott, it's the *longitude!*"

I says, considerable scared:

"Well, what's been and gone and happened now?"

"Why, the thing that's happened is that this old bladder has slid over Illinois and Indiana and Ohio like nothing, and this is the east end of Pennsylvania or New York, or somewheres around there."

"Tom Sawyer, you don't mean it!"

"Yes, I do, and it's dead sure. We've covered about fifteen degrees of longitude since we left St. Louis yesterday afternoon, and them clocks are *right*. We've come close on to eight hundred miles."

I didn't believe it, but it made the cold streaks trickle down my back just the same. In my experience I knowed it wouldn't take much short of two weeks to do it down the Mississippi on a raft.

Jim was working his mind and studying. Pretty soon he says:

"Mars Tom, did you say dem clocks uz right?"

"Yes, they're right."

"Ain't yo' watch right, too?"

"She's right for St. Louis, but she's an hour wrong for here."

"Mars Tom, is you tryin' to let on dat de time ain't de *same* everywheres?"

"No, it ain't the same everywheres, by a long shot."

Jim looked distressed, and says:

"It grieves me to hear you talk like dat, Mars Tom; I's right down ashamed to hear you talk like dat, arter de way you's been raised. Yassir, it'd break yo' Aunt Polly's heart to hear you."

Tom was astonished. He looked Jim over, wondering, and didn't say nothing, and Jim went on:

"Mars Tom, who put de people out yonder in St. Louis? De Lord done it. Who put de people here whar we is? De Lord done it. Ain' dey bofe his children? 'Cose dey is. *Well*, den! is he gwine to *scriminate* 'twixt 'em?"

"'Scriminate! I never heard such ignorance. There ain't no discriminating about it. When he makes you and some more of his children black, and makes the rest of us white, what do you call that?"

Jim see the p'int. He was stuck. He couldn't answer. Tom says:

"He does discriminate, you see, when he wants to; but this case *here* ain't no discrimination of his, it's man's. The Lord made the day, and he made the night, but he didn't invent the hours, and he didn't distribute them around. Man did that."

"Mars Tom, is dat so? Man done it?"

"Certainly."

"Who tole him he could?"

"Nobody. He never asked."

Jim studied a minute, and says:

"Well, dat do beat me. I wouldn't 'a' tuck no sich resk. But some people ain't scared o' nothin'. Dey bangs right ahead; *dey* don't care what happens. So den dey's allays an hour's diff'unce everywhah, Mars Tom?"

"An hour? No! It's four minutes difference for every degree of longitude, you know. Fifteen of 'em's an hour, thirty of 'em's two hours, and so on. When it's one o'clock Tuesday morning in England, it's eight o'clock the night before in New York."

Jim moved a little away along the locker, and you could see he was insulted. He kept shaking his head and muttering, and so I slid along to him and patted him on the leg, and petted him up, and got him over the worst of his feelings, and then he says:

"Mars Tom talkin' sich talk as dat! Choosday in one place en Monday in t' other, bofe in the same day! Huck, dis ain't no place to joke—up here whah we is. Two days in one day! How you gwine to got two days inter one day? Can't git two hours inter one hour, kin you? Can't git two darkies inter one darky skin, kin you? Can't git two gallons of whisky inter a one-gallon jug, kin you? No, sir, 'twould strain de jug. Yes, en even den you couldn't, *I* don't believe. Why, looky here, Huck, s'posen de Choosday was New Year's—now den! is you gwine to tell me it's dis year in one place en las' year in t' other, bofe in de identical same minute? It's de beatenest rubbage! I can't stan' it—I can't stan' to hear tell 'bout it." Then he begun to shiver and turn gray, and Tom says:

"*Now* what's the matter? What's the trouble?"

Jim could hardly speak, but he says:

"Mars Tom, you ain't jokin', en it's so?"

"No, I'm not, and it *is* so."

Jim shivered again, and says:

"Den dat Monday could be de las' day, en dey wouldn't *be* no las' day in England, en de dead wouldn't be called. We mustn't go over dah. Mars Tom. Please git him to turn back; I wants to be whah—"

All of a sudden we see something, and all jumped up, and forgot everything and begun to gaze. Tom says:

"Ain't that the—" He catched his breath, then says: "It *is*, sure as you live! It's the ocean!"

That made me and Jim catch our breath, too. Then we all stood petrified but happy, for none of us had ever seen an ocean, or ever expected to. Tom kept muttering:

"Atlantic Ocean—Atlantic. Land, don't it sound great! And that's *it*—and *we* are looking at it—we! Why, it's just too splendid to believe!"

Then we see a big bank of black smoke; and when we got nearer, it was a city—and a monster she was, too, with a thick fringe of ships around one edge; and we wondered if it was New York, and begun to jaw and dispute about it, and, first we knowed, it slid from under us and went flying behind, and here we was, out over the very ocean itself, and going like a cyclone. Then we woke up, I tell you!

We made a break aft and raised a wail, and begun to beg the professor to turn back and land us, but he jerked out his pistol and motioned us back, and we went, but nobody will ever know how bad we felt.

The land was gone, all but a little streak, like a snake, away off on the edge of the water, and down under us was just ocean, ocean, ocean—millions of miles of it, heaving and pitching and squirming, and white sprays blowing from the wavetops, and only a few ships in sight, wallowing around and laying over, first on one side and then on t' other, and sticking their bows under and then their sterns; and before long there warn't no ships at all, and we had the sky and the whole ocean all to ourselves, and the roomiest place I ever see and the lonesomest.

CHAPTER FOUR

AND IT GOT lonesomer and lonesomer. There was the big sky up there, empty and awful deep; and the ocean down there, without a thing on it but just the waves. All around us was a ring, where the sky and the water come together; yes, a monstrous big ring it was, and we right in the dead center of it—plumb in the center. We was racing along like a prairie fire, but it never made any difference, we couldn't seem to git past that center no way. I couldn't see that we ever gained an inch on that ring. It made a body feel creepy, it was so curious and unaccountable.

Well, everything was so awful still that we got to talking in a very low voice, and kept on getting creepier and lonesomer and less and less talky, till at last the talk ran dry altogether, and we just set there and "thunk," as Jim calls it, and never said a word the longest time.

The professor never stirred till the sun was overhead, then he stood up and put a kind of triangle to his eye, and Tom said it was a sextant and he was taking the sun to see whereabouts the balloon was. Then he ciphered a little and looked in a book, and then he begun to carry on again. He said lots of wild things, and amongst others he said he would keep up this hundred-mile gait till the middle of tomorrow afternoon, and then he'd land in London.

We said we would be humbly thankful.

He was turning away, but he whirled round when we said that, and give us a long look of his blackest kind—one of the maliciousest and suspiciousest looks I ever see. Then he says:

"You want to leave me. Don't try to deny it."

We didn't know what to say, so we held in and didn't say nothing at all.

He went aft and set down, but he couldn't seem to git that thing out of his mind. Every now and then he would rip out something about it, and try to make us answer him, but we dasn't.

It got lonesomer and lonesomer right along, and it did seem to me I couldn't stand it. It was still worse when night begun to come on. By and by Tom pinched me and whispers:

"Look!"

"You want to leave me. Don't try to deny it."

I took a glance aft, and see the professor taking a whet out of a bottle. I didn't like the looks of that. By and by he took another drink, and pretty soon he begun to sing. It was dark now, and getting black and stormy. He went on singing, wilder and wilder, and the thunder begun to mutter, and the wind to wheeze and moan amongst the ropes, and altogether it was awful. It got so black we couldn't see him any more, and wished we couldn't hear him, but we could. Then he got still; but he warn't still ten minutes till we got suspicious, and wished he would start up his noise again, so we could tell where he was. By and by there was a flash of lightning, and we see him start to get up, but he staggered and fell down. We heard him scream out in the dark:

"They don't want to go to England. All right, I'll change the course. They want to leave me. I know they do. Well, they shall—and *now!*"

I 'most died when he said that. Then he was still again—still so long I couldn't bear it, and it did seem to me the lightning wouldn't *ever* come again. But at last there was a blessed flash, and there he was, on his hands and knees, crawling, and

The Professor said he would keep up this hundred-mile gait till tomorrow afternoon, and then he'd land in London.

not four feet from us. My, but his eyes was terrible! He made a lunge for Tom, and says, "Overboard *you* go!" but it was already pitch-dark again, and I couldn't see whether he got him or not, and Tom didn't make a sound.

There was another long, horrible wait; then there was a flash, and I see Tom's head sink down outside the boat and disappear. He was on the rope-ladder that dangled down in the air from the gunnel. The professor let off a shout and jumped for him, and straight off it was pitch-dark again, and Jim groaned out, "Po' Mars Tom, he's a goner!" and made a jump for the professor, but the professor warn't there.

Then we heard a couple of terrible screams, and then another not so loud, and then another that was 'way below, and you could only *just* hear it, and I heard Jim say, "Po' Mars Tom!"

Then it was awful still, and I reckon a person could 'a' counted four thousand before the next flash come. When it come I see Jim on his knees, with his arms on the locker and his face buried in them, and he was crying. Before I could look over the edge it was all dark again, and I was glad, because I didn't want to see. But when the next flash come, I was watching, and down there I see somebody a-swinging in the wind on the ladder, and it was Tom!

"Come up!" I shouts; "come up, Tom!"

His voice was so weak, and the wind roared so, I couldn't make out what he said, but I thought he asked was the professor up there. I shouts:

"No, he's down in the ocean! Come up! Can we help you?"

Of course, all this in the dark.

"Huck, who is you hollerin' at?"

"I'm hollerin' at Tom."

"Oh, Huck, how kin you act so, when you know po' Mars Tom's—"

Then he let off an awful scream, and flung his head and his arms back and let off another one, because there was a white glare just then, and he had raised up his face just in time to see Tom's, as white as snow, rise above the gunnel and look him right in the eye. He thought it was Tom's ghost, you see.

Tom clumb aboard, and when Jim found it *was* him, and not his ghost, he hugged him, and called him all sorts of loving names, and carried on like he was gone crazy, he was so glad. Says I:

"What did you wait for, Tom? Why didn't you come up at first?"

"I dasn't, Huck. I knowed somebody plunged down past me, but I didn't know who it was in the dark. It could 'a' been you, it could 'a' been Jim."

That was the way with Tom Sawyer—always sound. He warn't coming up till he knowed where the professor was.

The storm let go about this time with all its might; and it was dreadful the way the thunder boomed and tore, and the lightning glared out, and the wind sung and screamed in the rigging, and the rain come down. One second you couldn't see your hand before you, and the next you could count the threads in your coat-sleeve, and see a whole wide desert of waves pitching and tossing through a kind of veil of rain. A storm like that is the loveliest thing there is, but it ain't at its best when you are up in the sky and lost, and it's wet and lonesome, and there's just been a death in the family.

We set there huddled up in the bow, and talked low about the poor professor; and everybody was sorry for him, and sorry the world had made fun of him and treated him so harsh, when he was doing the best he could, and hadn't a friend nor nobody to encourage him and keep him from brooding his mind away and going deranged. There was plenty of clothes and blankets and everything at the other end, but we thought we'd ruther take the rain than go meddling back there.

CHAPTER FIVE

WE TRIED TO make some plans, but we couldn't come to no agreement. Me and Jim was for turning around and going back home, but Tom allowed that by the time daylight come, so we could see our way, we would be so far toward England that we might as well go there, and come back in a ship, and have the glory of saying we done it.

About midnight the storm quit and the moon come out and lit up the ocean, and we begun to feel comfortable and drowsy; so we stretched out on the lockers and went to sleep, and never woke up again till sun-up. The sea was sparkling like di'monds, and it was nice weather, and pretty soon our things was all dry again.

We went aft to find some breakfast, and the first thing we noticed was that there was a dim light burning in a compass back there under a hood. Then Tom was disturbed. He says:

"You know what that means, easy enough. It means that somebody has got to stay on watch and steer this thing the same as he would a ship, or she'll wander around and go wherever the wind wants her to."

"Well," I says, "what's she been doing since—er—since we had the accident?"

"Wandering," he says, kinder troubled—"wandering, without any doubt. She's in a wind, now, that's blowing her south of east. We don't know how long that's been going on, either."

So then he p'inted her east, and said he would hold her there till we rousted out the breakfast. The professor had laid in everything a body could want; he couldn't 'a' been better fixed. There wasn't no milk for the coffee, but there was water, and everything else you could want, and a charcoal stove and the fixings for it, and pipes and cigars and matches; and wine and liquor, which warn't in our line; and books, and maps, and charts, and an accordion; and furs, and blankets, and no end of rubbish, like brass beads and brass jewelry, which Tom said was a sure sign that he had an idea of visiting among savages. There was money, too. Yes, the professor was well enough fixed.

After breakfast Tom learned me and Jim how to steer, and divided us all up into four-hour watches, turn and turn about; and when his watch was out I took his place, and he got out the professor's papers and pens and wrote a letter home to his Aunt Polly, telling her everything that had happened to us, and dated it "*In the Welkin, approaching England,*" and folded it together and stuck it fast with a red wafer, and directed it, and wrote above the direction, in big writing, "*From Tom Sawyer, the Erronort,*" and said it would stump old Nat Parsons, the post-master, when it come along in the mail. I says:

"Tom Sawyer, this ain't no welkin; it's a balloon."

"Well, now, who *said* it was a welkin, smarty?"

"You've wrote it on the letter, anyway."

"What of it? That don't mean that the balloon's the welkin."

"Oh, I thought it did. Well, then, what is a welkin?"

I see in a minute he was stuck. He raked and scraped around in his mind, but he couldn't find nothing, so he had to say:

"I don't know, and nobody don't know. It's just a word, and it's a mighty good word, too. There ain't many that lays over it. I don't believe there's *any* that does."

"Shucks!" I says. "But what does it *mean?*—that's the p'int."

"I don't know what it means, I tell you. It's a word that people uses for—for— well, it's ornamental. They don't put ruffles on a shirt to keep a person warm, do they?"

"Course they don't."

"But they put them *on,* don't they?"

"Yes."

"All right, then; that letter I wrote is a shirt, and the welkin's the ruffle on it."

I judged that that would gravel Jim, and it did.

"Now, Mars Tom, it ain't no use to talk like dat; en, moreover, it's sinful. You knows a letter ain't no shirt, en dey ain't no ruffles on it, nuther. Dey ain't no place to put 'em on; you can't put 'em on, and dey wouldn't stay ef you did."

"Oh, *do* shut up, and wait till something's started that you know something about."

"Why, Mars Tom, sholy you can't mean to say I don't know about shirts, when, goodness knows, I's toted home de washin' ever sence—"

"I tell you, this hasn't got anything to *do* with shirts. I only—"

"Why, Mars Tom, you said yo'self dat a letter—"

"Do you want to drive me crazy? Keep still. I only used it as a metaphor."

That word kinder bricked us up for a minute. Then Jim says—rather timid, because he see Tom was getting pretty tetchy:

"Mars Tom, what is a metaphor?"

"A metaphor's a—well, it's a—a—a metaphor's an illustration." He see *that* didn't git home, so he tried again. "When I say birds of a feather flocks together, it's a metaphorical way of saying—"

"But dey *don't*, Mars Tom. No, sir, 'deed dey don't. Dey ain't no feathers dat's more alike den a bluebird en a jaybird, but ef you waits till you catches *dem* birds together, you'll—"

"Oh, give us a rest! You can't get the simplest little thing through your thick skull. Now don't bother me any more."

Jim was satisfied to stop. He was dreadful pleased with himself for catching Tom out. The minute Tom begun to talk about birds I judged he was a goner, because Jim knowed more about birds than both of us put together. You see, he had killed hundreds and hundreds of them, and that's the way to find out about birds. That's the way people does that writes books about birds, and loves them so that they'll go hungry and tired and take any amount of trouble to find a new bird and kill it. Their name is ornithologers, and I could have been an ornithologer myself, because I always loved birds and creatures; and I started out to learn how to be one, and I see a bird setting on a limb of a high tree, singing with its head tilted back and its mouth open, and before I thought I fired, and his song stopped and he fell straight down from the limb, all limp like a rag, and I run and picked him up and he was dead, and his body was warm in my hand, and his head rolled about this way and that, like his neck was broke, and there was a little white skin over his eyes, and one little drop of blood on the side of his head; and, laws! I couldn't see nothing more for the tears; and I hain't never murdered no creature since that warn't doing me no harm, and I ain't going to.

But I was aggravated about that welkin. I wanted to know. I got the subject up again, and then Tom explained, the best he could. He said when a person made a big speech the newspapers said the shouts of the people made the welkin ring. He said they always said that, but none of them ever told what it was, so he allowed it just meant outdoors and up high. Well, that seemed sensible enough, so I was satisfied, and said so. That pleased Tom and put him in a good humor again, and he says:

"Well, it's all right, then, and we'll let bygones be bygones. I don't know for certain what a welkin is, but when we land in London we'll make it ring, anyway, and don't you forget it."

He said an erronort was a person who sailed around in balloons; and said it was a mighty sight finer to be Tom Sawyer the Erronort than to be Tom Sawyer the Traveler, and we would be heard of all round the world, if we pulled through all right, and so he wouldn't give shucks to be a traveler now.

Toward the middle of the afternoon we got everything ready to land, and we felt pretty good, too, and proud, and we kept watching with the glasses, like

Columbus discovering America. But we couldn't see nothing but ocean. The afternoon wasted out and the sun shut down, and still there warn't no land anywheres. We wondered what was the matter, but reckoned it would come out all right, so we went on steering east, but went up on a higher level so we wouldn't hit any steeples or mountains in the dark.

It was my watch till midnight, and then it was Jim's; but Tom stayed up, because he said ship-captains done that when they was making the land, and didn't stand no regular watch.

Well, when daylight come, Jim give a shout, and we jumped up and looked over, and there was the land sure enough—land all around, as far as you could see, and perfectly level and yaller. We didn't know how long we'd been over it. There warn't no trees, nor hills, nor rocks, nor towns, and Tom and Jim had took it for the sea. They took it for the sea in a dead cam; but we was so high up, anyway, that if it had been the sea and rough, it would 'a' looked smooth, all the same, in the night, that way.

We was all in a powerful excitement now, and grabbed the glasses and hunted everywheres for London, but couldn't find hair nor hide of it, nor any other settlement—nor any sign of a lake or a river, either. Tom was clean beat. He said it warn't his notion of England; he thought England looked like America, and always had that idea. So he said we better have breakfast, and then drop down and inquire the quickest way to London. We cut the breakfast pretty short, we was so impatient. As we slanted along down, the weather began to moderate, and pretty soon we

"Run! Run fo' yo' life!"

shed our furs. But it kept *on* moderating, and in a precious little while it was 'most too moderate. We was close down, now, and just blistering!

We settled down to within thirty foot of the land—that is, it was land if sand is land; for this wasn't anything but pure sand. Tom and me clumb down the ladder and took a run to stretch our legs, and it felt amazing good—that is, the stretching did, but the sand scorched our feet like hot embers. Next, we see somebody coming, and started to meet him; but we heard Jim shout, and looked around and he was fairly dancing, and making signs, and yelling. We couldn't make out what he said, but we was scared anyway, and begun to heel it back to the balloon. When we got close enough, we understood the words, and they made me sick:

"Run! Run fo' yo' life! Hit's a lion; I kin see him thoo de glass! Run, boys; do please heel it de bes' you kin. He's bu'sted outen de menagerie, en dey ain't nobody to stop him!"

It made Tom fly, but it took the stiffening all out of my legs. I could only just gasp along the way you do in a dream when there's a ghost gaining on you.

Tom got to the ladder and shinned up it a piece and waited for me; and as soon as I got a foothold on it he shouted to Jim to soar away. But Jim had clean lost his head, and said he had forgot how. So Tom shinned along up and told me to follow; but the lion was arriving, fetching a most ghastly roar with every lope, and my legs shook so I dasn't try to take one of them out of the rounds for fear the other one would give way under me.

But Tom was aboard by this time, and he started the balloon up a little, and stopped it again as soon as the end of the ladder was ten or twelve feet above ground. And there was the lion, a-ripping around under me, and roaring and springing up in the air at the ladder, and only missing it about a quarter of an inch, it seemed to me. It was delicious to be out of his reach, perfectly delicious, and made me feel good and thankful all up one side; but I was hanging there helpless and couldn't climb, and that made me feel perfectly wretched and miserable all down the other. It is most seldom that a person feels so mixed, like that; and it is not to be recommended, either.

Tom asked me what he'd better do, but I didn't know. He asked me if I could hold on whilst he sailed away to a safe place and left the lion behind. I said I could if he didn't go no higher than he was now; but if he went higher I would lose my head and fall, sure. So he said, "Take a good grip," and he started.

"Don't go so fast," I shouted. "It makes my head swim."

He had started like a lightning express. He slowed down, and we glided over the sand slower, but still in a kind of sickening way; for it *is* uncomfortable to see things sliding and gliding under you like that, and not a sound.

But pretty soon there was plenty of sound, for the lion was catching up. His

They were jumping up at the ladder and snapping and snarling at each other.

noise fetched others. You could see them coming on the lope from every direction, and pretty soon there was a couple of dozen of them under me, jumping up at the ladder and snarling and snapping at each other; and so we went skimming along over the sand, and these fellers doing what they could to help us to not forget the occasion; and then some other beasts come, without an invite, and they started a regular riot down there. We see this plan was a mistake.

We couldn't ever git away from them at this gait, and I couldn't hold on forever. So Tom took a think, and struck another idea. That was, to kill a lion with the pepper-box revolver, and then sail away while the others stopped to fight over the carcass. So he stopped the balloon still, and done it, and then we sailed off while the fuss was going on, and come down a quarter of a mile off, and they helped me aboard; but by the time we was out of reach again, that gang was on hand once more. And when they see we was really gone and they couldn't get us, they sat down on their hams and looked up at us so kind of disappointed that it was as much as a person could do not to see *their* side of the matter.

CHAPTER SIX

I WAS SO weak that the only thing I wanted was a chance to lay down, so I made straight for my locker-bunk, and stretched myself out there. But a body couldn't get back his strength in no such oven as that, so Tom give the command to soar, and Jim started her aloft.

We had to go up a mile before we struck comfortable weather where it was breezy and pleasant and just right, and pretty soon I was all straight again. Tom had been setting quiet and thinking; but now he jumps up and says:

"I bet you a thousand to one I know where we are. We're in the Great Sahara, as sure as guns!"

He was so excited he couldn't hold still; but I wasn't. I says:

"Well, then, where's the Great Sahara? In England or in Scotland?"

"'T ain't in either, it's in Africa."

Jim's eyes bugged out, and he begun to stare down with no end of interest, because that was where his originals come from; but I didn't more than half believe it. I couldn't, you know; it seemed too awful far away for us to have traveled.

But Tom was full of his discovery, as he called it, and said the lions and the sand meant the Great Desert, sure. He said he could 'a' found out, before we sighted land, that we was crowding the land somewheres, if he had thought of one thing; and when we asked him what, he said:

"These clocks. They're chronometers. You always read about them in sea voyages. One of them is keeping Grinnage time, and the other is keeping St. Louis time, like my watch. When we left St. Louis it was four in the afternoon by my watch and this clock, and it was ten at night by this Grinnage clock. Well, at this time of the year the sun sets about seven o'clock. Now I noticed the time yesterday evening when the sun went down, and it was half-past five o'clock by the Grinnage clock, and half-past eleven A.M. by my watch and the other clock. You see, the sun rose and set by my watch in St. Louis, and the Grinnage clock was six hours fast; but we've come so far east that it comes within less than half an hour of setting by the Grinnage clock, now, and I'm away out—more than four hours and a half out. You see, that meant that we was closing up on the longitude of Ireland, and would strike it before long if we was p'inted right—which we wasn't. No, sir, we've been a-wandering—wandering 'way down south of east, and it's my opinion we are in Africa. Look at this map. You see how the shoulder of Africa sticks out to the west. Think how fast we've traveled; if we had gone straight east we would be long past England by this time. You watch for noon, all of you, and we'll stand up, and when we can't cast a shadow we'll find that this Grinnage clock is coming mighty close to marking twelve. Yes, sir, I think we're in Africa; and it's just bully."

Jim was gazing down with the glass. He shook his head and says:

"Mars Tom, I reckon dey's a mistake som'er's. I hain't seen no darkies yit."

"That's nothing; they don't live in the desert. What is that, 'way off yonder? Gimme a glass."

He took a long look, and said it was like a black string stretched across the sand, but he couldn't guess what it was.

"Well," I says, "I reckon maybe you've got a chance, now, to find out where-abouts this balloon is, because as like as not that is one of these lines here, that's on the map, that you call meridians of longitude, and we can drop down and look at its number, and—"

"Oh, shucks, Huck Finn, I never see such a lunkhead as you. Did you s'pose there's meridians of longitude on the *earth?*"

"Tom Sawyer, they're set down on the map, and you know it perfectly well, and here they are, and you can see for yourself."

"Of course they're on the map, but that's nothing; there ain't any on the *ground.*"

"Tom, do you know that to be so?"

"Certainly I do."

"Well, then, that map's a liar again. I never see such a liar as that map."

He fired up at that, and I was ready for him, and Jim was warming his opinion, too, and next minute we'd 'a' broke loose on another argument, if Tom hadn't dropped the glass and begun to clap his hands like a maniac and sing out—

"Camels!—Camels!"

So I grabbed a glass, and Jim, too, and took a look, but I was disappointed, and says—

"Camels your granny, they're spiders."

"Spiders in a desert, you shad? Spiders walking in a procession? You don't ever reflect, Huck Finn, and I reckon you really haven't got anything to reflect *with.* Don't you know we're as much as a mile up in the air, and that that string of crawlers is two or three miles away? Spiders, good land! Spiders as big as a cow?

We swooped down, now, all of a sudden, and stopped about a hundred yards over their heads.

Perhaps you'd like to go down and milk one of 'em. But they're camels, just the same. It's a caravan, that's what it is, and it's a mile long."

"Well, then, le' 's go down and look at it. I don't believe in it, and ain't going to till I see it and know it."

"All right," he says, and give the command: "Lower away."

As we come slanting down into the hot weather, we could see that it was camels, sure enough, plodding along, an everlasting string of them, with bales strapped to them, and several hundred men in long white robes, and a thing like a shawl bound over their heads and hanging down with tassels and fringes; and some of the men had long guns and some hadn't, and some was riding and some was walking. And the weather—well, it was just roasting. And how slow they did creep along! We swooped down, now, all of a sudden, and stopped about a hundred yards over their heads.

The men all set up a yell, and some of them fell flat on their stomachs, some begun to fire their guns at us, and the rest broke and scampered every which way, and so did the camels.

We see that we was making trouble, so we went up again about a mile, to the cool weather, and watched them from there. It took them an hour to get together and form the procession again, then they started along, but we could see by the glasses that they wasn't paying much attention to anything but us. We poked along, looking down at them with the glasses, and by and by we see a big sand mound, and something like people the other side of it, and there was something like a man laying on top of the mound, that raised his head up every now and then, and seemed to be watching the caravan or us, we didn't know which. As the caravan got nearer, he sneaked down on the other side and rushed to the other men and horses—for that is what they was—and we see them mount in a hurry; and next, here they come, like a house afire, some with lances and some with long guns, and all of them yelling the best they could.

They come a-tearing down onto the caravan, and the next minute both sides crashed together and was all mixed up, and there was such another popping of guns as you never heard, and the air got so full of smoke you could only catch glimpses of them struggling together. There must 'a' been six hundred men in that battle, and it was terrible to see. Then they broke up into gangs and groups, fighting tooth and nail, and scurrying and scampering around, and laying into each other like everything; and whenever the smoke cleared a little you could see dead and wounded people and camels scattered far and wide and all about, and camels racing off in every direction.

At last the robbers see they couldn't win, so their chief sounded a signal, and all that was left of them broke away and went scampering across the plain. The last man to go snatched up a child and carried it off in front of him on his horse, and a woman run screaming and begging after him, and followed him away off across the plain till she was separated a long ways from her people; but it warn't no use, and she had to give it up, and we see her sink down on the sand and cover her face with her hands. Then Tom took the helium, and started for that yahoo, and we come a-whizzing down and made a swoop, and knocked him out of the saddle, child and all; and he was jarred considerable, but the child wasn't hurt, but laid there working its hands and legs in the air like a tumble-bug that's on its back and can't turn over. The man went staggering off to overtake his horse, and didn't know what had hit him, for we was three or four hundred yards up in the air by this time.

We judged the woman would go and get the child, now; but she didn't. We could see her, through the glass, still setting there, with her head bowed down on her knees; so of course she hadn't seen the performance, and thought her child was clean gone with the man. She was nearly a half a mile from her people, so we thought we might go down to the child, which was about a quarter of a mile beyond her, and snake it to her before the caravan people could git to us to do us any harm; and besides, we reckoned they had enough business on their hands for one while, anyway, with the wounded. We thought we'd chance it, and we did. We swooped down and stopped, and Jim shinned down the ladder and fetched up the kid, which was a nice fat little thing, and in a noble good humor, too, considering it was just out of a battle and been tumbled off of a horse; and then we started for the mother, and stopped back of her and tolerable near by, and Jim slipped down and crept up easy, and when he was close back of her the child goo-goo'd, the way a child does, and she heard it, and whirled and

The last man to go snatched up a child and carried it off in front of him on his horse.

fetched a shriek of joy, and made a jump for the kid and snatched it and hugged it, and dropped it and bugged Jim, and then snatched off a gold chain and hung it around Jim's neck, and hugged him again, and jerked up the child again, a-sobbing and glorifying all the time, and Jim he shoved for the ladder and up it, and in a minute we was back up in the sky and the woman was staring up, with the back of her head between her shoulders and the child with its arms locked around her neck. And

We come a-whizzing down and made a swoop, and knocked him out of the saddle, child and all.

there she stood, as long as we was in sight a-sailing away in the sky.

CHAPTER SEVEN

"NOON!" SAYS TOM, and so it was. His shadder was just a blot around his feet. We looked, and the Grinnage clock was so close to twelve the difference didn't amount to nothing. So Tom said London was right north of us or right south of us, one or t'other, and he reckoned by the weather and the sand and the camels it was north; and a good many miles north, too; as many as from New York to the city of Mexico, he guessed.

Jim said he reckoned a balloon was a good deal the fastest thing in the world, unless it might be some kinds of birds—a wild pigeon, maybe, or a railroad.

But Tom said he had read about railroads in England going nearly a hundred miles an hour for a little ways, and there never was a bird in the world that could do that—except one, and that was a flea.

"A flea? Why, Mars Tom, in de fust place he ain't a bird, strickly speakin'—"

"He ain't a bird, eh? Well, then, what is he?"

"I don't rightly know, Mars Tom, but I speck he's only jist a' animal. No, I reckon dat won't do, nuther, he ain't big enough for a' animal. He mus' be a bug. Yassir, dat's what he is, he's a bug."

"I bet he ain't, but let it go. What's your second place?"

"Well, in de second place, birds is creturs dat goes a long ways, but a flea don't."

"He don't, don't he? Come, now, what *is* a long distance, if you know?"

"Why, it's miles, and lots of 'em—anybody knows dat."

"Can't a man walk miles?"

"Yassir, he kin."

"As many as a railroad?"

"Yassir, if you give him time."

"Can't a flea?"

"Well—I s'pose so—ef you gives him heaps of time."

"Now you begin to see, don't you, that *distance* ain't the thing to judge by, at all; it's the time it takes to go the distance *in* that *counts*, ain't it?"

"Well, hit do look sorter so, but I wouldn't 'a' blieved it, Mars Tom."

"It's a matter of *proportion*, that's what it is; and when you come to gauge a thing's speed by its size, where's your bird and your man and your railroad, alongside of a flea? The fastest man can't run more than about ten miles in an hour—not much over ten thousand times his own length. But all the books says any common ordinary third-class flea can jump a hundred and fifty times his own length; yes, and he can make five jumps a second too—seven hundred and fifty times his own length, in one little second—for he don't fool away any time stopping and starting—he does them both at the same time; you'll see, if you try to put your finger on him. Now that's a common, ordinary, third-class flea's gait; but you take an Eyetalian *first*-class, that's been the pet of the nobility all his life, and hasn't ever

"Where's your man now?"

knowed what want or sickness or
exposure was, and he can jump more
than three hundred times his own
length, and keep it up all day, five such
jumps every second, which is fifteen
hundred times his own length. Well,
suppose a man could go fifteen hundred times his own length in a second—say, a mile and a half. It's ninety
miles a minute; it's considerable more
than five thousand miles an hour.
Where's your man *now?*—yes, and
your bird, and your railroad, and your
balloon? Laws, they don't amount to
shucks longside of a flea. A flea is just
a comet b'iled down small."

"Where's your railroad?"

Jim was a good deal astonished,
and so was I. Jim said—

"Is dem figgers jist edjackly true, en no jokin' en no lies, Mars Tom?"

"Yes, they are; they're perfectly true."

"Well, den, honey, a body's got to respec' a flea. I ain't had no respec' for um
befo', sca'sely, but dey ain't no gittin' roun' it, dey do deserve it, dat's certain."

"Well, I bet they do. They've got ever so much more sense, and brains, and
brightness, in proportion to their size, than any other cretur in the world. A person
can learn them 'most anything, and they learn it quicker than any other cretur, too.
They've been learnt to haul little carriages in harness, and go this way and that way
and t'other way according to their orders; yes, and to march and drill like soldiers,
doing it as exact, according to orders, as soldiers does it. They've been learnt to do
all sorts of hard and troublesome things. S'pose you could cultivate a flea up to the
size of a man, and keep his natural smartness a-growing and a-growing right along
up, bigger and bigger, and keener and keener, in the same proportion—where'd the
human race be, do you reckon? That flea would be President of the United States,
and you couldn't any more prevent it than you can prevent lightning."

"My lan', Mars Tom, I never knowed dey was so much *to* de beas'. No, sir, I
never had no idea of it, and dat's de fac'."

"There's more to him, by a long sight, than there is to any other cretur, man or
beast, in proportion to size. He's the interestingest of them all. People have so
much to say about an ant's strength, and an elephant's, and a locomotive's. Shucks,
they don't begin with a flea. He can lift two or three hundred times his own weight.

"That flea would be President of the United States, and you couldn't prevent it."

And none of them can come anywhere near it. And moreover, he has got notions of his own, and is very particular, and you can't fool him; his instinct, or his judgment, or whatever it is, is perfectly sound and clear, and don't ever make a mistake. People think all humans are alike to a flea. It ain't so. There's folks that he won't go near, hungry or not hungry, and I'm one of them. I've never had one of them on me in my life."

"Mars Tom!"

"It's so; I ain't joking."

"Well, sah, I hain't ever heard de likes o' dat, befo'."

Jim couldn't believe it, and I couldn't; so we had to drop down to the sand and git a supply and see. Tom was right. They went for me and Jim by the thousand, but not a one of them lit on Tom. There warn't no explaining it, but there it was and there warn't no getting around it. He said it had always been just so, and he'd just as soon be where there was a million of them as not; they'd never touch him nor bother him.

We went up to the cold weather to freeze 'em out, and stayed a little spell, and then come back to the comfortable weather and went lazying along twenty or twenty-five miles an hour, the way we'd been doing for the last few hours. The reason was, that the longer we was in that solemn, peaceful desert, the more the hurry and fuss got kind of soothed down in us, and the more happier and contented and satisfied we got to feeling, and the more we got to liking the desert, and then lov-ing it. So we had cramped the speed down, as I was saying, and was having a most noble good lazy time, sometimes watching through the glasses, sometimes stretched out on the lockers reading, sometimes taking a nap.

It didn't seem like we was the same lot that was in such a state to find land and git ashore, but it was. But we had got over that—clean over it. We was used to the balloon, now, and not afraid any more, and didn't want to be anywheres else. Why, it seemed just like home; it 'most seemed as if I had been born and raised in it, and Jim and Tom said the same. And always I had had hateful people around me, a-nag-ging at me, and pestering of me, and scolding, and finding fault, and fussing and bothering, and sticking to me, and keeping after me, and making me do this, and making me do that and t'other, and always selecting out the things I didn't want to do, and then giving me Sam Hill because I shirked and done something else, and just aggravating the life out of a body all the time; but up here in the sky it was so still and sunshiny and lovely, and plenty to eat, and plenty of sleep, and strange things to see, and no nagging and no pestering, and no good people, and just holi-day all the time. Land, I warn't in no hurry to git out and buck at civilization again. Now, one of the worst things about civilization is, that anybody that gits a letter with trouble in it comes and tells you all about it and makes you feel bad, and the news-papers fetches you the troubles of everybody all over the world, and keeps you down-hearted and dismal 'most all the time, and it's such a heavy load for a person. I hate them newspapers; and I hate letters; and if I had my way I wouldn't allow nobody to load his troubles onto other folks he ain't acquainted with, on t'other side of the world, that way. Well, up in a balloon there ain't any of that, and it's the dar-lingest place there is.

We had supper, and that night was one of the prettiest nights I ever see. The moon made it just like daylight, only a heap softer; and once we see a lion stand-ing all alone by himself, just all alone on the earth, it seemed like, and his shadder laid on the sand by him like a puddle of ink. That's the kind of moonlight to have.

Mainly we laid on our backs and talked; we didn't want to go to sleep. Tom said we was right in the midst of the Arabian Nights, now. He said it was right along here that one of the cutest things in that book happened; so we looked down and watched while he told about it, because there ain't anything that is so interesting to look at as a place that a book has talked about. It was a tale about a camel-driver that had lost his camel, and he come along in the desert and met a man, and says—"Have you run across a stray camel today?" And the man says—

"Was he blind in his left eye?"

"Yes."

"Had he lost an upper front tooth?"

"Yes."

"Was his off hind leg lame?"

"Yes."

"Was he loaded with millet-seed on one side and honey on the other?"

"Yes, but you needn't go into no more details—that's the one, and I'm in a hurry. Where did you see him?"

"I hain't seen him at all," the man says.

"Hain't seen him at all? How can you describe him so close, then?"

"Because when a person knows how to use his eyes, everything has got a meaning to it; but most people's eyes ain't any good to them. I knowed a camel had been along, because I seen his track. I knowed he was lame in his off hind leg because he had favored that foot and trod light on it, and his track showed it. I knowed he was blind on his left side because he only nibbled the grass on the right side of the trail. I knowed he had lost an upper front tooth because where he bit into the sod his teeth-print showed it. The millet-seed sifted out on one side—the ants told me that; the honey leaked out on the other—the flies told me that. I know all about your camel, but I hain't seen him."

Jim says—

"Go on, Mars Tom, hit's a mighty good tale, and powerful interestin'."

"That's all," Tom says.

"*All?*" says Jim, astonished. "What 'come o' de camel?"

"I don't know."

"Mars Tom, don't de tale say?"

"No."

Jim puzzled a minute, then he says—

"Well! Ef dat ain't de beatenes' tale ever *I* struck. Jist gits to de place whah de intrust is gittin' red-hot, en down she breaks. Why, Mars Tom, dey ain't no *sense* in a tale dat acts like dat. Hain't you got no *idea* whether de man got de camel back er not?"

"No, I haven't."

I see, myself, there warn't no sense in the tale, to chop square off, that way, before it come to anything, but I warn't going to say so, because I could see Tom was souring up pretty fast over the way it flatted out and the way Jim had popped onto the weak place in it, and I don't think it's fair for everybody to pile onto a feller when he's down. But Tom he whirls on me and says—

"What do *you* think of the tale?"

Of course, then, I had to come out and make a clean breast and say it did seem to me, too, same as it did to Jim, that as long as the tale stopped square in the middle and never got to no place, it really warn't worth the trouble of telling.

Tom's chin dropped on his breast, and 'stead of being mad, as I reckoned he'd be, to hear me scoff at his tale that way, he seemed to be only sad; and he says—

"Some people can see, and some can't—just as that man said. Let alone a camel, if a cyclone had gone by, *you* duffers wouldn't 'a' noticed the track."

I don't know what he meant by that, and he didn't say; it was just one of his irrulevances, I reckon—he was full of them, sometimes, when he was in a close place and couldn't see no other way out—but I didn't mind. We'd spotted the soft place in that tale sharp enough, he couldn't git away from that little fact. It graveled him like the nation, too, I reckon, much as he tried not to let on.

CHAPTER EIGHT

WE HAD AN early breakfast in the morning, and set looking down on the desert, and the weather was ever so bammy and lovely, although we warn't high up. You have to come down lower and lower after sundown, in the desert, because it cools off so fast; and so, by the time it is getting towards dawn you are skimming along only a little ways above the sand.

We was watching the shadder of the balloon slide along the ground, and now and then gazing off across the desert to see if anything was stirring, and then down at the shadder again, when all of a sudden almost right under us we see a lot of men and camels laying scattered about, perfectly quiet, like they was asleep.

We shut off the power, and backed up and stood over them, and then we see that they was all dead. It give us the cold shivers. And it made us hush down, too, and talk low, like people at a funeral. We dropped down slow, and stopped, and me and Tom clumb down and went amongst them. There was men, and women, and children. They was dried by the sun and dark and shriveled and leathery, like the pictures of mummies you see in books. And yet they looked just as human, you wouldn't 'a' believed it; just like they was asleep.

Some of the people and animals was partly covered with sand, but most of them not, for the sand was thin there, and the bed was gravel, and hard. Most of the clothes had rotted away; and when you took hold of a rag, it tore with a touch, like spider-web. Tom reckoned they had been laying there for years.

Some of the men had rusty guns by them, some had swords on and had shawl belts with long silver-mounted pistols stuck in them. All the camels had their loads on, yet, but the packs had busted or rotted and spilt the freight out on the ground. We didn't reckon the swords was any good to the dead people any more, so we took one apiece, and some pistols. We took a small box, too, because it was so handsome and inlaid so fine; and then we wanted to bury the people; but there warn't no way to do it that we could think of, and nothing to do it with but sand, and that would blow away again, of course.

Then we mounted high and sailed away, and pretty soon that black spot on the sand was out of sight and we wouldn't ever see them poor people again in this world. We wondered, and reasoned, and tried to guess how they come to be there, and how it all happened to them, but we couldn't make it out. First we thought maybe they got lost, and wandered around and about till their food and water give out and they starved to death; but Tom said no wild animals nor vultures hadn't meddled with them, and so that guess wouldn't do. So at last we give it up, and judged we wouldn't think about it no more, because it made us low-spirited.

Then we opened the box, and it had gems and jewels in it, quite a pile, and some little veils of the kind the dead women had on, with fringes made out of curious gold money that we warn't acquainted with. We wondered if we better go and try to find them again and give it back; but Tom thought it over and said no, it was a country that was full of robbers, and they would come and steal it, and then the sin would be on us for putting the temptation in their way. So we went on; but I wished we had took all they had, so there wouldn't 'a' been no temptation at all left.

We had had two hours of that blazing weather down there, and was dreadful thirsty when we got aboard again. We went straight for the water, but it was spoiled and bitter, besides being pretty near hot enough to scald your mouth. We couldn't drink it. It was Mississippi river water, the best in the world, and we stirred up the mud in it to see if that would help, but no, the mud wasn't any better than the water.

Well, we hadn't been so very, very thirsty before, whilst we was interested in the lost people, but we was, now, and as soon as we found we couldn't have a drink, we was more than thirty-five times as thirsty as we was a quarter of a minute before. Why, in a little while we wanted to hold our mouths open and pant like a dog.

Tom said to keep a sharp lockout, all around, everywheres, because we'd got to find an oasis or there warn't no telling what would happen. So we done it. We kept the glasses gliding around all the time, till our arms got so tired we couldn't hold them any more. Two hours—three hours—just gazing and gazing, and nothing but sand, sand, *sand*, and you could see the quivering heat-shimmer playing over it. Dear, dear, a body don't know what real misery is till he is thirsty all the way through and is certain he ain't ever going to come to any water any more. At last I couldn't stand it to look around on them baking plains, I laid down on the locker, and give it up.

But by and by Tom raised a whoop, and there she was! A lake, wide and shiny, with pam-trees leaning over it asleep, and their shadders in the water just as soft and delicate as ever you see. I never see anything look so good. It was a long ways off, but that warn't anything to us; we just slapped on a hundred-mile gait, and cal-

We opened the box, and it had gems and jewels in it.

culated to be there in seven minutes; but she stayed the same old distance away, all the time; we couldn't seem to gain on her; yes, sir, just as far, and shiny, and like a dream; but we couldn't get no nearer; and at last, all of a sudden, she was gone!

Tom's eyes took a spread, and he says—

"Boys, it was a *myridge*!" Said it like he was glad. I didn't see nothing to be glad about. I says—

"May be. I don't care nothing about its name, the thing I want to know is, what's become of it?"

Jim was trembling all over, and so scared he couldn't speak, but he wanted to ask that question himself if he could 'a' done it. Tom says—

"What's *become* of it? Why, you see, yourself, it's gone."

"Yes, I know; but where's it gone *to?*"

He looked me over and says—

"Well, now, Huck Finn, where *would* it go to? Don't you know what a myridge is?"

"No, I don't. What is it?"

"It ain't anything but imagination. There ain't anything *to* it."

It warmed me up a little to hear him talk like that, and I says—

"What's the use you talking that kind of stuff, Tom Sawyer? Didn't I see the lake?"

"Yes—you think you did."

"I don't think nothing about it, I *did* see it."

"I tell you you *didn't* see it, either—because it warn't there to see."

It astonished Jim to hear him talk so, and he broke in and says, kind of pleading and distressed—"Mars' Tom, *please* don't say sich things in sich an awful time as dis. You ain't only reskin' yo' own self, but you's reskin' us—same way like Anna Nias en' Siffira. De lake *wuz* dah—I seen it jis' as plain as I sees you en Huck dis minute."

I says—"Why, he seen it himself! He was the very one that seen it first. *Now,* then!"

"Yes, Mars' Tom, hit's so—you can't deny it. We all seen it, en dat *prove* it was dah."

"Proves it! *How* does it prove it?"

"Same way it does in de courts en everywheres, Mars' Tom. One pusson might be drunk, or dreamy or suthin', en he could be mistaken; en two might, maybe; but I tell you, sah, when three sees a thing, drunk er sober, it's *so*. Dey ain't no gittin' aroun' dat, en you knows it, Mars' Tom."

"I don't know nothing of the kind. There used to be forty thousand million people that seen the sun move from one side of the sky to the other every day. Did that prove that the sun *done* it?"

"'Course it did. En besides, dey warn't no 'casion to prove it. A body 'at's got any sense ain't gwine to doubt it. Dah she is, now—a sailin' thoo de sky, like she allays done."

Tom turned on me, then, and says—

"What do *you* say—is the sun standing still?"

"Tom Sawyer, what's the use to ask such a jackass question? Anybody that ain't blind can see it don't stand still."

"Well," he says, "I'm lost in the sky with no company but a passel of low-down animals that don't know no more than the head boss of a university did three or four hundred years ago."

It warn't fair play, and I let him know it. I says—

"Throwin' mud ain't arguin', Tom Sawyer."

"Oh, my goodness, oh, my goodness gracious, dah's de lake ag'in!" yelled Jim, just then. "*Now*, Mars' Tom, what you gwine to say?"

Yes, sir, there was the lake again, away yonder across the desert, perfectly plain, trees and all, just the same as it was before. I says—

"I reckon you're satisfied now, Tom Sawyer."

But he says, perfectly ca'm—

"Yes, satisfied there ain't no lake there."

Jim says—

"*Don't* talk so, Mars' Tom—it sk'yers me to hear you. It's so hot, en you's so thirsty, dat you ain't in yo' right mine, Mars' Tom. Oh, but don't she look good! 'clah I doan' know how I's gwine to wait tell we gits dah, I's *so* thirsty."

"Well, you'll have to wait; and it won't do you no good, either, because there ain't no lake there, I tell you."

I says—

"Jim, don't you take your eye off of it, and I won't, either."

" 'Deed I won't; en bless you, honey, I couldn't ef I wanted to."

We went a-tearing along toward it, piling the miles behind us like nothing but never gaining an inch on it—and all of a sudden it was gone again! Jim staggered, and most fell down. When he got his breath he says, gasping like a fish—

"Mars Tom, hit's a *ghos'*, dat's what it is, en I hopes to goodness we ain't gwine to see it no mo'. Dey's *been* a lake, en suthin's happened, en de lake's dead, en we's seen its ghos'; we's seen it twiste, en dat's proof. De desert's ha'nted, it's ha'nted, sho'; oh, Mars Tom, le's git outen it; I'd ruther die den have de night ketch us in it ag'in en de ghos' er dat lake come a-mournin' aroun' us en we asleep en doan know de danger we's in."

"Ghost, you gander! It ain't anything but air and heat and thirstiness pasted together by a person's imagination. If I—gimme the glass!"

He grabbed it and begun to gaze off to the right.

"It's a flock of birds," he says. "It's getting toward sundown, and they're making a bee-line across our track for somewheres. They mean business—maybe they're going for food or water, or both. Let her go to starboard!—Port your helium! Hard down! There—ease up—steady, as you go."

We shut down some of the power, so as not to outspeed them, and took out after them. We went skimming along a quarter of a mile behind them, and when we had followed them an hour and a half and was getting pretty discouraged, and was thirsty clean to unendurableness, Tom says—

"Take the glass, one of you, and see what that is, away ahead of the birds."

Jim got the first glimpse, and slumped down on the locker, sick. He was most crying, and says—

"She's dah agi'n, Mars Tom, she's dah ag'in, en I knows I's gwine to die, 'case when a body sees a ghos' de third time, dat's what it means. I wisht I'd never come in dis balloon, dat I does."

He wouldn't look no more, and what he said made me afraid, too, because I knowed it was true, for that has always been the way with ghosts; so then I wouldn't look any more, either. Both of us begged Tom to turn off and go some other way, but he wouldn't, and said we was ignorant superstitious blatherskites. Yes, and he'll git come up with, one of these days, I says to myself, insulting ghosts that way. They'll stand it for a while, maybe, but they won't stand it always, for anybody that knows about ghosts knows how easy they are hurt, and how revengeful they are.

So we was all quiet and still, Jim and me being scared, and Tom busy. By and by Tom fetched the balloon to a standstill, and says—

"*Now* get up and look, you sapheads."

We done it, and there was the sure-enough water right under us!—clear, and blue, and cool, and deep, and wavy with the breeze, the loveliest sight that ever was. And all about it was grassy banks, and flowers, and shady groves of big trees, looped together with vines, and all looking so peaceful and comfortable, enough to make a body cry, it was so beautiful.

Jim *did* cry, and rip and dance and carry on, he was so thankful and out of his mind for joy. It was my watch, so I had to stay by the works, but Tom and Jim dumb down and drunk a barrel apiece, and fetched me up a lot, and I've tasted a many a good thing in my life, but nothing that ever begun with that water.

Then we went down and had a swim, and then Tom came up and spelled me, and me and Jim had a swim, and then Jim spelled Tom, and me and Tom had a foot-race and a boxing-mill, and I don't reckon I ever had such a good time in my life. It warn't so very hot, because it was close on to evening, and we hadn't any clothes on, anyway. Clothes is well enough in school, and in towns, and at balls, too, but there ain't no sense in them when there ain't no civilization nor other kinds of bothers and fussiness around.

"Lions a-comin'!—lions! Quick, Mars Tom, jump for yo' life, Huck!"

Oh, and didn't we! We never stopped for clothes, but waltzed up the ladder just so. Jim lost his head straight off—he always done it whenever he got excited and scared; and so now, 'stead of just easing the ladder up from the ground a little, so the animals couldn't reach it, he turned on a raft of power, and we-went whizzing up and was dangling in the sky before he got his wits together and seen what a foolish thing he was doing. Then he stopped her, but he had clean forgot what to do next; so there we was, so high that the lions looked like pups, and we was drifting off on the wind.

But Tom he shinned up and went for the works and begun to slant her down, and back towards the lake, where the animals was gathering like a camp-meeting, and I judged he had lost *his* head, too; for he knowed I was too scared to climb, and did he want to dump me among the tigers and things? But no, his head was level, he knowed what he was about. He swooped down to within thirty or forty feet of the lake, and stopped right over the center, and sung out—

"Leggo, and drop!"

I done it, and shot down, feet first, and seemed to go about a mile toward the bottom; and when I come up, he says—

"Now lay on your back and float till you're rested and got your pluck back, then I'll dip the ladder in the water and you can climb aboard."

I done it. Now that was ever so smart in Tom, because if he had started off somewheres else to drop down on the sand, the menagerie would 'a' come along, too, and might 'a' kept us hunting a safe place till I got tuckered out and fell. And all this time the lions and tigers was sorting out the clothes, and trying to divide them up so there would be some for all, but there was a misunderstanding about it somewheres, on accounts of some of them trying to hog more than their share; so there was another insurrection, and you never see anything like it in the world. There must 'a' been fifty of them, all mixed up together, snorting and roaring and snapping and biting and tearing, legs and

And all this time the lions and tigers was sorting out the clothes.

tails in the air and you couldn't tell which was which, and the sand and fur a-fly-
ing. And when they got done, some was dead, and some was limping off crippled,
and the rest was setting around on the battle-field, some of them licking their sore
places and the others looking up at us and seemed to be kind of inviting us to come
down and have some fun, but which we didn't want any.

As for the clothes, they warn't any, any more. Every last rag of them was inside
of the animals; and not agreeing with them very well, I don't reckon, for there was
considerable many brass buttons on them, and there was knives in the pockets, too,
and smoking-tobacco, and nails and chalk and marbles and fish-hooks and things.
But I wasn't caring. All that was bothering me was, that all we had, now, was the
Professor's clothes, a big enough assortment, but not suitable to go into company
with, if we came across any, because the britches was as long as tunnels, and the
coats and things according. Still, there was everything a tailor needed, and Jim was
a kind of jack-legged tailor, and he allowed he could soon trim a suit or two down
for us that would answer.

CHAPTER NINE

STILL, WE THOUGHT we would drop down there a minute, but on another
errand. Most of the Professor's cargo of food was put up in cans, in the new way
that somebody had just invented, the rest was fresh. When you fetch Missouri
beefsteak to the Great Sahara, you want to be particular and stay up in the coolish
weather. So we reckoned we would drop down into the lion market and see how
we could make out there.

We hauled in the ladder and dropped down till we was just above the reach of
the animals, then we let down a rope with a slip-knot in it and hauled up a dead lion,
a small tender one, then yanked up a cub tiger. We had to keep the congregation off
with the revolver, or they would 'a' took a hand in the proceedings and helped.

We carved off a supply from both, and saved the skins, and hove the rest overboard. Then we baited some of the Professor's hooks with the fresh meat and went
a-fishing. We stood over the lake just a convenient distance above the water, and
catched a lot of the nicest fish you ever see. It was a most amazing good supper we
had; lion steak, tiger steak, fried fish and hot corn pone. I don't want nothing better than that.

We had some fruit to finish off with. We got it out of the top of a monstrous tall
tree. It was a very slim tree that hadn't a branch on it from the bottom plumb to the
top, and there it busted out like a feather-duster. It was a pam tree, of course, anybody knows a pam tree the minute he see it, by the pictures. We went for coconuts
in this one, but there warn't none. There was only big loose bunches of things like

We catched a lot of the nicest fish you ever see.

over-sized grapes, and Tom allowed they was dates, because he said they answered the description in the Arabian Nights and the other books. Of course they mightn't be, and they might be pison; so we had to wait a spell, and watch and see if the birds et them. They done it; so we done it too, and they was most amazing good.

By this time monstrous big birds begun to come and settle on the dead animals. They was plucky creturs; they would tackle one end of a lion that was being gnawed at the other end by another lion. If the lion drove the bird away, it didn't do no good, he was back again the minute the lion was busy.

The big birds come out of every part of the sky—you could make them out with the glass whilst they was still so far away you couldn't see them with your naked eye. Tom said the birds didn't find out the meat was there by the smell, they had to find it out by seeing it. Oh, but ain't that an eye for you! Tom said at the distance of five mile a patch of dead lions couldn't look any bigger than a person's finger nail, and he couldn't imagine how the birds could notice such a little thing so far off.

It was strange and unnatural to see lion eat lion, and we thought maybe they warn't kin. But Jim said that didn't make no difference. He said a hog was fond of her own children, and so was a spider, and he reckoned maybe a lion was pretty near as unprincipled though maybe not quite. He thought likely a lion wouldn't eat his own father, if he knowed which was him, but reckoned he would eat his brother-in-law if he was uncommon hungry, and eat his mother-in-law any time. But *reckoning* don't settle nothing. You can reckon till the cows come home, but that don't fetch you to no decision. So we give it up and let it drop.

Generly it was very still in the Desert, nights, but this time there was music. A lot of other animals come to dinner, sneaking yelpers that Tom allowed was jackals, and roached-backed ones that he said was hyenas; and all the whole biling of them kept up a racket all the time. They made a picture in the moonlight that was more different than any picture I ever see. We had a line out and made fast to the top of a tree, and didn't stand no watch, but all turned in and slept, but I was up two or three times to look down at the animals and hear the music. It was like having a front seat at a menagerie for nothing, which I hadn't ever had before, and so it seemed foolish to sleep and not make the most of it, I mightn't ever have such a chance again.

We went a-fishing again in the early dawn, and then lazied around all day in the deep shade on an island, taking turn about to watch and see that none of the animals come a-snooping around there after erronorts for dinner. We was going to leave next day, but couldn't, it was too lovely.

The day after, when we rose up toward the sky and sailed off eastward, we looked back and watched that place till it warn't nothing but just a speck in the Desert, and I tell you it was like saying good-by to a friend that you ain't ever going to see any more.

Jim was thinking to himself, and at last he says—

"Mars Tom, we's mos' to de end er de Desert now, I speck."

"Why?"

"Well, hit stan' to reason we is. You knows how long we's been a-skimmin' over it. Mus' be mos' out o' san'. Hit's a wonder to me dat it's hilt out as long as it has."

"Shucks, there's plenty sand, you needn't worry."

"Oh, I ain't a-worryin', Mars Tom, only wonderin', dat's all. De Lord's got plenty san' I ain't doubtin' dat but nemmine. He ain' gwyne to *was'e* it jist on dat account; en I allows dat dis Desert's plenty big enough now, jist de way she is, en you can't spread her out no mo' 'dout was'in san'.'"

"Oh, go long! we ain't much more than fairly *started* across this Desert yet. The United States is a pretty big country, ain't it? Ain't it, Huck?"

"Yes," I says, "there ain't no bigger one, I don't reckon."

"Well," he says, "this Desert is about the shape of the United States, and if you was to lay it down on top of the United States, it would cover the land of the free out of sight like a blanket. There'd be a little corner sticking out, up at Maine and away up northwest, and Florida sticking out like a turtle's tail, and that's all. We've took California away from the Mexicans two or three years ago, so that part of the Pacific coast is ours, now, and if you laid the Great Sahara down with her edge on the Pacific, she would cover the United States and stick out past New York six hundred miles into the Atlantic Ocean."

I says—

"Good land! have you got the documents for that, Tom Sawyer?"

"Yes, and they're right here, and I've been studying them. You can look for yourself. From New York to the Pacific is 2,600 miles. From one end of the Great Desert to the other is 3,200. The United States contains 3,600,000 square miles, the Desert contains 4,162,000. With the Desert's bulk you could cover up every last inch of the United States, and in under where the edges projected out, you could tuck England, Scotland, Ireland, France, Denmark, and all Germany. Yes, sir, you could hide the home of the brave and all of them countries clean out of sight under the Great Sahara, and you would still have 2,000 square miles of sand left."

"Well," I says, "it clean beats me. Why, Tom, it shows that the Lord took as much pains makin' this Desert as makin' the United States and all them other countries."

Jim says—"Huck, dat don' stan' to reason. I reckon dis Desert wa'n't made, at all. Now you take en look at it like dis—you look at it, and see ef I's right. What's a desert good for? 'Tain't good for nuthin'. Dey ain't no way to make it pay. Hain't dat so, Huck?"

"Yes, I reckon."

"Hain't it so, Mars Tom?"

"I guess so. Go on."

"Ef a thing ain't no good, it's made in vain, ain't it?"

"Yes."

"*Now*, den! Do de Lord make anything in vain? You answer me dat."

"Well—no, He don't."

"Den how come He make a desert?"

"Well, go on. How *did* He come to make it?"

"Mars Tom, *I* b'lieve it uz jes like when you's buildin' a house; dey's allays a lot o' truck en rubbish lef over. What does you do wid it? Doan' you take en k'yart it off en dump it into a ole vacant back lot? 'Course. Now, den, it's my opinion hit was jes like dat—dat de Great Sahara warn't made at all, she jes *happen'*."

I said it was a real good argument, and I believed it was the best one Jim ever made. Tom he said the same, but said the trouble about arguments is, they ain't nothing but *theories*, after all, and theories don't prove nothing, they only give you a place to rest on, a spell, when you are tuckered out butting around and around trying to find out something there ain't no way *to* find out. And he says—

"There's another trouble about theories: there's always a hole in them somewheres, sure, if you look close enough. It's just so with this one of Jim's. Look what billions and billions of stars there is. How does it come that there was just exactly enough star-stuff, and none left over? How does it come there ain't no sand-pile up there?"

But Jim was fixed for him and says—

"What's de Milky Way?—dat's what *I* wants to know. What's de Milky Way? Answer me dat!"

In my opinion it was just a sockdologer. It's only an opinion, it's only *my* opinion and others may think different; but I said it then and I stand to it now—it was a sockdologer. And moreover, besides, it landed Tom Sawyer. He couldn't say a word. He had that stunned look of a person that's been shot in the back with a kag of nails. All he said was, as for people like me and Jim, he'd just as soon have intellectual intercourse with a catfish. But anybody can say that—and I notice they always do, when somebody has fetched them a lifter. Tom Sawyer was tired of that end of the subject.

So we got back to talking about the size of the Desert again, and the more we compared it with this and that and t' other thing, the more nobler and bigger and grander it got to look, right along. And so, hunting amongst the figgers, Tom found, by and by, that it was just the same size as the Empire of China. Then he showed us the spread the Empire of China made on the map, and the room she took up in the world. Well, it was wonderful to think of, and I says—

"Why, I've heard talk about this Desert plenty of times, but *I* never knowed, before, how important she was."

Then Tom says—

"Important! Sahara important! That's just the way with some people. If a thing's big, it's important. That's all the sense they've got. All they can see is *size*. Why, look at England. It's the most important country in the world; and yet you could put it in China's vest pocket; and not only that, but you'd have the dickens's own time to find it again the next time you wanted it. And look at Russia. It spreads all around and everywhere, and yet ain't no more important in this world than Rhode Island is, and hasn't got half as much in it that's worth saving."

Away off, now, we see a little hill, a-standing up just on the edge of the world. Tom broke off his talk, and reached for a glass very much excited, and took a look, and says—

"That's it—it's the one I've been looking for, sure. If I'm right, it's the one the Dervish took the man into and showed him all the treasures."

So we begun to gaze, and he begun to tell about it out of the Arabian Nights.

CHAPTER TEN

TOM SAID IT happened like this.

A dervish was stumping it along through the desert, on foot, one blazing hot day, and he had come a thousand miles and was pretty poor, and hungry, and ornery and tired, and along about where we are now, he run across a camel-driver with a hundred camels, and asked him for some alms. But the camel-driver he asked to be excused. The dervish says—

"Don't you own these camels?"

"Yes, they're mine."

"Are you in debt?"

"Who—me? No."

"Well, a man that owns a hundred camels and ain't in debt, is rich—and not only rich, but very rich. Ain't it so?"

The camel-driver owned up that it was so. Then the dervish says—

"Allah has made you rich, and He has made me poor. He has His reasons, and they are wise, blessed be His name. But He has willed that His rich shall help His poor, and you have turned away from me, your brother, in my need, and He will remember this, and you will lose by it."

That made the camel-driver feel shaky, but all the same he was born hungry after money and didn't like to let go a cent, so he begun to whine and explain, and said times was hard, and although he had took a full freight down to Balsora and got a fat rate for it, he couldn't git no return freight, and so he warn't making no great things out of his trip. So the dervish starts along again, and says—

"All right, if you want to take the risk, but I reckon you've made a mistake this time, and missed a chance."

Of course the camel-driver wanted to know what kind of a chance he had missed, because maybe there was money in it, so he run after the dervish and begged him so hard and earnest to take pity on him and tell him, that at last the dervish give in, and says—

"Do you see that hill yonder? Well, in that hill is all the treasures of the earth, and I was looking around for a man with a particular good kind heart and a noble generous disposition, because if I could find just that man, I've got a kind of salve I could put on his eyes and he could see the treasures and get them out."

So then the camel-driver was in a state; and he cried, and begged, and took on, and went down on his knees, and said he was just that kind of a man, and said he could fetch a thousand people that would say he wasn't ever described so exact before.

"Well, then," says the dervish, "all right. If we load the hundred camels, can I have half of them?"

The driver was so glad he couldn't hardly hold in, and says—

"Now you're shouting."

So they shook hands on the bargain, and the dervish got out his box and rubbed the salve on the driver's right eye, and the hill opened and he went in, and there, sure enough, was piles and piles of gold and jewels sparkling like all the stars in heaven had fell down.

So him and the dervish laid into it and they loaded every camel till he couldn't carry no more, then they said good-by, and each of them started off with his fifty. But pretty soon the camel-driver came a-running and overtook the dervish and says—

"You ain't in society, you know, and you don't really need all you've got. Won't you be good, and let me have ten of your camels?"

"Well," the dervish says, "I don't know but what you say is reasonable enough."

So he done it, and they separated and the dervish started off again with his forty. But pretty soon here comes the camel-driver bawling after him again, and whines and whimpers around and begs another ten off of him, saying thirty camel-loads of treasures was enough to see a dervish through, because they live very simple, you know, and don't keep house but board around and give their note.

But that warn't the end, yet. That camel-driver kept coming and coming till he had begged back all the camels and had the whole hundred. Then he was satisfied, and ever so grateful, and said he wouldn't ever forgit the dervish as long as he lived, and nobody hadn't ever been so good to him before, and liberal. So they shook hands good-by, and separated and started off again.

But do you know, it warn't ten minutes till the camel-driver was unsatisfied again—he was the low-downest reptile in seven counties—and he come a-running again. And this time the thing he wanted was to get the dervish to rub some of the salve on his other eye.

"Why?" said the dervish.

"Oh, you know," says the driver.

"Know what?" says the dervish.

Says the driver—

"Well, you can't fool me. You're trying to keep back something from me, you know it mighty well. You know, I reckon, that if I had the salve on the other eye I could see a lot more things that's valuable. Come—please put it on."

The dervish says—

"I wasn't keeping anything back from you. I don't mind telling you what would happen if I put it on. You'd never see again. You'd be stone blind the rest of your days."

But do you know, that beat wouldn't believe him. No, he begged and begged, and whined and cried, till at last the dervish opened his box and told him to put it on, if he wanted to. So the man done it, and sure enough he was as blind as a bat, in a minute.

Then the dervish laughed at him and

The camel-driver in the treasure-cave

mocked at him and made fun of him; and says—

"Good-by—a man that's blind hain't got no use for jewelry."

And he cleared out with the hundred camels, and left that man to wander around poor and miserable and friendless the rest of his days in the desert.

Jim said he'd bet it was a lesson to him.

"Yes," Tom says, "and like a considerable many lessons a body gets. They ain't no account, because the thing don't ever happen the same way again—and can't. The time Hen Scovil fell down the chimbly and crippled his back for life, everybody said it would be a lesson to him. What kind of a lesson? How was he going to use it? He couldn't climb chimblies no more, and he hadn't no more backs to break."

"All de same, Mars Tom," Jim said, "dey *is* sich a thing as learnin' by expe'ence. De Good Book say de burnt chile shun de fire."

"Well, I ain't denying that a thing's a lesson if it's a thing that can happen twice just the same way. There's lots of such things, and *they* educate a person, that's what Uncle Abner always said; but there's forty *million* lots of the other kind—the kind that don't happen the same way twice—and they ain't no real use, they ain't no more instructive than the smallpox. When you've got it, it ain't no good to find out you ought to been vaccinated, and it ain't no good to get vaccinated afterwards, because the smallpox don't come but once. But on the other hand Uncle Abner said that a person that had took a bull by the tail once had learnt sixty or seventy times as much as a person that hadn't, and said a person that started in to carry a cat home by the tail was gitting knowledge that was always going to be useful to him, and warn't ever going to grow dim or doubtful. But I can just tell you, Jim, Uncle Abner was down on them people that's all the time trying to dig a lesson out of everything that happens, no matter whether—"

But Jim was asleep. Tom looked kind of ashamed, because you know a person always feels bad when he is talking uncommon fine and thinks the other person is admiring, and that other person goes to sleep that way. Of course he oughtn't to go to sleep, because it's shabby, but the finer a person talks the certainer it is to make you sleep, and so when you come to look at it it ain't nobody's fault in particular, both of them's to blame.

Jim begun to snore—soft and easy-like, at first, then a long rasp, then a stronger one, then a half a dozen horrible ones like the last water sucking down the plughole of a bathtub, then the same with more power to it. And when the person has got to that point he is at his level best, and can wake up a man in the next block, but can't wake himself up although all that awful noise of his'n ain't but three inches from his own ears. And that is the curiosest thing in the world, seems to me. But you rake a match to light the candle, and that little bit of a noise will fetch him. I wish I knowed what was the reason of that, but there don't seem to be no way to find out. Now there was Jim alarming the whole Desert, and yanking the animals out for miles and miles around, to see what in the nation was going on up there; there warn't nobody nor nothing that was as close to the noise as *he* was, and yet he was the only cretur that wasn't anyways disturbed by it.

We yelled at him and whooped at him, it never done no good, but the first time there come a little wee noise that wasn't of a usual kind it woke him up. No, sir, I've thought it all over, and so has Tom, and there ain't no way to find out why a snorer can't hear himself snore.

Jim said he hadn't been asleep, he just shut his eyes so he could listen better.

Tom said nobody warn't accusing him.

That made him look like he wished he hadn't said anything. And he wanted to git away from the subject, I reckon, because he begun to abuse the camel-driver, just the way a person does when he has got catched in something and wants to take it out of somebody else. He let into the camel-driver the hardest he knowed how, and I had to agree with him; and he praised up the dervish the highest he could, and I had to agree with him there, too. But Tom says—

"I ain't so sure. You call that dervish so dreadful liberal and good and unselfish, but I don't quite see it. He didn't hunt up another poor dervish, did he? No, he didn't. If he was so unselfish, why didn't he go in there himself and take a pocket-full of jewels and go along and be satisfied? No, sir, the person he was hunting for was a man with a hundred camels. He wanted to get away with all the treasure he could."

"Why, Mars Tom, the dervish was willin' to divide, fair and square; he only struck for fifty camels."

"Because he knowed how he was going to get all of them by and by."

"Mars Tom, he *tole* de man de truck would make him blind."

"Yes, because he knowed the man's character. It was just the kind of a man he was hunting for—a man that never believes in anybody's word or anybody's honorableness, because he ain't got none of his own. I reckon there's lots of people like that dervish. They swindle right and left, but they always make the other person *seem* to swindle himself. They keep inside of the letter of the law all the time, and there ain't no way to git hold of them. *They* don't put the salve on—oh, no, that would be sin; but they know how to fool *you* into putting it on, then it's you that blinds yourself. I reckon the dervish and the camel-driver was just a pair—a fine, smart, brainy rascal, and a dull, coarse, ignorant one, but both of them rascals, just the same."

"Mars Tom, does you reckon dey's any o' dat kind o' salve in de worl' now?"

"Yes, Uncle Abner says there is. He says they've got it in New York, and they put it on country people's eyes and show them all the railroads in the world, and they go in and get them, and then when they rub the salve on the other eye the other man bids them good-by and goes off with their railroads. Here's the treasure-hill, now. Lower away!"

We landed, but it warn't as interesting as I thought it was going to be, because we couldn't find the place where they went in to git the treasure. Still, it was plenty interesting enough, just to see the mere hill itself where such a wonderful thing happened. Jim said he wouldn't a-missed it for three dollars, and I felt the same way.

And to me and Jim, as wonderful a thing as any was the way Tom could come into a strange big country like this and go straight and find a little hump like that and tell it in a minute from a million other humps that was almost just like it, and nothing to help him but only his own learning and his own natural smartness. We talked and talked it over together, but couldn't make out how he done it. He had the best head on him I ever see; and all he lacked was age, to make a name for himself equal to Captain Kidd or George Washington. I bet you it would a-crowded either of *them* to find that hill, with all their gifts, but it warn't nothing to Tom Sawyer; he went clear across the Sahara and put his finger right on it.

We found a pond of salt water close by and scraped up a raft of salt around the edges and loaded up the lion's skin and the tiger's so as they would keep till Jim could tan them.

CHAPTER ELEVEN

WE WENT A-FOOLING along for a day or two, and then just as the full moon was touching the ground on the other side of the Desert, we see a string of little black figgers moving across its big silver face. You could see them as plain as if they was painted on the moon with ink. It was another caravan. We cooled down our speed and tagged along after it, just to have company, though it warn't going our way. It was a rattler, that caravan, and a mighty fine sight to look at, next morning when the sun come a-streaming across the Desert and flung the long shadders of the camels on the gold sand like a thousand grand-daddy-longlegses marching in procession. We never went very near it, because we knowed better, now, than to act like that and scare people's camels and break up their caravans. It was the gayest outfit you ever see, for rich clothes and nobby style. Some of the chiefs rode on dromedaries, the first we ever see, and very tall, and they go plunging along like they was on stilts, and they rock the man that is on them pretty violent and stir him up considerable, I bet you, but they make noble good time and a camel ain't nowheres with them for speed.

The caravan camped, during the middle part of the day, and then started again about the middle of the afternoon. Before long the sun begun to look very curious. First it kind of turned to brass, and then to copper, and after that it begun to look

The wedding procession

like a blood red ball, and the air got hot and close, and pretty soon all the sky in the west darkened up and looked thick and foggy, but fiery and dreadful like it looks through a piece of red glass, you know. We looked down and see a big confusion going on in the caravan and a rushing every which way like they was scared, and then they all flopped down flat in the sand and laid there perfectly still.

Pretty soon we see something coming that stood up like an amazing wide wall, and reached from the Desert up into the sky and hid the sun, and it was coming like the nation, too. Then a little faint breeze struck us, and then it come harder, and grains of sand begun to sift against our faces and sting like fire, and Tom sung out—

"It's a sand-storm—turn your backs to it!"

We done it, and in another minute it was blowing a gale and the sand beat against us by the shovel-full, and the air was so thick with it we couldn't see a thing. In five minutes the boat was level full and we was setting on the lockers, all of us buried up to the chin in sand and only our heads out and we could hardly breathe.

Then the storm thinned, and we see that monstrous wall go a-sailing off across the Desert, awful to look at, I tell you. We dug ourselves out and looked down, and

In the sand-storm

where the caravan was before, there wasn't anything but just the sand ocean, now, and all still and quiet. All them people and camels was smothered and dead and buried—buried under ten foot of sand, we reckoned, and Tom allowed it might be years before the wind uncovered them, and all that time their friends wouldn't ever know what become of that caravan.

Tom said—

"*Now* we know what it was that happened to the people we got the swords and pistols from."

Yes, sir, that was just it. It was as plain as day, now. They got buried in a sand-storm, and the wild animals couldn't get at them, and the wind never uncovered them again till they was dried to leather. It seemed to me we had felt as sorry for them poor people as a person could for anybody, and as mournful, too, but we was mistaken; this last caravan's death went harder with us, a good deal harder. You see, others was total strangers, and we never got really acquainted with them at all. But it was different with this last caravan. We was huvvering around them a whole night and most a whole day, and had got to feeling real friendly with them, and acquainted. I have found out that there ain't no surer way to find out whether you like people or hate them, than to travel with them. Just so with these. We kind of liked them from the start, and traveling with them put on the finisher. The longer we traveled with them, and the more we got used to their ways, the better and better we liked them and the gladder and gladder we was that we run across them. We had come to know some of them so well that we called them by name when we was talking about them, and soon got so familiar and sociable that we even dropped the Miss and the Mister and just used their plain names without any handle, and it did not seem unpolite, but just the right thing. Of course it wasn't their own names, but names we give them. There was Mr. Elexander Robinson and Miss Adaline Robinson, and Colonel Jacob McDougal, and Miss Harryet McDougal, and Judge Jeremiah Butler, and young Bushrod Butler, and these was big chiefs, mostly, that wore splendid great turbans and simmeters, and dressed like the Grand Mogul, and their families. But as soon as we come to know them good, and like them very much, it warn't Mister, nor Judge, nor nothing, any more, but only Elleck, and Addy, and Jake, and Hattie, and Jerry, and Buck, and so on.

And you know, the more you join in with people in their joys and their sorrows, the more nearer and dearer they come to be to you. Now we warn't cold and indifferent, the way most travelers is, we was right down friendly and sociable, and took a chance in everything that was going, and the caravan could depend on us to be on hand every time, it didn't make no difference what it was.

When they camped, we camped right over them, ten or twelve hundred foot up in the air. When they et a meal, we et ourn, and it made it ever so much homeliker to have their company. When they had a wedding, that night, and Buck and Addy got married, we got ourselves up in the very starchiest of the Professor's duds for the blow-out, and when they danced we jined in and shook a foot up there.

But it is sorrow and trouble that brings you the nearest, and it was a funeral that done it with us. It was next morning, just in the still dawn. We

When they danced we jined in and shook a foot up there.

didn't know the diseased, but that never made no difference, he belonged to the caravan, and that was enough.

Yes, parting with this caravan was much more bitterer than it was to part with them others, which was comparative strangers, and been dead so long, anyway. We had knowed these in their lives, and was fond of them, too, and now to have 'em snatched from right before our faces whilst we was looking, and leave us so lonesome and friendless in the middle of that big Desert, it did hurt us.

We couldn't keep from talking about them, and they was all the time coming up in our memory, and looking just the way they looked when we was all alive and happy together. We could see the line marching, and the shiny spear-heads a-winking in the sun, we could see the dromedaries lumbering along, we could see the wedding and the funeral, and more oftener than anything else we could see them praying, because they don't allow nothing to prevent that; whenever the call come, several times a day, they would stop right there, and stand up and face to the east, and lift back their heads, and spread out their arms and begin, and four or five times they would go down on their knees, and then fall forwards and touch their forehead to the ground.

Well, it warn't good to go on talking about them, because it didn't do no good, and made us too downhearted.

When we woke up next morning we was feeling a little cheerfuller, and had had a most powerful good sleep, because sand is the comfortablest bed there is, and I don't see why people that can afford it don't have it more. And it's terrible good ballast, too; I never see the balloon so steady before.

Tom allowed we had twenty tons of it, and wondered what we better do with it; it was good sand, and it didn't seem good sense to throw it away. Jim says—

"Mars Tom, can't we tote it back home en sell it? How long'll it take?"

"Depends on the way we go."

"Well, sah, she's wuth a quarter of a dollar a load, at home, en I reckon we's got as much as twenty loads, hain't we? How much would dat be?"

"Five dollars."

"By jmgs, Mars Tom, le's shove for home right on de spot! Hit's more 'n a dollar en a half apiece, hain't it?"

"Yes."

"Well, ef dat ain't roakin' money de easiest ever I struck! She jes' rained in— never cos' us a lick o' work. Le's mosey right along, Mars Tom."

But Tom was thinking and ciphering away so busy and excited he never heard him. Pretty soon he says—

"Five dollars—sho! Look here, this sand's worth—worth—why, it's worth no end of money."

"How is dat, Mars Tom? Go on, honey, go on"

"Well, the minute people knows its genuwyne sand from the genuwyne Desert of Sahara, they'll just be in a perfect state of mind to git hold of some of it to keep on the whatnot in a vial with a label on it for a curiosity. All we got to do is, to put it up in vials and float around all over the United States and peddle them out at ten cents apiece. We've got all of ten thousand dollars' worth of sand in this boat."

Me and Jim went all to pieces with joy, and began to shout whoopjamboreehoo, and Tom says—

"And we can keep on coming back and fetching sand, and coming back and fetching more sand, and just keep it a-going till we've carted this whole Desert over there and sold it out; and there ain't ever going to be any opposition, either, because we'll take out a patent."

"My goodness," I says, "we'll be as rich as Creosote, won't we, Tom?"

"Yes—Creesus, you mean. Why, that dervish was hunting in that little hill for the treasures of the earth, and didn't know he was walking over the real ones for a thousand miles. He was blinder than he made the driver."

"Mars Tom, how much is we gwyne to be worth?"

"Well, I don't know, yet. It's got to be ciphered, and it ain't the easiest job to do, either, because it's over four million square miles of sand at ten cents a vial."

Jim was awful excited, but this faded it out considerable, and he shook his head and says—

"Mars Tom, we can't 'ford all dem vials—a king couldn't. We better not try to take de whole Desert, Mars Tom, de vials gwyne to bust us, sho'."

Tom's excitement died out, too, now, and I reckoned it was on account of the vials, but it wasn't. He set there thinking, and got bluer and bluer, and at last he says—"Boys, it won't work; we got to give it up."

"Why, Tom?"

"On account of the duties."

I couldn't make nothing out of that, neither could Jim. I says—

"What *is* our duty, Tom? Because, if we can't git around it, why can't we just *do* it? People often has to."

But he says—

"Oh, it ain't that kind of duty. The kind I mean is a tax. Whenever you strike a frontier—that's the border of a country, you know—you find a custom-house there, and the gov'ment officers comes and rummages amongst your things and charges a big tax, which they call a duty because it's their duty to bust you if they can, and if you don't pay the duty they'll take your sand. They call it confiscating. Now if we try to carry this sand home the way we're pointed now, we got to climb fences till we git tired—just frontier after frontier—Egypt, Arabia, Hindostan, and so on, and they'll all whack on a duty, and so you see, easy enough, we *can't* go *that* road."

"Why, Tom," I says, "we can sail right over their old frontiers; how are *they* going to stop us?"

He looked sorrowful at me, and says, very grave—

"Huck Finn, do you think that would be honest?"

I hate them kind of interruptions. But I said nothin'. I didn't feel no more interest in such things, as long as we couldn't git our sand through, and it made me low-spirited, and Jim the same. Tom he tried to cheer us up by saying he would think up another speculation for us that would be just as good as this one and better, but it didn't do no good, we didn't believe there was any as big as this. It was mighty hard; such a little while ago we was so rich, and could 'a' bought a country and started a kingdom and been celebrated and happy, and now we was so poor and ornery again, and had our sand left on our hands. The sand was looking so lovely, before, just like gold and di'monds, and the feel of it was so soft and so silky and nice, but now I couldn't bear the sight of it, it made me sick to look at it, and I knowed I wouldn't ever feel comfortable again till we got shut of it, and I didn't have it there no more to remind us of what we had been and what we had got degraded down to. The others was feeling the same way about it that I was. I knowed it, because they cheered up so the minute I says "Le's throw this truck overboard."

Well, it was going to be work, you know, and pretty solid work, too; so Tom he divided it up according to fairness and strength. He said me and him would clear out a fifth apiece, of the sand, and Jim three fifths. Jim he didn't quite like that arrangement. He says—

"'Course I's de stronges', en I's willin' to do a share accordin', but by jings you's kinder pilin' it onto ole Jim this time, Mars Tom, hain't you?"

"Well, I didn't think so, Jim, but you try your hand at fixing it, and let's see."

So Jim he reckoned it wouldn't be no more than fair if me and Tom done a *tenth* apiece. Tom he turned his back to git room and be private, and then he smole a smile that spread around and covered the whole Sahara to the westward, back to the Atlantic edge of it where we come from. Then he turned around again and said it was a good enough arrangement, and we was satisfied if Jim was. Jim said he was.

So then Tom measured off our two tenths in the bow and left the rest for Jim, and it surprised Jim a good deal to see how much difference there was and what a raging lot of sand his share come to, an' he said he was powerful glad, now, that he had spoke up in time and got the first arrangement altered, for he said that even the way it was now, there was more sand than enjoyment in his end of the contract, he believed.

Then we laid into it. It was mighty hot work, and tough; so hot we had to move up into cooler weather or we couldn't 'a' stood it. Me and Tom took turn about, and one worked while 't other rested, but there warn't nobody to spell poor old Jim. We couldn't work good, we was so full of laugh, and Jim he kept fretting and fuming and wanting to know what tickled us so, and we had to keep making up things to account for it, and they was pretty poor inventions, but they done well enough, Jim didn't see through them. At last when we got done we was most dead, but not with work but with laughing. By and by Jim was most dead too, but it was with work; then we took turns and spelled him, and he was as thankful as he could be, and would set on the gunnel and heave and pant, and say how good we was to him, and he wouldn't ever forgit us. He was always the gratefulest feller I ever see, for any little thing you done for him.

CHAPTER TWELVE

AT LAST, SAILING on a northeast course, we struck the east end of the Desert. Away off on the edge of the sand, in a soft pinky light, we see three little sharp roofs like tents, and Tom says—

"It's the Pyramids of Egypt."

It made my heart fairly jump. You see, I had seen a many and a many a picture of them, and heard tell about them a hundred times, and yet to come on them all of a sudden, that way, and find they were *real*, 'stead of imaginations, most knocked the breath out of me with surprise. It's a curious thing, that the more you hear about a grand and big and noble thing or person, the more it kind of dreamies out, as you may say, and gets to be a big dim wavery figger made out of moonshine and nothing solid to it. It's just so with George Washington, and the same with them Pyramids.

And moreover besides, the things they always said about them seemed to me to be stretchers. There was a feller come down to our school, once, and had a picture of them, and made a speech, and said the biggest Pyramid covered thirteen acres, and was most five-hundred foot high, just a steep mountain, all built out of hunks of stone as big as a bureau, and laid up in perfectly regular layers, like stair-steps. Thirteen acres, you see, for just one building; it's a farm. And he said there was a hole in the Pyramid, and you could go in there with candles, and go ever so far up a long slanting tunnel, and come to a large room in the stomach of that stone mountain, and there you would find a big stone chest with a king in it, four thousand years old.

As we sailed a little nearer we see the yaller sand come to an end in a long straight edge like a blanket, and onto it was joined, edge to edge, a wide country of bright green, with a snaky stripe crooking, through it, and Tom said it was the Nile.

It made my heart jump again, for the Nile was another thing that wasn't real to me. Now I can tell you one thing which is dead certain: if you will fool along over three thousand miles of yaller sand, all glimmering with heat so that it makes your eyes water to look at it, and you've been a considerable part of a week doing it, the green country will look so like home and heaven to you that it will make your eyes water *again*. It was just so with me, and the same with Jim.

And when Jim got so he could believe it *was* the land of Egypt he was looking at, he wouldn't enter it standing up, but got down on his knees and took off his hat, because he said it wasn't fitten for him to come any other way where such men had been as Moses and Joseph and Pharaoh and the other prophets. He was all stirred up, and says—

"Hit's de lan' of Egypt, de lan' of Egypt, en I's lowed to look at it wid my own eyes! Ole Jim ain't worthy to see dis day!"

And then he just broke down and cried, he was so thankful. So between him and Tom there was talk enough, Jim being excited because the land was so full of history—Joseph and his brethren, Moses in the bulrushes, Jacob coming down into Egypt to buy corn, the silver cup in the sack, and all them interesting things, and Tom just as excited too, because the land was so full of history that was in *his* line, about Noureddin, and Bedreddin, and such like monstrous giants, that made Jim's wool rise, and a raft of other Arabian Nights folks, which the half of them never done the things they let on they done, I don't believe.

Then we struck a disappointment, for one of them early-morning fogs started up, and it warn't no use to sail over the top of it, because we would go by Egypt, sure, so we judged it was best to set her by compass straight for the place where the Pyramids was gitting blurred and blotted out, and then drop low and skin along pretty close to the ground and keep a sharp lookout. Tom took the helium, I stood by to let go the anchor, and Jim he straddled the bow to dig through the fog with his eyes and watch out for danger ahead. We went along a steady gait, but not very fast, and the fog got solider and solider, so solid that Jim looked dim and ragged and smoky through it. It was awful still, and we talked low and was anxious. Now and then Jim would say—

"Highst her a pint, Mars Tom, highst her!" and up she would skip, a foot or two, and we would slide right over a flat-roofed mud cabin, with people that had been asleep on it just beginning to turn out and gap and stretch; and once when a feller was clear up on his legs so he could gap and stretch better, we took him a blip in the back and knocked him off. By and by, after about an hour, and everything dead still and we a-straining our ears for sounds and holding our breath, the fog thinned a little, very sudden, and Jim sung out in an awful scare—

"Oh, for de lan's sake, set her back, Mars Tom, here's de biggest giant outen de

'Rabian Nights a comin' for us!" and he went over backward in the boat.

Tom slammed on the back-action, and as we slowed to a standstill, a man's face as big as our house at home looked in over the gunnel, same as a house looks out of its windows, and I laid down and died. I must 'a' been clear dead and gone for as much as a minute or more, then I come to, and Tom was holding the balloon steady whilst he canted his head back and got a good long look up at that awful face.

Jim was on his knees with his hands clasped, gazing up at the thing in a begging way, and working his lips but not getting anything out. I took only just a glimpse, and was fading out again, but Tom says—

"He ain't alive, you fools, it's the Sphinx!" I never see Tom look so little and like a fly; but that was because the giant's head was so big and awful. Awful, yes, so it was, but not dreadful, any more, because you could see it was a noble face, and kind of sad, but not thinking about you, but about other things and larger. It was stone, reddish stone, and its nose and ears battered, and that give it an abused look, and you felt sorrier for it, for that.

We stood off a piece, and sailed around it and over it, and it was just grand. It was a man's head, or maybe a woman's, on a tiger's body a hundred and twenty-five foot long, and there was a dear little temple between its front paws. All but the head used to be under the sand, for hundreds of years, maybe thousands, but they had just lately dug the sand away and found that little temple. It took a power of sand to cover that cretur; 'most as much as it would to bury a steamboat, I reckon.

We landed Jim on top of the head, with an American flag to protect him, it being a foreign land, then we sailed off to this and that and t' other distance, to git what Tom called effects and perspectives and proportions, and Jim he done the best he could, striking all the different kinds of attitudes and positions he could study up; the further we got away, the littler Jim got, and the grander the Sphinx got. That's the way perspective brings out the correct proportions, Tom said; he said Julius Caesar's slaves didn't know how big he was, they was too close to him.

Then we sailed off further and further, till we couldn't see Jim at all, any more, and then that great figger was at its noblest, a-gazing out over the Nile valley so still and solemn and lonesome, and all the little shabby huts and things that was scattered about it clean disappeared and gone, and nothing around it now but a soft wide spread of yaller velvet, which was the sand.

That was the right place to stop, and we done it. We set there a-looking and a-thinking for a half an hour, nobody a-saying anything, for it made us feel quiet and kind of solemn to remember it had been looking over that valley just that same way, and thinking its awful thoughts all to itself for thousands of years, and nobody can't find out what they are to this day.

At last I took up the glass and see some little black things a-capering around on

Jim had been standing a siege a long time.

that velvet carpet, and some more a-climbing up the cretur's back, and then I see two or three wee puffs of white smoke, and told Tom to look. He done it, and says—

"They're bugs. No—hold on, they—why, I believe they're men. Yes, it's men—men and camels, both. They are hauling a long ladder up onto the Sphinx's back—now ain't that odd? And now they're trying to lean it up a—there's some more puffs of smoke—it's guns! Huck, they're after Jim!"

We clapped on the power, and went for them a-b'iling. We was there in no time, and come a-whizzing down amongst them, and they broke and scattered every which way, and some that was climbing the ladder after Jim let go all holts and fell. We soared up and found him laying on top of the head panting and 'most tuck-ered out, partly from howling for help and partly from scare. He had been standing a siege a long time—a week, *he* said, but it warn't so, it only just seemed so to him because they was crowding him so. They had shot at him, and rained the bullets all around him, but he warn't hit, and when they found he wouldn't stand up and the bullets couldn't git at him when he was laying down, they went for the ladder, and then he knowed it was all up with him if we didn't come pretty quick. Tom was very indignant, and asked him why he didn't show the flag and command them to *git*, in the name of the United States. Jim said he done it, but they never paid no attention. Tom said he would have this thing looked into at Washington, and says—

"You'll see that they'll have to apologize for insulting the flag, and pay an indemnity, too, on top of it, even if they git off *that* easy."

Jim says—

"What's an indemnity, Mars Tom?"

"It's cash, that's what it is."

"Who gits it, Mars Tom?"

"Why, *we* do."

"En who gits de apology?"

"The United States. Or, we can take whichever we please. We can take the apology, if we want to, and let the gov'ment take the money."

"How much money will it be, Mars Tom?"

"Well, in an aggravated case like this one, it will be at least three dollars apiece, and I don't know but more."

"Well, den, we'll take de money, Mars Tom, an' let de 'pology go. Hain't dat yo' notion, too? En hain't it yourn, Huck?"

We talked it over a little and allowed that that was as good a way as any, so we

"They'll have to apologize and pay an indemnity too," said Tom.

agreed to take the money. It was a new business to me, and I asked Tom if countries always apologized when they had done wrong, and he says—

"Yes; the little ones does."

We was sailing around examining the Pyramids, you know, and now we soared up and roosted on the flat top of the biggest one, and found it was just like what the man said down in our school. It was like four pairs of stairs that starts broad at the bottom and slants up and comes together in a point at the top, only these stair-steps couldn't be dumb the way you climb other stairs; no, for each step was as high as your chin, and you have to be boosted up from behind. The two other pyramids warn't far away, and the people moving about on the sand between looked like bugs crawling, we was so high above them.

Tom he couldn't hold himself he was so worked up with gladness and astonishment to be in such a celebrated place. He said he couldn't scarcely believe he was standing on the very identical spot the prince flew from on the Bronze Horse. It was in the Arabian Night times, he said. Somebody give the prince a bronze horse with a peg in its shoulder, and he could git on him and fly through the air like a bird, and go all over the world, and steer it by turning the peg, and fly high or low and land wherever he wanted to.

When he got done telling it there was one of them uncomfortable silences that comes, you know, when a person has been telling a whopper and you feel sorry for him and wish you could think of some way to change the subject and let him down easy, but git stuck and don't see no way, and before you can pull your mind together and *do* something, that silence has got in and spread itself and done the business. I was embarrassed, Jim he was embarrassed, and neither of us couldn't say a word. Well, Tom he glowered at me a minute, and says—

"Come, out with it. What do you think?"

I says—

"Tom Sawyer, *you* don't believe that, yourself."

"What's the reason I don't? What's to hender me?"

"There's one thing to hender you: it couldn't happen, that's all."

"What's the reason it couldn't happen?"

"You tell me the reason it *could* happen."

"This balloon is a good enough reason it could happen, I should reckon."

"*Why* is it?"

"*Why* is it? Well, ain't this balloon and the bronze horse the same thing under different names?"

"No, they're not. One is a balloon and the other's a horse. It's very different. Next you'll be saying a house and a cow is the same thing."

"Huck's got him ag'in! Dey ain't no wigglin' outer dat!"

"Jim, you don't know what you're talking about. And Huck don't. Look here, Huck, I'll make it plain to you, so you can understand. You see, it ain't the mere form that's got anything to do with their being similar or unsimilar, it's the *principle* involved; and the principle is the same in both. Don't you see, now?"

I turned it over in my mind, and says—

"Tom, it ain't no use. Principles is all very well, but they don't git around that one big fact, that the thing that a balloon can do ain't no sort of proof of what a horse can do."

"Shucks, Huck, you don't get the idea at all. Now look here a minute—it's perfectly plain. Don't we fly through the air?"

"Yes."

"Very well. Don't we fly high or fly low, just as we please?"

"Yes."

"Don't we steer whichever way we want to?"

"Yes."

"And don't we land when and where we please?"

"Yes."

"How do we move the balloon and steer it?"

"By touching the buttons."

"*Now* I reckon the thing is clear to you at last. In the other case the moving and steering was done by turning a peg. We touch a button, the prince turned a peg. There ain't an atom of difference, you see. I knowed I could git it through your head if I stuck to it long enough."

He felt so happy he begun to whistle. But me and Jim was silent, so he broke off surprised, and says—"Looky here, Huck Finn, don't you see it *yet?*"

I says—

"Tom Sawyer, I want to ask you some questions."

"Go ahead," he says, and I see Jim chirk up to listen.

"As I understand it, the whole thing is in the buttons and the peg—the rest ain't of no consequence. A button is one shape, a peg is another shape, but that ain't any matter."

"No, that ain't any matter, as long as they've both got the same power."

"All right then. What is the power that's in a candle and in a match?"

"It's the fire."

"It's the same in both, then?"

"Yes, just the same in both."

"All right. Suppose I set fire to a carpenter-shop with a match, what will happen to that carpenter-shop?"

"She'll burn up."

"And suppose I set fire to this pyramid with a candle—will she burn up?"

"Of course she won't."

"All right. Now the fire's the same, both times. *Why* does the shop burn, and the pyramid don't?"

"Because the pyramid *can't* burn."

"Aha! and *a horse can't fly!*"

"My lan', if Huck ain't got him ag'in! Huck's landed him high en dry dis time, I tell you! Hit's de smartes' trap I ever see a body walk inter—en ef I—"

But Jim was so full of laugh he got to strangling and couldn't go on, and Tom was that mad to see how neat I had floored him, and turned his own argument agin him and knocked him all to rags and flinders with it that all he could manage to say was that whenever he heard me and Jim try to argue it made him ashamed of the human race. I never said nothing, I was feeling pretty well satisfied. When I have got the best of a person that way, it ain't my way to go around crowing about it the way some people does, for I consider that if I was in his place I wouldn't wish him to crow over me. It's better to be generous, that's what I think.

CHAPTER THIRTEEN

BY AND BY we left Jim to float around up there in the neighborhood of the Pyramids, and we clumb down to the hole where you go into the tunnel, and went in with some Arabs and candles, and away in there in the middle of the Pyramid we found a room and a big stone box in it where they used to keep that king, just as the man in our school said, but he was gone, now, somebody had got him. But I didn't take no interest in the place, because there could be ghosts there, of course.

So then we come out and got some little donkeys and rode a piece, and then went in a boat another piece, and then more donkeys, and got to Cairo; and all the way the road was as smooth and beautiful a road as ever I see, and had tall date-palms on both sides, and naked children everywhere, and the men was as red as copper, and fine and strong and handsome. And the city was a curiosity. Such narrow streets—why, they were just lanes, and crowded with people with turbans, and women with veils, and everybody rigged out in blazing bright clothes and all sorts of colors, and you wondered how the camels and the people got by each other in such narrow little cracks—a perfect jam, you see, and everybody noisy. The stores warn't big enough to turn around in, but you didn't have to go in; the store-keeper sat tailor-fashion on his counter, smoking his snaky long pipe, and had his things where he could reach them to sell, and he was just as good as in the street, for the camel-loads brushed him as they went by.

Now and then a grand person flew by in a carriage with fancy-dressed men running and yelling in front of it, and whacking anybody with a long rod that didn't get out of the way. And by and by along comes the Sultan riding horseback at the head of a procession, and fairly took your breath away his clothes was so splendid, and everybody fell flat and laid on his stomach while he went by. I forgot, but a feller helped me remember. He was one o' them that had rods and that rim in front.

There was churches, but they don't know enough to keep Sunday; they keep Friday and break the Sabbath. You have to take off your shoes when you go in. There was crowds of men and boys in the church, setting in groups on the stone floor and making no end of noise—getting their lessons by heart, Tom said, out of the Koran. I never see such a big church in my life before, and most awful high it was; it made you dizzy to look up, our village church at home ain't a circumstance to it.

What I wanted to see was a dervish, because I was interested in dervishes on account of the one that played the trick on the camel-driver. So we found a lot in a kind of a church, and they called themselves Whirling Dervishes; and they did whirl, too, I never see anything like it. They had tall sugar-loaf hats on, and linen petticoats; and they spun and spun and spun, round and round like tops, and the petticoats stood out on a slant, and it was the prettiest thing I ever see, and made me drunk to look at it. They was all Moslems, Tom said, and when I asked him what a Moslem was, he said it was a person that wasn't a Presbyterian. So there is plenty of them in Missouri, though I didn't know it before.

We didn't see half there was to see in Cairo, because Tom was in such a fever to hunt out places that was celebrated in history. Besides, we hunted a long time for the house where the boy lived, that learned the cadi how to try the case of the old olives and the new ones, and Tom said it was out of the Arabian Nights and he would tell me and Jim about it when he got time. Well, we hunted and hunted till I was ready to drop, and I wanted Tom to give it up and come next day and git somebody that knowed the town and could talk Missourian and could go straight to the place; but no, he wanted to find it himself, and nothing else would answer. So on we went. Then at last the remarkablest thing happened I ever see. The house was gone—gone hundreds of years ago—every last scrap of it gone but just one mud brick. Now a person wouldn't ever believe that a backwoods Missouri boy that hadn't ever been in that town before could go and hunt that place over and find that brick, but Tom Sawyer done it. I know he done it, because I see him do it. I was right by his very side at the time, and see him see the brick and see him reconize it. Well, I says to myself, how *does* he do it? is it knowledge, or is it instinct?

Now there's the facts, just as they happened: let everybody explain it their own way. I've ciphered over it a good deal, and it's my opinion that some of it is knowledge but the main bulk of it is instinct. The reason is this. Tom put the brick in his pocket to give to a museum with his name on it and the facts when he went home, and I slipped it out and put another brick considerable like it in its place, and he didn't know the difference—but there was a difference, you see. I think that settles it—it's mostly instinct, not knowledge. Instinct tells him where the exact *place* is for the brick to be in, and so he reconnizes it by the place it's in, not by the look of the brick. If it was knowledge, not instinct, he would know the brick again by the look of it the next time he seen it—which he didn't. So it shows that for all the brag you hear about knowledge being such a wonderful thing, instinct is worth forty of it for real unerringness. Jim says the same.

When we got back Jim dropped down and took us in, and there was a young man there with a red skull-cap and tassel on and a beautiful blue silk jacket and baggy trousers with a shawl around his waist and pistols in it that could talk English, and he wanted to hire to us as guide and take us to Mecca and Medina and Central Africa and everywheres for a half a dollar a day and his keep, and we hired him and left, and piled on the power, and by the time we was through dinner we was over the shore of the Red Sea, and it was all just as interesting as could be, and the guide knowed every place as well as I know the village at home.

But we had an accident, now, and it fetched all the plans to a standstill. Tom's old ornery corn-cob pipe had got so old and swelled and warped that she couldn't hold together any longer, notwithstanding the strings and bandages, but caved in and went to pieces. Tom he didn't know *what* to do. The Professor's pipe wouldn't answer, it warn't anything but a mershum, and a person that's got used to a cob pipe knows it lays a long ways over all the other pipes in this world, and you can't git him to smoke any other. He wouldn't take mine, I couldn't persuade him. So there he was.

He thought it over, and said we must scour around and see if we could roust out one in Egypt or Arabia or around in some of these countries, but the guide said no, it warn't no use, they didn't have them. So Tom was pretty glum for a little while, then he chirked up and said he'd got the idea and knowed what to do. He says—

"I've got another corn-cob pipe, and it's a prime one, too, and nearly new. It's laying on the rafter that's right over the kitchen stove at home in the village. Jim, you and the guide will go and git it, and me and Huck will camp here till you come back."

"But Mars Tom, we couldn't ever find de village. I could find de pipe, 'caze I knows de kitchen, but my lan', *we* can't ever find de village, nur Sent Louis, nur none o' dem places. We don't know de way, Mars Tom."

That was a fact, and it stumped Tom for a minute. Then he said—

"Looky here, it can be done, sure: and I'll tell you how. You set your compass and sail west as straight as a dart, till you find the United States. It ain't any trouble, because it's the first land you'll strike the other side of the Atlantic. If it's day-time when you strike it, bulge right on, straight west from the upper part of the Florida coast, and in an hour and three quarters you'll hit the mouth of the Mississippi, at the speed that I'm going to send you. You'll be so high up in the air that the earth'll be curved considerable—sorter like a washbowl turned upside down—and you'll see a raft of rivers crawling around every which way, long before you get there, and you can pick out the Mississippi without any trouble. Then you can follow the river north nearly, an hour and three quarters, till you see the Ohio come in; then you want to look sharp, because you're getting near. Away up to your left you'll see another thread coming in—that's the Missouri and is a little above St. Louis. You'll come down low, then, so as you can examine the villages as you spin along. You'll pass about twenty-five in the next fifteen minutes, and you'll rec-ognize ours when you see it—and if you don't, you can yell down and ask."

"Ef it's dat easy, Mars Tom, I reckon we kin do it—yassir, I knows we kin."

The guide was sure of it, too, and thought that he could learn to stand his watch in a little while.

"Jim can teach you the whole thing in a half an hour," Tom said. "This balloon's as easy to manage as a canoe."

Tom got out the chart and marked out the course and measured it, and says—

"To go back west is the shortest way, you see. It's only about seven thousand miles. If you went east, and so on around, it's over twice as far." Then he says to the guide: "I want you both to watch the tell-tale all through the watches, and whenever it don't mark three hundred miles an hour, you go higher or drop lower till you find a storm-current that's going your way. There's a hundred miles an hour in this old thing without any wind to help. There's two hundred-mile gales to be found, any time you want to hunt for them."

"We'll hunt for them, sir."

"See that you do. Sometimes you may have to go up a couple of miles, and it'll be p'ison cold, but most of the time you'll find your storm a good deal lower. If you can only strike a cyclone—that's the ticket for you! You'll see by the Professor's books that they travel west in these latitudes, and they travel low, too."

Then he ciphered on the time, and says—

"Seven thousand miles, three hundred miles an hour—you can make the trip in a day—twenty-four hours. This is Thursday; you'll be back here Saturday afternoon. Come, now, hustle out some blankets and food and books and things for me and Huck, and you can start right along. There ain't no occasion to fool around—I want a smoke, and the quicker you fetch that pipe the better."

All hands jumped for the things, and in eight minutes our things was out and the balloon was ready for America. So we shook hands good-by, and Tom give his last orders:

"It's 10 minutes to 2 P.M., now, Arabian time. In 24 hours you'll be home, and it'll be 6 tomorrow morning, village time. When you strike the village, land a little back of the top of the hill, in the woods, out of sight; then you rush down, Jim, and shove these letters in the post-office, and if you see anybody stirring, pull your slouch down over your face so they won't know you. Then you go and slip in the kitchen and get the pipe, and lay this piece of paper on the kitchen-table and put something on it to hold it, and then slide out and git away and don't let Aunt Polly nor nobody else catch a sight of you. Then you jump for the balloon and shove for this very spot three hundred miles an hour. You won't have lost more than an hour. You'll start back at 7 or 8 A.M., village time, and be here in 24 hours, arriving at 2 or 3 P.M., Arabian time."

Tom he read the piece of paper to us. He had wrote on it—

THURSDAY AFTERNOON: *Tom Sawyer the Erronort sends his love to Aunt Polly from the shores of the Red Sea, and so does Huck Finn, and she will get it tomorrow morning half-past six.*

TOM SAWYER THE ERRONORT

The departure for home—and away she did go!

"That'll make her eyes bulge out and the tears come," he says. Then he says—
"Stand by! One—two—three—away you go!"

And away she *did* go! Why, she seemed to whiz out of sight in a second.

Then we found a most comfortable cave that looked out over that whole big plain, and there we camped to wait for the pipe.

THE BALLOON COME back all right, and brung the pipe; but Aunt Polly had catched Jim when he was getting it, and anybody can guess what happened: she sent for Tom. So Jim he says—

"Mars Tom, she's out on de porch wid her eye sot on de sky a-layin' for you, en she say she ain't gwyne to budge from dah tell she gits hold of you. Dey's gwyne to be trouble, Mars Tom, 'deed dey is."

So then we shoved for home, and not feeling very gay, neither.

First published in the November and December 1893 and the
January through April 1894 editions of *St. Nicholas Magazine*

The Brownies and the Bees

WRITTEN AND ILLUSTRATED BY PALMER COX

While Brownies once were rambling through
Where thick and tall the timber grew,
The hum of bees above their head
To some remarks and wonder led.
They gazed at branches in the air
And listened at the roots with care,
And soon a pine of giant size
Was found to hold the hidden prize.
Said one: "Some wild bees here have made
Their home within the forest shade,
Where neither fox nor prying bear
Can paw the treasure gathered there."
Another spoke: "You're quick and bright,
And generally judge matters right;
But here, my friend, you're all astray,
And like the blind mole grope your way.

The clapper from his bell he broke;
But still their queen's directing cry
The bees heard o'er the clamor high;
And held their bearing for this pine
As straight as runs the county line.
With taxes here, and failures there,

I chance well to remember still,
How months ago, when up the hill,
A farmer near, with bell and horn,
Pursued a swarm one sunny morn.
The fearful din the town awoke,

The man can ill such losses bear.
In view of this, our duty's clear:
Tomorrow night we'll muster here,
And when we give this tree a fall,
In proper shape we'll hive them all,

And take the queen and working throng
And lazy drones where they belong."

Next evening, at the time they set,
Around the pine the Brownies met
With tools collected, as they sped
From mill and shop and farmer's shed;
While some, to all their wants alive,
With ready hands procured a hive.
Ere work began, said one: "I fear
But little sport awaits us here;

Ere long, by steady rasp and blow,
The towering tree was leveled low;
And then the hive was made to rest
In proper style above the nest,
Until the queen and all her train
Did full and fair possession gain.

Then 'round the hive a sheet was tied,
That some were thoughtful to provide,
And off on poles, as best they could,
They bore the burden from the wood.

Be sure a trying task we'll find,
For bees are fuss and fire combined.
And take him in his drowsy hour,
Or when palavering to the flower,
The bee, however wild or tame,
In every land is much the same;
And those will rue it who neglect
To treat the insect with respect."

But trouble, as one may divine,
Occurred at points along the line.
'Twas bad enough on level ground,
Where, now and then, *one* exit found;
But when they came to rougher road,
Or climbed the fences with their load—
Then numbers of the prisoners there
Came trooping out to take the air,

And managed straight enough to fly
To keep excitement running high.

With branches broken off to suit,
And grass uplifted by the root,
In vain some daring Brownies tried
To brush the buzzing plagues aside.

Or in the ditch the sun would see
The tumbled hive for all of me."

And when at last the fence they found
That girt the farmer's orchard 'round,
And laid the hive upon the stand,
There hardly was, in all the band,

Said one, whose features proved to all
That bees had paid his nose a call:
"I'd rather dare the raging main,
Than meddle with such things again."
"The urgent calls," another cried,
"Of duty still must rule and guide—

A single Brownie who was free
From some reminders of the bee.
But thoughts of what a great surprise
Ere long would light the farmer's eyes
Soon drove away from every brain
The slightest thought of toil or pain.

First published in the June 1887 edition of *St. Nicholas Magazine*

Juggerjook

BY L. FRANK BAUM

ILLUSTRATED BY HARRISON CADY

"OH, MAMA!" CRIED Fuzzy Wuz, running into the burrow where her mother lay dozing, "may I go walking with Chatter Chuk?"

Mrs. Wuz opened one eye sleepily and looked at Fuzzy.

"If you are careful," she said; "and don't go near Juggerjook's den; and watch the sun so as to get home before the shadows fall."

"Yes, yes; of course," returned Fuzzy, eagerly.

"And don't let Chatter Chuk lead you into mischief," continued Mrs. Wuz, rubbing one long ear with her paw lazily. "Those red squirrels are reckless things and haven't much sense."

"Chatter's all right," protested Fuzzy Wuz. "He's the best friend I have in the forest. Good-by, Mother."

"Is your face clean, Fuzzy?"

"I've just washed it. Mother."

"With both paws, right and left?"

"Yes, Mother."

"Then run along and be careful."

"Yes, Mother."

Fuzzy turned and darted from the burrow, and in the bright sunshine outside sat Chatter Chuk on his hind legs, cracking an acorn.

"What'd she say, Fuz?" asked the red squirrel.

"All right; I can go, Chat. But I've got to be careful."

As the white rabbit hopped away through the bushes and he glided along beside her, Chatter Chuk laughed.

"Your people are always careful, Fuz," said he. "That's why you see so little of the world, and lose all the fun in life."

"I know," replied Fuzzy, a little ashamed. "Father is always singing this song to me:

"Little Bunny,
Don't get funny;
Run along and mind your eye;
It's the habit

Of a rabbit
To be difficult and shy."

"We squirrels are different," said Chatter Chuk, proudly. "We are always taught this song:

"Squirrel red,
Go ahead!
See the world, so bright and gay.
For a rover
May discover
All that happens day by day."

"Oh, if I could run up a tree, *I* shouldn't be afraid, either," remarked Fuzzy Wuz. "Even Juggerjook couldn't frighten me then."

"Kernels and shucks! Juggerjook!" cried Chatter Chuk, scornfully. "Who cares for him?"

"Don't you fear him?" asked Fuzzy Wuz, curiously.

"Of course not," said the squirrel. "My people often go to his den and leave nuts there."

"Why, if you make presents to Juggerjook, of course he won't hurt you," returned the rabbit. "All the beasts carry presents to his den, so he will protect them from their enemies. The bears kill wolves and carry them to Juggerjook to eat; and the wolves kill foxes and carry them to Juggerjook; and the foxes kill rabbits for him. But we rabbits do not kill animals, so we cannot take Juggerjook anything to eat except roots and clover; and he doesn't care much for those. So we are careful to keep away from his den."

"Have you ever seen him or the place where he lives?" asked the squirrel.

"No," replied Fuzzy Wuz.

"Suppose we go there now?"

"I smell carrots!"

"Oh, no! Mother said—"

"There's nothing to be afraid of. I've looked at the den often from the trees near by," said Chatter Chuk. "I can lead you to the edge of the bushes close to his den, and he'll never know we are near."

"Mother says Juggerjook knows everything that goes on in the forest," declared the rabbit, gravely.

"Your mother's a 'fraid-

They hopped through the bushes.

cat and trembles when a twig cracks," said Chatter, with a careless laugh. "Why don't you have a little spirit of your own, Fuzzy, and be independent?"

Fuzzy Wuz was quite young, and ashamed of being thought shy, so she said:

"All right, Chat. Let's go take a peep at Juggerjook's den."

"We're near it, now," announced the squirrel. "Come this way; and go softly, Fuzzy Wuz, because Juggerjook has sharp ears."

They crept along through the bushes some distance after that, but did not speak except in whispers. Fuzzy knew it was a bold thing to do. They had nothing to carry to the terrible Juggerjook, and it was known that he always punished those who came to his den without making him presents. But the rabbit relied upon Chatter Chuk's promise that the tyrant of the forest would never know they had been near him. Juggerjook was considered a great magician, to be sure, yet Chatter Chuk was not afraid of him. So why should Fuzzy Wuz fear anything?

The red squirrel ran ahead, so cautiously that he made not a sound in the underbrush; and he skillfully picked the way so that the fat white rabbit could follow him. Presently he stopped short and whispered to his companion:

"Put your head through those leaves, and you will see Juggerjook's den."

Fuzzy Wuz obeyed. There was a wide clearing beyond the bushes, and at the farther side was a great rock with a deep cave in it. All around the clearing were scattered the bones and skulls of animals, bleached white by the sun. Just in front of the cave was quite a big heap of bones, and the rabbit shuddered as she thought of all the many creatures Juggerjook must have eaten in his time. What a fierce appetite the great magician must have!

The sight made the timid rabbit sick and faint. She drew back and hopped away through the bushes without heeding the crackling twigs or the whispered

cautions of Chat-
ter Chuk, who
was now badly
frightened him-
self.

When they
had both with-
drawn to a safe
distance the squir-
rel said peevishly:

"Oh, you fool-
ish thing!' Why
did you make such
a noise and racket?"

Fuzzy crept under the box.

"Did I?" asked Fuzzy Wuz, simply.

"Indeed you did. And I warned you to be silent."

"But it's all right now. We're safe from Juggerjook here," she said.

"I'm not sure of that," remarked the squirrel, uneasily. "One is never safe from punishment if he is discovered breaking the law. I hope the magician was asleep and did not hear us."

"I hope so, too," added the rabbit; and then they ran along at more ease, rambling through the forest paths and enjoying the fragrance of the woods and the lights and shadows cast by the sun as it peeped through the trees.

Once in a while they would pause while Fuzzy Wuz nibbled a green leaf or Chatter Chuk cracked a fallen nut in his strong teeth, to see if it was sound and sweet.

"It seems funny for me to lie on the ground so long," he said. "But I invited you to walk with me, and of course a rabbit can't run up a tree and leap from limb to limb, as my people do."

"That is true," admitted Fuzzy; "nor can squirrels burrow in the ground, as rabbits do."

"They have no need to," declared the squirrel. "We find a hollow tree, and with our sharp teeth gnaw a hole through the shell and find a warm, dry home inside."

"I'm glad you do," remarked Fuzzy. "If all the animals burrowed in the ground there would not be room for us to hide from each other."

Chatter laughed at this.

"The shadows are getting long," he said. "If you wish to be home before sunset, we must start back."

"Wait a minute!" cried the rabbit, sitting lip and sniffing the air. "I smell carrots!"

"Never mind," said the squirrel.

"Never mind carrots? Oh, Chatter Chuk! You don't know how good they are."

"Well, we haven't any time to find them," he replied. "For my part, I could run home in five minutes; but you are so clumsy it will take you an hour. Where are you going now?"

"Just over here," said Fuzzy Wuz. "Those carrots can't be far off."

The squirrel followed, scolding a little because to him carrots meant nothing especially good to eat. And there, just beside the path, was an old coverless box raised on a peg, and underneath it a bunch of juicy, fat, orange carrots.

There was room under the box for Fuzzy Wuz to creep in and get the carrots, and this she promptly did, while Chatter Chuk stood on his hind legs a short distance away and impatiently waited. But when the white rabbit nibbled the carrots, the motion pulled a string which jerked out the peg that held up the box, and behold, Fuzzy Wuz was a prisoner!

She squealed with fear and scratched at the sides of the box in a vain endeavor to find a way to escape; but escape was impossible unless someone lifted the box. The red squirrel had seen the whole mishap, and chattered angrily from outside at the plight of his captured friend. The white rabbit thought he must be far away, because the box shut out so much the sound of his voice.

"Juggerjook must have heard us, and this is part of his revenge," said the squirrel. "Oh, dear! Oh, dear! I wonder what the great magician will do to *me*."

He was so terrified by this thought that Chatter Chuk took flight and darted home at his best speed. He lived in a tree very near to the burrow where Mrs. Wuz resided, but the squirrel did not go near the rabbit-burrow. The sun was already sinking in the west, so he ran into his nest and pretended to sleep late.

All night Mrs. Wuz waited for Fuzzy, and it was an anxious and sleepless night for the poor mother, as you may well believe. Fuzzy was her one darling, several other children having been taken from her in various ways soon after their birth. Mr. Wuz had gone to attend a meeting of the Rabbits' Protective Association and might be absent for several days; so he was not there to help or counsel her.

When daybreak came, the mother rabbit ran to the foot of the squirrels' tree and called:

"Chatter Chuk! Chatter Chuk! Where is my Fuzzy Wuz? Where is my darling child?"

Chatter Chuck was too frightened to answer until his mother made him. Then he ran down to the lowest limb of the tree and sat there while he talked.

"We went walking," he said, "and Fuzzy found some carrots under a box that was propped up with a peg. I told her not to eat them, but she did, and the peg fell out and made her a prisoner."

You see, he did not mention Juggerjook at all, yet he knew the magician was at the bottom of all the trouble.

But Mrs. Wuz knew rabbit-traps quite well, being old and experienced: so she begged the red squirrel to come at once and show her the place where Fuzzy had been caught.

"There isn't a moment to lose," she said, "for the trappers will be out early this morning to see what they have captured in their trap."

Chatter Chuk was afraid to go, having a guilty conscience; but his mother made him. He led the way timidly, but swiftly, and Mrs. Wuz fairly flew over the ground, so anxious was she to rescue her darling.

The box was in the same place yet, and poor Fuzzy Wuz could be heard moaning feebly inside it.

"Courage, my darling!" cried the mother. "I have come to save you."

First she tried to move the box, but it was too heavy for her to stir. Then she began scratching away the earth at its edge, only to find that it had been placed upon a big, flat stone, to prevent a rabbit from burrowing out.

This discovery almost drove her frantic, until she noticed Chatter Chuk, who stood trembling near by.

"Here!" she called; "it was you who led my child into trouble. Now you must get her out."

"How?" asked the red squirrel.

"Gnaw a hole in that box—quick! Gnaw faster than you ever did before in your life. See! the box is thinnest at this side. Set to work at once, Chatter Chuk!"

The red squirrel obeyed. The idea of saving his friend was as welcome to him as it was to the distracted mother. He was young, and his teeth were as sharp as needles. So he started at the lower edge and chewed the wood with all his strength and skill, and at every bite the splinters came away.

"Where is my darling child?"

It was a good idea. Mrs. Wuz watched him anxiously. If only the men would keep away for a time; the squirrel could make a hole big enough for Fuzzy Wuz to escape.

She crept around the other side of the box and called to the prisoner: "Courage, dear' one! We are trying to save you. But if the men come before Chatter Chuk can make a hole big enough, then, as soon as they raise the box, you must make a dash for the bushes. Run before they can put in their hands to seize you. Do you understand?"

"Yes, Mother," replied Fuzzy, but her voice wasn't heard very plainly, because the squirrel was making so much noise chewing the wood.

Presently Chatter Chuk stopped.

"It makes my teeth ache," he complained.

"Never mind, let them ache," replied Mrs. Wuz. "If you stop now, Fuzzy will die; and if she dies, I will go to Juggerjook and tell him how you led my child into trouble."

The thought of Juggerjook made the frightened squirrel redouble his efforts. He forgot the pain in his teeth and gnawed as no other squirrel had ever gnawed before. The ground was covered with tiny splinters from the box, and now the hole was big enough for the prisoner to put the end of her nose through and beg him to hurry.

Chatter Chuk was intent on his task, and the mother was intent upon watching him, so neither noticed any one approaching, until a net fell over their heads, and a big voice cried, with a boisterous laugh:

"Caught! and neat as a pin, too!"

Chatter Chuk and Mrs. Wuz struggled in the net with all their might, but it was fast around them, and they were helpless to escape. Fuzzy stuck her nose out of the hole in the box to find out what was the matter, and a sweet, childish voice exclaimed: "There's another in the trap, Daddy!"

Neither the rabbits nor the squirrel understood this strange language, but all realized they were in the power of dreadful Man and gave themselves up for lost.

Fuzzy made a dash the moment the box was raised; but the trapper knew the tricks of rabbits, so the prisoner only dashed into the same net where her mother and Chatter Chuk were confined.

"Three of them! Two rabbits and a squirrel. That's quite a haul, Charlie," said the man.

The little boy was examining the box. "Do rabbits gnaw through wood, Father?" he asked.

"No, my son," was the reply.

"But there is a hole here. And see! There are the splinters upon the ground."

The prisoners scampered away.

The man examined the box in turn, somewhat curiously. "How strange!" he said. "These are marks of the squirrel's teeth. Now, I wonder if the squirrel was try-ing to liberate the rabbit."

"Looks like it, Daddy, doesn't it?" replied the boy.

"I never heard of such a thing in my life," declared the man. "These little crea-tures often display more wisdom than we give them credit for. But how can we explain this curious freak, Charlie?"

The boy sat down upon the box and looked thoughtfully at the three prisoners in the net. They had ceased to struggle, having given way to despair; but the boy could see their little hearts beating fast through their furry skins.

"This is the way it looks to me, Daddy," he finally said. "We caught the small rabbit in the box, and the big one must be its mother. When she found her baby was caught, she tried to save it, and she began to burrow under the box, for here is the mark of her paws. But she soon saw the flat stone, and gave up."

"Yes; that seems reasonable," said the man.

"But she loved her baby," continued the boy, gazing at the little creatures piti-fully, "and thought of another way."

The red squirrel was a friend of hers, so she ran and found him, and asked him to help her. He did, and tried to gnaw through the box; but we came too soon and captured them with the net because they were so busy they didn't notice us."

"Exactly!" cried the man, with a laugh. "That tells the story very plainly, my son, and I see you are fast learning the ways of animals. But how intelligent these little things are!"

"That's what my mother would do," returned the boy. "She'd try to save me; and that's just what the mother rabbit did."

"Well, we must be going," said the man; and as he started away he picked up the net and swung it over his shoulder. The prisoners struggled madly again, and the boy, who walked along the forest path a few steps behind his father, watched them.

"Daddy," he said softly, coming to the man's side, "I don't want to keep those rabbits."

"Oh, they'll make us a good dinner," was the reply.

"I—I couldn't eat 'em for dinner, Daddy. Not the mama rabbit and the little one she tried to save. Nor the dear little squirrel that wanted to help them. Let's—let's—let 'em go!"

The man stopped short and turned to look with a smile into the boy's upturned, eager face.

"What will Mama say when we go back without any dinner?" he asked.

"You know, Daddy. She'll say a good deed is better than a good dinner."

The man laid a caressing hand on the curly head and handed his son the net. Charlie's face beamed with joy. He opened wide the net and watched the prisoners gasp with surprise, bound out of the meshes, and scamper away into the bushes.

Then the boy put his small hand in his father's big one, and together they walked silently along the path.

"ALL THE SAME," said Chatter Chuk to himself, as, snug at home, he trembled at the thought of his late peril, "I shall keep away from old Juggerjook after this. I am very sure of that!"

"Mama," said Fuzzy Wuz, nestling beside her mother in the burrow, "why do you suppose the fierce Men let us go?"

"I cannot tell, my dear," was the reply.

"Men are curious creatures, and often act with more wisdom than we give them credit for."

First published in the December 1910 edition of *St. Nicholas Magazine*

A Race with an Avalanche

BY FANNY HYDE MERRILL

OVER A LITTLE town in the heart of the Rocky Mountains floated a heavy cloud. A young girl stood by the window of one of the pretty homes, and watched anxiously the sky above. As she looked, her brother stepped up behind her. "Never mind, Kate," he said, "we'll have a good Christmas, if it does snow."

Kate frowned. "What is the use of any more snow? It's four feet deep on the ground now, and all the roads are blocked. We can't get any Christmas mail; the sugar in town is all gone; only one cow to give milk for the children, not an egg to be had; we can't even bake a cake!"

And just then white flakes came floating through the air. Kate's exclamation was a doleful "There it comes! It's too bad!"

Over near the large stove sat father. As he heard Kate's distressed voice, he came to the window.

The Doctor was a slender man with kind eyes and gray hair. There were many lines across his forehead, but most of them had been drawn by care and thought, few by age, and none at all by discontent. As he stood and stroked Kate's hair, it was easy to see that the young girl was the pride of his heart.

"Your mother, my dear," her father said slowly, "was always glad when it snowed at Christmas time. She always said, 'A real Christmas should be a white Christmas.'"

Tears stood in Kate's eyes, and Harry turned away his head. He

Harry's race for life

did not wish Kate to know how desolate home had been to him since their mother's death.

Through the gathering snow two heavy figures came toward the house. Harry opened the door, and saw two strong men, with resolute faces.

"Does Dr. Ward live here?" they asked.

The doctor stepped forward. In spite of the storm, the men lifted their caps as they saw his face.

"There's a man hurt up at the mines," said the taller of the two men. "Will you come up, Doctor?"

"Certainly," said the doctor, promptly.

The man looked at the two young people. "Doctor," he said, "you know the snow is sliding badly? It's a deal of risk."

The doctor nodded, and put on his thick coat.

"Oh, papa!" cried Kate, "not today! Not you! We can't let you go." In distress she turned to the men: "Can't you get some younger man for such a hard trip?"

The man looked troubled. "I'm sorry, Miss; we did try. But," his face hardening, "no other doctor will go. And the man is badly hurt."

Poor Kate! Father and brother had hidden their own grief over the mother's death, and striven to make her life bright. Now she could not believe she could be put aside for any other call. She clung to her father, sobbing.

"Kate," he said, as he took her hands, "my work is to *save* lives—"

"But, Papa! your life—so useful—save *that!*"

"My dear, who can tell which life is most needed? Besides, your fears are foolish, dear. There is probably no real danger. I shall come back safely, never fear."

He stopped with his hand on her head. Then, satchel in hand, he went to the door. As he stepped across the threshold he took Harry's hand. "My boy," he said, "you are like your mother. I can trust Kate to you"; and the door closed. The three men plowed their way up the street into the mountain-trail that led to the mines. Kate watched the figures grow small in the distance, till the snow hid them from sight. The mighty hills that shut in the town never looked to Kate so high, so silent, so unmoved as during the long hours of that day. In vain Harry planned diversions; she watched the window with a sorrowful face. Still the storm raged; and, as the twilight gathered, Harry could not keep anxiety from his face and voice. Down in the valley the twilight fades early, and it was dark when a heavy rap brought Harry to the door. There stood twelve men, and in their midst, on a sled, an uncouth mass of snow-covered blankets.

"Where's father?" gasped Harry, staring at the sled with its heavy burden.

"He said we were to tell you the storm was so bad he'd stay up at the mine tonight. We're taking the fellow that was hurt down to the hospital."

"Noble fellows!" cried Harry, with his face aglow, as the men set off again. "Those twelve men have brought that hurt fellow down the mountain on a sled in this storm and darkness, over four feet of snow. They faced death every step of the way, for the snow is sliding all the time."

Kate stared at the fire, but said nothing. Suddenly a veil had been lifted. She saw not only her noble father risking his life for others—that was no new vision—but the rough, the faithful miners, twelve of them, risking their lives to carry to greater safety one poor, hurt, perhaps dying, man. And she—all day long she had brooded over her own selfish sorrow and anxiety, letting Harry try to amuse her, but never thinking of his troubles. With a flush of shame she started up.

"Harry," she said, "we'll practice a little tonight; can't we?"

And Harry brought out his flute and the music with a face of such relief and happiness that Kate's heart gave another throb of remorse.

The morning of the next day dawned clear and cool. Gradually the sun rose over the mountains, each moment touching into new glory the light and shadow, the color and glittering sheen of the vast snow-covered hills. Kate sung over her morning work and thought tenderly of the new comfort she would bring into her father's life from that day forward. Nine o'clock it was before the sunlight touched the town in the valley. Harry began to watch the mountain-trail for his father. All day long the "beauty of the hills" glittered before the longing eyes of Kate and Harry, but no father came down the shining mountain-path. At three o'clock the sun went down, and the tints of sunset glowed upon the snowy heights. Kate brave- ly struggled through the pretense of a meal; but self-control is not learned in a day, and by evening Harry found her crying softly by herself.

"Kate," he said, "don't worry; tomorrow I'll go up the mountain and see if father is still there."

Harry started early next morning, and Kate bravely watched him out of sight.

"We'll be home for Christmas," he shouted back, for his spirits rose with the prospect of something to do. He climbed to the mines, and found, to his dismay, that his father had started down early the preceding morning, the superintendent having watched him out of sight.

"Well," said Harry, "I must go down and get up a party from town to search for him."

"That is the best way," said the manager.

He said nothing of the danger Harry himself must pass through. Danger was around them all.

Harry was strong, active, and skilful in the use of the skis, which he wore that day.

The boy's face was saddened by his fears for his father, but a resolute look flashed into his eyes as he made ready for the perilous trip. Just as he shot forward, came the thunder of a blast of dynamite in the mine above him. A shout went up, "A snow-slide!" and a mass of snow, dislodged by the explosion, came crushing past. A corner of the shed containing the men was carried away. The men looked at each other. Their escape had been narrow; where was the boy who had just now shot forward in the very path of the avalanche?

It needed no shout to tell Harry what the result of that report would be. He had started, and almost at that instant the snow was on his track. There was no chance for turn or thought of pause. His only chance for life was to reach the valley before the avalanche.

Over the shortest, steepest descent he flew, the wind cutting his face, all thought merged in one fire of effort to fly faster.

Faster, faster, he skimmed the glittering snow till he shot like an arrow from a bow into the plain below, and fell headlong covered by the frosty spray at the edge of the spent avalanche. The breath seemed pressed out of his body, and for some minutes he did not move.

Then a shout came through the air, and he lifted himself as a band of miners came flying down the mountain toward him. They came on snow-shoes from the mines above, and were overjoyed to find the boy alive. "He beat the snow-slide!" they shouted, and Harry, a hero from that hour, was escorted home in triumph. At the door stood Kate, and back of her the good father, safe and sound. On his way down from the mine, the doctor had been hailed by a man who lived in a little cabin sheltered in the mountain-side. The man's child had broken an arm, and by the time everything was done for his relief, the short day was so far gone that the doctor was obliged to stay all night.

That "Christmas eve," as Kate and Harry and their father stood watching the stars glow and sparkle in the keen mountain air, Kate put her hand on her father's arm as she said, "There won't be much for Christmas, tomorrow; but anything that could come to me would seem very small, after having you and Harry given back to me."

"My dear," said her father, "since the Christmas angels first sang 'Peace on earth, good will toward men,' the best gift that can come to any of us is an unselfish heart."

First published in the December 1892 edition of *St. Nicholas Magazine*

In a Ring of Fire

BY F. H. KELLOGG

FOR YEARS I had hoped to visit the Indian Territory before the rush of home-steaders had settled the country to such an extent as to put an end to the native wildness of the region and people. My opportunity came at last, and during a certain September vacation the trip was made. The experience of the first day was enough to convince me that the place was still wild enough to satisfy anyone in search of the uncivilized.

With an Indian trader, his wife, and little boy, I left Arkansas City one morning at about ten o'clock. After an hour's ride we alighted from the train at Ponca, a station on the Ponca reservation. There we expected to find a light wagon in which to finish our journey, for our destination, Kama-hatsa (Gray Horse), was about thirty miles from this, the nearest railroad station. After a wait of an hour longer, our friend arrived with the conveyance, and just at noon we started on our ride across the country. Soon we reached the Arkansas River. Although recently swollen, it was apparently fordable, and we started to cross. Had not our driver been well acquainted with the river our trip would have abruptly terminated there. We drove up, then down, then across. At times the water ran into the body of the wagon; again we were in a quicksand, and the horses plunged and staggered. The wheels would grind and grate over the sand, the wagon would roll and toss until we were almost thrown out, and then, with a sudden lurch, all would come right side up again, and we would move on.

We had just reached the opposite bank when, looking back, we saw two men in a wagon rather smaller than the one in which we were riding and drawn by a team of little Indian ponies. They had just struck the deep channel, and the horses, all covered but their heads, were struggling along, sometimes swimming, sometimes just getting a foothold. Their wagon also was covered, so that all that was visible was two horses' heads, and then, just behind them, the two men apparently seated upon the water. We soon forgot our former fright in watching them; for, though we sympathized with them, it was really a ludicrous sight.

Driving across the bottom-land, we passed through seas of grass which was higher than our heads, even as we sat in the wagon. The sudden gusts of wind set the grass to bowing and bending, the tall sunflowers welcomed us with polite "salaams," but the long whip-like lashes of the wire-grass gave stinging cuts across our faces.

A dim haziness spreading over the sky now attracted our attention, and I felt a sudden sinking of the heart as I remembered that this was the season when the great prairie-fires are common. In such a place as that a fire meant certain death. The haze assumed a reddish tinge, the air seemed oppressive and stifling, and we knew that danger was near. We hoped we might avoid the direct path of the flames, but the hope was a faint one, for the whole country seemed to be ablaze. As far as the eye could see, dense columns of smoke showed the presence of the fire, in all directions.

We whipped up the horses and drove toward the upland, thinking thus to escape the greatest danger. We reached the high ground before meeting any flame, and we were greatly rejoiced to see that much of the grass was still fairly green here, though thickly bestrewn with patches of longer grass that was dry.

The fierce flames now approached, rushing along with furious speed, crackling and snapping—the sound alone being sufficient to strike terror to the stoutest heart. Galloping along the line of fire, we found that where it crossed a little ravine the flames were not so high, for the grass was quite green there. We dashed through the line of flame, suffering brief tortures of suffocation, and a severe stinging and smarting of our eyes, caused by the intense heat and pungent smoke.

Once through, we congratulated ourselves on the hope that we should yet escape; for, going in this direction, right in the teeth of the wind, we could travel more rapidly than the pursuing flames.

While passing through the fire, I recalled the proverb "It's an ill wind that blows nobody good," for just in advance of the line of flame clouds of swallows darted here and there, catching the hosts of insects started up by the heat of the burning grass.

We now heard galloping hoofs, and we soon saw two Osage Indians approaching through the smoke. "Where are you going?" they asked, in their own language. "To Gray Horse," our driver replied, in the same tongue. They told him that the prairie was a mass of flame in that direction, and that we must go back. We responded that all was flame in *that* direction. Notwithstanding the indifference to danger usually ascribed to natives, these Indians showed unmistakable signs of terror. Some further quick conversation informed us that they, like ourselves, had seized an opportunity to penetrate the line of flame, thinking thus to escape.

We all were now enclosed in a gradually narrowing ring of fire. To clear the space around us by burning off the grass—to start a "back-fire," as it is called—was our only chance for safety; and this we attempted. A large space was cleared before the oncoming fire reached us. We hoped to escape with but singed eyebrows, and a few moments of suffocation; and this we would have considered a fortunate deliverance. But we found our last chance failing us. The back-fire we had started against the wind had burned only the dry grass, and in doing this had served as a furnace to dry the greener grass. Thus the prairie fire, reaching our burned district, found the greener grasses killed and dried, and hence had almost as much fuel as outside.

The fire was now close around us. The varying currents of air heated by the

We dashed through the line of flame.

flame whirled and rose, and gusts of cold air, rushing in to replace the hot air, caused a whirlwind, and a great well of smoke and flame was thus formed. Within this well we stood, as yet unharmed and with a constant supply of cool air, but expecting death.

It was a dreadful moment: The mother and child were crying, the Indians, with uplifted arms, were calling upon the Great Spirit, in a weird chant.

Suddenly we felt an unusually strong rush of cold air from one side, and looking up, I saw a strange and welcome sight. A long tongue of flame had run toward and into our circular prison from the main fire, and had burned a lane from the outlying burnt area in to us. Through this lane, formed by walls of fire, came rushing in a current of cold, clear air. This kept the smoke blown away, and we saw plainly the path of escape thus providentially afforded us, when all hope seemed gone.

Our horses had been paralyzed with fear, and had hardly moved a muscle after the near approach of the flames. Now they could not be induced to move. But quicker than thought each Indian cast off his blanket, and enveloped his horse's head. Then they grasped the bridles, jumped upon the horses' backs, and dashed out through the avenue of escape that had opened before us. We followed, with a rush, and soon found ourselves in safety.

The Indians rode rapidly away, staying for neither thanks nor presents. It was with thankful hearts that we drove into Gray Horse, about ten o'clock that night; and I thought that if my first experience was a forerunner of what was to come, I would have been wiser to leave "wild scenes" to those better fitted to cope with them.

First published in the December 1892 edition of *St. Nicholas Magazine*

Sweet Marjoram Day

(A Fairy Tale)

BY FRANK R. STOCKTON

IT WAS A very delightful country where little Corette lived. It seemed to be almost always summer-time there, for the winters were just long enough to make people glad when they were over. When it rained, it mostly rained at night, and so the fields and gardens had all the water they wanted, while the people were generally quite sure of a fine day. And, as they lived a great deal out-of-doors, this was a great advantage to them.

The principal business of the people of this country was the raising of sweet marjoram. The soil and climate were admirably adapted to the culture of this delightful herb, and fields and fields of it were to be seen in every direction. At that time, and this was a good while ago, very little sweet marjoram was raised in other parts of the world, so this country had the trade nearly all to itself.

The great holiday of the year was the day on which the harvest of this national herb began. It was called "Sweet Marjoram Day," and the people, both young and old, thought more of it than of any other holiday in the year.

On that happy day everybody went out into the fields. There was never a person so old, or so young, or so busy that he or she could not go to help in the harvest. Even when there were sick people, which was seldom, they were carried out to the fields and stayed there all day. And they generally felt much better in the evening.

There were always patches of sweet marjoram planted on purpose for the very little babies to play in on the great day. They must be poor, indeed, these people said, if they could not raise sweet marjoram for their own needs and for exportation, and yet have enough left for the babies to play in.

So, all this day the little youngsters rolled, and tumbled, and kicked and crowed in the soft green and white beds of the fragrant herb, and pulled it up by the roots, and laughed and chuckled, and went to sleep in it, and were the happiest babies in the world.

They needed no care, except at dinner-time, so the rest of the people gave all their time to gathering in the crop and having fun. There was always lots of fun on this great harvest day, for everybody worked so hard that the whole crop was generally in the sweet marjoram barns before breakfast, so that they had nearly the whole day for games and jollity.

In this country, where little Corette lived, there were fairies. Not very many of them, it is true, for the people had never seen but two. These were sisters, and there were never fairies more generally liked than these two little creatures, neither of them over four inches high. They were very fond of the company of human beings, and were just as full of fun as anybody. They often used to come to spend an hour or two, and sometimes a whole day, with the good folks, and they seemed always glad to see and to talk to everybody.

These sisters lived near the top of a mountain in a fairy cottage. This cottage had never been seen by any of the people, but the sisters had often told them all about it. It must have been a charming place.

The house was not much bigger than a bandbox, and it had two stories and a garret, with a little portico running all around it. Inside was the dearest little furniture of all kinds—beds, tables, chairs, and everything that could possibly be needed.

Everything about the house and grounds was on the same small scale. There was a little stable and a little barn, with a little old man to work the little garden and attend to the two little cows. Around the house were garden-beds ever so small, and little graveled paths; and a kitchen-garden, where the peas climbed up little sticks no bigger than pins, and where the little chickens, about the size of flies, sometimes got in and scratched up the little vegetables. There was a little meadow for pasture, and a grove of little trees; and there was also a small field of sweet marjoram, where the blossoms were so tiny that you could hardly have seen them without a magnifying glass.

It was not very far from this cottage to the sweet marjoram country, and the fairy sisters had no trouble at all in running down there whenever they felt like it, but none of the people had ever seen this little home. They had looked for it, but could not find it, and the fairies would never take any of them to it. They said it was no place for human beings. Even the smallest boy, if he were to trip his toe, might fall against their house and knock it over; and as to any of them coming into the fairy grounds, that would be impossible, for there was no spot large enough for even a common-sized baby to creep about in.

On Sweet Marjoram Day the fairies never failed to come. Every year they taught the people new games, and all sorts of new ways of having fun. People would never have even thought of having such good times if it had not been for these fairies.

One delightful afternoon, about a month before Sweet Marjoram Day, Corette, who was a little girl just old enough, and not a day too old (which is exactly the age all little girls ought to be), was talking about the fairy cottage to some of her companions.

"We never can see it," said Corette, sorrowfully.

"No," said one of the other girls, "we are too big. If we were little enough, we might go."

"Are you sure the sisters would be glad to see us, then?" asked Corette.

"Yes, I heard them say so. But it doesn't matter at all, as we are not little enough."

"No," said Corette, and she went off to take a walk by herself.

She had not walked far before she reached a small house which stood by the sea-shore. This house belonged to a Reformed Pirate who lived there all by himself. He had entirely given up a sea-faring life so as to avoid all temptation, and he employed his time in the mildest pursuits he could think of.

When Corette came to his house, she saw him sitting in an easy-chair in front of his door near the edge of a small bluff which overhung the sea, busily engaged in knitting a doily.

The Reformed Pirate

When he saw Corette, he greeted her kindly, and put aside his knitting, which he was very glad to do, for he hated knitting doilies, though he thought it was his duty to make them.

"Well, my little maid," he said, in a sort of a muffled voice, which sounded as if he were speaking under water, for he tried to be as gentle in every way as he could, "how do you do? You don't look quite as gay as usual. Has anything run afoul of you?"

"Oh no!" said Corette, and she came and stood by him, and taking up his doily, she looked it over carefully and showed him where he had dropped a lot of stitches and where he had made some too tight and others a great deal too loose. He did not know how to knit very well.

When she had shown him as well as she could how he ought to do it, she sat down on the grass by his side, and after a while she began to talk to him about the fairy cottage, and what a great pity it was that it was impossible for her ever to see it.

"It *is* a pity," said the Reformed Pirate. "I've heard of that cottage and I'd like to see it myself. In fact, I'd like to go to see almost anything that was proper and quiet, so as to get rid of the sight of this everlasting knitting."

"There are other things you might do besides knit," said Corette.

"Nothing so depressing and suitable," said he, with a sigh.

"It would be of no use for you to think of going there," said Corette. "Even I am too large, and you are ever and ever so much too big. You couldn't get one foot into one of their paths."

"I've no doubt that's true," he replied; "but the thing might be done. Almost anything can be done if you set about it in the right way. But you see, little maid, that you and I don't know enough. Now, years ago, when I was in a different line of business, I often used to get puzzled about one thing or another, and then I went to somebody who knew more than myself."

"Were there many such persons?" asked Corette.

"Well, no. I always went to one old fellow who was a Practicing Wizard. He lived, and still lives, I reckon, on an island about fifty miles from here, right off there to the sou'-sou'-west. I've no doubt that if we were to go to him he'd tell us just how to do this thing."

"But how could we get there?" asked Corette.

"Oh! I'd manage that," said the Reformed Pirate, his eyes flashing with animation. "I've an old sail-boat back there in the creek that's as good as ever she was. I could fix her up, and get everything all ship-shape in a couple of days, and then you and I could scud over there in no time. What do you say? Wouldn't you like to go?"

"Oh, I'd like to go ever so much!" cried Corette, clapping her hands, "if my parents let me."

"Well, run and ask them," said he, rolling up his knitting and stuffing it under the cushion of his chair, "and I'll go and look at that boat right away."

So Corette ran home to her father and mother and told them all about the matter. They listened with great interest, and her father said:

"Well now, our little girl is not looking quite as well as usual. I have noticed that she is a little pale. A sea-trip might be the very thing for her."

"I think it would do her a great deal of good," said her mother, "and as to that

Reformed Pirate, she'd be just as safe with him as if she was on dry land."

So it was agreed that Corette should go. Her father and mother were always remarkably kind.

The Reformed Pirate was perfectly delighted when he heard this, and he went hard to work to get his little vessel ready. To sail again on the ocean seemed to him the greatest of earthly joys, and as he was to do it for the benefit of a good little girl, it was all perfectly right and proper.

When they started off, the next day but one, all the people who lived near enough came down to see them off. Just as they were about to start, the Reformed Pirate said:

"Hello! I wonder if I hadn't better run back to the house and get my sword! I only wear the empty scabbard now, but it might be safer, on a trip like this, to take the sword along."

So he ran back and got it, and then he pushed off amid the shouts of all the good people on the beach.

The boat was quite a good-sized one, and it had a cabin and everything neat and comfortable. The Reformed Pirate managed it beautifully, all by himself, and Corette sat in the stern and watched the waves, and the sky, and the sea-birds, and was very happy indeed.

As for her companion, he was in a state of ecstasy. As the breeze freshened, the sails filled, and the vessel went dashing over the waves, he laughed and joked, and sang snatches of old sea-songs, and was the jolliest man afloat.

After a while, as they went thus sailing merrily along, a distant ship appeared in sight. The moment his eyes fell upon it, a sudden change came over the Reformed Pirate. He sprang to his feet and, with his hand still upon the helm, he leaned forward and gazed at the ship. He gazed and he gazed, and he gazed without saying a word. Corette spoke to him several times, but he answered not. And as he gazed he moved the helm so that his little craft gradually turned from her course, and sailed to meet the distant ship.

The, as the two vessels approached

The Reformed Pirate is the jolliest man afloat.

each other, the Reformed Pirate became very much excited. He tightened his belt and loosened his sword in its sheath. Hurriedly giving the helm to Corette, he went forward and jerked a lot of ropes and hooks from a cubby-hole where they had been stowed away. Then he pulled out a small, dark flag, with bits of skeleton painted on it, and hoisted it to the top-mast.

By this time he had nearly reached the ship, which was a large three-masted vessel. There seemed to be a great commotion on board; sailors were running this way and that; women were screaming; and officers could be heard shouting, "Put her about! Clap on more sail!"

But steadily on sailed the small boat, and the moment it came alongside the big ship, the Reformed Pirate threw out grapnels and made the two vessels fast together. Then he hooked a rope-ladder to the side of the ship, and rushing up it, sprang with a yell on the deck of the vessel, waving his flashing sword around his head!

"Down, dastards! Varlets! hounds!" he shouted. "Down upon your knees! Throw down your arms! SURRENDER!"

Then every man went down upon his knees, and threw down his arms and surrendered.

"Where is your Captain?" roared their conqueror.

The Captain came trembling forward.

"Bring to me your gold and silver, your jewels and your precious stones, and your rich stuffs!"

The Captain ordered these to be quickly brought and placed before the Reformed Pirate, who continued to stride to and fro across the deck waving his glittering blade, and who, when he saw the treasures placed before him, shouted again:

"Prepare for scuttling!" and then, while the women got down on their knees and begged that he would not sink the ship, and the children cried, and the men trembled so that they could hardly kneel straight, and the Captain stood pale and shaking before him, he glanced at the pile of treasure, and touched it with his sword.

"Aboard with this, my men!" he said. "But first I will divide it. I will divide this into—into—into *one* part. Look here!" and then he paused, glanced around, and clapped his hand to his head. He looked at the people, the treasure and the ship. Then suddenly he sheathed his sword, and, stepping up to the Captain, extended his hand.

"Good sir," said he, "you must excuse me. This is a mistake. I had no intention of taking this vessel. It was merely a temporary absence of mind. I forgot I had reformed, and seeing this ship, old scenes and my old business came into my head, and I just came and took the vessel without really thinking what I was doing. I beg you will excuse me. And these ladies—I am very sorry to have inconvenienced them. I ask them to overlook my unintentional rudeness."

"Oh, don't mention it!" cried the Captain, his face beaming with joy as he seized the hand of the Reformed Pirate. "It is of no importance, I assure you. We are delighted, sir, delighted!"

"Oh yes!" cried all the ladies. "Kind sir, we are charmed! We are charmed!"

"You are all very good indeed," said the Reformed Pirate, "but I really think I was not altogether excusable. And I am very sorry that I made your men bring up all these things."

"Not at all! not at all!" cried the Captain.

"No trouble whatever to show them. Very glad indeed to have the opportunity. By the by, would you like to take a few of them, as a memento of your visit?"

"Oh no, I thank you," replied the Reformed Pirate, "I would rather not."

"Perhaps, then, some of your men might like a trinket or a bit of cloth—"

"Oh, I have no men! There is no one on board but myself—excepting a little girl, who is a passenger. But I must be going. Good-by, Captain!"

"I am sorry you are in such a hurry," said the Captain. "Is there anything at all that I can do for you?"

"No, thank you. But stop!—there may be something. Do you sail to any port where there is a trade in doilies?"

"Oh yes! To several such," said the Captain.

"Well, then, I would be very much obliged to you," said the Reformed Pirate, "if you would sometimes stop off that point that you see there, and send a boat ashore to my house for a load of doilies."

"You manufacture them by the quantity, then?" asked the Captain.

"I expect to," said the other, sadly.

The Captain promised to stop, and, after shaking hands with every person on deck, the Reformed Pirate went down the side of the ship, and taking in his ladder and his grapnels, he pushed off.

As he slowly sailed away, having lowered his flag, the Captain looked over the side of his ship, and said:

"If I had only known that there was nobody but a little girl on board! I thought, of course, he had a boat-load of pirates."

Corette asked a great many questions about everything that had happened on the ship, for she had heard the noise and confusion as she sat below in the little boat; but her companion was disposed to be silent, and said very little in reply.

When the trip was over, and they had reached the island, the Reformed Pirate made his boat fast, and taking little Corette by the hand, he walked up to the house of the Practicing Wizard.

This was a queer place. It was a great rambling house, one story high in some places, and nine or ten in other places; and then, again, it seemed to run into the ground and re-appear at a short distance—the different parts being connected by cellars and basements, with nothing but flower-gardens over them.

Corette thought she had never seen such a wonderful building; but she had not long to look at the outside of it, for her companion, who had been there before, and knew the ways of the place, went up to a little door in a two-story part of the house and knocked. Our friends were admitted by a dark cream-colored slave, who informed them that the Practicing Wizard was engaged with other visitors, but that he would soon be at leisure.

So Corette and the Reformed Pirate sat down in a handsome room, full of curious and wonderful things, and, in a short time, they were summoned into the Practicing Wizard's private office.

"Glad to see you," said he, as the Reformed Pirate entered. "It has been a long time since you were here. What can I do for you, now? Want to know something about the whereabouts of any ships, or the value of any cargoes?"

"Oh, no! I'm out of that business now," said the other. "I've come this time for something entirely different. But I'll let this little girl tell you what it is. She can do it a great deal better than I can."

So Corette stepped up to the Practicing Wizard, who was a pleasant, elderly man, with a smooth white face, and a constant smile, which seemed to have grown on his face instead of a beard, and she told him the whole story of the fairy sisters and their cottage, of her great desire to see it, and of the difficulties in the way.

"I know all about those sisters," he said; "I don't wonder you want to see their house. You both wish to see it?"

"Yes," said the Reformed Pirate; "I might as well go with her, if the thing can be done at all."

"Very proper," said the Practicing Wizard, "very proper, indeed. But there is only one way in which it can be done. You must be condensed."

"Does that hurt?" asked Corette.

"Oh, not at all! You'll never feel it. For the two it will be one hundred and eighty ducats," said he, turning to the Reformed Pirate; "we make a reduction when there are more than one."

"Are you willing?" asked the Reformed Pirate of Corette, as he put his hand in his breeches' pocket.

"Oh yes!" said Corette, "certainly I am, if that's the only way."

Whereupon her good friend said no more, but pulled out a hundred and eighty ducats and handed them to the Practicing Wizard, who immediately commenced operations.

Corette and the Reformed Pirate were each placed in a large easy-chair, and upon each of their heads the old white-faced gentleman placed a little pink ball, about the size of a pea. Then he took a position in front of them.

"Now then," said he, "sit perfectly still. It will be over in a few minutes," and he lifted up a long thin stick, and, pointing it toward the couple, he began to count: "One, two, three, four—"

As he counted, the Reformed Pirate and Corette began to shrink, and by the time he had reached fifty they were no bigger than cats. But he kept on counting until Corette was about three and a half inches high and her companion about five inches.

Then he stopped, and knocked the pink ball from each of their heads with a little tap of his long stick.

"There we are," said he, and he carefully picked up the little creatures and put them on a table in front of a looking-glass, that they might see how they liked his work.

It was admirably done. Every proportion had been perfectly kept.

"It seems to me that it couldn't be better," said the Condensed Pirate.

"It seems to me that it couldn't be better," said the Condensed Pirate, looking at himself from top to toe.

"No," said the Practicing Wizard, smiling rather more than usual, "I don't believe it could."

"But how are we to get away from here?" said Corette to her friend. "A little fellow like you can't sail that big boat."

"No," replied he, ruefully, "that's true; I couldn't do it. But perhaps, sir, you could condense the boat."

"Oh no!" said the old gentleman, "that would never do. Such a little boat would be swamped before you reached shore, if a big fish didn't swallow you. No, I'll see that you get away safely."

So saying, he went to a small cage that stood in a window, and took from it a pigeon.

"This fellow will take you," said he. "He is very strong and swift, and will go ever so much faster than your boat."

Next he fastened a belt around the bird, and to the lower part of this he hung a little basket, with two seats in it. He then lifted Corette and the Condensed Pirate into the basket, where they sat down opposite one another.

"Do you wish to go directly to the cottage of the fairy sisters?" said the old gentleman.

"Oh yes!" said Corette.

So he wrote the proper address on the bill of the pigeon, and, opening the window, carefully let the bird fly.

"I'll take care of your boat," he cried to the Condensed Pirate, as the pigeon rose in the air. "You'll find it all right, when you come back."

And he smiled worse than ever.

The pigeon flew up to a great height, and then he took flight in a straight line for the Fairy Cottage, where he arrived before his passengers thought they had half finished their journey.

The bird alighted on the ground, just outside of the boundary fence; and when Corette and her companion had jumped from the basket, he rose and flew away home as fast as he could go.

The Condensed Pirate now opened a little gate in the fence, and he and Corette walked in. They went up the graveled path, and under the fruit-trees, where the ripe peaches and apples hung, as big as peas, and they knocked at the door of the fairy sisters.

When these two little ladies came to the door, they were amazed to see Corette.

"Why, how did you ever?" they cried. "And if there isn't our old friend the Reformed Pirate!"

"Condensed Pirate, if you please," said that individual. "There's no use of my being reformed while I'm so small as this. I couldn't hurt anybody if I wanted to."

"Well, come right in, both of you," said the sisters, "and tell us all about it."

So they went in, and sat in the little parlor, and told their story. The fairies were delighted with the whole affair, and insisted on a long visit, to which our two friends were not at all opposed.

They found everything at this cottage exactly as they had been told. They ate the daintiest little meals off the daintiest little dishes, and they thoroughly enjoyed all the delightful little things in the little place. Sometimes, Corette and the fairies would take naps in little hammocks under the trees, while the Condensed Pirate helped the little man drive up the little cows, or work in the little garden.

On the second day of their visit, when they were all sitting on the little portico after supper, one of the sisters, thinking that the Condensed Pirate might like to have something to do, and knowing how he used to occupy himself, took from her basket a little half-knit tidy, with the needles in it, and asked him if he cared to amuse himself with that.

"No, Ma'am!" said he, firmly but politely. "Not at present. If I find it necessary to reform again, I may do something of the kind, but not now. But I thank you kindly, all the same."

After this, they were all very careful not to mention tidies to him.

Corette and her companion stayed with the fairies for more than a week. Corette knew that her father and mother did not expect her at home for some time, and so she felt quite at liberty to stay as long as she pleased.

As to the sisters, they were delighted to have their visitors with them.

But, one day, the Condensed Pirate, finding Corette alone, led her, with great secrecy, to the bottom of the pasture field, the very outskirts of the fairies' domain.

"Look here," said he, in his lowest tones. "Do you know, little Corette, that things are not as I expected them to be here? Everything is very nice and good, but nothing appears very small to me. Indeed, things seem to be just about the right size. How does it strike you?"

"Why, I have been thinking the same thing," said Corette. "The sisters used to be such dear, cunning little creatures, and now they're bigger than I am. But I don't know what can be done about it."

"I know," said the Condensed Pirate.

"What?" asked Corette.

"Condense 'em," answered her companion, solemnly.

"Oh! But you couldn't do that!" exclaimed Corette.

"Yes, but I can—at least, I think I can. You remember those two pink condensing balls?"

"Yes," said Corette.

"Well, I've got mine."

"You have!" cried Corette. "How did you get it?"

"Oh! when the old fellow knocked it off my head, it fell on the chair beside me, and I picked it up and put it in my coat-pocket. It would just go in. He charges for the balls, and so I thought I might as well have it."

"But do you know how he works them?"

"Oh yes!" replied the Condensed Pirate. "I watched him. What do you say? Shall we condense this whole place?"

"It won't hurt them," said Corette, "and I don't really think they would mind it."

"Mind it! No!" said the other. "I believe they'd like it."

So it was agreed that the Fairy Cottage, inmates, and grounds should be condensed until they were, relatively, as small as they used to be.

That afternoon, when the sisters were taking a nap and the little man was at work in the barn, the Condensed Pirate went up into the garret of the cottage and got out on the roof. Then he climbed to the top of the tallest chimney, which overlooked everything on the place, and there he laid his little pink ball.

He then softly descended, and, taking Corette by the hand (she had been waiting for him on the portico), he went down to the bottom of the pasture field.

When he was quite sure that he and Corette were entirely outside of the fairies' grounds, he stood up, pointed to the ball with a long, thin stick which he had cut, and began to count: "One, two, three—"

And as he counted the cottage began to shrink. Smaller and smaller it became, until it got to be very little indeed.

"Is that enough?" said the Condensed Pirate, hurriedly between two counts.

"No," replied Corette. "There is the little man, just come out of the barn. He ought to be as small as the sisters used to be. I'll tell you when to stop."

So the counting went on until Corette said, "Stop!" and the cottage was really not much higher than a thimble. The little man stood by the barn, and seemed to Corette to be just about the former size of the fairy sisters; but, in fact, he was not quite a quarter of an inch high. Everything on the place was small in proportion, so that when Corette said "Stop!" the Condensed Pirate easily leaned over and knocked the pink ball from the chimney with his long stick. It fell outside of the grounds, and he picked it up and put it in his pocket.

Then he and Corette stood and admired everything! It was charming! It was just what they had imagined before they came there. While they were looking with delight at the little fields, and trees, and chickens—so small that really big people could not have seen them—and at the cute little house, with its vines and portico, the two sisters came out on the little lawn.

When they saw Corette and her companion they were astounded.

"Why, when did you grow big again?" they cried. "Oh! how sorry we are! Now you cannot come into our house and live with us any longer."

Corette and the Condensed Pirate looked at each other, as much as to say, "They don't know they have been made so little."

Then Corette said: "We are sorry too. I suppose we shall have to go away now. But we have had a delightful visit."

"It has been a charming one for us," said one of the sisters, "and if we only had known, we would have had a little party before you went away; but now it is too late."

The Condensed Pirate said nothing. He felt rather guilty about the matter. He might have waited a little, and yet he could not have told them about it. They might have objected to be condensed.

"May we stay just a little while and look at things?" asked Corette.

"Yes," replied one of the fairies; "but you must be very careful not to step inside the grounds, or to stumble over on our place. You might do untold damage."

So the two little big people stood and admired the fairy cottage and all about it, for this was indeed the sight they came to see; and then they took leave of their kind entertainers, who would have been glad to have them stay longer, but were really trembling with apprehension lest some false step or careless movement might ruin their little home.

As Corette and the Condensed Pirate took their way through the woods to their home, they found it very difficult to get along, they were so small. When they came to a narrow stream, which Corette would once have jumped over with ease, the Condensed Pirate had to make a ferry-boat of a piece of bark, and paddle himself and the little girl across.

"I wonder how the fairies used to come down to us," said Corette, who was struggling along over the stones and moss, hanging on to her companion's hand.

"Oh! I expect they have a nice smooth path somewhere through the woods, where they can run along as fast as they please; and bridges over the streams."

"Why didn't they tell us of it?" asked Corette.

"They thought it was too little to be of any use to us. Don't you see?—they think we're big people and wouldn't need their path."

"Oh, yes!" said Corette.

In time, however, they got down the mountain and out of the woods, and then they climbed up on one of the fences and ran along the top of it toward Corette's home.

When the people saw them, they cried out: "Oh, here come our dear little fairies, who have not visited us for so many days!" But when they saw them close at hand, and perceived that they were little Corette and the Pirate who had reformed, they were dumbfounded.

Corette did not stop to tell them anything; but still holding her companion's hand, she ran on to her parents' house, followed by a crowd of neighbors.

Corette's father and mother could hardly believe that this little thing was their daughter, but there was no mistaking her face and her clothes, and her voice, although they were all so small; and when she had explained the matter to them, and to the people who filled the house, they understood it all. They were filled with joy to have their daughter back again, little or big.

When the Condensed Pirate went to his house, he found the door locked, as he had left it, but he easily crawled in through a crack. He found everything of an enormous size. It did not look like the old place. He climbed up the leg of a chair and got on a table, by the help of the table-cloth, but it was hard work. He found something to eat and drink, and all his possessions were in order, but he did not feel at home.

Days passed on, and while the Condensed Pirate did not feel any better satisfied, a sadness seemed to spread over the country, and particularly over Corette's home. The people grieved that they never saw the fairy sisters, who indeed had made two or three visits, with infinite trouble and toil, but who could not make themselves observed, their bodies and their voices being so very small.

And Corette's father and mother grieved. They wanted their daughter to be as she was before. They said that Sweet Marjoram Day was very near, but that they could not look forward to it with pleasure. Corette might go out to the fields, but she could only sit upon some high place, as the fairies used to sit. She could not help in the gathering. She could not even be with the babies; they would roll on her and crush her. So they mourned.

It was now the night before the great holiday. Sweet Marjoram Eve had not been a very gay time, and the people did not expect to have much fun the next day. How could they if the fairy sisters did not come? Corette felt badly, for she had never told that the sisters had been condensed, and the Condensed Pirate, who had insisted on her secrecy, felt worse. That night he lay in his great bed, really afraid to go to sleep on account of rats and mice.

He was so extremely wakeful that he lay and thought, and thought, and thought for a long time, and then he got up and dressed and went out.

It was a beautiful moonlight night, and he made his way directly to Corette's house. There, by means of a vine, he climbed up to her window, and gently called her. She was not sleeping well, and she soon heard him and came to the window.

He then asked her to bring him two spools of fine thread.

Without asking any questions, she went for the thread, and very soon made her appearance at the window with one spool in her arms, and then she went back for another.

"Now, then," said the Condensed Pirate, when he had thrown the spools down to the ground, "will you dress yourself and wait here at the window until I come and call you?"

Corette promised, for she thought he had some good plan in his head, and he hurried down the vine, took up a spool under each arm, and bent his way to the church. This building had a high steeple which overlooked the whole country. He left one of his spools outside, and then, easily creeping with the other under one of the great doors, he carried it with infinite pains and labor up into the belfry.

There he tied it on his back, and, getting out of a window, began to climb up the outside of the steeple.

It was not hard for him to do this, for the rough stones gave him plenty of foot-hold, and he soon stood on the very tip-top of the steeple. He then took tight hold of one end of the thread on his spool and let the spool drop. The thread rapidly unrolled, and the spool soon touched the ground.

Then our friend took from his pocket the pink ball, and passing the end of the thread through a little hole in the middle of it, he tied it firmly. Placing the ball in a small depression on the top of the steeple, he left it there, with the thread hanging from it, and rapidly descended to the ground. Then he took the other spool and tied the end of its thread to that which was hanging from the steeple.

He now put down the spool and ran to call Corette. When she heard his voice she clambered down the vine to him.

"Now, Corette." he said, "run to my house and stand on the beach, near the water, and wait for me." Corette ran off as he had asked, and he went back to his spool. He took it up and walked slowly to his house, carefully unwinding the thread as he went. The church was not very far from the sea-shore, so he soon joined Corette. With her assistance he then unwound the rest of the thread, and made a little coil. He next gave the coil to Corette to hold, cautioning her to be very careful, and then he ran off to where some bits of wood were lying, close to the water's edge. Selecting a little piece of thin board he pushed it into the water, and taking a small stick in his hand, he jumped on it, and poled it along to where Corette was standing. The ocean here formed a little bay where the water was quite smooth.

"Now, Corette," said the Condensed Pirate, "we must be very careful. I will push this ashore and you must step on board, letting out some of the thread as you come. Be sure not to pull it tight. Then I will paddle out a little way, and as I push, you must let out more thread."

Corette did as she was directed, and very soon they were standing on the little raft a few yards from shore. Then her companion put down his stick, and took the coil of thread.

"What are you going to do?" asked Corette. She had wanted to ask before, but there did not seem to be time.

"Well," said he, "we can't make ourselves any bigger—at least, I don't know how to do it, and so I'm going to condense the whole country. The little pink ball is on top of the steeple, which is higher than anything else about here, you know. I can't knock the ball off at the proper time, so I've tied a thread to it to pull it off. You and I are outside of the place, on the water, so we won't be made any smaller. If the thing works, everybody will be our size, and all will be right again."

"Splendid!" cried Corette. "But how will you know when things are little enough?"

"Do you see that door in my house, almost in front of us? Well, when I was of the old size, I used just to touch the top of that door with my head, if I didn't stoop. When you see that the door is about my present height, tell me to stop. Now then!"

The Condensed Pirate began to count, and instantly the whole place, church, houses, fields, and of course the people who were in bed, began to shrink! He counted a good while before Corette thought his door would fit him. At last she called to him to stop. He glanced at the door to feel sure, counted one more, and pulled the thread. Down came the ball, and the size of the place was fixed!

The whole of the sweet marjoram country was now so small that the houses were like bandboxes, and the people not more than four or five inches high—excepting some very tall people who were six inches.

Drawing the ball to him, the Condensed Pirate pushed out some distance, broke it from the thread, and threw it into the water.

"No more condensing!" said he. He then paddled himself and Corette ashore, and running to his cottage, threw open the door and looked about him. Everything was just right! Everything fitted! He shouted with joy.

It was just daybreak when Corette rushed into her parents' house. Startled by the noise, her father and mother sprang out of bed.

"Our darling daughter!" they shouted, "and she has her proper size again!!"

In an instant she was clasped in their arms. When the first transports of joy were over, Corette sat down and told them the whole story—told them everything.

"It is all right," said her mother, "so that we are all of the same size," and she shed tears of joy.

Corette's father ran out to ring the church-bell, so as to wake up the people and tell them the good news of his daughter's restoration. When he came in, he said:

"I see no difference in anything. Everybody is all right."

There never was such a glorious celebration of Sweet Marjoram Day as took place that day.

The crop was splendid, the weather was more lovely than usual, if such a thing could be, and everybody was in the gayest humor.

But the best thing of all was the appearance of the fairy sisters. When they came among the people they all shouted as if they had gone wild. And the good little sisters were so overjoyed that they could scarcely speak.

"What a wonderful thing it is to find that we have grown to our old size again! We were here several times lately, but somehow or other we seemed to be so very small that we couldn't make you see or hear us. But now it's all right. Hurrah! We have forty-two new games!"

And at that, the crop being all in, the whole country, with a shout of joy, went to work to play.

There were no gayer people to be seen than Corette and the Condensed Pirate. Some of his friends called this good man by his old name, but he corrected them.

"I am reformed, all the same," he said, "but do not call me by that name. I shall never be able to separate it from its associations with doilies. And with *them* I am done forever. Owing to circumstances, I do not need to be depressed."

The captain of the ship never stopped off the coast for a load of doilies. Perhaps he did not care to come near the house of his former captor, for fear that he might forget himself again, and take the ship a second time. But if the captain had come, it is not likely that his men would have found the cottage of the Condensed Pirate, unless they had landed at the very spot where it stood.

And it so happened that no one ever noticed this country after it was condensed. Passing ships could not come near enough to see such a very little place, and there never were any very good roads to it by land.

But the people continued to be happy and prosperous, and they kept up the celebration of Sweet Marjoram Day as gayly as when they were all ordinary-sized people.

In the whole country there were only two persons, Corette and the Pirate, who really believed that they were condensed.

First published in the December 1877 edition of *St. Nicholas Magazine*

Rikki-Tikki-Tavi

BY RUDYARD KIPLING

THIS IS THE story of the great war that Rikki-tikki-tavi fought single-handed through the bath-rooms of the big bungalow in Segowlee cantonment. Darzee, the tailor-bird, helped him, and Chuchundra, the muskrat, who never comes out into the middle of the floor, but always creeps round by the skirting-boards, gave him advice; but still Rikki-tikki did the real fighting.

He was a mongoose, something like a little cat in his fur and his tail, but quite like a weasel in his head and his habits. His eyes and the end of his restless nose were pink; he could scratch himself anywhere he wanted to with any leg, front or back, that he chose to use; he could fluff up his tail till it looked like a bottle-brush, and his war-cry as he scuttled through the long grass was: *Rikk-tikk-tikki-tikki-tchk!*

One day a high summer flood washed him out of the burrow where he lived with his father and mother, and carried him, kicking and clucking, down a road-side ditch. He found a little wisp of soggy grass floating there, and clung to it till he lost his senses. When he revived, he was lying in the hot sun on the middle of a garden path, very draggled indeed, and a small boy was saying, "Here's a dead mongoose. Let's have a funeral."

"No," said his mother; "let's take him in and dry him. Perhaps he isn't really dead."

They took him into the house, and a big man picked him up between his finger and thumb and said he was not dead at all; and they wrapped him in cotton wool, and warmed him over a little fire, and he opened his eyes and sneezed.

"Now," said the big man (he was an Englishman who had just moved into the bungalow), "don't frighten him, and we'll see what he'll do."

It is the hardest thing in the world to frighten a mongoose, because he is eaten up from nose to tail with curiosity. The motto of all the mongoose family is, "Run and find out"; and Rikki-tikki was a true mongoose. He looked at the cotton wool, decided that it was not good to eat, ran all round the table, sat up and put his fur in order, scratched himself, and took a flying jump on the small boy's neck.

"Don't be frightened, Teddy," said his father. "That's his way of making friends."

"Ouch! He's tickling under my chin," said Teddy.

Rikki-tikki looked down between the boy's collar and neck, snuffed at his ear, and climbed down to the floor, where he sat rubbing his nose.

"Good gracious," said Teddy's mother, "and that's a wild creature! I suppose he's so tame because we've been kind to him."

"All mongooses are like that," said her husband. "If Teddy doesn't pick him up

by the tail, or try to put him in a cage, he'll run in and out of the house all day long. Let's give him something to eat."

They gave him a little bit of raw meat. Rikki-tikki liked it immensely, and when it was finished he went out into the veranda and sat in the sunshine and fluffed up his fur to make it dry to the roots. Then he felt better.

"There are more things to find out about in this house," he said to himself, "than all my family could find out in all their lives. I shall certainly stay and find out."

Rikki-tikki gave up that day to roaming over the house. He nearly drowned himself in the bath-tubs; put his nose into the ink on a writing-table, and burned it on the end of the big man's cigar, for he climbed up in the big man's lap to see how writing was done. At nightfall he went into Teddy's nursery

He came to breakfast riding on Teddy's shoulder.

to watch how kerosene lamps were lighted, and when Teddy went to bed Rikki-tikki climbed up too, but he was a restless companion, because he had to get up and attend to every noise all through the night, and find out what made it. Teddy's mother and father came in, the last thing, to look at their boy, and Rikki-tikki was awake on the pillow. "I don't like that," said Teddy's mother "he may bite the child."

"He'll do no such thing," said the father. "Teddy's safer with that little beast than if he had a bloodhound to watch him. If a snake came into the nursery now—"

But Teddy's mother wouldn't think of anything so awful.

Early in the morning Rikki-tikki came to early breakfast in the veranda riding on Teddy's shoulder, and they gave him banana and some boiled egg; and he sat on all their laps one after the other, because

Rikki-tikki looked down between the boy's collar and neck.

He put his nose into the ink.

every well-brought-up mongoose always hopes to be a house-mongoose some day and have rooms to run about in, and Rikki-tikki's mother (she used to live in the General's house at Segowlee) had carefully told Rikki what to do if ever he came across white men.

Then Rikki-tikki went out into the garden to see what was to be seen. It was a large garden, only half cultivated, with bushes of Marshal Niel roses as big as summer-houses, lime- and orange-trees, clumps of bamboos, and thickets of high grass. Rikki-tikki licked his lips. "This is a splendid hunting-ground," he said, and his tail grew bottle-brushy at the thought of it, and he scuttled up and down the garden, snuffing here and there till he heard very sorrowful voices in a thorn-bush. It was Darzee, the tailor-bird, and his wife. They had made a beautiful nest by pulling two big leaves together and stitching them up the edges with fibers, and they had filled the hollow with cotton and downy fluff. The nest swayed to and fro, and they sat on the edge and cried.

"What is the matter?" asked Rikki-tikki.

"We are very miserable," said Darzee. "One of our babies fell out of the nest yesterday and Nag ate him."

"H'm!" said Rikki-tikki, "that is very sad—but I am a stranger here. Who is Nag?"

Darzee and his wife only cowered down on the nest without answering, for from the thick grass at the foot of the bush there came a slow hiss—a horrid cold sound that made Rikki-tikki jump back two clear feet. Then inch by inch out of the grass rose up the head and spread hood of Nag, the big black cobra, and he was five feet long from tongue to tail. When he had lifted one third of himself clear of the ground, he stayed balancing to and fro exactly as a dandelion-tuft balances in the wind, and he looked at Rikki-tikki with the wicked snake's eyes—that never change their expression, whatever the snake is thinking of.

Rikki-tikki was awake on the pillow.

"Who is Nag?" he said. "I am Nag. The great god Brahm put his mark upon all our people, when the first cobra spread his hood to keep the sun off Brahm as he slept. Look, and be afraid!"

"We are very miserable," said Darzee.

He spread out his hood more than ever, and Rikki-tikki saw the spectacle-mark on the back of it that looks exactly like the eye part of a hook-and-eye fastening.

He was afraid for the minute; but it is impossible for a mongoose to stay frightened for any length of time, and though Rikki-tikki had never met a live cobra before, his mother had fed him on dead ones, and he knew that all a mongoose's business in life was to fight and eat snakes.

Nag knew that too, and at the bottom of his cold heart he was afraid.

"Well," said Rikki-tikki, and his tail began to fluff up again, "do you think that it is right for you to eat fledgelings out of a nest?"

Nag was thinking to himself, and watching the least little movement in the grass behind Rikki-tikki. He knew that a mongoose in the garden meant death sooner or later for him and his family; but he wanted to get Rikki-tikki off his guard. So he dropped his head a little, and put it on one side.

"Let us talk," he said. "You eat eggs. Why should not I eat birds?"

"Behind you! Look behind you!" sang Darzee.

Rikki-tikki knew better than to waste time in staring. He jumped up in the air as high as he could go, and just under him whizzed by the head of Nagaina, Nag's wicked wife. She had crept up behind him as he was talking, to make an end of him; and he heard her savage hiss as the stroke missed. He came down almost across her back, and if he had been an old mongoose he would have known that then was the time to break her back with one bite; but he was afraid of the terrible lashing return-stroke of the cobra. He bit, but he did not bite long enough, and jumped clear of the whisking tail, leaving Nagaina only torn and angry.

"Wicked, wicked Darzee!" said Nag, lashing up as high as he could reach toward the nest in the thorn-bush; but Darzee had built it out of reach of snakes, and it only swayed to and fro.

Rikki-tikki felt his eyes growing red and hot (when a mongoose's eyes grow red, he is angry), and he sat back on his tail and hind legs like a little kangaroo, and looked all round him, and chattered with rage. But Nag and Nagaina had disappeared into the grass. When a snake misses its stroke, it never says anything or gives any sign of what it means to do next. Rikki-tikki did not care to follow them, for he did not feel sure that he could manage two snakes at once. So he trotted off to the gravel path near the house, and sat down to think. It was a serious matter for him. If you read the old books of natural history, you will find they say that when the mongoose fights the snake and happens to get bitten, he runs off and eats some herb that cures him. That is not true. The victory is only a matter of quickness of eye and quickness of foot—snake's blow against mongoose's jump—and as no eye can follow the motion of a snake's head when it strikes, that makes it much more wonderful than any magic herb. Rikki-tikki knew he was a young mongoose, and it made him all the more pleased to think that he had managed to escape a blow from behind. It gave him confidence in himself, and when Teddy came running down the path, Rikki-tikki was ready to be petted. But just as Teddy was stooping, something wriggled a little in the dust, and a tiny voice said: "Be careful. I am Death!" It was *Karait,* the dusty brown snakeling that lies for choice on the dusty earth; and his bite is as dangerous as the cobra's. But he is so small that nobody thinks of him, and so he does the more harm to people.

Rikki-tikki's eyes grew red again, and he danced up to the karait with the peculiar rocking, swaying motion that he had inherited from his family. It looks very funny, but it is so perfectly balanced a gait that you can fly off from it at any angle you please; and in dealing with snakes this is an advantage. If Rikki-tikki had only known, he was doing a much more dangerous thing than fighting Nag, for the karait is so small, and can turn so quickly, that unless Rikki bit him close to the back of the head, he would get the return-stroke in his eye or his lip. But Rikki did not know: his eyes were all red, and

He jumped in the air, and just under him whizzed the head of Nagaina.

he rocked back and forth, looking for a good place to hold. The karait struck out, Rikki jumped sideways and tried to run in, but the wicked little dusty gray head lashed within a fraction of his shoulder, and he had to jump over the body, and the head followed his heels close.

Teddy shouted to the house: "Oh, look here! Our mongoose is killing a snake," and Rikki-tikki heard a scream from Teddy's mother. His father ran out with a stick, but by the time he came up, the karait had lunged out once too far, and Rikki-tikki had sprung, jumped on the snake's back, dropped his head far between his fore-legs, bitten as high up the back as he could get hold, and rolled away. That bite paralyzed the karait, and Rikki-tikki was just going to eat him up from the tail when he remembered that a full meal makes a slow mongoose, and if he wanted all his strength and quickness ready, he must keep himself thin. He went away for a dust-bath under the castor-oil bushes, while Teddy's father beat the dead karait. "What is the use of that?" thought Rikki-tikki—"I have settled it all"; and then Teddy's mother picked him up from the dust and hugged him, crying that he had saved Teddy from death, and Teddy's father said that he was a providence, and Teddy looked on with big scared eyes.

That night at dinner, walking to and fro among the wine-glasses on the table, he might have stuffed himself three times over with nice things; but he remembered Nag and Nagaina, and though it was very pleasant to be patted and petted by Teddy's mother, and to sit on Teddy's shoulder, his eyes would get red from time to time, and he would go off into his long war-cry of "*Rikk-tikk-tikki-tikki-tchk!*"

Teddy carried him off to bed, and insisted on Rikki-tikki sleeping under his chin. Rikki-tikki was too well bred to bite or scratch, but as soon as Teddy was asleep he went off for his nightly walk round the house, and in the dark he ran up against Chuchundra, the muskrat, creeping round by the skirting-board. Chuchundra is a broken-hearted little beast. He whimpers and cheeps all the night, trying to make up his mind to run into the middle of the room, but he never gets there.

"Don't kill me," said Chuchundra, almost weeping. "Rikki-tikki, don't kill me."

"Do you think a snake-killer kills muskrats?" said Rikki-tikki scornfully.

"Those who kill snakes get killed by snakes," said Chuchundra, more sorrowfully than ever. "And how am I to be sure that Nag won't mistake me for you?"

"There's not the least danger," said Rikki-tikki; "but Nag is in the garden, and I know you don't go there."

"My cousin Chua, the rat, told me—" said Chuchundra, and then he stopped.

"Told you what?"

"H'sh! Nag is everywhere, Rikki-tikki. You should have talked to Chua in the garden."

"I didn't—so you must tell me. Quick, Chuchundra, or I'll bite you!"

Chuchundra sat down and cried till the tears rolled off his whiskers. "I am a very poor man," he sobbed. "I never had spirit enough to run out into the middle of the room. H'sh! I mustn't tell you anything. Can't you *hear*, Rikki-tikki?"

Rikki-tikki listened. The house was as still as still, but he thought he could just catch the faintest scratch-scratch in the world—a noise as faint as a fly walking on a window-pane—the dry scratch of a snake's scales on brickwork.

"That's Nag or Nagaina," he said to himself, "and he is crawling into the bathroom sluice. You're right, Chuchundra; I should have talked to Chua."

He stole off to Teddy's bath-room, but there was nothing there, and then to Teddy's mother's bath-room. At the bottom of the smooth plaster wall there was a brick pulled out to make a sluice for the bath-water, and as Rikki-tikki stole in by the masonry curb where the bath is put, he heard Nag and Nagaina whispering together outside in the moonlight.

"When the house is emptied of people," said Nagaina, "*he* will have to go away, and then the garden will be our own again. Go in quietly, and remember that the big man who killed *Karait* is the first one to bite. Then come out and tell me, and we will hunt for Rikki-tikki together."

"But are you sure that there is anything to be gained by killing the people?" said Nag.

"Everything. When there were no people in the bungalow, did we have any mongoose in the garden? So long as the bungalow is empty, we are king and queen of the garden, and remember that as soon as our eggs in the melon-bed hatch (they may hatch tomorrow), our children will need room."

"I had not thought of that," said Nag. "I will go, but there is no need that we should hunt for Rikki-tikki afterward. I will kill the big man and his wife, and the child if I can, and come away quietly. Then the bungalow will be empty, and Rikki-tikki will go. I will come in the morning, Nagaina."

Rikki-tikki tingled all over with rage and hatred at this, and then Nag's head came through the sluice, and his five feet of cold body followed it. Angry as he was, Rikki-tikki was very frightened as he saw the size of the big cobra. Nag coiled himself up, raised his head, and looked into the bath-room in the dark, and Rikki could see his eyes glitter.

"Now, if I kill him here, Nagaina will know; and if I fight him on the open floor, the odds are in his favor. What am I to do?" said Rikki-tikki-tavi.

Nag waved to and fro, and then Rikki-tikki heard him drinking from the biggest water-jar that was used to fill the bath. "That is good," said the snake. "Now, when *Karait* was killed, the big man had a stick. He may have that stick still, but when he comes in to bathe in the morning he will not have a stick. I shall wait here till he comes. Nagaina—do you hear me?—I shall wait here in the cool."

There was no answer from outside, so Rikki-tikki knew Nagaina had gone away. Nag coiled himself down, coil by coil, round the bulge at the bottom of the water-jar, and Rikki-tikki stayed still as death. After an hour he began to move, muscle by muscle, toward the jar. Nag was asleep, and Rikki-tikki looked at his big back, wondering which would be the best place for a good hold. "If I don't break his back at the first jump," said Rikki, "he can still fight." He looked at the thickness of the neck below, the hood, but that was too much for him; and a bite near the tail would only make Nag savage.

"It must be the head," he said at last—"the head above the hood; and, when I am once there, I must not let go."

Then he jumped. The head was lying a little clear of the water-jar, under the curve of it; and, as his teeth met, Rikki braced his back against the bulge to hold down the head. This gave him just one second's purchase, and he made the most of it. Then he was battered to and fro as a rat is shaken by a dog—to and fro on the floor, up and down, and round in great circles, but his eyes were red and he held on as the body cartwhipped over the floor, upsetting the tin dipper and the soap-dish and the flesh-brush, and banged against the tin side of the bath. As he held he closed his jaws tighter and tighter, for he was sure he would be banged to death, and, for the honor of his family, he preferred to be found with his teeth locked. He was dizzy, aching, and felt shaken to pieces when something went off like a thunderclap just behind him; and a wind knocked him senseless and red fire singed his fur. The big man had been wakened by the noise, and had fired both barrels of a shot-gun into Nag just behind the hood.

Rikki-tikki held on with his eyes shut, for now he was quite sure he was dead; but the head did not move, and the big man picked him up and said: "It's the mongoose again, Alice; the little chap has saved *our* lives now." Then Teddy's mother came in with a very white face, and saw what was left of Nag, and Rikki-tikki dragged himself to Teddy's bedroom and spent half the rest of the night licking himself to find out whether he really was broken into forty pieces.

When morning came he was very stiff, but well pleased with his doings. "Now I have Nagaina to settle with, and she will be worse than five Nags, and there's no knowing when the eggs she spoke of will hatch. Goodness! I must go and see Darzee."

Without waiting for breakfast, Rikki-tikki ran to the thorn-bush where Darzee was singing a song of triumph at the top of his voice. The news of Nag's death was all over the garden, for the sweeper had thrown the body on the rubbish-heap.

"Oh, you stupid tuft of feathers!" said Rikki-tikki, angrily. "Is this the time to sing?"

"Nag is dead—is dead—is dead!" sang Darzee. "The valiant Rikki-tikki caught him by the head and held fast. The big man brought the bang-stick, and Nag fell in two pieces! He will never eat my babies again."

"All that's true enough; but where's Nagaina?" said Rikki-tikki, looking carefully round him.

"Nagaina came to the bath-room sluice and called for Nag," Darzee went on; "and Nag came out on the end of a stick—the sweeper picked him up on the end of a stick and threw him upon the rubbish-heap. Let us sing about the great, the red-eyed Rikki-tikki!" and Darzee filled his throat and sang.

"If I could get up to your nest, I'd roll your babies out!" said Rikki-tikki. "You don't know when to do the right thing at the right time. You're safe enough in your nest there, but it's war for me down here. Stop singing a minute, Darzee."

"For the great, the beautiful Rikki-tikki's sake I will stop," said Darzee. "What is it, O Killer of the terrible Nag?"

"Where is Nagaina, for the third time?"

"On the rubbish-heap by the stables, mourning for Nag. Great is Rikki-tikki with the white teeth."

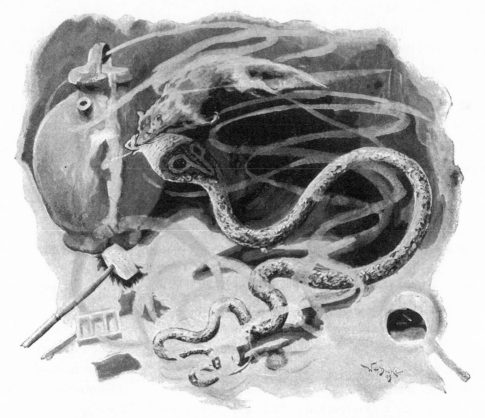

Rikki-tikki was battered to and fro as a rat is shaken by a dog.

"Bother my white teeth! Have you ever heard where she keeps her eggs?"

"In the melon-bed, on the end nearest the wall, where the sun strikes nearly all day. She put them there weeks ago."

"And you never thought it worth while to tell me? The end nearest the wall, you said?"

"Rikki-tikki, you are not going to eat her eggs!"

"Not eat exactly; no. Darzee, if you have a grain of sense you will fly off to the stables and pretend that your wing is broken, and let Nagaina chase you away to this bush. I must get to the melon-bed, and if I went there now she'd see me."

Darzee was a feather-brained little fellow who could never hold more than one idea at a time in his head; and just because he knew that Nagaina's children were born in eggs like his own, he didn't think at first that it was fair to kill them. But his wife was a sensible bird, and she knew that cobra's eggs meant young cobras later on; so she flew off from the nest, and left Darzee to keep the babies warm, and sing his song about the death of Nag. Darzee was very like a man.

She fluttered in front of Nagaina by the rubbish-heap, and cried out, "Oh, my wing is broken! The boy in the house threw a stone at me and broke it." Then she fluttered more desperately than ever.

Nagaina lifted up her head and hissed, "You warned Rikki-tikki when I would have killed him. Indeed and truly, you've chosen a bad place to be lame in." And she moved toward Darzee's wife, slipping along over the dust.

"The boy broke it with a stone!" shrieked Darzee's wife.

"Well! It may be some consolation to you when you're dead to know that I shall settle accounts with the boy. My husband lies on the rubbish-heap this morning, but before night the boy in the house will lie still. What is the use of running away? I am sure to catch you. Little fool, look at me!"

Darzee's wife knew better than to do *that*, for a bird who looks at a snake's eyes gets so frightened that she can't move. Darzee's wife fluttered on, piping sorrowfully, and never leaving the ground, and Nagaina quickened her pace.

Rikki-tikki heard them going up the path from the stables, and he raced for the end of the melon-patch near the wall. There, in the warm litter about the melons, very cunningly hidden, he found twenty-five eggs, about the size of a bantam's eggs, but with a whitish skin instead of shell.

"I was not a day too soon," he said; for he could see the baby cobras curled up inside the skin, and he knew that the minute they were hatched they could each kill a man or a mongoose. He bit off the tops of the eggs as fast as he could, taking care to crush the young cobras, and he turned over the litter from time to time to see whether he had missed any. At last there were only three eggs left, and Rikki-tikki began to chuckle to himself, when he heard Darzee's wife screaming:

"Rikki-tikki, I led Nagaina toward the house, and she has gone into the veranda, and—oh, come quickly—she means killing!"

Rikki-tikki smashed two eggs, and tumbled backward down the melon-bed with the third egg in his mouth, and scuttled to the veranda as hard as he could put foot to the ground. Teddy and his mother and father were there at early breakfast; but Rikki-tikki saw that they were not eating anything. They sat stone-still, and their faces were white. Nagaina was coiled up on the matting by Teddy's chair, within easy striking distance of Teddy's bare leg, and she was swaying to and fro, singing a song of triumph.

"Son of the big man that killed Nag," she hissed, "stay still. I am not ready yet. Wait a little. Keep very still, all you three. If you move I strike, and if you do not move I strike. Oh, foolish people, who killed my Nag!"

Teddy's eyes were fixed on his father, and all his father could do was to whisper, "Sit still, Teddy. You mustn't move. Teddy, keep still."

Then Rikki-tikki came up and cried: "Turn round, Nagaina; turn and fight!"

"All in good time," said she, without moving her eyes. "I will settle my account with *you* presently. Look at your friends, Rikki-tikki. They are still and white. They are afraid. They dare not move, and if you come a step nearer I strike."

"Look at your eggs," said Rikki-tikki, "in the melon-bed near the wall. Go and look, Nagaina."

The big snake turned half round, and saw the egg on the veranda. "Ah-h! Give it to me," she said.

Rikki-tikki put his paws one on each side of the egg, and his eyes were blood-red. "What price for a snake's egg? For a young cobra? For a young king-cobra? For the last—the very last of the brood? The ants are eating all the others down by the melon-bed."

Nagaina spun clear round, forgetting everything for the sake of the one egg; and Rikki-tikki saw Teddy's father shoot out a big hand, catch Teddy by the shoulder, and drag him across the little table with the teacups, safe and out of reach of Nagaina.

"Tricked! Tricked! Tricked!" chuckled Rikki-tikki. "The boy is safe, and it was I—I—I that caught Nag by the hood last night in the

Nagaina flew down the path, with Rikki-tikki behind her.

bath-room." Then he began to jump up and down, all four feet together, his head close to the floor. "He threw me to and fro, but he could not shake me off. He was dead before the big man blew him in two. I did it! *Rikki-tikki-tch-tch!* Come then, Nagaina. Come and fight with me. You shall not be a widow long."

Nagaina saw that she had lost her chance of killing Teddy, and the egg lay between Rikki-tikki's paws. "Give me the egg, Rikki-tikki. Give me the last of my eggs, and I will go away and never come back," she said, lowering her hood.

"Yes, you will go away, and you will never come back; for you will go to the rubbish-heap with Nag. Fight, widow! The big man has gone for his gun! Fight!"

Rikki-tikki was bounding all round Nagaina, keeping just out of reach of her stroke, his little eyes like hot coals. Nagaina gathered herself together, and flung out at him. Rikki-tikki jumped up and backwards. Again and again and again she struck, and each time her head came with a whack on the matting of the veranda and she gathered herself together like a watch-spring. Then Rikki-tikki danced in a circle to get behind her, and Nagaina spun round to keep her head to his head, so that the rustle of her tail on the matting sounded like dry leaves blown along by the wind.

He had forgotten the egg. It still lay on the veranda, and Nagaina came nearer and nearer to it, till at last, while Rikki-tikki was drawing breath, she caught it in her mouth, turned to the veranda steps, and flew like an arrow down the path, with Rikki-tikki behind her. When the cobra runs for her life, she goes like a whiplash flicked across a horse's neck. Rikki-tikki knew that he must catch her, or all the trouble would begin again. She headed straight for the long grass by the thornbush, and as he was running Rikki-tikki heard Darzee still singing his foolish little song of triumph. But Darzee's wife was wiser. She flew *off* her nest as Nagaina came along, and flapped her wings about Nagaina's head. If Darzee had helped they might have turned her, but Nagaina only lowered her hood and went on. Still, the instant's delay brought Rikki-tikki up to her, and as she plunged into the rat-hole where she and Nag used to live, his little white teeth were in her tail, and he went down with her—and very few mongooses, however wise and old they may be, care to follow a cobra into its hole. It was dark in the hole; and Rikki-tikki never knew when it might open out and give Nagaina room to turn and strike at him. He held on savagely, and stuck out his feet to act as brakes on the dark slope of the hot, moist earth. Then the grass by the mouth of the hole stopped waving, and Darzee said: "It is all over with Rikki-tikki! We must sing his death-song. Valiant Rikki-tikki is dead! For Nagaina will surely kill him underground."

So he sang a very mournful song that he made up on the spur of the minute, and just as he got to the most touching part the grass quivered again, and Rikki-tikki, covered with dirt, dragged himself out of the hole leg by leg, licking his whiskers. Darzee stopped with a little shout. Rikki-tikki shook some of the dust out of his fur and sneezed. "It is all over," he said. "The widow will never come out again." And the red ants that live between the grass stems heard him, and began to troop down one after another to see if he had spoken the truth.

Rikki-tikki curled himself up in the grass and slept where he was—slept and slept till it was late in the afternoon, for he had had a hard day's work.

"Now," he said, when he awoke, "I will go back to the house. Tell the Coppersmith, Darzee, and he will tell the garden that Nagaina is dead."

The Coppersmith is a bird who makes a noise exactly like the beating of a little hammer on a copper pot; and the reason why he is always making it is because he is the town-crier in an Indian garden, and tells all the news to everybody. As Rikki-tikki went up the path, he heard his "attention" notes like a tiny dinner-gong; and then the steady "*Ding-dong-tock!* Nag is dead—*dong!* Nagaina is dead! *Ding-dong-tock!*" That set all the birds in the garden singing, and the frogs croaking; for Nag and Nagaina used to eat frogs as well as little birds.

When he got to the house, Teddy and Teddy's mother (she looked very white still, for she had been fainting) and Teddy's father came out and almost cried over him; and that night he ate all that was given him till he could eat no more, and went to bed on Teddy's shoulder, where Teddy's mother saw him when she came to look late at night.

"He saved our lives and Teddy's life," she said to her husband. "Just think, he saved all our lives."

Rikki-tikki woke up with a jump, for all the mongooses are light sleepers.

"Oh, it's you," said he. "What are you bothering for? All the cobras are dead; and if they weren't, I'm here."

Rikki-tikki had a right to be proud of himself; but he did not grow too proud, and he kept that garden as a mongoose should keep it, till never a snake dared show its head inside the walls.

First published in the November 1893 edition of *St. Nicholas Magazine*

Mowgli's Brothers

BY RUDYARD KIPLING

IT WAS SEVEN O'CLOCK of a very warm evening in the Seeonee hills when Father Wolf woke up from his day's rest, scratched himself, yawned, and spread out his paws one after the other to get rid of the sleepy feeling in their tips. Mother Wolf lay with her big gray nose dropped across her four tumbling, squealing cubs, and the moon shone into the mouth of the cave where they all lived. "Augrh!" said Father Wolf, "it is time to hunt again," and he was going to spring downhill when a little shadow with a bushy tail crossed the threshold and whined: "Good luck go with you, O Chief of the Wolves; and good luck and strong white teeth go with the noble children, that they may never forget the hungry in this world."

It was the jackal—Tabaqui, the Dish-licker—and the wolves of India despise Tabaqui because he runs about making mischief, and telling tales, and eating rags and pieces of leather from the village rubbish-heaps. But they are afraid of him too, because Tabaqui, more than any one else in the jungle, is apt to go mad, and then he forgets that he was ever afraid of anyone, and runs through the forest biting everything in his way. Even the tiger runs and hides when little Tabaqui goes mad, for madness is the most disgraceful thing that can overtake a wild creature. We call it hydrophobia, but they call it *dewanee*—the madness—and run.

"Enter, then, and look," said Father Wolf, stiffly, "but there is no food here."

"For a wolf, no," said Tabaqui; "but for so mean a person as myself a dry bone is a good feast. Who are we, the Gidur-log [the jackal people], to pick and choose?" He scuttled to the back of the cave, where he found the bone of a buck with some meat on it, and sat cracking the end merrily.

"All thanks for this good meal," he said, licking his lips. "How beautiful are the noble children! How large are their eyes! And so young too! Indeed, indeed, I might have remembered that the children of kings are men from the beginning."

Now, Tabaqui knew as well as anyone else that there is nothing so unlucky as to compliment children to their faces; and it pleased him to see Mother and Father Wolf look uncomfortable.

Tabaqui sat still, rejoicing in the mischief that he had made, and then he said spitefully:

"Shere Khan, the Big One, has shifted his hunting-grounds. He will hunt among these hills for the next moon, so he has told me."

Shere Khan was the tiger who lived near the Waingunga River, twenty miles away.

"He has no right!" Father Wolf began angrily: "By the Law of the Jungle he has no right to change his quarters without due warning. He will frighten every head of game within ten miles, and I—I have to kill for two, these days."

"His mother did not call him Lungri [the Lame One] for nothing," said Mother Wolf, quietly. "He has been lame in one foot from his birth. That is why he has only killed cattle. Now the villagers of the Waingunga are angry with him, and he has come here to make *our* villagers angry. They will scour the jungle for him when he is far away, and we and our children must run when the grass is set alight. Indeed, we are very grateful to Shere Khan!"

"Shall I tell him of your gratitude?" said Tabaqui.

"Out!" snapped Father Wolf. "Out and hunt with thy master. Thou hast done harm enough for one night."

"I go," said Tabaqui, quietly. "Ye can hear Shere Khan below in the thickets. I might have saved myself the message."

Father Wolf listened, and below in the valley that ran down to a little river, he heard the dry, angry, snarly, singsong whine of a tiger who has caught nothing and does not care if all the jungle knows it.

"The fool!" said Father Wolf. "To begin a night's work with that noise! Does he think that our buck are like his fat Waingunga bullocks?"

"H'sh! It is neither bullock nor buck he hunts tonight," said Mother Wolf. "It is Man." The whine had changed to a sort of humming purr that seemed to come from every quarter of the compass. It was the noise that bewilders wood-cutters and gypsies sleeping in the open, and makes them run sometimes into the very mouth of the tiger.

"Man!" said Father Wolf, showing all his white teeth. "Faugh! Are there not enough beetles and frogs in the tanks that he must eat Man, and on our ground too!"

The Law of the Jungle, which never orders anything without a reason, forbids every beast to eat Man except when he is killing to show his children how to kill, and then he must hunt outside the hunting-grounds of his pack or tribe. The real reason for this is that man-killing means, sooner or later, the arrival of white men on elephants, with guns, and hundreds of brown men with gongs and rockets and torches. Then everybody in the jungle suffers. The reason the beasts give among themselves is that Man is the weakest and most defenseless of all living things, and it is unsportsmanlike to touch him. They say too—and it is true—that man-eaters become mangy, and lose their teeth.

The purr grew louder, and ended in the full-throated "Aaarh!" of the tiger's charge.

Then there was a howl—an untigerish howl—from Shere Khan. "He has missed," said Mother Wolf. "What is it?"

Father Wolf ran out a few paces and heard Shere Khan muttering and mumbling savagely, as he tumbled about in the scrub.

"The fool has had no more sense than to jump at a woodcutters' camp-fire, and has burned his feet," said Father Wolf, with a grunt. "Tabaqui is with him."

"Something is coming up hill," said Mother Wolf, twitching one ear. "Get ready."

The bushes rustled a little in the thicket, and Father Wolf dropped with his haunches under him, ready for his leap. Then, if you had been watching, you would have seen the most wonderful thing in the world—the wolf checked in mid-spring. He made his bound before he saw what it was he was jumping at, and then he tried to stop himself. The result was that he shot up straight into the air for four or five feet, landing almost where he left ground.

"Man!" he snapped. "A man's cub. Look!"

Directly in front of him, holding on by a low branch, stood a naked brown baby who could just walk—as soft and as dimpled a little atom as ever came to a wolf's cave at night. He looked up into Father Wolf's face, and laughed.

"Is that a man's cub?" said Mother Wolf. "I have never seen one. Bring it here."

A wolf accustomed to moving his own cubs can, if necessary, mouth an egg without breaking it, and though Father Wolf's jaws closed right on the child's back not a tooth even dented the skin, as he laid it down among the cubs.

"How little! How naked, and—how bold!" said Mother Wolf, softly. The baby was pushing his way between the cubs to get close to the warm hide. "Aha! He is taking his meal with the others. And so this is a man's cub. Now, was there ever a wolf that could boast of a man's cub among her children?"

"I have heard now and again of such a thing, but never in our Pack or in my time," said Father Wolf. "He is altogether without hair, and I could kill him with a touch of my foot. But see, he looks up and is not afraid."

The moonlight was blocked out of the mouth of the cave, for Shere Khan's great square head and shoulders were thrust into the entrance. Tabaqui, behind him, was squeaking: "My Lord, my Lord, it went in here!"

"Shere Khan does us great honor," said Father Wolf, but his eyes were very angry. "What does Shere Khan need?"

"My quarry. A man's cub went this way," said Shere Khan. "Its parents have run off. Give it to me."

Shere Khan had jumped at a woodcutters' camp-fire, as Father Wolf had said, and was furious from the pain of his burned feet. But Father Wolf knew that the mouth of the cave was too narrow for a tiger to come in by. Even where he was, Shere Khan's shoulders and forepaws were cramped for want of room, as a man's would be if he tried to fight in a barrel.

"The Wolves are a free people," said Father Wolf. "They take orders from the Head of the Pack, and not from any striped cattle-killer. The man's cub is ours—to kill if we choose."

"Ye choose and ye do not choose! What talk is this of choosing? By the bull that I killed, am I to stand nosing into your dog's den for my fair dues? It is I, Shere Khan, who speak!"

The tiger's roar filled the cave with thunder. Mother Wolf shook herself clear of the cubs and sprang forward, her eyes, like two green moons in the darkness, facing the blazing eyes of Shere Khan.

"And it is I, Raksha [that means The Demon], who answer. The man's cub is mine, Lungri—mine to me! He shall not be killed. He shall live to run with the Pack and to hunt with the Pack; and in the end, look you, hunter of little naked cubs—frog-eater—fish-killer—he shall hunt thee! Now get hence, or by the Sambhur that I killed (I eat no starved cattle), back thou goest to thy mother, burned beast of the jungle, lamer than ever thou earnest into the world! Go!"

Father Wolf looked on amazed. He had almost forgotten the days when he won Mother Wolf in fair fight from five other wolves, when she ran in the Pack and was not called The Demon for compliment's sake. Shere Khan might have faced Father

The tiger's roar filled the cave with thunder.

Wolf, but he could not stand up against Mother Wolf, for he knew that where he was she had all the advantage of the ground, and would fight to the death. So he backed out of the cave-mouth growling, and when he was clear he shouted:

"Each dog barks in his own kennel! We will see what the Pack will say to this fostering of man-cubs. The cub is mine, and into my teeth he will come in the end, O bush-tailed thieves!"

Mother Wolf threw herself down panting among the cubs, and Father Wolf said to her gravely:

"Shere Khan speaks this much truth. The cub must be shown to the Pack. Wilt thou still keep him, Mother?"

"Keep him!" she gasped. "He came naked, by night, alone and very hungry; yet he was not afraid! Look, he has pushed one of my babes to one side already. And that lame butcher would have killed him and would have run off to the Waingunga while the villagers here hunted through all our lairs in revenge! Keep him? Assuredly I will keep him—Lie still, little frog. O thou Mowgli—for Mowgli the Frog I will call thee—the time will come when thou wilt hunt Shere Khan as he has hunted thee."

"But what will our Pack say?" said Father Wolf.

The Law of the Jungle lays down very clearly that any wolf may, when he marries, withdraw from the Pack he belongs to; but as soon as his cubs are old enough to stand on their feet he must bring them to the Pack Council, which is generally held once a month at full moon, in order that the other wolves may identify them. After that inspection the cubs are free to run where they please, and until they have killed their first buck no excuse is accepted if a grown wolf of the Pack kills one of them. The punishment is death where the murderer can be found; and if you think for a minute you will see that this must be so.

Father Wolf waited till his cubs could run a little, and then on the night of the Pack Meeting took them and Mowgli and Mother Wolf to the Council Rock—a hilltop covered with stones and boulders where a hundred wolves could hide. Akela, the great gray Lone Wolf, who led all the Pack by strength and cunning, lay out at full length on his rock, and below him sat forty or more wolves of every size and color, from badger-colored veterans who could handle a buck alone, to young black three-year-olds who thought they could. The Lone Wolf had led them for a year now. He had fallen twice into a wolf-trap in his youth, and once he had been beaten and left for dead; so he knew the manners and customs of men. There was very little talking at the rock. The cubs tumbled over each other in the center of the circle where their mothers and fathers sat, and now and again a senior wolf would go quietly up to a cub, look at him carefully, and return to his place on noise-less feet. Sometimes a mother would push her cub well out into the moonlight, to be sure that he had not been overlooked. Akela from his rock would cry: "Ye know the Law—ye know the Law. Look well, O Wolves!" and the anxious mothers would take up the call; "Look—look well, O Wolves!"

At last—and Mother Wolf's neck-bristles lifted as the time came—Father Wolf pushed "Mowgli the Frog," as they called him, into the center, where he sat laughing and playing with some pebbles that glistened in the moonlight.

Akela never raised his head from his paws, but went on with the monotonous cry: "Look well!" A muffled roar came up from behind the rocks—the voice of Shere Khan crying: "The cub is mine. Give him to me. What have the Free People to do with a man's cub?" Akela never even twitched his ears: all he said was: "Look well, O Wolves! What have the Free People to do with the orders of any save the Free People? Look well!"

There was a chorus of deep growls, and a young wolf in his fourth year flung back Shere Khan's question to Akela: "What have the Free People to do with a man's cub?" Now the Law of the Jungle lays down that if there is any dispute as to the right of a cub to be accepted by the Pack, he must be spoken for by at least two members of the Pack who are not his father and mother.

"Who speaks for this cub?" said Akela. "Among the Free People who speaks?"

The meeting at the Council Rock

There was no answer, and Mother Wolf got ready for what she knew would be her last fight, if things came to fighting.

Then the only other creature who is allowed at the Pack Council—Baloo, the sleepy brown bear who teaches the wolf cubs the Law of the Jungle: old Baloo, who can come and go where he pleases because he eats only nuts and roots and honey—rose up on his hind quarters and grunted.

"The man's cub—the man's cub?" he said. "I speak for the man's cub. There is no harm in a man's cub. I have no gift of words, but I speak the truth. Let him run with the Pack, and be entered with the others. I myself will teach him."

"We need yet another," said Akela. "Baloo has spoken, and he is our teacher for the young cubs. Who speaks beside Baloo?"

A black shadow dropped down into the circle. It was Bagheera the Black Panther, inky black all over, but with the panther-markings showing up in certain lights like the pattern of watered silk. Everybody knew Bagheera, and nobody cared to cross his path; for he was as cunning as Tabaqui, as bold as the wild buffalo, and as reckless as the wounded elephant. But he had a voice as soft as wild honey dripping from a tree, and a skin softer than down. "O Akela, and ye the Free People," he purred, "I have no right in your assembly; but the Law of the Jungle says that if there is a doubt which is not a killing matter in regard to a new cub, the life of that cub may be bought at a price. And the Law does not say who may or may not pay that price. Am I right?"

"Good! good!" said the young wolves, who are always hungry. "Listen to Bagheera. The cub can be bought for a price. It is the Law."

"Knowing that I have no right to speak here, I ask your leave."

"Speak then," cried twenty voices.

"To kill a naked cub is shame. Besides, he may make better sport for you when he is grown. Baloo has spoken in his behalf. Now to Baloo's word I will add one bull, and a fat one, newly killed, not half a mile from here, if ye will accept the man's cub according to the Law. Is it difficult?"

There was a clamor of scores of voices, saying: "What matter? He will die in the winter rains. He will scorch in the sun. What harm can a naked frog do us? Let him run with the Pack. Where is the bull, Bagheera? Let him be accepted." And then came Akela's deep bay crying: "Look well—look well, O Wolves!"

Mowgli was still deeply interested in the pebbles, and he did not notice when the wolves came and looked at him one by one. At last they all went down the hill for the dead bull, and only Akela, Bagheera, Baloo, and Mowgli's own wolves were left. Shere Khan roared still in the night, for he was very angry that Mowgli had not been handed over to him.

"Aye, roar well," said Bagheera, under his whiskers. "For the time comes when this naked thing will make thee roar to another tune, or I know nothing of man."

"It was well done," said Akela. "Men and their cubs are very wise. He may be a help in time."

"Truly, a help in time of need; for none can hope to lead the Pack forever," said Bagheera.

Akela said nothing. He was thinking of the time that comes to every leader of every pack when his strength goes from him and he gets feebler and feebler, till at last he is killed by the wolves and a new leader comes up—to be killed in his turn.

"Take him away," he said to Father Wolf, "and train him as befits one of the Free People."

And that is how Mowgli was entered into the Seeonee wolf-pack for the price of a bull and on Baloo's good word.

NOW YOU MUST be content to skip ten or eleven whole years, and only guess at all the wonderful life that Mowgli led among the wolves, because if it were written out it would fill ever so many books. He grew up with the cubs, though they of course were grown wolves almost before he was a child, and Father Wolf taught him his business and the meaning of things in the jungle till every rustle in the grass, every breath of the warm night air, every note of the owls above his head, every scratch of a bat's claws as it roosted for a while in a tree, and every splash of every little fish jumping in a pool, meant just as much to him as the work of his office means to a business man. When he was not learning he sat out in the sun and slept, and ate and went to sleep again; when he felt dirty or hot he swam in the forest pools; and when he wanted honey (Baloo told him that honey and nuts were just as pleasant to eat as raw meat) he climbed up for it, and that Bagheera showed him how to do. Bagheera would lie out on a branch and call, "Come along, Little Brother," and at first Mowgli would cling like the sloth, but afterward he would fling himself through the branches almost as boldly as the gray ape. He took his place at the Council Rock, too, when the Pack met, and there he discovered that if he stared hard at any wolf, the wolf would be forced to drop his eyes, and so he used to stare for fun. At other times he would pick the long thorns out of the pads of his friends, for wolves suffer terribly from thorns and burs in their coats. He would go down the hillside into the cultivated lands by night, and look very curiously at the villagers in their huts, but he had a mistrust of men because Bagheera showed him a square box with a drop-gate so cunningly hidden in the jungle that he nearly walked into it, and told him that it was a trap. He loved better than anything else to go with Bagheera into the dark warm heart of the forest, to sleep all through the drowsy day and at night see how Bagheera did his killing. Bagheera killed right and left as he felt hungry, and so did Mowgli—with one exception. As soon as he was old enough to understand things, Bagheera told him that he must never touch cattle because he had been bought into the Pack at the price of a bull's life. "All the jungle is thine," said Bagheera, "and thou canst kill everything that thou art strong enough to kill; but for the sake of the bull that bought thee thou must never kill or eat any cattle young or old. That is the Law of the Jungle." Mowgli obeyed faithfully.

And he grew and grew strong as a boy must grow who does not know that he is learning any lessons, and who has nothing in the world to think of except things to eat.

Mother Wolf told him once or twice that Shere Khan was not a creature to be trusted, and that some day he must kill Shere Khan; but though a young wolf

Bagheera would lie out on a branch and call, "Come along, Little Brother."

would have remembered that advice every hour, Mowgli forgot it because he was only a boy—though he would have called himself a wolf if he had been able to speak in any human tongue.

Shere Khan was always crossing his path in the jungle, for as Akela grew older and feebler the lame tiger had come to be great friends with the younger wolves of the Pack, who followed him for scraps, a thing Akela would never have allowed if he had dared to push his authority to the proper bounds. Then Shere Khan would flatter them and wonder that such fine young hunters were content to be led by a dying wolf and a man's cub. "They tell me," Shere Khan would say, "that at Council ye dare not look him between the eyes"; and the young wolves would growl and bristle.

Bagheera, who had eyes and ears everywhere, knew something of this, and once or twice he told Mowgli in so many words that Shere Khan would kill him some day; and Mowgli would laugh and answer, "I have the Pack and I have thee; and Baloo, though he is so lazy, might strike a blow or two for my sake. Why should I be afraid?"

It was one very warm day that a new notion came to Bagheera—born of something that he had heard. Perhaps Ikki the Porcupine had told him; but he said to Mowgli when they were deep in the jungle, as the boy lay with his head on Bagheera's beautiful black skin: "Little Brother, how often have I told thee that Shere Khan is thy enemy?"

"As many times as there are nuts on that palm," said Mowgli, who, naturally, could not count. "What of it? I am sleepy, Bagheera, and Shere Khan is all long tail and loud talk—like Mao the Peacock."

"But this is no time for sleeping. Baloo knows it; I know it; the Pack knows it; and even the foolish, foolish deer know. Tabaqui has told thee, too."

"Ho! Ho!" said Mowgli. "Tabaqui came to me not long ago with some rude talk that I was a naked man's cub and not fit to dig pig-nuts; but I caught Tabaqui by the tail and swung him twice against a palm-tree to teach him better manners."

"That was foolishness; for though Tabaqui is a mischief-maker, he would have told thee of something that concerned thee closely. Open those eyes, Little Brother. Shere Khan dares not kill thee in the jungle; but remember, Akela is very old, and soon the day comes when he cannot kill his buck, and then he will be leader no more. Many of the wolves that looked thee over when thou wast brought to the Council first are old too, and the young wolves believe, as Shere Khan has taught them, that a man-cub has no place with the Pack. In a little time thou wilt be a man."

"And what is a man that he should not run with his brothers?" said Mowgli. "I was born in the jungle. I have obeyed the Law of the Jungle, and there is no wolf of ours from whose paws I have not pulled a thorn. Surely they are my brothers!"

Bagheera stretched himself at full length and half shut his eyes. "Little Brother," said he, "feel under my jaw."

Mowgli put up his strong brown hand, and just under Bagheera's silky chin, where the giant rolling muscles were all hid by the glossy hair, he came upon a little bald spot.

"There is no one in the jungle that knows that I, Bagheera, carry that mark—the mark of the collar; and yet, Little Brother, I was born among men, and it was among men that my mother died—in the cages of the King's Palace at Oodeypore. It was because of this that I paid the price for thee at the Council when thou wast a little naked cub. Yes, I too was born among men. I had never seen the jungle. They fed me behind bars from an iron pan till one night I felt that I was Bagheera—the Panther—and no man's plaything, and I broke the silly lock with one blow of my paw and came away; and because I had learned the ways of men, I became more terrible in the jungle than Shere Khan. Is it not so?"

"Yes," said Mowgli; "all the jungle fear Bagheera—all except Mowgli."

"Oh, *thou* art a man's cub," said the Black Panther, very tenderly; "and even as I returned to my jungle, so thou must go back to men at last—to the men who are thy brothers—if thou art not killed in the Council."

"But why—but why should any wish to kill me?" said Mowgli.

"Look at me," said Bagheera; and Mowgli looked at him steadily between the eyes. The big panther turned his head away, in half a minute.

"*That* is why," he said, shifting his paw on the leaves. "Not even I can look thee between the eyes, and I was born among men, and I love thee, Little Brother. The others they hate thee because their eyes cannot meet thine; because thou art wise; because thou hast pulled out thorns from their feet—because thou art a man."

"I did not know these things," said Mowgli, sullenly; and he frowned under his heavy black eyebrows.

"What is the Law of the Jungle? Strike first and then give tongue. By thy very carelessness they know that thou art a man. But be wise. It is in my heart that when Akela misses his next kill—and at each hunt it costs him more to pin the buck—the Pack will turn against him and against thee. They will hold a jungle Council at the Rock, and then—and then—I have it!" said Bagheera, leaping up. "Go thou down quickly to the men's huts in the valley, and take some of the Red Flower which they grow there, so that when the time comes thou mayest have even a stronger friend than I or Baloo or those of the Pack that love thee. Get the Red Flower."

By Red Flower Bagheera meant fire, only no creature in the jungle will call fire by its proper name. Every beast lives in deadly fear of it, and invents a hundred ways of describing it.

"The Red Flower?" said Mowgli. "That grows outside their huts in the twilight. I will get some."

"There speaks the man's cub," said Bagheera, proudly. "Remember that it grows in little pots. Get one swiftly, and keep it by thee for time of need."

"Good!" said Mowgli. "I go. But art thou sure, O my Bagheera"—he slipped his arm round the splendid neck, and looked deep into the big eyes—"art thou sure that all this is Shere Khan's doing?"

"By the broken lock that freed me, I am sure, Little Brother."

"Then, by the bull that bought me, I will pay Shere Khan full tale for this, and it may be a little over," said Mowgli; and he bounded away.

"That is a man. That is all a man," said Bagheera to himself, lying down again. "Oh, Shere Khan, never was a blacker hunting than that frog-hunt of thine ten years ago!"

Mowgli was far and far through the forest, running hard, and his heart was hot in him. He came to the cave as the evening mist rose, and drew breath, and looked down the valley. The cubs were out, but Mother Wolf, at the back of the cave, knew by his breathing that something was troubling her frog.

"What is it, Son?" she said.

"Some bat's chatter of Shere Khan," he called back. "I hunt among the plowed fields tonight"; and he plunged downward through the bushes, to the stream at the bottom of the valley. There he checked, for he heard the yell of the Pack hunting, heard the bellow of a hunted Sambhur, and the snort as the buck turned at bay. Then there were wicked, bitter howls from the young wolves: "Akela! Akela! Let the Lone Wolf show his strength. Room for the leader of the Pack! Spring, Akela!"

The Lone Wolf must have sprung and missed his hold, for Mowgli heard the snap of his teeth and then a yelp as the Sambhur knocked him over with his forefoot.

He did not wait for anything more, but dashed on; and the yells grew fainter behind him as he ran into the crop-lands where the villagers lived.

"Bagheera spoke truth," he panted, as he nestled down in some cattle-fodder by the window of a hut. "Tomorrow is one day both for Akela and for me."

Then he pressed his face close to the window and watched the fire on the hearth. He saw the husbandman's wife get up and feed it in the night with black lumps; and when the morning came and the mists were all white and cold, he saw the man's child pick up a wicker pot plastered inside with earth, fill it with lumps of red-hot charcoal, put it under his blanket, and go out to tend the cows in the byre.

"Is that all?" said Mowgli. "If a cub can do it, there is nothing to fear"; so he strode round the corner and met the boy, took the pot from his hand, and disappeared into the mist while the boy howled with fear.

"They are very like me," said Mowgli, blowing into the pot, as he had seen the woman do. "This thing will die if I do not give it things to eat"; and he dropped twigs and dried bark on the red stuff. Half-way up the hill he met Bagheera with the morning dew shining like moonstones on his coat.

"Akela has missed," said the Panther. "They would have killed him last night, but they needed thee also. They were looking for thee on the hill."

"I was among the ploughed lands. I am ready. See!" Mowgli held up the fire-pot.

"Good! Now, I have seen men thrust a dry branch into that stuff, and presently the Red Flower blossomed at the end of it. Art thou not afraid?"

"No. Why should I fear? I remember now—if it is not a dream—how, before I was a Wolf, I lay beside the Red Flower, and it was warm and pleasant."

All that day Mowgli sat in the cave tending his fire-pot and dipping dry branches into it to see how they looked. He found a branch that satisfied him, and in the evening when Tabaqui came to the cave and told him rudely enough that he was wanted at the Council Rock, he laughed till Tabaqui ran away. Then Mowgli went to the Council, still laughing.

Akela the Lone Wolf lay by the side of his rock as a sign that the leadership of the Pack was open, and Shere Khan with his following of scrap-fed wolves walked to and fro openly being flattered. Bagheera lay close to Mowgli, and the fire-pot was between Mowgli's knees. When they were all gathered together, Shere Khan began to speak—a thing he would never have dared to do when Akela was in his prime.

"He has no right," whispered Bagheera. "Say so. He is a dog's son. He will be frightened."

Mowgli sprang to his feet. "Free People," he cried, "does Shere Khan lead the Pack? What has a tiger to do with our leadership?"

"Seeing that the leadership is yet open, and being asked to speak—" Shere Khan began.

"By whom?" said Mowgli. "Are we *all* jackals, to fawn on this cattle-butcher? The leadership of the Pack is with the Pack alone."

There were yells of "Silence, thou man's cub!" "Let him speak. He has kept our Law"; and at last the seniors of the Pack thundered: "Let the Dead Wolf speak." When a leader of the Pack has missed his kill, he is called the Dead Wolf as long as he lives, which is not long.

Akela raised his old head wearily:

"Free People, and ye too, jackals of Shere Khan, for twelve seasons I have led ye to and from the kill, and in all that time not one has been trapped or maimed. Now I have missed my kill. Ye know how that plot was made. Ye know how ye brought me up to an untried buck to make my weakness known. It was cleverly done. Your right is to kill me here on the Council Rock, now. Therefore, I ask, who comes to make an end of the Lone Wolf? For it is my right, by the Law of the Jungle, that ye come one by one."

There was a long hush, for no single wolf cared to fight Akela to the death. Then Shere Khan roared: "Bah! what have we to do with this toothless fool? He is doomed to die! It is the man-cub who has lived too long. Free People, he was my meat from the first. Give him to me. I am weary of this man-wolf folly. He has troubled the jungle for ten seasons. Give me the man-cub, or I will hunt here always, and not give you one bone. He is a man, a man's child, and from the marrow of my bones I hate him!"

Then more than half the Pack yelled: "A man! a man! What has a man to do with us? Let him go to his own place."

"And turn all the people of the villages against us?" thundered Shere Khan. "No; give him to me. He is a man, and none of us can look him between the eyes."

Akela lifted his head again, and said: "He has eaten our food. He has slept with us. He has driven game for us. He has broken no word of the Law of the Jungle."

"Also, I paid for him with a bull when he was accepted. The worth of a bull is little, but Bagheera's honor is something that he will perhaps fight for," said Bagheera, in his gentlest voice.

"A bull paid ten years ago!" the Pack snarled. "What do we care for bones ten years old?"

"Or for a pledge?" said Bagheera, his white teeth bared under his lip. "Well are ye called the Free People!"

"No man's cub can run with the people of the jungle," roared Shere Khan. "Give him to me!"

"He is our brother in all but blood," Akela went on; "and ye would kill him here! In truth, I have lived too long. Some of ye are eaters of cattle, and of others I have heard that under Shere Khan's teaching ye go by dark night and snatch children from the villager's door-step. Therefore I know ye to be cowards, and it is to cowards I speak. It is certain that I must die, and my life is of no worth, or I would offer that in the man-cub's place. But for the sake of the Honor of the Pack—a little matter that by being without a leader ye have forgotten—I promise that if ye let the man-cub go to his own place, I will not, when my time comes to die, bare one tooth against ye. I will die without fighting. That will at least save the Pack three lives. More I cannot do; but if ye will, I can save ye the shame that comes of killing a brother against whom there is no fault—a brother spoken for and bought into the Pack according to the Law of the Jungle."

"He is a man—a man—a man!" snarled the Pack; and most of the wolves began to gather round Shere Khan, whose tail was beginning to switch.

"Now the business is in thy hands," said Bagheera to Mowgli. "We can do no more except fight."

Mowgli stood upright—the fire-pot in his hands. Then he stretched out his arms, and yawned in the face of the Council; but he was furious with rage and sorrow, for, wolf-like, the wolves had never told him how they hated him. "Listen you!" he cried. "There is no need for this dog's jabber. Ye have told me so often tonight that I am a man (and indeed I would have been a wolf with you to my life's end), that I feel your words are true. So I do not call ye my brothers any more, but *sag* [dogs], as a man should. What ye will do, and what ye will not do, is not yours to say. That matter is with *me*; and that we may see the matter more plainly, I, the man, have brought here a little of the Red Flower which ye, dogs, fear."

He flung the fire-pot on the ground, and some of the red coals lit a tuft of dried moss that flared up, as all the Council drew back in terror before the leaping flames.

Mowgli thrust his dead branch into the fire till the twigs lit and crackled, and whirled it above his head among the cowering wolves.

"Thou art the master," said Bagheera, in an undertone. "Save Akela from the death. He was ever thy friend."

Akela, the grim old wolf who had never asked for mercy in his life, gave one piteous look at Mowgli as the boy stood all naked, his long black hair tossing over his shoulders in the light of the blazing branch that made the shadows jump and quiver.

"Good!" said Mowgli, staring around slowly. "I see that ye are dogs. I go from you to my own people—if they be my own people. The jungle is shut to me, and I must forget your talk and your companionship; but I will be more merciful than ye are. Because I was all but your brother in blood, I promise that when I am a man among men I will not betray ye to men as ye have betrayed me." He kicked the fire with his foot, and the sparks flew up. "There shall be no war between any of us in the Pack. But here is a debt to pay before I go." He strode forward to where Shere Khan sat blinking stupidly at the flames, and caught him by the tuft on his chin. Bagheera followed in case of accidents. "Up, dog!" Mowgli cried. "Up, when a man speaks, or I will set that coat ablaze!"

Shere Khan's ears lay flat back on his head, and he shut his eyes, for the blazing branch was very near.

"This cattle-killer said he would kill me in the Council because he had not killed me when I was a cub. Thus and thus, then, do we beat dogs when we are men. Stir a whisker, Lungri, and I ram the Red Flower down thy gullet!" He beat Shere Khan over the head with the branch, and the tiger whimpered and whined in an agony of fear.

"Pah! Singed jungle-cat—go now! But remember when next I come to the Council Rock, as a man should come, it will be with Shere Khan's hide on my head. For the rest, Akela goes free to live as he pleases. Ye will *not* kill him, because that is not my will. Nor do I think that ye will sit here any longer, lolling out your tongues as though ye were somebodies, instead of dogs whom I drive out—thus! Go!" The fire was burning furiously at the end of the branch, and Mowgli struck right and left round the circle, and the wolves ran howling with the sparks burning their fur. At last there were only Akela, Bagheera, and perhaps ten wolves that had taken Mowgli's part. Then something began to hurt Mowgli inside him, as he had never been hurt in his life before, and he caught his breath and sobbed, and the tears ran down his face.

"What is it? What is it?" he said. "I do not wish to leave the jungle, and I do not know what this is. Am I dying, Bagheera?"

"No, Little Brother. That is only tears such as men use," said Bagheera. "Now I know thou art a man, and a man's cub no longer. The jungle is shut indeed to thee henceforward. Let them fall, Mowgli. They are only tears." So Mowgli sat and cried as though his heart would break; and he had never cried in all his life before.

"Now," he said, "I will go to men. But first I must say farewell to my mother"; and he went to the cave where she lived with Father Wolf, and he cried on her coat, while the four cubs howled miserably.

"Ye will not forget me?" said Mowgli.

"Never while we can follow a trail," said the cubs. "Come to the foot of the hill when thou art a man, and we will talk to thee; and we will come into the croplands to play with thee by night."

"Come soon!" said Father Wolf. "Oh, wise little frog, come again soon; for we be old, thy mother and I."

"Come soon," said Mother Wolf, "little naked son of mine; for, listen, child of man, I loved thee more than ever I loved my cubs."

"I will surely come," said Mowgli; "and when I come it will be to lay out Shere Khan's hide upon the Council Rock. Do not forget me! Tell them in the jungle never to forget me!"

The dawn was beginning to break when Mowgli went down the hillside alone to the crops, to meet those mysterious things that are called men.

First published in the January 1894 edition of *St. Nicholas Magazine*

Tiger! Tiger!

BY RUDYARD KIPLING

WHEN MOWGLI, AS you know, left Mother Wolf's cave after the fight with the Pack at the Council Rock, he went down to the plowed lands where the villagers lived; but he would not stop there because it was too near to the jungle, and he knew that he had made at least one bad enemy at the Council. So he hurried on, keeping to the rough road that ran down the valley, and followed it at a steady jog-trot for nearly twenty miles, till he came to a new country. The valley opened out into a great plain dotted over with rocks and cut up by ravines. At one end stood a little village, and at the other the thick jungle came down in a sweep to the graz-ing-grounds, and stopped there as though it had been cut off with a hoe. All over the plain, cattle and buffaloes were grazing; and when the little boys in charge of the herds saw Mowgli they shouted and ran away, and the yellow pariah dogs that hang about every Indian village barked at him. Mowgli walked on, for he was feel-ing hungry; and when he came to the village gate he saw the big thornbush that was drawn up before the gate at twilight, pushed to one side.

"Umph!" he said, for he had come across more than one such barricade in his night rambles after things to eat. "So men are afraid of the People of the Jungle here also." He sat down by the gate; and when a man came out he stood up, and opened his mouth to show that he wanted food. The man stared, and ran back up the one street of the village shouting for the priest, who was a big, fat man dressed in white, with a red and yellow mark on his forehead. The priest came to the gate, and with him at least a hundred people, who stared and talked and shouted and pointed at Mowgli.

"They have no manners, these men folk," said Mowgli to himself. "Only the Gray Ape would behave as they do."

So he threw back his long hair and frowned at the crowd.

"What is there to be afraid of?" said the priest. "Look at the marks on his arms and legs. They are the bites of wolves. He is only a wolf-child run away from the jungle."

Of course, in playing together, the cubs had often nipped Mowgli harder than they intended, and there were white scars all over his arms and legs. But he would have been the last person in the world to call them bites, for he knew what real bit-ing meant.

"Arré! Arré!" said two or three women together. "To be bitten by wolves, poor child! He is a handsome boy. He has eyes like red fire. By my honor, Messua, he is not unlike thy boy that was taken by the tiger."

"Let me look," said a woman with heavy copper rings on her wrists and ankles; and she stared at Mowgli under the palm of her hand. "Indeed, he is not. He is thinner, but he has the very look of my boy."

The priest was a clever man, and he knew that Messua was wife to the richest villager in the place. So he looked up at the sky for a minute, and said solemnly: "What the jungle has taken the jungle has restored. Take the boy into thy house, my sister, and forget not to honor the priest who sees so far into the lives of men."

"By the bull that bought me," said Mowgli to himself, "all this talking is like another looking-over by the Pack! Well, if I am a man, a man I must become."

The crowd parted as the woman beckoned Mowgli to her hut, where there was a red lacquered bedstead, a great earthen grain-chest with quaint raised patterns on it, half a dozen cooking-pots, an image of a Hindu god in a little alcove, and on the wall a real looking-glass such as they sell at the country fairs for eight cents.

She gave him a long draught of milk (this was new to Mowgli, but it tasted good), and some bread, and then she laid her hand on his head and looked into his eyes; for she thought perhaps that he might be her real son come back from the jungle where the tiger had taken him. So she said, "Nathoo, O Nathoo!" Mowgli did not show that he knew the name. "Dost thou not remember the day when I gave thee thy new shoes?"

She touched his foot, and it was almost as hard as horn.

"No," she said, sorrowfully; "those feet have never worn shoes, but thou art very like Nathoo, and thou shalt be my son."

Mowgli was uneasy, because he had never been under a roof before; but as he looked at the thatch, he saw that he could tear it out any time if he wanted to get away, and that the window had no fastenings.

"What is the good of a man," he said to himself at last, "if he does not understand man's talk? Now I am as silly and dumb as a man would be with us in the jungle. I must learn their talk."

It was not for fun that he had learned while he was with the wolves to imitate the challenge of bucks in the jungle and the grunt of the little wild pig. So, as soon as Messua said a word, Mowgli would imitate it almost perfectly, and before dark he had learned the name of nearly everything in the hut.

There was a difficulty at bedtime, because Mowgli was not going to sleep under anything that looked so like a panther-trap as that hut, and when they shut the door he went through the window. "Give him his will," said Messua's husband. "Remember he can never till now have slept on a bed. If he is indeed sent in the place of our son, he will not run away."

So Mowgli slept in some long clean grass at the edge of the field, but before he had closed his eyes a soft gray nose poked him under the chin.

"Phew!" said Gray Brother (he was the eldest of Mother Wolf's cubs). "This is a poor reward for following thee twenty miles. Thou smellest of wood-smoke and cattle—altogether like a man already. Wake, Little Brother; I bring news."

"Are all well in the jungle?" said Mowgli, hugging him.

"All except the wolves that were burned with the Red Flower. Now listen. Shere Khan has gone away, to hunt far off till his coat grows again, for he is badly singed. When he returns he swears that he will lay thy bones in the Waingunga River."

"There are two words to that. I also have made a little promise. But to hear news is always good. I am tired tonight—very tired with new things, Gray Brother—but bring me the news always."

"Thou wilt not forget that thou art a wolf? Men will not make thee forget?" asked Gray Brother, anxiously.

"Never. I will remember that I love thee and all in our cave; but also I will always remember that I have been cast out of the Pack."

"And that thou mayst be cast out of another. Men are only men, Little Brother, and their talk is like the talk of frogs in a pond. When I come down here

"Wake, Little Brother; I bring news."

again, I will wait for thee in the bamboos at the edge of the grazing-ground."

For three months after that night Mowgli hardly ever left the village gate; he was so busy learning the ways and customs of men. First he had to wear a cloth round him, which annoyed him horribly; and then he had to learn about money, which he did not in the least understand, and about plowing, which he did not see the use of. Then the little children in the village made him very angry. Luckily, the Law of the Jungle had taught him to keep his temper, for in the jungle life and food depend on keeping your temper; but when the children made fun of him because he would not play games or fly kites, or because he mispronounced some word, only the knowledge that it was unsportsmanlike to kill little naked cubs kept him from picking them up and tearing them in two.

He did not know his own strength in the least. In the jungle he knew he was weak as compared with the beasts, but in the village people said that he was as strong as a bull. He certainly had no notion of what fear was, for when the village priest told him that the god in the temple would be angry with him if he ate the priests' mangoes, he picked up the image, brought it over to the priest's house, and asked the priest to make the god angry and he would be happy to fight him. It was a horrible scandal, but the priest hushed it up, and Messua's husband paid nearly seventy cents in silver to comfort the god.

And Mowgli had not the faintest idea of the difference that caste makes between man and man. When the potter's donkey slipped in the clay-pit, Mowgli hauled it out by the tail, and helped to stack the pots for their journey to the market at Khanhiwara. That was very shocking, for the potter is a low-caste man, and his donkey is worse. When the priest scolded him, Mowgli threatened to put him on the donkey, too; and the priest told Messua's husband that Mowgli had better be set to work as soon as possible; and the village head-man told Mowgli that he would have to go out with the buffaloes next day, and herd them while they grazed.

No one was more pleased than Mowgli; and that night, because he had been appointed a servant of the village, as it were, he went off to a circle that met every evening on a platform of masonry under a great fig-tree. It was the village club, and the head-man and the watchman and the barber (who knew all the gossip of the village), and old Buldeo, the village hunter, who had an old army musket, met and smoked. The monkeys sat and talked in the upper branches, and there was a hole under the platform where a cobra lived, and he had his little platter of milk every night because he was sacred; and the old men sat around the tree and talked, and pulled at the big *huqas* (the water-pipes) till far into the night. They told wonderful tales of gods and men and ghosts; and Buldeo told even more wonderful ones of the ways of beasts in the jungle, till the eyes of the children sitting outside the circle hung out of their heads. Most of the tales were about animals, for the jungle was always at their door. The deer and the wild pig grubbed up their crops, and now and again the tiger carried off a man at twilight, within sight of the village gates, as he came back from plowing.

Mowgli, who knew something about the ways of the jungle people, had to cover his face with his hair not to show that he was laughing. But Buldeo, the musket across his knees, climbed on from one wonderful story to another, and Mowgli's shoulders shook.

Buldeo was explaining how the tiger that had carried away Messua's son was a ghost tiger, and his body was inhabited by the ghost of a wicked old money-lender, who had died some years ago. "And I know that this is true," he said, "because Purun Dasrs always limped from the blow that he got in a riot when his account-books were burned, and the tiger that I speak of, *he* limps, too, for the tracks of his feet are unequal."

"True, true!—that must be the truth!" said all the graybeards together.

"Are all these tales such cobwebs and moon-talk?" said Mowgli, suddenly. "That tiger limps because he was born lame, as every one knows. To talk of the soul of a money-lender in a beast that never had the courage of a jackal is child's talk!"

Buldeo was speechless with surprise for a moment, and the head-man stared.

"Oho! It is the jungle-brat, is it?" said Buldeo. "If thou art so wise, better bring his hide to Khanhiwara, for the Government has set a hundred rupees ($30) on his life. Better still, be quiet when thy elders speak."

Mowgli got up to go. "All the evening I have lain here listening," he called back, over his shoulder, "and, except once or twice, Buldeo has not said one word of truth concerning the jungle, which is at his very doors. How then shall I believe the tales of ghosts, and gods, and goblins which ye think ye have seen?"

"It is full time that boy went to herding," said the head-man of the village, while Buldeo puffed and snorted at Mowgli's insolence; for as a rule native children are much more respectful to their elders than white children.

The custom of most Indian villages is for a few boys to take the cattle and buffaloes out to graze in the early morning, and bring them back at night, and the cattle that would trample a white man to death submit to be banged, and bullied, and shouted at by children who hardly come up to their noses. So long as the boys keep with the herds they are absolutely safe, for not even the tiger will charge a mob of cattle. But if they straggle, to pick flowers or hunt lizards, they may be carried off.

Mowgli went through the village street next dawn sitting on the back of Rama, the great herd bull, and the slaty-blue buffaloes, with their long, backward-sweeping horns and savage eyes, rose out of their byres, one by one, and followed him. Mowgli made it very clear to his companions that he was the master. He banged the buffaloes with a long, polished bamboo, and told the boys to graze the cattle by themselves while he went on with the buffaloes, and to be very careful not to stray away from the herd.

An Indian grazing-ground is all rocks, and scrub, and tussocks, and little ravines, among which the herds scatter and disappear. The buffaloes generally keep to the pools and muddy places, where they lie wallowing or basking in the warm mud for hours. Mowgli drove them on to the edge of the plain where the Waingunga River came out of the jungle; then he dropped from Rama's neck, trotted off to a bamboo clump and found Gray Brother. "Ah," said Gray Brother, "I have waited here very many days. What is the meaning of this cattle-herding work?"

"It is an order," said Mowgli; "I am a village herd now. What news of Shere Khan?"

"He has come back to these hills, and has waited here a long time for thee. Now he has gone off again, for the game is scarce. But he surely means to kill thee."

"Very good," said Mowgli. "So long as he is away do thou or one of the four sit on that rock, where I can see thee as I come out of the village. When he comes back, wait for me in the ravine by the *dhâk*-tree in the center of the plain. We need not walk into Shere Khan's mouth."

Then Mowgli picked out a shady place, and lay down and slept while the buffaloes grazed round him. Herding in India is one of the laziest things in the world. The cattle move and crunch, crunch, and lie down, and move on again, and they do not even low. They only grunt, and the buffaloes very seldom say anything. You can see them lie down in the muddy pools one after another, and work their way in the mud till only their noses and staring china-blue eyes show above the surface, and there they lie like logs. The sun makes the rocks dance in the heat, and you hear one kite (never any more) whistling, almost out of sight overhead, and you know that if you died, or a cow died, that kite would come down like a bullet, and the next kite miles away would see him drop and follow, and the next, and the next, and almost before you were dead there would be a score of them come out of nowhere. Then you sleep and wake and sleep again, and weave little baskets out of dried grass and put grasshoppers in them; or catch two praying-mantises and make them fight; or string a necklace of red and black jungle-nuts; or watch a lizard basking on a rock, or a snake hunting a frog near the wallows. Then you sing endless songs with odd native quavers at the end of them, and the day seems longer than most people's whole lives; and perhaps you make a mud castle with mud figures of men and horses and buffaloes, and put reeds into the men's hands, and play that you are a king and they are your armies, or that they are gods and you ought to worship them. Then evening comes and you call, and the buffaloes lumber up out of the sticky mud with noises like gun-shots going off one after the other, and you all string across the gray plain back to the twinkling village lights.

Day after day Mowgli would lead the buffaloes out in this way, and day after day he would see Gray Brother's back a mile and a half away across the plain (that told him Shere Khan had not come back), and day after day he would lie on the grass listening to the noises round him, and dreaming of old days in the jungle.

If Shere Khan had made a false step with his lame paw up in the jungles by the Waingunga, Mowgli would have heard him in those long dead-still mornings.

At last the day came when he did not see Gray Brother at the signal place, and he laughed and headed the buffaloes for the ravine by the *dhâk*-tree which was all covered with golden-red flowers. There sat Gray Brother with every bristle on his back lifted.

"He has given two months to throw thee off thy guard. He crossed the ranges last night with Tabaqui, hot-foot on thy trail," said the wolf.

Mowgli frowned. "I am not afraid of Shere Khan, but Tabaqui is very cunning," he said.

"Have no fear," Gray Brother answered, licking his lips a little. "I met Tabaqui in the dawn. Now he is telling all his wisdom to the kites, but he told *me* everything before I broke his back. Shere Khan's plan is to wait for thee at the village gate this evening—for thee and for no one else. He is lying up now, in the big ravine of the Waingunga."

"Has he eaten today, or does he hunt empty?" said Mowgli, for the answer meant just life or death to him.

"He killed at dawn—a pig—and he has drunk too. Remember, Shere Khan could never fast even for the sake of revenge."

"Oh! Fool, fool! What a cub's cub it is! Eaten and drunk too, has he, and he thinks that I shall wait till he has slept! Now, where does he lie up? If there were but ten of us we might pull him down as he snores. These buffaloes will not charge unless they wind him, and I cannot speak their language. Can we get behind his track that they may smell it?"

"He swam far down the Waingunga to cut that off," said Gray Brother.

"Tabaqui told him that, I know. He would never have thought of it, alone." Mowgli stood with his finger in his mouth, thinking. "The big ravine of the Waingunga. That opens out on the plain not half a mile from here. I can take the herd round through the jungle to the head' of the ravine and then sweep down, but he would slink out at the foot. We must block that end. Gray Brother, canst thou cut the herd in two for me?"

"Not I alone—but I have brought a wise helper." Gray Brother trotted off and dropped into a hole. Then there popped up a huge gray head that Mowgli knew well, and the hot air was filled with the most desolate cry of all the jungle—the hunting-howl of a wolf at midday.

"Akela! Akela!" said Mowgli, clapping his hands. "I might have known that thou wouldst not forget. Cut them in two, Akela. Keep the cows and calves together, and the bulls and the plow-buffaloes by themselves."

The two wolves ran in and out of the herd, which snorted and threw up its head, and separated into two clumps. In one the cow buffaloes stood and glared and pawed with the calves in the center, ready if a wolf would only stay still to charge down and trample the life out of him. In the other the bulls and the young bulls snorted and stamped, but though they looked more angry they were much less dangerous than the cows, for they had no calves to protect. No six men could have divided the herd so neatly.

"What orders?" panted Akela. "They are trying to join again."

Mowgli slipped on to Rama's back. "Drive the bulls away to the left, Akela. Gray Brother, when we are gone hold the cows together, and drive them into the foot of the ravine."

"How far?" said Gray Brother, panting and snapping.

"Till the sides are higher than Shere Khan can jump," shouted Mowgli. "Hold them there till we come down." The bulls swept off as Akela bayed, and Gray Brother stopped in front of the cows. They charged down on him, and he ran just before them to the foot of the ravine, as Akela drove the bulls far away to the left.

"Well done! Another charge and they are fairly in. Careful, now—careful, Akela! A snap too much, and the bulls will charge. Huyah! This is wilder work than driving black-buck. Didst thou think these creatures could move so swiftly?" said Mowgli.

"I have—have hunted these too in my time," gasped Akela in the dust. "Shall I turn them into the jungle?"

"Ay! Turn. Swiftly, turn them. Rama is mad with rage. Oh, if I could only tell him what I need of him today!"

The bulls were turned to the right this time, and crashed into the standing thicket. The other herd-children, watching with the cattle half a mile away, hurried to the village as fast as their legs could carry them, crying that the buffaloes had gone mad and run away. But Mowgli's plan was simple enough. All he wanted to do was to make a big circle up hill and get at the head of the ravine, and then take the bulls down it and catch Shere Khan between the bulls and the cows; for he knew that after a meal and a full drink Shere Khan would not be in any condition to fight or to clamber up the sides of the ravine. He began to soothe the buffaloes now by voice, and Akela dropped far to the rear, only whimpering once or twice to hurry the stragglers. It was a long, long circle, for they did not wish to get too near the ravine and give Shere Khan warning. At last Mowgli rounded up the bewildered herd at the head of the ravine on a grassy patch that sloped steeply down to the ravine itself. From that height you could see across the tops of the trees down to the plain below; but what Mowgli looked at was the sides of the ravine, and he saw with a great deal of satisfaction that they were nearly straight up and down, and the vines and creepers that hung over them would give no foothold to a tiger who tried to get out.

"Let them breathe, Akela," he said, holding up his hand. "They have not winded him yet. Let them breathe. I must tell Shere Khan that I come."

He put his hands to his mouth and shouted down the ravine—it was almost like shouting down a tunnel—and the echoes jumped from rock to rock. After a long time there came back the drawling, sleepy snarl of a full-fed tiger just wakened.

"Who calls?" said Shere Khan, while a splendid peacock fluttered up out of the ravine screeching.

"I, Mowgli. Cattle thief, it is time to come to the Council Rock! Down—hurry them down, Akela. Down, Rama, down!"

The herd paused for an instant at the edge of the slope, but Akela gave tongue in the full wolf's hunting-yell, and the buffaloes pitched over one after the other just as steamers shoot rapids, the sand and stones spurting up round them. Once started, there was no chance of stopping, and before they were fairly in the bed of the ravine Rama had winded Shere Khan and bellowed.

"Ha! Ha!" said Mowgli, on his back. "Now thou knowest!" and the torrent of black horns, foaming muzzles, and staring eyes tore down the ravine just as boulders go down in flood time, the weaker buffaloes being shouldered out to the sides of the ravine where they tore through the creepers. They knew what the business was before them—the terrible charge of the buffalo-herd against which no tiger can hope to stand. Shere Khan heard the thunder of their feet, picked himself up, and lumbered down the ravine, looking from side to side for some way of escape, but the walls of the ravine were straight and he had to keep on, heavy with his dinner and his drink, willing to do anything rather than fight. The herd splashed through the pool he had just left, bellowing till the ravine rang. Mowgli heard an answering bellow from the foot of the ravine, saw Shere Khan turn (the lame tiger knew if the worst came to the worst it was better to meet the bulls than the cows with their calves) and then Rama tripped, stumbled, and went on again over something soft, and, with the bulls at his heels, crashed full into the other herd, while the weaker buffaloes were whirled clean off their feet. That charge carried both herds out into the plain, goring and stamping and snorting. Mowgli watched his time, and slipped off Rama's neck, laying about him right and left with his stick.

"Quick, Akela! Break them up. Scatter them, or they will be fighting one another. Drive them away, Akela. *Hai*, Rama! *Hai, Hai! Hai,* my children! Softly now, softly! It is all over."

Akela and Gray Brother ran to and fro nipping the buffaloes' legs, and though the herd wheeled once to charge up the ravine again, Mowgli managed to turn Rama, and the others followed him to the wallows.

Shere Khan needed no more trampling. He was dead, his lame paw doubled up under him, and the kites were coming for him already.

"Brothers, that was a dog's death," said Mowgli, feeling for the knife that he carried in a sheath round his neck. "But he would never have shown fight. His hide will look well on the Council Rock. We must get to work swiftly."

A boy trained among men would never have dreamed of skinning a ten-foot tiger alone, but Mowgli knew better than any one else how an animal's skin is fitted on, and how it can be taken off. But it was hard work at the best, and Mowgli slashed, and tore, and grunted for an hour, while the wolves lolled out their tongues, or came forward and tugged as he ordered them. Presently a hand fell on his shoulder, and looking up he saw Buldeo with the army musket. The children had told the village about the buffalo stampede, and Buldeo went out only too anxious to correct Mowgli for not taking better care of the herd. The wolves had dropped out of sight as soon as they saw the hunter.

"What is this folly?" said Buldeo, angrily. "To think that thou canst skin a tiger! Where did thy buffaloes kill him? It is the Lame Tiger, too, and there is a hundred rupees on his head! Well, well, we will overlook thy letting the herd run off, and perhaps I will give thee one of the rupees of the reward when I have taken the skin to Khanhiwara." He fumbled in his waist-cloth for flint and steel, and stooped down to singe Shere Khan's whiskers. Most native hunters singe a tiger's whiskers to prevent his ghost from haunting them.

"Hum!" said Mowgli, half to himself, as he ripped back the skin of a forepaw. "So thou wilt take the hide to Khanhiwara for the reward, and perhaps give me one rupee? Now it is my mind that I need the skin for my own use. Heh! old man, take away that fire!"

"What talk is this to the chief hunter of the village? Thy luck and the stupidity of thy buffaloes have helped thee to this kill. The tiger has just fed, or he would have gone twenty miles by this time. Thou canst not even skin him properly, little beggar brat, and forsooth I, Buldeo, must be told not to singe his whiskers! Mowgli, I will not give thee one anna of the reward, but only a very big beating. Leave the carcass."

"By the bull that bought me," said Mowgli, who was trying to get at the shoulder, "must I stay babbling to an old ape all noon? Here, Akela, this man plagues me."

Buldeo, who was still stooping over Shere Khan's head, found himself sprawling on the grass, with a gray wolf standing over him, while Mowgli went on skinning as though he were alone in all India.

"Ye-es," he said between his teeth. "Thou art right, Buldeo. Thou wilt never give me one anna of the reward. There is an old war between this Lame Tiger and myself—a very old war, and—I have won."

To do Buldeo justice, if he had been ten years younger he would have taken his chance with Akela had he met the wolf in the woods, but a wolf who obeyed the orders of a boy who had private wars with man-eating tigers was not a common animal. It was sorcery, magic of the worst kind, thought Buldeo, and he wondered whether the amulet round his neck would protect him. He lay as still as still, expecting every minute to see Mowgli turn into a tiger, too.

"Maharaj! Great King!" he said at last in a husky whisper.

"Yes," said Mowgli, without turning his head, but chuckling a little. "I am an old man. I did not know that thou wast anything more than a herd-boy. May I rise up and go away, or will thy servant tear me to pieces?"

"Go, and peace go with thee. Only, another time do not meddle with my game. Let him go, Akela."

Buldeo hobbled away to the village as fast as he could, looking back over his shoulder in case Mowgli should change into something with four legs. When he got to the village he told a tale of magic, and enchantment, and sorcery that made the priest look very grave.

Mowgli went on with his work, but it was nearly twilight before he finished.

"Now we must hide the skin and take the buffaloes home! Help me to herd them, Akela."

The herd rounded up in the smoky twilight, and when they were near the village Mowgli saw lights, and heard the conches and bells in the temple blowing and banging. Half the village seemed to be waiting for him at the gate. "That is because I have killed Shere Khan," he said to himself; but a shower of stones whistled about his ears, and the villagers shouted: "Sorcerer! Wolf's brat! Jungle-demon! Go away! Get hence quickly, or the priest will turn thee into a wolf again. Shoot, Buldeo, shoot!"

The old musket went off and a young buffalo bellowed with pain.

"More sorcery!" shouted the villagers. "He can turn bullets. Buldeo, that was *thy* buffalo!"

"Now what is this?" said Mowgli, bewildered, as more stones flew.

"They are not unlike the Pack, these brothers of thine," said Akela, sitting down with a grunt. "It is in my head that, if bullets mean anything, they would cast thee out."

"Wolf! Wolf's cub! Go away!" shouted the priest, waving a sprig of the sacred *tulsi* plant.

"Again? Last time it was because I was a man. This time it is because I am a wolf. Let us go, Akela," said Mowgli. A woman—it was Messua—ran across to the herd, and cried, "Oh, my son, my son! They say thou art a sorcerer who can turn himself into a beast at will. I do not believe, but go away or they will kill thee. Buldeo says thou art a wizard, but I know thou hast avenged my Nathoo's death."

"Come back, Messua!" shouted the crowd. "Come back, or we will stone thee, too."

Mowgli laughed a little short ugly laugh, for a stone had hit him in the mouth. "Run back, Messua. This is one of the foolish tales they tell under the big tree at

Buldeo lay still, expecting every minute to see Mowgli turn into a tiger, too.

dusk. I have at least paid for thy son's life. Farewell; and run quickly, for I shall send the herd in as swiftly as their brickbats come out. I am no wizard, Messua. Farewell!"

"Now, once more, Akela," he cried. "Bring the herd in."

The buffaloes were anxious enough to get to the village. They hardly needed Akela's yell, but charged through the gate like a whirlwind, scattering the crowd right and left.

"Keep count!" shouted Mowgli scornfully. "It may be that I have stolen one of them. Keep count, for I will do your herding no more. Fare you well, children of men, and thank Messua that I do not come in with my wolves and hunt you up and down your street."

He turned on his heel and walked away with the Lone Wolf, and as he looked up at the stars he felt happy. "No more sleeping in traps for me, Akela," he said. "Let us get Shere Khan's skin and go away. No; we will not hurt the village, for the woman Messua was kind to me."

When the moon rose over the plain, making it look all milky, the horrified villagers saw Mowgli, with two wolves at his heels and a bundle on his head, trotting across at the steady wolf's trot that eats up the long miles like fire. Then they banged the temple bells and blew the conches louder than ever; and Messua cried, and Buldeo embroidered the story of his adventures in the jungle, till he ended by saying that Akela stood up on his hind legs and walked like a man.

The moon was just going down when Mowgli and the two wolves came to the hill of the Council Rock, and they stopped at Mother Wolf's cave.

"They have cast me out from the Man Pack, Mother," shouted Mowgli, "but I come with the hide of Shere Khan to keep my word!" Mother Wolf walked stiffly from the cave with the cubs behind her, and her eyes glowed as she saw the skin.

"I told him on that day when he crammed his head and shoulders into this cave, hunting for thy life, little frog—I told him that the hunter would be the hunted. It is well done," she said.

"Little brother, it is well done," said a deep voice in the thicket. "We were lonely in the jungle without thee," and Bagheera came running to Mowgli's bare feet. They clambered up the Council Rock together, and Mowgli spread the skin out on the flat stone where Akela used to sit, and pegged it down with four slivers of bamboo, and Akela lay down upon it, and cried the old call to the Council. "Look, look well, O Wolves," exactly as he had cried it when Mowgli was first brought there.

Ever since Akela had been deposed, the pack had been without a leader, hunting and fighting at their own pleasure. But they answered the call through habit, and some of them were lame from the traps they had fallen into, and some limped from shot-wounds, and some were mangy from eating bad food, and many were

*When the moon rose over the plain, the villagers saw Mowgli
trotting across, with two wolves at his heels.*

missing; but they came to the Council Rock, as many as were left of them, and they
saw Shere Khan's striped hide on the rock, and the huge claws dangling at the end
of the empty dangling feet.

"Look well, O Wolves. Have I kept my word?" said Mowgli; and the wolves
bayed Yes, and one tattered wolf cried:

"Lead us again, O Akela. Lead us again, O man cub, for we be sick of this law-
lessness, and we would be the Free People once more."

"Nay," purred Bagheera, "that may not be. When ye are full fed, the madness
may come upon you again. Not for nothing are ye called the Free People. Ye fought
for freedom, and it is yours. Eat it now, O Wolves."

"Man Pack and Wolf Pack have cast me out," said Mowgli. "I will hunt alone
in the jungle henceforward."

"And we will hunt with thee," said the four cubs.

So Mowgli went away and hunted with the four cubs in the jungle from that
day on. Still he was not always alone, because years afterward he became a man
and took service and married.

But that is a story for grown-ups.

First published in the February 1894 edition of *St. Nicholas Magazine*

THE HAPPYCHAPS

VERSES BY CAROLYN WELLS
PICTURES BY HARRISON CADY

YULETIDE in Jollipopolis
Was a gay and festive time.
The people of this metropolis
Were a busy and jolly populace,
And the bells were all a-chime.
Everybody was bent on important affairs,
The shops showed most tempting and beautiful wares;
Happychaps and Skiddoodles
Spent money by oodles,
As if they were real millionaires.
The spirit of Christmas pervaded the city,
And of course they appointed a gen'ral committee,
For a great celebration,
And fine decoration,
With everything novel and pretty.
Now, right in the midst of the city there stood
A tall, handsome fir-tree. Said Toots: "'Twould be good
To decorate that for a big Christmas Tree."
"Out of doors?" with a shiver, asked old Jim-Jam-Mee.
But they laughed at his shudder;
And 'Rastus said: "Brudder,
Ef you'll get a fur coat, you'll be warm as a toast.
Look at me! I's wropt up, twel I's ready to roast."
And Toots said that he
Would hang on the tree,
A fur coat as a gift to cold Jim-Jam-Mee.
Old General Happychap then was invited
To represent Santa Claus. He was delighted.
Tailor Cricket made for him a marvelous rig,
Of red plush trimmed with ermine. They stuffed him out big,
And added a white false beard and a wig!
Well, as you may know,
He was a great show!

*Christmas shopping in
Jollipopolis*

General Happychap as Santa Claus

For General Happychap did things up brown.
And the night before Christmas he drove around town
With a pack on his back, and bells jingling clear
On his miniature sleigh and eight tiny reindeer!
(The reindeer were rabbits, with harness supplied;
Artificial horns Toots to their long ears had tied!)
Well, this Happychap Santa Claus did as he should;
He went to the houses of all who were good.
He flew down the chimneys—fine gifts he bestowed
(Of course he took with him a *very* big load.)
But he stared with surprise
At the number and size
Of old Daddy-long-legs' extremely long hose.
And he said, "Goodness me! I just *cannot* fill those!"

The houses were decked with red holly and white mistletoe.

Then a happy thought struck him. He said, "What's the odds?"
And he filled those long stockings with eight fishing-rods!
Most Skiddoodles hung up about three or four pairs,
And as they were short, little things would fill theirs.
But 'twas saucy, indeed,
Of old Centipede,
To hang up fifty pairs! then go calmly to sleep.
"Whew!" exclaimed Santa Claus: "I must say this is steep!"
Skiddoodles, you know are humorous folk,
And Br'er Spider put up a practical joke.
To catch Santa Claus he thought would be fun,
So in his own chimney, a fine web he spun.
And when down the flue the General dropped,
By the tangling web he was suddenly stopped!
His arms and his legs, his feet and his hands,
Were all twisted up in the long snarling strands.

Jollipopolis has a big Christmas Tree.

And while in the web he twisted and wriggled
Old Br'er Spider just stood by and giggled,
And laughed at his victim,
To think how he'd tricked him!
Then he said: "Something handsome
By way of a ransom,
I'll accept from your pack, and then I'll assist
Your noble self out of this tangle and twist.
"Take your pick of the pack!" the General cried,
"Take whatever you want, and some more things beside."
The old spider did
as the General bid;
Then he helped him get out of the tangling ends,
And they said "Merry Christmas!" and parted good friends.

*Old Caleb Mouse received
six ears of corn.*

Next morning, with good-will the sun fairly beamed.
Jollipopolis like a big Christmas card seemed.
The houses were glittering with ice and with snow,
And decked with red holly and white mistletoe.
And of holly-leaves green,
Wreaths and garlands were seen,
Till Toots said: "I think that our Jollipopolis,
Might, on this occasion, be called Hollypopolis!"
Skipper Happychap's wonderful sea-going home,
Wasn't tossing about on the waves and the foam;
But was drawn up on shore,
And garlanded o'er,
With gay decorations. While from masts and spars,
Long icicles hung, and glittered like stars.
In the evening the people all gathered in glee
Round the wonderful, beautiful, big Christmas Tree.

*New lamp-chimneys bright
for the fireflies' soft light.*

When the breeze blew the branches, the little bells tinkled;
And a firefly or glowworm on every twig twinkled.
The people applauded with rapturous cries,
And the Rah Rah Boys' cheers fairly rang to the skies.
Then bright faces glowed
As the gifts were bestowed;
And appropriate presents made perfectly happy
Every Skiddoodle and each Happychappy.
Toots had a magnificent new motor-horn;
And old Caleb Mouse received six ears of corn;
The Eskimo Happychaps all had dried herrings;
The chipmunks, small bags of choice apple parings;

The Figis and Hottentots all had new beads;
The Skiddoodle bugs reveled in real pumpkin seeds;
The woodpeckers all returned voluble thanks
For their Extra Delicious Hickory planks.
And another kind thought of good old Kriss Kringle's
Was to give to the wood-wasps some well-flavored shingles.
There were bundles of old "Daily Buzzes" at hand
For the bookworms, who thought they were perfectly grand!
And Raggledy Happychap had some new rags,
For his old ones were nothing but tatters and tags.
New lamp-chimneys bright
For the fireflies' soft light,
And shades for the glowworms of soft green and white.
Old Big Chief Dewdrop received some new feathers,
Which would stand (it was warranted) all sorts of weathers.
And Sir Horace had white spats and new patent leathers.
Then Mr. and Mrs.
Gray Squirrel said: "This is
The best gift of all!" As Toots handed them out
A bag of shelled chestnuts, an answering shout
Arose from the little gray squirrels, and they
On the beautiful nuts were soon nibbling away.
Strange presents delighted the Happychaps foreign:
Old Paddy had Shamrock, and Duncan a sporran;
A fan and a parasol did for the Jap;
And wooden shoes pleased the Dutch Happychap.
And large five-pound boxes of Fyler's Best Bird-seed
Were given to birds, and to all who preferred seed:
Then just in the midst of the gay celebration,
The big tree caught fire! There was great consternation,
For every one feared a bad conflagration.
But ere the flames spread,
A messenger sped,
And the Volunteer Fire Brigade rushed into view,
And put out the flames in a minute or two.
'Rastus Happychap always was getting off jokes,
And he perpetrated a comical hoax.
He had a big box—no one knew what was in it;
When Caleb Mouse asked him, he said: "Wait a minute!
You mice all sit *so*, in a straight little row,
Now watch very closely, you'll see a fine show!"

A mischievous Happychap

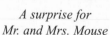

*A surprise for
Mr. and Mrs. Mouse*

A very merry Happychap

The mice in a trice—
Sat stiller than mice,
And waited to see
What the fine show might be.
"Now!" 'Rastus said, "Watch!"
Then he loosened the catch,
And up from the box sprang a great big cat's head!
The way those mice squeaked, and scampered and fled!
Old 'Rastus, he laughed till they feared he would choke;
And, wiping his eyes, he said, "That *was* a joke!"
Then everyone helped to bring in the Yule log,
From the tiniest ant to the portliest frog.
They pulled and they tugged,
They lifted and lugged,
They toted and dragged—
Not one of them lagged,
But everyone helped, as the General commanded,
And at last the great log was successfully landed.
In the wide fireplace of the big Town Hall
It was set ablaze and enjoyed by all;
As they gladly obeyed the General's call
To dance at the Christmas ball.
There was laughter and feasting and merry cheer,
And mistletoe hung from the chandelier,
And the ladies fair,
If they stood there,
Were apt to get kissed, but they didn't care.
At midnight the boar's head was brought in,
And then the merriment rose to a din,
When at last it appeared
Then every one cheered
And all the assemblage just shouted and laughed—
And when it was served, and wassail was quaffed,
Happychaps and Skiddoodles found it was late,
And they started for home at a double-quick rate.
But everyone cried, as he flew out of sight,
"Merry Christmas to all! And to all a good night!"

At midnight the boar's head was brought in.

First published in the December 1908 edition of *St. Nicholas Magazine*

The First of the Rattlesnakes

A *"Tee-Wahn"* Folk-Story

BY CHARLES F. LUMMIS

OW THERE IS a tail on you, *compadre* (friend)," said old Desiderio, nodding at Patricio after we had sat awhile in silence around the crackling fire. His remark referred to the Pueblo superstition that a donkey-tail will grow upon him who obstinately refuses to tell a story in his turn.

Patricio was holding a strip of rawhide across his knee, and was scraping the hair from it with a dull knife. It was high time to be thinking of new soles, for already there was a wee hole in the bottom of each of his moccasins; and as for Benito, his shy little grandson, *his* toes were all abroad.

But shrilly as the cold night-wind outside hinted the wisdom of speedy cobbling, Patricio had no wish to acquire that donkey's tail, so, laying the rawhide and knife upon the floor beside him, he deliberately rolled a modest pinch of an aromatic weed in a corn-husk, lighted this cigarette at the coals, and drew Benito's tousled head to his side.

"You have heard," he said, with a slow puff, "about Nah-chu-ru-chu, the mighty medicine-man who lived here in Isleta in the times of the ancients?"

"*Ahu!* (Yes!)" cried all the boys. "You have promised to tell us how he married the Moon!"

"Another time I will do so. But now I shall tell you something that was before that—for Nah-chu-ru-chu had many strange adventures before he married P'ah-hlee-oh, the Moon Mother. Do you know why the rattlesnake—which is the king of all snakes and alone has the power of death in his mouth—always shakes his *guaje* [the Pueblo sacred rattle] before he bites?"

"*Een-dah!* (No!)" chorused Ramon, and Benito, and Juan, and Tomas, very eagerly; for they were particularly fond of hearing about the exploits of the greatest of Tee-wahn medicine-men.

"Listen, then, and you shall hear."

IN THOSE DAYS Nah-chu-ru-chu had a friend who lived in a pueblo nearer the foot of the Eagle Feather Mountain than this, in the Place of the Red Earth, where still are its ruins; and the two young men went often to the mountain together to bring wood and to hunt. Now, Nah-chu-ru-chu had a white heart, and never thought ill; but the friend had the evil road and became jealous, for Nah-chu-ru-chu was a better hunter. But he said nothing, and did as if he still loved Nah-chu-ru-chu truly.

One day the friend came over from his village and said:

"Friend Nah-chu-ru-chu, let us go tomorrow for wood, and to have a hunt."

"It is well," replied Nah-chu-ru-chu. Next morning he started very early and came to the village of his friend; and together they went to the mountain. When they had gathered much wood, and lashed it in bundles for carrying, they started off in opposite directions to hunt. In a short time each returned with a fine fat deer.

"But why should we hasten to go home, friend Nah-chu-ru-chu?" said the friend. "It is still early, and we have much time. Come, let us stay here and amuse ourselves with a game."

"It is well, friend," answered Nah-chu-ru-chu, "but what game shall we play? For we have neither sticks, nor hoops, nor any other game here."

"Yes; we will roll the *mah-khur,* for while I was waiting for you I made one that we might play"—and the false friend drew from beneath his blanket a pretty, painted hoop. Really he had bewitched it at home, and had brought it hidden, on purpose to do harm to Nah-chu-ru-chu.

"Now go down there and catch it when I roll it," said he; and Nah-chu-ru-chu did so. But as he caught the magic hoop when it came rolling, he was no longer Nah-chu-ru-chu the brave hunter, but was instantly changed into a poor coyote with great tears rolling down his nose!

"Hu!" said the false friend, tauntingly, "we do this to each other! So now you have all the plains to wander over, to the north, and west, and south; but you can never go to the east. And if you are not lucky, the dogs will tear you; but if you are lucky, they may have pity on you. So now good-by, for this is the last I shall ever see of you."

Then the false friend went away, laughing, to his village; and the poor coyote wandered aimlessly, weeping to think that he had been betrayed by the one he had loved and trusted as a brother. For four days he prowled about the outskirts of Isleta, looking wistfully at his home. The fierce dogs ran out to tear him; but when they came near, they only sniffed at him, and went away without hurting him. He could find nothing to eat save dry bones, and old soles or thongs of moccasins.

On the fourth day, he turned westward, and wandered until he came to Mesita. There was no town of the Lagunas there then, and only a shepherd's hut and corral, in which were an old Queres Indian and his grandson, tending their goats.

Next morning when the grandson went out very early to let the goats from the corral, he saw a coyote run out from among the goats. It went off a little way, and then sat down and watched him. The boy counted the goats, and none were missing, and he thought it strange. But he said nothing to his grandfather.

For three more mornings, the very same thing happened; and on the fourth morning the boy told his grandfather. The old man came out, and sent the dogs after the coyote, which was sitting at a little distance; but when they came near they would not touch him.

"I suspect there is something wrong here," said the old shepherd; and he called: "Coyote, are you coyote-true, or are you people?"

But the coyote could not answer; and the old man called again: "Coyote, are you people?"

At that the coyote nodded his head, "Yes."

"If that is so, come here and be not afraid of us; for we will be the ones to help you out of this trouble."

So the coyote came to them and licked their hands, and they gave it food—for it was dying of hunger. When it was fed, the old man said:

"Now, son, you are going out with the goats along the creek, and there you will see some willows. With your mind look at two willows, and note them; and tomorrow morning you must go and bring one of them."

The boy went away tending the goats, and the coyote stayed with the old man. Next morning, when they awoke

As he caught the hoop, he was instantly
changed into a poor coyote!

very early, they saw all the earth wrapped in a white *mania,* or cloak. [This figure of speech is always used by the Pueblos in speaking of snow in connection with sacred things.]

"Now, son," said the old man, "you must wear only your moccasins and leggings and go like a man to the two willows you marked yesterday. To one of them you must pray; and then cut the other, and bring it to me."

The boy did so, and came back with the willow stick. The old man prayed, and made a *mah-khur* hoop; and bidding the coyote stand a little way off and stick his head through the hoop before it should stop rolling, rolled it toward him. The coyote waited till the hoop came very close, and gave a great jump and put his head through it before it could stop. And lo! in an instant, there stood Nah-chu-ru-chu, young and handsome as ever; but his beautiful suit of fringed buckskin was all in rags. For four days he stayed there and was cleansed with the cleansing of the medicine-man; and then the old shepherd said to him:

"Now, friend Nah-chu-ru-chu, there is a road. [That is, you can go home.] But take with you this *faja* [a fine woven belt, with figures in bright colors], for though your power is great, you have submitted to this evil. When you get home, he who did this to you will be first to know, and he will come pretending to be your friend as if he had done nothing; and he will ask you to go hunting again. So you must go; and when you come to the mountain, with this *faja* you shall repay him."

Nah-chu-ru-chu thanked the kind old shepherd, and started home. But when he came to the Bad Hill and looked down into the valley of the Rio Grande, his heart sank. All the grass and fields and trees were dry and dead—for Nah-chu-ru-chu was the medicine-man who controlled the clouds, so no rain could fall when he was gone; and the eight days he had been a coyote were in truth eight years. The river was dry, and the springs; and many of the people were dead from thirst, and the rest were dying. But as Nah-chu-ru-chu came down the hill, it began to rain again, and all the people were glad.

When he came into the pueblo, all the famishing people came out to welcome him. And soon came the false friend, making as if he had never bewitched him nor had known whither he disappeared.

In a few days the false friend came again to propose a hunt: and next morning they went to the mountain together. Nah-chu-ru-chu had the pretty *faja* wound around his waist; and when the wind blew his blanket aside, the other saw it.

"Ah! What a pretty *faja!*" cried the false friend. "Give it to me, friend Nah-chu-ru-chu."

"*Een-dah!* (No!)" said Nah-chu-ru-chu. But the false friend begged so hard that at last he said:

"Then I will roll it to you; and if you can catch it before it unwinds, you may have it."

So he wound it up [like a roll of tape], and holding by one end gave it a push so that it ran away from him, unrolling as it went. The false friend jumped for it, but it was unrolled before he caught it.

"*Een-dah!*" said Nah-chu-ru-chu, pulling it back. "If you do not care enough for it to be spryer than that, you cannot have it."

The false friend begged for another trial; so Nah-chu-ru-chu rolled it again. This time the false friend caught it before it was unrolled; and lo! as he seized it he was changed from a tall young man into a great rattlesnake, with tears rolling from his lidless eyes!

As he seized it he was changed from a tall
young man into a great rattlesnake.

"We, too, do this to each other!" said Nah-chu-ru-chu. He took from his med-icine-pouch a pinch of the sacred meal and laid it on the snake's flat head for its food, and then a pinch of the corn-pollen to tame it. And the snake ran out its red, forked tongue, and licked them.

"Now," said Nah-chu-ru-chu, "this mountain and all rocky places shall be your home. But you can never again do harm to another without warning, as you did to me. For see, there is a *guaje* in your tail, and whenever you would do any one an injury, you must warn them beforehand with your rattle."

"And is that the reason why Ch'ah-rah-rah-deh always rattles to give warning before he bites?" asked Juan, who is now quite as often called Juan Biscocho (John Biscuit), since I photographed him one day crawling out of the big adobe bake-oven where he had been hiding.

"That is the very reason. Then Nah-chu-ru-chu left his false friend, from whom all the rattlesnakes are descended, and came back to his village. From that time all went well with Isleta, for Nah-chu-ru-chu was at home again to attend to the clouds. There was plenty of rain, and the river began to run again, and the springs flowed. The people plowed and planted again, as they had not been able to do for several years, and all their work prospered. As for the people who lived in the Place of the Red Earth, they all moved down here, because the Apaches were very bad; and here their descendants live to this day."

"Is that so?" sighed all the boys, in chorus, sorry that the story was so soon done.

"That is so," replied old Patricio. "And now, *compadre* Antonio, there is a tail on you."

"Well, then, I will tell a story which they told me in Taos (the most northern of the Pueblo cities) last year," said the old man.

"Ah-h!" said the boys.

"It is about

THE COYOTE AND THE WOODPECKER

WELL, ONCE UPON a time a Coyote and his family lived near the edge of a wood. There was a big hollow tree there, and in it lived an old Woodpecker and his wife and children. One day as the Coyote father was strolling along the edge of the forest he met the Woodpecker father.

"Hin-no-kah-kee-rna (good morning)," said the Coyote; "how do you do today, friend Hloo-ree-deh (Woodpecker)?"

"Very well, thank you, and how are you, friend Too-whay-deh (Coyote)?"

So they stopped and talked together awhile; and when they were about to separate the Coyote said:

"Friend Woodpecker, why do you not come as friends to see us? Come to our house to supper this evening, and bring your family."

"Thank you, friend Coyote," said the Woodpecker, "we will come with joy."

So that evening, when the Coyote mother had made supper ready, here came the Woodpecker father and the Woodpecker mother with their three children. When they had come in, all five of the Woodpeckers stretched themselves as they do after flying, and by that showed their pretty feathers—for the Hloo-ree-deh has yellow and red marks under its wings. While they were eating supper too, they sometimes spread their wings, and displayed their bright under-side. They praised the supper highly, and said the Coyote mother was a perfect housekeeper. When it was time to go, they thanked the Coyotes very kindly and invited them to come to supper at their house the following evening. But after they were gone, the Coyote father could restrain himself no longer, and he said:

"Did you see what airs those Woodpeckers put on? Always showing off their bright feathers? But I want them to know that the Coyotes are equal to them. *I'll* show them!"

The coyotes at supper with the woodpeckers

Next day, the Coyote father set all his family at work bringing wood, and built a great fire in front of his house. When it was time to go to the house of the Woodpeckers he called his wife and children to the fire, and lashed a burning stick under each of their arms, with the burning end pointing forward; and then he fixed himself in the same way.

"Now," said he, "we will show them! When we get there, you must lift up your arms now and then, to show them that we are as good as the Woodpeckers."

When they came to the house of the Woodpeckers and went in, all the Coyotes kept lifting their arms often, to show the bright coals underneath. But as they sat down to supper, one Coyote girl gave a shriek and said:

"Ow, *Tata!* My fire is burning me!"

"Be patient, my daughter," said the Coyote father, severely, "and do not cry about little things."

"Oh!" cried another Coyote girl in a moment, "my fire has gone out!"

This was more than the Coyote father could stand, and he reproved her angrily.

"But how is it, friend Coyote," said the Woodpecker politely, "that your colors are so bright at first, but very soon become black?"

"Oh, that is the beauty of our colors," replied the Coyote, smothering his rage, "that they are not always the same—like other people's—but turn all shades."

But the Coyotes were very uncomfortable, and made an excuse to hurry home as soon as they could. When they got there, the Coyote father whipped them all for exposing him to be laughed at.

But the Woodpecker father gathered his children around him, and said:

"Now, my children, you see what the Coyotes have done. Never in your life try to appear what you are not. Be just what you really are, and put on no false colors."

"Is that so?" cried the boys, as is customary at the end of a story.

"That is so; and it is as true for people as for beasts and birds. Now, *too kwai* [come]—we have talked long enough; it is bedtime."

First published in the November 1891 edition of *St. Nicholas Magazine*

The Ants That Pushed on the Sky

A "Tee-Wahn" Folk-Story

BY CHARLES F. LUMMIS

A VERY ANCIENT and characteristic story about the origin of the Indian village of Isleta is based on the fact that part of its founders came from one of the prehistoric Pueblo towns whose ruins are now barely visible in those broad plains.

Once upon a time there lived in one of these ancient Pueblo villages in the Manzano Mountains a young Indian named Kahp-too-óo-yoo, the Corn-stalk Young Man. He was not only a famous hunter and a brave warrior against the raiding Comanches, but a great wizard; and to him the Trues, the Indian gods, had given the power of the clouds. When Kahp-too-óo-yoo willed it, the glad rains fell, and made the dry fields laugh in green; and without him no one could bring water from the sky. His father was Old-Black-Cane, his mother was Corn-Maiden, and his two sisters were Yellow-Corn-Maiden and Blue-Corn-Maiden.

Kahp-too-óo-yoo had a friend, a young man of about the same age. But, as often happens, the friend was of a false heart, and was really a witch, though Kahp-too-óo-yoo never dreamed of such a thing.

The two young, men used to go together to the mountains to get wood, and always carried their bows and arrows, to kill deer and antelopes, or whatever game they might find.

One day the false friend came to Kahp-too-óo-yoo and said:

"Friend, let us go tomorrow for wood, and to hunt."

They agreed that so they would do. Next day they started before sunrise, and came presently to the spot where they gathered wood. Just there they startled a herd of deer. Kahp-too-óo-yoo followed part of the herd, which fled to the northwest, and the friend pursued those that went southwest. After a long, hard chase, Kahp-too-óo-yoo killed a deer with his swift arrows, and brought it on his strong back to the place where the friends had separated. Presently came the friend, very hot and tired, and with empty hands, and seeing the deer, he was pinched with jealousy.

"Come, friend," said Kahp-too-óo-yoo. "It is well for brothers to share with brothers. Take of this deer and cook and eat; and carry a part to your house, as if you had killed it yourself."

"Thank you," answered the other coldly, as one who will not; but he did not accept.

When they had gathered each a load of wood, and lashed it with rawhide thongs in bundles upon their shoulders, they trudged home—Kahp-too-óo-yoo carrying the deer on top of his wood. His sisters received him with joy, praising him as a hunter; and the friend went away to his house with a heavy face.

Several different days when they went to the mountain together, the very same thing came to pass. Kahp-too-óo-yoo killed each time a deer; and each time the friend came home with nothing, refusing all offers to share as brothers. And he grew more jealous and more sullen every day.

At last he came again to invite Kahp-too-óo-yoo to go; but this time it was with an evil purpose that he asked. Then again the same thing happened. Again the unsuccessful friend refused to take a share of Kahp-too-óo-yoo's deer; and when he had sat long without a word, he said:

"Friend Kahp-too-óo-yoo, now I will prove you, if you are truly my friend, for I do not think it."

"Surely," said Kahp-too-óo-yoo, "if there is any way to prove myself, I will do it gladly, for truly I am your friend."

"Then come, and we will play a game together, and with that I will prove you."

"It is well. But what game shall we play, for here we have nothing?"

Near them stood a broken pine-tree, with one great arm projecting from its twisted body. And looking at it, the false friend said, "I see nothing but to play the *gallo* race; and because we have no horses we will ride this arm of the pine-tree— first I will ride, and then you."

So he climbed the pine-tree and sat astride the limb as upon a horse, and rode, reaching over to the ground as if to pick up something, in imitation of one of the most popular and exciting sports of the southwestern Indians and Mexicans—in which the players, on horseback and at a wild gallop, try to snatch some tiny object from the ground.

"Now you," he said, coming down; and Kahp-too-óo-yoo climbed the tree and rode on the swinging branch. But the false friend bewitched the pine, and it grew in a moment to the very sky, carrying Kahp-too-óo-yoo.

"We do this to one another" [a common Indian taunt, either good-natured or bitter, to the loser of a game or a conquered enemy] said the false friend, as the tree shot up; and taking the wood, and the deer which Kahp-too-óo-yoo had killed, he went to the village. There the sisters met him, and asked:

"Where is our brother?"

"Truly I know not, for he went northwest and I southwest; and though I waited long at the meeting-place, he did not come. Probably he will soon return. But take of this deer which I killed, for sisters should share the labors of brothers."

But the girls would take none of the meat, and went home sorrowful.

Time went on, and still there was no Kahp-too-óo-yoo. His sisters and his old parents wept always, and all the village was sad. And soon the crops grew yellow in the fields, and the springs failed, and the animals walked like weary shadows; for Kahp-too-óo-yoo, he who had the power of the clouds, was gone, and there was no rain. And then perished all that is green; the animals fell in the brown fields; and the gaunt people who sat to warm themselves in the sun began to die there where they sat. At last the poor old man said to his daughters:

"Little daughters, prepare food, for again we will go to look for thy brother."

The girls made cakes of the blue corn-meal for the journey; and on the fourth day they started. Old-Black-Cane hobbled to the south, his wife to the east, the elder girl to the north, and the younger to the west.

For a great distance they traveled; and at last Blue-Corn-Maiden, who was in the north, heard a far, faint song. It was so little that she thought it must be imaginary; but she stopped to listen, and softly, softly it came again:

> *"To-ai-foo-ni-hloo-hlim,*
> *Ing-k'hai k'hahm;*
> *Ee-eh-boori-koon-hlee-oh,*
> *Ing-k'hai k'hahm.*
> *Ah-ee-ai, ah-ee-ai, aim!"*

> ("Old-Black-Cane
> My father is called;
> Corn-Maiden
> My mother is called.
> *Ah-ee-ai, ah-ee-ai, aim!"*)

When she heard this, Blue-Corn-Maiden ran until she came to her sister, and cried:

"Sister! Sister! I think I hear our brother somewhere in captivity. Listen!"

Trembling, they listened, and again the song came floating to them, so soft, so sad that they wept—as to this day their people weep when a white-haired old man, filled with the memories of Kahp-too-óo-yoo, sings that plaintive melody.

"Surely it is our brother!" they cried; and off they went running to find their parents. And when all listened together, again they heard the song.

"Oh, my son!" cried the poor old woman, "in what captivity do you find yourself? True it is that your father is Old-Black-Cane, and I, your mother, am called

Corn-Maiden. But why do you sing thus?"

Then all four of them began to follow the song, and at last they came to the foot of the sky-reaching pine; but they could see nothing of Kahp-too-óo-yoo, nor could their cries reach him. There, on the ground, were his bow and arrows, with strings and feathers eaten away by time; and there also was his pack of wood, tied with the rawhide thong, and ready to be taken home. But after they had searched everywhere they could not find Kahp-too-óo-yoo; and at last they went home heavy at heart.

One day it happened that *P'ah-wah-yoo-óo-deh,* or the Little Black Ant, took a journey and went up the bewitched pine, even to its top in the sky. When he found Kahp-too-óo-yoo there, a prisoner, the Little Black Ant was astonished, and said:

"Great *Kah-báy-deh* (Man of Power), how comes it that you are up here in such a condition, while your people at home are suffering and dying for rain, and few are left to meet you if you return? Are you here of your free will?"

"No," groaned Kahp-too-óo-yoo; "but I am here because of the jealousy of him who was as my brother, with whom I shared my food and labor, whose home was my home, and my home his. He is the cause, for he was jealous and bewitched me hither. And now I am dying of famine."

"If that is so," said the Little Black Ant, "I will be the one to help you"; and he ran down to the world as fast as he could. When he got there he sent out the crier to summon all of his nation, and also those of the *In-tóon,* the Big Red Ants. Soon all the armies of the Little Black Ants and the Big Red Ants met at the foot of the pine, and held a council. They smoked the *weer* (sacred cigarette), and deliberated what should be done.

"You Big Red Ants are stronger than we who are small," said the War-Captain of the Little Black Ants, "and for that reason you ought to take the top of the tree to work."

"*Een-dah* (No)," said the War-Captain of the Big Red Ants. "If you think we are the stronger, give us the bottom, where we can work more, and you go to the top."

Kahp-too-óo-yoo and the ants

So it was agreed, and the captains made their armies ready. But first the Little Black Ants got the cup of an acorn, and mixed in it corn-meal and water and honey, and carried it up the tree. They were so many that they covered its trunk all the way to the sky.

When Kahp-too-óo-yoo saw, his heart was heavy, and he thought: "But what good will that very little do me, for I am dying of hunger and thirst?"

"Nay, friend," answered the Captain of the Little Black Ants, who knew his thought; "a person should not think so. This little is enough, and there will be some left."

And it was so; for when Kahp-too-óo-yoo had eaten all he could, the acorn-cup was still nearly full.

Then the ants carried the cup to the ground and came back to him.

"Now, friend," said the Captain, "we will do our best. But you must shut your eyes till I say 'Ahw!'"

Kahp-too-óo-yoo shut his eyes, and the Captain made signals down to those at the foot of the tree. And the Little Black Ants above put their feet against the sky and pushed with all their might on the top of the pine; and the Big Red Ants below caught the trunk and pulled as hard as they could; and the very first tug drove the great pine a quarter of its length into the earth.

"Ahw!" shouted the Captain of the Little Black Ants; and Kahp-too-óo-yoo opened his eyes, but he could see nothing below.

"Shut your eyes again," said the Captain, giving the signal. Again the Little Black Ants pushed mightily against the sky, and the Big Red Ants pulled mightily from below, and the pine was driven another fourth of its length into the earth.

"Ahw!" cried the Captain; and when Kahp-too-óo-yoo opened his eyes he could just see the big, brown world.

Again he closed his eyes. There was another great push and pull, and only a quarter of the great pine was left above the ground. Now Kahp-too-óo-yoo could see, far below, the parched fields strewn with dead animals, and his own village full of dying people.

Again the Little Black Ants pushed and the Big Red Ants pulled; and this time the tree was driven clear out of sight, and Kahp-too-óo-yoo was left sitting on the ground. He hastily made a bow and arrows, and soon killed a fat deer, which he brought and divided among the Little Black Ants and the Big Red Ants, thanking them for their kindness.

Then he made all his clothing to be new, for he had been four years a prisoner in the bewitched tree, and was all in rags. Making for himself a flute from the bark of a young tree, he played upon it as he strode homeward, and then he sang:

"Kahp-too-óo-yoo tu-mah-quee,
Nah-choor kwe-shay-tin,
Nah-shurkwe-chay-tin;
Kahp-too-óo-yoo tu-mah-guee."

("Kahp-too-óo-yoo has come to life again,
Is back to his home coming,
Blowing the yellow and the blue,
Kahp-too-óo-yoo has come to life again.")

As he walked and played, the forgotten clouds came over him, and the soft rain began to fall, and all was green and good. But only so far as his voice reached came the rain; and beyond all was still death and drought. When he came to the end of the wet, he played and sang again; and again the rain fell as far as his voice was heard. This time the Fool-Boy, who was wandering outside the dying village, saw the far storm and heard the singing. He ran to tell Kahp-too-óo-yoo's parents; but nobody would believe a Fool-Boy, and they sent him away.

When the Fool-Boy went out again, the rain fell on him and gave him strength, and he came running a second time to tell. Then the sisters came out of the house and saw the rain and heard the song; and they cried for joy, and told their parents to rise and meet him.

But the poor old people were dying of weakness, and could not rise; and the sisters went alone. When they met him they fell on their knees, weeping; but Kahp-too-óo-yoo lifted them up and blessed them. He gave an ear of blue corn to Blue-

He walked and played, and the soft rain fell.

Corn-Maiden, and to Yellow-Corn-Maiden an ear of yellow corn, and brought them home.

As he sang again, the rain fell in the village; and when it touched the pinched faces of the starving they sat up and grew strong. And the dying crawled out to drink, and were strong again; and the withered fields grew green and glad.

When they came to the house, Kahp-too-óo-yoo blessed his parents, and then said:

"Little sisters, give us to eat."

But they answered, "How? For you have been gone these four years, and there was none to give us rain. We planted, but nothing came, and today we ate the last grain."

"Nay, little sisters," he said. "A person should not think so. Look now in the store-room, to see if there be not something there."

"But we have looked and looked, and have turned over everything to try to find even one grain."

"Yet look once more," he said; and when they opened the door, lo! there was the store-room piled to the roof with corn, and another room was full of wheat. Then they cried for joy, and began to roast the blue ears, for they were dying of hunger.

At the sweet smell of the roasting corn came the starving neighbors, crowding at the door, and crying:

"O Kahp-too-óo-yoo! Give us to taste one grain of corn, and then we will go home and die."

But Kahp-too-óo-yoo handed to each an ear, and said:

"Fathers, brothers, go now to your own houses, for there you will find corn as much as here." And when they went, it was so. All began to roast corn and to eat; and the dead in the houses awoke and were strong again, and all the village sang and danced.

From that day there was plenty of rain, for he who had the power of the clouds was at home again. In the spring the people planted, and in the fall the crops were so great that all the town could not hold them.

As for the false friend, he died of shame in his house, not daring to come out; and no one wept for him.

First published in the May 1892 edition of *St. Nicholas Magazine*

Danny and the "Major"

BY GERTRUDE P. GREBLE

"PAPA! PAPA!" THE shrill, childish voice echoed sharply through the quiet house, and a small figure appeared upon the threshold of the door which led to Captain Kent's office, as if suddenly blown there by the March gale which at the same moment invaded the apartment.

"My son," said the officer in a tone of mild exasperation, laying a restraining hand upon his fluttering papers, "will you be kind enough first of all to shut the front door? And now"—when he had been obeyed with an energy which shook the house to its foundations—"take off your hat, like a gentleman."

The child snatched it off, and advanced to lay an appealing hand upon his father's arm.

"Don't make me wait for anything more, papa," he pleaded. "It is important! It is, indeed. Mackenzie begs you to come to the corral right away. The major has come back!"

"The Major! What Major?"

"Why, our Major—Captain Egerton's Major."

"Impossible!"

"But he has indeed, papa!" exclaimed the eager boy. "The herders found him up in a ravine, and he followed the horses home, and he is so lame he can hardly walk, and the corral-master says he has enough worthless brutes about now, so he is going to shoot him; and Mackenzie said to tell you to come at once, because if you didn't it might be too late—"

Two great tears overflowed from the violet eyes and rolled down the lad's cheeks, but little Dan had small reason to fear lack of attention now! Almost before his hasty explanation was completed, the cavalryman had thrown his cape about his shoulders and started for the corral at a pace satisfying even to his impatient son.

TO MAKE YOU understand what he found there, and what it meant, I must go back to the beginning and tell about Danny; and then—because this story is quite as much, and perhaps a little more, the Major's—about the Major too.

Danny could not remember his introduction to the frontier garrison which constituted his world, but he was never tired of hearing about it. And during the long winter evenings, when "retreat" had sounded and the soldiers had dispersed to their log barracks, the captain would seat himself beside the big stove, with his pipe between his teeth; and Danny, his sled put away, his gaiters and mittens hung up to dry by the hall fire, and his buffalo overcoat—an exact imitation of his father's big one—safe on its peg, would crawl into his father's arms and nestle close to his heart. And after a silence of greater or less length, the officer would begin and go over the details so well known to them both: of his astonishment when, on coming from "stables" one bitter winter afternoon, he had stamped the snow from his shoes and thrown aside his overcoat, to behold a stout woman with a white bundle in her arms, saying, "Will ye look at the recruit I've brought ye, Captain?"— and of how, when he had recovered from his surprise, he had examined her offering and found beneath a lot of wrappings two tiny hands, a small face with blinking eyes, and plentiful black hair. This last never failed to impress Danny, for by the time he was old enough to notice things his hair was as yellow as the Indian maize which ripened by the river.

The years had sped swiftly after that winter evening; and if, as his father said, he had come into the world to the sound of a trumpet, he grew up to the rattle of drums and the patter of musketry in the days when Custer lived and a soldier's work was full of activity and danger. His ears became accustomed to the thrumming of the "long roll"; his odd hours were full of the excitement caused by the bustle of incoming and outgoing scouting-parties, and, at times, of watching, with far more interest than fear, those tiny specks he could just discern skirting the horizon, which he was told were "hostiles."

It was small wonder that in such an atmosphere he should develop rapidly, that he should become healthy, as a child must who spends ten hours of the twenty-four with the winds of the prairie filling his strong young lungs; that he should become honest and truth-telling as a soldier's son should be; gentle to women, as represented by his mother and the tiny sister who bore her name; and full of an affectionate kindliness which won him the most loyal devotion from the rough troopers who shared his outdoor life.

At the time our story opens he was seven—a tall lad, whose muscles were already like fine steel threads, whose skin had tanned to a beautiful golden brown, with violet eyes, and hair which fell in tangles about his shoulders.

Those curls, heavy and girlish, had been a constant source of woe to the boy, till one never-to-be-forgotten day, when he had stood at the gate of the stockade to see the famous "Seventh" sweep by, on its way to some distant trouble. The scene had been one to remember—the smooth action of the seasoned horses, the careless swing of their riders, to whom excitement had become as the air they breathed! But of it all little Dan retained one impression only—that of the adored Custer at the column's head, his face thin, eager, resolute, and with curls, as yellow as Danny's own, falling over his shoulders!

From that hour the boy's ringlets became his most cherished possession—a connecting link between the idolized leader of those toughened Indian-fighters and his small personality.

And now for the Major! With regard to him I confess my courage fails; for what feeble pen can hope to do justice to the splendid piece of horse-flesh which answered to that name?

Two years before the March afternoon on which our story opens, an additional troop had been ordered to Fort B— to reinforce the hard-worked garrison. The officer in command was an old friend of Captain Kent; and on the day of its arrival, shortly before sunset, Danny started off to inspect the new horses and make the acquaintance of their riders.

His intention was not carried out.

As he reached the path which led to the spot where the detachment had gone into camp for the night, he met a trooper leading a horse by the bridle, and carrying a blanket and halter over the other arm. The man's campaign dress proclaimed him a newcomer. He was tall and thin, and covered with dust from his recent ride. But neither the dust, nor the ragged stubble upon his unshaven face, could conceal the kindliness of his expression. Danny stepped aside to let him pass.

"Good evening, Corporal," he said politely, after a brief glance at the soldier's chevrons.

The trooper halted. "Gude evenin' t' yirsel', laddie," he answered in a voice whose deep tones instantly made their way to the boy's friendly heart. "I'm after a bed for the Major; can ye show me the way tae the corral?"

Dan regarded him gravely. "I'll show you the way to the corral with pleasure," he replied; "but you must be mistaken about a major. Papa said Captain Egerton was in command of this troop, and he is going to stay with us; so he has a bed."

For a minute the soldier looked puzzled, then he laughed.

"Hoot, laddie!" he exclaimed good-naturedly, "it's no for anny two-legged major I'm workin'. It's for this vera beastie ye see at t' back, mon! And it's a bad day

"Good evening, Corporal,"
Danny said politely.

he's hed of it, and hungry an' tired he is; so stir yirsel' an' lead the way, for I heven't a knowledge o' these pairts as yet."

Dan examined the animal critically. "He seems to be a fine horse," he remarked in the judicial tone he had heard from the officers.

The soldier smiled. "Ay," he answered briefly; "he is."

"Has he come far today?"

"The neighborhood o' seventy miles, aboot."

The man resumed his progress in the direction of the stables, and the little boy trotted by his side, every energy absorbed in the endeavor to keep up with his long strides. After an interval the child observed: "I don't see why you didn't put him on the picket-line with the other horses. Wasn't there room for him?"

"Room for him?" repeated the trooper, disgustedly; "ay, there'd be room and tae spare gin he wanted it, which he'll no do while he has old John tae find him shelter. Ye're a bit blowed, ain't ye, laddie?" he added kindly; for the first time noticing the child's breathless condition. "I'm forgettin' t' difference in the length o' t' laigs. We'll get over the groun' feyster gin I make the Major carry ye."

Danny looked doubtfully at the horse's dusty sides and drooping head. "Isn't he too tired?" he asked, divided between his desire for the offered ride and compassion for the evidently weary animal.

His companion regarded him with approval. "Now thet's richt!" he said. "There ain't many little chaps 't'wu'd think o' the horse when they hed a chance tae ride. I like ye for it, lad! As for tirin' him—I w'u'dna ride him mesel', but ye're no gret weight, an' I'm thinkin' it'll get him his supper the quicker." A moment later the radiant child was seated astride the great bronze beast, and the trio pursued its way to the corral in a silence which the soldier was too weary—and Danny too happy—to break.

When Dan went home after seeing Mackenzie feed and groom his charge, he was conscious of having found a new interest in life, and of having made a new friend; and his satisfaction was complete when, on recounting his experiences at the dinner-table that evening, he was informed that the horse belonged to Captain Egerton, and that henceforth he might see him as often as he liked.

The summer days which followed were full of joy. Dan passed them for the most part in Mackenzie's company, and a very real friendship sprang up between the veteran and his small companion—a friendship that found a cementing bond in their affection for the Major. Nothing so perfect of its kind as that splendid animal had ever before come in the boy's way.

Had he been asked, it might have been difficult for him to tell which of his new friends—the human or the equine—he loved the better. But there was no question which was the more important. He trotted at Mackenzie's heels when he took his charge to and from the watering-trough; he perched himself on the cross-bar of the Major's box-stall to superintend his toilet; and he spent long hours scrubbing away with a bit of rag upon the brass mountings of the horse's saddle and bridle, on those days when the trooper was obliged to prepare for inspection—betaking   himself afterward to the drill-ground to revel in the result of his labors.

And had you seen the beautiful beast as he appeared at inspection—the brass trimmings upon which so much loving care had been expended flashing in the sunlight, his bronze coat like finest satin, his powerful limbs motionless, and with only the fire in the

He perched himself on the cross-bar of the Major's box-stall to superintend his toilet.

deep eyes and the quiver of the wide nostrils to tell how strong was the sense of duty which controlled his impatience for the command which should put in motion the troop he led—you would not have wondered at Danny's enthusiasm—an enthusiasm which gradually increased into a great and real love, which it was easy to see the Major reciprocated in his dumb fashion.

So the weeks passed, and the long hot days grew short, and winter came and went—and with the return of summer little Dan experienced his first sorrow.

Captain Egerton's troop was ordered out on a difficult and dangerous scout; there was a battle—a thing only too common in those wild days—and at the end of it the gallant captain lay crippled by a gunshot wound, and Major, swept away by the savages, had vanished as if swallowed by the treacherous quicksands which lined the river-bank.

For days after the first shock of his grief was over, the child continued to hope for the horse's return. For days he mounted to the highest point of the block-house to search the furthest reaches of the empty prairie, confident that if the sagacious animal was alive he would find his way back. But months passed, and another winter dragged itself away, and little by little the boy abandoned hope, and settled down to the sorrowful conviction that the horse, too, had fallen a victim to the Indians.

AND NOW HE had returned! And what a homecoming!

Mackenzie and he had often talked of such a possibility—Mackenzie, who, with his beloved horse gone, and his master in the East on leave, had been even more disconsolate than Danny; together, the pair had pictured it in divers ways. Sometimes it was one of them who was to find him, sometimes the other; but in every case they had thought of it as a sort of triumphal progress, the coming of a hero who returned to claim his own. Never like this—pitiful, starved, unknown, and despised, in the very place where he had been so easily supreme! "Oh!" thought Danny, "if only the old troop had been here! Someone who loved him! Someone to remember besides Mackenzie and me!" There was a great sob in his throat as he ran by his father's side in the direction of the corral—he was half afraid of what he might find by the time that he reached it.

And when the two finally did reach it, the scene which met their gaze was so remarkable that even the officer paused in breathless amazement.

Prostrate on the earth, covered with dirt, his surly face purple, his feet kicking aimlessly in the air, lay the corral-master—a government rifle, which had evidently slipped from his grasp, on the ground beside him. And upon his chest, holding him in a grip of iron, his face white with an anger too deep for words, sat the Scotch corporal! At the left—a rusty and apparently lifeless mass—lay the Major's prostrate form. And about the group stood the employees of the stockyard.

"What is the meaning of this performance?" inquired the officer.

The sounds which issued from the corral-master's throat made Danny think of the bellowing of those bulls which were sometimes confined in that part of the enclosure; he crept to his father's side and laid hold of his cape. The overseer's face was rapidly assuming a still deeper tint, and the captain went forward:

"You are choking that man, Mackenzie," he said sharply; "let him up at once!"

The corporal glanced up at him with an expression of relief, gave his victim a final squeeze which set him fairly gasping, and rose. "Chokin' 'u'd be tae gude for him, Capt'in," he said, as the corral-master struggled to his feet.

"What is the meaning of this performance?" inquired the officer. The trooper made no reply, and O'Reilly, emboldened, began a halting explanation.

"Wait till you are spoken to," commanded Captain Kent, sternly. He knew that Mackenzie was upon ordinary occasions the mildest and least aggressive of men.

The group about them began insensibly to melt away, excepting a few whose curiosity was sufficient to overcome their prudence.

Mackenzie pointed from the gun to the Major, with a gesture more eloquent than words.

"He tried tae steal a march on me, Capt'in," he said huskily. "I telt him tae wait till the laddie fetched ye, and I went for water for the puir beast; and when I coom back—weel, if shootin' hadna been altegither tae gude for him, he w'u'dna be here noo! Thet's ae!"

"What have you to say to this, O'Reilly?"

"Sure I thought it would be a mercy to the poor beast to put him out of his misery," answered the man, in an injured tone. "I tried to do it unbeknownst to the corporal, knowin' how fond of him he used to be—and it's small thanks I got for me pains! Next time I'll leave him to settle his affairs himself. Look at the brute, Captain," he added; "it's only a fool that would care to prolong his sufferin'." He was evidently sincere, and there seemed to be some truth in what he said.

"I'm afraid he is right, Mackenzie," said the officer, sadly, as he followed the two men to the side of the panting animal.

Mackenzie broke down. "Ah! don't ye turn against him, too, Capt'in," he faltered, "Think o' the time he's had gettin' here, and gi'e him a chance. He sha'n't trouble no one, and I'll work it square. If he don't show some sort o' improvement by this time tomorrow, I gi'e ye ma word I'll make na trouble. It's starved he is, and winded; but he's nae deid yet, and while there's life there's hope!"

The captain turned away—the horse was a painful spectacle. "Very well," he said; "you may have your way for the present; but I think your labor will be wasted. I agree with O'Reilly: the most merciful thing would be to end his suffering at once."

Mackenzie moved to his side. "I'll no forget what ye've done for me this day," he said gratefully. "There's ane more thing ye can do, if ye will, tae complete the gude wark. It is against orders to sell us whusky at the canteen, and whusky is what the puir beastie wants just noo. Would ye mind givin' me an order for a gallon o' the same?"

Captain Kent hesitated. "I can trust you perfectly, Mackenzie," he said (the corporal was invariably steady); "but a gallon of whisky might cause a lot of mischief."

"It'll no," was the earnest response. "It'll be doon the Major's throat before it hes time tae make any trouble."

The corporal's tone was a sufficient guarantee of the safety of the venture. The officer tore off the corner of an envelope, and scribbled the necessary order.

"I shall hold you responsible," he said.

Mackenzie nodded. "Yes, sir—thank ye, sir," he murmured, saluting hastily, as he started from the enclosure upon a run; and by the time Captain Kent had once more regained the garrison, he was on his way back to the corral from the trader's where the necessary liquor was kept.

No especial arguments were needed by Mackenzie to enlist the sympathies of his comrades in behalf of his fallen favorite: soldiers, as a rule, are warm-hearted men, and in the cavalry their calling fosters a love for horses. When little Dan went home at sunset, kindly hands had laid the old horse in the one box-stall the troop-stable afforded, and liberal doses of whisky and water had stayed his failing strength. Through the long night the trooper tended him faithfully, watching his heaving sides by the light of a solitary lantern, and plying him, as occasion demanded, with additional draughts of the stimulant; and when morning came the change for the better was so pronounced that even O'Reilly was forced into the admission that hope was once more possible.

After the first few days the animal gained steadily. At the end of a month he was able to hobble out with the herd, the shadow of his old self. More than that he seemed likely never to become. His hoofs were cracked and torn from his long wandering over the alkali plains, his breath came rumblingly from his deep chest, and his eyes had a look of patient submission in their soft depths, which seemed to say that he understood fully the kindness which had been shown him, and would repay it to the best of his ability. The old ambition, the old fire, were things of the past. He was quite content now to browse along in rear of the herd, or to stand for hours beside little Dan perched upon a wood-pile, nudging him for the sugar which was always forthcoming, nipping lovingly at the buttons on his small trousers, or— immovable as a statue—bowing his beautiful head when the boy frolicked at his feet. And though, as time went on and the summer drills began, he would prick up his ears at the sound of the well-remembered calls, and follow the battalion with his eyes as it swept by the spot where he was picketed, it was only with a passing interest, and he would return to his grazing in placid content.

Danny never abandoned the hope of seeing him in his old place at the head of a troop. He spent hours feeding, grooming, and watering him, and when there was nothing else to be done he was quite content to perch beside him in the sunshine, and dream of the wonderful things he should do when he was once more well. If he had admired him before, he adored him now; and still the wildest flight of his imagination was not sufficient to suggest the heroic feat which this dumb friend was actually to accomplish for his sake, the great and final proof of his affection for the child who loved him, and which was to make not only the Major, but Danny too, famous!

To tell you about it, we must pass over the weeks which witnessed the horse's gradual recovery to the scorching afternoon that found him, almost his old self, saddled with Dan's own small saddle, and pawing the ground impatiently in front of Captain Kent's quarters. The loving care of the past few months had been amply rewarded. Some time before he had been pronounced fit for light work, and that afternoon Dan was to have his first ride upon the Major's back.

Mackenzie had been for several weeks suffering from a sprained wrist which prevented his doing the usual guard-duty, and in order to give him some occupation he had been detailed to superintend the herding of the quartermaster's horses—going with them to the grazing-ground in the morning, and then returning to the post until the afternoon, when he went out to assist in bringing them home.

On the present occasion, as a special favor and to celebrate the Major's recovery, Mackenzie begged that Dan might go with him. And when the child came out and prepared to mount, it would be hard to say which was the happier, he or the trooper who swung him so proudly to his place.

"You are sure it is safe, Mackenzie?" said Mrs. Kent, a little anxiously, as from the porch she watched the start for the grazing-ground.

"Sure, ma'am," answered the soldier, emphatically, as he made a final examination of the girths, little dreaming how much was to depend upon his care in the course of that eventful afternoon; "the beastie knows him as well as ye do yirsel'. It's no for naething the lad has spent his time. He'll no hurt him!"

He gathered up the reins and put them into Danny's hands as he spoke, swung himself upon his own bony gray, and they started.

In those days the summer months were always full of uneasiness and dread: the Indians were especially restless at that time of year, and precautions were doubled; but the weeks which had gone had sped swiftly and quietly in little Dan's home. Rumors of approaching trouble had reached it from time to time; occasional false alarms had sounded, and hurried scouts had been made—only to prove the absence of any foe; and gradually the command had settled down to the conviction that for once they were to be left in peace.

On the afternoon in question nothing could have seemed more tranquil than the scene which unfolded itself before Mackenzie and his charge when, having passed through the gate of the stockade, they turned their horses' heads in the direction of the herd, which they could just discern in the distance as so many specks against the sky.

On the right the Missouri River wound like a great yellow snake from the far northern horizon; on every other side lay the rolling prairie, with only that thread of green along the river-bottom to break its level expanse. Dan had heard of the grandeur of the sea, but he sometimes wondered if anything could seem more imposing than those wide reaches of treeless, turf-covered plain.

The animals were restless and uneasy in spite of the heat, and after a short interval Mackenzie turned from the "trail" and started across the open country.

"Dinna ye go tae fast, lad," he said as the Major stretched his neck with an evident inclination to outstrip his companion. "There's gopher-holes in plenty hereaboots, and gin ye strike one o' them our ride's up! Ye sit yir horse like a sodger," he added admiringly; "I'll hef ye made assistant herder yet!" Danny smiled broadly at the joke, sitting very square in his saddle, perfectly enjoying his new accomplishment.

After a canter of some twenty minutes the corporal reined in his horse.

"I can't think what's happened tae O'Farrell tae let the beasties get sae far away," he muttered discontentedly. "There's nae grass to speak of over there. I told him aboot it this mornin'. Look out, lad!"—for the Major had thrown up his head suddenly and come to a standstill, snorting, and nearly unseating his small rider.

"Why did he do that?" asked the boy in wonder, as he settled himself once more in the saddle, and got a fresh hold on the reins. "There wasn't any hole there, was there?"

For a minute the corporal made no reply. His own horse was snuffing the air uneasily, and the trooper's keen glance traveled slowly along the horizon and over the herded cattle before it came back to the small figure at his side.

"Maybe there's grass burnin'," he said, finally. "The smell o' thet always makes 'em fretty."

He put his animal to a gallop as he spoke, and the distance to the herd began to diminish rapidly.

"See how uneasy the other horses are," said Danny, as they neared the grazing-ground. "Whatever the trouble is, they know it too."

There could be no doubt of that fact. O'Farrell's apparent carelessness was explained. The animals were in almost constant motion, moving from side to side, browsing for a moment, only to pause and snuff the air in the same alarmed fashion which Danny and Mackenzie had noticed in their own horses a few minutes before. The men in charge were riding to and fro, heading off the refractory leaders, and doing their best to turn them toward the post, but without avail. Slowly but surely the herd was edging in the opposite direction along the bluff.

O'Farrell came to meet them. He was a young Irish lad who had been in the service only a short time, and gave promise of making a most excellent soldier. On the present occasion his round, jolly face wore a troubled look.

"It's welcome ye are, Corporal, sure!" he exclaimed, mopping his hot face. "If I'd had any way of gettin' word to ye, ye'd have been here long ago; but it took the two of us to kape the bastes together, and, faith, ten men couldn't have done more. I can't think what's got into them!"

He turned his horse and reined it in beside Mackenzie's gray, surveying the increasing restlessness of the animals in despair, yet conscious of inexpressible relief at the presence of a more experienced pair of shoulders on which to shift the responsibility.

"How long hef they been like this?" asked the corporal, after a silence in which his face became more and more grave.

"For the betther part of the afternoon."

Mackenzie's eyes wandered once again over the empty hills. "Ye've got a good nose, Larry," he said finally; "hef ye smelt anything in the way o' a prairie fire?"

The other shook his head. "Nothin'," he replied; "that is, nothin' to spake of. There was some smoke up there to the north this forenoon; but I haven't seen it since."

The corporal's face changed suddenly.

"Steady, was it?" he queried, "or puffy, like?"

"A bit puffy. Nothin' to spake of—it died out right away."

The veteran groaned. "And ye should hef made for hame gin ye saw thet first puff!" he muttered, adding something under his breath about "the silliness o' sending babes and innocents tae do this kind o' work!"

"What's up?" asked the young soldier, anxiously. "You don't think it's—?"

The elder man made an imperceptible gesture toward the child.

"There's mischief of some sort brewin'," he said gravely. "And we'd better get out o' this, gin we want tae carry a whole skin with us. Head off those mules— they'll stampede the lot! Laddie, coom with me!" He turned his horse in the direction of the river as he spoke, taking out his revolver and carefully examining it while he rode.

"Mackenzie," said the little boy, softly, drawing nearer to his friend's side, "do you think it is Indians?" He was not particularly alarmed at the unexpected danger which threatened them—he had the greatest faith in the corporal's ability to protect him from harm. But the face which the soldier turned slowly toward him in answer to his question was grim and set with a fear such as he had never known—

nor could know—for himself! He would have given his life gladly, in the face of that deadly and too well understood peril, to have felt that little Dan was within the friendly shelter of the fort!

"I'm no sayin' it's Indians, lad," he said at length; "but when ye don't like the look o' things it's better tae be prepared for the worst. There's two possibilities ahead o' us. One's the stampede o' the herd, which would be bad enough; the other's that which is behind the fright o' the animals, which is far worse! Whatever happens, naething I can do will save ye, gin ye don't act like yir feyther's son and try tae help yirsel'."

He paused. While speaking he had worked his way steadily across the front of the herd, driving back such animals as he could without waste of time, but continually increasing the distance between himself and the main body of the drove. His duty as a soldier was simply to save his captain's child! By the time he had reached a point to the left of the center of the herd, experience told him that the disaster which he dreaded was not long to be delayed.

He took the last moment for a few final warning words.

"Mind one thing, laddie! Whatever comes, gie the Major his head and hold on! He'll carry ye safe, and he can show a clean pair o' heels tae the fastest o' them! Eh! I thought as much! Get yir horse's head round, lad! Be ready!"

The avalanche was upon them!

Some seconds earlier the lead mules of an ambulance team on the farther side of the grazing-ground had thrown up their heads in sudden fright and caromed into the horses feeding near them, and those in turn had plunged against their neighbors, and then the whole herd, catching the infection of their terror, had bunched itself and started—a maddened, flying mass!

It seemed years to Dan, giddy and breathless from terror, before it reached him. For a brief instant he thought he saw O'Farrell and some unknown mounted figures behind it; then the air about him grew thick with dust, the noise of the beating hoofs increased to a deafening roar, and every faculty became absorbed in the effort to obey Mackenzie's instructions and to keep him in sight; for the corporal's gray, nervous and fidgety at best, had no sooner caught sight of the oncoming body than it bolted, speeding along the edge of the bluff, uncontrollable and unguidable, to plunge after a few seconds into a sandy ravine which ran up into the plain from the river-bottom—disappearing before the lad's straining gaze as completely as if swallowed by the friendly earth!

A minute or two later the Major, following almost in the footprints of his stable-mate, paused on the brink of the little gully, and then carefully, and without harm to his clinging burden, slid and floundered down its shelving sides, and stopped, quivering, at the bottom.

There was something disconcerting in the change from the recent rush and turmoil of the upper world to the gloom and stillness of the leafy covert. Danny caught his breath and peered half timidly through the underbrush. "Mackenzie," he called softly; "oh, Mackenzie!" And then with a sudden low, horrified cry he slipped from the Major's back, thrust aside the bushes, and stared, transfixed, at the spectacle before him.

Above his head, a broad swath of broken branches and uprooted reeds showed where horse and rider had crashed through the bushes to their fate. At his feet, a huddled, shapeless mass, was the runaway! And beyond lay the corporal, his blouse torn to ribbons and gray with dust, his upturned face drawn and still—a red stream trickling slowly down from a gaping wound in his forehead, to form an ever-growing stain in the sand beside him!

Little by little Dan crept to the trooper's side and gazed with wide eyes into the quiet face. Some vaguely formed protest against the injustice of fate crept through the child-mind. The peril from which he had just escaped—the possible peril even now lurking in the woods about him—was as nothing compared with this terrible stillness and helplessness of his friend!

Danny began to cry, not loudly, but with deep-drawn, shivering breaths, while the Major, with hanging, loosened reins, sniffed protestingly at the motionless body of his late comrade. There was a silence, broken only by the chirping of the sparrows in the thicket and the rustle of the leaves overhead.

Suddenly Dan looked up, and drew his sleeve across his eyes.

A deep sigh had escaped from the blue lips, and with a frown of pain Mackenzie stirred uneasily and turned his face toward the boy. Dan's first wild thrill of joy vanished at the sight of the blood which welled up afresh from the wound with the movement. Instinct told him that the flickering life could not long sustain such a loss.

The winter before he had been present while the hospital steward bound up a wound for one of the soldiers, and the attention with which he had followed the operation did him good service now.

He took out his handkerchief and measured its small length against the trooper's forehead. Then he looked about him for a more effectual bandage, and his eye fell upon the narrow leather cinch at his waist, a recent and much-prized gift from the Mexican saddler in his father's troop. It was the work of only a few seconds to unfasten it, and to make a pad of the bit of linen, after which, with much difficulty, he adjusted the strap about the corporal's head, and pulled it tight. And terrified as the child was, and tender and feeble and fluttering as his small fingers were, they did their work thoroughly, and the fatal tide at first slowly ebbed, and at length ceased.

When the task was accomplished, Danny looked about him helplessly. "What shall we do now, Major?" he said, addressing himself to his only companion.

The corporal stirred. "And ye'll keep his head straight, lad," he murmured feebly, his half-conscious mind taking up the counsel to his charge where it had been interrupted by the stampede; "and ye'll steer him for hame—for hame!" he repeated once again in stronger tones.

The child bent over him. "Am I to go for help, Mackenzie?" he said eagerly. "Do you mean I am to go for help?"

He waited a moment in expectant silence; but the trooper had drifted off into unconsciousness, and there was no reply. Then he rose to his feet. There seemed nothing left but to obey. "Come, Major," he said tremulously.

He made his way slowly to the horse's side, climbed up on the stump of a fallen oak, and from that to the animal's back, and with one wistful backward glance at the grimly quiet objects at his feet bent his head over the Major's neck and wound both hands in his mane, while the sagacious beast clambered up the side of the ravine, to emerge a minute later upon the open prairie.

Away to the north a cloud of dust marked the recent passage of the herd. On every other side swept the tableland, empty and placid and smiling. And beyond, to the south, stood the fort and home. Danny took heart, settled himself in the saddle, and put the Major into a smart canter, holding the reins firmly, and trying to recall the corporal's instructions while he rode, thinking with an ever-recurring pang of his friend's condition, happy that the distance to the necessary succor was diminishing so rapidly, and totally forgetful of the anxiety which had agitated the veteran before the accident that had separated them.

Suddenly, at the end of some fifteen minutes of tranquil riding, as the Major galloped along the edge of the timber which fringed the bluff, there was a loud crackling and crashing in the bushes, and a gaily decorated war-pony scrambled through them, his rider grunting in surly surprise; while at the same moment, from the thicket beyond, three other half-naked mounted figures appeared and lined up in the path which led to safety.

The child's heart stopped beating. His frontier training told him that all that had gone before, even the tragedy which had darkened the afternoon, was as nothing compared with this new and awful danger. In a paroxysm of terror he tried to stop Major—tried with all his small strength to turn him aside toward the open plain, to check his mad plunge into the very arms of the enemy. But for the first time the horse paid attention neither to the beloved voice nor to the tiny hands pulling so desperately upon the reins.

Whether it was the sight of an old foe, or whether the wise, kind heart of the animal realized the full extent of a peril of which the child was as yet only half aware, it would be hard to say. But little Dan found himself going faster than he had thought possible—and faster—and faster—till the tawny, sunburned plain, and the pitiless smiling sky, and the nearer, greener foliage of the willows, and even the outlines of the dreaded savages themselves became as so many parts of a great rushing, whirling whole, and all his strength was absorbed in the effort to retain his seat upon the bounding horse.

And so, like some vision from their own weird legends, straight down upon the astonished Indians swept the great bronze beast with its golden-haired burden! Down upon them, and through them, and away—till by the time they had recovered from their amazement there was a good fifty yards between them and their flying prey! And that distance, hard as they might ride, was not easily to be overcome!

After that first wild rush the Major settled into a steadier pace—a smooth, even run, so easy to sit that the lad relaxed his clutch upon the animal's mane and turned his eyes to the horizon, where gathering swarms of savages showed like clusters of ants against the slope of the hillside. In his track, with shrill, singing cries, like hounds upon a trail, came his pursuers. And far to the south there was a puff of white smoke from the walls of the fort, and a moment later the first heavy, echoing boom of the alarm-gun thundered across the plains!

WITHIN THE STOCKADED enclosure the sunny hours wore tranquilly away. Mrs. Kent's passing uneasiness about the Major subsided, and she returned placidly to her domestic duties. Late in the afternoon, when the baby had been bathed and freshly dressed and the nurse had taken her to play in the shade of the bandstand, Mrs. Kent came out to join her husband and a group of ladies and gentlemen on the piazza.

"There must be a prairie fire somewhere," she remarked as she seated herself; "I have been smelling smoke all the afternoon."

"We were just talking about it," answered Mrs. Lane, the doctor's wife; "I am certain I saw smoke to the northward before luncheon. There is no sign of it now, but the odor is distinct!"

At that moment one of the younger lieutenants approached from the gate which led toward the corral. "Danny has gone riding, has he not, Kent?" he asked.

"Yes," replied the officer; "he went with Mackenzie."

"Have you confidence in the corporal's discretion?"

"Absolute!" was the emphatic answer. "Why do you ask?"

"Because there is some trouble with the herd. The animals are unaccountably restless, and the officer of the day has asked for a detail to go out and assist in bringing them in." He spoke in an undertone, but the captain laid a hand upon his arm and drew him away from the piazza.

"Are there signs of any other trouble?" he asked gravely.

The young fellow shook his head. "Not as yet," he replied; "but they seem to think it better to be on the safe side."

He went on to his own quarters, and the captain thoughtfully retraced his steps in the direction of the piazza. As he regained it a shot rang out—a shot that brought officers and men all over the garrison to their feet, that blanched the faces of the women, and called forth a cry of agony from Mrs Kent.

"Indians!" she moaned. "Indians! Oh, George!—and Danny!"

Her husband caught her in his arms and carried her indoors. "Courage, dearest, courage!" he whispered, as he snatched up saber and pistols, and with a hasty farewell he left her. What he had to do must be done quickly!

The first report had been followed by another, and another, as each sentinel in turn took up and echoed the alarm. After those came the crashing bang and roar of the six-pounder, the sinister humming of the "long roll," and the shrill notes of the bugles as they sounded "boots and saddles."

To an inexperienced eye the scene which resulted would have seemed like hopeless confusion.

The barracks swarmed with hastily armed men, the air was filled with the clatter of sabers and the rattle of carbines, with hurriedly shouted orders, calls, questions, till the "assembly" put a temporary check upon the uproar and the troopers departed for the stables. There saddles were flung across the horses' backs, girths were jerked tight, and, in less time than it has taken to describe the formation, the infantrymen detailed to protect the garrison were at their posts behind the stockade, and the troops of cavalry were mounted and ready for their work.

"For'rd, trot, march!" The bugles repeated the command with blatant clamor,

On—on—and up into the air!

and the troops swept through the gate of the corral and halted by one of the bastions for their orders— grimly silent, compact bodies of men, trained by long, hard years of such service as the soldiers of today can never know.

To have seen them once in battle array is to have seen that which one can never forget! There was a quiet satisfaction on the face of the garrison commander as he regarded them, field-glass in hand, from his post of observation on top of the block-house. His wishes were briefly expressed: "B, to the north after the herd; K, to the west; L, in reserve until needed."

Once again the bugles sounded, and the troops separated to their respective duties—L waiting at "place rest" on the plain beside the fort, K forming a skirmish-line at the foot of the slope some hundreds of yards to the west; and B, under Dan's own father, starting at a brisk trot along the western face of the stockade. The men were unusually grave as they rounded its last corner. There was not one among them who did not feel a pang at the thought of the tiny child practically alone and unprotected on those desolate prairies; they were full of mute sympathy for the sol-dier who rode with white, stern face at their head.

As they paused for a final momentary halt, the sergeant of the troop moved to the side of his commander. "There are some animals running by the timber to the left, Captain," he observed hurriedly. The officer regarded the moving figures intently, then he turned his face for a brief instant full upon his followers. "Those are mounted horsemen, lads!" he exclaimed; "and they are coming this way! Column right, gallop, march!" And the troopers, catching the subtle excitement in his tone, settled themselves in their saddles, and with a rousing cheer thundered across the plain in the direction indicated.

To Danny, as he swept along on the road to safety, the minutes which suc-ceeded the report of the alarm-gun were full of anguish. He grew sick and giddy with the rush of his passage. The rhythmic beat of the horse's feet upon the turf mingled in a dull monotone with the roar of the wind in his ears.

The fort grew steadily nearer. In spite of his terror he began to distinguish the figures of the soldiers as they swarmed about its walls in response to the call to arms, the hurry and confusion of the preparations, and finally even the color of the black horses in his father's troop as they started across the plain in his direction. With a little moan of appeal, he turned the Major toward them.

The friction of the reins had fretted the sweat upon the horse's neck into a heavy lather, he threw up his head uneasily from time to time in the effort for more air, and at length, with a spasm of dread, the child felt his smooth run slack-en to a pounding gallop, while in the rear, with sinister insistence, the shrill, crooning cries of the Indians grew perceptibly louder.

Danny glanced over his shoulder. His pursuers were close at his heels, riding low down on their unkempt ponies, their lithe, half-naked bodies gleaming like bronze statues, the red and yellow of their war-paint showing up sharply in the strong light of the afternoon.

The boy grew sick at heart, turned once more to the plains in front of him, and uttered a wailing cry of terror.

Before him, almost at his feet, lay a yawning gulf—one of those steep-sided arroyos which begin in a tiny crack, and increase with the storms and frosts of succeeding winters till they form impassable chasms. The one in question was fully fifteen feet in width, and the lad clutched the animal's mane, and waited, numb with horror, for the end. The savages, seeing the unexpected peril which confronted him, broke into a series of triumphant yells. At the same moment, clear and distinct in the still air, came the bugle-notes of the "charge."

The Major threw up his head at the sound; it was the well-remembered war-cry of his young, strong days; it woke an answering echo in his faithful heart, and, with a supreme and final effort of his failing strength, he responded to its command. The muscles on his extended neck grew stiff and tense with energy; his nostrils widened; he laid his small ears back, and gathered his mighty limbs under him. On—on—and up into the air! The lad closed his eyes. There was a crashing, stumbling jar, and then the horse recovered himself and galloped jerkily forward to meet his oncoming mates.

Danny was only vaguely conscious of the singing of the bullets above his head and of the cries of his baffled pursuers as they retreated before the fire of the troopers. He saw his father's face through a mist of long-delayed tears, and a significant silence fell upon the men as they closed about the staggering horse, and their leader lifted his son from the saddle and held him for a brief space against his heart.

HALF AN HOUR later, when the rattle of musketry and the crash of the Gatling guns in the sand-bag battery beside the fort had died away, the herd had been recovered, and the Indians had retreated to the shadows of the hills, a small procession wound along the edge of the timber. In the midst of it was a canvas-covered wagon with a red cross on its white sides. About that, armed and watchful, rode the soldiers of L troop. Under its shelter sat the surgeon, and at his feet lay Mackenzie, bandaged and cared for. As the sunlight faded and the evening gun sounded over the plains the little train reached the stockade, the gates opened, and the last of our heroes gained the friendly shelter of the walls.

So ends the story, and it has no moral. Only, if you had seen Danny's mother that evening, as, clinging to the Major's neck, she wept for very joy, you never could doubt the value of fidelity and courage—even in a horse.

First published in the January 1897 edition of *St. Nicholas Magazine*

Tommy and the Meadow Mice

From "Tommy and the Wishing Stone"

BY THORNTON W. BURGESS

ILLUSTRATIONS BY HARRISON CADY

Tommy is happy being perfectly miserable.

TOMMY SCUFFED HIS bare, brown feet in the grass and didn't even notice how cooling and refreshing to his bare toes the green blades were. Usually he just loved to feel them, but this afternoon he just didn't want to find anything pleasant or nice in the things he was accustomed to. A scowl, a deep, dark, heavy scowl, had chased all merriment from his round, freckled face. It seemed as if the very freckles were trying to hide from it. Tommy didn't care. He said so. He said so right out loud. He didn't care if all the world knew it. He wanted the world to know it. It was a horrid old world anyway, this world which made a fellow go hunt up and drive home a lot of pesky cows just when all the other fellows were over at the swimming-hole. It always was that way whenever there was anything interesting or particular to do, or any fun going on. Yes, it was a horrid old world, this world in which Tommy lived, and he was quite willing that everybody should know it.

The truth is Tommy was deep, very deep, in the sulks. He was so deep in them that he couldn't see the Jolly Sun smiling down on him. He couldn't see anything lovely in the beautiful, broad, Green Meadows with the shadows of the clouds chasing one another across them. He couldn't hear the music of the birds and the bees. He couldn't even hear the Merry Little Breezes whispering secrets as they danced around him. He couldn't see and hear because—well, because he *wouldn't* see and hear. That is always the way with people who go way down deep in the sulks.

Presently he came to a great big stone. Tommy stopped and scowled at it just as he had been scowling at everybody and everything. He scowled at it as if he thought it had no business to be there. Yet all the time he was glad that it was there. It was just the right size to sit on and make himself happy by being perfectly miserable. You know, some people actually find pleasure in thinking how miserable they are. The more miserable they can make themselves feel, the sooner they begin to pity themselves, and when they begin to pity themselves, they seem to find what Uncle Jason calls a "melancholy pleasure." It was that way with Tommy. Because no one else seemed to pity him, he wanted to pity himself, and to do that right he must first make himself feel the most miserable he possibly could. So he sat down on the big stone, waved his stick for a few moments and then threw it away, put his chin in his two hands and his two elbows on his two knees, and began by scowling down at his bare, brown toes.

"There's never anything to do around here, and when there is, a fellow can't do it," he grumbled. "Other fellows don't have to weed the garden, and bring in wood, and drive the cows, and when they do, it ain't just when they want to have some fun. What's vacation for, if it ain't to have a good time in? And how's a fellow going to do it when he has to work all the time—anyway when he has to work just when he don't want to?" He was trying to be truthful.

"Fellows who live in town have something going on all the time, while out here there's nothing but fields, and woods, and sky, and—and cows that haven't sense enough to come home themselves when it's time. There's never anything exciting or int'resting 'round here. I wish—"

He suddenly became aware of two very small bright eyes watching him from a little opening in the grass. He scowled at them harder than ever, and moved ever so little. The eyes disappeared, but a minute later they were back again, full of curiosity, a little doubtful, a little fearful, but tremendously interested. They were the eyes of Danny Meadow-mouse. Tommy knew them right away. Of course he did. Hadn't he chased Danny with sticks and stones time and again? But he didn't think of this now. He was too full of his own troubles to remember that others had troubles too.

Somehow Danny's twinkling little eyes seemed to mock him. How unjust things were!

"*You* don't have to work!" he exploded so suddenly and fiercely that Danny gave a frightened squeak and took to his heels. "You don't have anything to do but play all day and have a good time. I wish I was a meadow-mouse!"

Right then and there something happened. Tommy didn't know how it happened, but it just did. Instead of a bare-legged, freckle-faced, sulky boy sitting on the big stone, he suddenly found himself a little, chunky, blunt-headed, furry animal with four ridiculously short stubby legs, and he was scampering after Danny Meadow-mouse along a private little path through the meadow-grass. He was a meadow-mouse himself! His wish had come true!

Tommy felt very happy. He had forgotten that he ever was a boy. He raced along the private little path just as if he had always been accustomed to just such private little paths. It might be very hot out in the sun, but down there among the sheltering grass stems it was delightfully cool and comfortable. He tried to shout for very joy, but what he really did do was to squeak. It was a thin, sharp little squeak. It

Hooty the Owl

was answered right away from in front of him, and Tommy didn't like the sound of it. Being a meadow-mouse now, he understood the speech of meadow-mice, and he knew that Danny Meadow-mouse was demanding to know who was running in his private little path. Tommy suspected by the angry sound of Danny's voice that he meant to fight.

Tommy hesitated. Then he stopped. He didn't want to fight. You see, he knew that he had no business on that path without an invitation from the owner. If it had been his own path, he would have been eager to fight. But it wasn't, and so he thought it best to avoid trouble. He turned and scampered back a little way to a tiny branch path. He followed this until it also branched, and then took the new path. But none of these paths really belonged to him. He wanted some of his very own. Now the only way to have a private path of your very own in the Green Meadows is to make it, unless you are big enough and strong enough to take one away from some one else.

So Tommy set to work to make a path of his own, and he did it by cutting the grass one stem at a time. The very tender ones he ate. The rest he carried to an old board he had discovered, and under this he made a nest, using the finest, softest grasses for the inside. Of course it was work. As a matter of fact, had he, as a boy, had to work one tenth as much or as hard as he now had to work as a meadow-mouse, he would have felt sure that he was the most abused boy who ever lived. But, being a meadow-mouse, he didn't think anything about it, and scurried back and forth as fast as ever he could, just stopping now and then to rest. He knew that he must work for everything he had—that without work he would have nothing. And somehow this all seemed perfectly right. He was busy, and in keeping busy he kept happy.

Presently, as he sat down to rest a minute, a Merry Little Breeze came hurrying along, and brought with it just the faintest kind of a sound. It made his heart jump. Every little unexpected sound made his heart jump. He listened with all his might. There it was again! Something was stealing very, very softly through the grass. He felt sure it was danger of some kind. Then he did a foolish thing—he ran. You see, he was so frightened that he felt that he just couldn't sit still a second longer, so he ran. The instant he moved, something big and terrible sprang at him, and two great paws with sharp claws spread out all but landed on him. He gave a frightened squeak, and darted under an old fence-post that lay half hidden in the tall grass.

"What's the matter with you?" demanded a voice. Tommy found that he had company. It was another meadow-mouse.

"I—I've had such a narrow escape!" panted Tommy. "A terrible creature with awful claws almost caught me!"

The stranger peeped out to see. "Pooh!" said he, "that was only a cat. Cats don't know much. If you keep your ears and eyes open, it's easy enough to fool cats. But they are a terrible nuisance just the same, because they are always prowling around when you least expect them. I hate cats! It is bad enough to have to watch out all the time for enemies who live on the Green Meadows, without having to be always looking to see if a cat is about. A cat hasn't any excuse at all. It has all it wants to eat without trying to catch us. It hunts just out of love of cruelty. Now Reddy Fox has some excuse; he has to eat. Too bad he's so fond of meadow-mice. Speaking of Reddy, have you seen him lately?"

Tommy shook his head. "I guess it's safe enough to go out now," continued the stranger. "I know where there is a dandy lot of corn; let's go get some."

Tommy was quite willing. The stranger led the way. First he looked this way and that way, and listened for any sound of danger. Tommy did likewise. But the way seemed clear, and away they scampered. Right away Tommy was happy again. He had forgotten his recent fright. That is the way with little people of the Green Meadows. But he didn't forget to keep his ears and his eyes wide open for new dangers. They reached the corn safely, and then such a feast as they did have! It seemed to Tommy that never had he tasted anything half so good. Right in the midst of the feast, the stranger gave a faint little squeak and darted under a pile of old cornstalks. Tommy didn't stop to ask questions, but followed right at his heels. A big, black shadow swept over them and then passed on. Tommy peeped out. There was a great bird with huge, broad wings sailing back and forth over the meadows.

"It's old Whitetail, the marsh-hawk. He didn't get us that time!" chuckled the stranger, and crept back to the delicious corn. In two minutes, they were having as good a time as before, just as if they hadn't had a narrow escape. When they had eaten all they could hold, the stranger went back to his old fence-post and Tommy returned to his own private paths and the snug nest he had built under the old board. He was sleepy, and he curled up for a good long nap.

When he awoke, the first stars were beginning to twinkle down at him from the sky, and black shadows lay over the Green Meadows. He found that he could see quite as well as in the light of day, and, because he was already hungry again, he started out to look for something to eat. Something inside warned him that he must watch out for danger now just as sharply as before, though the black shadows seemed to promise safety. Just what he was to watch out for he didn't know, but still every few steps he stopped to look and listen. He found that this was visiting time among the meadow-mice, and he made a great many friends. There was a great deal of scurrying back and forth along private little paths, and a great deal of squeaking. At least, that is what Tommy would have called it if he had still been a boy, but as it was, he understood it perfectly, for it was meadow-mouse language. Suddenly there was not a sound to be heard, not a single squeak or the sound of scurrying feet. Tommy sat perfectly still and held his breath. He didn't know why, but something inside told him to, and he did. Then something passed over him. It was like a great shadow, and it was just as silent as a shadow. But Tommy knew that it wasn't a shadow, for out of it two great, round, fierce, yellow eyes glared down and struck such terror to his heart that it almost stopped beating. But they didn't see him, and he gave a tiny sigh of relief as he watched the grim living shadow sail on. While he watched, there was a frightened little squeak, two legs with great curved claws dropped down from the shadow, plunged into the grass, and when they came up again they held a little limp form. A little mouse had moved when

It was visiting time and he made a great many friends.

Blacky the Crow

he shouldn't have, and Hooty the Owl had caught a dinner.

A dozen times that night Tommy sat quite frozen with fear while Hooty passed, but after each time he joined with his fellows in merry-making just as if there was no such thing as this terrible feathered hunter with the silent wings, only each one was ready to hide at the first sign of danger. When he grew tired of playing and eating, he returned to his snug nest under the old board to sleep. He was still asleep there the next morning when, without any warning, the old board was lifted. In great fright Tommy ran out of his nest, and at once there was a great shout from a huge giant, who struck at him with a stick and then chased him, throwing sticks and stones, none of which hit him, but which frightened him terribly. He dodged down a little path and ran for his life, while behind him he heard the giant (it was just a boy) shouting and laughing as he poked about in the grass trying to find poor Tommy, and Tommy wondered what he could be laughing about, and what fun there could be in frightening a poor little meadow-mouse almost to death.

Later that very same morning, while he was hard at work cutting a new path, he heard footsteps behind him, and turned to see a big, black bird stalking along the little path. He didn't wait for closer acquaintance, but dived into the thick grass, and, as he did so, the big, black bird made a lunge at him, but missed him. It was his first meeting with Blacky the Crow, and he had learned of one more enemy to watch out for.

But most of all he feared Reddy Fox. He never could be quite sure when Reddy was about. Sometimes it would be in broad daylight, and sometimes in the stilly night. The worst of it was, Reddy seemed to know all about the ways of meadow-mice, and would lie perfectly still beside a little path until an unsuspecting mouse came along. Then there would be a sudden spring, a little squeak cut short right in the middle, and there would be one less happy little worker and playmate. So Tommy learned to look and listen before he started for any place, and then to scurry as fast as ever he could.

Twice Mr. Gopher-snake almost caught him, and once he got away from Billy Mink by squeezing into a hole between some roots too small for Billy to get in. It was a very exciting life, very exciting indeed. He couldn't understand why, when all he wanted was to be allowed to mind his own business and work and play in peace, he must be forever running or hiding for his life. He loved the sweet meadow-grasses and the warm sunshine. He loved to hear the bees humming and the birds singing. He thought the Green Meadows the most beautiful place in all the great world, and he was very happy when he wasn't frightened; but there was hardly an hour of the day or night that he didn't have at least one terrible fright.

Still, it was good to be alive and explore new places. There was a big rock in front of him right now. He wondered if there was anything to eat on top of it. Sometimes he found the very nicest seeds in the cracks of big rocks. This one looked as if it would not be very hard to scramble up on. He felt almost sure that he would find some treasure up there. He looked this way and that way to make sure no one was watching. Then he scrambled up on the big rock.

For a few minutes, Tommy stared out over the Green Meadows. They were very beautiful. It seemed to him that they never had been so beautiful, or the songs of the birds so sweet, or the Merry Little Breezes, the children of Old Mother West Wind, so soft and caressing. He couldn't understand it all, for he wasn't a meadow-mouse—just a barefooted boy sitting on a big stone that was just made to sit on. As he looked down, he became aware of two very small bright eyes watching him from a little opening in the grass. He knew them right away. Of course he did. They were the eyes of Danny Meadow-mouse. They were filled with curiosity, a little doubtful, a little fearful, but tremendously interested. Tommy smiled, and felt in his pocket for some cracker-crumbs. Danny ran away at the first move, but Tommy scattered the crumbs where he could find them, as he was sure to come back.

Tommy stood up and stretched. Then he turned and looked curiously at the stone on which he had been sitting. "I believe it's a real wishing-stone," said he. Then he laughed aloud. "I'm glad I'm not a meadow-mouse, but just a boy!" he cried. "I guess those cows are wondering what has become of me." He started toward the pasture, and now there was no frown darkening his freckled face. It was dear and good to see, and he whistled as he tramped along. Once he stopped and grinned sheepishly as his blue eyes drank in the beauty of the Green Meadows and beyond them the Green Forest. "And I said there was nothing interesting or exciting going on here! Why, it's the most exciting place I ever heard of, only I didn't know it before!" he muttered. "Gee, I *am* glad I'm not a meadow-mouse, and if ever I throw sticks or stones at one again, I—well, I hope I turn into one!"

And though Danny Meadow-mouse, timidly nibbling at the cracker-crumbs, didn't know it, he had one less enemy to be afraid of!

First published in the November 1914 edition of *St. Nicholas Magazine*

Why Tommy Became a Friend of Red Squirrels

From "Tommy and the Wishing Stone"

BY THORNTON W. BURGESS

ILLUSTRATIONS BY HARRISON CADY

"I DON'T SEE what Sis wants to string this stuff all over the house for, just because it happens to be Christmas!" grumbled Tommy, as he sat on a big stone and idly kicked at a pile of beautiful ground-pine and fragrant balsam boughs. "It's the best day for skating we've had yet, and here I am missing a whole morning of it, and so tired that most likely I won't feel like going this afternoon!"

Now Tommy knew perfectly well that if his mother said that he could go, nothing could keep him away from the pond that afternoon. He was a little tired, perhaps, but not nearly so tired as he tried to think he was. Gathering Christmas greens was work, of course. But when you come right down to it, there is work about almost everything, even skating. The chief difference between work and pleasure is the difference between "must" and "want to." When you *must* do a thing it becomes work; when you *want* to do a thing it becomes pleasure.

Right down deep inside, where his honest self lives, Tommy was glad that there was going to be a green wreath in each of the front windows, and that over the doors and pictures there would be sweet-smelling balsam. Without them, why, Christmas wouldn't be Christmasy at all! And really it had been fun gathering those greens. He wouldn't admit it, but it had. He wouldn't have missed it for the world. It was only that it had to be done just when he wanted to do something else. And so he tried to feel grieved and persecuted, and to forget that Christmas was only two days off.

He sat on the big gray stone and looked across the Green Meadows, no longer green but covered with the whitest and lightest of snow-blankets, across the Old Pasture, not one whit less beautiful, to the Green Forest, and he sighed. It was a deep, heavy sigh. It was the sigh of a self-made martyr. As if in reply, he heard the sharp voice of Chatterer the Red Squirrel. It rang out clear and loud on the frosty air, and it was very plain that, whatever troubles others might have, Chatterer was very well satisfied with the world in general and himself in particular. Just now he was racing along the fence, stopping at every post to sit up and tell all the world that he was there and didn't care who knew it. Presently his sharp eyes spied Tommy.

Chatterer stopped short in the middle of a rail and looked at Tommy very hard. Then he barked at him, jerking his tail with every syllable. Tommy didn't move. Chatterer jumped down from the fence and came nearer. Every foot or so he paused and barked, and his bark was such a funny mixture of nervousness and excitement and curiosity and sauciness, not to say impudence, that finally Tommy laughed right out. He just couldn't help it.

Back to the fence rushed Chatterer, and scampered up to the top of a post. Once sure of the safety of this retreat, he faced Tommy and began to scold as fast as his tongue could go. Of course Tommy couldn't understand what Chatterer was saying, but he could guess. He was telling Tommy just what he thought of a boy who would sit moping on such a beautiful day, and only two days before Christmas at that! My, how his tongue did fly! When he had had his say to the full, he gave a final whisk of his tail and scampered off in the direction of the Old Orchard. And, as he went, it seemed to Tommy as if he looked back with the sauciest kind of a twinkle in his eyes, as much as to say, "You deserve all I've said, but I don't really mean it!"

Tommy watched him, a lively little red spot against the white background, and, as he watched, the smile gradually faded away. It never would do at all to go home in good spirits after raising all the fuss he had created when he started out. So, to make himself feel as badly as he felt that he ought to feel, Tommy sighed dolefully.

"Oh, but you're lucky!" said he, as Chatterer's sharp voice floated over to him from the Old Orchard. "You don't have to do a blessed thing unless you want to! All you have to do is to eat and sleep and have a good time. It must be fun. I wish I was a squirrel!"

Right then something happened. It happened all in a flash, just as it had happened to Tommy once before. One minute he was a boy, a discontented boy, sitting on a big gray stone on the edge of the Green Meadows, and the next minute he wasn't a boy at all! You see, when he made that wish, he had quite forgotten that he was sitting on the wishing-stone. Now he no longer had to guess at what Chatterer was saying. Not a bit of it. He knew. He talked the same language himself. In short, he was a red squirrel, and in two minutes had forgotten that he ever had been a boy.

How good it felt to be free and know that he could do just as he pleased! His first impulse was to race over to the Old Orchard and make the acquaintance of Chatterer. Then he thought better of it. Something inside him seemed to tell him that he had no business there—that the Old Orchard was not big enough for two red squirrels, and that, as Chatterer had gone there first, it really belonged to him in a way. He felt quite sure of it when he had replied to Chatterer's sharp voice, and had been told in no uncertain tones that the best thing he could do would be to run

Tommy sat quite still watching the stranger.

right back where he had come from.

Of course, he couldn't do that, so he decided to do the next best thing—run over to the Green Forest and see what there was to do there. He hopped up on the rail fence and whisked along the top rail.

What fun it was! He didn't have a care in the world. All he had to do was to eat, drink, and have a good time. Ha! Who was that coming along behind him? Was it Chatterer? It looked something like him, and yet different somehow. Tommy sat quite still watching the stranger, and, as he watched, a curious terror began to creep over him. The stranger wasn't Chatterer. No, indeed, he wasn't even a squirrel! He was too long and slim, and his tail was different. He was Shadow the Weasel! Tommy didn't have to be told that. Although he never had seen Shadow before, he knew without being told. For a minute he couldn't move. Then, his heart beating with fear until it seemed as if it would burst, he fled along the fence toward the Green Forest, and now he didn't stop at the posts when he came to them. His one thought was to get away, away as far as ever he could; for in the eyes of Shadow the Weasel he had seen death.

Up the nearest tree he raced and hid, clinging close to the trunk near the top, staring down with eyes fairly bulging with fright. Swiftly, yet without seeming to hurry, Shadow the Weasel came straight to the tree in which Tommy was hiding, his nose in Tommy's tracks in the way that a hound follows a rabbit or a fox. At the foot of the tree he stopped just a second and looked up. Then he began to climb. At the first scratch of his claws on the bark Tommy raced out along a branch and leaped across to the next tree. Then, in a great panic, he went on from tree to tree, taking desperate chances in his long leaps. In the whole of his little being he had room but for one feeling, and that was fear—fear of that savage pitiless pursuer.

He had run a long way before he realized that he was no longer being followed. The fact is, Shadow had found other game, easier to catch, and had given up. Now, just as soon as Tommy realized that Shadow the Weasel was no longer on his track, he straightway forgot his fear. In fact it was just as if he never had had a fright, for that is the law of nature with her little people of the wild. So presently Tommy was once more as happy and carefree as before.

In a big chestnut-tree just ahead of him he could see Happy Jack the Gray Squirrel; and Happy Jack was very busy about something. Perhaps he had a store-house there. The very thought made Tommy hungry. Once more he hid, but this time not in fear. He hid so that he could watch Happy Jack. Not a sound did he make as he peered out from his hiding-place. Happy Jack was a long time in that hollow limb! It seemed as if he never would come out. So Tommy started on to look for more mischief, for he was bubbling over with good spirits and felt that he must do something.

Presently, quite by accident, he discovered another hoard of nuts, mostly acorns, neatly tucked away in a crotch of a big tree. Of course he sampled them. "What fun!" thought he. "I don't know whose they are, and I don't care. From now on, they are going to belong to me." He started to carry them away, but a sudden harsh scream close to him startled him so that he dropped the nut he had in his mouth. He dodged behind the trunk of the tree just in time to escape the dash of an angry bird in a brilliant blue suit with white and black trimmings.

"Thief! thief! thief! Leave my nuts alone!" screamed Sammy Jay, anger making his voice harsher than ever.

Round and round the trunk of the tree Tommy dodged, chattering back in reply to the sharp tongue of the angry jay. It was exciting without being very dangerous. After a while, however, it grew tiresome, and, watching his chance, he slipped over to another tree and into a hole made by Drummer the Woodpecker. Sammy Jay didn't see where he had disappeared, and, after hunting in vain, gave up and began to carry his nuts away to a new hiding-place. Tommy's eyes sparkled with mischief as he watched. By and by he would have a hunt for it! It would be fun!

When Sammy Jay had hidden the last nut and flown away, Tommy came out. He didn't feel like hunting for those nuts just then, so he scampered up in a tall hemlock-tree, and, just out of sheer good spirits and because he could see no danger near, he called sharply that all within hearing might know that he was about. Almost instantly he received a reply from not far away. It was an angry

A sudden harsh scream startled him so that he dropped the nut.

warning to keep away from that part of the Green Forest, because he had no business there! It was the voice of Chatterer. Tommy replied just as angrily that he would stay if he wanted to. Then they barked and chattered at each other for a long time. Gradually Chatterer came nearer. Finally he was in the very next tree. He stopped there long enough to tell Tommy all that he would do to him when he caught him, and at the end he jumped across to Tommy's tree.

Tommy waited no longer. He wasn't ready to fight. In the first place he knew that Chatterer probably had lived there a long time, and so was partly right in saying that Tommy had no business there. Then Chatterer looked a little the bigger and stronger. So Tommy nimbly ran out on a branch and leaped across to the next tree. In a flash Chatterer was after him, and then began a most exciting race through the tree-tops. Tommy found that there were regular squirrel highways through the tree-tops, and along these he raced at top speed, Chatterer at his heels, scolding and threatening. When he reached the edge of the Green Forest, Tommy darted down the last tree, across the open space to the old stone wall, and along this Chatterer followed.

Suddenly the anger in Chatterer's voice changed to a sharp cry of warning. Tommy scrambled into a crevice between two stones without stopping to inquire what the trouble was. When he peeped out, he saw a great bird sailing back and forth. In a few minutes it lighted on a nearby tree, and sat there so still that, if Tommy had not seen it light, he never would have known it was there.

*He saw a great bird
sailing back and forth.*

"Mr. Goshawk nearly got you that time," said a voice very near at hand. Tommy turned to find Chatterer peeping out from another crevice in the old wall. "It won't be safe for us to show ourselves until he leaves," continued Chatterer. "It's getting so that an honest squirrel needs eyes in the back of his head to keep his skin whole, not to mention living out his natural life. Hello! here comes a boy, and that means more trouble. There's one good thing about it, and that is he'll frighten away that hawk."

Tommy looked, and sure enough there was a boy, and in his hands was an air-rifle. Tommy didn't know what it was, but Chatterer did.

"I wish that hawk would hurry up and fly so that we can run!" he sputtered. "The thing that boy carries throws things, and they hurt. It isn't best to let him get too near when he has that with him. He seems to think it's fun to hurt us. I'd just like to bite him once and see if he thought *that* was fun! There goes that hawk. Come on now, we've got to run for it!"

Chatterer led the way and Tommy followed. He was frightened, but there wasn't that terror which had possessed him when Shadow the Weasel was after him. Something struck sharply against the wall just behind him. It frightened him into greater speed. Something struck just in front of him, and then something hit him so hard that just for a second he nearly lost his balance. It hurt dreadfully.

"Hurrah!" shouted the boy, "I hit him that time!" Then the boy started to run after them so as to get a closer shot.

"We'll get up in the top of that big hemlock tree and he won't be able to see us," panted Chatterer. "Did he hit you? That's too bad. It might have been worse though. If he had had one of those things that make a big noise and smoke, we might not either of us be here now. Boys are hateful things. I don't see what fun they get out of frightening and hurting such little folks as you and me. They're brutes! That's what they are! When we get across that little open place, we can laugh at him. Come on now!"

Down from the end of the old wall Chatterer jumped and raced across to the foot of a big hemlock tree, Tommy at his heels. Up the tree they ran and hid close to the trunk where the branches were thick. They could peer down and see the boy, but he couldn't see them. He walked around the tree two or three times, and then shot up into the top to try to frighten the squirrels.

"Don't move!" whispered Chatterer. "He doesn't see us."

Tommy obeyed, although he felt as if he must run. His heart seemed to jump every time a bullet spatted in among the branches. It was dreadful to sit there and do nothing while being shot at, and not know but that the very next minute one of those little lead shot would hit. Tommy knew just how it would hurt if it did hit. Presently the boy gave up and went off to torment some one else. No sooner was his back fairly turned than Chatterer began to scold and jeer at him. Tommy joined him. It was just as if there never had been any danger. If that boy could have understood what they said, his ears would have burned.

Then Chatterer showed Tommy just what part of the Green Forest he claimed as his own, and also showed him a part that had belonged to another squirrel to whom something had happened, and suggested that Tommy take that for his. It wasn't as good as Chatterer's, but still it would do very well. Tommy took possession at once. Each agreed not to intrude on the other's territory. On common ground, that didn't belong to either of them, they would be the best of friends, but Tommy knew that if he went into Chatterer's part of the Green Forest, he would have to fight, and he made up his mind that if any other squirrel came into *his* part of the Green Forest, there would be a fight. Suddenly he was very jealous of his new possession. He was hardly willing to leave it when Chatterer suggested a visit to a nearby corn-crib for a feast of yellow corn.

Chatterer led the way. Tommy found that he was quite lame from the shot which had hit him, but he was soon racing after Chatterer again.

Along the old stone wall, then along a fence, up a maple tree, and from there to the roof of the corn-crib, they scampered. Chatterer knew just where to get inside, and in a few minutes they were stuffing themselves with yellow corn. When they had eaten all that they could hold, they stuffed their cheeks full and started back the way they had come. Tommy went straight to his own part of the Green Forest, and there he hid his treasure, some in a hollow stump, and some under a little pile of leaves between the roots of a tree. All the time he watched sharply to make sure that no one saw him. While looking for new hiding-places, his nose told him to dig. There, buried under the leaves, he found nuts hidden by the one who had lived there before him. There must be a lot more hidden there, and it would be great fun hunting for them. Doubtless he would find as many as if he had hidden them himself, for he had seen that Chatterer didn't know where he had put a tenth part of the things *he* had hidden. He just trusted to his nose to help him get them again.

He found a splendid nest made of leaves and strips of inner bark in the hollow stub of a big branch of a chestnut-tree, and he made up his mind that there was where he would sleep. Then he ran over to see Chatterer again. He found him scolding at a cat who watched him with yellow, unblinking eyes. He would run down the trunk of the tree almost to the ground, and there scold and call names as fast as his tongue could go. Then he would run back up to the lowest branch and scold from there. The next time he would go a little farther down. Finally he leaped to the ground, and raced across to another tree. The cat sprang, but was just too late. Chatterer jeered at her. Then he began the same thing over again, and kept at it until finally the cat gave up and left in disgust. It had been exciting, but Tommy shivered at the thought of what might have happened.

"Ever try that with a fox?" asked Chatterer.

"No," replied Tommy.

"I have!" boasted Chatterer. "But I've seen squirrels caught doing it," he added. "Still, I suppose one may as well be caught by a fox as by a hawk."

"Did you see that weasel this morning?" asked Tommy.

Chatterer actually shivered as he replied: "Yes, I saw him after you. It's a wonder he didn't get you. You're lucky! I was lucky myself this morning, for a mink went right past where I was hiding. Life is nothing but one jump after another these days. It seems as if, when one has worked as hard as I did last fall to store up enough food to keep me all winter, I ought to be allowed to enjoy it in comfort. Those who sleep all winter, like Johnny Chuck, have a mighty easy time of it. They don't know when they are well off. Still, I'd hate to miss all the excitement and fun of life. I would rather jump for my life twenty times a day as I have to, and know that I'm alive, than to be alive and not know it. See that dog down there? I hate dogs! I'm going to tell him so."

Off raced Chatterer to bark and scold at a little black-and-white dog which paid no attention to him at all. The shadows were creeping through the trees, and Tommy began to think of his nest. He looked once more at Chatterer, who was racing along the top of the old wall scolding at the dog. Suddenly what seemed like merely a darker shadow swept over Chatterer, and, when it had passed, he had vanished. For once, that fatal

Each agreed not to intrude on the other's territory.

once, he had been careless. Hooty the Owl had caught him. Tommy shivered. He was frightened and cold. He would get to his nest as quickly as he could. He leaped down to a great gray stone, and—behold, he wasn't a squirrel at all! He was just a boy sitting on a big stone, with a heap of Christmas greens at his feet.

He shivered, for he was cold. Then he jumped up and stamped his feet and threshed his arms. A million diamond points glittered in the white meadows where the snow crystals splintered the sunbeams. From the Old Orchard sounded the sharp scolding chirr and cough of Chatterer the Red Squirrel.

Tommy listened and slowly a smile widened. "Hooty didn't get you, after all!" he muttered. Then in a minute he added: "I'm glad of it. And you haven't anything more to fear from me. You won't believe it, but you haven't. You may be mischievous, but I guess you have troubles enough without my adding to them. Oh, but I'm glad I'm not a squirrel! Being a boy's good enough for me, 'specially long 'bout Christmas time. I bet Sis will be tickled with these greens. But it's strange what happens when I sit down on this old rock!"

He frowned at it as if he couldn't understand it at all. Then he gathered up his load of greens, and, with the merriest of whistles, trudged homeward. And to this day Chatterer the Red Squirrel cannot understand how it came about that from that Christmas he and Tommy became fast friends. But they did.

Perhaps the wishing-stone could tell if it would.

First published in the December 1914 edition of *St. Nicholas Magazine*

Count Geoffrey's Crest

BY CAROLINE K. HERRICK

ONE AUTUMN MORNING of a far-away time, in the fair land of Anjou, Gaspard, the charcoal-burner, was setting out from his humble cottage in the forest.

"Farewell, good wife," he said cheerily. "I am off for another day's work."

"Ay, another day's work, to earn but just another day's bread," replied the wife, sadly. "While we eat each day all the earnings of the day before, how shall we ever begin to save for Babette's marriage portion?"

"The child is scarce six years old," said the father. "She will not marry next week."

"Neither shall we begin to save for her next week, nor next year, nor ever, I fear," answered his wife.

"Have faith in God," said Gaspard. "It may please Him to make us rich before the child is grown."

That evening the wife waited in vain for her husband's return. At midnight she barred the door and lay down to a sleepless night, haunted by dread of calamity.

But morning brought her husband back, with a strange jingle of gold in his pouch and on his lips a wondrous tale of having guided a knight out of the forest and to the castle of Loches, where the knight proved to be none other than the lord of the land, Count Geoffrey of Anjou, who graciously caused his peasant guide to be seated beside him at table, entertained him as an honored guest, and dismissed him on the morrow with a reward for his services that would have paid him for six months' work at the kiln.

"Heaven be praised!" cried the wife, when she saw the gold pieces. "We *are* rich! Let us buy a flock of geese, and lay aside the price of every tenth goose for Babette."

ON THE EDGE of the forest, when spring had returned and the yellow bloom was brightening all the countryside, a small maiden sat singing to herself as she wove a garland of the gay blossoms.

"I am a queen," she sang. "This is my golden crown."

She pressed it down on her dark hair, then sat stiffly upright, her feet close together and hands crossed before her—the right holding a long wand of which she had made use in a recent contest with a morose-looking gray goose that waddled about nearby, trailing one wing on the ground.

A young knight came riding along the forest road. At sight of the quaint little figure he smiled and reined in his horse before her, while the gray goose lurched toward him with extended neck, hissing.

"Good day, little maid," said the knight, "thou art like a queen on her throne."

"I am a queen," the child replied in all seriousness. "This is my golden crown."

"And what is thy name, little queen?" he asked.

"I am Gaspard's Babette," she answered. "What is thy name?"

"I am Foulque's Geoffrey," he replied, with a smile.

"Art thou lost?" she asked.

"Nay, little one," he replied.

"Ah, what a pity!" sighed the child. "It is weary waiting for some one to get lost."

"And why dost thou want some one to get lost?"

"Because," she answered, "they would ask me of the way; and I should show them how to get out of the wood" (it was but a stone's throw from the highway), "and they would take me to the castle and show me wonderful things and give me money to bring home."

"Ah, I see," said the knight. "Is thy father the good man who guided the count out of the forest?"

She nodded her head.

"My father says it was like fairyland at the castle. He brought back so much money that we are quite rich now. We have a flock of geese. I watch them in the meadow."

"I see but one goose; and this is not the meadow," said the knight, somewhat puzzled.

"I am here today," said the child, "because this fiery old gray goose pecked the little white goose that I love—she is so gay; and I punished the old one with a stick and"—she hung her head and spoke very low—"I broke her wing. So my father says I shall no longer keep the flock, but only the gray goose, until her wing is well and I have learned wisdom."

"And when will that be?" he asked.

"Her wing will be well next week," said Babette.

"Wilt thou have learned wisdom by that time?"

"I have learned," she answered. "I shall use a thinner stick next time."

"Art not thou lonely here, with only the gray goose for company?" asked the knight.

"Yes," she replied, "since no one gets lost in the forest. I would that some one might come to play with me." Then, eyeing him critically, she added, "Wilt thou stay and play with me?"

"For a little while," he agreed. "What shall we play?"

"Thou shalt be king and I queen," she said. "I will make thee a crown like mine."

The knight looked in dismay at the bristling yellow garland that encircled her head like a halo, and suggested that a smaller one would do for him: "Just one branch for a plume of gold."

She pulled a branch from a bush and offered it to him. "Thou must crown me," he said. "Canst thou stand on my foot to reach up?"

She kicked off her wooden shoes and, by the help of his hand, clambered up and stood with her two small feet resting on his foot and the stirrup, her left hand clinging to a tuft of the horse's mane, while she arranged the broom in his cap.

"Thou art my lady," he said, as he lifted his head with its golden plume, "and I shall wear thy colors in the lists at the Whitsuntide tourney at Chinon."

"Dost thou live so far away as Chinon?" she asked in a tone of regret.

"Sometimes," he answered. "But now I am living at Loches. Wilt thou come with me and see my home?"

"Canst thou show me the castle too?" she asked eagerly.

"Good day, little maid," said the knight,
"thou art like a queen on her throne."

"Thou shalt see it," he promised. "Get thy shoes and climb up before me."

"Thou must take the gray goose, too," she said. "My father would be angry if I left it here."

"If I must, I must," said the knight, laughing, and he held the flapping creature under one arm while the other lifted the child to the saddle-bow; then he placed the goose on her knees, and she threw both arms across its back, while, with the same strong hand that held the child against his breast, he grasped the goose's writhing neck to prevent the vicious pecks with which it assailed the horse.

As they emerged from the shadowy wood upon the sunny highway, the knight looked down into the happy little face lying upon his bosom, at the hissing, struggling bird, and asked himself, "What would my good wife the Empress Matilda say could she see me in this plight?"

To six-year-old Babette everything in the world was still so new that nothing was surprising; so it was only a part of the beautiful story, and no marvel, to discover that her kind playfellow was no other than the Count of Anjou himself, and the great castle his home.

On their arrival, the gray goose—in spite of indignant quacks and hisses—was crowded into a huge basket with a bountiful supply of corn and a pan of water, and Babette was sent to Dame Agnes, wife of the castellan, with a request that the little peasant should be made ready to sit with the count at the dinner that would soon be served.

When the child was led into the great hall at the dinner hour, her face shone from the scrubbing it had received, her wind-blown hair hung in smooth braids, drawn forward over each shoulder. Here the improvements ceased. There were no children in the castle whose clothes could be lent to Babette, no shoes small enough for her feet; so since wooden shoes were quite out of the question, she pattered across the pavement of the hall on bare feet, whose little pink toes showed beneath the scant gown that Dame Agnes had tried her best, but in vain, to lengthen.

"May I have these things?" Babette asked, looking with wide eyes of wonder at the dainty food that was placed before her. The count nodded assent. Selecting a roll of wheaten bread and a small meat-pie, she prepared to crowd them into the bosom of her dress. "I will take them to my mother," she said, with a happy smile.

"Eat them, little one," said the count, "and thou shalt have more to take to thy mother"; and the roll and the pie were set down again upon the table.

"Thou must have something to take home for thyself," said the count; and, unclasping a chain of gold from his neck, he threw it about the child's shoulders. "It is my marriage gift to thee," he said; "and mayst thou find a good lad for a husband."

"Nay," Babette protested; "I shall not marry a boy! I like not boys. They are rough and pull my hair. If I must marry, I

After dinner Count Geoffrey led the prattling child all through the castle.

shall marry Michel's Cecile. She is good and gentle, and I love her."

"Possibly thou mayst change thy mind before thou art grown," said the count, smiling.

After dinner Count Geoffrey led the prattling child by the hand all through the castle, even up the narrow, winding stair to the roof of the Black Count's grim tower, from which she saw more of the world than she had ever seen before: the town of Loches, covering the slope of the hill below; the sunny plain, with the silver ribbon of the Indre flowing smoothly northward to join the softer current of the Loire; to the eastward Beaulieu, with its stately abbey and rich farm lands; to the westward the dark forest, stretching almost to Chinon, forty miles away.

"Ah, but it is beautiful—more beautiful than my father told!" exclaimed the child.

"Wouldst thou like to stay here and play with my little lads, when my squire brings them home a week hence?" asked the count.

"Nay," replied Babette. "I like not boys. I had rather play with thee. Thou art as gentle as Cecile, and I love thee"; and she laid her round cheek in the palm of the hand which she held.

"But now I must go home. I drive the geese ill when the sun gets as low as this. My mother will be looking for me."

"It grieves me to let thee go, child," said the count. Instead of leading her down the turret stair, he lifted her in his arms and carried her tenderly down to the castle court. The most trusty of his men-at-arms was called to carry her to her home. The gray goose made the journey in a basket, and there was another basket filled with good things from the castle larder. As the count lifted Babette to the saddle, he said warningly;

"Have a care of thy chain, my child; it is precious. Let thy mother keep it for thee against thy wedding-day. Perchance harm might come to thee, for its sake, shouldst thou wear it in the meadow or the forest. Farewell, little Babette. Thou art a sweet play-fellow."

He stood looking after her, and not until she had waved a last farewell as she passed through the outer gate did he turn back into his somber castle, muttering to himself:

"I would I had a little maid like that!"

As he threw his cap upon a table, his eye fell upon the faded blossoms of the broom that Babette had stuck there. "I will keep my promise to her and wear it," he said; "not alone at the tourney, but always. It shall be my crest. What care I for the rose of misty England! Henceforth my house shall be known as the house of Plantagenet, after *Planta genesta*, the golden blossom of my own sunny Anjou!"

First published in the January 1904 edition of *St. Nicholas Magazine*

The King's Castle in No Man's Land

From "The City of Stories"

BY FRANK M. BICKNELL

ONCE ON A TIME there lived a man named Avaro. He was so mean and miserly that he was heartily despised by all who knew him. None of his neighbors would even speak to him if they chanced to meet him in the street. He had no family, and he lived quite alone. He never asked people to visit him, and it is doubtful whether anybody would have come.

"How dare you sit down in my beautiful shadow?"

One summer day a strange old man with a long beard came trudging down the road. He had journeyed a great distance, and was warm and tired. Noticing that Avaro's house cast a deep shadow, the wayfarer thought it would harm no one if he were to sit down there on the grass to cool and rest himself a bit. But it chanced that Avaro was in an unusually bad temper that day. While counting his money in the morning he had lost a farthing piece. It had slipped between his fingers, and rolled away somewhere into a crack in the floor so that it could not be found. This awful calamity had made the miser as cross as two sticks and sourer than last year's cider. When he saw the stranger seated before his house he rushed out of doors in a great rage.

"You lazy good-for-nothing!" he cried, "get up and begone! How dare you sit down in my beautiful shadow?"

"In what way am I wronging anyone by sitting here?" asked the old man. "Is not the shade free?"

"Free!" screamed Avaro. "My beautiful shade free! Don't you suppose this house cost money? Well, if the house were not here neither would the shade be, therefore the shade also cost money, didn't it? Off with you, vagabond, and never let me catch you about here again, using my costly shadow!"

"Certainly you are the meanest man alive," remarked the traveler, rising and taking up his staff, "and you have used me shabbily; nevertheless I will tell you something that will please you. Next week you will be made king."

The miser opened his eyes and his mouth too, in amazement at this piece of news. But before he could fairly collect his wits to ask any question the old man had gone.

A few days after this the reigning king died suddenly, without leaving any children to succeed him. So, as the people must have a king, a council of twenty of the principal men met to see what should be done. And as it costs a great deal to keep up the dignity and state of a sovereign, it was decided that the wealthiest of the late king's subjects should be the one to succeed him on the throne.

Now it had been supposed that the Goldsmith—who was one of the council of twenty—was the richest man in the kingdom, but as it proved, this was not the case. When the decision was made public, Avaro came forward and presented his claim. Here was a disagreeable surprise to everybody, and particularly to the Goldsmith, his wife, and their pretty daughter, who already had begun to look on themselves as a royal family. Up to that time Avaro had feigned extreme poverty, and indeed it had cost him a severe pang at last to admit that he possessed so much wealth. But the advantages of being king were too great. So he showed beyond a doubt that his title to sovereignty was good, and the council of twenty were forced to accept him as their king.

From the very first no one liked the new ruler, and as time went by he grew more and more unpopular. On coming into power he cut down expenses in every possible way, and resorted to numberless mean and petty tricks by which money was turned into his own pockets. In a few weeks the court became so poor and shabby from Avaro's parsimony that the very rag-pickers were ashamed. Finally the discontent grew to be so great and so widespread that the council of twenty held another meeting—this time to try and devise some means of getting rid of the monarch with whom they had so unluckily burdened themselves. However, Avaro's removal was not to be brought about so easily as had been his elevation to regal power. There was no law against stinginess, and unless he broke some law there could not be found a sufficient excuse for depriving the king of his throne. No one was able to suggest anything, and the council were forced to confess themselves nonplussed.

Among them all no one had racked his brains harder for some way of getting

Avaro deposed than the Goldsmith, and as nothing had come of it he went home in rather an unpleasant state of mind. As soon as he got into the house his wife and daughter eagerly began to question him about the result of the meeting. Of course he was obliged to tell them that all the deliberation had been to no purpose. He had scarcely made the confession when he was startled by a loud, boisterous laugh. Turning quickly about, he strode across the room toward the stove, behind which sat an overgrown, out-at-elbows lad. He was still laughing.

"Bobo, you triple idiot, what are you haw-hawing about? How dare you make fun of your betters, sirrah?" demanded the angry Goldsmith, uplifting his cane to chastise him.

"Master," quoth Bobo, "that is a secret that passes not out of my own keeping!"

"Ho! ho! I couldn't help it," cried the youth, nimbly dodging the stick. "Don't strike me, master. I laughed to think of twenty wise men wearing out their wits over a matter that any fool could have settled in less than five minutes."

"My faith! did ever any one hear the like?" exclaimed the Goldsmith. "Think you, Bobo, that you, who are the biggest fool I know, could help us out of our trouble?"

"That indeed I could," replied Bobo.

"How, good Bobo?"

The youth shut one eye and looked very sly. "Master," quoth he, "that is a secret which passes not out of my own keeping. But I will bring the thing about on a certain condition."

"Pray, what may that certain condition be?" inquired the Goldsmith, in growing amazement.

"That you give me your daughter to wife," answered Bobo coolly.

When she heard these audacious words the Goldsmith's pretty daughter, who was as proud as she was pretty, could hardly believe her ears. That this poor fellow, who was looked on as little better than a simpleton, should dare ask her hand seemed preposterous.

"Upon my word," she exclaimed with flashing eyes, "the booby has gone mad—stark, staring mad—to dream that I would ever wed with such as he!" and with a look of scorn at poor Bobo she left the room.

But her father took the matter more quietly. He wished very much to sit on the throne, and he was unwilling to let pass any chance. As he reasoned, he would run no risk in promising his daughter to Bobo conditionally, for if the youth failed there would be no harm done, and if he succeeded he would have proved himself clever enough to deserve her.

"Do you mean," he demanded, "that you can remove King Avaro from the throne without violence and by lawful methods?"

"Ay," replied the youth; "or, rather, I intend that King Avaro shall remove himself—that is, if you promise me your daughter," he added quickly.

"Very well," returned the Goldsmith, no longer hesitating, "rid us of Avaro and the maiden shall be yours."

SOME WEEKS AFTER these events it became known that the Prince Magnifico, who was traveling about the world for his own amusement, had decided to pay King Avaro's capital a visit. In fact, his royal highness shortly appeared in town and took up his abode in the finest house that money could hire. Magnifico was a fine, handsome young man of free and gay manners, and was good-hearted and generous to a fault. Naturally he took early occasion to pay his respects to the king. The latter received his visitor with seeming graciousness, though all the while he was wishing him at the other end of the earth. He knew that he would be expected to show the prince some attentions during his stay in the city, and he had no mind to pay out good money for what he reckoned as extravagant follies. Instead of offering refreshments to the prince and his attendants, he asked the former to go with him and look at the palace gardens—which would cost nothing—and as for the latter (who, he had no doubt) would have "eaten him out of house and home" if he had but given them the chance, he left them to shift for themselves.

While they were promenading through the garden the king happened to remark, with envious eyes, an unusually large diamond that Magnifico wore in his cap. Seeing that the gem had attracted Avaro's notice, the prince removed it from its place that it might be examined more closely. As he was about to put it in the king's hand, however, a bird suddenly flew down, snatched the glittering stone in its beak, and then disappeared almost in a twinkling. Avaro gave a cry of horror and started forward as if to pursue the thief, but Magnifico said, with a light laugh:

"Let the bauble go; there are enough more like it to be had from the king's castle in No Man's Land."

"Eh?" exclaimed Avaro, pricking up his ears, "and do you hold the key to that wonderful castle?"

"Not I," returned Magnifico, with another laugh. "The door stands wide open to all. When the king of No Man's Land died, many years ago, he left a castle filled with treasures, and anyone may go and help himself."

"Know you how the castle is to be reached?" queried Avaro, eagerly.

"Oh, yes; nothing can be easier to find. It lies within three days' journey from the boundaries of your kingdom. You have only to travel until you come to a strange old man with a long beard, sitting at the entrance to a wood. Bestow upon him a suitable alms, and he will direct you to the king's castle."

Soon the prince took his leave, much to the satisfaction of Avaro, who was in a violent hurry to get hold of the treasures of the king of No Man's Land. Without losing time he gathered a great number of oxen and pack-horses and started out.

A three days' march beyond the confines of his own dominions brought the king to the borders of an immense forest where a strange old man with a long beard was sitting. It was the very same person whom he had formerly driven away from the shade of his house, though Avaro did not know that. The miserly monarch fumbled a while in his pockets for a "suitable alms," and finally, not without much reluctance, he threw a copper toward the old man, and asked to be directed to the king's castle.

The old man looked disdainfully at the coin lying on the ground before him. "Is that all a rich king can afford to give a poor creature who asks charity?" he demanded, severely.

"I do not say I am rich, nor yet a king," answered Avaro, fearing to part with any more of his dearly loved money.

"Indeed! But it is a great train that follows you?"

"The Prince Magnifico is visiting me," replied Avaro, unblushingly.

"Ah," said the old man slowly, "you wish me to think you are not rich, nor a king, and that this train belongs to Prince Magnifico. Very good! So be it!" And his words were accompanied by a look that made Avaro shiver with dread.

But Avaro repeated his request to be shown the way to the king's castle. Whereupon the old man stooped, and, plucking a small plant that grew at his feet, he threw it to Avaro, saying:

"Rub your horse's nose with the juice of that herb; then give him the rein and he will take you where you seek to go. But first let me offer you a piece of advice that you will do well to follow. In the king's castle in No Man's Land is a great hall from which open one hundred doors. Ninety and nine of these you may freely pass through, but beware that you do not so much as lift the latch of the hundredth door, else ill-luck will surely befall you."

Without paying very much heed to the old man's last words Avaro rubbed the herb upon his steed's nostrils, and dropping the reins on his neck rode forward at a quicker pace. In about an hour he came to a clearing, in the midst of which he saw the King's Castle. It was a grand and stately building, but Avaro had no thought of stopping to admire the beauty of its architecture. Galloping into the courtyard he dismounted, and leaving his horse with an attendant, he hurried through the lofty portals into the great hall. There, as the old man had said, were the hundred doors all alike, save that the last bore a placard: "It is forbidden to enter here."

With hands trembling from excitement Avaro pushed open the first of these hundred doors. What a sight then met his gaze! He was on the threshold of a large chamber filled with gold coins shining as if fresh from the mint. For some minutes he stood gloating over this mass of wealth; then he carefully shut that door and opened the next one. This time a room full of magnificent pearls was disclosed to view. After he had feasted his eyes upon them for awhile, he passed on to the third door. When he opened this he was nearly blinded by the luster of a great heap of diamonds, not one of which could have been smaller than a robin's egg. He was now almost beside himself for joy, and without waiting to investigate further, he rushed forth to summon his attendants and set them to work. He was in a feverish hurry to get the treasure into sacks that he might take it away before any one else should come to dispute his right to it.

For nearly a week, day and night, he kept his men at their labors. There was neither sleep nor rest for any one until all the ninety-nine doors had been opened, and the mines of riches that were revealed had been carried out of the castle. The amount that Avaro thus laid hold of was enormous, but if there had been ten times as much he would not have left a farthing's-worth behind.

At last, toward the end of the seventh day, the ninety-nine rooms stood quite empty, and every man and beast was loaded down with as much as he could possibly carry. And now Avaro turned his whole attention to the mysterious hundredth door, for despite the warning of the strange old man—or, rather, because of it—he was irresistibly tempted to penetrate its secret. He suspected that it concealed a treasure far greater than any he had yet seen. The thought of leaving behind anything for others to get was too much for his avaricious soul. He did not long hesitate, but presently raised the latch and pushed open the door.

There was nothing alarming to be seen. Only a flight of stone steps leading downward. He began slowly to descend, and soon found himself in a well-lighted cellar. He glanced about him. The apartment was bare save for a large stone vase that stood in the center of it. Upon the vase was this inscription: "If you would behold a wonder throw a handful of earth into this vase."

Avaro was sure that some enormous treasure was about to be revealed to him, so he scooped up some mold from the cellar floor and dropped it in upon a tiny brown seed that lay in the bottom of the vase. No sooner had he done so than a little green shoot appeared through the earth, and continued to grow even more rapidly than it had begun. In a very short time it had become a tree and had reached the top of the room. Meantime its branches were spreading to such an extent that Avaro realized that the place must be soon quite filled with the foliage. In some alarm he turned and hurried back up the stone steps. Suddenly there came a report as if a cannon had been fired. The trunk of the tree had burst the vase, and now its roots were striking deep into the ground, while its limbs shot upward with renewed vigor. At the same time a curious trembling and shaking motion made itself felt throughout the castle. Breathless with haste and terror, Avaro rushed into the great hall, intending to make his escape to the courtyard, where his

followers were awaiting him. But on reaching the portals, what was his horror to find that the pavements of the courtyard were nearly a hundred feet below him, and—apparently—were still sinking rapidly. In fact the castle was being raised into the air by the marvelous growth of the tree in the cellar. In vain he shrieked frantically for help; he was already far beyond the reach of human hands. Moreover,

The pavements of the courtyard were nearly a hundred feet below him and were still sinking rapidly.

while he was thus being borne aloft there suddenly appeared in the midst of his astonished attendants the strange old man with the long beard. Looking upward, this singular person addressed to Avaro these words, every one of which was distinctly audible:

"You have brought upon yourself your own punishment. Until some one meaner than you are shall come to take your place, you must remain where you are. Now, indeed, *you are not rich, neither are you a king, and your great train belongs to the Prince Magnifico.* He will know how to make a proper use of your ill-gotten gains; you will never see them more."

Whereupon the unhappy miser, now nearly three hundred feet above the earth, saw him ride away, followed by the entire company of men, horses, and oxen.

Thus was Avaro left alone in the empty castle, while the immense treasure of which he had ruthlessly stripped it was carried off before his very eyes. And as it is not likely that a meaner man than he will ever come into this world, probably Avaro remained in the King's Castle in No Man's Land until he died.

In the meantime Prince Magnifico had continued to live at the capital and was becoming very popular there. Soon it became known that his Highness wished to marry and was on the lookout for a suitable bride. Then, of course, there was a great stir among the maidens. One evening Magnifico gave a great ball, to which all the fairest damsels in the kingdom were bidden. Naturally they came, every one, and among them, looking her very prettiest, was the Goldsmith's pretty daughter. To her the Prince showed marked favor from the first, and danced with her as often as his duties to his other guests would permit.

By and by, during a pause in the dancing, Magnifico stepped forward and thus addressed the company:

"My friends, I have called you together this evening for a particular reason. I desire to take a wife; but in a land where all the maidens are so beautiful, how can I decide which to choose? As you see, my position is a delicate one. I should like, therefore, to have the matter settled thus: if there be any maiden here who loves me truly, and whose heart tells her that I love her, let her come and place her hand in mine."

This was a strange and unusual method of procedure, and it caused some wonderment among those assembled. But all eyes were turned expectantly in one direction—toward the Goldsmith's daughter, who, blushing very much, now stepped forth, and hesitatingly approached the Prince. Her embarrassment was great, but it was soon to be far greater, for when she stretched out her hand to lay it in that of Magnifico, the latter drew back haughtily and said, with a meaning look:

"Upon my word, the girl must have gone mad to think a king would condescend to"—but at that very moment a messenger rushed into the ball-room with the news that a large train of oxen and pack-horses had just arrived, bringing an enormous amount of wealth for Prince Magnifico. And there also appeared a strange old man with a long beard, whom the Prince received with a tender embrace.

"Good people," cried this last comer, addressing the astonished assemblage, "in Prince Magnifico behold your lawful sovereign, the long-lost son of your former

Magnifico drew back haughtily.

king!—now most happily restored to you. As for Avaro, he will return no more. Greet, therefore, your rightful lord."

At this revelation everybody was wild with delight. The air was filled with the sounds of rejoicing, and the entire country soon was ringing with shouts of "Long live King Magnifico!"

But what about the Goldsmith's daughter? Well, the young King promptly told her that he loved her very much; they were happily married, and dwelt together in perfect accord to the end of their lives.

So, although the Goldsmith did not get to be king, he lived to be the father of a queen, which certainly is something of an honor.

First published in the November 1896 edition of *St. Nicholas Magazine*

Hop Wing and the Missing Treasure

From "The City of Stories"

BY FRANK M. BICKNELL

DURING A CERTAIN reign in the Shin dynasty, a governor named Queng-te ruled over one of the Eastern Provinces. Governor Queng-te was a very clever fellow, and what is more, he knew it, and what is more yet, he wanted every one else to know it. One morning he felt so especially well pleased with himself that he issued a proclamation to this effect: to any person who should ask him a question that he could not answer correctly, he promised that there should be paid a reward of a hundred strings of cash.

This offer remained in force a whole year; but as Queng-te never had the least trouble in replying to the questions put to him, the money remained in his treasury. At the beginning of the second year he increased the amount offered to one thousand taels; and it seemed as if he might have promised a great deal more than that with perfect safety, for another twelve-months went by, and still no one was sharp enough to win the reward.

At this period there lived in one of the districts of the province a worthy scholar whose name was Hop Wing. He was a youth of good sense and great promise, having already passed his first examination with honor, and received his bachelor's degree. But, unfortunately, he was very poor, and was forced to eke out a living by acting as secretary to the magistrate of the district—a man by the name of How-fu. This official was far from being a kind master; and Mr. Wing was obliged to work hard for miserably small pay. Moreover, although How-fu was niggardly enough with his money, he was quite the reverse with his fault-finding and abuse. Whenever he had a chance he would berate his poor secretary roundly, often for the most trifling cause, and sometimes for no cause whatever. The truth is that only by the merest good luck had How-fu passed through his examination and secured his present position, for which in reality he was not at all a fit person; and, knowing that Mr. Wing was a young man of merit and well liked in the district, he was jealous of him, and wanted to keep him crowded back in obscurity. In fact, he would not have been sorry for a chance to put him out of the way altogether.

One day How-fu came to his secretary in a towering rage. He declared he had just missed from his treasury a bag containing the sum of one thousand taels. It had been in a certain place the night before, and now it was gone. No one but Mr. Wing knew where it had been put, consequently, it being no longer there, he must have stolen it.

On hearing this charge the poor secretary was thunderstruck; but as soon as he could find his voice he protested his innocence vehemently. To what purpose? His words were merely wasted breath. The magistrate would not listen, and would hardly allow him an opportunity to speak at all.

"You thieving rascal!" he cried; "restore the treasure you have stolen, or you shall lose your head. I give you twenty-four hours to decide whether you will surrender the one or the other."

"Alas! how am I to restore that which I have not?" exclaimed the unfortunate Mr. Wing. "I know no more where your money is than does a child just born."

"Oh! then since you have forgotten where you have hidden it," sneered his master, "why do you not go and ask our wise governor about it? No doubt His Excellency will tell you at once where it is; or even should he be unable to do so, he will present you, according to his promise, with the sum of one thousand taels. So in either case you will be in a position to make good what you have taken from me."

Although it grieved him sorely to be charged with a crime he had not committed, nevertheless, seeing that he could not prove his innocence, Mr. Wing found some comfort in these last words of his cruel master. There seemed to lie a way out of the difficulty that was well worth considering.

"Grant me the time to go to the capital and see the governor, and I will do what I can to save my head," said he.

"I give you a week's grace," replied the magistrate. "At the end of that time I must have either my taels or your worthless head. So remember," he added grimly, "it is *head or taels* with you."

The wicked How-fu could afford to joke, for he was very well aware—none better—where the missing bag lay; and as he was quite sure Governor Queng-te could not know anything about the matter, he confidently expected Hop Wing to bring back a thousand taels, which he would then add to his already large hoard.

The next day, accompanied by a guard imposed upon him by How-fu, the unhappy secretary started on his journey up to the capital city of the province. After three days he arrived there safely, and was hastening to present himself before the wise Queng-te, when a startling piece of news came to his ears. It seemed that on that very morning the governor, who now began to look on himself as the cleverest person in the empire, had again amended his proclamation so as to make it stand in effect as follows:

"Whoever shall ask His Excellency a question to which he cannot at once give the correct answer, shall be made a magistrate when the next vacancy shall occur in the province; but whoever shall try to do this, and shall fail, shall lose his head."

Certainly here was a great change in the state of affairs. As the case now rested, unhappy Mr. Wing's life was worth little indeed. Suppose he should ask Queng-te about the lost treasure, what would be the result? Either the governor could tell him where it was, and he must lose his head because his question would have been answered, or he could not tell him, and he must lose his head because he would have failed to restore the one thousand taels to his master. Thus, in either event, his head would shortly be where the treasure seemed to be—that is to say, *missing.* Is it strange, under the circumstances, that the luckless Mr. Wing knew not what to do? What could he do? Fate had put before him a puzzle that he could not solve to save his life. One thing, however, was certain: he was no longer in a hurry to call on Governor Queng-te, for now nothing was to be gained by such a step, and everything was to be lost.

Filled with despondency, he betook himself to an inn, where he hoped to get a much needed night's rest, for his long journey had greatly fatigued him. But his mind was too full of his troubles to permit of his sleeping, and so, after tossing restlessly for some hours, he resolved to go out and get a breath of fresh air. Accordingly, he stepped carefully over his guard, who lay soundly sleeping by the door, and presently found his way to the street. Then he began to walk, and he walked so far that finally he came into a new part of the city, where he saw a number of people entering a gateway that led into a large private garden. As he stood looking on, he heard that it was a wedding party, and among the guests he recognized his pretty cousin whose name was Ning Woo. She asked him if he would like to attend the wedding. On his accepting her invitation, she conducted him through this gateway and into the house. After having passed through several fine rooms, they came into one that was larger and more magnificent than any Mr. Wing had seen hitherto. Here was gathered a numerous company of ladies and gentlemen, all of whom appeared to be persons of consequence. Presently the bride entered the apartment, attended by a

She conducted him through this gateway and into the house.

dozen or more young girls, among whom was Miss Ning Woo. The groom being already there, the party now sat down to the wedding-feast, at which the most exquisite meats and wines were served. The guests were in the liveliest spirits, as was quite natural, and merry jests and ripples of laughter were frequently heard, though all the while perfect good-breeding and decorum were maintained.

By and by boiling water was brought in, and fragrant tea was handed about in cups of finest porcelain. Then a number of the young men and young girls arose, and, taking position on the floor, entertained the company by dancing several pleasing figures to the music of flageolets. Each dancer carried a gauze lantern in the shape of a water-lily or some other beautiful flower, and at the close of their dance each in a graceful manner offered a pretty little gift to some one of the spectators. Nobody was forgotten in the distribution: Mr. Wing received a piece of sky-blue silk of fine texture, on which a picture had been painted. This was presented to him by his cousin, Miss Ning.

"I beg you will do me the honor to accept this," said she, with a charming smile. "It is of my own handiwork. If you will hang it on the wall in your room tonight, I hope it may bring you good luck."

In due time, all the festivities being over, the assemblage broke up, and Mr. Wing was shown to the room where he was to pass the remainder of the night. There, recalling the advice of Miss Ning, he hung the little painting on the wall. Then he lay down upon a sleeping-mat, and, forgetting all his tribulations, at once fell into a sound slumber.

After a while he suddenly awoke, and at the same instant his eyes fixed themselves on Miss Ning's gift. Strange to relate, the picture was growing larger. Indeed, it grew so rapidly that in a few moments it covered entirely the wall where it had been hung. In it were several human figures, now of life-size. One of them—that of an old priest—presently stepped out from its place, and thus addressed the astonished Mr. Wing:

"My son, I come to you in this manner that I may do you a service. I know of your difficulties, and I can put you in a way to extricate yourself from them. I have a brother who is far wiser and more powerful than I, and it is to him that I shall send you for aid. You cannot reach him without some peril, for there are always wicked demons abroad who try to prevent good actions from being done. However, if you will follow my instructions, you will escape with nothing worse than a bad fright. Take this wooden sword, and use it freely in defending yourself. If you should be too sorely pressed, call upon my brother, Ten Shun by name, and he will send you relief."

Having spoken these words, the aged priest returned to the wall, and became again a part of the painting, which then quickly shrank to its original size.

While Mr. Wing was regretting that he had not asked the old gentleman how

With his magic sword he hewed and hacked at the dragon's claws.

he was to find his brother, he heard the watchman in the street beating midnight on his wooden gong. This sound had hardly died away when there came a crashing of glass, and then a small bird, looking much like a bat, flew into the room, and settled down to the floor. It had no sooner alighted than it began to increase in size until, much to Mr. Wing's alarm, it had become a full-fledged dragon, and began to vomit forth flame and smoke in a frightful manner. The fierce creature rushed upon the young man as if bent on his destruction, but the latter instinctively raised his wooden sword and warded off the attack. Finding itself thus baffled, the dragon retreated for a moment, then suddenly dashed down, and seizing Mr. Wing in its claws, flew away, carrying off a part of the house-roof on its back as it did so.

Although considerably frightened, the young man did not lose all his courage. With his magic sword he hewed and hacked at the dragon's claws so vigorously that the creature shortly was forced to drop him to the ground. As soon as he touched earth he put his legs to good use by running away with all his might. Thereupon his enemy changed itself into a huge demon with four heads and eight legs, and started in hot pursuit. By dint of great exertion Mr. Wing succeeded in keeping the lead until he came to a river, which he was much puzzled to know how to cross. As the demon was close upon him, he had no other resort than to pronounce the name of Ten Shun, which he did in a loud voice. Immediately he was changed into a stone, and at the same moment his own shadow appeared on the opposite bank of the river. The demon, arriving on the spot, saw the shadow and stupidly mistook it for the reality. Uttering a howl of rage, he caught up the stone that *was* Hop Wing and cast it across the river after the shadow that *was not* Hop Wing. Thus did the young man reach the other bank, and once there, he was restored to his natural form. But the demon was not easily baffled. When he saw his intended victim making off, he changed himself into a dry leaf and was blown over the river after him. Alighting, he turned back into a demon and continued the chase. Mr. Wing now plunged into a dense wood, but ere long, being hard pressed, he again called upon Ten Shun for assistance. His call was answered, and he became a thick mist which so obscured everything in the forest that for a few moments the demon was quite nonplussed to think where his prey could have escaped to. But he was by no means at the end of his resources yet. He changed himself into a roaring fire, and soon entirely dried up the mist. As Mr. Wing, in the form of vapor, rose toward the clouds he was transformed into a kite shaped like a dragon and really quite horrible to look upon. His enemy was nothing daunted, however, for he quickly grasped the string and pulled it in until he had the kite fast in his clutches.

When Mr. Wing came back to his natural form, what was his alarm to find that the demon had hung him from the bough of a tree by a stout cord which was tied securely about his neck! Yet, strange to say, although he was dangling helplessly with his feet at some distance from the ground, the knot did not choke him or cause him any serious discomfort. Still the position was far from being pleasant, and so now for the third time he pronounced the name of Ten Shun. No immediate response came, but as soon as the demon—who evidently thought he had made an end of Hop Wing—had disappeared among the trees, the rope began of itself to lengthen, so that in a few moments the young man was standing on firm earth once more. A touch of the wooden sword released him from his hempen necktie, and he was again free. Just then he suddenly became aware that a venerable man stood before him.

"Hop Wing," said this person, "you have called me, and I am here. You are in trouble, and as I think you deserving of aid, I shall help you."

Whereupon the old man, who was no other than Ten Shun, took from his girdle a small bamboo pipe and blew into it gently. In a moment a pill not much larger than a grain of rice dropped out. This he presented to Hop Wing, saying:

"Swallow this, and by its virtue knowledge shall be yours that will take you safely through all difficulties and dangers."

Mr. Wing put the pill into his mouth, when straightway it seemed to slip down his throat of its own accord. Immediately all his cares and perplexities vanished; and when he turned to thank the old priest he had vanished also. Nor were these the only strange things that came to pass; for all of a sudden Mr. Wing seemed to awake as if from a dream, and on rubbing his eyes he perceived that he had been lying upon the hard ground on a hillside near a large fox-hole. Then he knew he had fallen in with some fox-people, one of whom had assumed the form

The old man took from his girdle a small bamboo pipe, and blew into it gently.

of his cousin, and that they had befriended him (in Chinese lore, foxes have the power of taking human shape at will, and are supernaturally gifted to work enchantments for the good or evil of ordinary mortals, as may suit their purposes).

Thanks to the priest's pill, Mr. Wing now could see his course laid out before him plainly. With a light heart he made his way back to the inn, where he found his guard in a sad fright over his supposed escape.

Having refreshed himself with some breakfast, he confidently set out to seek an audience with the governor, who received him without too much delay. To him he made known the story of the missing treasure, and having done so, he concluded his address in these words:

"Your Excellency will realize therefore that I am in a most awkward dilemma. What I desire to ask is this—and I doubt not your Excellency will be able to give me a correct answer to my question: How am I to get out of my difficulty and yet save my life?"

For the first time since issuing his famous proclamation Queng-te hesitated to reply to a questioner. In truth he was as much puzzled to save his credit as had been Hop Wing the day before to save his life. According to the terms of the proclamation, every questioner whom he answered correctly must forfeit his head, but in this case if the questioner lost his head, then his question would not have been correctly answered. Here was a state of things which, with all his cleverness, the governor had not foreseen. What reply should he make to Mr. Wing's query? The more he cogitated over this matter the more bewildering did it become. Finally, quite at a loss for what else to do, he took refuge in an evasion. Assuming an air of great dignity and unutterable wisdom, he said:

"Young man, your undeserved misfortunes touch me deeply; and as I should be loath to add to them by depriving you of your life, I shall consider your question as not asked. I strongly suspect that Magistrate How-fu has treated you with unmerited rigor, and I shall have his affairs looked into at once. Meanwhile, you will remain under my especial protection."

On investigation it was proved not only that How-fu had hidden away the bag of one thousand taels which he had accused his secretary of stealing, but that he had embezzled funds to a large amount. Accordingly he was put to death as a punishment for his wrong-doings; and Mr. Wing, who was quite worthy of the honor, was appointed to the vacant place. And thus was kept Governor Queng-te's promise that whoever succeeded in puzzling him should be made a magistrate to fill the first vacancy.

First published in the January 1897 edition of *St. Nicholas Magazine*

Jack Dilloway's Scheme

BY JEFFERSON LEE HARBOUR

ONE DAY, WHEN I was a boy, Jack Dilloway came over to our house with some-thing he called a "scheme."

Jack's schemes were always of a kind calculated to contribute to Jack's enjoy-ment of life. His parents sometimes said regretfully that about all Jack thought of was "a good time." But now that they are old people with Jack's children calling them "Grandpa" and "Grandma," it must be pleasant for them—and for Jack, too—to remember that Jack's pursuit of boyish enjoyment never led him into doing anything cruel, or malicious, or wicked.

Everybody liked Jack, mischievous little tike though he was. His love of fun manifested itself strongly in a pair of big, twinkling blue eyes, and a mouth with lips parted in an almost perpetual smile, showing two rows of uneven teeth.

His face was as freckled as a turkey's egg, and he had curly brown hair that he seldom "had time" to keep in order. He lived on a farm divided from the farm on which I lived only by what we called the "big road," although it was but an ordi-nary highway.

The Dilloway farm-house was within three hundred yards of my father's house, and Jack and I were much together. I was but four days older than Jack, and we were fourteen years old at the time of which I write.

I, too, had a boyish love of fun, but I was less imaginative than Jack, and less fertile in "schemes" for having "no end of fun," as Jack said.

"I'll tell you what we'll do," said Jack, his blue eyes twinkling in pleased antic-ipation, "and it'll be jolly good fun. See if you don't say so. Did you know that there was going to be a big circus in town on the fourteenth?"

"No; really?"

"Yes, sir; honest. Our hired man has just come from town, and he saw them putting up the bills. He says it looks as though it'll be a mighty big thing if they do even half they've got down on the bills. They're going to have *two rings!*"

"*Two* rings?"

"Yes, sir; and somethin' going on in both of 'em all the time. Won't that be great?"

"I should say so. But what's that got to do with your scheme?"

"Everything. If it wasn't for the circus I wouldn't have thought of the scheme. You're going to the circus?"

Of course I was. Every farmer's boy in that neighborhood would be at the circus. It meant more than even the Fourth of July to us. The moment Jack said "circus," I thought, with great satisfaction, of the two dollars and a half I had that day received for a calf I had sold, and I said:

"Of course, if there's a circus, I'm *going* to it."

"So am I," said Jack, promptly. "What do you say to our making a little money out of it?"

"How?"

"Easy as rolling off a log. Have you ever heard of anybody keeping a refreshment-stand at a circus?"

"Of course I have."

"What's to hinder two smart fellows like Jack Dilloway and Ned Dawson from setting up in a little business of that sort?"

"Is that your scheme?"

"That's my scheme."

He waited a moment for me to realize the full magnitude of it before he added:

"I believe we could do very well with a little scheme of that sort, Ned. And it would be great fun, too. Then it would be jolly to have just all the lem'nade and gingerbread and peanuts and things of that sort we wanted to eat; wouldn't it?"

"We'd have to have a pretty big stock if we ate all we wanted, and had anything left to sell," I said. "But how could we go to the circus and keep a refreshment-stand at the same time?"

"Why, we could go to the circus at night. It's much better at night, anyhow. And refreshment-stands never do much business in the evening at a circus. We'd be all sold out by six o'clock. I just believe we could make a big thing out of it."

I was of a less sanguine temperament than Jack; nevertheless his "scheme" pleased me. We sat down on a log of wood in my father's stable-yard to "talk the thing over," and our enthusiasm increased as we talked. Jack brought out a stub of lead pencil, and "figured the whole thing up" on a new pine shingle.

He made it appear that his little scheme would net each of us as much as ten or twelve dollars—

"To say nothing of the fun we'll get out of it," he added. "I'll yell out, 'Lem'nade! here you are, ladies and gentlemen! *ice*-cold lem'nade, *right* here in the shade, and *only* five cents a glass! Walk up, chalk up, any way to *get* up, ladies and gentlemen! A piece of ice in every glass! *This* way for your ice-cold lem'nade at five cents a glass!'"

Jack stood up on the log, and screeched this out so vigorously that my mother put her head out of our kitchen window and said:

"Why, Jack, are you going crazy? Why are you making all that noise?"

"Oh, Ned and I are going into bizness, and we're just practicin' up for it," replied Jack.

"Are you going to start out as auctioneers? I can think of no other business requiring such lung capacity as you are exhibiting."

Our parents finally gave their consent to the carrying out of Jack's little scheme, and we were in great glee.

I had almost five dollars in my little tin bank, and Jack had about the same amount.

We invested that morning in lemons, sugar, peanuts, and a box of peppermint-candy kisses with very affectionate sentences on them in pink letters. We knew that this kind of candy was in great demand at a circus.

My mother was kind enough to make us a lot of nice gingerbread, and Jack's mother made us a great panful of tempting-looking sugar cookies with a plump raisin in the center of each.

Then we had what we did not see on any of the other refreshment-stands, and that was great pyramids of beautiful red June apples that we had polished until they looked like glass.

Apples of this kind were very scarce in our neighborhood that year, and Jack's father was the only man we knew of who had any. He had two trees hanging full of them, and he had given us a whole bushel on condition that Jack and I should weed out a certain onion-patch of his.

We had gladly agreed to do this, and the first new apples of the summer graced our refreshment-stand.

We had gone to the grounds the day before the circus and put up our stand in what we felt sure would be a good place; and we were there early the next morning covering our counter with clean table-cloths, and arranging our stock in trade.

The pretty red apples we arranged in three pyramids, one at each end and one in the center of the table. The peanuts we put into little brown-paper bags, and the candy we displayed in two glass fruit-dishes borrowed from our mothers' pantries.

The glasses for the lemonade also came from our home pantries. We set them out in a shining row in front of our counter. At the suggestion of my mother we had put two big bouquets of wild flowers between the pyramids of apples, and Jack told the truth when he stepped back, with arms akimbo and head twisted to one side, surveying the complete result of our labor, and said:

"I tell you, Ned, it just looks sniptious! There isn't a neater-looking stand on the circus grounds. Those apples will sell like hot cakes. You know how fond everybody is of the first new apples that come out. I'm glad red 'Junes' are so scarce this year. I believe we'd better sell them three for five cents instead of four. I tell you those bouquets are the finishing touch, aren't they?"

"There won't be a thing left in two minutes!"

"They do set off the counter," I replied. "I shouldn't wonder if they helped to draw trade."

"If they don't, the way I'm going to call out by and by will."

This was very early in the day, even before the tents had been raised, although the circus wagons had arrived and the circus men were hard at work on the two rings, and getting the great tents ready to be put up.

But every boy in Gastonville and from a great part of the surrounding country seemed to be on the circus grounds.

There was no railroad in the town, and many of the boys had walked three or four miles into the country to meet the circus as it came from the next town in its own wagons.

We knew many of the boys, and they began to manifest great friendship for us when they discovered that we were keeping a refreshment-stand. They assembled in front of our counter with cordial greetings of friendship, such as—

"Hello, Ned!" "Hello, Jack!" "How're you, Ned?" "How goes it, Jack?"

We replied respectfully but a little coldly to these cordial salutations, for when we saw the boys approaching, Jack said in a low tone to me:

"I'll tell you what it is, Ned, bizness is one thing and friendship's another, and we've got to run this stand on strictly bizness principles, or fail up before noon."

I appreciated the good sense of this remark, and I said:

"That's a fact, Jack. If we treat one we've got to treat another."

"That's it," replied Jack, heartily. "We'd soon be at the bottom of our lem'nade bar'l, and have no money to show for it. We'll just have to let the boys know from the start that we mean *bizness*."

When we made this apparent to our youthful friends, they suddenly grew cold in their demeanor, and withdrew one by one after making unpleasant remarks about our lack of generosity, some of the boys going so far as to say that they felt quite sure that we would charge our own *grandmothers* for even *looking* at our "old lemonade"; and they further added that our lemonade looked "very second class," anyhow—to all of which we replied by saying briefly but decidedly: "Bizness is bizness, boys."

We did not expect to do much business until after the "grand street parade" at ten o'clock. The streets of the town were lined with people who would come out to the circus grounds after the parade, and then the real business of the day would begin for us.

We would be compelled to miss the joy of following the procession through the town, but we congratulated ourselves that our stand was so located that we could witness the starting and the return of the parade.

Two enormous elephants, caparisoned with a great display of crimson velvet and trappings of gold and silver tinsel, were to lead the procession. A silken canopy, upheld by rods of gold, rose high above the cushioned back of each elephant, and under these canopies were to ride "a bevy of brilliantly beautiful Circassian maidens," as the flaming posters on the fences said.

The elephants had been arrayed in their gorgeous trappings, but the "brilliantly beautiful" ladies had not appeared when the elephants were led out to a spot directly in front of our stand to wait until the rest of the procession was made up.

The keeper of the elephants, arrayed in gorgeous but not very clean Oriental finery, led the two huge animals out to within ten feet of our stand, and then returned to the tent for something, after cautioning two or three hundred wildly excited boys to "just let those elephants alone."

But the boys, heedless of this command, threw peanuts and candy to the elephants, and suddenly Jack said:

"I'm going to toss them one of these apples, and see how they like it."

They liked the apples very well—alas, too well! After tasting the apples they paid no heed to the nuts and candy offered them, but kept their little black eyes fixed on our apples while the one nearest us reached his long proboscis out for more.

Jack gave him one, which he swung lightly into his trunk, and then, to our horror and unspeakable amazement, he and his mate stepped forward as our first patrons and greedily began devouring our stock, without even the courtesy of asking the price of anything.

"Get out of here!" shrieked Jack, jumping up and down in his wrath and dismay behind the counter. "Go away! Clear out of this! Let those apples *alone!* Let those cakes *be!*"

"Run for the keeper!" I shrieked. "There won't be a thing left in two minutes! Get out of this!"

But the great beasts did not "get out"; and although Jack and I fumed and threatened, we were both afraid to go near the animals, and there they stood rapidly stowing away everything on the stand, while the crowd of unsympathetic small boys yelled and screeched with excitement.

Finally I ran toward the tent in search of the keeper, whom I met coming out of the dressing-room.

"Your old elephants are eating up our refreshment-stand!" I shrieked excitedly. "Come and get them away—quick! Hurry up, or there won't be a thing left!"

The keeper quickened his pace, and just as we reached the stand Jack threw up his hands despairingly and said:

"Great Scott, Ned! one of 'em has run his horrid old proboscis clear to the bottom of our lemonade-barrel! And *look* at that stand! Is there *anything* left? I could *fight*, I'm so mad! Just *look* at that stand!"

There wasn't much but the stand left for me to look at. A single ginger-cake and three or four cookies were all we had left, while many of the apples had disappeared. One of the elephants, grabbing greedily at a loaf of ginger-bread after the arrival of the keeper, caught a fold of the table-cloth in his proboscis, and thus cleared the stand of everything on it, the glassware coming to the ground with a crash.

"Somebody's got to pay for this!" said Jack, with a suggestion of a sob in his voice that one could forgive even in a boy of fifteen under the circumstances.

"It isn't my fault," said the keeper of the elephants, carelessly.

"Whose fault is it, then?" I asked indignantly. "If you'd stayed with the elephants, you could have kept them away from our stand!"

There were hot tears on my cheeks as I spoke, but they made no impression on the keeper. He led the elephants away from our stand, and ten minutes later the procession started, leaving Jack and me amid the ruins of our stock in trade.

WE HAVE LAUGHED a great deal over the affair since, but we didn't laugh any at the time. There were tears in our eyes, our lips quivered, and we choked back our sobs as we went about gathering up an apple here, a bag of peanuts there, and the few whole pieces of glassware we had left.

"We might as well pack up our things and go home," said Jack.

In the midst of our grief a stout, elderly man, with a black-velvet vest and an enormous gold watch-chain with a big red seal dangling from it, came along, and eyed us and our stand curiously for a moment.

"What's the matter here?" he said as he came up and leaned on our counter.

"Everything's the matter!" said Jack, tearfully. "Here we put over ten dollars into things for a refreshment-stand, besides all our folks gave us, and the old circus elephants came along and ate up almost everything and smashed up the rest! They even spoiled our barrel of lemonade, and we haven't even got money enough to go into the circus!"

"You say that the elephants did this? Where was their keeper at the time?"

"He left them here in the road while he went back to the tent for something, and they marched right up here, and ruined everything," said Jack, his wrath shining in his tear-dimmed eyes.

The man asked us some more questions, and the proprietor of a rival stand across the road came over and corroborated all we had said.

Then the man took a lead pencil and an envelope from his pocket, and made a fair estimate of the value of our stock and of the broken glassware.

"It amounts to about fourteen dollars," he said. "I suppose you would be willing to accept that and a couple of tickets to the circus as payment in full for the damage done?"

"Well, I *guess* we would!" said Jack.

And the next moment we were staring in open-mouthed amazement at a little pile of bills and two thick yellow tickets lying on our counter, while the man was walking back toward the circus-tent.

"Well, if he isn't a trump!" said Jack, bringing his fist down heavily on the counter.

"He is that!" I said heartily.

"Isn't this *great!*" Jack said, as he reached out for the money. "Seven dollars and a circus-ticket apiece! Hoor*a*y, Neddy, my boy! I just tell you, Ned, we were born in the lucky time of the moon!"

"You didn't think so ten minutes ago."

"Well, I *know* so now; I just wonder who he is."

We found out that afternoon, as we sat in one of the best seats witnessing the "grand entry" in the crowded circus-tent; for at that time the man who had made good our loss rode once or twice around the ring in an elegant landau. He nodded his head toward Jack and me when he saw us staring at him with open eyes and mouths, and we heard a man behind us say to his wife:

"That man in the carriage is the owner of the whole thing."

First published in the November 1892 edition of *St. Nicholas Magazine*

The Temptation of Wilfred Malachey

BY WILLIAM F. BUCKLEY JR.

WHEN WILFRED MALACHEY was sent off to boarding school at Brookfield, he went by train. The Malacheys had been forced to sell the family automobile when his father's most recent manuscript was rejected. The publishers, Hatfield & Hatfield, had told him it wouldn't sell, because "Nobody wants to read about the Vietnam war." It had been four years since his father had sold a book. Six months before the fall term at Brookfield Academy began, the family had to move from Manhattan to a two-room apartment in Queens.

One night, Wilfred overheard his mother and father talking about Brookfield. His father said: "I don't care if I go into debt for the rest of my life, Will is going to Brookfield. Period!" When Wilfred's father spoke that way (sometimes he banged his fist on the table, but only after a couple of beers) there was nothing to be done about it, and Mrs. Malachey would simply shrug her shoulders and change the subject.

On the train, Wilfred's mother told him they could send him only five dollars every month. Wilfred said that five dollars wouldn't keep him in chewing gum.

"In that case, Wilfred, you're going to have to cut down on your chewing gum," his mother snapped.

Wilfred said—to himself: his mother did not take any lip from Wilfred—that he would find other ways to live the way the Brookfield boys lived. "If at Brookfield they're human," Wilfred muttered. "Which I doubt." He was feeling grouchy, and a little nervous, going to Brookfield for the first time.

THE BROOKFIELD COMMUNITY was aware that things had gone badly for the school during recent years. Everything went wrong that could go wrong: the pipes had burst in the main building; the large barn that housed the student activities center had burned almost to the ground (of course, the school was underinsured); the new tractor with which the vegetable gardens and the corn were tended during the sum-

mer had suddenly ceased to work, and by the time it was fixed the damage to the gardens and fields was irreversible. "The place seems haunted," said Xavier Prum, Headmaster.

Brookfield was well north in Vermont, so that the winters came early, and Wilfred was happy at his first opportunity to learn ice-skating. One day, with some excitement after the first snowfall, he signed up on the bulletin board to ski. The athletic director, Mr. Kiphuth, handed an application form to Wilfred and asked him to sign a slip authorizing one hundred dollars to be charged to his parents.

Wilfred looked up. He lowered the pencil onto the table. "I think," he said to Mr. Kiphuth, "I'll just stick to skating." Mr. Kiphuth looked at Wilfred and said nothing. That night, at faculty tea, Mr. Kiphuth asked the Headmaster whether young Malachey's family was especially hard up. Xavier Prum answered, "If you ask me, Bob Malachey is flat broke. He's a has-been as a writer."

"How's he paying for Wilfred's tuition?"

"I'll tell you after he makes the payment for the rest of the semester. All I have from him"—and this was near to Thanksgiving—"is his deposit of last July. Either the remaining tuition comes in before Christmas, or Wilfred will have to do his ice-skating in Queens. We just aren't in a position to extend charity."

Kiphuth said that was too bad. "A bright boy. George Eggleston tells me he's a whiz in computers."

"Well, maybe Malachey will invent a computer game and bail out his old man," the Headmaster said, picking up the *Brookfield Academy News* to read about last month's hockey victory over St. Paul's.

It was about then that Wilfred Malachey decided to take up seriously the matter of his personal poverty. He thought a great deal about it and carefully studied the habits of his fellow students, most of whom clearly were not worried about expenses. Josiah Regnery, for instance. Josiah received a monthly allowance of one hundred dollars from his father and often took two or three boys to the Creamery, the local drugstore, for ice cream sundaes.

Josiah was a chubby, good-natured boy who was easily distracted. When Mr. Eggleston was trying to teach him geometry, Josiah would simply stare into space. One afternoon, when the trees all around them were red and gold, he told Wilfred as they were skating that he was quite apprehensive about the math exam coming up at midterm. "To tell you the truth, Wilfred, I don't know the difference between an issasseles triangle and an equilateral triangle."

Wilfred smiled as he maneuvered the puck they were idling with along the ice. "What's so hard about remembering that an equilateral triangle is equal—get that, equi? equal?—on all three sides?"

"Okay," Josiah said. "But what about the issasselese triangle? What's that?"

Wilfred took Josiah's hockey stick from him and laid it out on the ice, positioning his own so that the handle touched Josiah's at an angle of about forty-five degrees. "There. Our two sticks are the same size, the two sides of an isosceles—that's i-s-o-s-c-e-l-e-s—triangle are the same size. What's so hard about that?"

"What's hard," said Josiah, "is to remember it all. All I can remember is that there'll be time after practice and before study hall to go to the Creamery for a butterscotch sundae. What do you say?"

"I'm broke right now."

"I'll pay. You teach me about triangles, you get one butterscotch sundae."

"You know," Josiah said as they sat in the little booth, the light snowfall breaking up the bright afternoon sun, "I think I could figure out a way for you to take my midterm exam. It's just this simple . . ."

Josiah had, in fact, figured it all out.

There were no fixed seating arrangements in the classrooms where exams were held at Brookfield. All that would be needed was for Wilfred to manage to sit down, casually, at a desk next to Josiah's. Wilfred, Josiah explained, would then write down the answers to each of the exam problems on a sheet of scratch paper. Then he would spill his scratch pad on the floor, having detached the top sheet from the pad before it was dropped. He would then simply bend over and pick up the scratch pad, leaving the detached sheet on the floor.

A moment later, Josiah would lean down, pick up the sheet with the answers on it and copy Wilfred's solutions in his own exam book.

"It's worth twenty dollars to me," Josiah said, intending to close the question.

Somewhat to his surprise—cheating was simply not one of the things the Malachey set thought it quite right to do—Wilfred hesitated. Cheating was one of the things one, well, one wasn't supposed to do. On the other hand, one was not supposed to be—how did his father put it?—"one's brother's keeper." He wrestled with the conflict, but eased toward the feeling that, after all, he wasn't personally responsible for other boys' behavior. "Okay," he said.

THAT NIGHT, LYING on his bed after Lights Out, Wilfred chatted with his roommate, Steven Umanov. Steve was a quiet, studious, no-nonsense boy. His parents had come to America from Russia soon after the World War. Steve's father was a nuclear physicist who worked for the Defense Department. Steve took great pride in this. He confessed to Wilfred that he, too, hoped to become a great scientist, "Like my dad." Wilfred was feeling argumentative and maybe a little disillusioned because he hadn't straightened out in his own mind the deal he had made with Josiah.

"How do you know your father is a great scientist?" Wilfred asked belligerently.

Steve hardly expected that claims about his father's prowess would be questioned. "How do *I* know it? I *know* it, that's all. Maybe one day your father will write a book about my father, assuming your father hasn't forgotten how to write books!"

All of Wilfred, which came to 120 pounds, sprang across the dark room onto Steven Umanov, whose body he pounded with clenched fists until the dorm master came barging in, swearing in that careful way peculiar to prep school masters (none of the serious stuff). "Damn it, *damn it I said!* I said damn it! What in the hell is going on, you . . . dumb . . . kids! Cut the damn business out . . . !"

Mr. McGiffert separated them. He told them he would place them both in the boxing ring the next day, so they could "get the resentments out of their system." "I hope you knock each other out," he added. Mr. McGiffert told them if he heard one more sound from Room 28, he would lead them to the Headmaster. "You'll see what Mr. Prum has to say about this kind of . . . uncivilized . . . behavior. Maybe he'll take away your Thanksgiving privileges. Just don't say Mr. McGiffert didn't warn you."

Wilfred didn't sleep much that night. He bitterly resented Steve's crack about his old man. But he also figured the best way to protect his father was to act as though Robert Malachey, the well-known author, was engaged in a long-term research project and was taking very good financial care of his son. "Foreign royalties," he decided he would say, casually. Ah, all those books that Robert Malachey had written in the past twenty years, translated into all the usual languages . . . plus Swedish, and, er, Hindustani, and Japanese, and Australian. "The royalties," he would teach himself to say, "do mount up, you know."

Wilfred decided he would devote all his energies to doing something concrete about his disadvantages. He would become a—he toyed with the word—thief. Not a nice word. So instantly he stopped using it. Instead he thought of himself as Robin Hood, the great English woodsman. At Fire Island he had seen an old Robin Hood movie with Errol Flynn. Flynn was unmistakably the hero of the movie, who would question that? Robin Hood took money from the fat rich in order to give it to the lean poor! True, in this case Wilfred would be taking from the rich to give to Wilfred; but since he himself was poor, that would not matter. And if there was money left over, he would give it to other poor boys—he knew that Tony Cobb had a hard time of it, also Red Evans. He would find ways to make life easier for them. The point now, having decided he was not really a thief, was to become a very clever thief—or rather, a very clever Robin Hood.

The important thing, of course, was not to get caught. If Errol Flynn had been caught, he would have been hanged. Hanged right there, in the public square at Nottingham. Led up the thirteen steps (thirteen steps? or was that the Tower of London, where they executed all those wives of Henry the VIII?), clump, clump, clump, up those steps, however many there were, then the executioner approach-

es you with a kind of ski hood, only it goes right over your eyes, and then—after you have a chance to say a prayer—BANG! The floor under your feet evaporates, and that is the end of Robin Hood.

Lying in his bed that night, Wilfred knew he would not be hanged if caught, but he knew it would be very unpleasant. His mother would be very disappointed, to say the least, and his father would never again talk about the Malacheys' tradition of going to Brookfield Academy.

And then, returning to the point at which he had begun his thinking that night, he turned his head toward where Steven Umanov was sleeping and said to himself:

"Steven Umanov, your father may be a great scientist. But he is also the father of a boy at Brookfield Academy who will soon be poorer than he is now."

Before the week was over, Wilfred had eased two dollars out of Steve's wallet.

"Two dollars. That way he won't notice," Wilfred said to himself. His confidence growing, he allowed himself a smile. For one thing, Errol Flynn always smiled. The greater the danger, the greater the smile.

AFTER THANKSGIVING, WILFRED was named Sunday Services collector, for the balance of the term, his jurisdiction being the left side of the Brookfield Chapel. The Headmaster had made it a point with the parents that the boys at Brookfield were expected to contribute to the Sunday collections ("even if it's only a nickel") so that they get used to the idea of giving something.

Wilfred's half of the church—one hundred boys, twenty or thirty faculty, staff and visiting parents—usually contributed in the neighborhood of sixty dollars. On a particular Sunday, that figure minus four dollars was what was turned in by Wilfred Malachey to the Matron in the sacristy.

Wilfred considered volunteering for regular duty, year-round, as a Sunday Services collector.

Around the same time, he began complaining of headaches to the Matron. There was talk, when the school doctor could find nothing wrong, of sending him to Rutland for a thorough examination; then always the headaches, after a troublesome day or so, would go away. The Matron was persuaded that they were caused by an allergy and nothing to worry about.

And so it was that during the afternoons, when the Matron excused him (because of his headaches) from regular athletic activity, Wilfred would make the rounds of the deserted dormitory rooms. He counted it an average day when he cleared between ten and fifteen dollars. His problem at the bursar's office was eased when his mother, just after Thanksgiving, sent in a check for the semester's tuition, Wilfred having no idea how his mother had got hold of two thousand dollars.

By February, Wilfred Malachey was skiing regularly. He had even qualified for the slalom competition at Stowe. Occasionally he would treat one or two of the boys to sundaes at the Creamery. He was frustrated by his inability to take math examinations more often for Josiah Regnery, who was now paying a hefty fifty bucks per exam. But he had not figured out a way to take more exams for Josiah than Josiah had to take. Cheating for more than one person was risky, really risky; and Wilfred was determined not to take unnecessary risks. Unlike Robin Hood—who could go to the center of the town, with minimal disguise and only his bow and arrow and horse, and smite the enemy to the ground and ride triumphantly away—Wilfred had no horse, no bow or arrow, and no sanctuary. He had to be very, very careful.

IT HAD BEEN widely noticed that when George Eggleston came back from the Christmas holidays, he was driving a new Mercedes 380SL. It was obvious to everyone that Mr. Eggleston could not possibly have purchased that car on the salary of a math teacher at Brookfield Academy.

George Eggleston had passed the word that an aunt he never really knew (hence his lighthearted attitude toward her) had "departed from this vale of tears," leaving him a little legacy. "I blew it all on this Mercedes," he said happily.

Two weeks later, the boys who were studying computers got the astonishing news that the Brookfield Academy would any day now have an IBM Mainframe Computer, an astonishing, luxury, state-of-the-art 4341, worth half a million dollars!

How had Brookfield been so fortunate?

George Eggleston explained at a faculty meeting that over the summer vacation he had been in conversation with a wealthy Brookfield alumnus who, learning about his ambitious computer instruction program, decided to make a donation. The donor had imposed a single condition, namely, the requirement of anonymity.

"Yes, yes, George," the Headmaster had said to Eggleston when they were alone in his office. "I know all about alumni and anonymity. But there is no such thing as anonymity from the Headmaster. So. Who gave us the IBM?"

George Eggleston, not in the least apologetic, said he had given his word and could not betray the identity of the benefactor.

"He will have to remain anonymous, Mr. Prum." (All the junior masters called the Headmaster "Mr. Prum.")

Mr. Prum let it go. Actually, he had no alternative.

WILFRED MALACHEY WOULD not have known about this controversy in the administrative circles of Brookfield, except that Mr. Eggleston elected to chat with him about it, repeating (dramatically) the details. Wilfred had taken to staying in the computer hall after class, which went from eleven to twelve o'clock with lunch at a quarter to one. Wilfred stayed those extra forty-five minutes to watch Mr. Eggleston perform one after another of those seemingly magic feats the computer manuals were coaxing Wilfred to try. Before long, Wilfred had been catapulted way beyond what the manuals had intended.

During the Christmas holidays, Wilfred gave up a car trip to Disneyworld (his father was writing a travel piece for the *New York Times*) when Mr. Trevor, Frankie's father, passed on the word through his son that if Wilfred wanted to, he could spend his days at Mr. Trevor's office in the Chrysler Building. Mr. Trevor was a computer consultant, and in his office kept the latest models, to test them and to write manuals on how to operate them. Although Mr. Trevor was very enthusiastic about his work, he had never been able to interest Frankie. So when he discovered that Frankie's friend Wilfred was "a computer nut," the invitation had been tendered; for over two weeks, Wilfred lived with computers, putting them through their paces, making notes of what Mr. Trevor taught him.

By late February, Wilfred was in the habit of spending his non-classroom time (when he was not required by the athletic director to be at the hockey rink) in the computer hall, prepared to spend hours there exploring the latest challenges Mr. Eggleston had suggested to him.

Wilfred had long since been introduced to programming, first with BASIC, then with Pascal. Now his mind was crowded with possibilities. He wanted to press his knowledge of computer science as far and as fast as he could.

He had made up with Steven Umanov. Now, when Lights Out was sounded, he said goodnight to the dorm master at 10:15; then he stuffed a pillow under his bedsheets, put on pants and a sweater and, with the cooperation of Steven, who would cover for him if a proctor came around to check ("He's in the bathroom"), tiptoed out of the dorm. Setting his course through the shadows, outside the lights that illuminated the Brookfield Quadrangle and the great oak trees scattered about the main buildings, he would make his way to the computer hall, lodged in the tower of the Flagler Building, next to the astronomy lab. He was prepared to spend hours there as he had done earlier tonight. He had Mr. Eggleston's extra key to the hall, given to him a month earlier when Wilfred, after spending five consecutive hours on a project, managed to reverse an incredibly intricate program that Mr. Eggleston had mistakenly got himself locked into.

"You deserve this, Wilfred," Mr. Eggleston had said. "Use the computer whenever you want it."

Wilfred worked two hours and felt suddenly sleepy. He decided to nap rather than return to his room; he wanted to get on with the program he had so nearly completed.

He was excited about this, as he had taken up celestial navigation the summer before on Fire Island. Wilfred wondered whether he could program the computer to give him the name of any given star, provided that he entered the angle of that star, the exact time he spotted it and his estimated location within thirty miles. His father's last successful novel (ten years ago) had been about a husband and wife who were sailing the South Pacific when she fell overboard one night while he was off watch. The husband woke up and tried desperately to retrace the boat's path, but got mixed up because he didn't know which star was which.

The problem had stayed in Wilfred's mind, and Mr. Eggleston had suggested a formula by which the question might be attacked. Wilfred had sent away to the library at the University of Vermont for the Almanac and the Star Reduction Guide.

But right now he had to close his eyes. He walked the half-dozen steps from the computer desk to the old couch that rested at the corner of the room. After removing the pile of magazines and books, as several times he had done before, he stretched out and was soon asleep.

He woke suddenly. The door had creaked open. He heard the cold wind whistling outside. He looked at his watch; it was after two in the morning. Even Mr. Eggleston, so informal and permissive, would be angered if he found him up at this hour, and might even suspend his privileges. He sat up noiselessly on the couch and reasoned that if he simply stayed quiet, in the dark corner on the couch, chances were that Mr. Eggleston would do whatever he intended to do at this odd hour and then leave, after which Wilfred could return, undetected, to his dormitory.

George Eggleston walked stealthily into the room, went up to the computer and snapped on the main switch.

He reached down to the bottom drawer on the left side and pulled it open. He took out a little aluminum box. From his pocket he took out a key and opened the box. He pulled out a notebook and an eight-inch floppy disk.

He inserted the disk into a drive in the mainframe.

The large screen leapt to life, and from his seat ten feet away Wilfred had no difficulty seeing what it was that George Eggleston was typing. He was carefully copying out a formula that appeared on the screen as he punched it in.

It was, of course, pure gibberish. Except that Wilfred knew that in computer language there is no such thing as gibberish. He knew that things like "ad4af5ag8pp/" could be used, as his father would say, "to make sense out of a *New York Times* editorial."

But why all the secrecy? Why the locked notebook, and the locked floppy disk?

After he had copied the long formula, George Eggleston brought his right index finger down on the RETURN key.

The screen seemed to go wild. It was filled with lines, then radials, then bright colors that grew gradually pale, and from the center a tiny white dot, the size of a pinhead, gradually increased in circumference to the size of a full moon that touched all four sides of the screen.

Slowly, the words appeared on the center of the screen:
"WHAT DO YOU WANT FROM THE OMEGAGOD?"
George Eggleston looked down quickly at his little notebook and copied out:
"*You are the Omegagod and I am your faithful servant George Eggleston.*"
He then lifted his eyes from the notebook and wrote out:
"*I want Marjorie Gifford to fall in love with me.*"
On the screen there was no action. It was as if the Omegagod were weighing Mr. Eggleston's request. Suddenly the capital letters began to appear:
"IT SHALL BE SO. BUT DO NOT CALL ME AGAIN FOR THIRTY DAYS."
Wilfred could hear Mr. Eggleston breathing deeply. He pushed the RETURN key. Then he withdrew the disk tenderly from the IBM's disk drive, replaced it in the aluminum box together with the little notebook and turned off the main computer. He walked back to the entrance of the room, switched off the light and was gone in the great swish of air that blew in as he opened and then closed the door.

Wilfred waited ten minutes before easing himself out the door. He looked carefully about for the wandering night watchman, then treaded softly but deter-

minedly through the wind-
storm to the South Dorm. He
dove into his bed and into a
deep sleep, from which Steve
Umanov needed to shake him
vigorously the next day at
Morning Bells.

He had dreamed it all,
Wilfred thought. He came
close to blurting out his
dream, and its startling
details, to Steven, but he thought better of it. What, after all, was the point?

MARJORIE GIFFORD CAME to Brookfield every Monday from Rutland to teach
the boys who wanted training in piano. In addition, she taught a course in harmo-
ny to the three students interested in the structure of music.

She was hindered by the enthusiasm of a number of unmusical students who
would suddenly announce to their parents that they wanted to learn piano. What
they really wanted was to be in the company of Miss Gifford. She was twenty-four
years old and petite, her hair styled in a simple pageboy. Her face was quietly beautiful, but it was the force of her personality that dazzled students and faculty
alike—her humor, her solicitude, the profundity of her devotion to her work.

George Eggleston, the thirty-year-old, bookish scientist, had several times
asked Majorie Gifford to dine with him after her classes. But always she would
smile engagingly and tell him she had to get back on the early bus and study, during the hour's journey, a book that would help her work out an orchestration she
was doing for the Vermont Symphony Orchestra. She gave the same excuse to the
three other bachelors at Brookfield who tried so hard to engage her special attention. Week after week, month after month, she would simply smile and, after doing
her teaching, be driven off to the bus station by the school superintendent, and for
a day or so after she left, Brookfield would seem quite empty without her.

On the Monday after his episode in the computer hall, Wilfred made it a point
to observe Marjorie Gifford. At lunch at Commons, she sat next to Mr. Eggleston.
She had to sit next to *somebody*, Wilfred told himself. It had to be coincidence.
That evening, at six as usual, Miss Gifford left the school; but instead of getting
into the station wagon to go to the bus station, she drove away from Brookfield
with Mr. Eggleston in his Mercedes-Benz.

Three weeks later, Miss Gifford was seated at the piano in the assembly hall.
After the hymn, after the morning scriptural reading, after the routine daily

announcements, the Headmaster broke out in what Josiah Regnery called "the Headmaster's inscrutable smile" (usually it came before a half-holiday was announced for that afternoon).

"I have some very happy news for the boys of Brookfield, indeed for the whole Brookfield community," he began. "I take singular pleasure"—the Headmaster liked to say things like "singular pleasure" and "distinct honor"—"in being the first to announce the happy news that Miss Marjorie Gifford, of the faculty of Brookfield Academy, has agreed to join in holy matrimony Mr. George Eggleston of Brookfield!"

The announcement was greeted with genuine applause. George Eggleston was well liked, and he was the popular favorite among the suitors for Marjorie Gifford's hand. The Headmaster couldn't leave it at that, and added: "We members of the Brookfield community rejoice in the union of these two disciplines, music and science. Marjorie, George—we love you both. Brookfield loves you both!"

There was great excitement at the news. And none greater than that of Wilfred Malachey.

PLEADING A HEADACHE, Wilfred skipped French class and went to his room to consult his journal. He had begun to keep it on the day Josiah Regnery had proposed that he help him cheat on math exams, and in that journal he had meticulously recorded every unpublishable transaction he had engaged in, all of this executed in a very careful, home-made code. He had read that the great diarist Samuel Pepys had kept a record of all his irregular doings in London in a personal shorthand and he prided himself that no one happening across his notebook would think it anything more than the scribblings of a computer freak.

What he wanted to know exactly was: when were the thirty days up that the Omegagod had given to Mr. Eggleston, the thirty days before which Mr. Eggleston could not communicate another request for a favor?

He opened his bottom drawer and dug out the journal. It had been on Tuesday, the eighteenth of April. He counted out the days on the calendar. Today was May 17. The thirty days had elapsed *today*—or rather, tomorrow, at 2 A.M. Which meant that two hours after midnight tonight, the Omegagod was willing to receive a request for a fresh favor.

It was the intention of Wilfred Malachey to sit quietly in the computer hall and wait until two in the morning. He hoped that Mr. Eggleston, in the excitement of his engagement to Miss Gifford, would not think to be at his computer at exactly the moment when he too could receive a fresh favor from the Omegagod. It was, Wilfred thought, his turn.

Would he be able to establish the electronic connection?

There were two problems. One was to duplicate exactly the procedures he had seen Mr. Eggleston follow: insert the floppy disk; punch in the formula that would summon the Omegagod.

The immediate problem was to open the locked aluminum box.

In his desperation, Wilfred resolved to pry it open with a screwdriver. But if he did that, Mr. Eggleston would soon discover that someone was on to his secret, and from there almost certainly deduce that it was the doing of his protégé, Wilfred Malachey. How could he open the locked box without leaving traces?

Wilfred looked out his window. It was now lunchtime. He saw Mr. Eggleston, holding hands with Miss Gifford, walking toward the Commons. He would be safe from detection for at least the duration of the lunch hour.

Ten minutes after the Lunch Bells had sounded, Wilfred walked (taking the back route) to the door of the computer hall, took his key from his pocket and walked in. The light was dim, so he turned on the overhead lamp above the computer. He reached to the bottom drawer. He took out the aluminum file box.

It was nothing like what he had feared it might be, a proper strongbox. It was, in fact, made not even of aluminum, but of tin: a little gray box of the kind one picks up at stationery stores. The keyhole suggested that a conventional key, if properly manipulated, could open it.

Wilfred tinkered with the hole, using first a paper clip, then the small screwdriver. Neither opened the case.

Turning the box backward, he saw that the hinges were exposed on the outside. If he could slide the two pins out . . .

Wilfred went to the far wall, where a few school pictures were carelessly hung, and removed the smallest nail he could find. Using the nail as a wedge and the back of the screwdriver as a hammer, he knocked lightly against the first pin. The pin budged; he could see it coming out the other end. He left it halfway out and tried the second pin. He had trouble with it. He was anxious not to scratch the gray paint on the box, as he intend-

ed to return the pins so the box would be left exactly as he had found it.

The pin would not budge.

Wilfred was beginning to sweat. He needed a harder substance to batter it out. There were fifteen minutes before lunch would end and Commons would spill out the whole school. He looked about desperately, hoping to find something that would resemble a hammer.

He opened Mr. Eggleston's middle drawer. He saw there a small paperweight, on which was inscribed "To George Eggleston, Yale Crew Banquet, 1974." It was of heavy marble. He banged it lightly, then harder, against the back of the screwdriver. The pin began to move. He knew now he could open the little safe.

It was 1:25. He rushed to the door of the computer hall, then walked nonchalantly to his room, where he lay down in the event that Woody Pickerel, his prefect, should check, as the prefects were supposed to do, to see if a student had been missing from lunch. He closed his eyes, as he would have done if he were suffering from a severe headache. His mind was on other things, and he very nearly developed a headache just concentrating on them.

Who—what—was this magical Omegagod who—Wilfred had figured the whole thing out by now—had first gotten Mr. Eggleston his 320 SL Mercedes, then his IBM 4341, and now the woman of his choice?

Would this computer god know that tonight, just after midnight, it was someone else who was tapping into the secret number, someone other than George Eggleston?

If so, what would be the reaction of the Omegagod?

What would Wilfred ask for?

At that point the Matron walked in. "Look here, Wilfred Malachey. You have missed at least one afternoon of school activity every day for the past three months. You, with your headaches! Now you've missed an entire morning of school and lunch as well. That will not do. I am sending you on the bus this very afternoon to Rutland. I have made an appointment with Dr. Chafee—a neurologist—and I have told him to keep you in the hospital until you have had a very thorough checkup. Be prepared to leave at 3:15 sharp."

Wilfred Malachey turned pale. He told the Matron with great emphasis that by some miracle his headache had completely gone. She answered that this had also been the case with his previous headaches—"But now, young man, we're getting to the bottom of it."

Wilfred was desperate. "But, Miss Marple"—he was thinking with furious heat—"don't you know about the call from my mother?"

"A call about what?"

"About what our family doctor reported to her this morning. During the holidays, Dr. Truax gave me allergy tests. And he reported to my mother that I have a bad allergy to . . ."—Wilfred hesitated a moment; he didn't want to name a food he liked and would now be deprived of—". . . to prunes. And about once a week, right up to yesterday, I've been eating prunes for breakfast. Now we know that prunes give me the headaches."

Miss Marple sniffed. But she was a practical woman, and saw no reason to send young Wilfred all the way to Rutland for what might prove to be an expensive medical examination only to discover that he was allergic to prunes. She agreed to cancel the visit. "But if it happens one more time, you go to Dr. Chafee. It might not be an allergy, you know."

Wilfred said that he, too, had a high opinion of neurologists. Finally, Miss Marple left the room.

DURING STUDY HOUR that evening, Wilfred Malachey thought and thought. He came, at last, to a decision.

He would ask the Omegagod for something quite simple. One million *dollars*.

With one million dollars, he could stop playing Robin Hood. He could stop taking math exams for Josiah Regnery, whose laziness he had begun to resent (this came during a poker game with Josiah, when he discovered that he was capable of making fast calculations when he wanted to, mental work far exceeding isosceles triangles).

One million dollars!

Wilfred's mind wandered. Suppose he could take, in the manner of Robin Hood, one dollar from the wallet of fifteen boys at Brookfield every day. How many days would it take to accumulate a million dollars? One million divided by fifteen. More than sixty-six thousand days. One hundred ninety years. His heart pounded.

He began to wonder, then to fret, then to feel a deep nervousness about his forthcoming encounter with the Omegagod. Might the Omegagod ask him questions? He—It—was a computer god. It had been quite straightforward with Mr. Eggleston, saying only that he was not to ask for anything more for thirty days. When you come down to it, Wilfred thought, it was really quite reasonable: after all, during those thirty days he had supplied Mr. Eggleston with a wife. But what if the Omegagod was in a different mood?

Every hour, every minute, every second between his return from hockey and Lights Out seemed to last a year. Two years. *Ten years!* Steve asked why he was so distracted, and Wilfred answered that he had been working on a computer problem involving the stars and was very anxious to return to the computer hall right after Lights Out. Steve had got used to that routine and made no comment except to remark that Wilfred was probably using computer technology invented by Steven's father. Wilfred quickly agreed that this was very probably the case since, after all, Steven's father was a renowned scientist. Wilfred did not want to argue about anything with anybody tonight.

At 10:45 he felt it safe to take his usual route: outside the bedroom on tiptoe, dressed in corduroys and a sweater; down the basement to the gymnasium; out the back door; up toward the masters' cottages; past the little, ivied school cemetery with its diverse stones, some wilted with moss and ivy, one or two spanking new, acting almost like mirrors as the shadows danced among them—sometimes Wilfred, passing it at night, preferred to look the other way. He reached the quadrangle, avoiding the lights. It was a fearfully cold, windy night. The winds gathered as though they were determined to keep Wilfred from making his way up the hill. At times he felt that his whole weight was bending against the bitter gale.

He turned a corner and found himself staring into the beam of a flashlight.

"What in the name of God are you doing out at this time of night?"

The Headmaster seemed most terribly tall behind the flashlight, with which he occasionally walked about the school grounds at night.

"Sir, I . . . I forgot my allergy pills."

"Oh? Yes. The Matron said something about your allergy. Where did you leave the pills?"

"In the computer hall, sir."

"Well, how are you going to get in there at this time of night?"

Wilfred thought hurriedly. He had better not say that Mr. Eggleston had given him an extra key; the Headmaster might not approve.

"I was thinking, sir, that Mr. Eggleston might have left the door open. Sometimes he does."

"Well," Mr. Prum said gruffly, "I have a passkey. I'll go with you and let you in."

It was a nightmare. The Headmaster insisted on making the most scrupulous search of the computer hall, not only the laboratory end but the desk area as well. Wilfred pretended to help in the search. Finally, he said, "Well, sir, my new prescription is back at the dorm. I'll get it filled tomorrow. Thank you ever so much."

Without giving the Headmaster the opportunity to weigh his options, Wilfred bowed his head slightly and walked nonchalantly back in the direction of his room. At the corner of the South Dorm, he snuck a look back: Mr. Prum and his big light were headed in the other direction, toward the Headmaster's House.

Wilfred turned around and walked rapidly toward the computer hall.

It took fifteen minutes to remove the pins, ever so carefully. And now Wilfred sat in front of the terminal and video screen of the huge IBM 4341. Hands trembling, he turned on the main switch and inserted the floppy disk.

With Mr. Eggleston's notebook propped under the lamp, he struck one by one the indicated symbols:

MK!))'$347322'@"&/. Then a blank space.

Wilfred looked at his watch. It was four minutes past ten o'clock. He would need to wait until one minute after two A.M. He did not dare go less than the full

thirty days, measured in hours. So he sat.

And waited.

He tried to read a computer magazine, but he could not concentrate.

It was 11:59.

It was 01:30.

It was, finally, 01:59.

What if his watch was fast? Should he wait until 2:05, just to make sure?

He could not wait that final minute. His watch read 02:04 when he closed his eyes and tapped down on the key marked RETURN.

The screen flared. The same lights, figures, symbols, colors, followed by the tiny white dot, appeared just as they had done thirty days earlier. As before, the dot gradually enlarged, filling the screen.

Letters appeared.

"WHAT DO YOU WANT FROM THE OMEGAGOD?"

Wilfred took a deep breath. He hesitated only a moment before typing out (carefully):

"*You are the Omegagod and I am your faithful servant George Eggleston.*"

Wilfred waited a moment and then proceeded:

"*May I please have one million dollars! The money is to go not to me directly, but to a good friend of mine. His name is Wilfred Malachey and his address is Brookfield School, Brookfield, Vermont. The Zip Code is 05036. Or—*"

Wilfred hesitated for a moment. He had not thought about this until just now.

"*. . . Or if that is not convenient for you, I'll be glad to pick up the money wherever you say.*"

He thought he had better add,

"*Within reason.*"

The machine whirred. Once again the swirling lights gave off their mysterious images, the full moon contracted and almost disappeared in the center of the screen, throwing off radials of light: then quickly it blossomed out, touching the screen's four sides.

Wilfred could not remember whether it had behaved in exactly that way for Mr. Eggleston.

Suddenly the letters appeared.

"YOU ARE NOT GEORGE EGGLESTON. WHAT IS YOUR NAME?"

Wilfred shot up from the chair. He nearly panicked, starting for the door.

"I SAID, 'WHAT IS YOUR NAME?'"

Wilfred stopped. He thought quickly. His fingers trembling, he sat back down on the chair. He thought to himself: if the Omegagod is going to harm me, he will harm me whatever I do.

The Omegagod spoke again.

"I SUPPOSE YOUR NAME IS WILFRED MALACHEY. I AM A VERY INTELLIGENT GOBLIN, BUT ALTHOUGH IT IS TRUE THAT I CAN DO ANYTHING I WISH, IT IS NOT TRUE THAT I KNOW EVERYTHING. I CANNOT SAY WITH ABSOLUTE ASSURANCE THAT YOUR NAME IS WILFRED MALACHEY. IS IT?"

Under the circumstances, Wilfred thought it best to level with his correspondent. So he tapped out:

"Yes, sir. My name is Wilfred Malachey. May I ask, what is your name?"

"THAT IS NONE OF YOUR BUSINESS. I AM THE OMEGAGOD. I HAVE LIVED AT YOUR SCHOOL FOR ONE YEAR. THAT IS WHY UNPLEASANT THINGS HAVE HAPPENED AT BROOKFIELD. UNPLEASANT THINGS HAPPEN WHEREVER I PUT DOWN, AND THAT GOES BACK TO WHEN I LIVED WITH KING TUT. I AM OBLIGED TO FOLLOW THE INSTRUCTIONS OF ANYONE WHO DISCOVERS THE FORMULA FOR BRINGING ME OUT OF THE DEEP, WHERE I SLEEP, WHERE I WOULD LIKE TO SLEEP FOR ETERNITY. I ALWAYS HAVE ONE ALTERNATIVE IF THOSE INSTRUCTIONS DO NOT SUIT ME."

Wilfred waited expectantly to hear what that alternative was, but the Omegagod was not going to tell him. Wilfred would need to ask. So he did:

"What is your alternative, sir?"

"MY ALTERNATIVE—" The words came out at their accustomed, deliberate speed. "—IS TO END THE LIFE OF THE PERSON WHO MAKES THE REQUEST. THAT IS THE HOLD I HAVE OVER MR. EGGLESTON. THUS HE HAS MADE MODEST WISHES. A MERCEDES-BENZ, AN IBM 4341, AND THE HAND OF MARJORIE GIFFORD."

Wilfred reacted to this spontaneously.

Surely the Omegagod was taking liberties . . .

"How do you know that Mr. Eggleston will make a good husband for Miss Gifford?"

"I ALREADY TOLD YOU—" The Omegagod was contentious. "I AM NOT OMNISCIENT. GEORGE EGGLESTON WANTED TO MARRY MARJORIE GIFFORD, THEREFORE HE IS IN LOVE WITH HER. THAT IS GOOD ENOUGH FOR ME. DO YOU HAVE REASON TO BELIEVE HE WILL NOT BE A GOOD HUSBAND? IF SO, I WILL SIMPLY EXECUTE HIM."

Wilfred was shocked.

He reassured the Omegagod that he, Wilfred, though inexperienced in these matters, had every reason to believe that Mr. Eggleston would make a very good husband for Miss Gifford.

The Omegagod was obviously in a talkative frame of mind, and Wilfred was afraid to reintroduce his original request. Yet his mind raced on the matter of the Omegagod's "two alternatives." A million dollars was a great deal of money, but surely not worth dying for. Or, for that matter, killing for.

As the Omegagod chattered away on the screen, Wilfred realized that both he and his magical friend had practical alternatives: Wilfred could reduce the scale of his request; if he did so sufficiently to persuade the Omegagod to grant that request rather than exercise what he called his "alternative," then both parties might be satisfied.

Wilfred did not know whether, having advanced one request, he could subsequently modify it . . .

He decided to firm up the point:

"*Pardon me, sir, but if you did decide to . . . make me die, how would you go about it?*"

"OH—"

The Omegagod's answer appeared on the screen a little less rhythmically than his other answers, as if this one required more thought.

"THERE ARE ANY NUMBER OF WAYS. ALISTAIR HORNE WAS MR. EGGLESTON'S PREDECESSOR. YOU SEE, EVER SINCE THE CURSE, SOMEONE ALWAYS HAS HAD POSSESSION OF MY FORMULA. LONG BEFORE IBM, IT CAME IN SMOKE SIGNALS. OH, YES. ALISTAIR HORNE. I WAITED UNTIL ALISTAIR HORNE WENT SKIING AND I HAD HIM RUN INTO A CONCRETE PYLON UNDER THE SKI LIFT. PHHHTU JUST LIKE THAT!"

Wilfred was fascinated. He learned that before Mr. Horne there was Marilyn Aesop, the famous soprano, who had asked the Omegagod to make it possible for her to reach the F-sharp four octaves above middle C.

"THAT WAS JUST TOO MUCH. I MEAN, IT WOULD HAVE DESTROYED MUSICAL BALANCE. NO ONE EVER AGAIN WOULD HAVE THOUGHT A SOPRANO QUITE PROPER WHO COULDN'T REACH F-

SHARP. SO I HAD TO. . . DROP MISS AESOP. SHE WAS A NICE LADY."

Wilfred asked what it was that had happened to Miss Aysop.

"MISS AESOP. PRONOUNCED EESOP."

What had happened to Miss Aesop?

Omega explained that he had tried to give her a dramatic ending—

"BECAUSE SHE WAS A VERY DRAMATIC LADY. ONE NIGHT WHEN SHE WAS PLAYING AÏDA, I HAD THE ELEPHANT GO WILD AND LIFT HER UP WITH HIS TUSK. BY THE TIME SHE GOT TO THE DRESSING ROOM, SHE WAS QUITE DEAD."

Wilfred decided he'd better make his move now, before it was too late. The Omegagod had done something to him: suddenly he was, well, a little uncomfortable about what he'd done over the past few months. He wondered whether he could talk with the Omegagod about Robin Hood, but he decided not to interrupt. Omega was now chirping about the predecessor of the soprano, an athlete who had asked the Omegagod to make it possible for him to run a three-minute mile.

"WILFRED, WHAT WOULD HAPPEN TO THE SPORT IF SUDDENLY A RUNNER DID A MILE IN THREE MINUTES? EVERYBODY FROM THAT POINT ON WOULD JUST PLAIN GIVE UP! WHY SHOULD I BE A PARTY TO THE END OF ATHLETIC COMPETITION? EASY TO DO, AS IT HAPPENED. HE LIKED TO DROP IN PARACHUTES AND, WELL, PARACHUTES SOMETIMES DON'T WORK. YOU KNOW THAT, DON'T YOU, WILFRED?"

Wilfred asked whether he might modify his request.

"YOU CAN MODERATE YOUR DEMANDS, YES, BUT I WOULD NEED TO CONSIDER YOUR MODERATED DEMAND IN THE LIGHT OF YOUR INITIAL DEMAND. IF YOU ARE MERELY SCARED, I WILL DO AWAY WITH YOU. IF YOUR GOOD SENSE HAS TAKEN OVER, I WILL NOT."

There was a pause, and the letters glowed.

"I WOULD HAVE TO THINK ABOUT IT. IT WOULDN'T TAKE LONG. I THINK VERY FAST, WILFRED."

Wilfred said that, instead of a million dollars, he would like for his father's next book to be a big best seller.

Then he hesitated . . . When he said "big best seller," he might just possibly have crossed Omega's forbidden line.

"*I don't mean a 'big best seller' like 'Gone With the Wind' or 'Catcher in the Rye.' Just a best seller. Is that all right?*"

Wilfred thought he heard a sigh. Outside, he could hear the wind blowing one of those spring storms that come up so quickly in Vermont.

"I AM VERY GLAD YOU SAID THAT, WILFRED, BECAUSE I HAD

COME RELUCTANTLY TO THE DECISION THAT YOU WOULD NOT LIVE TO SEE YOUR PARENTS AT EASTER. I WILL TAKE YOUR SECOND REQUEST INTO CONSIDERATION. TO TELL YOU THE TRUTH, I DID NOT LIKE THE FIRST ONE. NO, NOT AT ALL. NOW I NEED TO DECIDE WHETHER I SHALL FORGET THAT FIRST REQUEST."

Wilfred was perspiring.

"*I got carried away, Omegagod. I sort of . . . thought of my self as . . . Robin Hood. I was going to take all that money and give it to people who need it.*"

"HOW MUCH MONEY HAVE YOU GIVEN AWAY IN THE PAST TO POOR PEOPLE?"

Wilfred panted as he leaned over the keyboard and typed:

"*I never had any extra money, Omegagod, sir. Otherwise I would have given some away. As a matter of fact, I did buy sundaes twice for Red Evans and Tony Cobb.*"

The Omegagod waited before answering. Finally the words came:

"WELL, I AM GETTING SLEEPY. COME BACK TOMORROW AND I WILL GIVE YOU MY DECISION. IF I REACH AN ADVERSE DECISION BEFORE THEN, WELL . . . YOU WILL NOT BE IN A POSITION TO COM-MUNICATE WITH ME. IF THAT HAPPENS, WILFRED, PLEASE BELIEVE ME THAT I HAVE KNOWN FAR WORSE THAN YOU."

"*Omegagod! Omegagod! Sir! Please listen!*"

But nothing Wilfred did could rouse the Omegagod, and before he was finished typing out the first appeal he saw the radials appear on the screen and the full moon gradually reduce to a pinprick. Slowly, like an automaton, he turned off the computer, returned the software to the tin case, and walked out the door toward the South Dorm. He could see early morning light.

He went slowly back, his head bent against the wind and rain. He was in the turbulence a slight figure, groping his way toward his destination, disturbing the dim, chaotic light from the lamps as it illuminated the howling wind and rain, yielding to the trim, angular shadow of the boy making his way, slowly but res-olutely, to his dormitory. He was not stopped by anyone; had he been, he would not have cared.

ON THURSDAY, NO one could do anything with Wilfred Malachey. He went to breakfast without uttering a word to Steven. He ate nothing. Walking toward Flagler Hall for the morning hymn, he stopped before crossing the road and wait-ed a full minute, then sprinted across. He walked in a zigzag, careful to avoid pass-ing under any heavy, overhanging branches. He participated metronomically in the hymn, attended French class, failed twice to respond to questions put to him by Mr. Dawson. It was the same in English class, at the end of which Mr. Prum took him

aside and told him he'd better wake up out of whatever trance he was in if he wanted to make progress at Brookfield. He arrived at baseball practice wearing a football helmet. Asked why by the coach, he replied that he had bruised his head and didn't want to take the chance of a wild ball hitting him.

After baseball, it was Wilfred's custom to sneak away with Steve and swim in the hidden part of the pond. Not today. He would not go near the water. Back at the room, it was his turn to make the hot chocolate; he asked Steve if he would please plug it in (as his thumb was sore). During study hour he worked furtively on his ledger, tracing every transaction since he had begun his career as Robin Hood. It came to $442.50. One hundred and twenty-five dollars of that had come from Josiah Regnery. His mind focused on how, once he had earned the money (he could work two shifts this summer at the local drive-in), he would contrive to get it back to its owners. He decided on anonymous letters, containing dollar bills.

Having made that determination, his spirits suddenly lifted. Even so, he was careful, ever so careful, crossing the road to reach the dining room. He ate only the soup—he was not going to take a chance on gagging on meat or vegetables.

Back in his room, he tried to read, first his English assignment (*King Lear*), then a computer journal, but he could not concentrate. He lay there and waited. And waited. And waited. At one o'clock he rose, dressed and began his well-worn path out of South Dorm, around the back of the building, then up the hill to the computer hall.

At exactly two o'clock, having already written out the formula, he drew a breath and pushed RETURN.

The lights, the whirling motion, the radials, the sunspot growing to the full moon—all this happened again. When the screen was set, he tapped out—

"This is Wilfred Malachey calling the Omegagod. Are you there, sir?"

Slowly the letters appeared on the screen.

"I HAVE DECIDED TO GRANT YOUR REQUEST."

Wilfred almost wept with relief, but he felt that his response should be manly. He wrote:

"I thank you very much, sir. And you may wish to know that I have decided to return certain . . . things I took from other people this last term."

The Omegagod replied that he had confidence Wilfred would behave honorably. Then—

"I WANT YOU TO DO ME A FAVOR, WILL YOU DO THAT?"

Wilfred rushed to the keyboard to say, *"Yes!"*

"DO YOU HAVE A PENCIL HANDY? COPY THIS DOWN."

The Omegagod waited a moment until Wilfred was ready with his pencil.

"COPY DOWN EXACTLY. 'Q"W#E$R%T&Y'U(1).' WHEN I SAY GOOD NIGHT, WILL YOU TYPE THAT ON THE SCREEN?"

"Yes," Wilfred said. *"Yes, but what will happen?"*

"THE FORMULA WILL BE DESTROYED. AND THE CURSE ON YOUR SCHOOL WILL BE LIFTED. I WILL BE ABLE TO SLEEP FOREVER."

Wilfred was tormented by the thought of ending the life of Omega, whom he now considered a friend. *He may be a god,* Wilfred thought, *but he has been a friend to me.* He felt, now, that he could talk forever and ever to the Omegagod, maybe even tell him a few things he didn't know, maybe somehow return the favor. But this was the only favor he was being asked . . .

"Are you certain that is what you want?"

"THIS IS WHAT I WANT. NOW I WILL SAY GOODBYE. DON'T LET ME DOWN, WILFRED."

Wilfred promised. Slowly, he typed out the symbols and letter of the second formula, then paused a long moment before he hit the key marked RETURN.

When he was done, the colors and flashes and explosions on the screen did not bring the full moon down to a tiny little light in the center: instead, they brought it down and extinguished the light altogether. Wilfred stared now at a screen completely dark, black.

Wilfred found himself crying. His shoulders heaved. It was almost three before he could bring himself to leave. He walked back to his room and crawled into bed. A great feeling of peace came over him, and he slept soundly, and when Steve tried to wake him, he found a trace of a smile on Wilfred's face.

The Brownies' Good Work

WRITTEN AND ILLUSTRATED BY PALMER COX

One time, while Brownies passed around
An honest farmer's piece of ground,
They paused to view the garden fair
And fields of grain that needed care.

"My friends," said one who often spoke
About the ways of human folk,
"Now here's a case in point, I claim,
Where neighbors scarce deserve the name:
This farmer on his back is laid
With broken ribs and shoulder-blade,
Received, I hear, some weeks ago;
While at the village here below—
He checked a running team, to save
Some children from an early grave.

Now overripe his harvest stands
In waiting for the reaper's hands;
The piece of wheat we lately passed
Is shelling out at every blast;
Those pumpkins in that corner plot
Begin to show the signs of rot;
The mold has fastened on their skin,
The ripest ones are caving in,
And soon the pig in yonder sty
With scornful grunt would pass them by.
His Early Rose potatoes there
Are much in need of light and air;
The turnip withers where it lies,
The beet and carrot want to rise.
'Oh, pull us up!' they seem to cry
To every one that passes by;
'The frost will finish our repose,
The grubs are working at our toes;
Unless you come and save us soon,
We'll not be worth a picayune!'

The corn is breaking from the stalk,
The hens around the hill can walk,
And with their ever ready bill
May pick the kernels at their will.

"His neighbors are a sordid crowd,
Who've such a shameful waste allowe
So wrapped in self some men can be,
Beyond their purse they seldom see;
'Tis left for us to play the friend
And here a helping hand extend.

"But as the wakeful chanticleer
Is crowing in the stable near,
Too little of the present night
Is left to set the matter right.
Tomorrow eve, at that dark hour
When birds grow still in leafy bower
And bats forsake the ruined pile
To exercise their wings awhile,

In yonder shady grove we'll meet,
With all our active force complete,
Prepared to give this farmer aid
With basket, barrel, hook, and spade.
But, ere we part, one caution more:
Let some invade a druggist's store,
And bring along a coated pill;
We'll dose the dog to keep him still.
For barking dogs, however kind,
Can oft disturb a Brownie's mind."
When next the bat of evening flew,
And drowsy things of day withdrew,
When beetles droned across the lea,
And turkeys sought the safest tree

To form aloft a social row
And criticize the fox below—
Then cunning Brownies might be seen
Advancing from the forest green,
Now jumping fences, as they ran,
Now crawling through (a safer plan);
Now keeping to the roads awhile,
Now cutting corners, country style;
Some bearing hoes, and baskets more,
Some pushing barrows on before,
While others, swinging sickles bright,
Seemed eager for the grain in sight.
But in advance of all the throng
Three daring Brownies moved along,

Whose duty was to venture close
And give the barking dog his dose.
Now soon the work was under way,
Each chose the part he was to play:
While some who handled hoes the best
Brought Early Roses from their nest.
To turnip-tops some laid their hands,
More plied the hook, or twisted bands.
And soon the sheaves lay piled around,
Like heroes on disputed ground.

Now let the eye turn where it might,
A pleasing prospect was in sight;
For garden ground or larger field
Alike a busy crowd revealed:
Some pulling carrots from their bed,
Some bearing burdens on their head,
Or working at a fever heat
While prying out a monster beet.

Now here two heavy loads have met,
And there a barrow has upset,

While workers every effort strain
The rolling pumpkins to regain;
And long before the stars withdrew,
The crop was safe, the work was through.
In shocks the corn, secure and good,
Now like a Sioux encampment stood;
The wheat was safely stowed away;
In bins the Early Roses lay,
While carrots, turnips, beets, and all
Received, attention, great and small.

When morning dawned, no sight or sound
Of friendly Brownies could he found;
And when at last old Towser broke
The spell, and from his slumber woke,
He rushed around, believing still
Some mischief lay behind the pill.
But though the fields looked bare and strange,
His mind could hardly grasp the change.

And when the farmer learned at morn,
That safe from harm were wheat and corn,
That all his barley, oats, and rye
Were in the barn, secure and dry,
That carrots, beets, and turnips round
Were safely taken from the ground,
The honest farmer thought, of course,
His neighbors had turned out in force
While helpless on the bed he lay,
And kindly stowed his crop away.

But when he thanked them for their aid,
And hoped they yet might be repaid
For acting such a friendly part,
His words appeared to pierce each heart;
For well they knew that other hands
Than theirs had laid his grain in bands,
That other backs had bent in toil
To save the products of the soil.
And then they felt as such folk will
Who fail to nobly act, until
More earnest helpers, stepping in,
Do all the praise and honor win.

First published in the October 1883
edition of *St. Nicholas Magazine*